Command

In the wake of the troubled campaigns in Afghanistan and Iraq, military decision-making appears to be in crisis and generals have been subjected to intense and sustained public criticism. Taking these interventions as a starting point, Anthony King examines the transformation of military command in the twenty-first century. Focusing on the army division, King argues that a phenomenon of collective command is developing. In the twentieth century, generals typically directed and led operations personally, monopolizing decision-making. They commanded individualistically, even heroically. As operations have expanded in range and scope, decision-making has multiplied and diversified. As a result command is becoming increasingly professionalized and collaborative. Through interviews with many leading generals and vivid ethnographic analysis of divisional headquarters, this book provides a unique insight into the transformation of command in Western armies.

Anthony King is Chair of War Studies in the Politics and International Studies Department at Warwick University. His most recent publications include *The Combat Soldier* (2013) and, as editor, *Frontline* (2015). He has acted as a mentor and adviser to the British Army and the Royal Marines for over a decade and worked as one of General Carter's special advisers in the Prism Cell in Regional Command South, Kandahar, in 2009–10.

Command

The Twenty-First-Century General

Anthony King
University of Warwick

CAMBRIDGE
UNIVERSITY PRESS

University Printing House, Cambridge CB2 8BS, United Kingdom

One Liberty Plaza, 20th Floor, New York, NY 10006, USA

477 Williamstown Road, Port Melbourne, VIC 3207, Australia

314–321, 3rd Floor, Plot 3, Splendor Forum, Jasola District Centre,
New Delhi – 110025, India

79 Anson Road, #06-04/06, Singapore 079906

Cambridge University Press is part of the University of Cambridge.

It furthers the University's mission by disseminating knowledge in the pursuit of
education, learning, and research at the highest international levels of excellence.

www.cambridge.org
Information on this title: www.cambridge.org/9781108476409
DOI: 10.1017/9781108642941

© Anthony King 2019

First published 2019

Printed in the United Kingdom by TJ International Ltd, Padstow, Cornwall

A catalogue record for this publication is available from the British Library.

Library of Congress Cataloging-in-Publication Data
Names: King, Anthony, 1967– author.
Title: Command : the twenty-first-century general / Anthony King,
University of Warwick.
Description: Cambridge : Cambridge University Press, 2019.
Identifiers: LCCN 2018038867 | ISBN 9781108476409 (hardback) |
ISBN 9781108700276 (paperback)
Subjects: LCSH: Command of troops–History–21st century. |
BISAC: HISTORY / Military / General.
Classification: LCC UB210 .K49 2019 | DDC 355.3/3041–dc23
LC record available at https://lccn.loc.gov/2018038867

ISBN 978-1-108-47640-9 Hardback
ISBN 978-1-108-70027-6 Paperback

CONTENTS

FIGURES

TABLES

PREFACE

It would be convenient to claim that a book on command exemplified its own subject matter and that, with military precision, I followed a clear, coherent research plan from the very start. The reality was quite different. Having completed *The Combat Soldier* in 2012 (published the following year), I fully intended to return to the topic of warfare and the armed forces but only after I had completed a long-contemplated project on social theory and on the question of social change, in particular. In 2004, I had published a book on social theory which had advocated a 'hermeneutic', 'interactionist' and, ultimately, Durkheimian sociology against various individualist, idealist and realist currents in contemporary sociological thinking. My 2004 theory book raised an obvious question: how is it possible to explain long-range historical trends without recourse to the very underlying structural factors which I had explicitly denied in *The Structure of Social Theory*? It seems to me an interesting problem and one which I began to return to in 2012 and early 2013. As part of this work, I eventually published an article on the work of Gabriel Tarde as an early articulation of my thoughts on social change.

However, in the spring of 2013, it became clear that the British Army was reorganizing itself quite radically following the Iraq and Afghanistan interventions; it was re-investing in the division, a latterly neglected formation. It also became obvious that my own contacts in the British Army were particularly good at that time. It became apparent that I should reverse the order of the projects and commit myself to the study of the army division, not least because if I waited at least three years until after the completion of the projected monograph on social change, it would be so much more difficult to re-establish the relations on which good ethnography relies. Consequently, relegating the social theory project, I chose to study the division, and specifically the divisional headquarters, with the encouragement of Hew Strachan.

By the summer of 2013, then, I had a topic. However, although I knew I was interested in the divisional headquarters, I had no real concept of what I wanted to study. Indeed, embarrassingly, it took me a year to determine that the project was even about command at all. I now look on my obtuseness with some amazement; what are military headquarters, after all, but machines for command? It seemed remarkable that it had taken me so long to understand that the project was about command. It took me many further months to develop a concept of collective command, which is the central argument of this monograph. Once I had a clear concept, the research fell rapidly into place, although there was a great deal of work to do in order to refine the theory and to collate sufficient evidence to make my claims remotely plausible – against some pretty well-founded objections from professional soldiers and scholars. The book's genesis was rather like a confused counter-insurgency operation than a grand Napoleonic campaign, then. I had no clue what I was doing at the beginning and only developed a clear concept of my objective retrospectively, after much struggle and many mistakes. This book emerged through a very messy, even confused, iterative process, eventually crystallizing into an account of military transformation which is, I hope, clear and interesting, even if readers disagree with the argument.

It was in the course of developing the project and, specifically, the argument for the rise of a command collective that the evident parallels with my previous works on the armed forces became clear. Indeed, the parallels with *The Combat Soldier* were entirely accidental but, although they potentially supported my analysis, somewhat disturbing to me when they became apparent. It is, perhaps, true that scholars eventually keep making the same argument over and over again. As my work on divisional command proceeded, it became clear that I was unwittingly writing a trilogy about contemporary military transformation. This trilogy started with my first volume on the armed forces, *The Transformation of Europe's Armed Forces*, published in 2011, followed by *The Combat Soldier* and to be completed by this current volume, *Command*. The central themes of this trilogy and each of its constituent volumes are professionalization and the transformation of Western armed forces in the twenty-first century. Each book attempts to highlight the distinctiveness of Western forces today in contrast to the previous century.

Command is plainly concerned with warfare and the armed forces. However, while the book tries to explore the lifeworld of command in ethnographic detail, it is obvious that the work is concerned with much more than military command. It is concerned with organizational and social transformation much more widely, with the military taken as a focus of analysis. Indeed, in the course of completing the book, the question of command and leadership became more salient than I could ever have imagined when I started work on it. In the last decade, the West has descended into an ever-deepening crisis. Economically, Western Europe and the United States have yet to recover from the banking collapse of 2008; debt repayments continue and, in most countries, the economy has not yet returned to pre-crash levels. At the same time, inequalities between the richest and the poorest have widened to generate increasing popular resentment against elites, generally. The economic crisis has been compounded by increasing strain over immigration, which has affected Western populations differentially. Whether legal or not, this immigration has ignited intense reactions. Finally, the campaigns in Afghanistan and especially Iraq, which are widely presumed to have been failures, have compounded the alienation, not least because in Europe the current immigration crisis is a direct result of Western policy towards Iraq, Syria and Libya. Political leaders are seen to have failed to protect European citizens from unsustainable waves of immigrants. This multifarious crisis has encouraged the resurgence of extremist political views, especially – but not only – on the right. In Europe, far-right groups, like Marine Le Pen's *Front Nationale* and *Alternative für Deutschland*, have gained significant electoral support. In the United States, the irresistible rise of Donald Trump reflects the same frustration, fear and resentment.

The West is suffering a series of multiple shocks of an order which may perhaps eventually match the Thirty Years War, the end of the *Ancien Régime* in the late eighteenth century or the Depression of the 1930s. The West is, then, afflicted by a genuine crisis which is not internal to the political system. However, although the political system and especially the current model of political authority and leadership have not caused this crisis, they have played a contributing role. Specifically, the crisis has been exacerbated by popular frustrations at the perceived failures of political leaders to listen to ordinary people and to address their concerns about the economy and migration. This frustration was demonstrated palpably in the United Kingdom when, on 23 June 2016, the EU Referendum was held. On that day, 52 per cent of those who voted chose to leave the EU. In fact, in England, the proportion of those voting out was far higher. In Boston, Lincolnshire, for instance, 75 per cent of the electorate voted against the EU; barring London and a few metropolitan areas, England overwhelmingly demanded Brexit. Although predicted by some of the polls, the result – especially its scale – shocked the British political establishment and, indeed, many public and private institutions in the United Kingdom which were committed to Europe.

The concerns of those who voted out were real but the rhetoric which surrounded the Brexit campaign was instructive. A loathsome yet critical figure here was Nigel Farage, who, amid a series of lies and distortions both about the EU and also what Brexit would achieve, made a very important claim: 'We want our country back'. In stark contrast to the Remainers' anodyne campaign, the phrase brilliantly evoked the popular mood. For Farage, an exit from the EU constituted a reaffirmation of traditional national, Parliamentary sovereignty, in which the United Kingdom once again had total authority to make and enforce its own laws and policies. Farage rejected globalization and the unelected elites located in multinational corporations, and especially in Brussels, who manage and promote it. Politically, Farage wanted a return to an ideal of twentieth- or even nineteenth-century democracy.

On 8 November 2016, in an almost unprecedented act, the US elected Donald Trump, a billionaire businessman, to the presidency. There were evident affinities between his election and Brexit. His rise has been predicated on the apparent failure of the Washington system to protect normal working Americans from the economic and migratory depredations of globalization. Trump promised to re-assert American political sovereignty, cleansing it of the foreign influences which have putatively infected and corrupted it: 'to make America great again'. The connection between the two plebiscites was widely noted. Indeed, on 24 August 2016, Nigel Farage gave a speech at a presidential rally for Trump in which he drew an immediate parallel between Brexit and the Trump election: 'We did it – we made June 23 our independence day when we smashed the establishment. We reached those people who have never voted in their lives but believed they could take back control of their country, take back control of their borders, and get back their pride and self-respect'. He advocated that Trump's supporters form a 'people's army' and do the same in the United States. Trump responded: 'On June 23, the people of Britain voted to declare their independence – which is what we're also looking to do, folks – from their international government'. Populist politicians across the West are increasingly envisioning a return to a political past, when national authority was invested in an elected representative body.

The dislocations, which have been precipitated by globalization, have to be recognized. For many, especially those at the lower end of the socio-economic scale, they have been very serious. Moreover, many of the criticisms of national government articulated by Farage and Trump are valid. Indeed, some of Farage's concerns about the EU are well-founded. The EU has failed to manage the economic crisis since 2008; much of southern Europe is still in a desperate condition, with conditions seen to have been imposed by Germany. It has also failed to manage the current immigration crisis. The Commission is inefficient and has been involved in an unfortunate level of corruption. Confronting a crisis it was never constructed to face, the EU has failed to manage the situation. However, the proposal of Farage and Trump that history can be underdone and that it is possible to return to a previous and apparently more comforting political form is deluded and dangerous. It is incorrect to believe that the EU is a simply supranational organization whose purpose has been to rob properly independent nation-states of their sovereignty. Rather, the EU has evolved as a complex, multi-layered political structure in response to the needs and wishes of its member states themselves, to comprise of inter-governmental, supranational and regional levels. Precisely because the EU has become so central to each of the member states, it is not always easy to discern where domestic state institutions end, especially in foreign and home offices, and where the EU begins.

Sovereignty, and therefore political power and authority, has become highly complex and diffuse in twenty-first-century Europe – and in the international order more widely. The international system is no longer Newtonian, consisting of only a few elements whose causal interrelations are relatively simple and predictable. The EU and the global order itself have become a quantum political reality. They are infuriating as such. Yet, while sovereignty has been shared and political decision-making diffused outwards across borders, it does not represent the end of the nation-state or the end of national sovereignty. Rather, national sovereignty is no longer as absolute as it once was. It has been relativized, distributed and shared. Even within individual nation-states, a disaggregation of power is observable as government and individual departments operate through new configurations and alliances.

It is at this point that the wider relevance of this study of military command and especially a theory of collective command might become relevant. The army division is, in comparison to the nation-state or the EU, only a very small and simple organization. However, like those organizations, the process of globalization has forced a radical reconfiguration of its structure. In response to this new organizational structure and the new operations in which the division has emerged, a new and highly professionalized practice of command has begun to be institutionalized, which I have called 'collective command'; commanders have shared decision-making authority, integrating subordinates, staff and partners into the process of leadership. The appearance of collective command in the division seems to be suggestive. In particular, just as command has been distributed in an army division, so may political power be in the process of dispersion in the twenty-first-century state. The EU represents precisely this disaggregation and redistribution of authority and power. Even more than Foucault knew, power is becoming capillary, running along a complex arterial system of multiple interconnections. Sovereignty is shared; in order to exercise independent national sovereignty, cooperation with other states is required. Paradoxically, to maximize national sovereignty, it is increasingly necessary to share it.

Accordingly, although the likes of Farage and Trump exaggerate the pristineness of twentieth-century sovereignty, political leaders are certainly no longer in control of government in the way they once were. They must interact, collaborate and cooperate with other leaders internationally and increasingly transnationally in order to achieve their political goals. They must form partnerships and networks. In this way, although their jobs are quite different, there is a similarity between today's political leaders and their generals. Successful political leaders often have to operate with partners and allies, tying intricate transnational systems together. They must be more adept at collaboration, cooperation and diplomacy. This certainly means that they cannot just stop immigration or the economic crisis – if they ever could. However, this new paradigm of political leadership does not represent the collapse of representative democracy – although it complicates it dramatically. It certainly cannot be cured by a return to the past. States can disengage from each other to reaggregate their putatively pristine power only at great cost, as the UK discovered as it negotiated Brexit. Political leaders, more than ever, need to be able to construct alliances and teams, coordinating agents, partners and proxies not only in their own states but in others. Political power has become collective, dispersed and distributed.

Farage and Trump offer a quite different vision of leadership as a solution to the crisis of globalization. In line with their return to an apparently simpler past, these individuals promote an atavistic ideal of leadership. In particular, although Farage has recurrently resigned when threatened with any role involving political responsibility, they advocate a millenarian image of politics which involves the appearance of a pure political leader, untainted by the establishment and political party. They see the solution to the complexity of global politics in the personality of an individual saviour, mobilizing ethno-nationalist resentments. In his narcissism, Donald Trump seems to believe that he represents the incarnation of political – and perhaps cultural – purity, capable of independently redeeming America from the forces of globalization. The simplicity of the political message and the security it promises are evidently attractive to many people.

Yet, it may be an illusion. The age of the individual leader, to use Yves Cohen's word, seems to be over. The complexity of today's world system may require a more subtle model of leadership, especially if democracy is to be preserved. In the west, heroic, individual leaders seem to be less helpful. Indeed, messianic leaders of this kind might be regarded with deep suspicion. Rather, the intricate interdependencies between democratic states recommend a more modest and collaborative politician. International order demands professional and competent leaders, capable of building consensus and coordinating alliances and teams, deferring and disseminating authority to deputies and subordinates. It may require politicians who are capable of, what Max Weber called, the 'strong and slow boring of hard boards' together. It is here that the analysis of divisional commanders, perhaps, becomes illustrative. For all their allure, politics today may not require the egotistical charisma of the most famous twentieth-century generals, like Matt Ridgway, Bernard Montgomery or Erwin Rommel. It may prefer the apparently more mundane, professional skills of defining a mission with precision and, then, building a command team to accomplish it. The best leaders today may not be heroes or saviours but teachers, coaches and team players. Command collectives, not individualists, may be needed. This book tries to tell the story of the emergence of a new kind of leadership for the twenty-first century.

ACKNOWLEDGEMENTS

It is probably appropriate and perhaps necessary that authors are held solely responsible for their work – and receive the credit for it. Even the most dedicated writer would find motivation difficult if no personal recognition was to be gained from the Sisyphean effort of writing. Yet, one does not need to be a sociologist to know that, in the end, a work of any length is a collaborative rather than individual effort. There is no doubt that this book could never have been written without the assistance, guidance and support of numerous individuals, to each one of which I am deeply indebted.

I started the research for this book in the spring of 2013, while I was a Visiting Fellow at All Souls College. It is, therefore, predictable that Hew Strachan, who held the Chichele Chair in the History of Warfare at that time, played a crucial role in encouraging me to take on a study of the divisional headquarters, even though I had absolutely no clue of where it would lead. Yet, our discussions in his rooms, when he persuaded me it was both viable and potentially relevant, were the catalyst for this project.

Once I began the project, I quickly became reliant upon the British Army, who supported the project and facilitated access throughout, even though they were bemused at how long it could take to write a book. I am grateful to Charles Heath-Saunders at the Ministry of the Defence for managing the contract. It is important to state a formal disclaimer: UK MOD review of this work has been undertaken for security purposes only and should not be construed as endorsement.

In the British Army itself, the project could not have been started without the initial support of the Chief of the General Staff, General Sir Nick Carter, and the subsequent extraordinary hospitality of the 3 UK Division. It says a lot about the professional competence and personal confidence of the successive commanders of this division, James Cowan, Patrick Sanders and Nick Borton, that they allowed me to wander around their command, wasting their own and their staff's time, at will. I am profoundly grateful to each of them. Their staff were themselves universally accommodating and engaging throughout the project and I enjoyed my time with them immensely. I am especially thankful to Zac Stenning, Gerry Ewart-Brookes, Jo Butterfill, Andrew Stewart, James Bowder, Philip Clark, Nick MacGinlay, Mark Croft, Laurence Roche, Toby Till, Jeremy Pughe-Morgan, Alex Nixon, Nick Mackenzie, Annabel Felton, Tom Parsons, Austin Pearce, Alistair Aitken and Karl Ford. Giles Hill and Charles Collins were extremely generous with their time at 1 UK Division.

The project also involved research trips to some important American and French divisions. These could not have occurred without the generosity of a number of individuals. I would not have been able to visit 82nd Airborne Division without the help of Giles Hill, in particular, and Richard Clarke, James Learmont, Catherine Wilkinson, and Brendan Fox; I am grateful to each of them. Doug Chalmers was hugely helpful in allowing me to visit III Corps in Fort Hood; I am also grateful to him and to Helen for some Texan hospitality and a memorable, if occasionally disturbing, fishing trip with his friend, Bubba. Thierry Lion and Stephane Vasseur facilitated my visit to Etat Major de Force 1 in Besancon. I would not have been able to visit 1st Marine Division without the support of Dan O'Donoghue, Al Litster, Martin Twist and Durward 'Woody' Page; I am particularly grateful to the latter for also organizing a brief surf at Carlsbad – where I caught a still-remembered wave. It was an honour to talk to James Mattis, Richard Natonski, Paul Kennedy, Dan O'Donoghue and Clarke Lethin, who were all very patient with their time. Mungo Melvin's advice was invaluable, especially on Operation Granby.

It will be no surprise that I relied on a number of academic colleagues to help me with this project. Lawrence Freedman, Jonathan Boff, Huw Bennett, Niall Barr, Douglas Delaney, Eric Bergerud, Douglas Porch and Dennis Showalter all provided some very wise counsel in each of their areas of expertise, recommending literature and, in some cases, sending me their work. I could not have done without their advice. There is no possibility that I would have been able to interview James Mattis or Rupert Smith without the help of Frank Hoffman and Mirjam Grandia Mantas.

I am grateful to a number of archives, including the National Archive, Kew; NARA, Washington, DC; the Army Heritage and Education Centre, Carlisle, PA; Bayerisches Hauptsstaatarchiv, Abteilung Kriegsarchiv, Munich; Service Historique de la Défence, Chateau Vincennes, Paris; the US Marine Historical Division, Quantico; the Imperial War Museum Library, London; and the Joint Services Command and Staff College Library, Shrivenham. I hope that these invaluable resources will remain free and accessible to public usage. I am especially grateful to Fred Allison and Annette Ammerman at Quantico and to Sue Barrett and Aaron Cripps at Shrivenham, who were incredibly patient with my irritating requests.

The project could not have been completed without significant financial support from the Economic and Social Research Council, which funded the project, 'The Post-Heroic General: military command in the 21st century', ES/N007859/1; indeed, they have supported every previous project in which I have been involved. Academics may like to complain about the ESRC but my entire research career has been dependent on their patronage, which I have always found to be faultless.

During the course of this project, I moved from Exeter University to Warwick University to take up the post of Chair in War Studies. I spent nineteen very happy years at Exeter and I made some very good friends at that institution. In terms of this project, I am particularly grateful to Hannah Pike, Rosamund Davies, Claire Packman and Paul Woolnough in supporting my application to the ESRC; I remain guilty about leaving for Warwick, having won the award. My move to Warwick coincided with a period of study leave for this grant and, although I have been in the privileged position of being employed by Warwick but not actually starting to teach for the university, I have found my new department to be extremely collegial; it has been a privilege to get to know some impressive new colleagues. I am extremely grateful to the support of Nick Vaughan Williams, Jackie Smith, Jade Perkins, Jill Pavey and Gary Fisher. Indeed, I could not have put on the conference 'Command in the 21st Century' in September 2017 without the assistance of Jackie Smith, Jade Perkins and Jill Pavey.

The quality of a piece of prose is normally determined by the number of revisions between the first and final drafts. This process can be assisted by the intervention of sympathetic but critical readers. I could not have been better served by some good friends; Christopher Dandeker, Randall Collins and Andrew Dorman all read the manuscript and provided excellent and detailed feedback on it. I am especially grateful to Patrick Bury here, whose transition from professional soldier and combat veteran to scholar I have been lucky enough to oversee. He provided perceptive comments on the manuscript, while affirming the potential value of the project at a moment when I was troubled by doubts.

I presented some of the material from the book and especially from Chapter 12 in a number of seminars over the last twelve months. Each one of these was hugely helpful in refining my argument and suggesting that there might be a wider interest in the topic. The following all organized valuable seminars for me to present my work: Sinisa Malesevic at University College Dublin; Jeffrey Alexander, Philip Smith, their postgraduate seminar series at the Center for Cultural Sociology and Scott Boorman at Yale; Huw Bennett at Cardiff; Megan Mackenzie and Colin White at Sydney; Daniel Marston at the Australian National University; Paul Muldoon at Monash, Pascal Vennesson at Nanyang Technical University, Singapore; and Charles Turner at Warwick. I am grateful to them and the audiences at those talks. I must also thank Michael Williams, Joshua Judd and Jacqui McIver, Rob and Hils Thomson, Paula and Justin Breheny and Mark and Sue Breheny for putting me up while I was giving some of these talks.

Finally, as I completed this book, I became unwell. My family helped me recover. I was also deeply touched by the care of some good friends: Jim Pyne, Charles Lloyd, Tim Edmunds, Christopher Dandeker, Rob Johnson, Alex Ellis, Tim Gibbons, Euan Ambrose, Sophie Otton and Simon Thompson.

1 COMMAND IN THE TWENTY-FIRST CENTURY

In the notes of his conversations with Philip Stanhope on 2 November 1831, the Duke of Wellington gave his assessment of Napoleon Bonaparte: 'I used to say of him that his presence on the field made the difference of forty thousand men'.[1] Later, in 1836, he qualified this equation: 'It is very true that I have said that I considered Napoleon's presence in the field equal to 40,000 men in the balance. This is a very loose way of talking; but the idea is a very different one from that of his presence at a battle being equal to a reinforcement of 40,000 men'.[2] Napoleon was not worth a corps of soldiers; rather, his value as a commander lay in the intellectual and moral influence he exerted over his armies. Wellington famously argued that the principle skill of a commander lay in the art of deduction: 'All the business of war, and indeed all the business of life, is to endeavour to find out what you don't know by what you do; that's what I called "guessing what was at the other side of the hill"'.[3] Napoleon, perhaps more than any other commander of his age, possessed an extraordinary ability to calculate these probabilities and to predict his enemies' actions. In assessing the military significance of Napoleon, Wellington was, of course, making a wider point about the importance of command in

[1] Philip Stanhope, *Notes of Conversations with the Duke of Wellington*, 2 November 1831 (New York: Longmans Green and Co, 1888), 9.
[2] Ibid., 18 September 1836, 81.
[3] Louis J. Jennings (ed.), *The Croker Papers: The Correspondence and Diaries of the Late Right Honourable John Wilson Croker, LL.Dm F.R.S, Secretary of the Admiralty from 1809 to 1830*, Vol. III (1884), 276.

war. A commander's ability to anticipate, to organize and to motivate was vital to the conduct of war. The outcome of battles and campaigns depended upon it.

Carl von Clausewitz invested command with equal significance. Command is a – perhaps, *the* – major theme of *On War*; the work seems primarily to have been written as a handbook of strategy for future commanders-in-chief. Indeed, while Clausewitz certainly also had Frederick the Great in mind, the third chapter of the first book, 'On Military Genius', is a thinly veiled encomium to Napoleon, 'the God of War himself'.[4] It identifies some of characteristics required of a commander in the age of modern war, which Napoleon fully embodied. While the politician concentrated on policy and, therefore, required highly developed powers of reason, the general operated in the arena of probability and chance. To survive in this opaque and confusing domain, a commander required two basic qualities: 'If the mind is to emerge unscathed from this relentless struggle with the unforeseen, two qualities are indispensable: *first, an intellect that, even in the darkest hour, retains some glimmerings of inner light which leads to the truth; and second, the courage to follow this faint light wherever it may lead.* The first of these qualities is described by the French term, *coup d'oeil*, the second is determination'.[5] Wellington associated command with vision. It is noticeable that light is recurrently drawn upon by Clausewitz as a metaphor of command. Commanders illuminate the darkness and, in doing so, they light the way for their soldiers; they act as beacons in two senses. It is obvious from Clausewitz's prose that he regarded command as indispensable to military operations. Military endeavours required a commander who identified clear and achievable goals, anticipated the difficulties and frictions they involved and, despite inevitable setbacks, was able to inspire the confidence of the troops.

Command Crisis

Wellington and Clausewitz speak from a now-distant and foreign era. Much of what they wrote has become obsolete in all but historical

---

[4] Carl von Clausewitz, *On War*, translated by Michael Howard and Peter Paret (Princeton, NJ: Princeton University Press, 1984), 583.
[5] Ibid., 102.

terms. Clausewitz's comments on 'attacks on swamps, flooded areas and forests', for instance, are of little contemporary relevance. Yet, despite all the prodigious advances in military technology and the transformation of warfare itself, the observations of Clausewitz and Wellington about command remain as valid as ever. Even in the twenty-first century, military command remains of paramount importance. Battlefield success still relies upon generalship. Indeed, many of the fundamental skills of command remain the same as they were in the Napoleonic era. Above all, penetrating the fog of battle, commanders still need to be able to identify clear and achievable objectives and to calculate the probability of success. Command remains critical to military operations and combat effectiveness today.

Indeed, the recent campaigns in Iraq and Afghanistan have demonstrated only the enduring importance of command to military operations. In response to the disappointments of those campaigns and proving the continuing validity of Wellington's and Clausewitz's interventions, command has been the object of intense scrutiny over the last fifteen years, in both America and Europe. Concern, even calumny, about the failures of command has been frequent and strident. Of course, much of the debate has focused exclusively on civilian leadership. The Bush and Obama administrations have been roundly criticized for their strategic incompetence in their respective 'Wars on Terror'; Bush foolishly invaded Iraq, fomenting a sectarian civil war which has de-stabilized the Middle East,[6] while Obama precipitately withdrew from the theatre, facilitating the rise of ISIS and the collapse of Syria.[7] Yet, military command and individual generals have themselves been the object of widespread and deep public concern. For many commentators, military command has demonstrably and specifically failed in the last decade. Generals stand accused. In an increasingly multi-polar and mediatized world, they have been unable to identify or to execute coherent strategies. They have failed to display precisely the qualities which Wellington and Clausewitz most prized in a general. Rather than illuminating the darkness, they seem to have been as confused by recent conflicts as their political masters.

---

[6] Thomas Ricks, *Fiasco: the American Adventure in Iraq* (London: Penguin, 2006).
[7] David Kilcullen, *Blood Year: Islamic State and the Failures of the War on Terror* (London: Hurst, 2016).

These criticisms have predictably been most pronounced in the United States, where an entire genre has developed criticizing generalship.[8] This literature is far too voluminous to consider at any length. However, the work of Tom Ricks exemplifies many of the criticisms. As a leading war correspondent and military journalist, Ricks has been particularly excised by the problem of military command itself – and its failings. His monograph on command, *The Generals*, begins with a pointed dedication, 'For those who died following poor leaders', and an epigraph, 'There are no bad soldiers, only bad generals'. The implication is very clear. The 'fiasco' in Iraq could not be blamed on Bush and Washington alone; America's generals were culpable too. Consequently, Ricks examines American generalship from the Second World War to identify individual failings and recurrent structural problems. Thus, Tommy Franks, Ricardo Sanchez and George Casey are subjected to very severe personal admonition.[9] Yet, the malady is deeper. For Ricks, America's command problems have constituted a profound corruption of the system which General George Marshall had implemented in the Second World War. Crucially, although a number of US officers have been relieved from duty in the course of the post-9/11 wars in Iraq

---

[8] E.g., Seymour Hersch, *Chain of Command: the road from 9/11 to Abu Ghraib* (London: HarperCollins, 2009); Bob Woodward, *Plan of Attack* (London: Pocket Books, 2004); Bob Woodward, *Bush at War* (London: Pocket Books, 2003); Bob Woodward, *State of Denial* (London: Pocket Books, 2006); Tom Ricks, *The Gamble* (London: Penguin, 2009); Fred Kaplan, 'Challenging Generals', in Robert Taylor, William Rosenbach and Erik Rosenbach (eds), *Military Leadership* (Boulder, CO: Westview, 2008); Greg Jaffe, *The Fourth Star: four generals and the epic struggle for the future of the US Army* (New York: Three Rivers Press, 2009); Linda Robinson, *Tell Me How This Ends: General David Petraeus and the Search for a Way out of Iraq* (New York: Public Affairs, 2008); Fred Kaplan, *The Insurgents: David Petraeus and the Plot to Change the American Way of War* (London: Simon and Schuster, 2014). Dan Bolger, *Why We Lost: a general's inside account of Iraq and Afghanistan* (New York: First Mariner Books, 2015); Paul Yingling, 'A Failure in Generalship', in Robert Taylor, William Rosenbach and Erik Rosenbach (eds), *Military Leadership* (Boulder, CO: Westview, 2008): Harry Laver and Jeffry Matthews (eds), *The Art of Command* (Lexington, KY: University of Kentucky Press, 2008); Eliot Cohen, *Supreme Command* (London: Simon and Schuster, 2002); Kimberley Kagan, *The Eye of Command* (Ann Arbor, MI: University of Michigan Press, 2006); Eliot Cohen and John Gooch, *Military Misfortunes; the anatomy of failure in war* (New York: Vintage, 1991); Andrew Bacevich, *The New American Militarism: how Americans are seduced by war* (Oxford: Oxford University Press, 2013); Andrew Bacevich, *Washington Rules: America's path to power* (New York: Metropolitan Books, 2010).

[9] Ricks, *The Generals: American military command from World War II to today* (London: Penguin, 2012), 413.

and Afghanistan, in most cases, according to Ricks, these reliefs have been primarily political, initiated and enacted not from within the military but by civilian leaders and the White House itself. There has been only one exception. During 1st Marine Division's advance on Baghdad, James Mattis, the divisional commander, relieved one of his Regimental Combat Team commanders. Precisely because it was so unusual, the sacking 'made page-one news'.[10] However, Ricks claims that for the most part commanders have not been relieved because the armed forces have been too weak, self-interested or cowardly to remove their own officers. The Service Chiefs have devolved themselves from their professional responsibilities with disastrous results.

The command crisis in America may be the most internationally prominent because of the country's superpower status. Yet, it is far from unique. On the contrary, equivalent discussions are evident in Europe and no more so than in the United Kingdom. Indeed, British concerns about military command have reached a level of intensity in the last decade which may even have exceeded American interventions. There are some evident reasons for this. Britain's armed forces have not only been committed to complex expeditionary counter-insurgencies, with all their attendant ambiguities and contradictions, but they have been deployed in support of an American-led mission. As a medium-sized military power and America's closest ally, the United Kingdom felt impelled to contribute to costly foreign missions in Iraq and Afghanistan which were not in the immediate national interest. Caught between alliance obligations and public scepticism, the United Kingdom's campaigns in Afghanistan and Iraq have been fraught with controversy from the very start. Public concerns about the quality of military leadership have been radically compounded. Over the last decade numerous publications have appeared published by leading scholars, journalists and officers criticizing British commanders.[11]

---

[10] Ibid., 405.

[11] E.g., Tim Edmunds and Anthony Forster, 'Out of Step: the case for change in the British armed forces', *Demos* 2007; Paul Cornish and Andrew Dorman, 'Blair's wars and Brown's budgets: from Strategic Defence Review to strategic decay in less than a decade', *International Affairs* 85 (2) March 2009: 247–61; Paul Cornish and Andrew Dorman, 'National defence in the age of austerity', *International Affairs* 85(4) July 2009: 733–5; Hew Strachan, *The Direction of War: contemporary strategy in historical perspective* (Cambridge: Cambridge University Press, 2013); Richard North, *Ministry of Defeat* (London: Continuum, 2009); James Fergusson, *One million bullets* (London: Bantam, 2008); Stephen Grey, *Operation Snakebite* (London: Penguin,

The public disquiet about political and military leadership, of course, reached its apogee in Britain on 6 July 2016 with the long-awaited publication of the Chilcot Inquiry into the Iraq War. The inquiry had sat for seven years, longer than the military intervention itself, to produce a 2.6-million-word report. It is the most comprehensive statement of command failure yet to be produced. The report admonished Tony Blair for rashly committing the United Kingdom to follow the US into Iraq before properly assessing the necessity for military action and its likely outcome. Yet, military commanders were also reprimanded for their failure to respond to the changing situation in Basra, to communicate the dangers to their political leaders and for committing themselves to a simultaneous campaign in Helmand in breach of defence planning guidelines. For instance, Air Chief Marshall Jock Stirrup, the Chief of the Defense Staff, in the crucial

2009); *The Economist*, 'Losing Their Way', 31 January 2009, www.economist.com/node/13022177; *The Times*, 'The Officers' Mess', 9 June 2010, 2; David Betz and Anthony Cormack, 'Iraq, Afghanistan and British strategy', *Orbis*, Spring 2009, 319–36; Theo Farrell and Stuart Gordon, 'COIN Machine: the British military in Afghanistan', *RUSI Journal* 154(3) 2009: 18–25; Peter Mansoor, 'The British Army and the Lessons of the Iraq War', *British Army Review* 147, Summer 2009: 11–15; Daniel Marston, ' "Smug and Complacent?" Operation TELIC: the need for critical analysis', *British Army Review* 147, Summer 2009: 16–23; Andrew Mackay and Steve Tatham, 'Behavioural Conflict: from general to strategic corporal, complexity, adaptation and influence', *The Shrivenham Papers*, 9 December 2009, 31; Paul Newton, Paul Colley and Andrew Sharpe, 'Reclaiming the Art of British Strategic Thinking', *RUSI Journal*, February/March 155(1) 2010: 47; Public Administration Committee, *Who Does UK National Strategy?*, www.publications.parliament.uk/pa/cm201011/cmselect/cmpubadm/435/43502.htm; Anthony King, 'Military Command in the Last Decade', *International Affairs* 87(2) 2011, 377–96; Anthony King, 'Understanding Helmand: British military campaign in Afghanistan', *International Affairs* 86(2) 2010: 311–32; Lawrence Freedman, *Strategy* (Oxford: Oxford University Press, 2015); Tim Bird and Alex Marshall, *Afghanistan: how the west lost its way* (New Haven, CT: Yale University Press, 2011); Robert Egnell and David Ucko, *Counter-Insurgency in Crisis* (New York: Columbia University Press, 2015); Jonathan Bailey, Richard Iron and Hew Strachan, *British Generals in Blair's Wars* (Farnham: Ashgate, 2013); Christopher Elliott, *High Command: British military leadership in the Iraq and Afghanistan wars* (London: Hurst, 2015); Sons of the Iron Lady, 'Donkeys led by Lions', *British Army Review* 150, 55–8. www.wapentakes.co.uk/donkeys.pdf; Frank Ledwidge, *Losing Small Wars: British military failure in Iraq and Afghanistan* (New Haven, CT: Yale University Press, 2011); Ben Barry, *Harsh Lesson: Iraq, Afghanistan and the changing character of war* (London: IISS, 2017); John Kiszely, *Anatomy of a Campaign: the British fiasco in Norway 1940* (Cambridge: Cambridge University Press, 2017).

period between 2006 and 2010,[12] was singled out for special censure by the Chilcot Inquiry.[13] He recommended an option of drawdown in Basra in 2006, unaware that a British withdrawal would have disastrous consequences for the city and severe reputational consequences with American allies: 'ACM Stirrup's proposed remedy of continued drawdown and managing public opinion did not mitigate the risk of strategic failure he described'.[14] The public criticism of a senior British officer was almost unprecedented.

Although its predicament may have been more accentuated than most, the United Kingdom is by no means alone in Europe in having suffered a command crisis in the last decade. Similar disquiet has been evident in the Netherlands,[15] Denmark,[16] France[17] and Germany.[18]

Western command is suffering a legitimation crisis, then; indeed, for some, generalship has palpably failed. However, despite all the often bitter complaints about generals over the last fifteen years, not one commentator, whether civilian, academic or military, has questioned the enduring relevance of military command. On the contrary, the central presumption underlying all these interventions is not that military command has become irrelevant in the twenty-first century but, on the contrary, that command remains as indispensable to military effectiveness as it ever was. The condemnation of a legion of failures does not in any way suggest that generalship is obsolete today. On the contrary, command is regarded as vital to military success in the twenty-first century as it was in the Napoleonic wars. Generals have been calumniated not because their utility is now questioned but, on the

---

[12] Tony Zinni and Tony Koltz, *Leading the Charge: leadership lessons from the battlefield to the boardroom* (London: Palgrave Macmillan, 2009), 51.

[13] www.iraqinquiry.org.uk/media/247921/the-report-of-the-iraq-inquiry_executive-summary.pdf, 106.

[14] www.iraqinquiry.org.uk/media/247921/the-report-of-the-iraq-inquiry_executive-summary.pdf, 105.

[15] Mirjam Grandia Mantas, *Deadly Embrace: the Decision Paths to Uruzgan and Helmand* (Doctoral Dissertation, University of Leiden, 2015), 181.

[16] www.theguardian.com/film/2010/jun/03/armadillo-danish-documentary-afghanistan.

[17] Pascal Vennesson, 'Cohesion and Misconduct: The French Army and the Mahé Affair', in Anthony King (ed.), *Frontline: combat and cohesion in the twenty-first century* (Oxford: Oxford University Press, 2015).

[18] www.spiegel.de/international/germany/kunduz-bombing-affair-german-colonel-wanted-to-destroy-insurgents-a-669444.html.

contrary, because they have failed to fulfil their duty. Generals have been criticized precisely because they have lacked the acuity advocated by Wellington and Clausewitz. Even today, command retains the primacy with which Wellington and Clausewitz invested it in the early nineteenth century.

The Transformation of Command

There is little doubt that military commanders have made very considerable mistakes in the last decade. There have been many cases of poor decision-making; a coherent strategy has often been lacking and campaigns have been periodically mismanaged. Yet, while in no way excusing these individual errors, generals have found themselves in an unenviable predicament. Since the turn of the century, generals have confronted distinctively challenging operational and organizational conditions. Indeed, command itself has been undergoing a significant transformation. In many cases, generals, attuned to twentieth-century expectations, have struggled to adapt to the new conditions in which they have been ordered to operate.

Generals may have struggled to command campaigns in Iraq and Afghanistan but senior officers have become increasingly aware of the new challenges they face. Indeed, some generals have suggested that the very practice of command is in transition; in the face of increased operational and organizational complexity, decision-making has begun to evolve. Consequently, alongside the vivid discourses on command failure, a second sub-literature has begun to appear in the last decade on the transformation of military command itself. Tony Zinni's book, *Leading the Charge*, published in 2009, is a highly pertinent example of this emergent genre. Tony Zinni served for forty years in the US Marine Corps, including tours in Vietnam in the late 1960s.[19] He retired as a four-star general, having served as the Commander of US Central Command. As a result of his long military experience, he has been exercised by command failures in the last decade. Significantly, Zinni does not criticize or blame particular civilian or military leaders in his book, nor does he deconstruct the contradictions in Western strategy

---

[19] Tom Clancy with Anthony Zinni, *Battle Ready* (London: Pan, 2005).

or in civil–military relations. Rather, he attributes much of the current crisis to more fundamental organizational problems in leadership itself.

Specifically, Zinni claims that leadership is currently in transition. The practice of generalship has changed and, in many cases, the problems of the last decade have been the result of a failure to respond to these new challenges: 'Virtually all organizations are becoming too complex and involved for single, directive approaches to leading'.[20] Existing command models, derived from the twentieth century, have become increasingly obsolete in the face of new global problems. Precisely because organizations and operations have become more complex and dispersed, traditional, heroic models of leadership, designed for vertically integrated organizations, have become obsolete.

Zinni argues that, if there is to be any improvement in the quality of military command, a new model of 'participatory leadership' is required which actively seeks to engage with and maximize a network of peers and subordinates: 'We no longer build a leadership hierarchy in a cutting edge modern organization. Instead, we build leadership *networks* that make the business of leading institutionalized and multidirectional. Leadership is no longer only vertical, working from the top down. It is distributed, pervasive, invited from all members, and instilled in the culture of successful enterprises'.[21] For Zinni, because of the increasing complexity of operations and the expanding span of command, the armed forces must embrace participatory leadership: 'Leaders who are organizing combat commands, like leaders of organizations everywhere, have realized that our fast-changing world requires new approaches and new thinking'.[22] Team-building is now essential. Zinni maintains that certain leadership characteristics are requisite in the current era. However, 'good character alone is no longer enough to define a good leader'; he defines eleven new characteristics which will allow the new leader to understand the situation and to collaborate with others so that problems can be resolved collectively. For Zinni, command has become a collaborative, joint enterprise.

Zinni's work is certainly significant and it has attracted a wide readership. However, in the English language, General Stanley

---

[20] Tony Zinni and Tony Koltz, *Leading the Charge: leadership lessons from the battlefield to the boardroom* (London: Palgrave Macmillan, 2009), 51.

[21] Ibid., 101–2.

[22] Ibid., 132.

McChrystal has surely made the most important contemporary statement about the changing character of command in the twenty-first century. McChrystal commanded the US Joint Special Operations Command in Iraq from 2003 to 2008 and subsequently commanded NATO's International Security Assistance Force in Afghanistan in 2009–10, before being relieved by Barack Obama in controversial circumstances. McChrystal is widely admired as one of the finest military commanders of the current era. His two recent publications, *My Share of the Task* and *Team of Teams*, document this reformation of command.

Team of Teams is particularly relevant here. It situates McChrystal's personal experience of Joint Special Operations Command in Baghdad in a wider historic context to show that the evolution of this command was consistent with general patterns of organizational transformation in the twenty-first century. In particular, McChrystal claims that the hierarchies which were developed in the twentieth century for industrial warfare have become archaic in the face of hybrid opponents. According to McChrystal, twentieth-century warfare was complicated; it involved the coordination of massive, homogeneous forces. This was administratively demanding – and a mistake could be catastrophic. By contrast, in the twenty-first century, military problems have become 'complex': 'Being *complex* is different from being complicated. Things that are *complicated* have many parts but those parts are joined, one to the next in relatively simple ways ... Complexity, on the other hand, occurs when the number of *interactions* between components increases dramatically – the interdependences that allow viruses and bank runs to spread; this is where things quickly become unpredictable'.[23] The elements of a complex system are heterogeneous, interconnected with each other in multiple ways.

While commanding in Baghdad, McChrystal discovered that the armed forces, which he had known throughout his career, were ill-adapted for complex, multi-dimensional operations. They were configured for mass two-dimensional fights: 'In the course of this fight, we had to unlearn a great deal of what we thought we knew about how war – and the world – worked. We had to tear down familiar organizational structures and rebuild them along completely different lines, swapping our sturdy architecture for organic fluidity, because

---

[23] Stanley McChrystal, *Team of Teams* (London: Penguin, 2015), 57.

it was the only way to confront a rising tide of complex threats'.[24] McChrystal had to construct a network to fight one. It was no longer enough simply to be better at mass industrial warfare; a paradigm shift was required in the execution of military operations. The development of this new organizational form required a revision of old hierarchies and allegiances. In particular, McChrystal had to break down the local tribal loyalties in the armed forces and, especially, within the Special Operations Forces community.

The reform of command itself was central to McChrystal's reconfiguration. In place of an imperious individual commander directing operations from above, decision-making had to be devolved outwards and downwards. Echoing Zinni's argument about leadership, McChrystal became not so much the pinnacle of an organizational hierarchy but rather a node at the centre of a network. Consequently, McChrystal recognized that, even as a commander, he could not know everything. On the contrary, he emphasized the importance of 'shared consciousness', which 'helped us understand and react to the inter-dependence of the battlefield'.[25]

> Being woken to make life-or-death decisions confirmed my role as a leader, and made me feel important and needed – something most managers yearn for. But it was not long before I began to question my value to the process. Unless I had been tracking the target the previous night, I would usually know only what officer told me that morning … My inclusion was a rubber stamp that slowed the process, and sometimes caused us to miss fleeting opportunities.[26]

Indeed, traditional models of leadership had become obsolete and obstructive: 'The heroic "hands-on" leader whose personal competence and force of will dominated battlefields and boardrooms for generations had been overwhelmed by accelerating speed, swelling complexity, and interdependence'.[27] McChrystal empowered commanders at the local level to prosecute missions on the basis of shared understanding and collective initiative.

---

[24] Ibid., 20.
[25] Ibid., 202.
[26] Ibid.
[27] Ibid., 225.

Substantially because of McChrystal's writings, the question of command reform is perhaps most advanced in the United States. Yet, similar discussions are observable elsewhere. There have been a number of publications in the United Kingdom by retired generals which echo the remarks of Zinni and McChrystal. General Lord David Richards has become a prominent figure here. Richards was, perhaps, the foremost officer of his generation, commanding forces in East Timor, Sierra Leone and Afghanistan, before going on to be appointed both Chief of the General Staff and Chief of the Defence Staff. On the basis of these wide experiences, like Zinni and McChrystal, Richards has suggested that command today has become 'more complicated' because the commander 'has to deal with a range of actors'; commanders have to manage complex inter-service and inter-agency operations.[28] Consequently, traditional dirigist systems of leadership have become outmoded and Richards did not practice them. Rather, the commander 'has to be an entrepreneurial networker and communicator rather than a dictator'.[29]

Richards is not alone among British generals in believing that the practice of command has changed. General Sir Richard Shirreff, who commanded the Multinational Division South East (Basra) in the scarring period of 2006–7, has affirmed some enduring features of command. He insists that high command is still about setting a personal example and that 'it is up to the commander to decide how he wants to do things, not the staff'.[30] However, he also acknowledges evident differences: 'What has changed is that generalship now requires more than the ability to command and control purely military capabilities'.[31] Since success in war depends on the achievement of unity of purpose with other non-military players, command, according to Sherriff, involves new skills, characteristics and techniques. British discussions of the evolution of command may be somewhat underdeveloped in comparison with America; concepts of teamwork, shared consciousness and interdependence are absent. Yet, the broad parallels are evident.

---

[28] General Sir David Richards, 'The Art of Command in the Twenty-First Century: reflections of three commands', in Julian Lindlay-French and Yves Boyer (eds), *The Oxford Handbook of War* (Oxford: Oxford University Press, 2012), 346, 356.

[29] Ibid., 350. See also See Also General David Richards *Taking Command* (London: Headline, 2014).

[30] General Sir Richard Shirreff, 'Conducting Joint Operations', in Julian Lindlay-French and Yves Boyer (eds), *The Oxford Handbook of War* (Oxford: Oxford University Press, 2012), 382, 383.

[31] Ibid., 384.

It might be argued that, as retired generals, Zinni, McChrystal or Richards have a distorted perspective. Their texts might be read as not entirely reliable self-vindications. Yet, their analysis of the evolution of command has been recently supported by Gary Klein, a more junior officer. He concurs with Zinni and McChrystal that in the face of radical organizational transformation, traditional models of command are becoming obsolete: 'Complex environments require different leadership and decision-making techniques than succeeding in simple or complicated environments'. Crucially, Klein proposes that, 'decision-making researchers in a number of different fields believe that experimentation and collaboration are keys to success in the complex domain'. Instead of prescribing one course of action for their subordinates, effective commanders today have to identify a clear but broad direction of travel to guide followers.

However, Klein is concerned that despite the requirement for a new system of command, military atavism has impeded change:

> It is unlikely that many Army leaders would describe their current leadership environment as a networked phenomenon. Whether it is deliberate or not, the Army's current leadership paradigm and doctrine encourage Soldiers to view leadership through a leader-centric, hierarchical lens. Leaders issue orders to their subordinates and subordinates must express 'loyalty, subordination, [and] respect for superiors.' *Army Leadership*[32] describes leadership using the leader-centric Army leadership requirements model.

Klein recommends thoroughgoing reform: 'To enable collaboration, leaders and staffs must be capable of forming more flat, distributed organizations in addition to traditional hierarchical models'. Closely echoing Zinni, Klein emphasizes the creation of newly empowered followers: 'In the near term, leaders can encourage networked leadership and collaboration by increasing their emphasis on followership. They must educate their subordinates about and demonstrate qualities of good followers'.[33] Effective commanders will train, develop and empower their subordinates to make decisions. His recommendations

---

[32] *ADRP 6-22: Army Leadership* (Washington, DC: Department of the Army, 2012).
[33] Gary Klein, 'Overcoming complexity through collaboration and follower-based leadership', *Small Wars Journal*, 2017, http://smallwarsjournal.com/jrnl/art/overcoming-complexity-through-collaboration-and-follower-based-leadership.

for a more collaborative, devolved system of leadership and decision-making are compatible with the observations of Zinni and McChrystal.[34]

The work of Zinni, McChrystal and Klein suggests that military command is moving rapidly away from 'heroic' individualism, typical of the twentieth century, to a more professionalized, collective practice. It is very noticeable that the emergent lexicon of command today contrasts markedly with traditional definitions of leadership. New concepts like 'shared consciousness', 'collaboration', 'teamwork', 'empowerment' and 'interdependence' all suggest a very significant reform of command. Command may, indeed, be in crisis, as many commentators have argued. However, if Zinni, McChrystal and Klein are right, command may, more significantly, be in transition. The very institution of command seems to have evolved in the last decade so that the fundamentals of decision-making, management and leadership have changed. Generals should certainly be subject to public scrutiny and their poor decisions criticized. Yet, perhaps many of the commentators have themselves failed to appreciate sufficiently the extent of this transformation. Like the generals they reprimand, they too may still presume an obsolescent definition of command.

Command Regimes

Zinni, McChrystal and Klein document the transformation of command in the twenty-first century. They outline the reconfiguration of command hierarchies, as collaboration, collectivism and professionalism have displaced more traditionally directive and centralized practices. Nowhere do these authors employ the term, but it might be argued that their work operates around the concept of two command regimes. A command regime refers to a broadly stable paradigm of leadership when a characteristic practice of decision-making is widely institutionalized by the armed forces. In particular, each of these writers identifies an important transition between command in the twentieth and twenty-first centuries, to whose understanding they want to contribute. Effectively, they are trying to make sense of the shift from one command regime to another.

---

[34] See also Hans Hasselbladh, 'Command and the War Machine', in Karl Yden (ed.), *Directions in Military Organizing* (Stockholm: Förswvarshögskolan, 2005), 39–62.

Their attempt to map this transition is important. However, in positing the historical existence and evolution of command regimes, Zinni, McChrystal and Klein are, in fact, drawing on a much wider literature. A number of scholars have addressed precisely this question of the historical development and transformation of command regimes. Martin van Creveld and John Keegan are particularly pertinent here. They, for instance, seek to explore how the institution of command has changed over a very long historical period from antiquity to the present. They attempt to periodize command, showing how particular regimes of command, involving a demonstrable repertoire of practices, emerge in different eras, primarily in response to operational and organizational problems.

John Keegan, for instance, claims that while command displays some common features, generalship necessarily reflects the cultures in which it arises:

> Commonality of traits and behaviours I certainly see in
> commanders of all periods and places. But even more strongly
> do I perceive that the warfare of any one society may differ
> so sharply from that of another that commonality of trait
> and behaviour in those who direct it is overlaid altogether in
> importance by difference in the purposes they serve and the
> functions they perform.[35]

Reflecting immediate historical conditions, Keegan identifies five types of command: heroic (Alexander), anti-heroic (Wellington), un-heroic (Grant), false-heroic (Hitler) and post-heroic (the nuclear age). However, although hugely suggestive, in the end, Keegan's analysis of these command types collapses, for the most part, into a descriptive biography of each individual commander. It fails to deliver the genuine sociology of command which it promises.

Van Creveld is more successful in delineating command regimes. He organizes his analysis into two periods: Stone Age command and modern command. Quickly dismissing Stone Age command, van Creveld is primarily interested in showing how modern command has evolved. He plots how the emergence of headquarters and staff systems in the eighteenth century facilitated command on increasingly

---

[35] John Keegan, *The Mask of Command* (London: Pimlico, 1999), 1.

complex and expansive campaigns. This is an important work but it also has some shortcomings as an investigation of command. It lacks the ethnographic and empirical detail of individual, historical studies. Decisively, it is compromised by van Creveld's approbation of one specific form of command over all others: namely, mission command, the de-centralization of decision-making initiative to subordinates. He sees the Roman legions, Napoleon's marshals, Moltke's army commanders, Ludendorff's storm troops and Ganesh's divisional commanders in 1967 as the ideals here. In each case, they embodied the self-evidently superior principle of mission command.[36] The ahistorical advocacy of mission command, putatively unchanging across the ages, eventually vitiates van Creveld's work. Nevertheless, his basic concept that command can be understood only in organizational – not personal – terms and that stable and identifiable command regimes exist is instructive. It has, of course, been followed by Zinni, McChrystal and Klein.

Other scholars have also argued for the existence of recognizable regimes of authority. Yves Cohen's recent work on leadership represents a seminal contribution to this literature and it is immediately relevant to the study of command regimes. He claims that the period, from the late nineteenth century up to 1940, constituted the age of the 'leader' and he tries to document this regime in detail.[37] As a result of the increased scale of industrial production and growing international competition in this era, a new class of managers or leaders emerged to plan, direct and coordinate production. These managers developed new bureaucratic systems to control workers in pursuit of efficiency. The rise of the industrial manager was, according to Cohen, paralleled by developments in two other sectors: the military and politics. Cohen appositely notes that the rise of the leader was substantially a moral phenomenon aimed at motivating workers, soldiers and citizens, even as elaborate administrative systems were developed to organize them; 'The industrial revolution as much as mass politics and mass war made actors feel impelled to recompose and develop hierarchies which were known to have nothing in common with those

---

36 Martin van Creveld, *Command in War* (Cambridge, MA: Harvard University Press, 1985), 270.

37 Yves Cohen, *Le Siècle des Chefs: une histoire transnationale du commandement et de l'autorité (1890–1940)* (Paris: Editions Amsterdam, 2013).

of the aristocratic Ancien Regime'.[38] Cohen claims that underlying socio-political forces demanded a new kind of leadership in these three sectors. Consequently, a broadly stable regime of leadership across civilian, political and military spheres is identifiable in the first half of the twentieth century.

Significantly, at the end of his work, Cohen considers contemporary leadership in the twenty-first century. In the light of rapidly changing social conditions, he considers whether a new regime of leadership might not be emerging in the global era. Cohen considers the role of leaderless movements, like the Arab Spring in Tunisia in 2011, as a way of contemplating these changing patterns of leadership: 'Social movements are equally the sites of a search for alternatives to the traditional hierarchies of the rational and organizational epoch of the twentieth century'.[39] Cohen suggests that, in the face of globalization, the heroic, hierarchical and, indeed, often authoritarian leadership of the twentieth century is being superseded by flatter networks in which collaboration and partnership are more adaptive. Cohen's remarks are deliberately suggestive; his work focuses on the twentieth century. However, at this point, he begins to address the transformation of leadership and consider the emergence of an alternative regime of command today. Like Keegan and van Creveld, he identifies two distinct command regimes: one in the twentieth century and another in the current era.

When Zinni, McChrystal and Klein discuss command regimes, they are then contributing to a much wider literature which also recognizes the existence of historic paradigms of authority. Their work is an important starting point. Crucially, they highlight the distinctiveness of contemporary command; they demonstrate that, in fact, a major rupture has taken place in the practice of command itself. As serving offices, they have actually experienced this transition. However, their work invites further, more detailed and systematic research. It could be strengthened empirically and conceptually by the application of academic rigour. Zinni's prose is a journalistic and rhetorical plea for a new form of leadership rather than a detailed and evidenced investigation of command practice itself; it is a manifesto rather than a sustained inquiry into command. While McChrystal's work is deeply

---

[38] Ibid., 41.
[39] Ibid., 817.

informative and draws on some relevant literature, it is based ultimately on only one empirical example: Joint Special Operations Command (JSOC) in Baghdad. Precisely because the conventional forces typically imitate the Special Operations Forces, the analysis of JSOC is likely to anticipate wider changes. Nevertheless, the distinctiveness of Special Operations and the unique mission of JSOC in Baghdad would recommend some caution about the immediate replicability of McChrystal's findings, especially since the author is likely to put himself in the best possible light. Similarly, Klein's analysis is based primarily on the interpretation of contemporary US military doctrine. As such, it cannot be dismissed but in order to understand the contemporary command regime and its origins with precision, a deeper investigation is required.

This book builds upon the work of Zinni, McChrystal, van Creveld, Keegan and Cohen to develop a theory of contemporary command; it analyzes the displacement of twentieth-century command by a twenty-first-century regime. It tries to dissect the distinctive practice of contemporary command. In this way, in line with the pleas of Zinni and McChrystal, it attempts to explore the potential rise of participatory, network leadership in the armed forces of the Western powers today. It broadly confirms the central arguments of Zinni and McChrystal that increased operational and organizational complexity has propelled the emergence of professionalized command teams in place of individual commanders, personally blessed with *coup d'oeil*. However, it introduces an alternative lexicon to Zinni, McChrystal or Klein, knowingly derived from sociology. Specifically, this book argues that in the twenty-first century, in the face of increased complexity, 'collective command' has emerged to replace a more individualist practice of twentieth-century command. Today, command collectives, consisting of commanders, their deputies, subordinates and staff bound together in dense, professionalized decision-making communities, has displaced previously more individualized, intuitive systems. The book is organized around these fundamental concepts, which will be defined in greater detail below and then exemplified and illustrated throughout the text.

Of course, this investigation of command regimes in the twentieth and twenty-first centuries makes no attempt to analyze command at every level; it does not claim to be comprehensive. Such an endeavour would be impossible. Command is exercised at the very highest strategic level down to the small unit. It would be quite impractical to attempt to examine command in all its manifestations from supreme commanders down to combat leaders. While commanders might be united in their responsibilities, the practice of command at each level is clearly quite different. Coherence demands a narrower focus. Consequently, this study concentrates purely on the command of army and marine divisions, combined arms formations of approximately 20,000 troops. This study examines the 'two-star' major-general. It examines how major-generals have commanded divisions in the twentieth century and how they command them today.

The Scope

Although the rationale will be discussed at greater length in the following chapter, the divisional level of command is identified as the object of study because the division has both been the basic formation for warfare since the First World War and is currently being regenerated once again. In the light of Iraq and Afghanistan, the major Western powers – the US, UK, France and Germany – have begun to implement changes at this command level. Specifically, the US Army, followed by the British, French and, finally, German armies, have sought to restore the divisional level of command.[40] The division is at the centre of contemporary army transformation, therefore. Indeed, this renovation of the division is substantially a response to the perceived command failings in Iraq and Afghanistan that have been excoriated in public debates. The division is currently being reformed so that commanders will be able to conduct future operations more successfully. This study of divisional command addresses, therefore, a critical military reform. It concentrates exclusively on the divisional level. However, precisely because the division is the site of significant adaptation, it may provide a particularly advantageous vantage point for the study of command more widely.

Focusing on the division, this book examines two command regimes: one in the twentieth century, the second in the twenty-first. The first regime emerged in response to industrial warfare in the First World War and persisted until just after the end of the Cold War: from 1914 to 1991. This regime was itself displaced after the Cold War,

---

[40] The details of this restoration will be discussed in Chapter 2.

as new operational and organizational conditions arose, initially in the 1990s. Its contours became particularly apparent in the first and second decades of the twenty-first century, especially in the course of operations in Iraq and Afghanistan and the subsequent reorganization of the division. These twin regimes are the poles around which the book revolves. Specifically, the book contrasts the way in which divisions are commanded and coordinated in combat today in contrast with the previous century. While acknowledging continuities, this work tries to show the radical – but often unacknowledged – differences between command practices of the twentieth and twenty-first centuries. It argues that command today is historically distinctive.

As Zinni and McChrystal acknowledge, in the twentieth century military operations were large but mechanically simple operations. Consequently, individual commanders, supported by a very small staff, were invested with sole decision-making authority to define and manage missions; command was broadly individualist. Conditions are radically different now. The scope of command has expanded. Divisions and divisional operations have become increasingly heterogeneous, involving the deep integration of diverse joint and multinational elements; the geographic, temporal and functional span of command has also increased in complexity. Military missions have become deeply politicized and, even at a low level, military force has to be applied with precision and proportion. Consequently, in order to address increased coordination problems, generals have been forced to distribute their decision-making authority to empowered subordinates, forming executive teams, closely united around a common understanding of the mission. While generalship has always necessarily involved a cooperative element, in the twenty-first century, military command has become collective to a degree which has rarely, if ever, been seen before; decision-making has now become a professionalized, ensemble activity. As command points have proliferated, it has been necessary to increase the capacity for decision-making in the division and integrate it across echelons. Highly professionalized command collectives have emerged, displacing a formerly more individualist, instinctual system of command. Command collectives, involving dense confederations of commanders, partners, deputies and subordinates, have begun to manage complex, heterogeneous contemporary operations.

Clearly, to argue that military command has been transformed since the end of the Cold War, and in the last two decades in particular, is to propose a controversial thesis. A theory of collective command is potentially radical – even unwelcome. At the same time, military traditions and even the self-perception of officers and generals, who often like to project a heroic self-image, resist the concept of change. To argue for command as a historic practice, against the inherent individual qualities of a general, is challenging for many. It replaces a celebration of revered personal martial qualities, like intelligence, bravery, courage and nobility, with an emphasis on the more mundane mechanics of command itself. Indeed, even in the course of the research, the concept of a command collective met with considerable resistance, not least from some generals themselves. Some saw the argument for collective command as undermining their autonomy and responsibility – even their duty.

In interviews during the research, both James Mattis and David Petraeus, among the most famous and successful generals of the modern era, both questioned the idea that command could be shared. They rejected a concept of collective command and asserted a traditional concept of individual command responsibility:

> I disagree if you are trying to do decision-making in boards. The enemy will dance around you.[41]
> There is one commander. He is the guy. Everyone else is in support of him.[42]

Their subordinates often concurred. One Marine officer, who had served with Mattis in the 1st Marine Division in Iraq, decried any idea of sharing command: 'If the commander is not invested in ownership of the mission, there is no vision. If he is just a board member, the mission does not get actualized'.[43] In the United Kingdom, officers often took a similar view. Rupert Smith, for instance, one of the foremost British generals of his generation, commanding a division in the Gulf War in 1991 to become Deputy SACEUR during the Kosovo War, also rebuffed the idea of collective command as an aberration: 'I accept that the processes you are describing may be happening. But they shouldn't be'.[44]

---

[41] General James Mattis, interviewee 113, personal interview, 4 June 2016.

[42] General David Petraeus, interviewee 096, personal interview, 7 January 2016.

[43] OF-6, Brigadier General, US Marine Corps, interviewee 100, personal interview, 22 March 2016.

[44] General Sir Rupert Smith, interviewee 087, personal interview, 7 October 2015.

All these officers have a point. Since generals are still the primary decision-makers and divisional tactics have remained recognizably similar, there are undeniable constants. So there are evident empirical objections to a theory of collective command. There are also ethical objections that the concept seems to divest commanders of their inalienable legal and moral responsibility for the actions they order. However, notwithstanding evident historical continuities and the controversy of its central thesis, this book aims to demonstrate that a new regime of command has appeared in the early twenty-first century. The presumptions of continuity prevent the armed forces and civil society itself from understanding the character of military command and, therefore, its capabilities, requirements and, crucially, limitations. The aim of this book is analyze military command – not to criticize generalship or individual commanders.

Of course, the parameters of this book are limited. It focuses only on the divisions of the major Western powers: America, Britain, France and Germany. Writing in the twenty-first century, this is potentially problematic. Jeremy Black, for instance, has consistently warned military historians about Western ethnocentrism. He has properly advocated the requirement for a global perspective.[45] This study potentially falls short of Black's injunction; it avowedly looks only at Western forces. However, some defence might be made here. It is impossible to study everything; some boundaries must be put in place. Moreover, necessary empirical boundaries do not always imply inevitable, still less catastrophic, conceptual limitations. In his seminal work on leadership, Yves Cohen examines leadership only in France, America, Germany and Russia. Yet, no one could claim that his work was invalidated by this limited comparative focus. On the contrary, although he focuses only on four states, Cohen's work has much deeper resonance. The regime of leadership, which he identifies in the first half of the twentieth century, is not only deeply significant in itself but it has evident relevance for the other parts of the globe, although Asian, African and South American hierarchies assumed their own differentiated forms. This study is fully aware of the dangers of Occidentalism but adopts a similar position to Cohen. In order to attain a sufficient level of depth, it concentrates on four major powers with a view to providing some

---

[45] Jeremy Black, *War: a short history* (London: Continuum, 2010), 163–7.

insight into command globally. Indeed, at the end of the book, the cases of China and Russia are briefly assessed in order to determine whether the transformation of command evident in the West is also observable elsewhere.

The book has a second necessary limitation; it focuses only on land warfare. The division is an army and marine formation and, consequently, the fascinating question of the transformation of maritime and air command is excluded from most of this study. It is simply impossible to provide an evidentially adequate account of the transformation of command in all three services. However, although it cannot pretend to be a genuine solution, at the very end of the book, the evolution of naval and air command is considered briefly. At this point, it is suggested that while the strategic mission of each service remains quite different, informing singular organizational cultures and structures, command of maritime and air forces has indeed undergone very significant reforms since the end of the Cold War. These developments are not the exact equivalent of the emergence of collective command at the divisional level in land warfare but there seem to be evident parallels. This analysis is cursory but it suggests that complementary changes may be taking place. If this is the case, then the exclusive attention to land warfare may have a wider pertinence.

This book is an analysis of military command – specifically at the divisional level. However, since the armed forces are an important part of the state, this book plainly has a much wider purpose. It necessarily speaks to the wider questions of social organization, leadership and, ultimately, to power. Over the past decade, social scientists from the across the disciplines have become increasingly interested in the transformation of public and private organizations. In place of homogeneous, vertically integrated hierarchies, heterogeneous networks – often global in scope – have begun to appear. Of immediate relevance to this study, organizational studies scholars have plotted the transformation of corporate hierarchies. Michael Hammer and James Champy have analyzed – and indeed advocated – the evolution of the American company in the face of changing markets, increased competition and technological change. They have demanded that companies reorganize existing divisions of labour into flatter, more flexible and responsive networks: 'The reality that organizations have to confront, however, is that the old ways of doing business – the division of labour around which companies have been organized since Adam Smith first articulated the principle – simply don't work any more'.[46] They are not alone: Rosabeth Moss Kanter has also recommended radical corporate restructuring.[47] More recently, Keith Grint has promoted the 'arts of leadership' over obsolete, dirigist twentieth-century models of management.[48]

Meanwhile, social and political scientists from across the disciplines have attempted to analyze and describe the many complex changes which have occurred to social, political and economic structures. They have traced the transformation of states and public sector organizations, business and industry in the commercial sector or the restructuring of class, ethnic and gender orders. Indeed, it might be argued that ultimately all recent social scientific scholarship is but an attempt to understand the dynamics of globalization. Modes of solidarity, social and political hierarchies, methods of organizing and, even, power itself are all changing. No consensus has emerged about its implications and is unlikely to. Yet, a new lexicon is emerging which has tried to capture these reconfigurations. Major academic figures have proposed concepts such as 'the interaction ritual chain',[49] 'the civil sphere',[50] the 'workshop',[51] the 'sphere'[52] or the 'Actor-Network' to define emergent social forms.[53] This book has avoided the beguiling

[46] Michael Hammer and James Champy, *Re-Engineering the Corporation: a manifesto for business revolution* (London: Nicholas Brealey, 1995), 19.

[47] Rosabeth Moss Kanter, *The Change Masters: corporate entrepreneurs at work* (London: Unwin, 1987); *When Giants Learn to Dance: mastering the challenges of strategy, management and careers in the 1990s* (London: Unwin, 1990).

[48] Keith Grint, *The Arts of Leadership* (Oxford: Oxford University Press, 2001).

[49] Randall Collins, *Interaction Ritual Chains* (Princeton, NJ: Princeton University Press, 2004); *The Sociology of Philosophies* (London: Belknap Press, 2000); *Violence: a Micro-Sociology* (Princeton, NJ: Princeton University Press, 2008).

[50] Jeffrey Alexander, *The Civil Sphere* (Oxford: Oxford University Press, 2008).

[51] Richard Sennett, *The Craftsman* (London: Penguin 2009); Richard Sennett, *Together: the rituals, the pleasures and politics of cooperation* (London: Penguin, 2013).

[52] Peter Sloterdijk, *Globes: macrospherology* (Cambridge, MA: MIT Press, 2014); *Bubbles: microspherology* (Los Angeles, CA: Semiotext(e); Cambridge, MA: Distributed by the MIT Press, 2011).

[53] Michel Callon, 'Some elements of a sociology of translation: domestication of the scallops and the fisherman of St Brieuc Bay', in John Law (ed.), *Power, Action and Belief* (London: Routledge and Kegan Paul, 1986); Bruno Latour and Michel Callon, 'Unscrewing the Big Leviathan: how actors macro-structure reality and how sociologists help them do so?' in K. Knorr-Cetina and A. Cicourel (eds), *Advances*

metaphors of scholars like Peter Sloterdijk and Bruno Latour and has adopted a more empirical approach. In order understand changing power structures, it seeks to plot the precise reform of practice through the close observation of one lifeworld. Nevertheless, it is self-consciously trying to address these wider debates about globalization and the transformation of power.

This book is, then, an attempt to contribute to these debates about contemporary social transformation through the detailed study of one specialist area: military command. It explores the changing application of military force, evolving in parallel to social and civil power. It traces the emergence of highly tuned command teams to prosecute contemporary operations and the professionalization of their decision-making. It dissects the rise of concentrated, condensed nodes of executive military authority. Since command is intimately associated with the distribution and application of power, this book can also be read obliquely as an analysis of the transformation of power much more generally. Through the sociological analysis of divisional command, this work aims to contribute much more widely to the comprehension of the exercise of power in the twenty-first century. In particular, this work addresses the transformation of one aspect of state-military power. The armed forces are a unique organization which alone, even with the declining power of the state, retain the monopoly of legitimate violence. Nevertheless, the way the armed forces exercise military power may usefully illustrate the dynamics of power in Western society today more widely.

This book is an anatomy of military command. It describes the emergence of new regime of military command in the twenty-first century. Especially towards the end, when the intricate staff methods of the new divisional headquarters are discussed, the book traverses terrain which seems to be a very long distance from Wellington or Clausewitz, writing after the Napoleonic Wars. The differences between these eras are, indeed, profound. Yet, all the dramatic innovations which have been instituted at the divisional level are still designed for one purpose, which both Wellington and Clausewitz would immediately recognize; they are but attempts to allow commanders to see the battlefield more

in *Social Theory and Methodology* (London: Routledge Kegan Paul, 1981); Bruno Latour, *Reassembling the Social* (Oxford: Oxford University Press, 2005).

clearly and, therefore, to make better decisions. Although the point is often obscured by the complex apparatus of management, command still fundamentally involves seeing over the over side of the hill. It is simply that the geography of hill, what is over it and the way of seeing it has changed. This book documents that transformation.

2 THE DIVISION

The Restoration of the Division

To select the army division as the focus for an analysis of command in the twenty-first century may seem arbitrary. For most of the twentieth century, armies had eight command echelons, from army groups of 500,000 troops to infantry platoons of thirty. As respectively the largest and smallest, either the army group or the platoon could be studied as a unit of command. Intermediate commands at corp, brigade or battalion level might equally well serve as a focus for the investigation of command. The division is but one level of command, of no more intrinsic importance than any other. Indeed, in the recent past, it was deemed to be of much less significance than the brigade or corps level.[1] There was a period at the beginning of the twenty-first century when the division seemed to be obsolete as a tactical command echelon; Western powers were reducing it to an administrative role, while the brigade became the favoured formation. Some explanation is clearly required to justify the selection of the division as the sole object of investigation in a book about twenty-first-century command.

It is certainly true that the division faced a decline after the Cold War. In the late 1990s and early 2000s, Western armies committed themselves to a radical military transformation – even a revolution. At this point, large formations like the division seemed obsolete. Western

---

[1] Anthony King, *The Transformation of Europe's Armed Forces: from the Rhine to Afghanistan* (Cambridge: Cambridge University Press, 2011).

armies, led by the United States, began to recognize the potential of new digital communications and surveillance systems as part of the so-called Revolution in Military Affairs.[2] New digital communications systems and associated weaponry allowed ground forces to begin to operate at ranges and with a precision that was once inconceivable. Forces, organized into far smaller formations, could disperse because they could rely, with increasing certainty, on ever-more-accurate support from airpower and long-range artillery. The sheer size of the division – with its 20,000 troops – seemed otiose. Armies no longer required mass to generate combat power. In addition, after the collapse of the Soviet Union, the strategic environment changed radically. The West's primary concern was no longer the territorial defence of the Inner German border; the central requirement for Western land forces was increasingly deemed to be rapid global deployability. In the light of both of these developments, the division began to look unnecessarily cumbersome. It could not deploy quickly and its units were not easily interchangeable with other units and formations. Accordingly, in the late 1990s, the brigade, of about 5000 soldiers, began to be identified as the optimal combined arms formation for the new wars in which the US and its allies were increasingly engaged.

There was, of course, extensive analysis and discussion about this reorientation of the army away from the division to the brigade. Douglas MacGregor's work, *Breaking the Phalanx*, was one of the earliest and most influential here. In that work, MacGregor, a retired major-general, dismissed the structure of the US Army in the 1990s and argued that the large divisional phalanxes, so essential to the mass interstate warfare of the twentieth century, were now obsolete. Indeed, divisions were so vulnerable that they had become a liability. He advocated the creation of lighter, more strategically and tactically mobile forces, organized into brigade-sized units, which would exploit the potential of network-centric warfare. They would be deployed more quickly but would also be militarily more powerful because they could coordinate a diversity of ground and air fires.[3] For

---

[2] Patrick Morgan, 'The Impact of the Revolution in Military Affairs', *Journal of Strategic Studies* 23(1) 2000: 132–9; William Owens, 'Creating a US Military Revolution', in T. Farrell and T. Terriff (eds), *The Sources of Military Change* (London: Lynne Rienner, 2002); Colin Gray, *Strategy for Chaos: revolution in military affairs and the evidence of history* (London: Frank Cass, 2002).

[3] Douglas Macgregor, *Breaking the Phalanx* (London: Praeger, 1997), 4

MacGregor, as his title suggested, the supersession of the industrial division by the 'empowered' brigade represented an organizational transformation no less significant than the replacement of the Greek phalanx by the Roman legion. In place of one immobile dense mass, Macgregor envisaged an agile force of dispersed but interconnected, mutually supporting maniples: 'Rather than relying on the cumbersome mobilization and mass firepower arrangements of the Cold War, this work suggests reorganizing the Army into mobile combat groups positioned on the frontiers of American security, ready to act quickly and decisively, primed to move with the minimum of preparation'.[4]

In the early 2000s, the American Army implemented many of the changes which Macgregor discussed. Divisions remained but, where they had once actively commanded their brigades on operations providing them with the critical supporting assets, they became only administrative frameworks for networked Brigade Combat Teams. Brigade Combat Teams became the critical level of command; artillery, communications and logistic assets, once held at divisional level, were reapportioned down to the brigade level. On the direction of the Army Chief of Staff, General Peter Shoomaker, the brigade became an independent task-force commanding all its own supporting elements.[5] At the same time, these new brigades were organized on a modular basis so that any of their sub-units could be reassigned to another brigade; they were all organized and equipped in the same way. As John Bonin and Telford Crisco observed: 'Modularity is a new organizational paradigm … it requires self-contained organizations that can plug into and unplug from unit formations with minimal need for augmentation and reorganization'.[6]

The US Army, naturally, instituted the modular brigade far more completely than any of its allies. Nevertheless, although lacking resources, the British and French army and marine forces were also influenced by the idea of the empowered brigade. From the early

---

[4] Ibid.

[5] William Donnelly, *Transforming an Army at War: designing the modular force* (Washington, DC: US Army Centre of Military History, 2007), 19; Also, John Brown, *Kevlar Legions; the transformation of the US Army, 1989–2005* (Washington, DC: US Army Centre of Military History, 2011); John McGrath, *The Brigade: a history* (Ft Leavenworth, KS: Combat Studies Institute Press, 2004), 131–2; John Wilson, *Maneuver and Firepower; the evolution of divisions and separate brigades* (Honolulu, HI: University Press of the Pacific, 2001).

[6] John Bonin and Telford Crisco, 'The Modular Army', *The Military Review*, March–April 2004: 21–7.

2000s, the British invested in the brigade level and, especially, in their two rapid reaction forces, 16 Air Assault and 3 Commando Brigades. The French retained divisions as territorial and administrative head-quarters but its divisions were reduced to brigades, actively – but perhaps somewhat artificially – sustaining divisional traditions and histories.[7] At this point, the division, as a distinctive level of command, seemed to be if not dead, then at least moribund.

There were undoubtedly many advantages to the modular brigade. It was a means of implementing distributed operations, which continues to inform military doctrine today, and it facilitated the introduction of some advanced technologies. Nevertheless, its shortcomings became apparent in the course of the long Iraq and Afghan campaigns. A brigade headquarters might be able to coordinate air support and other fires but, as a relatively small organization, it was unable to synchronize all the other increasingly important elements of contemporary operations. It was not designed to coordinate information operations, indigenous security forces, multinational allies, political engagement with local leaders or, decisively, to sustain a long campaign. A brigade headquarters was simply insufficiently staffed to provide these critical supporting functions. Consequently, the brigade level of command became increasingly inadequate for contemporary operations.

Against expectation, the division re-emerged as an indispensable echelon of command in Iraq and Afghanistan. The Western division has experienced a renaissance. Moreover, after the withdrawal from Afghanistan in 2014, the United States Army reversed its modular brigade policy. Because of constant deployments and the attachment of non-organic units to divisions, senior officers in the US Army expressed concern that the coherence of the Army was a risk: 'During Iraqi Freedom, we could not keep the US divisions organized as single formations. They became modular. We broke responsibility and authority within the division; there was no intent, no task and purpose. Everything, every structure fell apart. It was horrific'.[8] Irrespective of their specialisms, divisional headquarters deployed to command any units assigned to them; divisional training cycles, command structures and cohesion collapsed. Since the emergent threats were increasingly

---

[7] Anthony King, *The Transformation of Europe's Armed Forces* (Cambridge: Cambridge University Press, 2011).

[8] Anonymous source, US Army, 23 June 2016.

identified as Russia, Iran, China and North Korea, all of whom possessed very large, conventional forces, the restoration of America's divisions seemed essential after Iraq and Afghanistan.

Consequently, from 2014, the US Army reconstituted its divisions and sought to re-invest in the authority of the divisional commander; it engaged in a major programme of reform. As a result, the division has been re-invigorated. The US Army has reorganized its ten deployable divisions: 1st Infantry Division (the Big Red One), 1st Armoured Division (the Old Ironsides), 1st Cavalry Division, 2nd Infantry Division, 3rd Infantry Division, 4th Infantry Division, 25th Infantry Division, 10th Mountain Division, 101st Airborne (Air Assault) Division and 82nd Airborne Division. The ten divisions of the US Army underwent a major overhaul as they were restructured and re-equipped. These developments are absolutely central to this study and will be discussed at length from Chapter 10. Brigades remained small and agile, with appropriately lean headquarters, dedicated exclusively to the immediate tactical battle, while divisions supported and sustained that close fight, while conducting deep operations in the present and planning the campaign out over the next days and, in fact, weeks and months. Consequently, the command capacity of the division was increased by the modernization and expansion of its headquarters and staff. In addition to the re-empowerment of divisional commanders and the expansion of their headquarters, critical assets, like artillery and signals, which had been distributed among brigades in the period 1995–2005, were reassigned to the division. For instance, in 2015, a divisional artillery commander and dedicated divisional artillery headquarters was re-instituted in 82nd Airborne Division, reversing the previous policy in which divisional assets had been distributed down to the Airborne Brigade Combat Teams.[9]

Predictably, the American Army has led the restoration of the division but the process has been followed closely by its allies. It is particularly marked in the United Kingdom. As discussed in Chapter 1, Iraq and Afghanistan were deeply controversial for the UK and commentators highlighted numerous shortcomings in British command. However, the consensus among senior commanders in the British Army was that one of the principal reasons for the UK's great

---

[9] OF-4, Lieutenant-Colonel, US Army, interviewee 060, personal interview, 21 April 2015; OF-3, Major, US Army, interviewee 077, personal interview, 21 April 2015.

difficulties in both Helmand and Iraq was the erosion of the army division as a command echelon. Many senior officers argued that the problems in Helmand were principally due to attempting to command the operation from the brigade level. The Task Force Helmand headquarters was, consequently, overwhelmed by its mission as neither brigade commanders nor their staffs had the experience or resources to direct a campaign of that complexity. The results were predictable. Yet, for many senior officers, operations in Iraq were no better since the British-led Multinational Division (South-East) with responsibility for Basra was not a truly divisional headquarters either. As one officer observed of the British debacles in the period 2006 to 2009:

> How did it happen? The army forgot about what the divisional level was for. This started to be compounded by Multinational Division (South-East) with one [divisional headquarters] over one [brigade]. It had difficulty in understanding the different role between the two- and one-star levels. And then this was compounded over in Afghanistan where we wanted to deploy a divisional headquarters but lost the argument. The net result was a brigade headquarters, which is a tactical unit of manoeuvre with a headquarters of 230 staff, that wasn't going to do manoeuvre. It was trying to fulfill all the functions of the level above, on what was a fast-moving battlefield. There was an assumption you could jump from the operational level to the tactical level without any impact on the tactical level. It spawned a Brigade HQ which was really a division and to get that you ended up with a Brigade commander looking up and out and not down and in.[10]

Another British general summarized the situation bluntly: 'It was laughable that Britain thought they could run a campaign at brigade level in Helmand'. He concluded: 'We did ourselves a disservice'.[11] Indeed, another senior officer worried that the Army had effectively abandoned divisional operations: 'The British Army has effectively lost its capacity at the divisional level because it has given up the structures,

---

[10] OF-8, Lieutenant-General, British Army, interviewee 050, personal interview, 15 January 2014.

[11] OF-8, Lieutenant-General, British Army, interviewee 042, personal interview, 2 October 2014.

training, logistical support and sustainability required to manoeuvre in the way the Russians did during the invasion of Georgia'.[12]

As a result of this military crisis in the first decade of the twenty-first century, the British army began to restore the division. The renovation of the division in the UK was further reinforced by the experiences of General Nick Carter, the current Chief of the Defence Staff, when he commanded ISAF's Regional Command South, in Kandahar in 2009–10. There, General Carter experienced something of an epiphany. He recognized the indispensability of the divisional level in modern twenty-first-century military campaigns: 'The brigade level of command has predominated in the UK's recent operational experience, to the extent that the divisional level is in danger of slipping from collective military consciousness. This is a significant problem which arises from a failure to recognize that UK brigade-level operations in Iraq and Afghanistan have taken place in, and relied upon, a divisional framework of command and enablement'.[13] For Carter, the multidimensionality of contemporary warfare rendered the divisional level of command indispensable once again. Only the divisional level of command could coordinate the various military, political, informational, coalition and civilian elements of a contemporary operation: 'Each level in the command hierarchy is very different from the next and has a key role to play in the delivery of effect. Nowhere is the distinction greater than between the brigade and the division'.[14]

The Iraq and Helmand experiences have galvanized the British Army. They provoked a profound reconsideration of the command architecture of the field army, precipitating a re-investment in the divisional level, in contrast to the 1990s when the brigade seemed the optimal formation. From 2010, Nick Carter became a principal advocate of the divisional level in Britain and, once he was appointed to Commander Field Army in 2011 and then Chief of the General Staff in 2014, he prioritized the division as part of the 'Army 2020' reforms

---

[12] General Sir Richard Shirreff, 'Conducting Joint Operations', in Julian Lindley-French and Yves Boyer (eds), *The Oxford Handbook of War* (Oxford: Oxford University Press, 2012), 379.

[13] Lieutenant General Nick Carter, 'The Divisional Level of Command', *British Army Review* 157, Summer 2013: 7.

[14] Ibid., 8.

he pioneered.[15] He re-emphasized the importance of the division and, stripping staff and assets away from the brigade level, he reassigned them to the divisional level. From the end of the Cold War, the UK had always maintained two standing divisions: 1 and 3 UK Divisions. The Army would certainly have preferred to maintain both of these divisions fully. However, this commitment became increasingly difficult under the policy of austerity, following the financial crisis of 2008. In the last decade, the Army has had to make some severe cuts. Consequently, under Army 2020, 3 UK Division became the formation-level headquarters of the British Army's Reaction Force, responsible for intervention and divisional manoeuvre; 1 UK Division, meanwhile, commanded the Adaptive Force, coordinating the deployment of small mentoring teams as part of a programme of preemptive defence engagements. Therefore, 3 UK Division became the only remaining British division committed to war-fighting; it is, in effect, the only remaining full standing division in Britain. Nevertheless, it represents a significant investment and an important reversal of policy.

The British Army overtly re-emphasized the divisional level because of its scarring experiences in Iraq and Afghanistan. However, the pressures of coalition politics should not be ignored here, especially since the UK lacks many of the basic resources to deploy and fight a full division. In this context, Britain's divisional reforms make sense only in the light of the Alliance; they rely on American resources to be able to operate. The British Army recognized that the US Army was regenerating its divisions following Iraq and Afghanistan and, as America's closest ally, it seems probable that even without the impetus of Nick Carter's experiences in Afghanistan, the UK would have followed the US to re-invest in the divisional level. In order to cooperate with the US Army effectively, the British Army has often tried to adopt compatible structures and doctrine. Accordingly, as the American Army division began to be re-identified as the decisive level of land commander, it would have impeded interoperability if the UK had continued to prioritize the brigade. It is no coincidence that improved interoperability has been a central element of the divisional restoration in the UK. In particular, since 2013, 3 UK Division has been explicitly trained to fight as a British Division within a US corps.

---

[15] The British Army, *Transforming the British Army: an update – July 2013,* www.army .mod.uk/documents/general/Army2020_Report_v2.pdf.

Even though France experienced nothing like the traumas of Iraq or Afghanistan in the last ten years, the French Army has been imitating its closest peers and partners, the UK and America, to renovate its own divisions. A very similar alliance pressure seems to have been working on the French Army. Since Nicholas Sarkozy's decision to reintegrate French forces into NATO military structures,[16] the French have made extensive efforts to align themselves with the US and UK. Indeed, the bi-lateral Anglo-French Defence Treaty of 2010 represented a turning point in these relations.[17] Committed primarily to standing deployments in former colonies in Africa since the end of the Cold War, the French army has prioritized the battalion or brigade level until very recently. The African commitments required the roulement of relatively small forces into that theatre on stabilizing missions, augmented by emergency forces. Consequently, although organized on a divisional basis, the division, as an active command echelon, in the French Army had been more marginal since the 1990s. However, since 2012, the French Army, following the US example and operating closely with the British Army, has completely reconstructed the divisional level. In place of standing territorial divisions, the French Army has created two divisional commands, *État Major de Force 1* (in Besancon) and *État Major de Force 3* (in Marseilles), to act as deployable two-star headquarters on future missions.[18] In 2015, brigades were assigned permanently to these divisional commands for the first time since 1961. As with the UK, the French is seeking to increase interoperability at the divisional level, primarily through its participation in the Combined Joint Expeditionary Force.[19] This force involves the creation of a bi-lateral headquarters comprised of staff from *Etat Major de Force 1* and 3 UK Division. This is a UK-French divisional construct but, through NATO, it has also aligned the French Army with the US.

---

[16] *The French White Paper on Defence and National Security* (New York: Odile Jacob, 2008); www.mocr.army.cz/images/Bilakniha/ZSD/French%20White%20Paper%20on%20Defence%20and%20National%20Security%202008.pdf; www.css.ethz.ch/content/dam/ethz/special-interest/gess/cis/center-for-securities-studies/pdfs/CSS-Analyses-46.pdf.

[17] www.gov.uk/government/news/uk-france-defence-co-operation-treaty-announced–2.

[18] In English, EMF 1 and 3 would be called 1 Division and 3 Division. The irony that both the remaining divisions of the French and British Armies have the same numeric designation has not been unnoticed by French and British officers.

[19] www.gov.uk/government/news/uk-france-defence-co-operation-treaty-announced–2; www.gov.uk/government/news/uk-and-france-launch-rapid-deployment-exercise.

Until 2016, the German Army was behind its peers in restoring the division. From 1990, the Bundeswehr budget declined significantly to below 2 per cent of GDP, dropping to below 1.2 per cent from 2014.[20] Military intervention also remains a sensitive topic. As a result, the Germany Army has engaged in divisional restructuring, which has animated its main allies only belatedly. It did not initially participate in the multinational Combined Joint Expeditionary Force exercises in which Britain, France and the US have been participating since 2013. However, since 2016, in response to the increased Russian threat and in recognition of the growing bonds between the other three major Western powers, a reinvigoration of the Bundeswehr is currently underway. The Defence Minister, Ursula von der Leyen, has been forthright in her expansive, expeditionary and war-fighting ambitions for the Bundeswehr. As part of this programme, in 2014, the Bundeswehr was reorganized into three combat divisions: a light intervention division, *Division Schnelle Kräfte* (Rapid Reaction Division),[21] and two armoured divisions, 1 and 10 Panzer Divisions. These divisions have just begun to be reconstituted as the decisive formations for land warfare.[22] Although certainly available for European defence, *Division Schnelle Kräfte* has been designed for potentially global deployment. By contrast, 1 Panzer has been assigned responsibility for the defence of the Baltics and northern Europe, while 10 Panzer has been assigned to southern Germany. In the case of 1 Panzer, the division has been committed to the deep integration of Dutch forces into the formation, even while it restructures itself for hybrid warfare. This integration is likely to retard its operational development considerably. However, the Bundeswehr is beginning to re-invest at the divisional level in order to realign itself with its allies; the German divisions are actively looking to create partnerships with 82nd Airborne and with 3 UK Division, for instance.

A divisional reformation is evident across the Western alliance, then; all four major Western powers have committed their armies to it. Accordingly, in the last five years, as forces have withdrawn from

---

[20] http://data.worldbank.org/indicator/MS.MIL.XPND.GD.ZS?locations=DEhttps://www.economist.com/blogs/graphicdetail/2017/02/daily-chart-11.

[21] The division is comprised of paratroopers and Special Operations Forces and is essentially an air assault division.

[22] Presentation, 1 Panzer to 3 UK Division, Bulford, 31 August 2016, Fieldnotes, Vol. VI, 54–6.

Afghanistan, the American, British, French and German armies have collaboratively sought to reaffirm the divisional level of command, with increased doctrinal significance and enhanced levels of resourcing and training. Specifically, they have recognized that complex operations require an enhanced command capacity which, they argue, is best located at the divisional, 'two-star' level. Other Western powers, such as Canada, Italy and the Netherlands, have not been uninterested in this re-empowerment of the army division. They have placed exchange officers in the divisional headquarters of the major powers and have contributed to exercises; 3 UK Division, for instance, has had Canadian and Italian officers in important staff functions in the headquarters throughout its period of regeneration. The Netherlands has adopted a more radical strategy. Recognizing that it cannot sustain an armoured capability independently, the Dutch army has fully integrated its 43 Mechanized Brigade into 1 Panzer Division and its 11 Airmobile Brigade into the *Division Schnelle Kräfte*; the Dutch intend to fight in German divisions under German command on any future operation.[23] The smaller powers are contributing to the divisional restoration, restructuring their forces in the light of it. However, the smaller Western powers do not have sufficiently large armies to operate at the divisional level; their forces are simply too small to deploy, sustain and fight a division. Nevertheless, across the NATO alliance, land forces are currently prioritizing the division as the preferred formation for land warfare.

Precisely because the major Western powers are all reinvesting in the division and specifically seeking to enhance its command capacity for future operations, this formation offers a singularly fertile object for the analysis of the contemporary transformation of command. Indeed, the division is the current focus for the evolution of land command in all these forces. Because this echelon is seen as critical in future hybrid operations, Western armies have been conducting a series of experiments at the divisional level, testing alternative systems of control and communication. The reorganization of divisional command provides a unique insight into the way operations have been, are and will be commanded. The division is, of course, not the only level of command, still less is it the only interesting echelon. The study of any command level would certainly illustrate contemporary

---

[23] Ibid.

transformation as well. Yet, because the divisional level has itself been privileged by Western armies, it provides an especially pertinent object of contemporary study.

However, before the analysis of divisional command can begin properly, it is necessary to define precisely what an army division is. Some detailed consideration of the history of the division as a military formation is necessary. This study is organized around a comparison of twentieth- and twenty-first-century divisional command. Yet, such a comparison is coherent only if the army division has some organizational continuity throughout this period. If today's division shares nothing in common with its forebear, comparison becomes fruitless; generals in the two eras have commanded quite different entities. It is, therefore, imperative to show that the division constitutes a unified object of study from the First World War to the present. A brief description of the origins of the division and, above all, an account of the emergence of the modern combined-arms division is required. This will show that for all the division's considerable adaptations, it remains the same basic formation which crystallized on the Western Front.

The Divisional Principle

The division is currently being renewed as Western armies preferred formation but, in fact, the division, as a military formation, has a long history. In a famous essay, Michael Roberts claimed that a military revolution occurred in Europe between 1560 and 1660 as a result of increasing potency of firepower on the battlefield and the emergence of standing armies.[24] Whether 'revolution' is the appropriate term, European armies certainly evolved very significantly between the sixteenth and eighteenth centuries. Above all else, they became simply much bigger than their feudal predecessors. As a result of this growth, an important reorganization of the army began to be observable from the middle of the eighteenth century. Frederick II the 'Great' of Prussia was an important figure here. In addition to imposing an extraordinary discipline on his troops and developing new 'oblique order' tactics during the Seven Years' War, he also began to divide his army into

---

[24] Michael Roberts, 'The Military Revolution, 1560–1660', in Michael Roberts (ed.), *Essays in Swedish History* (London: Arnold, 1967), 56–81.

large sub-units – 'divisions' – since it was simply too large to man-oeuvre as a single host.[25] The creation of divisions facilitated the control and administration of the Prussian Army. Frederick the Great may have 'invented' the division. However, the division is more commonly thought to have been properly institutionalized as the preferred military formation in France following the Seven Years' War. The introduction of the division was part of a wide-ranging programme of reforms instituted by Marshal De Broglie, especially following the humiliations of that war: 'The divisional principle was applied by Maurice de Saxe, but the divisional principle was definitely adopted in 1759 by Marshall de Broglie'.[26]

Comte Jacques de Guibert was one of the most influential figures in debates about French Army reform at this time and his *Essaie Général de Tactique* remains a critical and insightful resource about the origin of the division. Although Guibert favoured limited wars fought by a small professional army, inspired by patriotic ideals, he advocated the division as an appropriate organizational form: 'It is not possible to move in one single column, because the immense elongation of this column would slow the march, increase the fatigue of the troops and put one in danger of being beaten and thrown back, before it can form up'.[27] Guibert recommended that generals divide their armies into equal parts, each of which marched as an independent column on its own line of advance.

> If attempting to organize a machine, one makes it with too many
> moving parts or parts which are too weak, one complicates the
> details of this machine and diminishes its power. If one makes
> it insufficiently numerous and too solid, it becomes susceptible
> to inaction, be it of force or of speed. It is the same with an
> army. If in composing its divisions with too few troops, one
> forms a great number of divisions, one falls into complication.
> One lacks the men capable of commanding these divisions.
> One has the difficulty of combining so many movements. If one
> composes divisions with too many troops, one forms an army

---

[25] Christophy Duffy, *War in the Age of Enlightenment* (London: Routledge and Kegan Paul, 1982).

[26] Jean Colin, *L'Éducation Militaire de Napoleon* (Paris: Librairie Militaire R. Capelet and Cie, 1900), 50.

[27] Comte Jacques de Guibert, *Essai général de tactique* (Paris: Economica, 2004), 150.

> with too small a number of divisions, each one of them remains too massive and too heavy, and the operation does not fulfill its objective, which is to lighten and to energize.[28]

For Guibert, properly constituted divisions had evident operational advantages; they simplified marches and accelerated the speed with which an army could assume its battle formation. At the same time, a division was still powerful enough to defend itself so that it could not be defeated in detail. The division could form the 'head of the army' capable of fighting independently: 'Each of them [division] was capable of receiving an enemy's blow without being crushed by it and gain time for others'.[29] Consequently, Guibert regarded the divisional principle as a 'fundamental principle' of warfare.

It is precisely at this moment, when the division was invented, that distinctly modern command emerged as a military institution. Since the enlarged armies of the eighteenth century operated over hitherto-unanticipated tracts of space and time and were now separated into divisions, they presented new organizational problems; coordination became difficult. The range of military operations and the size of armies required more than just traditional combat leadership. While combat leadership was a ubiquitous feature of human history and the great captains like Alexander, Caesar or Gustavus were outstanding generals, Guibert implied that command, rather than mere leadership, was a distinctively modern creation, the progeny of the Enlightenment. It is no coincidence that as Guibert discussed the divisional principle, he also described the emergence of a new 'science of generalship'. This science was not primarily interested in battle tactics, though they were surely not irrelevant, but involved, rather, the analysis of the march; it was a 'science of the choice of positions and knowledge of the country'.[30] This science of grand manoeuvre – that is, *command* – did not exist much before Guibert's lifetime and was closely associated with the Guibertian concept of *coup d'oeil*: a general's ability to guess the enemy's intentions and to exploit the tactical opportunities presented by the terrain. Here command involved not simply tactical combat leadership, but rather the operational coordination of armies.

---

[28] Ibid., 152–3.
[29] Jean Colin, *The Transformation of War*, translated by L. Pope-Hennessy (London: Hugh Rees, 1912), 208.
[30] Guibert, *Essai général*, 55.

It is noticeable that, in battle, commanders no longer led their troops from the front but coordinated their forces from the rear: 'Not until the second half of the seventeenth century did commanders habitually start taking their place behind, rather than in front, of their men, and Frederick the Great was probably the first commander in chief regularly depicted as wearing a suit of linen rather than of armour'.[31]

The division had profound implications for land warfare but it is important, of course, not to overstate its military significance in the late eighteenth century. Guibert regarded an army of 60,000 to 70,000 as optimal. This force would be organized into about 80 battalions divided into three divisions, right, left and centre. Each division consisted of 24 battalions, commanded by a lieutenant general, with a second lieutenant general under him, and assisted by three marshals de camp.[32] However, the reality was rather different; the division was not always a formal military formation. In the late eighteenth century, divisions were normally formed on the basis of operational requirement. By the time of the Revolutionary Wars, a division in the French Army consisted of two demi-brigades: 'However, because this reorganization was carried out while the campaigns were still in progress and because trained officers were still lacking, the brigade never came into existence. Instead a number of demi-brigades were placed under the command of a single general officer who was given the title of a general of the division'.[33] Moreover, although the division tended to have a standardized form of two demi-brigades and several artillery batteries, its composition varied; Messena's Army of the Danube in 1799 included a division of 11,232 men and another one of 4668 soldiers.[34] Although adopted by European armies, the division was not yet a fully standardized formation.

Indeed, as the French Revolutionary Army increased in size, the divisional principle was partly superseded by the creation of Napoleon's *Corps D'Armée*. Divisions played a critical in Napoleon's earlier battles, like Montenotte, Lodi, Arcola and Rivoli in 1796.[35] Thereafter, the corps, consisting of several divisions, became the prime

---

[31] Van Creveld, *Command in War*, 17.
[32] Guibert, *Essai général*, 175.
[33] Steven Ross, 'The Development of the Combat Division in Eighteenth-Century French Armies', *French Historical Studies* 4(1) Spring 1965: 90.
[34] Ibid., 93.
[35] David Chandler, *The Campaigns of Napoleon* (New York: Macmillan Publishing), 64, 76, 97.

formation of the *Grande Armée*. Napoleon's Corps operated in unison to ensnare opponents through grand manoeuvres of the kind seen at Austerlitz or Jena. Genuine operational command was exercised at the corps level, as Marshal Davoût's victory at Auerstedt demonstrates. On that battlefield, he defeated the main force of the Prussian Army with his Third Corps, while Napoleon simultaneously triumphed over a smaller force at Jena.[36]

The Modern Division

The army division was an eighteenth-century invention and, notwith-standing Napoleon's corps system, the division remained a fundamental formation in the French and German armies throughout the nineteenth century. Divisions were prominent in the Franco-Prussian War.[37] Divisions also played a crucial role in the Confederate and Union armies during the American Civil War; the climax of the Battle of Gettysburg occurred on 3 July 1863 when Major General Pickett's division of 12,500 soldiers advanced against Union forces on Cemetary Ridge. Divisions played a prominent role throughout the nineteenth century, then. However, Western armies in the nineteenth century organized themselves into specialist infantry, cavalry and artillery divisions. These forces certainly cooperated with each other but the division in this period was not a fully integrated formation of infantry and artillery. At the Battle of St. Privat-Gravelotte, the grandfather of Field Marshal Erich von Manstein, who commanded a corps, 'addressed some pretty harsh words to one battery for unlimbering too far from the enemy'; they were not in the firing line.[38] This episode showed that artillery and infantry divisions were not yet united. The combined arms formation which united infantry and artillery had not yet appeared.

The division began to modernize towards the end of the century. After the Franco-Prussian war, both German Imperial and French Armies were reorganized.[39] The improvements in the range, rapidity

---

[36] H.C.B. Rogers, *Napoleon's Army* (London: Ian Allan, 1974), 138.
[37] Michael Howard, *The Franco-Prussian War* (London: Routledge, 2000).
[38] Erich von Manstein, *Lost Victories* (Minneapolis, MN: Zenith, 2004), 189.
[39] Douglas Porch, *March to the Marne: the French Army 1871–1914* (Cambridge: Cambridge University Press, 1981); Eric Brose, *Kaiser's Army: the politics of military technology in Germany during the machine age, 1870–1918*

and accuracy of artillery was one of the critical developments here. Eventually, with significant resistance from traditionalists, these technical developments led to an increase in the amount of artillery pieces which both armies fielded, though the French fell badly behind in heavy artillery. Later, during the first decade of the twentieth century, French and German armies perfected techniques of defilade artillery fire. Instead of bringing field artillery up to the firing line in close support of the infantry, the artillery dispersed into concealed positions, well behind the infantry, from which it fired indirectly onto the enemy, coordinated by wireless: 'the gloriously long lines of cannons that won at Sedan – and were reproduced for decades at maneuvers – had to yield to smaller groups of batteries that took advantage of cover while advancing with the infantry'.[40] Indeed, the French noted with consternation that Germany had fully adopted indirect fire in 1910.[41] By the start of the First World War, indirect fire was the preferred way of employing artillery by all the belligerents.

The emergence of long-range, indirect fire was an important moment in the evolution of the army division. As artillery ranges increased, it became necessary to integrate artillery and the infantry ever more closely. Because they were no longer co-located in or just behind the firing line, divisional commanders needed to ensure that the guns supported their troops, while the artillery had to be assigned targets which it could no longer immediately identify. The modern combined arms division emerged as armies tried to exploit the potential of indirect fire in support of the infantry. The period immediately before the First World War was plainly important but the war itself was decisive. During the course of that conflict, as the infantry's dependence on artillery became clear, the combined arms division became thoroughly institutionalized. More and more artillery was assigned to the infantry division, which, therefore, became ever more integrated.

(Oxford: Oxford University Press, 2001); Dennis Showalter, 'From Deterrence to Doomsday Machine: the German way of war, 1890–1914', *Journal of Military History* 64(3) July 2000: 679–710; Dennis Showalter, 'Army and Society in Imperial Germany: the pains of modernization', *Journal of Contemporary History* 18(4) October 1993: 583–618.
[40] Brose, *Kaiser's Army*, 147–8.
[41] Ibid., 149.

In 1914, for instance, each German division had its own battalion of light field howitzers, consisting of 72 guns and howitzers.[42] The French army division's artillery regiment had 36 guns.[43] Nevertheless, in both cases, the French and German division was still overwhelmingly an infantry formation at the start of the war. The opening engagements of the First World War, when huge masses of French and German infantry collided during the Battle of the Frontiers with devastating casualties, demonstrated that the combined arms divisions was still in its infancy. Marshal Joseph Joffre criticized the French Army for its failure to integrate artillery with the infantry: 'I told the armies to be more prudent in their attacks and above all to pay more attention to inter-arm coordination'.[44] Combined arms cooperation was insufficiently developed in the German Army too. In the battle at the Sambre-Meuse angle, German infantry complained that their artillery failed to interdict enemy fire and, worse, was responsible for many friendly casualties. The German infantry was equally guilty of failing to cooperate; it advanced so heedlessly that troops were often confused for the enemy by their own artillery.[45] The Western Front demanded a profound reformation; combined arms action became utterly essential. By 1918, for instance, the French Army division had been reduced from four to three infantry regiments, while a heavy artillery group was added.[46] By the end of the war, combined arms action was the norm with infantry and artillery united in the division.

The British experience was not dissimilar. The British Army had fielded divisions during the Napoleonic War. The 3rd Division fought at Waterloo and British divisions were formed for the Crimea and Boer Wars. However, committed primarily to imperial policing until after 1900, the British Army only established permanent divisions after the Haldane Reforms of 1906. Instructively, the Field Service Regulations of 1909 provided no guidance on their role or employment. Between 1909 and 1913, however, there was substantial discussion of the division in *The Journal of the Royal United Services Institute* by serving officers. Problems of signals, artillery, engineering and the use of mechanical transport within the division were all discussed.

---

[42] Robert Citino, *The German Way of War: from the Thirty Years War to the Third Reich* (Lawrence, KS: University of Kansas Press, 2005), 208.

[43] www.chtimiste.com/regiments/divisioncestquoi.htm.

[44] Porch, *March to the Marne*, 223.

[45] Borse, *Kaiser's Army*, 199.

[46] www.chtimiste.com/regiments/divisioncestquoi.htm.

One observer claimed that 'the influences which have been and are gradually transforming a division from a mere collection of units into an organized "higher unit" were apparent'.[47] Like the Germans and the French, the British Army was beginning to develop a concept of the combined arms division just before the First World War. Yet, in the course of the war, the combined arms division became established as the primary formation.

Although Western armies had incorporated artillery into their infantry divisions before the First World War, the genuinely combined arms formation was fully established only during this conflict, then. The infantry division of the First World War became a combined arms formation consisting of approximately 20,000 soldiers, with an upper limit of about 27,000 and a lower limit of some 10,000. Typically, these troops were organized into three infantry brigades (or regiments), consisting of three or four battalions each, supported by an artillery brigade, a battalion of engineers, a logistics battalion and a squadron of signallers; divisions also contained a number of other specialist units, such as medics and machine guns. Clearly, there were many variations on this basic structure. The US Army adopted the square division of four regiments with four battalions each.[48] However, the basic pattern of the modern division was clear; it consisted of about three brigades supported by other arms and services. Crucially, it united artillery and infantry under a single command.

The First World War had demonstrated the absolute priority of firepower on the battlefield, demanding a profound reformation of tactics.[49] The machine-gun was of evident importance here and many of the accounts of the war focus on its devastating effects but advances in artillery were even more decisive. Long-range artillery, providing indirect fire-support, transformed the battlefield, multiplying the space and lethality of the killing zone geometrically.[50] The question

---

[47] Paul Latawski, 'A Historical Perspective of the Division in the British Army', Army Field Manual Vol. 1, Part 1A, *Divisional Tactics*, 4.9; Ashley Jackson, 'The evolution of the division in British military history', *RUSI Journal* 152(6) 2007: 78–81.

[48] Kedzior, *Evolution and Endurance*, 8–10; Wilson, *Maneuver and Firepower*, 39–73; Donnelly, *Transforming an Army at War*, 3.

[49] John English and Bruce Gudmundsson, *On Infantry: the military profession* (Westport, CA: Praeger, 1994).

[50] Shelford Bidwell and Dominic Graham, *Fire-Power: The British Army – Weapons and Theories of War, 1904–1945* (Barnsley: Pen and Sword, 2004); Patrick Griffith,

of infantry-artillery cooperation became, therefore, one of the most pressing on the Western Front. It was here that the division became so significant because it was specifically designed to integrate infantry and artillery under a single command: 'the chief role of the divisional commander consists in combining the action of the artillery and infantry'.[51] The modern division uniquely incorporated an artillery brigade permanently into its order of battle, whose batteries' prime role was to support the infantry brigades in attack and defence. Clearly, combined arms action had been a consistent feature of warfare since the emergence of firepower in the sixteenth century. Yet, a permanent combination of arms had not standardized much before the First World War. The modern division institutionalized this combination. The division was, then, a command solution to an organizational problem.

The establishment of the combined arms division as the prime formation of war can be very clearly seen with the sudden proliferation of doctrinal publications during the war. Here, 1916 might be taken as a decisive year. By then, the belligerents had already been fighting for nearly a year-and-a-half and the realities of the Western Front, with its industrialized firepower and mass armies, were becoming apparent. By the end of 1916, France, Germany and Britain had all been involved in major battles at Verdun or the Somme. Moreover, as armies expanded and casualties attrited the officer corps, there was an increasingly pressing requirement to accelerate the promotion of officers to command and staff jobs within newly formed divisions. Doctrine became a means of disseminating new practices.

The French Army played a pioneering role for the Allies in developing divisional doctrine. In January 1916, the French General Headquarters North and North-East issued *Instruction sur le combat offensif des grandes Unités*, followed in October 1917 by *Instruction sur l'action offensive des grandes Unités dans la Bataille*. These manuals were adopted by the British Army, which issued a translation of the French instructions, *Summary of the French Instructions for Higher Formations in the Attack*, in July 1916, as the Somme offensive opened. Eventually, the British Army produced its own divisional doctrine issuing *Instructions for the Training of Divisions* (SS 135)

Battle Tactics of the Western Front (New Haven, CT: Yale University Press, 1994), 134–58.
[51] General Staff, *Summary of French Instructions*, 6.

in 1916, updated as *The Training and Employment of Divisions* (SS 135) in early 1918, to be superseded in turn by *The Division in Attack* and the *The Division in Defence* later in the year. SS 135 has been widely recognized as a seminal publication for the British Army, demonstrating that it had finally embraced large-scale, continental warfare. The commonwealth forces, including Indian, West African, Canadian, Australian, New Zealand and South African troops, that fought under British command in the First World War adhered to this doctrine.

The German Army produced similar publications, including the 1908 *Field Service Regulations*. During the war, they published new doctrines which addressed the special conditions of industrial warfare. *Ausbildung fur Infanterie* was very important especially in establishing modern platoon tactics, which would be practiced by stormtroopers. However, in November 1916, Hindenburg issued another significant memorandum, 'Command in War and the General Staff'. Of immediate relevance to the divisional level, other publications, such as *Sammelheft der Vorschriften für den Stellungskrieg* (*Collected Instructions for Trench Warfare*), were more important. The keystone Part 8, *Grundsätze für die Führung in der Abwehrschlacht im Stellungskriege* (*Principles for Command of the Defensive Battle in Trench Warfare*), was released on 1 December 1916 and, although the problem for the Germans was defence rather than attack, its recommendations echoed contemporaneous British and French doctrine very closely.[52] It included sections dedicated to the division: 'Infantry divisions are the combat units for the defensive battle as well; their mission is to direct combat command, guaranteeing inter-arm cooperation for close and deep tasks'.[53] After the War in 1921, the Reichswehr published *Führung und Gefecht der Verbundenen Waffen* (*Command and Combat of the Combined Arms*), which collated many of the command lessons learnt on the Western Front. It was aimed at commanders at regimental level and higher. As the title suggested, its leitmotif was the combination of artillery and infantry *en masse*. German doctrine made it eminently clear that the division had become a critical formation for land warfare.

---

[52] Jonathan Boff, *Haig's Enemy: Crown Prince Rupprecht and Germany's War on the Western Front* (Oxford: Oxford University Press, 2018), 146-7.

[53] Chef des Generalstabbes des Feldherres, *Grundsätze für die Führung in der Abwehrschlacht im Stellungskriege* (Berlin: Reichsdruckerie, 1917), 11.

The US Army was unprepared for combat on the Western Front. Since the Civil War, excepting the Spanish-American war, it had been primarily involved in policing and border actions against Native Americans and Mexico. Accordingly, the United States had no experience of, nor any doctrine for, large formation warfare. They drew on existing British Army divisional doctrine and, because the American forces were placed in French sectors under French higher command, French doctrine. In fact, the connections between the US and French Army were deep, arising ultimately from alliances during the War of Independence and the 1812 War. Relations between West Point and St Cyr were close and the US Army had already adopted some important practices from the French, including the organization of headquarters. However, the First World War catalyzed this long-standing relationship. For instance, the British Army's translation of *Instruction sur le combat offensif des grandes unités* was edited and reissued by the US Army War College in May 1917 and the US Army employed French divisional doctrine from that time onwards. Although latecomers, the US Army quickly recognized the divisional level as critical.

The twentieth-century division fused infantry and artillery, then. However, the cooperation of these two arms demanded a series of further innovations. The divisional commander had to integrate infantry and artillery but 'he cannot do this unless he has good information'. In addition, 'the full power of the artillery' was possible only 'when they are well supplied'.[54] Combined arms operations at the divisional level, therefore, required intelligence and logistics capabilities. Consequently, 'the whole effort of the staff' was dedicated to 'obtaining accurate information', 'combining the action of the infantry and artillery' and 'organizing the chain of supplies'.[55] In addition, divisional commanders needed to be able to communicate with their units, construct defensive positions and prepare routes for the attack. In order for a division to function properly, it therefore required signallers and engineers. Significantly, although they could sometimes help the infantry directly, the engineers' chief duty was 'to improve communications, to allow the advance of the artillery and to facilitate supplies'.[56] For the first time, a division united all the major combat functions at scale under a single

[54] General Staff, *Summary of French Instructions*, 6.
[55] Ibid.
[56] Ibid., 11.

command. Although combined arms divisions had already existed for about a decade, 1916 might be identified as the true genesis of the modern Western division.

Generals were well aware of the importance of the division. In a famous passage, General William Slim, who commanded the British 14th Army in Burma during the Second World War, identified the division as one of the most rewarding commands, precisely because this formation was autonomous: 'It was good fun commanding a division in the Iraq desert. It is good fun commanding a division anywhere. It is one of the four best commands in the Service – a platoon, a battalion, a division and an army... A division because it is the smallest formation that is a complete orchestra of war and the largest in which every man can know you'.[57] The division was an efficient way of distributing, organizing and commanding critical enabling assets in the Army.

Moreover, although large, the division did not merely unite all the functions of war but was also able to inspire the affection of troops, who often identified strongly with it. The division had a genuine corporate identity. The American Army, for instance, recognized the division as distinctive formation in both senses:

> It is the largest permanent unit. It is the largest organization in which officers learn to know one another well enough for form a closely knit organization. It is the smallest unit that is composed of all the essential arms and services, that is designed to be tactically and administratively self-sustaining, and can conduct, by its own means operations of general importance. It can strike and penetrate effectively, move readily, and absorb reinforcing units easily. It is the organization which officers and men love and cherish and about which their recollections cluster in aftertimes. It is therefore the unit which promotes morale and a spirit of service. It forms a whole that should never be broken up.[58]

If the infantry platoon was the basic unit of combat, the division had become the elementary cell of land warfare. Plainly, a modern division in the twentieth century could not fight a campaign alone but it was

---

[57] Field Marshal Viscount Slim, *Defeat into Victory* (London: Cassell, 2009), 3.
[58] The Chief of Staff, *A Manual for Commanders of Large Units Vol 1 Operations* (Washington, DC: US Government Printing Office, 1930), 39.

able to conduct major actions without external support. It had all the capabilities required to fight and sustain an intense combined arms battle.

The Evolution of the Division

The combined arms division emerged during the First World War and was thoroughly institutionalized into doctrine in 1916. Of course, it underwent numerous adaptations, evolutions and transformations thereafter. The First World War witnessed the invention of a modern infantry division and the demise of the cavalry division. However, by the 1930s, new specialized divisions began to emerge alongside the infantry division. The first of these innovations was the armoured division and, in Germany, the mechanized (*Panzer-Grenadier*) division, consisting of tanks and vehicle-borne infantry. At a similar time, the airborne division was developed as a specialist infantry formation by the Wehrmacht, to be imitated by the Allies after its successful use in early Blitzkreig campaigns. In addition, the amphibious marine division was also created during the Second World War. Finally, in the 1960s, the US Army developed the Air Assault Division, based on the new mobility provided by the helicopter. Having been strongly advocated by General Howze, 1 Cavalry Division was the first formation to conduct air assault operations in Vietnam. By the late 1960s, Western forces had therefore developed six types of combined arms division: infantry, airborne, air assault, marine, armour and mechanized. Each of these divisions had different capabilities and requirements. The functional differences between these divisions have to be recognized.

At the same time, in addition to the multiplication of divisional types, Western armies experimented with divisional structures throughout the twentieth century. The American adaptations were the most pronounced. The US Army used a square division in the First World War but, finding it too large and cumbersome, reverted in the inter-war era to the triangular division.[59] In the 1950s, this triangular division was transformed into the 'pentomic' division. Consisting of five independent battle-groups, the pentomic division was intended to

[59] Richard Kedzior, *Evolution and Endurance: the US Army Division in the twentieth century* (Santa Monica, CA: Arroyo Center, Rand, 2000), 9–16.

be more survivable on the nuclear battlefield. There was a strong reaction against the pentomic division[60] in the 1960s and it was replaced by the Reorganization Objectives, Army Division (ROAD), which essentially reintroduced the triangular structure.[61] In the 1970s, a triple-capability division (Tri-Cap) was tested briefly but the US Army eventually returned to a conventional heavy division under Division 86 and a new light division of 10,000 troops.[62] Finally, in the 1990s, the US Army introduced a project, called Division XXI, which attempted to capitalize on the potential of informational technology.[63] Divisional amendments continue to this day; they will be discussed later. European armies did not institute such formal or radical changes to divisional structure during the Cold War as the US Army. Rather, French, British and German divisions underwent slow but constant evolution throughout the twentieth century as these powers experimented with alternative force structures.[64]

The basis structure of the army division and the character of divisional operations endured throughout the twentieth century, notwithstanding the emergence of specialized divisions after the First World War. However, naturally, the existence of a recognizable divisional paradigm in this period should not obscure some important developments that began to occur in the late 1970s and 1980s. These reformations of Western military doctrine and the conduct of land warfare were materially relevant to the army division of the late Cold War period and to the subsequent transformation of divisional operations in the twenty-first century. After the Vietnam War, the US Army (and Marine Corps) sought to reform themselves in the face of the disaster which had befallen them in South East Asia. Conscription was abolished and the army became an all-volunteer professional force. At the same time, in the face of Soviet threat and in the light of the fact that, as a professional force, the army was now much smaller than it had been in the '50s and '60s, the US Army began to develop a new

---

[60] Andrew Bacevich, *The Pentomic Era* (Washington, DC: National Defence University Press, 1986); Kedzior, *Evolution and Endurance*, 23–7.

[61] Ibid., 29.

[62] Kedzior, *Evolution and Endurance*, 35–40.

[63] Ibid., 43.

[64] Latawski, 'A Historical Perspective of the Division in the British Army', 4.19–4.21; Dennis Showalter, 'The Bundeswehr of the Federal Republic of Germany', in Lewis Gann (ed.), *The Defense of Western Europe* (London: Croom Helm, 1987), 225, 237–8.

doctrine. Instead of fighting an attritional battle against its enemies, and especially against the Warsaw Pact countries, the US Army introduced a new 'manoeuvrist' approach in which it would offset its numerical inferiority with deep strikes executed at an unexpectedly high tempo. Having begun to explore the possibility of Active Defence in the late 1970s, the 1982 edition of the Army's Field Manual 100–5 institutionalized Air-Land Battle. The doctrine was substantially informed by studies of Israeli actions on the Suez Canal during the Yom Kippur War, when the IDF had successfully responded to a surprise attack with a retaliatory deep strike which unhinged the Egyptian forces. Under this doctrine, air power was to be integrated into the land battle to strike follow-on Soviet formations.

Significantly, Air-Land Battle also involved a reform of military command; it introduced the concept of 'mission command'. Under this philosophy, subordinate commanders were liberated to act on their own initiative in line with their Commander's Intent but without direct supervision.[65] Mission command implied a distribution of command authority and the emergence of network of interdependent commanders of the type which would begin to become very evident after 2000. However, right up to the Gulf War, divisions were still configured for mass, industrial warfare on small lineal fronts. Mission command will be discussed more fully in Chapter 5.

Plainly, the division assumed several different forms during the twentieth century and each evolved in its own way. In the 1980s, there was an important reformation of command which had implications for the division. It would be wrong to underplay the division's diversity. Yet, for all its evident diversity, the modern division displayed the same fundamental structure throughout the twentieth century; it typically consisted of three manoeuvre units supported by artillery and other services. Crucially, the main role of the division was to unite artillery and infantry or armour under a single command. In every case, the division was designed to orchestrate mass fire and manoeuvre. As

[65] Richard Lock-Pullan, 'An inward-looking time', *Journal of Military History* 67(2) 2003: 483–512; Richard Swain, 'Filling the void; the operational art and the US Army', in Brian McKercher and Matthew Hennessy (eds), *The Operational Art* (Westpoint, NY: Praeger, 2006), 147–73; Saul Bronfield, 'Did Tradoc Outmanoeuvre the manoeuvrists? A Comment', *War and Society* 27(2) 2008: 111–25; Robert Leonard, *The Art of Maneuver* (New York: Ballantine Books, 1991).

such, the division, which emerged in the trenches of the Western Front, remained the basic unit of land warfare throughout what the historian, Eric Hobsbawm, called the 'short' twentieth century; from 1914 to 1991, the division endured. Up to the very end of the Cold War, divisions of a recognizably similar structure to that of the First World War constituted the elementary form of land combat. Whatever the divisional type, the command problem was the essentially same: the coordination of infantry or armour and artillery at scale. It was notable how similar the command and headquarters of the division remained through the entire period. The fundamental continuity of divisional operations and their command systems during the twentieth century is, perhaps, best exemplified by a NATO exercise in May 1980. On that exercise, former Wehrmacht generals Hermann Balck and F.W. von Mellenthin, who had last fought in 1945, were employed as players, tasked to defend a divisional sector of the US Corps against a simulated Warsaw Pact attack. They had no difficulty whatsoever in conducting operations some 40 years after their last command appointments: 'The old Wehrmacht hands made it look easy as they crippled two enemy tank divisions and counter-attacked to the West Germany border'.[66] Despite evident revisions, the basic function and structure of the division endured throughout the century. Even today, there are evident continuities.

From 1916 to 2016

The modern combined arms division was designed as a response to an organizational problem which Western forces faced in the First World War. It was a means of coordinating mass infantry and artillery. By unifying manoeuvre units and fire under a single commander, Western armies sought to maximize the combat effectiveness of their forces in the face of the industrial conditions on the Western Front. The division solved a coordination problem. If 1916 is symbolically taken as the year of origin of the combined arms division, the current divisional restoration was initiated almost precisely a century later. For all the

[66] Showalter, 'The Bundeswehr of the Federal Republic of Germany', 236.

very great differences between a contemporary division and a modern, twentieth-century one, the restoration of the division today has evident parallels with the initial creation of the combined arms division. In 1916, the division was institutionalized in order to integrate artillery and infantry; it sought to unite them under a single commander. Today's reform of the division is also fundamentally a command solution to an organizational problem. It is a way of coordinating new forces and capabilities. In the twenty-first century, Western armies have found that they do not need to coordinate only artillery and infantry but also to integrate them with air power, helicopters, drones, information, cyber, electronic, psychological and political operations. In the light of this proliferation of functions, the division has once again been identified as the optimal level for the command of land warfare. It is the location where traditional combined arms action can be fused with new military and non-military functions. Of course, the challenge of coordination is more heterodox today. Yet, just as in 1916, Western armies have decided that the various functions which contribute to combat effectiveness can be best united at the divisional level. If the modern combined arms division was a response to the demands of mass industrial warfare, the twentieth-century division should be seen as a potential solution to the challenges of post-industrial, globalized conflict.

This book takes these two command reforms as its starting point; the first in 1916 brought the combined arms division formally into being, the second, in the twenty-first century, has restored and reformed it. The book consequently aims to compare divisional command in the short twentieth century (1914–1991) with contemporary divisional command in the early twenty-first century (1992–2018), focusing especially on the period from 2003 to the present. This study seeks to illustrate the distinctive practice of command today, then, by contrasting it with twentieth-century generalship. This book examines the contemporary transformation of command. Specifically, it describes the emergence of an increasingly professionalized and collective system of command, in place of a relatively individualistic one. Building on Zinni, McChrystal and Klein, the analysis dissects the morphology of command today. However, this comparison is possible because, despite all the evident developments, the division retains its fundamental structure. It still consists of three manoeuvre brigades and a brigade of artillery. The central problem at the heart of the division remains the coordination of mass fire and movement against a peer opponent. The dramatic advances in military technology should not conceal an enduring reality at the heart of divisional operations. It is possible to trace the evolution of command from the First World War to the present precisely because the basic pattern of the division, and the fundamental problem it was designed to resolve, remains broadly commensurate.

3 DEFINING COMMAND

Decision-Making

It is very easy to talk about command but it has typically been more difficult to define it. In his widely read work on command, Martin van Creveld neatly highlights the problem.

> The exercise of command in fact involves a great many things, not all of which can be clearly separated from each other. There is, in the first place, the gathering of information on the states of one's own forces – a problem that should not be underestimated – as well as on the enemy and on such external factors as the weather and the terrain. The information having been gathered, means must be found to store, retrieve, filter, classify, distribute and display it. On the basis of the information thus processed, an estimate of the situation must be formed. Objectives must be laid down and alternative methods for attaining them worked out. A decision must be made. Detailed planning must be got under way. Orders must be drafted and transmitted, their arrival and proper understanding by the recipients verified. Execution must be monitored.[1]

Documenting an array of practices and procedures, the passage usefully clarifies the impediments to a simple definition of command. Precisely because command is such a diverse practice, it defies easy classification.

[1] van Creveld, *Command in War*, 6–7.

However, having accepted the complexity of command, the passage contains one crucial phrase: 'A decision must be made'. At this point, van Creveld identifies the principal function of command: decision-making. Commanders are uniquely invested with the authority to make decisions about what their subordinates are to do. Here, van Creveld accords with long-standing military doctrine: 'Command is the authority which an individual in military service lawfully exercises over subordinates by rank of assignment ... Decision as to the specific course of action is the responsibility of the commander alone'.[2] Contemporary doctrine confirms the point: 'Command embraces authority, responsibility and accountability. It has a legal and constitutional status – codified in Queen's Regulations. It is also vested in a commander by their superior. Authority enables an individual to influence events and order subordinates to implement decisions'. [3] Command is decision-making, then.

However, of course, commanders do not make decisions about everything. Rather, their decision-making is concentrated on two critical areas, as van Creveld makes clear:

> First, command must arrange and coordinate everything an army needs to exist – its food supply, it sanitary service, its system of military justice, and so on. Second, command enables the army to carry out its proper mission, which is to inflict the maximum amount of death and destruction on the enemy within the shortest possible period of time and at minimum loss to itself; to this part of command belong, for example, the gathering of intelligence and the planning and monitoring of military operations.[4]

For van Creveld, command involves decisions about the administration of an army and its operations. The two responsibilities of command refer to function and output. In both cases, the purpose of command, as a decision-making capacity, is to increase military effectiveness through the coordination of forces.

---

[2] Chief of Staff, *Field Service Regulations* (Washington, DC: US Government Printing Office, 1941), 23–4.
[3] Ministry of Defence, *Joint Doctrine Publication 0-01 Joint Operations* (Shrivenham: Development, Concepts and Doctrine Centre, 2011), 3.
[4] Martin van Creveld, *Command in War*, 6.

The point has been affirmed by other scholars. For instance, in his mainly polemical work on the failures of generalship, the psychologist Norman Dixon defines command in a way which is entirely compatible with van Creveld; 'the ideal senior commander may be viewed as a device for receiving, processing and transmitting information in a way which will yield maximum gain for minimum cost'.[5] In order to achieve this purpose, 'the senior commander makes decisions'. Dixon illustrates command with a flow diagram in which generals receive information about their own and their enemies' forces, on the basis of which input they make either 'heroic, managerial or technical' decisions about the use of their troops. Dixon rightly notes that, while the basic decision-making function of command is simple, the execution of command is complex in practice. 'Noise' – the fog of war – constantly threatens coherent decision-making; information about the situation is wrong or incomplete. Alternatively, the psychology of generals impedes proper assessment of the situation and, therefore, coherent decision-making. Whether his analysis of the psychopathologies of generalship is correct, Dixon, like van Creveld, usefully identifies decision-making as the defining characteristic of command. Whether good or bad, commanders make decisions about the deployment and use of their forces in order to achieve their missions. Specifically, command decisions refer to the coordination of forces and, in the division, primarily to inter-arm cooperation between artillery and infantry.[6]

Command, Management and Leadership

Command may, indeed, be best defined as decision-making authority but this can only be a starting point. It is necessary to identify the precise nature of specifically military decision-making more closely. One of the greatest difficulties here is to establish the relative meanings of the terms 'command', 'management' and 'leadership'. This triad is almost always

---

[5] Norman Dixon, On The Psychology of Military Incompetence (London: Pimlico, 1994), 28.

[6] See also Ryan Grauer, Commanding Military Power: organizing for victory and defeat on the battlefield (Cambridge: Cambridge University Press, 2016). Defining command in terms of the number of subordinates, the degree of centralization and the communications systems, Grauer takes an alternative, more formalistic approach than that pursued here.

invoked together. Indeed, the concepts of command, management and leadership are often conflated with each other; sometimes they are even confused. Consequently, it is necessary to differentiate command definitively from the closely related concepts of management and leadership and to establish the precise interrelationship between them. At this point, defining command becomes rather more challenging. Indeed, scholars and practitioners have often struggled to clarify terms here.

Edgar Puryear's popular work on generalship illustrates some of the typical problems very clearly. Rather than identifying the specific functions of command, management and leadership, Puryear has consistently conflated command with leadership and, indeed, with the qualities of the individual commander, irrespective of institutional and operational contexts. Thus, in his analysis of celebrated American commanders in the Second World War – Eisenhower, MacArthur and Marshall – Puryear provides a psychology of command; successful command is to be located in the personality of the general. The subtitle of his work suggests this conflation of command and leadership: *19 Stars: a study in military character and leadership*. For Puryear, command and leadership are interchangeable because both are a reflection of a general's personality. Consequently, Puryear's work is organized around a series of character traits critical to effective leadership, such as altruism, patience, dedication, duty, honour, country, selflessness, decision and courage: 'There is absolutely nothing which can take the place of the qualities in a man which are referred to as character. Generals such as George Washington, Robert E. Lee, John J. Pershing, Stonewall Jackson, to mention but a few, are remembered not only as great field leaders but as generals whose character transcended the ways they fought'.[7] In the end, Puryear reduces command to leadership. His idealized commanders were successful because they were able to inspire and motivate. The questions of executive authority and management are wholly ignored in his work.

Yet, the armed forces themselves are not always helpful here either since they recurrently conflate the concepts of command, management and leadership. Declarations such as, 'command is inseparable from leadership'[8] are very common in military doctrine, without

---

[7] Eric Puryear, *19 Stars: A study in military character and leadership* (Novato, CA: Prisidio, 1981), 289.
[8] Chief of Staff, *Field Service Regulations*, 23.

either being fully defined. Indeed, military doctrine has sometimes compounded the problem. There, command is linked to 'control', so officers talk of 'command and control' or 'C2' as a single entity. The following passage illustrates some of the difficulties of establishing a clear relationship between these elements:

> Commanders influence the outcome of battles, campaigns, and engagements by assigning missions; prioritizing and allocating resources; assessing and taking risks; deciding when and how to make adjustments; committing reserves; seeing, hearing, and understanding the needs of subordinates and seniors; and guiding and motivating the organization toward the desired end. In battle, command is being with soldiers, sharing their hardships, feeling their pride – and often their pain – and continuing to think and act to accomplish the mission with the least cost to them.[9]

This passage vividly depicts both the importance of command to the conduct of war and also the central functions of a commander. Commanders must identify the mission and assign the tasks but they must also motivate their troops by example. Most of the major functions of command are described but the passage is conceptually confusing. Command, management and leadership are intertwined in the prose. The elements are conflated and the managerial functions are rather overwhelmed by the more emotive appeal to leadership.[10] Although less pronounced than Puryear's work, there is a tendency to merge command and leadership.

In the light of these confusions, it is clearly necessary to distinguish command, management and leadership with the greatest clarity and precision. At this point, military scholarship becomes less useful; it is typically more concerned with causal explanation and the analysis of individual command performance. By contrast, organizational studies become more pertinent because the discipline is concerned with analyzing the general characteristics of organizations. Consequently, the

---

[9] Headquarters, Department of the Army, FM 100–5 Operations, June 1993, 2–14. I cite this passage as the very final statement of command in the (short) twentieth century by the US Army, written soon after the Gulf War and before the new strategic and organizational challenges of the global era became apparent.

[10] See Jim Storr, The Human Face of War (London: Continuum, 2009) for a criticism of command and control concepts.

clarification of concepts, which can be applied across examples, is of central importance. However, even here, a careful selection of the relevant texts is necessary. Much of the literature in organizational studies focuses on the function of the organization itself, its historical development and how the structure of an organization affects behaviours both within and outside the organization. The work of Peter Selznick, Alvin Gouldner, Peter Blau, Amitai Etzioni or James Burnham is all seminal in this regard.[11] They demonstrated the sometimes pathological social effects of organizations on managers, employees and wider society. However, they do not explicitly address the concepts of command, management and leadership.

It is necessary to turn to the scholarship dedicated exclusively to the executive function. There is a potential disadvantage here since this work tends to be less critical. Nevertheless, it is here that the concepts of command, leadership and management are discussed with greatest clarity. One of the seminal texts in this tradition was Henri Fayol's celebrated 1916 work on management. There, Fayol discusses the issue of 'command' at length. He notes that 'management and command are very closely linked'.[12] However, while management refers to the function of 'foresight, organization, coordination and control', 'command may be treated separately'.[13] Specifically, Fayol defines command as serving a motivational function: 'For every manager, the object of command is to get the optimum return from all employees of his unit in the interest of the whole concern'.[14] For Fayol, command refers to motivation. Other scholars would reserve Fayol's term, 'command', for leadership. Consequently, while Fayol certainly provides an important statement about management and his work is directly relevant to the question of military command, his definitions are consequently somewhat at odds with contemporary usage. He uses

---

[11] Peter Selznick, *TVA and the Grass Roots: a study in the sociology of formal organizations* (New York: Harper Torchbooks, 1966); Alvin Gouldner, *Patterns of Industrial Bureaucracy* (London: Collier Macmillan, 1954); Peter Blau, *On the Nature of Organizations* (London: John Wiley and Sons, 1974); Peter Blau, *The Dynamics of Bureaucracy: a study of interpersonal relations in two government agencies* (Chicago: University of Chicago Press, 1955); Amitai Etzioni, *Complex Organizations: on power, involvement and their correlates* (Glencoe, NY: Free Press, 1961); James Burnham, *The Managerial Revolution* (New York: Day, 1941).

[12] Henri Fayol, *General and Industrial Management* (London: Pittman, 1971), 5.

[13] Ibid.

[14] Ibid., 97.

the term 'management' to denote practices which most other scholars have defined as command, while 'command' denotes what many would call leadership. It is convenient to look to other scholars at this point.

The work of Peter Drucker is the most immediately relevant here. Drucker dedicated his sixty-year career to the study of the executive function, which included close observation of and discussions with numerous senior executives. He developed perhaps the best understanding of what the role involved. Moreover, he is particularly pertinent to this study because he repeatedly recognized the similarities between civilian management and military leadership. His definition of the executive function was intended to be applicable cross-sectorally to both civilian and military spheres. There is an obvious criticism to be made of Drucker. It is certainly true that Drucker's work is not critical about the executive function in the way that other organizational scholars, like Selznick, Gouldner or Blau, have been. Drucker's work is primarily directed at identifying an ideal and improving the performance of executives, rather than pointing up the pathologies of the role. However, precisely because Drucker's definition is so comprehensive and clear, it constitutes an ideal starting point for understanding command.

Drucker typically begins his analysis with apparently obvious, even self-evident, observations whose implications he pursues to draw profound and illuminating conclusions. Thus, his definition of the executive function is sparse: 'The executive is, first of all, expected to *get the right things done*'.[15] Apparently banal, this statement usefully identifies the central executive function. Executives exist in large, complex organizations to administer and organize the workforce in order to maximize output. An executive who fails to perform this role is useless. Clearly, the executive function involves many practices. However, across all sectors, an executive has the monopoly over one unique responsibility, which echoes van Creveld's observations: 'Decision-making is only one of the tasks of an executive. It usually takes but a small fraction of his time. But to make decisions is the *specific* executive task. Decision-making therefore deserves special treatment in a discussion of the effective executive. Only executives make decisions ... Effective executives, therefore, make effective decisions'.[16] Drucker

---

[15] Peter Drucker, *The Effective Executive* (Oxford: Butterworth Heinemann, 1997), 1.
[16] Ibid., 95.

affirms his definition: 'Whatever a manager does, he does through making decisions'.[17] The point is crucial. Executives are distinguished from all other employees because they alone are accorded the authority to make and implement decisions about the organization. The point applies directly to the armed forces; as both the scholarly literature and military doctrine affirms, the unique and distinguishing function of commanders is that they make decisions. Specifically, generals make decisions about the deployment and usage of force; they manage the application of violence.

For Peter Drucker, there were obvious reasons why an executive was given decision-making responsibility: 'The manager is the dynamic, life-giving element in every business. Without his leadership, the "resources of production" remain resources'.[18] For Drucker, effective management maximized the potential of an organization. Good management improved the productivity of workers not primarily by making them work harder or longer, but by coordinating the efforts of the whole organization. Good management enhanced the efficiency of a company by increasing the cohesiveness and cooperativeness of the employees.[19] Similarly, in the armed forces, command has been a means of generating cohesion. Generals are invested with the authority to give orders to maximize combat effectiveness. Orders are a means of creating organizational order.

According to Drucker, 'effective executives do not make a great many decisions. They concentrate on the important ones'.[20] Crucially, they must answer the fundamental question: 'What is our business?'.[21] They must identify the core mission of their organization. Using the examples of Alfred Vail and Alfred Sloan, Drucker identified additional elements implied by this primary executive decision. Deciding 'what is our business' required 'a clear rationalization that the problem was generic and could be solved only through a decision which established a rule, a principle'. This decision is the reference point for every subsequent decision. In addition, this initial definitional decision presumes certain 'boundary conditions'; the decision of what 'our business is'

---

[17] Peter Drucker, *The Practice of Management* (Heinemann: London, 1969), 345.

[18] Ibid., 3.

[19] Chester Barnard, *The Functions of the Executive* (Cambridge, MA: Harvard University Press, 1953).

[20] Drucker, *The Effective Executive*, 95.

[21] Peter Drucker, *Management* (London: Heinemann, 1988), 71.

presumes certain market and organizational conditions, only under which it continues to be valid. It is vital that these conditions are identified and monitored so that the mission remains valid and achievable. 'The second major element in the decision-making process is the clear specification as to what the decision has to accomplish'.[22]

Drucker's prime examples may indeed be giants of American industry, like General Motors and AT&T, but his account of the executive function applies immediately to military commanders. Indeed, his discussion of the boundary condition issue is illustrated by a discussion of the Schlieffen plan. The Schlieffen Plan was designed so that Germany could fight 'a war on both the eastern and the western fronts without having to splinter her forces'. The crucial boundary condition of the Schlieffen Plan was that the more powerful Western allies would be defeated first so that Germany could fight two successive campaigns, each with adequate forces. In the event, these boundary conditions were not met. Germany had to fight two concurrent campaigns for which it did not have the troops: 'Schlieffen had himself kept the boundary conditions clearly in his mind. But his successors were technicians rather decision-makers and strategists. They jettisoned the basic commitment underlying the Schlieffen Plan, the commitment not to splinter the German forces. They should have dropped the Schlieffen Plan. Instead they kept it but made its attainment impossible'.[23] The result was a disaster. In establishing a mission, boundary conditions are vital.

Following Drucker's argument, the primary duty of all military commanders is, like their executive peers in the civilian world, to decide what their business is; it is to identify a mission. As Clausewitz observed: 'The first, the supreme, the most far-reaching act of judgment that the statesman and commander have to make is to establish by that test the kind of war on which they are embarking; neither mistaking it for, nor trying to turn it into, something that is alien to its nature'.[24] Mission definition is clearly most important and difficult at the strategic level, as Clausewitz noted. Yet, the requirement to establish 'what our business is' is no less a duty for divisional commanders. In this case, it is their duty to define the specific mission of their division.

---

[22] Drucker, *The Effective Executive*, 109.
[23] Ibid., 111.
[24] Clausewitz *On War*, 88.

Divisional commanders must establish the precise goal of their formation that acts as the reference point – the boundary condition – for all
subsequent decisions and actions. Indeed, in his notes to the 21st Army
Group, written in November 1944, aimed especially at his divisional
commanders, General Bernard Montgomery prioritized mission definition as the primary responsibility of the commander: 'A war is won
by victories in battle. No victories will be gained unless commanders
will sort out clearly in their own minds those essentials which are vital
for success and will ensure that those things form the framework on
which all action is based'.[25] Montgomery's language is naturally quite
different to Drucker's prose. Yet, the concept is commensurate. Like
Drucker, Montgomery insisted that successful command involved the
identification of a mission and its boundary conditions. By identifying
the mission, commanders not only unified all their forces into a single
enterprise but they provided for themselves an intellectual framework
by which they could appraise intelligence and information. They had
some criteria to distinguish the militarily significant data from mere
fog and noise.

Command is constituted by decision-making. Specifically, the
'first, supreme and most far-reaching' decision of a divisional commander is to define the basic mission of the division and to organize,
deploy and fight that force in pursuit of that mission. In point of fact,
it is questionable whether it is optimal to define this act of mission
definition merely as a form of decision-making. Certainly, a decision is
clearly involved, but the term 'decision-making' reduces a constitutive
act of interpretation to a routine matter of opting between already-
existing choices. Mission definition is, in fact, more than the mere
selection of pre-existing options. In order to determine the mission,
commanders must define their situation; they must correlate the higher
direction they have received with what the enemy is trying to do, the
terrain and the forces they have at their disposal. They must understand
the relationship between, at least, four elements – task, enemy, terrain
and forces. Mission definition requires, then, a complex interpretation
whereby the elements of the situation are causally interconnected to
produce one coherent solution – a mission. Committing to such a definition is clearly a decision; selection is involved. Nevertheless, mission

---

[25] 21st Army Group, *Some Notes on the Conduct of War and the Infantry Division in
Battle* (Belgium, November 1944), 5.

definition is far more than a mere administrative decision about the allocation of resources; it is an existential act which defines the collective purpose of the force under command. There is, of course, a very large literature about how executives and military commanders define missions erroneously due to psychological faults or organizational pressures.[26] Some of these will be drawn upon in the analysis of actual decision-making processes in the army division. However, even scholars who are most critical of the decision-making process, like James March and Johan Olson, would not dispute the claim that mission definition is a critical executive function. Their criticism is only that organizations normally define missions wrongly.

Mission definition is the prime executive act of the military commander, then. It has a unique status. However, this act of definition presumes and will eventually demand, as Drucker makes eminently clear, a prodigious investment of time and effort. The effective executive 'converts the decision into action', 'building into the decision all the actions required to carry it out'.[27] This is the domain of normal, routine decision-making. Drucker notes that 'while thinking through the boundary conditions is the most difficult step in decision making, converting the decision into effective action is usually the most time-consuming one'.[28] The act of business definition – the supreme executive act – presumes the mundane under-labour of management. No matter how brilliant a general might be in theory, the real test of command is the execution of the mission. Commanders must manage, administer and direct their human and material resources to accomplish a mission. In a force of any size, this is challenging. At the divisional level, for instance, commanders must organize and coordinate some 20,000 personnel, thousands of vehicles and weapons in typically difficult geographic and climactic conditions, facing an opponent actively seeking to disrupt them. Even the simplest decision necessarily involves a multiplicity of administrative sub-decisions about how the mission is to be achieved in practice. Overlooking any one of these minor decisions or making an incorrect decision about an apparently trivial issue might have catastrophic repercussions for a military

---

[26] E.g., Irving Janis, *Group Think: psychological studies of policy decisions and fiascos* (Boston: Houghton Mifflin Company, 1982).

[27] Drucker, *Effective Executive*, 103.

[28] Ibid., 114.

operation. As Clausewitz noted: 'Everything in war is very simple, but the simplest thing is difficult'.[29]

Management of the mission accordingly includes a bewildering range of specific activities, as van Creveld described. However, management involves three fundamental administrative requirements. First, the subordinate tasks need to be defined; every single activity that a military formation needs to complete, including manoeuvre, firepower, logistics and communication, has to be identified. Second, these tasks need to be prioritized in order of importance, assigned to particular sub-units and sequenced. A detailed plan is required which defines all of these tasks, their assignment and their sequencing. Finally, the commander has to supervise or 'control' the tasks in real time in the light of inevitable alterations due to internal organizational frictions and situational changes, which include the weather and, of course, enemy action. The larger the force and the more complex the mission, the more onerous the task of management becomes. Headquarters and the staff have emerged specifically as a response to the problem of managing military campaigns. Crucially, while the staff are not executives in Drucker's sense – they have no command authority – the staff become utterly critical in organizing, administering and controlling these tasks. Command involves, then, two crucial features: the definition of the mission and the management of the mission (and all the tasks it involves).[30]

There is a third inalienable dimension to command. Much of Peter Drucker's work concentrates, appropriately enough, on the cognitive dimension of the executive function; this is, after all, its defining feature. Nevertheless, Drucker does not regard organizations as only functional entities, nor executives as a merely rational function. On

---

[29] Clausewitz, *On War*, 119.

[30] In practice, there is some overlap between command and management. This pragmatic conflation becomes apparent in the course of an operation when the tasks have to be coordinated in real time. At this point, commanders often have to re-orient their forces. They have to re-adjust the tasks or, indeed, in a crisis, give their troops completely new ones in the face of unanticipated enemy action. Generals have to order their subordinates to complete new tasks urgently; they must *command* them in the general sense of the word. Indeed, on occasion, a new mission must be defined rapidly. As generals exercise their decision-making authority *in extremis*, command and management can elide. Yet, while practically there is certainly no clear divide between mission definition and its management, conceptually the functions are separable, with command superior and prior to management.

the contrary, in *The Practice of Management* he discusses 'the spirit of the organization'. Perhaps surprisingly since his ostensible concern is efficiency and, therefore, profit, he claims that 'morality, to have any meaning at all, must be the principle of action'.[31] Drucker, plainly, is not advocating that companies adopt a system of universalistic ethics. Rather, by morality, he means that organizations must have a collective sense of identity and purpose. The US Marine Corps and the Royal Navy self-evidently embody the morality which Drucker describes; they have *esprit de corps*. Moral managers are ones who ask, in the first instance, neither for remuneration nor focus on their own perform- ance, but simply on their contribution: 'What can I contribute that will significantly affect the performance and results of the institutions I serve?'[32] Above all, a moral organization is one whose members pursue collective rather than selfish ends. By moral, Drucker refers to activity which addresses the collective goals of the organization, not the interests of the individual workers or managers.

Drucker rarely uses the word 'leadership' in his writing. This seems to be partly because he is deeply sceptical of the term. Against widespread sanctification of leadership in business literature, he insists that, in fact, it 'has little to do with "leadership qualities", and even less to do with "charisma". It is mundane, unromantic and boring. Its essence is performance'.[33] For him, leadership is not his- trionic; it involves ensuring that high performance is required, pro- motion systems are rational and jobs are rewarding. It is defined by consistency. Nevertheless, although he disparages its more utopian proponents, leadership is plainly of paramount importance to Drucker for very good reasons. Without effective leadership, employees will not be motivated to work for the common good. They will not feel obliged to contribute to corporate goals or to fulfil the mission which the executive has defined as the organization's business. Without leader- ship, employees will prioritize their immediate self-interest. Leadership is a critical part of the executive function, then, and, of course, it is an essential element of command. Indeed, on the battlefield, leadership assumes a priority which it does not normally have in civilian life. In

---

[31] Drucker, *The Practice of Management*, 144.
[32] Drucker, *Effective Executive*, 44.
[33] Peter Drucker, *Managing for the Future* (Oxford: Butterworth Heinemann, 1992), 100.

the face of the unique dangers of combat, commanders must motivate their troops not just to work, but to fight – and, potentially, to die. The leadership function becomes critical.

It is essential that the special character of military organizations is fully recognized. Nevertheless, by drawing on management literature, it is possible to begin to define that often elusive and difficult concept – command. Command is an executive decision-making function. It involves one decisive and unique responsibility: mission definition. However, because a commander is responsible for mission definition, command necessarily incorporates two further executive functions: the management of the mission and its designated tasks, and leadership – the motivation of subordinates. Management and leadership are critical to command. However, command, as mission definition, constitutes the superior, encompassing element because issues of management and leadership will be determined by how the commander has already defined the mission. Mission definition – the unique act of command – must be primary.

The Morphology of Command

Command consists of three intimately connected functions: mission definition, mission management and mission motivation. Of course, in practice, the three elements are inseparable. Troops are often best motivated by a commander who is capable of defining and managing missions competently. The management of a mission will substantially influence how a commander can define a division's objectives. Yet, command, management and leadership are always present and, conceptually, separable and identifiable. However, over time, the morphology of command oscillates so that the elements of the trinity assume a different significance. As van Creveld and Keegan argued, in some periods of history, combat leadership becomes primary; in others, management becomes more important. Consequently, although informed by wider cultural and social norms, the practice of command is substantially determined by operational and organizational circumstance. Dysfunctional command systems, which are constructed purely according to arbitrary cultural preferences or political interests, will be incapable of directing military operations; they will not endure. Consequently, the morphology of command is likely to correspond to operational and organizational conditions. As those conditions change, so do the practice of command and the interrelation of its three elements. This reconfiguration of the command trinity gives rise to distinctive historical regimes of command.

Van Creveld maintains that a pre-modern command regime – which consisted almost entirely of combat leadership – existed for millennia and that there was little difference between the command of the Roman legion and the late-Medieval crusade.[34] This is a simplification. Although combat leadership was a persistent theme, it is now clear that there were very significant differences within Western systems of command in antiquity and the middle ages.[35] Moreover, he ignores global differences during the era of agrarian civilization entirely; he implies that Western, Asian, Oriental and pre-colonization American leaders all commanded in the same way. In reality, command has been far more diverse than van Crevold allows. Nevertheless, command is not random, nor has command assumed an infinite number of morphologies. Identifiable regimes of command have emerged and persisted for significant periods. Van Creveld may exaggerate when he identifies a Stone Age command regime which lasted for millennia, but it is not unusual for a particular system of command to remain stable for decades, sometimes even for a century or more. As large organizations, the armed forces tend to evolve slowly and, consequently, warfare assumes a recognizable pattern in historical eras. Stable organizational and operational conditions generate coherent methods of command, but as these conditions change new regimes of command emerge.

The following chapters analyze the transformation of command from 1914 to the present. The object is to show that, continuities notwithstanding, the morphology of divisional command has changed very significantly in the last twenty years. Throughout the short twentieth and early twenty-first centuries, divisional command has always involved the trinity of command, management and leadership. However, in contrast to the twentieth century, mission definition, management and leadership involve distinct practices today and the balance between the elements and their relative significance has changed. In particular, mission definition has become a more complex, subtle task for divisional commanders in the early twenty-first century,

---

[34] Van Creveld, *Command in War*.
[35] E.g., Christopher Teyerman, *How to Plan a Crusade* (London: Allen Lane, 2015).

while mission management has become an increasingly onerous burden for which greater decision-making capacity has been required; deputies, devolution and revised staff systems have been developed to assist commanders. Finally, the challenge of leadership has changed.

This analysis of the morphology of command and its three elements is necessary because it is often presumed, on the basis of assertion, that either command today is fundamentally different from the past or that nothing at all has changed. Neither position is satisfactory. There are both continuities and ruptures and it is essential to identify both. In each case, insufficient attention has been paid to the three elements of command. Only a close empirical analysis of the practice of divisional command between 1914 and the present can provide this level of detail. Of course, a fine-grained examination of divisional command in the twentieth and twenty-first centuries cannot be definitive; no empirical study can be. However, this study aims to describe a sufficiently broadly evidenced account of command across this era, on a variety of operations, to make the case for a distinctive command regime in the twenty-first century. It aims to plot the evolution of command morphology over the last century.

This book compares two regimes of command. It makes a simple, perhaps, bold argument. In the twentieth century, the fundamental simplicity of divisional operations allowed a single commander to oversee and direct missions with little assistance from staff or subordinates. The division was a homogeneous organization which could be commanded more or less effectively through the agency of a single general. As operational conditions have changed and the division has become a more complex, heterogeneous organization, the role of the commander has also evolved. Commanders have been presented with prodigious problems of coordination; cohesion has become more difficult. Consequently, it is to be expected that the particular ways in which commanders define, manage and then lead their divisions have also adapted. The central claim of this book is that in order to conduct divisional operations in the twenty-first century, divisional commanders can no longer monopolize decision-making. They have been forced to distribute their authority, especially in the domain of mission management. In short, they have been required to construct highly integrated, professionalized command collectives, capable of enacting diverse decisions across the division simultaneously. Of course, in their work on leadership, cited in the first chapter, Tony Zinni, Stanley McChrystal and David Richards alluded to precisely this shift. They outlined a more collaborate and integrated system of command in comparison with the twentieth century. However, while deeply suggestive, neither ever reached a level of conceptual accuracy or empirical breadth about what precisely this new regime of command involved. In the early twenty-first century, the armed forces have sought to ensure combat effectiveness through the creation of command teams which are able to fulfil all the decision-making functions associated with the execution of a mission.

4 TWENTIETH-CENTURY OPERATIONS

The modern division was institutionalized by the four major Western powers in the First World War as an organizational response to industrial, interstate warfare. The combined arms division remained the elementary formation for land warfare from 1914, and especially 1916, until the end of the Cold War. It was a 'full orchestra of *war*'. Its primary mission was always high-intensity combat. Any analysis of divisional command should, therefore, begin with a consideration of the army division on conventional war-fighting operations in this period, the short twentieth century. Consequently, the following three chapters examine divisional command in conventional interstate warfare, for which the modern division was invented. By the end of Chapter 6, the aim is to demonstrate the existence of a distinctive twentieth-century command regime and elucidate the reasons for its existence in warfighting operations. It will be argued that the practice of command from the First World War to the Gulf War in 1991 might be described as individualist, with divisional commanders personally monopolizing the decision-making process.

However, although the division was invented and principally used for high-intensity warfare in the twentieth century, it is, of course, insufficient to look only at conventional operations. Divisions were frequently involved in counter-insurgency and stabilization operations during the same period. It is imperative to include these operations in the sample, especially since they are likely to challenge the central argument of the book most strongly. Consequently, having delineated the practice of command on conventional operations, Chapter 7 examines divisional command on the classic counter-insurgency campaigns of the 1950s and 1960s in Kenya, Algiers and Vietnam. In this way, the next four chapters explore the morphology of command in the twentieth century. They identify the way in which divisional commanders defined their formations' missions, managed them and then led their troops on both warfighting and also counter-insurgency operations. They attempt to show that a common practice of command was evident across the period, irrespective of the type of operation.

The Mission

Although divisions were large organizations of some 20,000 troops engaged in intense industrial warfare, it is important not to exaggerate the essential difficulty of divisional operations in the twentieth century. On the contrary, the range of a divisional operation throughout the twentieth century was always strikingly narrow. The size of divisional fronts across the period, 1914 to 1991, illustrates the character of conventional divisional operations very well. Fronts are, by their nature, very simple and easy to measure. They, therefore, provide a particularly lucid way of describing divisional operations and their evolution over the whole period.

On the Western Front in the First World War, French doctrine stated that a divisional front extended between 1500 and 2500 metres.[1] The British Army broadly accepted these figures. While the number of infantry battalions was not irrelevant, the frontage was substantially determined by the range of artillery. In effect, a division held a line which allowed it to deploy all its artillery regiments to maximum effect. If a front were less than 1500 metres away, the divisional artillery had to be deployed in echelon, reducing the range at which it could provide supporting fire to the infantry; over 2500 metres and the artillery support was insufficiently dense. In defence, divisional fronts expanded a little. For instance, German doctrine specified that: 'The

---

[1] Grand Quartier Général des Armées de l'Est, *Instruction sur le combat offensif des grandes unités* (Paris: Imprimerie du service géographique de l'armée, 26 janvier 1916), 23; General Staff, *Summary of the French Instructions for Higher Formations in the Attack* (Washington, DC: Government Printing Office, 1918), 21. In translation, the US Army used imperial measurements; a divisional front was between 1650 and 2700 yards.

breadth of a divisional sector on the frontline in a defensive battle is to amount to between approximately 2500 metres to 3000 metres'.[2] Even in defence, a divisional front was plainly very small, though.

During the Second World War, as artillery improved, a divisional front almost doubled. In Normandy, for instance, which was a particularly congested battle-space until the breakout in late July, a typical divisional frontage was 4000 to 5000 yards. In addition, precisely because war was conducted on fronts, the depth of any divisional attack was extremely limited. British divisional doctrine in 1942 stated that 'a penetration of 3000 - 5000 yards will be about the limit a division can expect to achieve with its own resources'.[3] Consequently, during the Second World War, a divisional assault typically took place in an area of less than nine square miles.

Even by the very end of the Cold War in Germany, the divisional front had not increased that much. Indeed, serving soldiers highlighted the continuity with the First World War. One senior British officer who had served in the Cold War observed: 'The divisional level in the Cold War was a tactical organization committed to the close battle. It was unable to engage the enemy beyond its organic contact weapons. The division of the late 1980s had little more visibility on the battlefield than World War I. In the Cold War, you had a frontage of about 12 kilometres and a depth of your divisional artillery'.[4] He continued: 'In the Cold War, the divisional area was relatively small. In Germany, we had a confined frontage and space; 20 to 30 kilometres [in defence]. Movement would be made by night and there was about an hour drive between headquarters. It was all well within the HF [high-frequency radio] range of the vehicles'. At the end of the Cold War, divisional fronts had certainly been extended, then, but not radically so.

There were, of course, some exceptions to these standard divisional fronts. In Korea, for instance, divisional frontages expanded somewhat, especially before the Chinese intervention in November 1950. Notoriously, during the Chosin Campaign in November and

[2] Chef des Generalstabes des Feldherres, *Grundsätze fur die Führung in der Abwehrschlacht im Stellungskriege*, 13.

[3] CINC Home Forces, *Doctrine for the tactical handling of the division and the armoured division: Part I: Introduction; Part II: The Division; Part III: The Armoured Divison* (October 1942), 7.

[4] OF-8, Lieutenant-General (retired), British Army, interviewee 042, personal interview, 2 October 2014.

December 1950, 1st Marine Division became very dispersed, much to the consternation of its commander, Major-General Oliver Prince Smith. When his corps commander, Edward Almond, ordered him into a precipitate advance to the Yalu in mid-November, Smith complained that his division was spread over seventy miles, from Hugaru-Ri in the north to Wonsan in the south. At the height of the Chosin campaign after the Chinese intervention on 27 November, his formation was deployed along a corridor of thirty miles, from Yungdam-ni in the north to Chinghung-ni in the south. Eventually, Smith drew up 1 Marine Regiment to Koto-ri to reduce his lines to twenty miles as he executed his famous extraction operation. He disliked this extenuation of his division along a very vulnerable road, but it was eventually not entirely out of line with normal divisional operations of the time.[5]

There were other exceptions. Fronts became very large for Allied and Axis forces in the North African campaign of 1940–1942.[6] This was typical in desert warfare characterized by wide-open spaces. During the Gulf War in 1991, when the armoured and mechanized divisions of the US-led coalition again advanced across an almost-featureless and uninhabited desert optimal for manoeuvre warfare,[7] divisional frontages were extended considerably. For instance, the front of 24th Infantry Division, which was designated as the main effort of the XVIII Airborne Corps' campaign, was approximately forty kilometres.[8] However, 24th Infantry Division's front was unusually wide because it attacked on the western flank, where combat densities were very low. Moreover, the division's brigades attacked much smaller specific objectives; the actual battlefronts were narrow.[9]

---

[5] Lynn Montross and Nicholas Canzona, *The Chosin Reservoir Campaign* (Washington, DC: Headquarters USMC, 1957); Brigadier General Edwin Simmons, *Frozen Chosin: US Marines at Changjin Reservoir*; Gail Shisler, *For Country and Corps: The life of Oliver P. Smith* (Annapolis, MD: Naval Institute Press, 2009), 178–202; Clifton La Bree, *The Gentle Warrior: General Oliver Prince Smith, USMC* (Kent, OH: Kent State University Press, 2001).

[6] Niall Barr, *The Pendulum of War* (London: Pimlico, 2005).

[7] 'Due to the flat terrain in this area observation and the fields of fire will be excellent': Major Jason Kamiya, *A History of 24th Mechanised Division Combat Team during Operation Desert Storm* (Fort Stewart, GA: 24th Mechanised Division, 1992).

[8] Charles Lane Toomey, *XVIII Airborne Corps in Desert Storm: from planning to victory* (Central Point, OR: Hellgate, 2004), 237, 335.

[9] OF-7, Major-General retired, British Army, interviewee 139, personal interview, 30 May 2017. Based on 1 Division frontage.

Similarly, in the desert, the depth of the assault was also considerably extended. 24th Infantry Division advanced 413 kilometres from their line of departure on the Kuwait Border to the Rumaylah Oil Fields between the 24 and 28 February 1991.[10] A British officer who served in the Gulf with 1 UK Division confirmed the point: 'In the Gulf War, these ranges stretched to 50 or 100 kilometres. Communications were stretched and there was far more use of satellite'.[11] The introduction of rocket systems and aviation had also increased the depth of the divisional battlefield to about 100 kilometres beyond the frontline troops. Nevertheless, even with the exception of the Gulf War, divisional frontages between 1914 and 1991 were small. In the closer, more heavily populated terrain of Northern Europe,[12] a divisional front was, then, approximately 10–15 kilometres in attack, with a depth of rarely more than 10 kilometres, and 30 kilometres in defence; a division required 150 square kilometres in which to hide.[13]

The fact that divisions were assigned small fronts was highly significant in command terms. Not only did it simplify mission definition but it also circumscribed combat operations within a very narrow zone. Although divisions were susceptible to air strikes or guerrilla action in their rear area, the combat zone was restricted. Indeed, in his discussion of the division, General Rupert Smith, who commanded 1 UK Division in the Gulf War, claimed that one of the essential prerequisites of a division was the fact that while its forward elements were engaged with the enemy, it was sufficiently large to have substantial forces out the range of enemy artillery fire.[14] For Smith, 'this [depth] allows considerable freedom of action for combat power'.[15] Smith's point is important. While the divisional commander was certainly exercised by administrative problems in the rear area, divisional operations were simplified by the existence of small fronts. Because the depth of the battlefield was

[10] Kamiya, *A History of 24th Mechanised Division Combat Team*; Charles Lane Toomey, *XVIII Airborne Corps in Desert Storm: from planning to victory* (Central Point, OR: Hellgate, 2004), 334–5.

[11] OF-7, Major-General retired, interviewee 139, personal interview, 30 May 2017.

[12] See Gordon Sullivan and Jim Dubik, *Envisioning Future Warfare* (Fort Leavenworth, KS: Army Command and General Staff College Press, 1995), 12. They tabulate the increased distribution of forces from antiquity to the Gulf, though they forget that force densities in the Gulf were unusually low because of the environment.

[13] Rupert Smith, 'The Division', *British Army Review* 144, 1990: 78.

[14] Ibid., 77.

[15] Ibid.

short and the distance between logistical bases and the frontline small, problems of coordination were substantially reduced. Three hundred and sixty-degree, rear-area security and the problems of extended lines of communication, which would become critical framing issues for the twenty-first-century commander, were a relatively minor issue in the twentieth century. Offensive or defensive operations took place on very circumscribed frontages with limited depths. Divisional commanders fought a close battle in immediate support of and, indeed, often directly supervising their brigades. The spatial problem remained simple, limited and unidirectional. Mission definition ultimately involved a decision about the deployment of manoeuvre brigades along a single axis of advance. It was noticeable that Major-General Barry McAffrey, commander of 24th Infantry Division during Operation Desert Storm, was able to exhort his troops with a simple instruction just before the operation: 'Go North! We are never coming back. If you do not know what to do, keep moving north – on to the valley'.[16]

Of course, managing divisional operations was complicated. They involved many troops, vehicles and weapon systems. However, on any mission, there were only a few subordinate units which had to be deployed and coordinated. Typically, as noted in Chapter 2, a twentieth-century division fought with three manoeuvre units, which it supported with a brigade of artillery, a battalion of engineers and so on. There were only a few points of command. Moreover, subordinate units were overwhelmingly homogeneous national army units – or marine units in a United States Marine Corps division – assigned organically to the division. Divisions were discrete, tightly integrated vertical hierarchies which coordinated their own forces. Multinationality was rarely an issue. In addition, while tactical air defence was often a very significant concern for divisions, corps and armies usually assumed responsibility for air interdiction at the higher tactical and operational levels. In the twentieth century, divisions engaged in combined not joint warfare; air-land integration was very limited at the divisional level. Rather, from the First World War, the central problem was how to combine artillery and infantry or, later, armour: 'At every echelon, the principal preoccupation of command is to direct and combine all available fires, with a view to support the infantry'.[17] Divisional commanders coordinated

---

[16] Toomey, *XVIII Airborne Corps in Desert Storm*, 336.
[17] Ministère de la Guerre, *Instruction Provisoire du 6 October 1921 sur L'Emploi Tactique des Grandes Unités* (Paris: Charles-Lourauzelle and Co, 1924), 98.

functionally homogeneous forces, over whom they exercised formal authority.

Of course, there were some exceptions. Divisional commanders from the First World War sometimes employed reconnaissance aircraft; John Monash, the commander of 3rd Australian Division in 1917, was innovative in his use of them. By the Second World War, most armoured divisions had a small permanent air reconnaissance capacity. Air-land integration was particularly advanced in 1st Marine Division in Korea. In Korea in 1950, a Marine Air Wing supported O.P. Smith's 1st Marine Division. 1st Marine Division conducted an unusually integrated, joint operation at the divisional level for the twentieth century. It constitutes an important counter-example. Yet, the problems of air-ground coordination were very limited in Korea.[18] Even in 1st Marine Division, there was no close, multi-layered coordination of the type which has become conventional divisional business today.[19] In each case, air power acted in support of the division but almost independently of it in tactical terms. Its coordination was not a command problem at the divisional level.

The emergence of the helicopter and air assault operations from the 1960s certainly complicated operations at the divisional level. In addition to their complex logistic burdens, helicopters increased the range of operations and raised the question of tactical air-space management at the divisional level for the first time. The air assault division presaged the increasingly complex character of military operations in the twenty-first century. However, in the era of mass lineal warfare, air assault neither fundamentally altered the dynamics of the battlefield nor the problems of mission definition. Helicopters acted as the division's flying artillery or troop carriers on a lineal battlefield, operating over limited ranges. As Chapter 7 will show, the 9th Infantry Division in the Mekong Delta in 1968, for instance, had little problem in coordinating their own aviation.[20] The problems of truly joint and integrated operations, with highly complex air-space management issues, which would become so important in the twenty-first century, were not an issue for divisional commanders in the twentieth century. Specifically, as Western doctrine from 1916 emphasized, inter-arm cooperation

[18] Major-General O.P. Smith, United States Marine Corps Historical Division, Oral History Transcript 11–12 June 1969 by Benis M. Frank of the Historical Division, at General Smith's home in Los Altos, CA, 293.

[19] See Chapter 9.

[20] See Chapter 7.

was the divisional commander's principle concern. Even in armoured, mechanized and air assault divisions to the end of the Cold War, this issue remained primary. The most important command decision was how to deploy manoeuvre units and support them with the division's own artillery. Divisional commanders sought to generate mass combat power with their own assigned forces in tightly circumscribed areas.

Commanders were also little troubled by the problem of precision which would become such a vital concern in the twenty-first century. The careful synchronization of artillery fire with air power was unnecessary. The massive size of the enemy and the limitations of weapons technology for much of the twentieth century precluded excessive concern about accuracy. In addition, few political constraints operated in interstate warfare at this time. Divisional commanders were not usually concerned about civilian casualties or collateral damage.

From 1914 to 1991, then, homogeneous divisions fought land battles on narrow fronts. Moreover, in the twentieth century, divisions were exclusively tactical formations, which were subordinate to corps and army commanders. Consequently, divisional commanders were substantially given missions which typically referred to action in the next twenty-four hours. Western doctrine from 1916 highlighted the point. For instance, *Instruction sur le combat offensif des grandes unités* noted: 'In order to conduct their reconnaissance, it is essential that the divisional commander has received from the corps commander; his mission (axis and objectives); his zone of action; additional means placed at his disposal: notably heavy artillery and trench artillery'.[21] On this account, the divisional commander's role was bounded. Not only were the zones of action highly circumscribed and the objectives assigned but the general parameters of an operation had already been substantially established before the divisional commander had made any significant contribution. Decision-making was, then, limited in scope to a series of immediate actions in close proximity. Typically, a division conducted one action in a limited area every twenty-four hours.

None of this detracts from the difficulties of commanding high-intensity operations against near-peer enemies, against whom

---

[21] Grand Quartier Général des Armées de l'Est, *Instruction sur le combat offensif des grandes unités* (Paris: Imprimerie du service géographique de l'armée, 26 janvier 1916), 7; General Staff, *Summary of the French Instructions for Higher Formations in the Attack* (Washington, DC: Government Printing Office, 1918).

defeat was eminently possible. Command in the twentieth century was, of course, an onerous responsibility. Casualties were exceptionally heavy and commanders were only too aware of this burden upon them. One of the most successful divisional commanders of the First World War, John Monash, observed to his wife: 'I leave you to imagine a sense of responsibility which weighs upon one'.[22] Yet, the intensity of warfare in this period also paradoxically simplified decision-making for generals. Precisely because of the tempo and intensity of the fight in which heavy casualties were accepted, rapid, individual decisions, even if they were not perfect, were more likely to be successful, or at least to minimize casualties, than carefully cogitated, complicated courses of action. Highly refined decision-making was not required. Simplicity was repeatedly emphasized in Western military doctrine throughout the period: 'Every commander must know what is happening and must impress on his troops that refraining from doing anything or neglect is a worse mistake than the incorrect selection of a course of action'.[23] The point applied particularly to divisional commanders; without the ability to make rapid decisions, they risked failure and removal. Since speed, not accuracy, was of paramount importance, empowering a single commander to make decisions autonomously represented a sensible organizational solution.

In the light of the small frontages and the primacy of mass combined arms rather than joint, precision fires, the problem of mission definition was significantly simplified for any divisional commander. From 1914 to 1991, divisions fought under compatibly circumscribed operating conditions. The fundamental problem was one of scale, not scope. In the language of Stanley McChrystal, then, divisional operations of the twentieth century were complicated, not complex. They involved the integration of functionally homogeneous elements on simple tasks over short tracts of time and space. Divisional commanders were expected to conduct large-scale manoeuvres with their own assigned forces, maximizing their performance through the internal coordination of their units.

---

[22] Tony MacDougall, *The War Letters of General Monash* (Sydney: Duffy Snellgrove, 2002), Monash to his wife, 29 April 1917, 137.

[23] Heeres Division 487, *Führung und Gefecht der Verbundenen Waffen*, 1921, 7.

Mission Definition

Right to the end of the Cold War, as the Gulf War showed, division operations remained recognizably similar; divisions attacked or defended objectives on small fronts. The relative simplicity of the divisional mission facilitated the problem of mission definition. Receiving their mission from their corps or army commander, divisional commanders defined only its precise character themselves, negotiating details with their superiors. Indeed, the 1916 *Instruction sur le combat offensif des grandes unités* described how divisional commanders should define a divisional mission. Once he had received his mission from the corps commander, the divisional commander was expected to reconnoitre the zone of action 'accompanied by his artillery commander, engineer commanders and his headquarters; followed by other brigade and regimental commanders'. Divisional commanders – and their staff – then engaged in detailed intelligence analysis using photographs, observations from trenches and observations posts and aeroplanes.[24] At this point, they were able to define the precise mission. Before any work was conducted, the commander issued a plan of operations which established 'the object to be attained'.[25] This was all significant work. Nevertheless, mission definition itself was not onerous. A divisional commander in the twentieth century, and especially in the classic era of the First and Second World Wars, had only a few realistic options from which to choose. An objective, normally assigned by higher command, was identified. A divisional commander was responsible for the method of attack, within typically constrained parameters. The commander normally chose to attack either with one brigade up and two in reserve, or with two brigades up and one in reserve. Artillery, engineers, signals and logistics were assigned to support this manoeuvre.

One of the most famous examples of how quickly a divisional commander could define and execute a mission was Hermann Balck, commander of 11 Panzer Division, on the Chiri River in Russia on 18–19 December 1942. He demonstrated both the great skill required of a divisional commander and the fundamental simplicity of the problem.

---

[24] Grand Quartier Général des Armées de l'Est, *Instruction sur le combat offensif des grandes unités*, 5; General Staff, *Summary of the French Instructions*.
[25] Ibid.

In the course of the battle on the Chiri, he was ordered to mount an immediate divisional counter-attack against a strong Russian incursion from the north into Wehrmacht lines. The chief of staff of XLVIII Corps, Colonel von Mellenthin, radioed Balck: 'Suspend current attack. Russian forces broken through in-depth 20 kilometers further west'. Initially Balck dismissed the order: 'Fine we will clean up right here first and then we will take care of the other problem'. However, Mellenthin impressed the urgency of the mission on Balck: 'No, General, this time it is more than critical. 11 Panzer Division must go there immediately, every second counts'.[26] Balck extracted his division from the defensive operation to which it was committed, and redeployed it during the night for an assault eastwards against the left flank of Russian forces.

> So we halted our attack, refueled immediately, and distributed rations. I issued the warning order: 'Get ready to move in direction of Nizhree-Kalinouksi. Twenty kilometre march distance. Drive with headlights on. On 19 December in the morning you will be deployed as follows: the 111th Panzer Grenadier Regiment secures right flank against Nizhree and Kalinouski; the 115th Panzer Regiment penetrates enemy left flank; the 110th Panzergrenadier Regiment deploys on Line A-B against Russian attack, artillery... etc.'[27]

110 Panzer Grenadier Regiment blocked to the south of the Russian force, while 115th Panzer Regiment attacked its right (eastern) flank. Finally, 111th Panzer Grenadier Regiment, the right flank of Balck's division, attacked from the north, into the Russian rear. The operation, planned and executed within twenty-four hours, was an astounding victory; the division destroyed some 107 Russian tanks in this single action. With reason, von Mellenthin subsequently described Balck as 'one of our most brilliant leaders of armour'.[28] It was a well-conceived and well-executed mission, demonstrating a highly trained and cohesive division. Yet, while an outstanding command performance, the decisions which Balck had to make were bold but simple. He blocked

---

[26] Hermann Balck, *Order in Chaos* (Lexington, KS: University of Kansas Press, 2015), 270.

[27] Ibid., 270.

[28] F.W. von Mellenthin, *Panzer Battles*, translated by H. Betzler (London: Futura 1979), 304.

with his left and middle regiments, while his right flank, 111th Regiment, enveloped the enemy's rear. The fact that he could conceive and execute the mission so quickly demonstrates the relative simplicity of defining a divisional mission in the era of industrial warfare.

The problem of mission definition remained very similar through to the end of the twentieth century. In the Gulf in 1991, even though the frontage and depth of his attack was very large, Major-General Barry McAffrey's 24th Infantry Division initially advanced across the line of departure with all his three brigades – 197th, 1st and 2nd – up. However, at Phase Line Colt, 45 kilometres from the line of departure, the division assumed its attack formation; 2nd Brigade echeloned in behind 1st brigade on the right, while 197th Brigade advanced on the left.[29]

Mission definition was not genuinely complex, therefore. Instructively, throughout the twentieth century, divisions planned even major operations in days, rather than weeks or months. There were, of course, exceptions. The dense positional warfare of the First World War demanded extensive planning. The major offensives on the Western Front in the First World War, such as at Vimy or Messines Ridges, took a relatively long time to prepare. For instance, at the beginning of the Third Battle of Ypres in 1917, Plumer's Second Army issued its operation order on 10 and 19 May to the II Anzac Corps, which, in turn, gave its orders on 15 May to Major-General John Monash, commander of 3rd Australian Division. Twelve days later, on 27 May, having consulted closely with his brigade commanders, Monash distributed his 'Magnum Opus', the Divisional Operation Plan for Messines Ridge, although he also managed to issue thirty-six circulars before the attack itself on 7 June 1917.[30] 3rd Australian Division took about three weeks to plan Messines, then; from 15 May to 7 June. This was unusually long for a divisional operation; Monash was a very careful commander and trench warfare demanded extensive preparation. Throughout the period, there were other examples when divisions expended significant time in planning. In the Gulf War, 24th Infantry Division prepared for approximately three months

[29] Kamiya, *A History of 24th Mechanised Division Combat Team*.

[30] James Edmonds, *Military Operations in France and Belgium 1917 Volume II: 7 June – 10 November* (London: HMSO, 1948), 32; Charles Bean, *The Australian Imperial Force Volume IV: 1917* (Sydney, NSW: Angus and Robertson, 1933), 576–7.

for a four-day operation, although at the divisional level the actual planning took much less time. Most of the three months before G-Day on 24 February 1991 was spent moving into position and conducting Operation Desert Shield.

Yet, normally, the period of planning at the divisional level was far more limited, even on decisive operations. For instance, although the US Army's 82nd Airborne Division had been preparing for the Overlord assault since they arrived in England in the autumn of 1943, their precise mission was planned quickly and very belatedly. The mission of securing the western flank of the beachhead and protecting Utah Beach was initially divided into regimental tasks by February 1944; 505th Parachute Infantry Regiment were to land west of St Sauveur, seizing the town and bridge, and 508th were to seize Hill 110 while 507th protected the northern flank. However, from February onwards, Hill 110 proved to be a 'worry' since it was covered in anti-parachute obstacles. As a result, 'about a week before our movement to the departure airfields, the drop zones of all elements of 82nd Airborne were moved about ten miles east of St-Sauveur-le-Vicomte'.[31] The drop on Hill 110 was never made as, only days before the invasion, the Division was given a new mission of landing on both sides of the Merderet River in order 'to seize, clear and secure the general area of Neuville-au-Plain, St Mere Eglise, Chef du Pont, Etienville, Amreville'.[32] It is instructive that the Division's most important mission was planned so quickly. It demonstrates that divisional operations were difficult but not essentially complex enterprises in this era. Because the issue was only one of internal coordination over a limited time and space, missions could be defined and redefined relatively quickly.

82nd Airborne's mission in Operation Market Garden demonstrated the point even more clearly. On 16 August 1944, James Gavin was appointed divisional commander of the 82nd Airborne, after Matt Ridgway had been promoted to commander of the XVIII Airborne Corps. Gavin was the youngest major-general in the US Army and his first operation was Market Garden in the Netherlands only a month later. This was a hugely challenging operation for 82nd Airborne. Not only was Gavin a new commander but he also had a very inexperienced divisional staff, which was the youngest in the European

[31] James Gavin, *On to Berlin* (New York: Bantam, 1985), 94.
[32] Ibid., 98.

theatre of Operations. The new chief of staff, Bob Weinecke, was only a lieutenant-colonel, while three of his four branch chiefs were majors.[33] As a staff, they lacked experience, had not worked together before and had only a month to prepare for the operation, even though Nijmegen was the division's most difficult operation.

The division's objective consisted of a large triangle with the Wyler–Groesbeck–Mook road at the base, the Wyler–Nijmegen road to the east and the Mook–Nijmegen road to the west. Because of the size of the objective, 'there would be huge gaps in the perimeter'.[34] In addition, the division had to seize the bridge over the Maas River at Grave, take and hold the Groesbeek heights and secure at least one of four crossings over the Maas–Waal Canal before seizing the bridge at Nijmegen. The Division was ordered to complete four major tasks in a large area. Indeed, after the planning conference, Lieutenant-Colonel Bob Weinecke observed that 'We'll need two divisions to do all that'. Gavin did not disagree but observed: 'There it is and we're going to have to do it with one'.[35] Gavin was well aware of the challenges:

> Some very difficult decisions had to be made concerning when and where the landings to take place. We had learned, from the very beginning in Sicily, that it is better to land near an objective and take heavy landing losses rather than have to fight on the ground to get it. On the other hand, we had so many objectives over such an extensive area – approximately twenty-five miles – that complete loss of control of the division might take place the very moment the landings occurred if careful judgement was not exercised in allocating troops to particular objectives.[36]

It is notable that Gavin regarded a twenty-five-mile area as especially large for an infantry division at that time. Nevertheless, even with his inexperienced staff, Gavin defined the mission for Nijmegen rapidly. Indeed, the whole operation was planned in less than two weeks. In the end, Gavin assigned a parachute infantry or glider regiment to each of the division's four major objectives and gave them their supporting

---

[33] T. Michael Booth and Duncan Spencer, *Paratrooper: the life of General James Gavin* (Philadelphia, PA: Casemate, 212).

[34] Gavin, *On to Berlin*, 145–6.

[35] Guy Lofaro, *The Sword of St Michael: the 82nd Airborne Division in World War II* (Cambridge, MA: Da Capo, 2011), 298.

[36] Gavin, *On to Berlin*, 147.

assets. It was a problematic plan but Gavin had few other options. Even this mission was not ultimately that difficult to define; execution would be another matter.[37]

Administration

Divisional operations may have been tactically simple and mission definition, therefore, relatively facile. However, it is important to recognize the sheer scale, and therefore the difficulty, of administering divisional operations in the twentieth century. The management of divisional operations – 'control' in military terminology – was onerous. After all, a major-general commanded a 'full orchestra of war'. It was necessary to identify, assign, sequence and prioritize the tasks of all the division's units and then to coordinate them. This was intensely demanding work, requiring detailed planning and real-time coordination. It was imperative that divisional commanders identify all the tasks which the mission presumed and that they conducted those tasks properly.

Twentieth-century military doctrine demonstrates the administrative burden of this work. From the First World War – and especially from 1916, when manuals first began to appear – divisional doctrine emphasized the importance of comprehensive and coherent administration, providing excellent evidence about the specific managerial requirements of commanding a division. The French Army's 1916 *Instruction sur le Combat Offensif des Grandes Unités* is one of the first examples here. That manual prescribed the process of mission management in detail. Once divisional commanders had been given their mission by their corps commander, they were, as noted above, expected to develop a plan on the basis of their reconnaissance and to issue an operation plan (*Le plan d'engagement*). In the first instance, the operation plan defined the mission, 'the goal of the operation, the objectives of the Division (resulting from the orders of the Corps

---

37 At the strategic level, General Douglas MacArthur's intervention into Korea with the Inchon landings seems to demonstrate a similarly individualist method, recognition-primed decision model. See Pascal Vennesson and Amanda Huan, 'The General's Intuition: Overconfidence, Pattern Matching, and the Inchon Landing Decision', *Armed Forces & Society*, 2017, http://o-journals.sagepub.com.pugwash.lib.warwick.ac.uk/doi/pdf/10.1177/0095327X17738771, 1–23.

Commander)'.[38] The operation plan also included an immediate specification of the tasks and their coordination. Tellingly, *Instruction* moved quickly from mission definition to mission management; the real test of divisional command lay in the coordination of the assets and units to achieve this mission. Accordingly, having recorded 'the goal of the operation', *Instruction* gave a detailed, itemized list of all the tasks which the commander had to identify and assign:

a) the goal of the operation, the objectives of the division (following the order from the corps commander)
b) the location of the particular objectives to be attacked by subordinate units;
c) the disposition of forces, according to the results to be attained;
d) the coordination to be achieved, in concert with neighbouring units;
e) emplacement of artillery; field, heavy and trench artillery;
f) the zone of attack of each brigade;
g) the use of reserves;
h) eventually, the employment of gas clouds, special high explosives of all types, mine warfare.[39]

The plan of attack was followed by a plan for the preparation of the ground – *le plan d'amenagement definitif de terrain* – which consisted of:

a) a clarification of the earthworks which have to be built or completed: saps, shelters, weapons positions, communications, supply dumps, aid posts, etc.; and an evaluation of the coordination of logistical support.
b) deciding on observation and command posts;
c) complete the plan of communications to be established; telephone, optics, T.S.F [radio], signal, runners, pigeons, etc...;
d) complete the plan of the execution of work, determination of the order of priority, disposition of tasks among the units, transport etc.[40]

There were further tasks which were required for the operation plan to be viable:

[38] État Major Grand Quartier des Armées de l'Est, *Instruction sur le combat offensif des grandes unités*, 5.
[39] Ibid., 5–6.
[40] Ibid., 6

a) the destruction, by precise artillery fire, of enemy artillery;
b) the verification by the General and his headquarters, of the execution of all the orders in preparation for the operation;
c) moral preparation.[41]

A major attack was a complicated management problem, then.

British Army doctrine echoed *Instruction* closely. Indeed, although perhaps less prescriptive and more discursive, British Army doctrine from the First World War similarly recorded the tasks which the divisional commander had to complete before an operation. SS 135, *Instructions for the Training of Divisions*, was, of course, a central resource here. It advocated that before an attack, every unit had to be thoroughly trained and prepared to fulfil its function, including infantry, artillery, machine-guns, trench mortars, tanks, cavalry, the air force, signal communications, engineers and medical services. A divisional commander had to assign and coordinate the tasks of these ten specialized functions.[42] SS 135 went on to describe how the forces had to be deployed with a view to protecting the formation's flanks, identifying a reserve and 'carefully allotting' the sectors of attack. Good intelligence needed to be gathered and secrecy maintained by careful preparation, including the camouflaging of supply dumps. The later 1918 edition, *The Division in the Attack*, specified that commanders also needed to decide upon new artillery positions for the attack to extend the range of their guns, the accommodation of troops, their assembly positions, the selection and preparation of headquarters, rations, signals communications, including cable, visual, pigeons, message carrying rockets, wireless and runners, mounted orderlies, messenger dogs and, finally, the accommodation of signals personnel.[43] Of course, the coordination of the artillery with the infantry and, therefore, the fireplan was utterly critical but divisional commanders also had to assign tasks to their machine guns, engineers and supply units.

German doctrine in the First World War was concerned primarily with the defensive battle. Yet, the administrative demands here were prodigious too. For instance, the first chapter of *Grundsätze für die Führung in der Abwehrschlacht im Stellungskriege*, 'General

---

[41] Ibid., 6.
[42] The General Staff, *The Division in the Attack*, 1918, SS 135 (Shrivenham: Strategic and Combat Studies Institute), 15–19.
[43] The General Staff, *The Division in the Attack*, 29–35.

Principles of Combat Leadership', begins with a list of fifteen conditions which generals had to ensure before the start of an engagement. These included: working out what weapons, ammunition and equipment the troops needed; the construction of lines of communication and the preparation of the deployment of troops to battle; confirming specific divisional and regimental sectors and so on.[44]

The Headquarters

It is quite clear from British, German and French doctrine that, by 1916, the modern division had begun to generate substantial managerial burdens; 20,000 troops had to be directed, organized, coordinated and sustained. In the late eighteenth and nineteenth century, a divisional commander had a miniscule staff, consisting of several aides, normally organized in an informal and ad hoc way.[45] However, during the First World War, the demands of combined arms operations had propelled the administrative burden to a new level. Consequently, divisional headquarters emerged as a permanent institution with a standardized structure, a dedicated staff and established staff procedures in the armies of all the major Western powers for the first time during the First World War. The emergence of the standing divisional headquarters was an extremely important moment in military history, with profound implications for modern command. An understanding of the structure of the divisional headquarters and its national variations at this time is necessary. This is particularly the case because one of the most striking and important changes to the division in the twenty-first century is the reorganization of the divisional headquarters. The significance of the contemporary reforms for command becomes apparent only when contrasted with the structure of a divisional headquarters in the previous era.

The French divisional headquarters of the First World War era was organized on the Napoleonic staff system, consisting of four 'Bureaus': the First (personnel), the Second (intelligence), the Third

---

[44] Chef des Generalstabes des Feldherres, *Grundsätze für die Führung in der Abwehrschlacht im Stellungskriege*, 2–3
[45] See Paul Baron Thiebault, *The Memoirs of Baron Thiebault (Late Lieutenant General in the French Army) Volume I and II* (Memphis, TN: General Books, 2012).

(operations) and the Fourth (logistics). It is significant that the French Division had no plans cells; divisions conducted missions rather than operations or campaigns. They operated in a time span of hours and days, normally planning missions for the next day. In addition, the commander was assisted by an artillery commander with his own brigade headquarters, which generated fireplans, and an engineer commander, who developed the engineering plan. Although this structure underwent some adaptation and personnel expansion in the course of the twentieth century, the French divisional headquarters retained this basic structure. Consequently, although it was supported by a larger headquarters company and signals detachment, the core of the headquarters was extremely small. The commander was assisted by a deputy commander and an artillery commander (both brigadier-generals), a chief of staff and a chief engineer (both colonels) and four lieutenant-colonels for each of the bureaus – eight senior officers in all. The bureaus themselves consisted of small teams of junior lieutenants and captains. In all, a divisional headquarters in the French Amy in the First World War headquarters consisted of just over twenty staff officers; this expanded to nearly fifty in the Second World War.

Later during the Cold War, the French divisional headquarters expanded significantly. In the Gulf War, for instance, the French Army deployed a single division, 6 Light Armoured Division, which fought out on the far-western flank, to the left of 24th Infantry Division. The division attacked on two separate axes with two brigade-sized forces, assigned respectively to the west and east. According to one source, the headquarters of 6 Light Armoured Division consisted of 500 personnel.[46] This seems unlikely to have referred to the number of staff officers, since the French national headquarters commanded by Général de corps d'armee Michel Roquejeoffre, above 6 Light Armoured Division commanding Operation Daguet as a whole, consisted of only 350 staff.[47] The figure, therefore, presumably includes all the supporting headquarters company with its protection details. It seems likely that the actual staff of the division numbered between 100 and 200, like equivalent US and British divisions. In order to conduct this operation, the commander of 6 Light Armoured Division created to two small command posts, Rouge and Vert, each of which was responsible for

[46] https://fr.wikipedia.org/wiki/Opération_Daguet.
[47] Toomey, *XVIII Airborne Corps in Desert Storm*, 345, 349.

the western or eastern brigades. During the two-day attack, General de Brigade Janvier moved between the two headquarters, depending on which axis was the main effort. It is notable that the two command posts were commanded by lieutenant-colonels rather than full colonels or brigadiers. The relatively low rank of the commanding officers suggests that the command posts were very small. Throughout the twentieth century, French divisional headquarters were small, attaining a size of about 100 staff officers only at the very end of the Cold War.

During the First World War, the US Army division adopted the French headquarters system because, in addition to long-standing connections, its formations fought mainly under French command. It retained this Napoleonic system throughout the twentieth century and, indeed, even in the contemporary divisional headquarters the traces of the original structure are plainly evident, as many of the cells retain the same name and function. Accordingly, the US Army Division from 1917 onwards was organized into four cells, G1 through to G4, each with the same function as the equivalent French Bureau. Like the French Army, American divisional headquarters in the first half of the twentieth century were small. In 1939, the US Army's consolidated table for the infantry division recorded a wartime complement of thirty-one officers: one major-general (the commander), one colonel (the chief of staff), twelve lieutenant-colonels (SO1s), four branch chiefs and eight others, six majors (SO2s), eight captains (SO3s) and three lieutenants. To this number might be added the headquarters of the artillery brigade, consisting of one brigadier and his staff, and the chief engineer (a colonel) with his.[48]

Of course, an American divisional headquarters required additional personnel, including non-commissioned officers and enlisted men, for its support but the staff was diminutive. By 1945, the US divisional headquarters had increased to forty-two officers, with the addition of a brigadier as assistant divisional commander and an additional colonel as assistant chief of staff. At this point, there were only eleven lieutenant-colonels but the number of majors and captains had increased to ten and eleven, respectively, with one post open to either a major or captain.[49] The increase in majors (SO2s) and captains (SO3s)

---

[48] The War Department, *Table of Organization No.7 The Infantry Division Consolidated Table*, 1 September 1939, 2.
[49] War Department, *Table of Organization Infantry Division*, 24 January 1945, 2–3.

implied an increase in administrative load, matched by a slightly higher rank profile at the top of the division. Nevertheless, the divisional headquarters had plainly changed very little. Although an armoured division organized itself into two and, later, three combat commands in the Second World War, its headquarters had the same basic structure and personnel; it was organized into cells, G1 to G4, although the G3 cell included a small air cell.[50]

The American Army Division evolved slowly in the second half of the twentieth century, gradually expanding in numbers and cells. By 1959, an infantry division could be augmented by G5, a civil affairs branch, which was not always activated.[51] In the 1980s, the G5 civil affairs branch was redesignated as a permanent plans branch, by which time the divisional headquarters consisted of approximately 100 staff officers. During the Gulf War, for instance, 24th Infantry Division consisted of five branches and approximately 150 staff officers.[52] Like the French Army, the US Army headquarters underwent significant but limited expansion in terms of structure and personnel between the First World War and the end of the Cold War.

The British Army, and therefore all its commonwealth divisions, in the First and Second World Wars and in Korea organized divisional headquarters on a different system. Instead of the Napoleonic staff system, the headquarters was organized into three branches: the General Staff (G), Adjutant General (A) and Quartermaster General (Q). The G branch was responsible for intelligence and operations; the A and Q branches together dealt with administration. In line with the British Army tradition of commander-led operations, the divisional headquarters had less representation at the higher ranks. There was no chief of staff. The crucial officer in the headquarters was the General Staff Officer 1 (GSO1), the lieutenant-colonel in charge of operations in the G (operations) branch. There were some extremely famous individuals who fulfiled this role in both the First and the Second World Wars; Lieutenant-Colonel Bernard Montgomery, for instance, finished the First World War as GSO1 in 47th Division; Lieutenant-Colonel

---

[50] War Department, *Armored Command Field Manual FM 17–100: the Armored Division* (Washington, DC: US Government Printing Office, 1944), 4.

[51] US Army, *Infantry Division Special Text 7-100-1* (Fort Leavenworth, KS: US Army Command and General Staff College), 5.

[52] It has been difficult to affirm this figure precisely. This figure is an estimate based on the size of 1 UK division.

Roy Urquhart served as the GSO1 of the 51st Highland Division from 1942 until the summer of 1943, before being rapidly promoted to command the 1st Airborne Division on Market Garden in September 1944. After the Second World War, the G branch consisted of eight officers: an operations cell comprising the GSO1, assisted by a GSO2 (a major) and two GSO3s (both captains), and an intelligence cell with one GSO3 and three GSO3 liaisons officers.[53] A and Q cells were united as the staff and services branch under the command of a lieutenant-colonel, the assistant adjutant (AA) and quartermaster general (QMG), who was responsible for all administration within the division. On the staff side, the AA and QMG was supported by a deputy assistant adjutant and a deputy assistant quarter master general, both majors, with one or two captains as staff officers. The services side also included a chaplain and medical, education, military police, catering and welfare officers.

Of course, as in the French headquarters, the artillery and engineering commanders played a crucial role in the British division. Initially the chief artillery officer was only considered an adviser to the divisional commander. The artillery commander was titled the Brigadier-General Royal Artillery to indicate this role but, in 1917, the BGRA was redesignated as the General Officer Commanding Royal Artillery (GOCRA) and later, in the 1930s, Commander Royal Artillery, to denote the genuine command authority which he held; the Commander Royal Engineers was similarly empowered.[54] Both had their own small headquarters. A British divisional headquarters in the First and Second World Wars was marginally smaller than its US equivalent, then; it consisted of about forty officers. A more obvious difference was the rank profile of the headquarters; there was only one brigadier general (the Commander Royal Artillery, CRA) and one full colonel (the Commander Royal Engineers, CRE), reflecting the British army's command-led culture and the primacy of brigade commanders over the staff.

The British divisional headquarters initially seems to have been very different from the French and American model. Yet, both in terms of function and personnel, it was, in fact, always closely compatible.

---

[53] War Office, *The Armoured Division in Battle*, 1952, 67.
[54] Kenneth Radley, *We Lead, Others Follow: the First Division 1914–1918* (St Catherines, ON: Vanwell Publishing, 2006), 92–3.

The British G branch corresponded closely with the French Second and Third Bureaus or the American G2 and G3 branches, while the A and Q branches were equivalent to First and Fourth Bureaus or the G1 and G4 cells; G dealt with operations and intelligence, A and Q with personnel and logistics. Not only was the headquarters functionally commensurate but there is little evidence to suggest that their performance differed significantly. In each case, the twentieth-century British and French or US headquarters coordinated the units within the division with equal efficiency – or inefficiency. Moreover, in the 1960s, as part of the NATO alignment process, the British Army adopted the Napoleonic staff system, which, by then, had effectively become the American rather than the French staff system. British divisions replaced the G, A and Q branches with G1 to G4 cells. As with the United States, the British division increased in size and structure in the second half of the twentieth century. By the end of the Cold War, a divisional headquarters consisted of five major branches, G1 to G5, and was comprised of approximately seventy officers.[55]

The German divisional headquarters demonstrated a strikingly similar evolution. In the First and Second World Wars, the German Army employed a distinctive staff system; the staff were divided into Führung (G), Quartiermeister (QM) and Adjutantur (A) – operations, logistics and administration.[56] The core of a German divisional headquarters, and by far the most important officer, was the Ia. The Ia was a lieutenant-colonel or a major on the General Staff who organized the Ia (or operations) branch; the Roman numeral designated its importance. It was the prime branch in the headquarters and the Ia, the leading staff officer. The German Ia was the equivalent of the British GSO1 but, in addition to controlling operations, the Ia assumed some command responsibilities and was also potentially able to take the commander's role if the latter were incapacitated, injured or killed; 'The General Staff Officer is in all matters concerning combat action the sole adviser of the Divisional commander'.[57] The Ia was, then, a GSO1, a chief of staff and an assistant divisional commander in one; 'at the divisional level the first GSO (Ia), although not a chief of the general staff, carried out

[55] See Chapter 5.
[56] Albert Seaton, *The German Army, 1933–45* (London: Weidenfeld and Nicolson, 1982), 98.
[57] Christian Stachelbeck, *Militärische Effektivität im Ersten Weltkreig: Die 11 Bayerishe Infanteriedivision 1915 bis 1918* (Paderborn: Ferdinand Schoningh, 2010), 43-4.

many of the same duties'. For instance, in the 11 *Bayerische Infanterie Division*, the staff-trained Prussian Ia Wilhelm Ritter von Leeb[58], who was highly regarded as 'brilliant' by the Commander General Paul Ritter von Kneussl, assumed the role of de facto chief of staff from February 1916.[59] Given his crucial role and the necessity for close partnership, the commander and the Ia were often appointed in pairs, moving on together.[60]

The I branch also included an Ib, a supply officer, who was the only other General Staff officer in the headquarters, and a Ic, an intelligence officer. The Ia was known as the 'first general staff officer', the chief of supply was the 'second' and the chief of intelligence was the 'third'.[61] The Adjuntantur (personnel, G1 or A branch) was designated as IIa, b and c and had only specialist officers appointed to it, not General Staff officers.[62] In addition to the main staff branches, the chaplaincy, medical and veterinary branches were also represented in headquarters. Of course, the divisional headquarters also incorporated the artillery and engineer headquarters.

As with their peers, the German divisional headquarters of the first half of the twentieth century was very small. For instance, in the First World War, the headquarters 11 *Bayerishe Infanterie Division* consisted in total of forty officers, 300 NCOs and 300 horses.[63] The enlisted troops acted as clerks, runners or they supported the headquarters and provided protection. In the Second World War, the headquarters staff remained more or less the same: fewer than fifty staff officers. The Wehrmacht – and SS military units – were dissolved in 1945 and when the Bundeswehr was established in 1955 the new German divisions adopted the headquarters structure of their American allies and mentors. The I, II, III branch system was replaced with the American G1 to G4 structure with an equivalent staffing model. The German divisional headquarters remained small throughout the Cold War, however.

---

[58] Leeb would go onto to become a field marshal in the Wehrmacht in the Second World War.

[59] Stachelbeck, *Militärische Effectivität in Ersten Weltkrieg*, 44.

[60] Seaton, *The German Army*, 99.

[61] Ibid., 98.

[62] Ibid., 98.

[63] Stachelbeck, *Militärische Effectivität in Ersten Weltkrieg*, 43.

As divisional instructions throughout the era make eminently clear, twentieth-century warfighting divisions were large organizations whose coordination was difficult. There were numerous units whose multiple functions had to be integrated for any operation to succeed; in order to synchronize the artillery fireplan with the infantry or armoured brigades' manoeuvre, numerous preparatory issues had to be addressed. Nevertheless, this survey of French, German, British and American division structure from 1914 to 1991 demonstrates two important points.

First, from the outset, the headquarters of the combined arms division might have taken three different forms: the Napoleonic, G or I structure. Yet, functionally and structurally, these organizational structures were always closely compatible. In order to operate effectively, the division had to coordinate six essential functions: manoeuvre, fire, intelligence, communications, supplies and accommodation. While their organizational structure differed somewhat, British, German, French and American headquarters all reflected these same functions and the cells themselves were, in fact, extremely similar. In every case, the headquarters was effectively divided into two main functional areas: operations (including intelligence) and logistics (itself divided into the management of personnel and the administration of supplies). Precisely because the organizational problems were much the same, by 1917, the major Western powers had converged on a common pattern of divisional management which endured to the end of the Cold War.

Second, throughout the twentieth century, the divisional headquarters were small; they consisted of about forty officers during the first half of the twentieth century, in the First and Second World Wars and in Korea, increasing to about 100 staff by the end of the Cold War and in the Gulf War of 1991. Even so, they remained lean and functionally limited organizations, adding only one cell – the G5 plans cell – by the end of this period. The functional simplicity and smallness of the divisional headquarters affirms an important point about military operations during the twentieth century. It has already been established that the definition of a divisional mission was relatively straightforward in the era of mass armies. While the management of a divisional mission was more administratively demanding, it would be wrong to exaggerate its complications, even in the positional warfare of the First World War when very significant preparations had to be conducted if strong enemy defences were going to be successfully breached. From

1914 to the Gulf War in 1991, small divisional headquarters repeatedly planned and executed multiple operations, often with resounding success. Even when divisions failed, there was no suggestion that the headquarters structure was at fault or that they were organizationally inadequate to the managerial task of coordinating a division. In this period, divisional commanders could define their formations' missions quickly and with relative ease and they could manage the tasks which those missions involved with a very small staff, organized into a simple branch structure. Typically, while monopolizing the executive responsibility of decision-making, divisional commanders relied on one principal staff officer who organized administrative details with the staff.

Staff Work

The divisional headquarters, with its standing staff, was designed to manage large-scale and complicated military operations. Consequently, a series of bureaucratic practices – and associated artefacts – also emerged alongside the standing headquarters to facilitate administration. Although these procedures have been rather overlooked – paperwork is, after all, not very interesting – they are very important to the understanding of twentieth-century command. Andrew Godefroy has noted the importance of efficient and detailed administrative procedure to military success in the First World War. In his analysis of the Canadian general Arthur Currie, Godefroy examines the Battle of Mount Sorrel, Currie's first major operation as commander of the 1st Canadian Division. A brigade attack on this objective had failed on 3 June 1916 because of poor preparation. Consequently, when ordered to mount another assault, Currie 'insisted on being given sufficient time to conduct proper battle procedure'.[64] With 'his penchant for meticulous intelligence preparation', every detail of the new German defence positions was identified and, on 6 June, when he issued his Operation Order, he had a highly developed target list. As a result of this careful staff work, the attack was a success, despite terrible weather.[65]

[64] Andrew Godefroy, 'The advent of the set piece attack: Major General Arthur Currie and the Battle of Mount Sorrel 2–13 June 1916', in Andrew Godefroy (ed.), *Great War Command: historical perspectives on Canadian Army Leadership*, 1914–18 (Kingston, ON: Canadian Defence Press, 2010), 14.
[65] Ibid., 14–15.

It was impossible to coordinate divisional activities without a coherent means of managing tasks and controlling subordinate units. In the fog of battle, some reliable method was required which imposed order on the formation. In particular, commanders had to know where their troops and the enemy were and what they were doing and to be able tell their units what to do clearly, precisely and efficiently. Staff work fulfilled these two vital functions; it collated information about the units in the division and communicated orders to them. There were two decisive innovations in the First World War which allowed the headquarters and its staff to fulfil these functions: the tactical operations centre with its the situation map and the written operations order. These practices became so imbedded into the headquarters and so routinized that they might even be termed as institutions in their own right. They were crucial to command.

The Tactical Operations Centre

A number of terms have been applied to the divisional operations room: 'Divisional Tactical Operations Centre', 'Situation Room' or 'War Room'. The specific title is not significant. In each case, the operations room was established as the critical command node of the division during the First World War; it was the 'nerve centre'.[66] Located in a farmhouse or some other convenient building a short distance from the frontline, or more rarely in a dug-out, it consisted essentially of two elements: the situations map and a communications system (typically telephones and radios). The divisional tactical operations centre was not a total novelty in 1914. Command posts and head-quarters had been in existence for at least 150 years. However, they had not normally been formalized at the divisional level. The purpose of the tactical operations centre was to monitor current operations and prepare, on the basis of immediate developments, for future ones. The situations map was absolutely critical here and, during the First World War, the detailed map became standard equipment for a division.

---

[66] Department of the Army, *FM 17–100 Armored Division and Combat Command* (Washington, DC: US Government Printing Office, 1949), 42; *US Army Infantry Division Special Text 7-100-1* (Fort Leavenworth, KS: US Army Command and General Staff, 1959), 8.

German doctrine in the First World War stressed that divisional staffs had a responsibility to ensure that information about the
position of friendly and enemy troops was complete and accurate[67] on
this map:

> The collation of intelligence on maps of different types and scales
> and their allocation is dealt with in the main in relation with
> the map and survey branches at the General and Army Higher
> Commands. Yet other echelons – divisions, artillery commanders
> and conditionally even regiments and battalions – produce special
> maps and printed sketches on the basis of intelligence reports for
> their own purposes.[68]

Of course, European cartography was always intimately related to
military requirements. From the eighteenth century, increasingly large-
scale military operations could be planned and coordinated only
by reference to accurate maps and, of course, Napoleon depended
upon them. However, both the scale of the maps in usage and also
the division's reliance on them was novel. Before the First World
War, divisional commanders had been in immediate proximity with
their brigades; they had led rather than commanded them. Moreover,
the map was now augmented by overlying traces or 'talcs' (made of
grease-proof paper or acetate) which depicted the precise position of
friendly and enemy positions, trench lines and guns. The map became
the central collective reference point in the operations room for the
GSO1, Ia or G3. In addition to the central operations map, each staff
section maintained its own 'situation map': 'In divisions and higher
units, each staff section keeps a situation map constantly up to date
showing graphically thereon such data as pertains to the activities of
the section'.[69]

In his memoir of his service as a clerk in the G3 cell of 82nd
Airborne Division's headquarters in Sicily, Normandy and Holland,
Sergeant Len Lebenson described how he and some colleagues were
responsible for the maintenance of the division's situation map. In

---

[67] Chef des Generalstabes des Feldherres, *Grundsätze für die Führung in der Abwehrschlacht im Stellungskriege*, 17.
[68] Ibid., 18.
[69] War Department, *Staff Officers' Field Manual: Part 1 Staff Data* (Washington, DC:
US Government Printing Office, 1932), 16.

Normandy, the divisional command post was set up in a small tent in an orchard near St Mere Eglise and the technology was very simple. The map of the immediate area was mounted on a board and Lebenson marked the position of the regiments and battalions with sheets of grease-proof paper that lay over the map. Every day, these overlays were updated.

> When we were reunited as a group, our routine centred around the map, daily reports, the issuance and receipt of orders, and the keeping of the all-important journal. The time for each day's Situation Report was fixed at midnight. Each of the lower formations (Regiments etc.) was required to get their reports to us by midnight so that they could be collated and brought into the Division's nightly report.

On the basis of these reports, Lebenson and his colleagues produced fifty copies of the situation map to be distributed to the division. They also amended their own operations map in the headquarters.

> Another duty, which I have referred to before, was the maintenance of the Operations Map. On a piece of plywood about 4-foot square, we would assemble a 1:25,000 scale map which covered the immediate battlefield. This map came in sections which we would thumbtack to the board, all of it to covered by a sheet of acetate. Writing on this surface was by way of grease pencil, one of our most precious commodities. On the scale of the map, one half inch would equal slightly less than 1,100 feet, and two and a half inches would roughly equal a mile. (In that scale the whole of the United States would cover the area of the size of two football fields.) The position of our Division would be represented more or less in the centre of the map with room to have the neighbouring units shown on each of our flanks ... The map used to plot battle plans and the first item to be viewed by visitors, was my responsibility.[70]

This is an interesting passage. It reveals that for all the prodigious weaponry at a division's disposal, one of its most precious pieces of equipment was the humble grease pencil. Without a device to mark the positions of the division's and enemy's positions on the map, it

---

[70] Len Lebenson, *Surrounded by Heroes* (Philadelphia, PA: Casement, 2007), 128–9.

was more or less impossible to command the division. It was impossible to see where forces were deployed, what enemies they faced and, therefore, what might be an appropriate plan. In addition to the map, and as Lebenson's statement clarifies, the headquarters simultaneously kept a journal or diary which recorded all major events and a log of messages.

Consequently, the operations room, with its situation map and record-keeping, assumed a standardized form from the First World War.[71] The central purpose of the situation map was to generate a shared situational understanding of the division's dispositions. In this way, by recording all the relevant information from across the division, these documents explicitly aimed to facilitate decision-making. They enabled commanders to visualize the battlefield and, therefore, to be able to decide how best to deploy their forces. The operations room with its situation map was a vital command tool.

Despite remarkable developments in military technology, the map remained essential to command right up to the end of the Cold War. During the Gulf War, for instance, Major-General Barry McAffrey, commander of 24th Mechanised Division, was punctilious about the maps in his divisions tactical operations centres. He 'demonstrated an intense interest in maps, regarding them as precise tools of command':

> He specified the finest details of map assembly, marking and display. He was concerned about the thickness of the plexiglass covering them, the selection of target reference points, the details of map accuracy. He wanted place names and roads highlighted, and he specified how unit symbols would be displayed. He wanted all maps standardized throughout all command posts. In practice, he often moved his eyes to a point within inches of the map, studying it in great detail and making key decisions based upon the information depicted upon it.[72]

Apparently mundane bureaucratic devices like the map were actually critical to modern command.

---

[71] War Department, *Staff Officers' Field Manual: Part I Staff Data* (Washington, DC: US Government Printing Office, 1932), 15–16.
[72] Toomey, *XVIII Airborne Corps in Desert Storm*, 61.

Staff Work

In addition to the operations centre, other decision-making tools were invented at the same time. Specifically, standard procedures were developed in the First World War and institutionalized thereafter about how a division should plan and order an operation. In its planning, a divisional headquarters had to analyze the situation which confronted it and then instruct its troops what to do. This process quickly assumed a standard, bureaucratized format. Indeed, the operation plan and order assumed a form which remained stable for the entire century.

In the American Army, the planning process was called an 'estimate' and involved a five-stage process:

> In a general way, any commander making an estimate of
> the situation follows in his train of thought the sequence
> outlined below:
>
> (1) *Mission* – He considers the mission assigned to him by the higher authority or deduced by him from instructions from that source.
> (2) *Relative strength* – He considers the factors affecting the combat strength of his own and the enemy's forces.
> (3) *Enemy intentions* – He fully considers the probable enemy mission and the plans open to the enemy.
> (4) *Possible plans* – He fully considers the plans open to himself in view of his mission, the existing tactical situation and his strength and dispositions as compared to that of the enemy.
> (5) *Decision* – Having considered the above points, he formulates, in general terms only, the plan he adopts. This is the decision.[73]

The British Army used the term 'appreciation' rather than 'estimate' to describe the analytical process which informed decision-making. Yet, terminology aside, the procedure which the British institutionalized was equivalent to the US methods. Accordingly, a British Army appreciation involved four principal steps:

(1) The object to be attained.
(2) Factors which affect the attainment of the object.

---

[73] War Department, *Staff Officers' Field Manual: Part 1 Staff Data*, 28. The paragraphs have been abridged in citation so that only the first line of each is given.

(3) The course of action open to the writer and to the enemy.
(4) The plan.[74]

Significantly, British doctrine, like American, emphasized mission definition: 'the bed rock of an appreciation is the correct definition of the "object" to be attacked'.[75] The instructions continued to specify the precise factors which a headquarters must consider: time and space, weather, time of year, phases of the moon, security, communications, water supply, etc.[76]

Once a division had conducted an estimate and developed a plan, it then had to order its subordinate units to execute this plan. The order, and especially the standard written order, facilitated command. The written order ensured that the commander and staff officers completed a routinized, analytical process in which they were forced to consider all the factors at work and the functions which needed to be fulfilled; it prevented the omission of critical considerations, such as supply or engineering works. The standardization also reduced the chances of misunderstanding and confusion on the part of subordinate units because instructions assumed a predictable form.

The 1918 edition of the British Army's SS 135, *The Division in the Attack*, usefully records this systemization. Having issued a warning order, 'the divisional staff should then work out the necessary details to give effect to the plan outlined in the memorandum, and should issue them in a series of "Instructions"', which included further details about the work required to organize the attack, the divisional defensive system, the assembly areas, the artillery plan, the employment of machine guns and so on.[77] Finally, an operation order consisting of five central elements was issued:

a) such information on the enemy as will affect the recipients of the orders;
b) information with regard to other troops who are to take part in the attack, including the general objective of the corps and of the divisions on the flanks etc.;
c) a brief summary of the intentions of the divisional commander;

---

[74] War Office, *Operations: military training pamphlet No. 23 Part III – Appreciations, orders, intercommunications and movements* (London: HMSO, 1939), 1.
[75] Ibid., 2.
[76] Ibid., 2.
[77] The General Staff, *The Division in the Attack*, 37–8.

d) the objective of the division and the objectives of the assaulting brigades;

e) the particular instructions to those to whom the order is issued.[78]

The standardization of the written order was widespread. For instance, in 1932, the US Army instructed staff that a formal field order should include a heading, a date, a map reference and the distribution of the troops, followed by five critical paragraphs:

1. Information
2. The decision and general plan.
3. Tactical instructions to subordinate units.
4. Administrative instructions.
5. Provisions for the maintenance of signal communication.
    (a) *Paragraph 1* contains such information of the enemy and friendly troops as subordinates should know in order that they may cooperate effectively in the performance of their tasks.
    (b) *Paragraph 2* contains the general plan of the commander or so much thereof as embodies his decision and the general plan for the employment of the command as a whole to meet the immediate situation.
    (c) *Paragraph 3* gives a definite task to each of the several combatant factions of the command in order to carry out the main plan outlined in *Paragraph 2*.
    (d) *Paragraph 4* contains administrative instructions.
    (e) *Paragraph 5* contains instructions providing for the maintenance of signal communications.[79]

The five-paragraph order described by US doctrine in the 1930s subsequently became the standard NATO orders format and remains in use to this day.

As already noted, artillery, and therefore the fireplan, became critical in the First World War: 'Since on the fire plan depends the success of the operation, it will be the main consideration of the divisional commander with advice from the CRA'.[80] Moreover, precisely because so much artillery was required, developing a fireplan involved a very significant administrative effort: 'The problem of the concentration

---

[78] Ibid., 39.

[79] War Department, *Staff Officers' Field Manual: Part I – Staff Data*, 1932, 31–2. The descriptive paragraphs have been shortened to record only their first sentence in each case.

[80] War Office, *The Infantry Division in Battle*, 1950, 34.

of artillery is complicated by preliminary work which has to be carried out on the gun positions and on the dumping of ammunition, and by the difficulty of concealing these positions from enemy air reconnaissance'.[81] Even before they could fire, the headquarters had to site the guns carefully and organize for their supply. In addition, commanders had to decide whether they wanted a barrage or timed concentrations. In addition, there were other considerations: 'the fireplan must pass well beyond the objective' and 'in order to make the fireplan flexible and to be able to deal quickly with unforeseen vicissitudes of battle, it is necessary to have a proportion of the artillery firing in depth which can be taken off the fireplan on call without interfering with the basic plan'.[82]

The result was a very detailed document, attached to the main orders and involving two elements: a written order to the artillery batteries, designating specific fire missions (targets, timings and firing rates) for the operation, and a map-trace to overlay the batteries' own situation maps. For a creeping barrage, this trace depicted a successive series of lines which represented actual positions on the ground. Artillery units fired into the target boxes beyond each line for a set period of time and then lifted the barrage to the next line; with limited communications, this was the most effective way of generating mass fire. Like the written order, the fireplan was a precise standardized method developed in order to overcome the complex management problem of concentrating the artillery and coordinating its fire with the infantry.

A Problem of Scale

It is clear from all this evidence that divisional operations in twentieth century were demanding. Mission definition could be challenging. It was certainly not always obvious how best to select, conceive and execute an operation. Commanders had to consider a number of factors, such as ground, enemy, weather, combat ratios, logistics and neighbouring forces, in order to assess the probability of whether their divisions could succeed. They had to have accurate intelligence on the enemy, an excellent understanding of the tactical environment and the capabilities of their own forces and how best to exploit them. The

---

[81] Ibid.
[82] Ibid., 35.

possibility of heavy casualties and defeat were ever-present and exerted inordinate psychological pressures on them.

At the same time, the management of divisional operations was plainly onerous. Standing headquarters, permanent staff and standardized administrative processes rapidly became essential: operations centres, estimates, appreciations, orders and fireplans were all institutionalized into doctrine in 1916. The aim of these innovations was to ensure that all the necessary tasks required to fulfil a mission were addressed and that the units ordered to complete them were coordinated with each other. This standardization was necessary because the scale of divisional operations was so large that errors were very likely, especially since commanders and staff were often inexperienced and sometimes untrained. The managerial challenges presented by a combined arms division should not be underestimated; they were prodigious and many of the problems, being administrative, could be resolved only through standardized bureaucratic methods. The divisional headquarters was a novel modern invention, then. It would be wrong to ignore the crucial administrative reforms which lay at the heart of divisional operations from the First World War onwards. They constitute remarkable and historically important innovations which facilitated the prosecution of mass industrial warfare for the first time. However, it is also important not to misunderstand their significance.

Despite their scale and seriousness, divisional operations remained functionally simple mechanical problems throughout the period. Missions were lineal. They were conducted on small fronts, over relatively short distances, involving a few subordinate units, normally organic to the division; typically, divisional commanders coordinated three manoeuvre brigades with an artillery brigade supported by signals, engineers and logistics battalions. In attack, the options were very limited. Effectively, at the divisional level, the definition of the mission required three decisions: the objective, the direction of attack and the attack formation (two or one brigades up). Moreover, the parameters of any mission were already usually established or at least suggested by the corps commander, constraining these three decisions from the outset. As a result, mission definition, although hugely important, was not complex. Good commanders identified their divisions' missions very quickly.

Administration could be more troublesome. Numerous functions had to be fulfilled; specialized units had to be assigned a series of tasks. However, because of the constrained nature of operations and the homogeneity of the force, even this challenge was not excessive. Instructively, commanders managed their missions with a small staff, using a few basic artefacts: a map, a trace and the written order. Moreover, from 1914 right up to 1991, the structure of the divisional headquarters remained stable and its expansion limited; in eight decades, the staff approximately doubled from under fifty in the First World War to about 100 in the Gulf. This slow expansion of the staff is significant. It shows that not only was the fundamental problem of divisional operations compatible throughout the period but also that their challenges were not excessive. Commanders needed some assistance in managing operations but the extent of that staff support was limited.

Although this chapter is intended as a preliminary investigation of the challenge of divisional operations, it is possible, at this point, to make some preliminary observations about command in the twentieth century. Commanders had to direct homogeneous forces on tactically simple, limited but very dangerous missions over a small area. It was important to ensure that all the necessary tasks of which a mission was comprised were considered. Commanders had to complete a comprehensive inventory of preparations if they were to avoid incurring massive casualties. However, mission definition and mission management were bounded. The management of a divisional operation was, therefore, a problem of scale, rather than scope.

It is possible to summarize some of the implications of this chapter. The distinctive problem of divisional operations generated a recognizable form of decision-making across the twentieth century. With the assistance of a small staff to help them with management, divisional commanders were central to all decision-making; they defined the mission and continued to play a key role in its management, supervising the tasks. It is, of course, too early to claim that command in the twentieth century was individualist. This chapter is intended purely to introduce and to frame the issue of divisional command. However, notwithstanding the emergence of a standing headquarters, a permanent staff and professional staff procedures, it may be possible to suggest that the outlines of an individualist system of decision-making might nevertheless be evident from the analysis. Of course, focusing on the general problem of divisional operations and describing the emergence of the combined arms division, this chapter can in no way prove the existence of such a command regime. To understand twentieth-century command, it is necessary to examine specific commanders in detail to appreciate how they actually directed divisional operations and made decisions in combat. The next chapter will focus on precisely this issue. It will try to establish the argument that a distinctively individualist regime of command was evident in the short twentieth century, as a response to the specific operational problems which a division presented at that time.

5 TWENTIETH-CENTURY COMMAND

It is relatively easy to describe the general outlines of conventional divisional operations in the twentieth century and, of course, it is explanatory important to establish these basic organizational parameters. Divisional command was a response to these conditions. However, this description can only be preliminary. In order to understand divisional command in the twentieth century and, more, to argue that a coherent regime of command was discernible across this era, it is necessary to go into far greater detail. It is necessary to look at how generals actually commanded their divisions in this period.

There are several possible ways of doing this. Military historians have often focused on individual commanders. The historiography of the First World War, for instance, is replete with important studies of this kind. For instance, the centrepiece of Geoffrey Powell's biography of General Herbert Plumer is an account of his command of the 2nd British Army during the First World War. In particular, Powell documents that Plumer's close relationship with his chief of staff, Charles 'Tim' Harington, his use of command conferences to confirm his plans, his constant visits to his subordinates and his own close personal eye for details were critical to his success.[1] Powell convincingly shows that, despite his crusty appearance, Plumer was in fact a highly effective, modern commander.

Similarly, in their work on Henry Rawlinson, Robin Prior and Trevor Wilson take this approach even further. They use the example

---

[1] Geoffrey Powell, *Plumer: the soldier's general* (Barnsley: Pen and Sword, 2004), 155–7.

of Rawlinson to show how command practices developed during the First World War as the armed forces adapted to the new industrial conditions which faced them. Specifically, they are interested in exploring the problems of command at the army level, between high strategic command and the experiences of the soldiers themselves.[2] Prior and Wilson frequently pass individual judgement on Rawlinson as a commander. For instance, they assess his performance at his first battle at Neuve Chapelle in the following way:

> What all this shows is that Rawlinson in the planning stages of his first battle, had acquitted himself less than satisfactorily. He had shown good sense concerning fundamental principles: most of all the principle that infantry movements required powerful artillery support. But he had proved tardy in his own formulation of a plan embodying this principle, and had been content to promulgate the questionable schemes of a subordinate.[3]

However, although these studies focus on individual generals, their purpose is not simply biographical. They are attempts to demonstrate wider command methods. Christian Stachelbeck's study of Major-General Paul Ritter von Kneussl and the 11 Bavarian Infantry Division in the First World War is a notable recent example of this.[4] He uses Kneussl's experiences with this division to illustrate how command became modernized in the face of the exigencies of industrial warfare. He also shows how Kneussl, educated and socialized in nineteenth-century traditions, struggled to accept the de-centralization of control demanded on the Western Front.

In a collected volume on command on the Western Front, Gary Sheffield and Dan Todman have drawn on individual cases to develop a systematic account of the evolution of command in the First World War. Thus, for instance, Todman explores the structure of General Headquarters, with its General Staff, Quartermaster General and Adjutant General branches, to show how this structure and the officers in it influenced battle plans.[5] Other individual studies, such as those on

---

[2] Robin Prior and Trevor Wilson, *Command on the Western Front: the military career to Sir Henry Rawlinson 1914–18* (Barnsley: Pen and Sword, 2004), 394.

[3] Ibid., 29.

[4] Stachelbeck, *Militärische Effectivität im Ersten Weltkrieg*.

[5] Dan Todman, 'The Grand Lamasery Revisited: General Headquarters on the Western Front, 1914–18', in Gary Sheffield and Dan Todman (eds), *Command and Control on the Western Front: the British Army's experience 1914–18* (Staplehurst: Spellmount, 2004).

John Monash, Douglas Haig, Erwin Rommel, Matt Ridgway or 'Bert' Hoffmeister, adopt a similar strategy. Their central purpose is to assess each of these generals as a commander in order to illustrate the historical practice of command more widely.

Historians have employed individual case studies of particular generals to illustrate the practice of command in a specific period, then. The individual commander exemplifies a wider regime. Of course, historians are absolutely right to use individual case studies. In order to understand command, it is necessary to examine particular commanders. There is no generic or abstract institution of command, only its multiple manifestations by particular generals. Command exists only when it is exercised in particular times and places by specific commanders. The only evidence to be found on command is in particular individual cases, then. Moreover, only by examining individual cases in detail, is it possible to reach a level of analytical adequacy in relation to decision-making.

This study follows the historical method; it is based on individual case studies of a selection of particularly prominent divisional commanders. However, unlike much of the historiography of command, the following chapters do not seek to analyze command in one war but across the twentieth century as a whole. Its purpose is to identify a coherent regime of command from 1914 to 1991. There is clearly a significant problem of sample selection here. Specifically, it is necessary to generate a sample which is rich and wide enough to be considered representative. The cases have to be of a sufficient level of detail so that they are in themselves persuasive and, yet, diverse enough to be able to represent what is a potentially huge sample. This is not particularly easy. In the Second World War alone, Germany raised 250 divisions, Britain 62, America 89 and, in 1940, France 117 divisions. From 1914 to 1991, the Western powers raised many hundreds of divisions and they conducted thousands of operations in the First and Second World Wars, Korea and the Gulf War and on numerous counter-insurgency campaigns in Malaya, Kenya, Algeria and Vietnam. Any of these divisions and their commanders might be the object of investigation but it is also difficult to be certain which might be indicative of wider patterns.

Representativeness is plainly a challenge. Moreover, at some point, given a sample of this size, an element of arbitrariness has to be admitted. For every general who has been selected for analysis, there are many hundreds who were not. In some cases, random factors, such as previous knowledge, personal interest or the availability of material, played a role in the selection of particular generals. However, four principles have been followed in order to try and generate a sample which might be sufficiently diverse to be convincing. First, although the division may have been invented for conventional warfare, the following case studies include both warfighting and also counter-insurgency operations. This chapter and the following one discuss the issue of divisional command in conventional manoeuvre operations, while Chapter 7 draws on three case studies to examine the character of counter-insurgent command in the twentieth century. Second, where possible, commanders from all four major Western powers have been analyzed. It is vital to demonstrate that the appearance of a new regime is not a peculiar cultural adaptation limited to one country, but is a general organizational response to new conditions. Third, although by no means comprehensive, the sample includes examples from most divisional types: infantry, airborne, air assault, armoured, mechanized and marine divisions. Fourth, cases have been drawn from across the period 1914 to 1991. In this chapter in particular, there has been a conscious effort to include examples from the beginning, middle and end of the era: the First World War, the Second World War and the Gulf War. While recognizing definite developments in divisional operations, especially after 1970, the discussion of examples from the beginning and the very end of the era is essential if a claim about a distinctive command regime is to be maintained. It is necessary to show that for all the advances in military technology, the basic problem which confronted divisional commanders in the Gulf War and their solutions to them were closely compatible with those of their predecessors.

The sample is intended to be representative, then. Nevertheless, its limitations have to be admitted. No study can be truly comprehensive and this one does not claim to be. It attempts to identify two broad regimes of command on the basis of a sample of sufficient diversity, breadth and detail to be convincing. Of course, based on an inductive method, in which a general explanation has been developed on a necessarily limited empirical basis, the theory of command proposed here can only ever be more or less plausible. There might always be cases which disprove it. It is certainly true that in the twentieth century some generals were more collaborative than others, anticipating some of the collective, professional practices which have become the norm today. The theory of collective command cannot have the apodictic certainty of a logical argument. However, by analyzing the divisions of four major powers on two very different kinds of operation over the last century, an attempt has been made to generate a persuasive sample on the basis of which it might be possible to claim the existence of two distinctive command regimes.

Focusing on conventional warfighting, this chapter and the following one consider a series of individual generals in an attempt to argue for a broadly stable paradigm of command in the short twentieth century among the major powers and across different kinds of division. To this end, this chapter examines the cases of John Monash (1917), Bernard Montgomery (1940), Erwin Rommel (1940) and Rupert Smith (1991).[6] The following chapter will consider the question of combat leadership before, concluding with an analysis the command of counter-insurgency operations in the twentieth century. In those discussions, the cases of Matthew Ridgway, James Gavin, Jay MacKelvie, Charles Bullen-Smith, George Erskine, Jacques Massu and Julian Ewell will be discussed. There is little surprise about the selection of these commanders. In most cases, these generals are very famous. However, precisely because of their celebrity, there is a good archive of evidence about them, allowing for a sufficiently detailed comparative analysis to be conducted on them. Each of the case studies will analyse each of these commanders in terms of the principal executive functions: mission definition, mission management and leadership. The central claim of this chapter, focusing on the first two functions, will be that, notwithstanding the rise of the standing divisional headquarters with its staff and the planning tools developed from the First World War, decision-making was monopolized by the individual commanders in the twentieth century, often on the basis of their own intuition and by means of direct and personal intervention. Commanders defined divisional missions individually and, in fact, assumed the principal role

---

[6] These cases have been supported by additional studies on a number of other divisional commanders, who do not appear except in passing in the text – namely, Hermann Balck, Philippe Leclerc, Douglas Wimberley and Oliver Prince Smith.

in managing the mission with the assistance of a principal staff officer and a small staff.

John Monash

This study ostensibly focuses on the four major Western powers. It is rather unusual, then, to begin the analysis of divisional command in the twentieth century with the case of John Monash. Monash was a native of neither Britain, France, Germany nor America; he was an Australian who commanded Australian forces in the First World War. Some justification must be made for his selection, therefore. As a subject of the British Empire, he always served under British command, following British doctrine and methods closely. Consequently, although not British by nationality, he exemplifies divisional command in the British Expeditionary Force at that time. Indeed, his was recognized by General Douglas Haig as one of his exceptional commanders and was subsequently knighted by King George V. Moreover, as a celebrated early example of divisional command, he is highly useful in illustrating the distinctive practice of command in the early twentieth century. Indeed, Charles Bean, the official Australian army historian, highlighted Monash's modern qualities: 'he was, above all things, the first twentieth century general, a man with petrol in his veins and a computer in his head'.[7] Bean was, in fact, pointedly critical of Monash. At various moments he questioned his courage and seemed even to imply that Monash was a physical coward, even while emphasizing his evident qualities: 'That Monash was in some respects an outstandingly capable commander was well recognized in staff circles, but though a lucid thinker, a wonderful organizer, and accustomed to take endless pains, he had not the physical audacity that Australian troops were thought to require in their leaders'.[8] Elsewhere, Bean openly racialized his barbed praise: 'His Jewish blood gave him an outstanding capacity for tirelessly careful organization'.[9] Despite Bean's imputations,

---

[7] Geoffrey Serle, *John Monash: a biography* (Melbourne, VIC: Melbourne University Library, 2002), 382.

[8] C.E.W. Bean, *The Australian Imperial Force in France Vol VI: 1918* (Sydney, NSW: Angus and Robertson, 1942), 195.

[9] C.E.W. Bean, *The Australian Imperial Force in France Vol IV: 1917* (Sydney, NSW: Angus and Robertson, 1933), 562.

Monash exemplified a new kind of commander who emerged in the context of industrial warfare. Moreover, not only did he display some critical features of modern military command, but the material on Monash, in official histories, in the archives, his own autobiography and biographies, also recommends him as a focus of attention. His practice of command has been analyzed at great depth, facilitating the task of interpretation here very greatly. Despite his nationality, he is, therefore, a highly pertinent example of divisional command, not least because there is extensive primary and secondary material about his experiences.

Having commanded a brigade in Gallipoli, John Monash was appointed to command 3rd Australian Division in 1916. He eventually joined Plumer's 2nd Army in the spring of 1917 and fought at Messines and the subsequent Third Battle of Ypres. He was promoted to commander of 1 Australian Corps early in 1918. This analysis will focus on his command of 3rd Australian Division in 1917, especially at the Battle of Messines in June. Monash was certainly advantaged in his appointment as commander of 3rd Australian Division. Monash's divisional staff was 'very fine' and had been carefully selected by General Birdwood: Lieutenant Colonel Jackson (GSO1), Brigadier Grimwade (Command Royal Artillery) and Captain Pyke (Deputy Adjutant and Quarter Master General (AQMG)) were very competent officers.[10] In addition, Monash was lucky to be assigned to Plumer's 2nd Army. General Plumer and his chief of staff Charles Harington were the most effective and efficient command team in the BEF and the staff work of their headquarters was excellent. Monash was also perhaps advantaged to enter the war as many of the lessons of positional warfare had been learnt. Monash, for instance, paid close attention to the Canadian attack at Vimy in April 1917 and visited General Currie, who had become a proficient exponent of contemporary tactics, infantry-artillery cooperation and the limited operation. Monash was not an innovator, then. He did not genuinely invent any new techniques or tactics. However, he displayed a rare gift for recognizing the potential of various adaptations and of exploiting their potential by using them systematically.

---

[10] P.A. Pedersen, *Monash as Military Commander* (Melbourne, VIC: Melbourne University Press, 1985), 144.

Chapter 4 described the particular difficulties of mission definition and mission management for the twentieth-century division. Although missions were normally relatively simple to define, the administrative details were very significant. At Messines, for instance, Monash received his mission from the 2nd Army and it required little refinement or cogitation from Monash. The management of this operation was quite different, however, and it is here that Monash demonstrated his virtuosity. Monash was deeply conscious of the organizational challenges involved in modern divisional operations. In his letters to his wife, Monash lyrically described his conception of command and its problems:

> I wonder if it is possible for you to realize the scope and scale and dynamic splendour of a modern battle. No mere words can convey any idea of it, or of the complexity of the organization and administrative detail required to coordinate the action of 20,000 people and all the different weapons, guns, howitzer, trench-mortars, bombs, rifle machine-guns, tanks, aeroplanes, balloons, mines, etc.[11]

It is little wonder that he understood military operations as a vast engineering problem.

Monash's plan for Messines displayed an extraordinary pedancy. Yet, Monash was no mere dry bureaucrat. Monash had a rare facility to visualize terrain accurately, merely from his study of maps and photographs, and to imagine the units of his division advancing together in time and space. He was able to envisage military operations as a living machine:

> In every battle plan, whether great or small, it is necessary first of all to map out the whole of the intended action of the Infantry, at any rate on the general lines indicated above. When that has been done the next step is to work backwards, and to test the feasibility of each body of infantry being able to reach the allotted point of departure, punctually, without undue stress on of the troops, and without crossing or impeding the line of movement of any other body of infantry.[12]

---

[11] MacGougall, *War Letters of General Monash*, 136–7.
[12] Monash, *The Australian Victories in France*, 92.

This is an important and illuminating statement. In it, Monash dissects the command problem, which he confronted. In the first instance, Monash had to define a mission; he had to identify the infantry objectives. These objectives determined every other consideration, providing the boundary conditions for his subsequent planning. In fact, as this passage suggests, the identification of the infantry objectives was not particularly difficult and it was, in fact, often given to him by his corps commander. Monash's responsibility as a divisional commander lay primarily in managing the operation. Having visualized the objectives, Monash dissected every part of it so that he was able to identify and assign all the tasks which were required to accomplish it. Every successful division in the First World War had to have detailed staff work. The difference in 3rd Australian Division was that Monash, as the commander, not only monitored his staff's work closely but, in fact, did most of it himself.

Monash's first major operation was the assault on the Messines Ridge in June 1917, the opening phase of the Third Battle of Ypres; 3rd Australian Division were positioned on the right flank of 2nd Army. Monash appropriately called his plan for the attack his 'Magnum Opus' and, with all its subordinate instructions, it was six inches thick. The plan for Messines was remarkable.

Monash planned missions down to the company and, indeed, 'particularizing in some cases the employment of platoons'.[13] Before Messines, while Brigadier Jobson's scheme for the 9th Brigade battle rarely mentioned platoons and Brigadier McNicoll's 10th Brigade plan not at all, 'Monash considered them frequently, devoting each battalion's frontage by the number of platoons'.[14] He outlined platoon tasks, explained the criteria for consolidation and prescribed the length of new trenches to be dug as well as the number of tools.[15] Indeed, his GSO1, Lieutenant Colonel Jackson, who was himself an excellent officer, admitted Monash did 'a lot of work personally', while others claimed that 'Monash regarded his GSO1 as his G clerk' and advised John Gellibrand to draft his own order on taking charge of 3rd Division.[16] Before Messines, for instance, Monash personally plotted

[13] Serle, *John Monash*, 285.
[14] Pedersen, *Monash as Military Commander*, 162.
[15] Ibid., 161.
[16] Pedersen, *Monash as Military Commander*, 217.

the exact location of enemy trenches from aerial photographs.[17] Indeed, Charles Harington, to whom Monash had presented a copy of the Magnum Opus on 4 June, was astounded by the document, both amazed and disturbed by his attention to minutiae: 'I never saw such a document – wonderful detail but not his job. He would tell you which duckboard needed repairing but never in his life went near a front-line trench'.[18]

The command conference became an important forum in which Monash resolved all management issues. Before Messines, Monash employed the divisional conference as a crucial method of command, bringing commanders and staff together as a group: 'I want to leave nothing to chance … so we are going to talk these matters out to finish and we will not separate until we have a perfect mutual understanding among all concerned'.[19] During these conferences, he described the operation in detail from start to finish, outlining every subordinate action, often without notes. As a corps commander at Hamel the following year, Monash explained his method: 'At these [conferences] I personally explained every detail of the plan and assured myself that all present applied an identical interpretation to all orders'.[20] The lucidity of his expositions amazed – and delighted – his audiences. At the same time Monash was ruthless in confirming the work of his staff and subordinates. He attended conferences with sheets of paper with up to 100 questions for his staff; he crossed off each question in pencil and then eventually struck through the whole sheet when all of the issues had been answered.

Monash employed his conferences to allow his subordinate commanders to articulate concerns and for horizontal issues between commanders to be worked out, though, in fact, they are not recorded in the archive. However, the primary function of the conference was for Monash to impose his vision upon his commanders. For instance, when he became a corps commander he recorded that his first task was to 'acquire a moral ascendency' over his senior commanders and staff and 'to secure domination complete over their thoughts'.[21] For Monash, command was not a collaborative, dialogic activity. Rather,

[17] Ibid., 166.
[18] Ibid., 165
[19] Ibid., 168.
[20] Monash, *The Australian Victories in France*, 51.
[21] Serle, *John Monash*, 379.

his subordinates had to be disciplined and united around his monolithic vision of how every detail was to be executed: 'Messines, Broodseinde and Passchendaele showed Monash as a forceful, even bullying battle-field commander'.[22] Whether Monash was actually a bully is open to question. Yet, he exerted a pronouncedly directive, authoritarian form of control over all his subordinates, including his staff and his brigade commanders. As his AAQMG, Lieutenant Colonel Mynors Farmar noted: 'General Monash as a leader is a genius and the thought he has given to every detail inspires every man in the Division with confidence'.

Monash invested a huge amount of effort in the definition of the mission and the preparation for it. He was obsessive in his manage-ment of every detail of the mission before it was executed. However, although his managerial skills were, perhaps, his most original, Monash also thought deeply about how to coordinate operations once they were underway. Once an operation started, Monash always situated himself in his command post; he believed that it was the only place from which an operation could be managed. Monash was criticized by Charles Bean and others for never visiting the frontline to assess the situation and to provide some support and leadership to his subordinates. For Bean, the problems on the Hindenburg Line in 1918, for instance, would have been avoided had Monash gone forward. Yet, precisely because Monash conceived of military operations as an engineering problem, he asserted, as an absolute principle, the requirement for the higher commander to remain in his headquarters. The headquarters was the only place on the battlefield where the divisional commander was in communication with his various units and, therefore, where he could coordinate infantry manoeuvre with artillery fire. He had an unwavering belief that it was not merely advisable but the active duty of the commander to stay in his headquarters; it was the only place 'where I can have before me, at all time, a complete picture of what is going on and ... can at all times reach every possible subordinate'.[23]

In order to ensure that he did indeed have as complete a situ-ational awareness of operations as possible, Monash made some not-able innovations. It has often been claimed that higher-formation

---

[22] P.A. Pedersen, 'General Sir John Monash: corps commander on the Western Front', in D.M. Horner (ed.), *The Commanders: Australian military leadership in the 20th century* (Sydney, NSW: Allen and Unwin Press, 1984), 101.

[23] Ibid., 101.

generals had no idea of the progress of battle once the assault had begun. In order for Monash's principle of staying in his headquarters to be justified, he had to be certain that he was in communication with his frontline troops – or as certain as he could be. He utilized the standard method of multiplying communications systems so that should one system fail – as it undoubtedly would – another system would provide him with current information. He expended considerable administrative effort on ensuring that his telephone lines, the best form of communication, were secured by being buried sufficiently deeply. He tasked his engineers properly before an operation. In addition, he developed a system of liaison officers, with their own communications systems, to accompany brigades and to report back on the situation to the headquarters. Finally, and most creatively, he developed an airborne communications technique. He organized observation 'contact aircraft' to follow attacks, with the navigator marking the progress of the attack on a map which was then rolled into a map-case. The planes would then drop the cases at pre-designated fields near Monash's headquarters, to which they would be brought by a cyclist. At Messines, for instance, Monash received notifications from contact aircraft every five minutes. Against the image of isolated and impotent generals, Monash's claim that he was best able to command from his headquarters do not seem unjustified.

Monash was highly unusual as commander – even unique among all his peers, not just in the First World War but throughout the twentieth century. He utterly monopolized all decision-making in terms of both mission definition and management. This suggests that Monash is a very bad example of divisional command in the twentieth century. He was inimitable; as evidence of the practice of command, he is misleading. However, it would be a mistake to dismiss Monash in this way. First, as the discussion of headquarters and divisional doctrine in the previous chapter demonstrated, divisional operations in the twentieth century were complicated; they involved multiple elements which had to coordinated and synchronized. Before an attack a commander had to complete a checklist of tasks. Divisions were large organizations. Yet, their missions and their fundamental workings were mechanical; they were limited and simple. There were indeed many tasks to supervise, as SS 135 clarified. Yet, Monash's division comprised three infantry brigades and an artillery brigade which operated in a small geographic area over a very limited period. Monash was unusually compulsive in his control of operations. Yet, in his very extremity, the remarkable and important thing he demonstrates is that in the era of industrial warfare, and especially in the first half of the twentieth century, a divisional commander could not only define the mission but actually manage it more or less personally. Monash proves that a military operation was a fundamentally simple undertaking. It may not have been John Monash's job to write a plan down to the last duckboard. Yet, he was able to do it, without it in anyway impairing his ability to successfully command the division as a whole. Certainly, had most divisional commanders attempted such a level of control over their forces, they would have failed. They would not have been able to retain a picture of the mission as a whole while concentrating on the administrative details. They required the support of a small staff.

Monash was certainly unusual in having the facility to do both and to allow his overall sense of the mission to inform his analysis of the detail. Yet, he demonstrated that in early the twentieth century, divisional command could be exercised by a single individual, with the support of a very small and, in Monash's case, totally subordinated staff. In a paradoxically bureaucratic way, Monash displayed a certain heroism in his command of 3rd Australian Division. He regarded it as his sole duty to ensure that attacks were properly prepared in order to save the lives of his men and he went to extraordinary personal lengths to fulfil this duty. Monash's unusual intelligence and his remarkable industriousness allowed him to dominate the managerial problem of positional warfare; he was personally able to conduct all the administrative work identified by SS 135 and impose his solutions on this staff and subordinates. Bureaucratic standardization allowed him to monopolize command almost entirely, rather than undermining his individual autonomy as the sole decision-maker.

Erwin Rommel

Monash was unusual; he had a rare intellect and, until August 1918, he commanded under conditions of extreme positional warfare. Consequently, his intense concentration on administration and, in particular, his personal ability to dominate staff work were peculiar and specific. However, it is clearly necessary to triangulate Monash with other commanders. Above all, it is necessary to consider divisional command in conditions of open, mechanized warfare. Outstanding commanders are again useful here. Through this analysis, it will be possible to build up a picture of how divisional operations were commanded in the twentieth century. Erwin Rommel is pertinent here both because he commanded an armoured division during the Battle of France in 1940 but also because he was in many ways the absolute antithesis of Monash; while Monash was a military bureaucrat, Rommel was a combat leader in the heroic mould.[24] Consequently, he offers a useful contrast to Monash, though, significantly, his highly individualistic method of command, in which he monopolized all the significant decisions, had an interesting resonance with Monash's own techniques.

As a result of the patronage of Adolf Hitler, Rommel was given command of 7th Panzer Division for the invasion of Poland in 1939 and France in 1940.[25] According to the plan, Rommel's division was given only a subordinate role in the French campaign. The invasion of France in 1940, Fall Gelb, involved three army groups. In the north, General Bock's Army Group B would attack into Belgium just south of Brussels along the conventional and expected line of assault. Their role was to draw Allied forces forward into Flanders. Army Group C, commanded by General von Leeb, would assault the northern end of the Maginot line, fixing French forces there. However, the main thrust would come from Gunther von Rundstedt's Army Group A on an axis through the Ardennes. This Army Group aimed to make a 'sickle stroke' across northern France to the coast, cutting off the Allied armies. For the invasion of France, Rommel's 7th Panzer Division was assigned to General Hoth's XV Corps along with the 5th Panzer Division. This corps was the main striking force of Gunther von Kluge's Fourth Army on the northern flank of Gerd von Rundstedt's Army Group A; its task was to seize a bridgehead over the Meuse in order to seize Dinant. However, although part of the decisive force, neither Hoth's XV Corps nor Rommel's 7th Panzer Division were denoted as the 'main effort' or *Schwerpunkt* of the attack by German higher command. Before

---

[24] Karl-Heinz Frieser, *The Blitzkrieg Legend* (Annapolis, MD: Naval Institute Press, 2005), 230.

[25] Alaric Searle, 'Rommel and the Rise of the Nazis', in Ian Beckett (ed.), *Rommel Reconsidered* (Mechanisburg, PA: Stackpole, 2014), 23.

the operation, Ewald von Kleist's Panzer Group, with Guderian's XIX Corps and Reinhardt's XLI Corps, was ordered to seize Sedan and Montherme.[26] As the heavier force, on the southern flank of Army Group A, they were originally conceived as having the most important mission; Hoth's Corps' role was only to cover their right flank.[27]

However, despite his designated mission, Rommel played an unexpectedly prominent role. Against orders, Rommel determined that the division was to advance as quickly as possible into the enemy's rear. He entirely ignored the directives of his superiors or the needs of his adjacent units, whom in fact he exploited to his own advantage. After starting on 10 May 1940, Rommel's division had advanced beyond Arras by 21 May and was thirty miles in front of the main line of German forces on a tiny salient; it was so deep in enemy territory that the formation earned the title of the 'Ghost' or 'Phantom' Division.[28] Rommel angered and worried his superiors. Indeed, his operations caused general higher command to slow the advance and, after the campaign, Hitler personally admitted to Rommel that he had been worried about him. Rommel seems to have displayed extraordinary licence in defining his division's mission – a rapid, even precipitate advance – oblivious to his orders.

Rommel's decision-making was certainly extraordinarily rapid in France in 1940. Rommel – by accident or design – implemented what became established as a central principle of armoured warfare in the twentieth century. Avoiding strongpoints and exploiting gaps and flanks, Rommel sought to exploit the velocity of his armoured division. In this way, he thrust his force deep into the enemy's rear in order to engender a general collapse, disregarding his own flanks and maintaining a constant momentum.[29] However, this was not a deeply complex mission requiring extensive coordination. It was noticeable that Rommel was an inexperienced tank commander; he lacked the expertise to conduct complex armoured manoeuvres. At the outset of the First World War, Rommel was an infantry platoon commander in

[26] Kenneth Macksey, *Rommel: Battles and Campaigns* (New York: Da Capo Press, 1997), 28.

[27] Claus Telp, 'Rommel and 1940', in Ian Beckett (ed.), *Rommel Reconsidered* (Mechanisburg, PA: Stackpole, 2014), 32.

[28] Desmond Young, *Rommel* (London: Collins, 1950), 69.

[29] Ronald Lewin, *Rommel as Military Commander* (New York: Barnes and Noble, 1968), 11.

a Württemberger infantry battalion, fighting in France before being promoted and transferred to Romania and thence to Italy, where he participated in the Battle of Caporetto. Rommel was a hugely capable combat leader, then, and was awarded the highest decoration for valour in the German army, the *Pour le Mérite*. After the war, he published his memoirs – *Infantry Attacks* – which established him as a celebrity in Germany and abroad. Rommel was a physically brave combat leader and a superb tactician, implementing modern platoon tactics well before they were supposedly invented by the storm-troops in 1915 and 1916.[30] However, despite his evident abilities as an infantry commander, Rommel was not staff-trained, was never on the German General Staff and had no experience of armoured warfare. He was only appointed to 7th Panzer against the considerable scepticism of senior officers. Moreover, perhaps as a result of his experiences in the infantry, Rommel's military thinking was initially conservative. He showed no interest in innovations in armoured warfare in the 1930s and rejected the ideas of Guderian and others.[31] It was only later, during the Polish campaign, that Rommel recognized the true potential of armoured warfare.[32] However, Rommel fought his division with a rare boldness rather than any great sophistication; his manoeuvres were much simpler than Balck's at the Chiri.

He was aided in this by the structure of his division. In 1939, Rommel's 7th Panzer division was a recently converted light division. Unusually, it consisted of only a single three-battalion tank regiment, 25th Panzer Regiment, and a vehicle-borne infantry brigade. The relative lightness of his division, with only two manoeuvre units, may partially explain the aggressive – even reckless – way in which Rommel was able to fight the formation. With only one tank regiment to fight, he had a flexibility and mobility which the commanders of pure panzer divisions, like Hermann Balck, did not; he had far less forces to coordinate and to administer. The 25th Panzer Regiment was the sole spearhead of his attacks, on which Rommel focused the mission, while 7th Infantry Brigade tended to fall behind the action to become a minor actor in operations. Essentially, Rommel punched 25th Panzer

---

[30] Basil Liddell Hart, *The Other Side of the Hill: Germany's generals, their rise and fall, with their own accounts of military events 1939–1945* (London: Cassell and Co, 1948), 58.

[31] K.-H. Frieser, *The Blitzkrieg Legend*, 224.

[32] Ibid.

Regiment through French defences as quickly as possible, leaving his own division, and indeed the rest of the Wehrmacht, to follow. He fought his division as a reinforced armoured regiment. It was remarkable what he achieved with it, but it rather simplified the problem of command for him.

At the same time, as a result of his experiences in the First World War, Rommel had astutely recognized the influence of moral factors in close-quarters combat. In most cases, forces were not physically destroyed in battle; their morale collapsed in the face of a demonstration of overwhelming firepower and determination. On his assaults in the Isonzo theatre in October 1917, Rommel captured 9000 Italians with only 150 men. Rommel properly recognized that mass-conscript armies, with inadequate training, were highly susceptible to shock and panic, precipitated by the aggressive, even excessive, use of firepower, especially in the opening engagements. Accordingly, although he had insufficient time to train 7th Panzer Division properly for the French Campaign, he instituted an important combat principle. Against official doctrine, which emphasized ammunition preservation, he instructed his combat units to use profligate firepower when they first encountered the enemy:

> I have found again and again that in encounter attacks, the day goes to the side that is first to plaster its opponent with fire. The man who lies low and awaits develops usually comes off second best. Motor cyclists at the head of a column must keep their machine-guns at the ready and open fire the instant an enemy shot is heard. This applies even when the exact position of the enemy is unknown, in which case the fire must simply be sprayed over enemy-held territory. Observation of this rule, in my experience, substantially reduces one's own casualties.[33]

Like Ardant du Picq, Rommel fully recognized the potent effect of fire; the mere noise of the guns and the fall of shot, even if totally ineffective, were simultaneously intimidating to the enemy and encouraging for friendly troops. Although it was not always followed, Rommel instituted a standard operating procedure in 7th Panzer Division; forces were to open fire immediately on contact with the enemy. Throughout the French campaign, Rommel complained that his

---

[33] Basil Liddell Hart, *The Rommel Papers* (London: Arrow, 1987), 7.

units failed to implement this instruction and were reluctant to fire; he repeatedly had to order his subordinates to open fire.[34] At the very end of the advance on the Channel, as they approached St Valery, Rommel reprimanded one of his tank commanders: 'I told a tank commander what I thought of him for not opening fire'.[35]

Rommel was a capable and bold commander. His corps commander, General Hoth, himself declared that Rommel 'explored new paths in the command of a Panzer Division'.[36] His experimentations with velocity and fire were certainly important. However, the mission which he gave his Panzer division in France was not complex. He ordered the division simply to advance on its axis against enemy defences as quickly as it could, relying on its own organic assets and, above all, the shock of 25th Panzer Regiment to penetrate the front. Rommel himself may have been exceptional in many ways but, while astonishingly successful, 7th Panzer's mission was not incompatible with the general pattern of twentieth-century warfare. Rommel fought the division on a very narrow front, engaging in a series of close fights against a wavering opposition.

Rommel supervised operations directly. However, it would be quite wrong to presume that Rommel was a mere combat leader of a traditional type, unaware of the administrative complexities of the modern division. Rommel did not eschew the requirement for some bureaucratic methods, nor was he ignorant of the problems of large-scale coordination. He too employed bureaucracy, using it as a guide and aide for his command – though, like these other commanders, bureaucracy was employed to support his command rather than to share decision-making responsibilities. Bureaucracy became a means by which he ensured his monopoly over decision-making.

This pragmatic use of bureaucracy is demonstrated by Rommel's own administrative reforms. Rommel made an administrative innovation of lasting importance for divisional command. In the course of the French campaign, Rommel implemented the concept of the *Stosslinie* (literally assault line), which is probably most accurately translated into contemporary military lexicon as 'phase line'. The

[34] Ibid., 75; Telp, 'Rommel and 1940', 48.
[35] Liddell Hart, *The Rommel Papers*, 61.
[36] Dennis Showalter, *Patton and Rommel: men of war in the twentieth century* (New York: Berkley Caliber, 2006), 200.

Stosslinie was an imaginary line which Rommel drew on the map for his manoeuvre units, artillery and potential air support. It represented a temporary objective. Once the *Stosslinie* had been established, Rommel ordered his manoeuvre units to advance upon it and his artillery to fire on it in immediate support of the attack. Moreover, because the *Stosslinie* was an imaginary objective, Rommel could send orders clearly over the radio because the enemy could only guess the objective of the attack.[37]

In his memoirs, Rommel usefully recorded the use of the *Stosslinie* as he advanced towards Avenses from the Meuse:

> It was my intention to ride with 25th Panzer Regiment so that
> I could direct the attack from up forward and bring in artillery
> and dive-bombers at the decisive moment. To simplify the
> wireless traffic – over which highly important messages often
> arrived late, due to the necessity of encoding – I agreed to a 'line
> of thrust'[38] (*Stosslinie*) with the Ia and the artillery commander.
> Starting point for this line was taken as the Rosée church and
> finishing point Froidchapelle church. All the officers marked the
> lines on their maps. If I now wanted artillery fire on, for instance,
> Philippeville, I simply radioed: 'Heavy artillery fire immediate,
> rounds eleven.[39]

Although the derivation of the idea is uncertain, it might be claimed that Rommel's *Stosslinie* was taken from a First World War artillery fireplan. A creeping barrage consisted of a series of imaginary target lines on which the artillery was successively cued; each one of these lines was, in effect, a *Stosslinie* because the infantry attacked immediately behind the bombardment securing each line in turn. The *Stosslinie* may not have been entirely original, then. Nevertheless, the *Stosslinie* was a brilliantly simple managerial device which facilitated close cooperation between manoeuvre units and fire support in the division with minimal effort and instruction; it required no explanation. Moreover, it demonstrated that while his talents lay primarily at the tactical level as a combat leader, Rommel was fully aware of the critical organizational

---

[37] Telp, 'Rommel and 1940', 51.
[38] This is Liddell Hart's translation. Telp translates Stosslinie more plausibly as a 'phase line'.
[39] Liddell Hart, *The Rommel Papers*, 15.

problem of divisional command: the fusion of manoeuvre and fire-power at scale. The *Stosslinie* allowed Rommel to coordinate the critical elements of his division, even as he led from the front, improvising incessantly in the face of new threats and opportunities.

Rommel has been frequently accused of neglecting the wider requirements of his division and especially its logistic needs. The main evidence of his neglect of his duties as a divisional command is the breakdown in relations with his Ia, Major Heidkaemper. There was an undignified argument between them.[40] It would be difficult to deny that Rommel took enormous risks with his division and was negligent in communicating to his headquarters. However, it is also important to recognize that Rommel was not concerned with the management of his division in a normal sense. When in contact with the enemy on an offensive operation, he ignored more or less entirely the logistical concerns of his formation; he was quite unlike Monash in this. He concentrated exclusively on the close fight. Yet, it would be wrong to claim that he became simply an infantry platoon leader, as some have suggested. Even while taking over command from his subordinates, personally ordering troops to fire on targets he had identified, he maintained a wider awareness. It might be more accurate to interpret Rommel's method not as a wilful neglect of his administrative duties, but a deliberate prioritization of the decisive mission of his division. Rommel repeatedly assumed direct command over subordinate units at critical moments. Indeed, it is significant that he was irritated by Heidkaemper's failure to do what seemed to him obvious; to ensure that the division simply followed Rommel's lead so that they were in a position to support him when the need arose. In a letter to his wife, he complained precisely about Heidkaemper's inability to follow the obvious course of action:

> I'm having a lot of trouble with my Ia just at the moment ... This young General Staff Major, scared that something might happen to him and the Staff, stayed some 20 miles behind the front and, of course, lost contact with the fighting troops I was commanding up near Cambrai. Instead of rushing everything up forward, he went to Corps HQ, upset people there and behaved as if the command of the division was no longer secure. And he

---

[40] Kenneth Macksey, *Rommel: battles and campaigns* (New York: Da Capo, 1997), 35.

still believes to this day that he performed a heroic deed. I'll have to make a thorough study of the documents so as to put the boy in his place.[41]

For Rommel, the administration of the division was self-evident; support units needed to march to the sound of the guns. Precisely because Rommel conceived military operations in this way, he did not see the requirement for long orders, conferences and discussions. Effectively, the divisional rear should also orient itself to the *Stosslinie* and to Rommel himself, following the combat units as closely as possible on their lines of advance.

During the French Campaign, Rommel, to Heidkaemper's frustration, certainly ignored normal procedure; he was careless about his divisional rear area, higher command and adjacent units. Nevertheless, he was able to command one of the most remarkable divisional manoeuvres of the twentieth century almost single-handedly. It cannot be forgotten that whatever the complaints about Rommel, he was outstandingly successful; his command method demonstrably worked in May 1940. Rommel demonstrated not only that mission definition was essentially simple but that even the management of an operation was within the capabilities of a single individual at this time. Precisely because it was optimal to make and to execute decisions quickly and coherently, it was organizationally advantageous to have a commander imposing himself entirely on fighting elements of his formation. Rommel focused on the close fight. In an admittedly quite different way to Monash, Rommel demonstrated a highly individualist approach to divisional command, in which he monopolized decision-making, personally commanding, managing and leading operations.

Bernard Montgomery

Monash and Rommel are deeply interesting cases. Despite commanding different formations in different wars and under radically divergent conditions, they illustrate individualist command at its extreme, either through their close personal administration or their extraordinary

[41] Ibid., 86.

combat leadership of their respective divisions. The question they pose is whether they were unrepresentative outliers or whether their methods, while unusual, were broadly compatible with the norm of twentieth-century command? At this point, other generals, who adopted rather more conventional methods, need to be considered.

General Bernard Montgomery was one of the most successful divisional commanders in the Second World War. He provides a good insight into more normal, perhaps even optimal, methods of managing a division at this time. Montgomery has, unfortunately, become a highly controversial general in the historiography of the Second World War. His performance as Commander 8th Army and, in particular, as Commander 21st Army Group in Europe has been frequently denigrated. Ironically, his own vanity and reckless self-promotion has undermined his reputation. In fact, Montgomery was a very competent general and there is no question that he was a highly talented divisional commander, almost certainly the best of his generation in Britain. It is worth remembering that there were few more experienced soldiers in Europe or America at the start of the Second World War. Montgomery had fought throughout the First World War on the Western Front, first as a platoon commander when he led a charge, brandishing a sword, at Le Cateau on 26 August 1914 and, later, as a staff officer at battalion, brigade and finally divisional level.[42] He had then served in Ireland during the War of Independence and Palestine during the Arab Revolt, where he commanded 8th Division, before being appointed to 3rd Division in 1939.[43] He commanded 3rd Division through the Battle of France, until he was promoted to Corps Command at the very end of the campaign on 30 May 1940.

The performance of Montgomery's 3rd Division in this battle provides a discrete and instructive example of divisional command in the twentieth century. It is particularly useful because Montgomery was renowned among his peers for his ruthless professionalism, at a time when many preferred a more gentile approach: 'He behaved in fact in a way that most of his gentlemanly predecessors would have found impossible and many of his contemporaries considered intolerable. But

[42] Nigel Hamilton, *Monty: the making of a general 1887–1942* (London: Hamish Hamilton, 1981), 87.
[43] Ibid.

then, Montgomery was no gentleman – that was his great strength'.[44] In his professionalism, Montgomery was closer to his twenty-first-century successors, than perhaps many of his contemporaries. He is, therefore, a very useful comparator. He demonstrates how a highly professional general sought to command in the mid-twentieth century.

Montgomery's 3rd Division deployed to France in September 1939 and was eventually assigned to a sector south of Lille in preparation for a likely German attack in the spring. When the Germans attacked on 10 May 1940, the 3rd Division was ordered forward to the Dyle River, west of Louvain, but, having been involved in fighting on that line, played an important role in the retreat to Dunkirk. 3rd Division made an orderly retreat, countering German attacks and preserving the British line. Despite the catastrophe, the performance of 3rd Infantry Division during this campaign was exemplary. Montgomery himself was totally imperturbable even in the face of disaster and, on reaching Dunkirk, Montgomery's corps commander, General Alan Brooke, noted that 3rd Division had suffered far less casualties than his other divisions.[45]

This study must determine the methods which Montgomery employed to ensure that his division was so effective and to consider whether they were compatible with those of Monash and Rommel. Montgomery's command method involved two basic elements. First, having come straight from Palestine and fully aware of the likelihood of a war with Germany, Montgomery trained 3rd Infantry Division hard. From September 1940, when it was deployed to France, Montgomery subjected the division to a series of increasingly demanding exercises, which did not merely practice divisional manoeuvre in general but imitated the specific actions which Montgomery thought it was most likely that his formation would be ordered to conduct when the Germans invaded: 'If the Belgians were attacked, we were to move forward and occupy a sector astride Louvain behind the River Dyle. I trained the division for this task over a similar distance moving westwards, i.e. backwards into France'.[46] However, Montgomery also wisely predicted

[44] Michael Howard, 'Leadership in the British Army in the Second World War: some personal observations', in Gary Sheffield (ed.), *Leadership and Command: the Anglo-American Military Experience since 1861* (London: Brassey's, 2002), 126.

[45] Hamilton, *Monty*, 382.

[46] Bernard Montgomery, *The Memoirs of Field Marshal the Viscount Montgomery of Alamein, K.G.* (St James Place, London: Collins, 1958), 58.

that, having advanced to this river line, 3rd Division would be required to retreat in contact with German forces – one of the most difficult of all military manoeuvres. These exercises concluded on 30 March 1940 with a final scenario in which 'Jumboland' (Belgium) was invaded. 3rd Division practised advancing to defend a river line and, then, in the course of exercise, retreating in contact with the enemy.[47] Montgomery emphasized night marches during these exercises: 'We became expert at long night moves and then occupying a defensive position in the dark and by dawn being fully deployed and in all respects ready to receive an attack. This is what I felt we might have had to do; and it was'.[48] Unlike Monash, Montgomery could not plan precisely what his division would do but, on the basis of astute judgement, he prepared his formation for the most likely scenario and ensured that they were capable of conducting the manoeuvres which would be necessary.

Montgomery was also assiduous about staffwork. It is noticeable that the division's all-important march tables for these movements were comprehensive and very detailed. They listed all the division's units and assigned each a route, a destination and timings.[49] Consequently, by the time the war broke out, 3rd Infantry Division was a cohesive organization able to execute a series of drills with precision:

> My division did everything that was demanded of it; it was like a ship with all sails set in a rough sea, which rides the storm easily and answers to the slightest touch on the helm. Such was my 3rd Division. There were no weak links; all the doubtful commanders had been eliminated during the previous six months of training. The Division was like a fine piece of steel.[50]

Montgomery maximized his division's combat effectiveness by ensuring that only commanders who could follow his orders immediately and accurately remained in post; they had to be able to execute their manoeuvres in a timely and ordered manner. Anyone who failed was removed.

This intense training regime accelerated decision-making in the division for Montgomery. Before the campaign, the division was already

[47] 3rd Division, The Battle of France, WO 167/218 TNA.
[48] Montgomery, The Memoirs, 58-9.
[49] 3rd Division, The Battle of France, WO 167/218 TNA.
[50] Montgomery, The Memoirs, 61.

attuned to a series of established drills which subordinate commanders were competent enough to execute immediately, on Montgomery's orders. The importance of this preparation became evident during the campaign and it was especially notable on the critical day of 27 May when the division was ordered to conduct a 'most difficult operation'. The division was ordered to withdraw from its position in the line and then, sidestepping the 4th, 5th and 50th Divisions, move northwards to a new position three miles north of Ypres.[51] Montgomery described the action in the following way:

> I was ordered to sidestep the division to the left of the British front and fill in a gap which had opened between the 50th Division and the Belgians. It involved a night move of the whole division within a couple of thousands yards of the 5th Division front, where a fierce battle had been raging all day and was still going on. If this move had been suggested by a student at Staff College in a scheme, he would have been considered mad. The movement went without a hitch.[52]

Montgomery was never one to suggest that anything he had commanded had gone less than brilliantly. However, Alan Brooke himself praised the movement: 'It was a task that might well have shaken the stoutest of hearts, but for Monty it might just have been a glorious picnic! He told me exactly how he was going to do it, and was as usual exuberant in confidence.'[53] The operation exemplified a critical element of Montgomery's method of managing operations. He imposed on his formation a series of manoeuvre drills which the division could execute on order. It reduced coordination problems considerably for him as commander. As Nigel Hamilton noted: 'There was every reason, however, for Bernard to feel his 3rd Division could perform such a night withdrawal. Had the Division not already rehearsed the movement time after time on exercises, and again and again in battle, withdrawing successfully from the Dyle to the Dendre, from the Dendre to the Escaut, and from the Escaut to the French frontier defences from which they had first sallied forth on 10 May?'[54]

---

[51] Hamilton, *Monty*, 379.
[52] Montgomery, *The Memoirs*, 61.
[53] Hamilton, *Monty*, 379.
[54] Ibid., 379.

The drill was certainly essential to Montgomery's ability to manage 3rd Division operations but it did not explain his success completely. Clearly, operations could not be reduced entirely to drills. Local circumstances and unexpected events required his supervision and lower-level decision-making; he had to manage the division constantly throughout the battle. At this point, his staff became vital. In particular, his GSO1, Lieutenant-Colonel Victor Brown, Royal Marines, proved an important aide for Montgomery. Brown was killed in tragic circumstances on the night of 29 May, when he was shot accidentally by a sentry.[55] Montgomery trusted Brown to enact his plans and it was perhaps fortunate for Montgomery that the 3rd Division were already evacuating Dunkirk when he was killed. Montgomery was himself promoted to command of II Corps a day after Brown's death.

Montgomery developed a robust command system with Brown. Montgomery dominated all decision-making but he devolved administrative functions and details to Brown and his staff:

> It was during this campaign that I developed the habit of going to bed early, soon after dinner. I was out and about on the front all day long, saw all the subordinate commanders, and heard their problems and gave decisions and verbal orders. I was always back in the Divisional H.Q. about tea-time [4pm], and would see my staff and give order for the night and the next day. I would then have dinner and go to bed, never to be disturbed except in crisis.[56]

It is worth considering Montgomery's daily routine in great depth. During the battle, Montgomery gave his orders to Brown in the evening before dinner; he retired while his staff worked up the orders and administrative details. It is instructive how much rest Montgomery gave himself, especially in comparison with his successors in the twenty-first century; he ensured he had a full night's sleep and, indeed, finished work in the early evening. The fact that he could retire for so long demonstrated that a divisional commander had to make few decisions; the problem of coordination was considerably simpler at this time than it would become. Montgomery was quite untroubled by the endless

[55] 3rd Division, 'The Battle of France', WO 167/218 TNA.
[56] Montgomery, *The Memoirs*, 61.

negotiations and meetings which tormented divisional commanders in Iraq and Afghanistan.

The following day, while his staff were still refining the details of that day's operations and receiving information and orders from Corps, Montgomery visited his units to confirm that his subordinate commanders were doing what they were ordered and that his orders were still valid. At the same time, he was naturally keeping himself aware of the real situation on the front and the likely crisis points the following day, supervising his subordinates and giving them immediate direction. He then returned to the headquarters with this information, on the basis of which he issued orders for the next day, that his staff again worked up. Clearly, Montgomery's staff and especially Victor Brown were critical to this system of command. Unlike Monash, Montgomery did not – and would not – attend to detailed questions of administration or the material issue of orders; they were completed and signed off by Brown. Quite unlike Rommel, he did not ignore them. Montgomery commanded the division alone and he ensured that he was always in close contact with his subordinate commanders and current operations. However, he devolved the administration of the division to his staff and especially his GSO1.

Montgomery was an outstanding divisional commander. He dominated his division no less powerfully than Monash or Rommel and, in unfavourable circumstances, was at least as successful as these virtuosic commanders. He exercised a powerfully individualized system of command. However, in contrast with Rommel and Monash, it might also be claimed that he instituted a highly directive but less individualized system of command. This system relied upon Montgomery, of course; he was at the centre of all decision-making. However, through extensive preparation, drills and the selection of disciplined subordinates, Montgomery created an integrated command system where the entire division was united around and animated by his intention. He ensured that his subordinates were able to actualize his will. Consequently, although Montgomery was very much a twentieth-century divisional commander, monopolizing a rapid decision cycle of limited scope, he anticipated some of the elements of collective command which would become so prominent in the twenty-first century.

Other exceptional commanders adopted a very similar system to Monash. The example of Hermann Balck, commander of 11th Panzer Division, was discussed briefly in the previous chapter.

The celebrated French general Philippe Leclerc, who commanded the *2e Division Blindée* (2nd Armoured Division) in Normandy and the European campaign, is also worth considering briefly. In each case, those commanders spent most of the days out with their units, returning to their headquarters in the evening to confirm the situation and to give orders. Like Montgomery, they relied on one principal and highly competent aide; Balck on his Ia, Major Kienetz,[57] and Leclerc on his intelligence officer, Colonel Repiton-Préneuf.[58] Most divisional commanders were, however, average. They served their time in command and then, even if promoted, disappeared from history.[59] They were neither brilliantly successful nor disastrously unsuccessful. However, although these commanders lacked the facility of a general like Montgomery, they implemented a system which was more broadly compatible with this method than with those of unusual commanders like Rommel and Monash. They relied on an aide and staff procedure to ensure that they were able to manage divisional operations.

Monash and Rommel appear to have been extreme in monopolizing command. Montgomery might represent a more typical accommodation, then. Yet, even in the case of the more collaborative divisional commanders, Montgomery plainly dominated the decision-making process. He defined the division's missions and made the critical decisions about the deployment of forces, while supervising the implementation of their orders closely. He left only subordinate managerial responsibilities to his principal staff officers and, by integrating his subordinates into his decision-making, ensured that they fulfilled his intentions.

It has been argued above that Rommel exemplified a distinctively individualistic method of command in the Battle of France. He instructively demonstrated that at this time, a divisional commander could conduct a battle almost single-handedly. However, despite Heidkaemper's complaints, Rommel may have been a more conventional commander than is often assumed and, therefore, closer to

---

[57] Balck, *Order in Choas*, 251.

[58] William Mortimor-Moore, *Free France's Lion: the life of Philippe Leclerc, de Gaulle's Greatest General* (Philadelphia: Newbury, 2011); Dominique Forget, *Le General Leclerc et la 2e DB 1944–5* (Bayeux: Heimdal, 2008), 123–6.

[59] David French, 'Colonel Blimp and the British Army: British Divisional Commanders in the War against Germany, 1939–45', *English Historical Review* 111(444) November 1996: 1182–1201.

Montgomery than is sometimes assumed. Like them, he monopolized decision-making, defining the mission and managing the critical parts of it perfectly, using his staff and headquarters to provide him with administrative support. Moreover, Rommel's apparent negligence of administrative issues in France in 1940 may have been a deliberate response to the particular operational situation which confronted him. As he crossed the Meuse, Rommel seemed to have sensed that the French Army was fragile and that a general collapse was possible; a highly aggressive assault, which seemed wildly dangerous, might actually generate extraordinary results and avoid the positional slaughter of the First World War. In this situation, Rommel chose to ignore his rear area to concentrate all his command efforts on the immediate tactical fight.

It is noticeable that later, as he confronted the highly organized mass artillery and airpower of the Allies, his concept of operations changed radically. In debates about the defence of Europe against the invasion, he dismissed the notion of Blitzkrieg warfare and criticized senior Wehrmacht generals used to fighting on the Russian Steppes against less-sophisticated opponents for whom infantry casualties were irrelevant.

> At one time they [German senior commanders] looked on mobile warfare as something to keep clear of at all costs, but now that our freedom of manoeuvre in the West is gone, they're crazy after it. Whereas, in fact, it's obvious that if the enemy once gets his foot in, he'll put every anti-tank gun and tank he can into the bridgehead and let us beat our heads against it, as he did at Medenine. To break through such a front you have to attack slowly and methodically, under cover of massed artillery, but we, of course, thanks to the Allied air forces, will have nothing there in time. The day of the dashing cut-and-thrust tank attack of the early war years is past and gone.[60]

Had Rommel been a divisional commander in Italy, Normandy and the subsequent battles for Germany, it seems highly unlikely that he would have commanded in the same way in which he did in France in 1940. It is probable that he would have been far more careful in his preparations, focusing on administrative details, coordination and preparation in a way which was irrelevant during the Battle of

---

[60] Liddell Hart, *The Rommel Papers*, 468.

France when the priority was to exploit the opportunities for a break-through. In short, he would probably have adopted the more methodical methods of more conventional divisional commanders. While monopolizing decision-making, Rommel might have commanded with the close assistance of an aide and a small staff and, through his subordinate commanders, united together in a cohesive executive group. This command system in which the commander played a critical role not only in mission definition but also everyday mission management – and personal leadership – was an understandable response to the organizational problem which confronted the twentieth-century division. It appears to have been well-adapted to the problem of scale, which defined divisional operations at the time.

Rupert Smith

With the possible exceptions of the Falklands War or Grenada, Western forces were not engaged in conventional, high-intensity divisional operations after the mid-1950s.[61] Of course, the US was committed heavily to Vietnam until 1973, and its operations there will be discussed in Chapter 7. However, although periodically intense, US forces in Indochina were primarily involved in pacification operations against guerrillas there rather than conventional operations against a peer. For the rest of the Cold War, Western divisions were involved in conventional deterrence, primarily in Europe. Consequently, there is only one example of manoeuvre warfare at the divisional level from after the Korean War to the very end of the period in 1991: the Gulf War. In order to attempt to demonstrate the existence of a regime of command throughout the short twentieth century, it is clearly necessary to consider this example. Indeed, it conveniently punctuates the period. The Gulf War might be seen as the last expression of twentieth-century, mass warfighting. During this war, the land forces of the US-led coalition effectively implemented a ground offensive, which they had been practising in West Germany for about a decade. In effect, the coalition's brief assault into Iraq indicates what NATO forces would

---

[61] Although the last major divisional actions took place in the Korean War, which ended in 1953, Suez in 1956 and Dien Bien Phu in 1954 might be taken as examples of high-intensity warfighting when divisional-sized Western forces were engaged.

have attempted along the Inner German border had conflict broken out with the Warsaw Pact in the 1980s.

After the Gulf War, of course, the strategic situation changed dramatically. The West became increasingly committed to peace-keeping, peace-enforcement and then full-scale counter-insurgency operations, first in the Balkans and then in Afghanistan, Iraq and beyond. Notwithstanding important developments in the late 1970s and 1980s, which will be discussed below, from the mid-1990s, the Western approach to military operations changed as a result of the so-called Revolution in Military Affairs and further reductions in force size. The Gulf War represents, then, the very last genuine war of the short twentieth century; a Western-dominated coalition of almost half-a-million troops conducted a sweeping manoeuvre with hundreds of tanks. It was far more reminiscent of the North African Campaign in the Second World War than subsequent operations in which Western forces were engaged in the early twenty-first century. The Gulf War is an ideal example for understanding command in this era. Indeed, in order to establish the argument for a twentieth-century command regime, it is useful and probably essential to consider this campaign.

Despite the evidential importance of the Gulf War, there are also some disadvantages to this campaign which have to be admitted. Although the war as a whole lasted approximately two months, ground combat lasted only four days. The coalition launched air strikes onto Iraq on 6 January 1991. Thirty-seven days later, at 0400 on 24 February, the ground war started with coalition forces attacking across the international border into Kuwait and Iraq itself. On 28 February, a ceasefire was called, although most Iraqi opposition had dissolved by the previous day. Moreover, the fighting was cursory and grossly one-sided. Iraqi equipment was vastly overmatched by coalition weap-onry; in many cases, American and British tanks were able to destroy enemy tanks, before Iraqi soldiers could even see their opponents, still less engage them. Iraqi tactics were no match for the profession-alism of Western forces. After weeks of air bombardment, Iraqi troops were badly demoralized and, in many cases, gave up without a fight. The brevity and inequality of much of the combat contrasts markedly with the experiences of divisional commanders in the First and Second World Wars, where operations extended over days and weeks against often fearsome opposition. Nevertheless, the Gulf War is the only avail-able example of true divisional warfare from this period. Moreover, despite the mismatch, there were some significant engagements in the four-day land battle. No example is ever perfect and, accepting its shortcomings, the Gulf War is a valid and illuminating case. Indeed, in his work on combat power, Stephen Biddle employed the Gulf War and, specifically, the now-celebrated Battle of 73 Easting as a highly pertinent example of combat readiness.[62] He compares this action with Operation Michael in 1918 and Operation Cobra in 1944.

Although this study focuses exclusively on command rather than combat effectiveness, it adopts Biddle's strategy. It employs the Gulf War to exemplify divisional command at the end of the twentieth century, comparing this campaign with divisional operations, already discussed, from the First and Second World Wars. There is a problem of selection here. In the Gulf War, the Coalition consisted of twelve Western divisions; ten American, one British and one French. Some of the American forces have been the focus of substantial attention. In addition to 3 Armored Cavalry Regiment's action at 73 Easting, 24th Infantry Division has also been the subject of some detailed studies.[63] This study explores the example of the 1 (UK) Armoured Division. This division is selected because, while it has not been the subject of so much international interest, it was involved significant fighting. Moreover, partly because it was the only British division involved in the war, there is a useful literature on it, augmented by the personal availability of its commander, Major-General Rupert Smith, and his plans officer. Moreover, as noted in the previous chapter, precisely because Smith was such a competent commander, he represents something of an ideal case study at the very end of the Cold War. Indeed, his plans officer, who worked closely with him throughout the campaign, described him as 'the most influential officer after General Bagnall since World War II'.[64] He was perhaps not unbiased. Yet, Smith's superior, General Sir Peter de la Billiere, concurred; he claimed that Smith had 'exceptional qualities'.[65] He exemplified divisional command at its optimum

---

[62] Stephen Biddle, *Military Power* (Princeton, NJ: Princeton University Press, 2004).

[63] E.g., Toomey, *XVIII Airborne Corps in Desert Storm.*

[64] OF-7, Major-General retired (SO2 Plans 1 Armoured Division, 1990–1), British Army, interviewee 139, 'Enduring Operational Lessons from a Divisional Perspective', Lecture, 3 UK Division Higher Staff Formation Trainer, 17 September 2014, Fieldnotes Vol. II, 42–7.

[65] General Sir Peter de la Billiere, *Storm Command: a personal account of the Gulf War* (London: HarperCollins, 1995), 127.

at the very end of the Cold War. Consequently, the evidence about the command of 1 Armoured Division is sufficiently detailed from which to draw some wider conclusions about command.

As with the previous studies, it will, of course, be necessary to try and examine Smith's method of command in detail. However, before that analysis can begin, it is necessary to situate the Gulf War and Smith's own practice of command within a wider historical context. This context was briefly mentioned in Chapter 2. After Vietnam, the US Army had abolished conscription and introduced new doctrine. By the mid-1980s, this doctrine had crystallized into AirLand Battle, which sought to offset Russian numerical advantages in deep air attack and the introduction of a new command philosophy. The British Army was certainly influenced by changes in American doctrine but, in the early 1980s, General Nigel Bagnall, Commander of NATO's Northern Army Group in Germany, also began to develop his own operational ideas, in close consultation with the American and German armies. He sought to exploit air power in order to detach the first Soviet echelon from its forward elements. Eventually, having held the initial Soviet attack, Bagnall sought to implement a deep counter-strike, commanded at the operational level, against Soviet follow-on forces. The doctrine became known as Follow-on-Forces-Attack. His successor General Martin Farndale extended this doctrine and in an important exercise, Certain Strike, in 1987 demonstrated NATO's ability to mount such a counter-stroke.[66]

Later in the 1980s and on the basis of these developments, General Bagnall, by then promoted to Chief of the General Staff, reorganized British Army education, notably with the introduction of the Higher Command and Staff Course, and introduced new doctrine, *Design for military operations: British Military Doctrine*, in 1989. This publication represented an important transformation for the British Army. In line with US and NATO reforms, British Military Doctrine advocated two fundamental revisions of contemporary practices. First, against a traditional, attritional approach which concentrated forces frontally on enemy strengths, *Design for*

---

[66] General Sir Nigel Bagnall, 'Concepts of Land/Air Operations in the Central Region: I', *RUSI Journal* 129(3) 1984: 59–62; General Sir Martin Farndale, 'Counter Stroke: Future Requirements', *RUSI Journal* 130(4) 1987: 6–10.

Operations introduced the 'manoeuvrist approach'. This operational concept sought to exploit enemy vulnerabilities, massing combat power against them. The doctrine envisaged only holding an enemy attack, while unhinging it through bold, deep strikes – manoeuvres – against the enemy rear. In order to effect such a counter-strike, *British Military Doctrine* introduced 'mission command', as a new philosophy in the British Army. In place of a dirigist system of command, which had disputably characterized the British Army in the twentieth century, *Design for Operations* formally recommended the empowerment of subordinates. Commanders were instructed to give their subordinates missions which expressed the commander's intentions, rather than detailed tasks. In the face of unexpected circumstances, subordinates were free to fulfil that mission, as they judged best within constraints. Mission command was seen as a way of exploiting opportunities on a deep battlefield, accelerating decisions to compensate for numerical inferiority.

Rupert Smith was appointed to the command of 1 Armoured Division within this fertile context, just after the publication of *Design for Military Operations*. As an intellectual, knowledgeable and highly competent officer, he sought to implement the manoeuvrist approach in the Gulf War. 1 Armoured Division was deployed under VII Corps, the main effort of the Coalition attack, positioned on its eastern flank.[67] Smith was given a very clear mission by his corps commander: 'My mission was to protect the Corps flank by destroying the enemy's tactical reserve'.[68] It was a clear, discrete and nominally simple mission, which involved an attack into Iraq and then Kuwait towards Kuwait City. In addition to the length of the assault, it involved evident difficulties: 'The enemy might be moving about and I had to go for the ones threatening the Corps as they moved against the Republican Guard'.[69] In the event, 1 Armoured Division eliminated almost three Iraqi armoured divisions and took 7000 prisoners[70] as VII Corps fought a

---

[67] In addition to being on the main effort, 1 Armoured Division was subordinated to VII Corps rather than to the US Marines, under whom 7th Armoured Brigade had initially been subordinated due to concerns about excessive casualties. De la Billière, *Storm Command*, 93–4.

[68] Major-General Rupert Smith, 'The Gulf War: the land battle', *RUSI Journal* 137(1) 1992: 4.

[69] Ibid.

[70] De la Billiere, *Storm Command*, 299.

series of major engagements at designated objectives, which became known later as the Battle of 73 Easting and the Battle of Norfolk.

Having been given his mission, Smith identified precisely what it involved: 'The first thing I had to decide was how to fight the Division'.[71] He began to conduct this analysis in the Autumn of 1990, long before 1 Armoured Division deployed and, indeed, he had even conducted his reconnaissance. However, very early, Smith made an important decision, in line with emergent British doctrine. He decided to fight 'the Division in Depth rather than Width'. Smith was aware that he would not receive any reinforcements during the operation and only he could reinforce success or failure. Moreover, especially because his brigades were relatively small, he did not want to risk his whole force simultaneously. He also had to ensure that his formation was still showing national intent to the end of the campaign, by being involved in 'the kill'. He concluded, therefore: 'I had to organise to fight and fight in such a way that we had best chance of enduring a long fight. To do this I thought it best to fight lots of little fights quickly over period, rather than a few big ones over the same period'. Smith, therefore, decided to concentrate his forces, focus them on a narrow frontage and economize elsewhere: 'I would focus the power of the Division'.

In order to concentrate his forces, and in line with the *Design for Military Operations*, Smith organized his mission into three discrete elements: the Depth Battle, the Contact Battle and the Rear. The division would fight the deep battle with its air, intelligence and artillery assets, while the brigades fought a series of sharp engagements against Iraqi units. Smith would find and strike the enemy's reserve, while his brigades eliminated them in sequence, one brigade attacking while the other replenished itself. He characterized the divisional battle in the following way: 'The committal of appropriately grouped brigades, usually sequentially to the contact battle in concert with the Depth Fire Battle, being fought by the Artillery Group under the Commander Royal Artillery'.[72] In retrospect, Rupert Smith recognized the novelty of his concept of operations: 'I was the first to do it in 1990–1. I fought simultaneously the deep, contact and rear'.[73] Later, from Chapter 10, the importance of these concepts of deep, close and rear for divisional

[71] Smith, 'The Gulf War', 1.
[72] Ibid.
[73] General Sir Rupert Smith, interviewee 087, personal interview, 9 October 2015.

operations and their command in the twenty-first century will become apparent.

1 Armoured Division was a somewhat unusual formation in the Gulf War. It consisted of only two manoeuvre formations: 7th Armoured and 4th Armoured Brigades, commanded respectively by Brigadiers Patrick Cordingley and Chris Hammerbeck. This simplified command very substantially, facilitating a binary scheme of manoeuvre with one brigade leapfrogging the other in a series of sequential engagements. In the event, 7th Armoured Brigade, the heavier formation, assaulted enemy forces at Objectives Bronze, Copper South, Brass, Steel and Tungsten, while 4th Brigade attacked Objective Copper North, Platinum and Lead. However, the simplification of manoeuvre was offset by additional forces. Smith had an enlarged Divisional Artillery Group, with multiple-launch rocket systems (MLRS), which he divided into two groups, a reconnaissance regiment and, distinctively, an aviation regiment; this regiment consisted of seventy-two Lynx and support helicopters.[74] Indeed, Smith understood his division as consisting of twelve brigades or groups in all. In addition to the elements already specified, his command also consisted of an American artillery brigade (142 Field Artillery Brigade), an engineer brigade, a signal group, two logistic groups and a medical group. The US 142 Field Artillery Brigade, which provided General Support Reinforcing Fires, was hugely important in creating a sufficient density of fires. The 1 Armoured Division was a more complex, multi-functional formation than the standard mid-twentieth-century division such as Rommel's 7th Panzer or Montgomery's 3rd Division, therefore; it was moving towards the genuinely joint, multi-dimensional division of the twenty-first century. In contrast to Rommel or Montgomery, Smith also had to integrate fires and aviation to a much greater depth; MLRS had a range of thirty-two kilometres. While the close fight remained very similar, the depth of the divisional battle had extended.

As a result of these changes, Smith's headquarters also began to assume a somewhat different form to a conventional twentieth-century command post. The requirement to divide operations from plans became apparent. Consequently, an independent plans branch was created staffed by an SO2 and SO3 (a major and a captain), while two small operations branches were created for each of the two

---

[74] www.tim-thompson.com/gwob7corps.html.

headquarters.[75] However, significant though these changes were, they should not be overstated. 1 UK Division's headquarters in the Gulf War was bigger than a mid-twentieth-century divisional headquarters but it was by no means excessive. It was staffed by seventy-six officers, staffing G1 through G4 branches; although there was a small planning cell, there was no formal G5 branch. A further 100 personnel of all ranks, including clerks, signallers etc. supported the headquarters. Even this was regarded as too large.[76] For the operation itself, Smith organized the headquarters into main and rear headquarters. Each had a duplicate and all were armoured and completely mobile. Main headquarters consisted of a birdtable in an eighteen-foot by twenty-one-foot tent, with twelve command vehicles around it. Smith was able to staff his main headquarters and its duplicate so that only his principal staff officers and he had to move when he changed headquarters. Smith also had a smaller rover group but he used it only once to move, from the breach to join the main headquarters in the rear of 7 Brigade, and it was not deemed worthwhile. Smith commanded the whole operation from a small main headquarters, then, and its alternate, rotating between them as the brigades themselves leap-frogged forward. The headquarters moved six times in the course of the operation; more than once a day. It is worth emphasizing the size of Smith's headquarters. Each one consisted of about forty officers. As his plans officer noted: '1 Armoured Division had a very small command and staff'. Indeed, it worked on the aphorism that 'small is beautiful'. Despite the extension of his battle, his headquarters was of a size and structure which would have been recognizable to Montgomery.

As noted, Smith conceived the battle as a sequence of brigade fights; in the event 4 and 7 Brigades would punch against enemy forces on designated objectives, in turn. However, because the division could not know the precise location of the enemy until immediately before each action, Smith could not write a detailed plan for the whole

[75] OF-7, Major-General (retired), British Army, OF-7, Major-General retired (SO2 Plans 1 Armoured Division, 1990–1), interviewee 139, email communication, 29 March 2018.

[76] OF-7, Major-General (retired), British Army, OF-7, Major-General retired (SO2 Plans 1 Armoured Division, 1990–1), interviewee 139, 'Enduring Operational Lessons from a Divisional Perspective', Lecture, 3 UK Division Higher Staff Formation Trainer, 17 September 2014, Fieldnotes, Volume II, 44. In peacetime, 1 UK Division's establishment was forty-five officers and forty-six all ranks.

operation. Although Smith knew that the attack would involve actions against a series of objectives, his staff produced a plan only for the initial breach: 'We produced a most detailed order which took us to the Line of Departure and it covered the transit of the Breach and the Passage of Lines with 1st Infantry Division'.[77] The Headquarters also produced an operational overlay of boundaries, objectives and phase lines – the 'target matrix' – which allowed subsequent radio and written fragmentary orders to be issued effectively. This work organized the battle-space to expedite the coordination of the subsequent battle. Smith confessed: 'I did not think I could be any more specific than this because I would not know the situation until the ground battle started'.[78] Indeed, even on G-Day, Smith had not decided the order of march through the breach, still less which brigade was to attack which objective.[79] Consequently, although Smith did issue a series of succinct verbal orders in the course of the battle, the operation was conducted by reference to some operation directives which Smith had distributed to his division in the Autumn: 'In principle I set out to command by issuing Directives rather than detailed orders'.[80]

Since they were an essential means of managing the mission, it is worth considering Smith's directives in some detail. For instance, on 30 November 1990, Smith issues his Operation Directive 1, called 'Training for War'. The central element of this important directive was that effective manoeuvre relied on drills. Each commander was held responsible for training and rehearsing drills and procedure. If the division's units were to respond quickly and cohesively to a dynamic situation, they had to have already been committed to a set of pre-established tactics which could be executed instantly by everyone on order. The directive prioritized manoeuvre and specified that commanders should train their subordinates two levels down so that they could make appropriate plans to facilitate it.

Smith also impressed a mentality on his division: 'It is very important that we establish throughout the Division an attribute of mind that is robust'. Smith did not simply mean that his commanders and troops should be determined, though of course they had to be.

---

[77] Smith, 'The Gulf War: the land battle', 4.
[78] Ibid.
[79] Ibid.
[80] Ibid.

By robust, he referred rather to the fact that every unit in the division and all commanders should fully understand their specific mission all the time; 'if you don't understand at the unit level what the division does, you get lost'. Units could get disoriented by failing to understand their role in the division at any given moment. By developing a detailed understanding of the operation, anchored in specific drills, Smith sought to create a formation which could respond to an inevitably changing situation because all the units knew what they were trying to achieve and how to do so. They were imbued with Smith's Intent. To ensure that his forces could implement his directives, Smith subjected them to intense training in theatre, culminating in two full-scale divisional rehearsals which were very realistic – so realistic, in fact, that one unit thought it was under Iraqi attack.[81]

Smith went to some effort to try to improve his subordinates' decision-making by actively training them in command. For instance, Smith's Operation Directive 2, 'Offensive Action', explicitly sought to train commanders about how they should make decisions. This directive emphasized the importance of seizing and holding the initiative by aggressive action. Decisiveness was imperative. However, effective command relied on Smith's subordinates identifying and declaring a 'main effort'. This could not be something ethereal and abstract but had to be a specific outcome and a precise location where a decision was to be sought.

Smith adopted many of the practices which Montgomery employed in France in 1940. He imposed a clear operating concept on his division and trained them rigorously to implement a series of drills on order. However, while there were parallels, the command arrangements for this operation were distinctive. Smith commanded from a highly mobile headquarters from which to control the operation, coordinating close, deep and rear areas. Crucially, Smith, devolved considerable decision-making responsibility down to the commanders of 4th and 7th Brigades. Similarly, he assigned his Reconnaissance and Aviation Regiments and any air that he was apportioned to his Commander Royal Artillery so that he could fight the deep battle; 'there was little

---

[81] OF-7, Major-General retired (SO2 Plans 1 Armoured Division, 1990–1), British Army, interviewee 139, 'Enduring Operational Lessons from a Divisional Perspective', Lecture, 3 UK Division Higher Staff Formation Trainer, 17 September 2014, Fieldnotes Vol. II, 42–7.

point in having MLRS and all those A10s, if I was not attacking accurately'.[82] On a fast-moving battlefield in which communications might be difficult, these commanders were empowered to make independent decisions on the basis of their initiative: 'I set out to lower decision levels, thus reducing the need for information to flow upwards and speeding action'.

In addition, Smith's staff assisted him with the administration of the operation, as Montgomery did. His Chief of Staff, Colonel John Reith, and his Deputy Chief of Staff Graham Dewar, played a critical role, commanding the Main and Rear Headquarters respectively so that Smith could focus on the operation.[83] His headquarters issued Warning Orders twelve hours before each attack, after which the battle was run on radio orders.[84] The staff issued traces for the final objectives as they appeared, supplemented by written Fragmentary Orders. However, distinctively, Smith's staff also actively helped him with decision-making. For instance, Smith repeatedly asked his staff: 'Do I need to make a decision?' The staff had to understand the substance of each decision so that could advise Smith properly: 'Everyone in the headquarters had to know what a decision was – and to write them down'. The atmosphere inside his headquarters was distinctive, therefore. One officer noted: 'I was proud to be his SO2 Plans and to be able to recommend decisions to him. Of course, the GOC retained the sole right to say whether the decision was right or wrong'.[85] In this way, Smith actively implemented a system of mission command. 1 Armoured Division might be described as a loosely coupled system, in which Smith designed and supervised the operation closely but where management decisions about specific tasks and actions were devolved downwards. To this end, the Commander Royal Artillery, the Chief of Staff and the Deputy Chief of Staff were essential parts of the Smith system.

Some elements of Smith's command were certainly novel. He fought a deep battle well beyond the forward line of his troops. He

---

[82] Smith, 'The Gulf War: the land battle', 2.
[83] The fact that John Reith was a Parachute Regiment officer like Rupert Smith might have helped to create a close professional bond between them.
[84] Smith, 'The Gulf War: the land battle', 5.
[85] OF-7, Major-General retired (SO2 Plans 1 Armoured Division, 1990–1), British Army, interviewee 139, 'Enduring Operational Lessons from a Divisional Perspective', Lecture, 3 UK Division Higher Staff Formation Trainer, 17 September 2014, Fieldnotes Vol. II, 44.

actively sought to implement mission command in order to facilitate manoeuvre within his division. He wanted subordinate commanders to be operating in a framework in which they could seize opportunities through rapid local decisions. Incorporating his staff into the decision-process, he did not monopolize managerial decisions, like Monash, or subject his subordinates to the close personal supervision of Montgomery, for instance. In this way, Smith certainly represents something of a transitional case. The devolution of authority to subordinates and the attempt to distribute decision-making, while simultaneously aligning it more closely across command echelons, presaged central changes which would occur in the twenty-first century.

Yet, there were also very close parallels with other twentieth-century commanders. Like Montgomery, Smith trained his division to execute a sequence of specific, pre-established drills. Despite the increased depth of the battlefield, 1 Armoured Division's operations consisted of a series of simple, circumscribed actions, which involved the coordination of tanks, armoured vehicles and artillery. The functions of the division were limited, then. Indeed, although Smith commanded an aviation regiment, he had only two manoeuvre brigades. Moreover, as the operation proceeded, it became increasingly difficult for Smith to command entirely in the way he had hoped.

Rupert Smith is an important example, right at the end of the period. He represents the culmination of twentieth-century command before the Revolution in Military Affairs and the new wars of the early twenty-first century. It is important to recognize some important innovations which Smith implemented. His command demonstrated some novel features, which would come to full fruition in the early twenty-first century: above all, the deep, joint battle and mission command. Yet, in many ways, Smith was a conventional commander. 1 Armoured Division's mission was simple and unilineal; it was a rapid advance in an uncongested battlespace against a conventional enemy. The risks were considerable but the central problem was circumscribed. Smith resolved this problem by identifying a very clear mission and establishing parameters for its accomplishment with the greatest precision. He impressed a series of drills on his forces to be executed on order and imposed an operational framework on his commanders, so they knew what decisions they could make.

Smith initially gives his commanders an unusually high degree of autonomy. However, it seems likely that had the operation continued, he might have had to assume closer managerial responsibility for the mission and to supervise his brigade commanders more closely. Smith was eventually unable to fight the deep battle and had, like a conventional commander, to focus ultimately on the close fight: 'after about 100 kilometres I had ceased to acquire targets for myself and abandoned the Deep Battle'.[86] Indeed, it seems likely that had the ground campaign continued longer than four days, Smith might have had to assume an even more conventional role in managing the mission. This was noticeable as the division approached Kuwait City and the battlefield became more congested and confused; 4 Brigade fired on the tail elements of 7 Brigade. In response to friendly fire incidents like this, Smith issued orders on paper, with traces, for the final objectives so that each headquarters had a record of what the Division was trying to do. Indeed, there were some suggestions that the commander of one of Smith's brigades was not fulfilling his intent satisfactorily. Had the war gone on any longer, this commander would probably have been subjected to ever closer inspection by Smith. In short, had Operation Granby lasted more than four days, Smith might have become even more like his twentieth-century predecessors, compelled to supervise the management of operations and the close battle personally.

Individual Commanders

The modern combined arms division was a twentieth-century invention, as significant to warfare as the multi-divisional corporation was to business and industry. In comparison with the divisions of the previous centuries, it was a complicated organization consisting of multiple functions. Especially during the First World War, industrial firepower demanded increasingly sophisticated methods of command. Crucially, in order to overcome the enemy's firepower, the division had to coordinate its combat forces so that manoeuvre units and artillery were seamlessly unified. Divisional commanders had to achieve this coordination over hitherto-inconceivable ranges; the artillery was able to fire well beyond the line of sight and the infantry and later armour had to disperse much more widely in the attack in order to protect itself. Combined arms operations presented a significant organizational

---

[86] Smith, 'The Gulf War: the land battle', 2.

challenge, which the division and its headquarters was substantially created to resolve.

The distinctive challenges of mass industrial warfare must be recognized. Divisional headquarters, with staff, bureaucratic procedures and apparatus – maps, orders, fireplans – were constructed as a means of managing the modern military operation. These innovations were very significant and represented a major reform of military command. They represented important steps in professionalizing command. The management of a divisional mission was onerous, then. It consisted of numerous tasks which had to be identified, prioritized, sequenced and assigned to units, which had then to be coordinated and synchronized. Consequently, standardized bureaucratic practices and specialist expert knowledge both about military operations and staff procedure became essential at the divisional level from 1914 onwards.

Yet, the fundamental command problem was linear and functionally simple. Even during the Gulf War, it involved the deployment of the division's own troops on a narrow front against a limited objective. Administrative burdens arose because of the scale of operations, not the span of command. Consequently, the best divisional commanders, like Rommel, Montgomery, Monash or Smith, personally decided what was to be done very quickly; mission definition was rapid. The headquarters certainly then played a vital role in the management of the mission. Yet, the evidence considered in this chapter suggests that these divisional commanders continued to dominate the decision-making process in terms of the management and supervision of operations as well. They were able to do this because operations occurred in such close proximity and there were usually only one or two major decisions relating to their own forces on any one day. The best commanders were also able to decide upon unexpected amendments to their plans, which they implemented through communications directly to their subordinates or through their headquarters. This individualized decision-making process, personally dominated by the commander, represented an adequate and, perhaps, even optimal adaptation. Individualized decision-making was quick and consistent. In the outlying cases of Rommel and Monash, these generals effectively colonized the entire command procedure of mission definition and management. More typically, as Montgomery or Smith show, some commanders in the twentieth century could be less monopolistic. They devolved important managerial and administrative tasks to their staff, relying upon a single principal staff officer, the Ia, the chief of staff, the G3 or the GSO1, while training their subordinates to enact their orders automatically. Yet, they retained exclusive decision-making responsibility and monitored their subordinates closely. Smith is certainly an interesting, transitional case here, for, having begun Operation Granby, employing a system of mission command which presaged the twenty-first century, he tended towards a more traditional system of control as the operation continued.

It may be useful to summarize the argument of this chapter. In the twentieth century, competent individual divisional commanders were at the heart of two executive functions; they defined the mission and, with the support of a principal staff officer, managed it. Of course, as Drucker noted, the management function is always collective; no single executive could perform all the work required of the office. Even Rommel and Monash could not have commanded without Lieutenant Colonel Jackson, Major Heidkaemper and a small headquarters. Yet, in relative terms, command in this era, despite its bureaucratization, functioned through the individual agency of the general. Decision-making authority was invested in the agency of the divisional commander and competent generals ensured that they were personally able to make the critical decisions about the management of current operations; and that they oversaw their subordinates closely. The creation of a standing headquarters and staff and the bureaucratization of administration facilitated rather than eliminated individualized decision-making. Of course, towards the end of the era, a transition was evident. Under the philosophy of mission command, Rupert Smith began to explore the possibilities of a professionalized, quasi-collective system of command. Yet, even in this case and especially as the operation continued, he exemplified a practice of command which had more in common with Montgomery than with his successors in the following decades. He defined a simple mission and was then able to supervise its management closely, with the help of a small staff.

6 LEADERSHIP

Combat Motivation

So far, only the command functions of mission definition and management have been considered. It was argued that, in both areas, commanders were responsible for mission definition and tended to monopolize decision-making, with the assistance of a small staff to assist in management issues. It might be claimed that an individualist practice of command predominated. The evidence seems to be minimally suggestive that a distinctive regime of command endured throughout the century. However, before a final assessment of divisional command on conventional operations in the twentieth century can be made, the practice of leadership, the third executive function, in this period needs to be examined. This chapter examines leadership methods in the twentieth century in order to determine whether they too displayed a compatibly individualist character.

It was noted in Chapter 3 that, since combat motivation is essential, leadership is always important in the army. However, because armies in the twentieth century were predominantly citizen forces, leadership was particularly significant. In some cases, such as Kitchener's armies in the First World War, soldiers volunteered for service. Yet, the vast majority of the soldiers from 1914 to 1991 were conscripts, compelled to serve. Indeed, even when citizens volunteered it was often in the knowledge that a draft was already in place or would be introduced later. Of course, there was a decline in the mass-conscript army in the last third of the twentieth century.[1] Britain abolished conscription entirely in 1960 and the United States followed in 1973; their divisions in the Gulf War were totally professional. However, France and Germany did not abandon conscription till after the Cold War, in 2002 and 2014, respectively.

The armies of the major Western powers in the twentieth century were overwhelmingly citizen forces, then. Consequently, troops, including junior officers and non-commissioned officers, often lacked training and experience.[2] The twentieth-century division consisted of a small cadre of professional officers and NCOs in command of a mass of citizen soldiery of often inadequate training and sometimes questionable motivation. The problems were particularly pronounced in liberal democracies which did not insist upon political fanaticism or impose harsh sanctions on troops who were unwilling to fight. Despite the contemporary furore around the application of death penalties in the First World War, capital punishment was used sparingly by France, Britain and America. Citizen soldiers represented a prodigious leadership challenge, then. They had to be encouraged to fight. Indeed, Michael Howard, who served as a British Army infantry officer in the Second World War, has noted these difficulties: 'if they [conscripts] come from complex, urban and rather unmilitary societies such as the United States and the United Kingdom, they will require very careful handling indeed'.[3] During the twentieth century, the leadership challenge was very significant, then.

There was a further problem in terms of motivation which accentuated the importance of leadership. Not only were troops often fighting against their will but battlefield conditions were intensely demoralizing. Above all, the casualty rates were extremely high. In

---

[1] Catherine Kelleher, 'Mass Armies in the 1970s: the debate in Western Europe', *Armed Forces & Society* 5(1) 1978: 3–30; Michel Martin, 'Conscription and the Decline of the Mass Army in France, 1960–75', *Armed Forces & Society* 3(3) 1977: 355–406; Karl Haltiner, 'The Decline of the Mass Army', in Caforio, G. (ed.), *Handbook of the Sociology of the Military* (London: Kluwer/Plenum, 2003); Karl Haltiner, 'The Definite End of the Mass Army in Western Europe?' *Armed Forces & Society* 25(1) 1998: 7–36.

[2] See Anthony King, *The Combat Soldier: infantry tactics and cohesion in the twentieth and twenty-first centuries* (Oxford: Oxford University Press, 2013).

[3] Michael Howard, 'Leadership in the British Army in the Second World War: some personal observations', in Gary Sheffield (ed.), *Leadership and Command: the Anglo-American Military Experience since 1861* (London: Brassey's, 2002), 121.

the First World War, it was routine for battalions to withdraw a small cadre of officers and NCOs who might be able to reconstitute the unit should casualties be heavy. In effect, armies recognized the possibility that in any assault, a battalion might effectively be wiped out. In the Second World War, the daily casualty rate for the US Army, for instance, was 144 times what it was in Iraq and Afghanistan.[4] Of course, some care needs to be taken with these figures. Armies were much larger in the past than on recent operations and so the proportionate casualty rate was often more compatible than these figures initially suggest. For instance, British infantry units operating in Sangin, Helmand between 2006 and 2010 experienced casualty rates of about one in ten in any six-month tour; they would incur between sixty and ninety casualties, with between ten and twenty soldiers killed. Of course, because of body armour and advances in medical care, the proportion of soldiers who died of their wounds declined dramatically. Casualty rates in Normandy for an infantry unit were not often that much greater, though many more died than were wounded. However, of course, the entire Normandy campaign only lasted two months and units were often in the line for relatively short periods. Casualty rates in the major wars of the twentieth century were, then, significantly higher than in recent operations in Iraq and Afghanistan. Even taking into account advances medical care and protection, the reasons were simple. In the First and Second World Wars and in Korea, to a somewhat lesser extent, the major Western powers were fighting against an opponent of more or less equal combat power. Consequently, belligerents were able to inflict severe casualties on each other. In addition to the high casualty rates, citizen soldiers were often under-prepared for combat and lacked unit cohesiveness; they were, consequently, very vulnerable to enemy fire.

Therefore, in this situation, leadership was critical in the twentieth century. Indeed, given the relative simplicity of military operations, it might even be argued that the central contribution of a divisional commander was not so much in terms of mission definition and mission management, but in motivation. Since no great subtlety was typically required in the execution of military operations, success

---

[4] Robert Maginnis, *Deadly Consequences: how cowards are pushing women into combat* (Washington, DC: Regnery Publishing Inc., 2013), 40. In Iraq, 1.8 US soldiers were killed a day, in comparison with 260 in the Second World War.

was often determined substantially by the motivation of the troops. It was noticeable that in the First World War, the French and British high command substantially assessed the leadership of their generals by the number of casualties which their formations could endure. A general who failed to take an objective without having taken severe casualties was at severe risk of 'de-gumming'; he had failed to enforce high morale. Leadership was seen to be of paramount importance. This chapter addresses the question of leadership in the twentieth century. It tries to show that a highly individualist – indeed, heroic – model of leadership was developed in this period as the optimal way of motivating citizen soldiers. The chapter begins by identifying a distinctive theory of leadership before going on to explore the actual practice of leadership on the battlefield. In the last three chapters, attention has been focused primarily on outstanding commanders. The analysis of leadership practice will begin to describe failed divisional commanders in the twentieth century.

The Theory of Leadership

Before the First World War and, indeed, right up to the Second World War, Western armies were very well aware of the problems presented by industrial warfare. They fully recognized that the tendency for inertia and even disintegration was pronounced in citizen armies in the face of increasingly lethal firepower. It was not at all obvious how to ensure the participation of soldiers in combat when the chances of being killed and wounded were so high. There were a number of solutions which were proposed to this problem; tactical innovation and indoctrination became very important. However, there was also a rich and distinctive current of military thinking on leadership in all four major Western powers from the First World War onwards, reaching a high point around the middle of the century between the 1930s and 1950s. This literature identified personal leadership as a – perhaps the – principal means of overcoming the moral problems created by industrial warfare. Leadership was seen as the best means of inculcating high morale and, thereby, overcoming inertia.

In France, this leadership discourse was very strong. The French Army committed itself to a doctrine of *l'attaque à outrance* in the late nineteenth century in response to its defeat in the Franco-Prussian War.

It saw the failure in that war in terms of morale, which a commitment to all-out attack was designed to remedy. France could best be defended if its soldiers were imbued with a heightened sense of patriotism. Consequently, the French Army committed itself to all-out attack in all circumstances, whatever the cost. The bayonet charge was celebrated as the embodiment of national will.

The nascent disciplines of sociology and psychology and the scholarship of Garde Tarde and Gustav Le Bon, in particular, played an important role in these discussions about morale. Both Tarde and Le Bon argued that the alienation and *anomie* of advanced industrial society could be overcome only through the influence of potent charismatic leaders who could mesmerize the masses.[5] Salvation lay in the hierarchical control of the masses. Influenced by these writings, French doctrine before the First World War prioritized authority and obedience in the service of *La Patrie*.[6] At the same time, it idealized, even sanctified, individual leadership which could control and channel the collective enthusiasms of the masses.

Yet, even during the War, French military writing emphasized the importance of leadership. For instance, The French Army's 1916 *Instructions sur le Combat Offensif des Grand Unités* included an important section on leadership and morale: 'The moral preparation of the troops should be carried out simultaneously with material preparation. It is obtained by daily personal action of all commanders, particularly the GOC [General Officer Commanding] division'.[7] This concept of leadership was affirmed even after the First World War in military doctrine. The French Army's 1921 Provisional Instructions claimed: 'The leader of large units establishes his authority over his subordinates by the confidence he inspires in them, the firmness of his character, his professional and more quality ... he must know his troops'.[8] The 1924 Instructions continued the theme. It demanded that a commander must prepare his unit for combat by putting his troops

---

[5] Emmanuel Saint-Fuscien, *À Vos Ordres? La relations d'autorité dans l'armée française de la Grand Guerre* (Paris: Edition de l'Ecole des hautes etudes en sciences sociales, 2011), 175.

[6] Ibid., 28–9.

[7] General Staff, *Summary of the French Instructions for Higher Formations*, May 1917, 9.

[8] Ministère de la Guerre, *Instruction Provisoire du 6 October 1921 sur L'Emploi Tactique des Grandes Unités* (Paris: Charles-Lavauzelle and Co, 1924), 45.

in the best possible condition. Discipline was important here but leadership was vital: 'He develops constantly in them sentiments of duty, honour and patriotism. The commander establishes his authority by the firmness of his character, by his professional and moral qualities'.[9] In the inter-war period, General G. Rouquerol's work *Le Troiseme Corps D'Armée* and Leon Dumoncel's *Essai de Mémento Tactique* both affirmed the essential importance of close personal contact with the troops and exemplary leadership.[10] For the French Army, combat motivation was critical to combat effectiveness and citizen soldiers required exemplary personal leaders to inspire them in combat.

In Britain, pre-war debates about military effectiveness, often informed by the experiences of the Boer War, similarly highlighted the superiority of moral factors. Consequently, the British Army endorsed a concept of exemplary individual leadership before and during the First World War:

> Victory can only be won as a result of offensive action. The success of an offensive campaign depends upon the degree to which the attack troops possess: i) will to go forward ii) skill to go forward ... The inculcation of the will to go forward depends on a close study of the characteristics of troops. Leaders must understand their men, so as to be able to develop in them those qualities of temperament or race which have made the different sections of our nation such formidable fighters in the past and which make them so still ... If this spirit of determination is to reach its full development, there must by sympathy and comradeship between officers and men ... This is the true meaning of moral[e]; it lies at the root of all achievement and endurance in war by soldiers in a free state.[11]

In Britain, leadership was regarded as critical.

It might be thought that the slaughter of the First World War demonstrated the fallaciousness of these apparently facile concepts about leadership and morale. In fact, in the decades immediately after

---

[9] Ministère de la Guerre, *Instruction Provisoire sur le Service en Campagne. 20 October 1924. Annex No.1 à l'Instrution Provisoire sur l'emploi tactique des Grandes Unités* (Paris: Charles-Lavauzelle and Co, 1924), 30.

[10] Yves Cohen, *Le Siècle des chefs: Une histoire transnationale du commandement et de l'autorité (1890–1940)* (Paris: Editions Amsterdam, 2013), 603.

[11] The General Staff, *The Division in the Attack*, 13.

the First World War, deep concerns were expressed by officers who had served on the Western Front about the lack of leadership they had seen in the trenches. Most notably, Captain Basil Liddell Hart and Major General J.F.C. Fuller wrote extensively on generalship in the inter-war period partly as a result of their experiences in the Great War. Fuller was a regular army officer who had served during the First World War and had, by the 1920s, became one of its prime intellectuals, publishing copiously up to the Second World War. He was responsible for new infantry doctrine in the 1920s and subsequently played a major role in the development of armour in the British Army in the 1930s. Basil Liddell Hart had served as a subaltern on the Western Front until he was wounded. He retained his reserve commission but became a journalist; by 1925, he was one of the most influential military commentators in Britain.[12] As a result of their mutual interest in reforming and modernizing the British Army, Liddell Hart and Fuller developed a close, though sometimes tense, relationship. However, in tandem, they produced a series of seminal texts on leadership in the 1920 and 1930s. Crucially, they both claimed that the catastrophes of the First World War were primarily caused by a failure of leadership. Even though both writers rejected the crude tactics of the First World War, they also maintained that personal leadership was the only true antidote to mass mechanization.

Fuller was perhaps the more prominent figure here, writing a number of important texts in the 1920s and 1930s on generalship. One of his most influential works during this period was the famous pamphlet *Generalship: its diseases and their cure,* published in 1933. Fuller opens the work with a satirical vignette in which the life of a wounded colonel is saved by the removal of his brain, on the grounds

[12] Azar Gat, 'Liddell Hart's theory of armoured warfare: revising the revisionists', *Journal of Strategic Studies* 19(1) March 1996: 1–30; Azar Gat, 'The hidden sources of Liddell Hart's Strategic Ideas', *War in History* 3(3) 1996: 293–308; Azar Gat, 'British Influence and the evolution of the panzer arm: myth or reality? Part I', *War in History* 4(2) 1997: 150–73; Azar Gat, 'British Influence and the evolution of the panzer arm: myth or reality? Part II', *War in History* 4(3) 1997: 316–38; Azar Gat, *A History of Military Thought: from Enligthenment to Cold War* (Oxford: Oxford University Press, 2001); John Mearsheimer, *Liddell Hart and the Weight of History* (London: Brassey's Defence Publishers, 1988); Alex Danchev, *Alchemist of War: the life of Basil Liddell Hart* (London: Weidenfeld and Nicolson, 1988); Brian Holden Reid, *JFC Fuller: military thinker* (London: Macmillan, 1987); Brian Bond, *Liddell Hart: a study of his military thought* (London: Cassell, 1977).

that he will not require this organ once he is promoted to general. Yet, the purpose of the work is serious; Fuller delineated the kind of leadership that he believed was required on the industrial battlefield. For Fuller, the First World War demonstrated a catastrophic absence of leadership in combat: 'The more mechanical become the weapons with which we fight, the less mechanical must be the spirit which controls them'.[13] Indeed, Fuller thought that industrial society itself required moral leadership: 'What the world of today is lacking in is courage, the valour of leadership and the self-sacrifice of those in command. This is, I think, the essence of the above quotation [Lieutenant-Colonel Head, *A Glance at Gallipoli*]; neither a nation nor an army is a mechanical contrivance, but a living thing, built of flesh and blood and not of iron and steel'.[14] Fuller complained that the signal error of generals in the First World War was that they were not seen by their troops. They failed to develop a relationship with them or share in their suffering.

As evidence of the moral importance of personal and exemplary leadership, Fuller described the collapse of the British front in March 1918. Generals and staffs packed up and retreated: 'I for one watched it'. He recorded only one exception: 'The exception I witnessed myself, a divisional commander in the picket line with his men and everyone was confident and smiling. He was doing nothing outside showing himself, yet his presence acted like a charm – it maintained confidence. He was a man who knew the value of moral cement'.[15] As Stephen Wesbrook has proposed, on a modern battlefield, citizen soldiers could not be motivated by coercive threats or calculative rewards; the dangers were too great.[16] The soldier had to be inspired by shared values, personal commitment and example. It was the general's role to embody those ideals:

> As late as the South African War, personal contact between the general and the firing line was normally maintained; but when the [First] World War broke out, so intellectually unprepared were higher commanders, that they were at once sucked into

[13] J.F.C. Fuller, *Generalship: its diseases and their cure* (London: Faber and Faber, 1933), 14.

[14] Ibid., 13–14.

[15] Ibid., 15.

[16] Stephen Wesbrook 'The Potential for Military Disintegration' in S. Sarkesian (ed.), *Combat Effectiveness and Cohesion* (London: Sage, 1980), 244–78.

the vortex of impersonal command which had been rotting
generalship on the continent for forty years ... As the general
became more and more bound to his office and, consequently,
divorced from his men, he relied for contact not upon the
personal factor but the mechanical telegraph and telephone.[17]

In their work on Grant and Sherman, whom they saw as a 'prototype of
a most modern age',[18] Fuller and Liddell Hart respectively emphasized
the importance of the personality above the technical skill of these
commanders: 'It was the personality of the American generals, more so
than their knowledge, which stood them in such good stead.'[19] Fuller
and Liddell Hart were the most prominent English contributors to
inter-war debates about leadership but they were by no means unusual
in Britain in their advocacy of personal leadership.[20] On the contrary,
they exemplified a widely held belief that the alienation of industrial
warfare could be overcome only by close social communion between
the general and the soldier. Leadership was decisive.

In the United States, personal leadership was also seen as critical to combat motivation. Thus, as cited in Chapter 2, the *Manual
for Commanders of Large Units* stressed the affective bonds between
troops within the division: 'It is the organization which officers and
men love and cherish and about which their recollections cluster in
aftertimes'.[21] The commander played a crucial role in generating this
morale through enjoining a sense of collective identity and purpose.
For instance, the 1941 Field Service regulations noted that 'during the
decisive phase of battle, the place of the commander is near the critical
point of action. A commander influences the course of the subsequent
action by his leadership, by the use of his reserves, by the concentration

---

[17] Ibid., 28–9. See also Basil Liddell Hart, *Sherman: soldier, realist, American* (Cambridge, MA: Da Capo Press, 1993); J.F.C. Fuller, *The Generalship of Ulysses S Grant* (Cambridge, MA: Da Capo Press, 1929), viii–ix.

[18] Basil Liddell Hart, *Sherman: soldier, realist, American* (Cambridge, MA: Da Capo Press, 1993), 430; also Fuller *The Generalship of Ulysses S Grant*, viii.

[19] J.F.C. Fuller, *The Generalship of Ulysses S Grant* (Cambridge, MA: Da Capo Press, 1929), 9.

[20] In his 1939, 'Lees Knowles Lecture Cambridge' on *Generals and Generalship*, General Wavell reaffirmed many of these themes. General Archibald Wavell, *Generals and Generalship: the Lee Knowles Lectures delivered at Trinity College, Cambridge 1939* (New York: Macmillan, 1941).

[21] The Chief of Staff, *A Manual for Commanders of Large Units, Volume 1 Operations* (Washington, DC: US Government Printing Office, 1930).

of his artillery and supporting fires'.[22] Clearly, the US Army recognized the technical aspects of command but morale leadership was plainly viewed to be equally as important as the purely executive functions of command in the 1940s.

It is noticeable that the US Army saw the commander playing no less a leadership role after the Second World War. Thus, even in the 1950s, US Army armoured doctrine still stressed the importance of personal leadership on a nuclear battlefield in the most advanced technical and mechanized formations. For instance, in discussing the location of the divisional commander in combat, 1958 doctrine observed: 'His [the commander's] presence at the crucial point of combat should serve to inspire the confidence of the troops and junior leaders and encourage the maximum effort from subordinate commanders'.[23] Clearly, Western doctrine had long recommended that commanders go forward in order to ascertain the tactical situation. The moral function was vital, even in an armoured division, when the force was mounted in tanks and could not physically see the commander. Nevertheless, even in this situation the American divisional commander was believed to be able to generate an appreciable moral influence.

In Germany, the question of leadership was no less prominent in the twentieth century. Indeed, in his monograph on leadership in the first part of the twentieth century, Yves Cohen has demonstrated the ways in which it eventually assumed a toxic form in the 1930s and 1940s. It is difficult to avoid the pernicious concepts promulgated by Adolf Hitler. *Mein Kampf*, of course, celebrated the principle of personal leadership to an extreme. Although he does not seem to have read either Tarde or Le Bon, some of his sub-Nietzschean language echoes their own views on leadership. For Hitler, only an individual leader could save the masses and ensure that a nation fulfilled its historic destiny: 'The receptivity of the masses is very limited, their intelligence is small, but their power of forgetting is enormous. In consequence of these facts, all effective propaganda must be limited to a very few points and must harp on these in slogans until the last member of the public understands what you want him to understand

---

[22] Chief of Staff Field, *Service Regulations Operations FM 100–5* (Washington, DC: US Government Printing Office, 1941), 29.
[23] Headquarters Department of the Army, *The Armored Division and Combat Command FM 17–100* (1958), 18.

by your slogan.'[24] Hitler may represent the corruption of leadership in the twentieth century and the ends to which he mobilized the German people were despicable. Yet, his insights into its importance and its mechanics were not entirely out of line with contemporary thinking.

Indeed, as Yves Cohen shows, the concept of *Führertum*, leadership, was deeply ingrained in German culture at this time and was the subject of considerable scholar inquiry.[25] Although a democrat, Weber, for instance, wrote extensively about the question of political leadership and domination before his death in 1922; his work was subsequently hugely influential in ways of which he would not have approved.[26] As in Britain and France, military doctrine also underscored the importance of leadership. The 1921 *Führung und Gefecht der Verbundenen Waffen* includes significant sections on command which prescribe the specific duties of a general. However, leadership was an important theme too. This manual asserted that in pursuit of the fruits of victory and the elimination of the enemy, 'the tiredness of the troops can never be an excuse' for inaction. Similarly, in defence, 'resistance to the last man must be demanded'.[27] Clearly, in a situation of this extremity, more than executive competence was required. Leadership was necessary: 'The commander must attend to the care and trust of his troops. A strong will and firm character are in addition to knowledge and ability a requirement'.[28] *Truppenführung* of 1933 demonstrated a similar balance. The technical decision-making of the commander was central but moral leadership was of equal importance: 'The personal influence of the commander on his troops is vitally important. He must position himself close to the combat units'.[29]

A vivid discourse about leadership is observable across the major powers during the first half of the twentieth century, then. In each case, Western armies recognized the special challenge of industrial warfare. A concept of personal exemplary leadership was idealized as the most effective means of encouraging reluctant citizen soldiers

---

[24] Adolf Hitler, *Mein Kampf* (London: Pimlico, 1992), 165.
[25] Yves Cohen, *Le Siècle des chefs: Une histoire transnationale du commandement et de l'autorité (1890–1940)* (Paris: Editions Amsterdam, 2013), 137–47.
[26] Ibid., 128–35.
[27] Heeres Division 487, *Führung und Gefecht der Verbundenen Waffen*, 10.
[28] Ibid., 7.
[29] Bruce Condell and David Zabecki, *On the German Art of War: Truppenführung* (Mechanicsburg, PA: Stackpole, 2009), 36.

on an industrial battlefield. Generals were expected not merely to command their troops but to lead them morally and, if necessary, physically. Commanders had to identify closely with their troops and form affective bonds of solidarity with them so their soldiers would fight for *them*.

The Practice of Leadership

The existence of such a deep and rich international literature on leadership is significant in and of itself. It is evidence of a historically distinctive command culture. However, this writing was not merely an abstract ideal. On the contrary, divisional commanders throughout this period actively sought to embody the ideal of leadership which Fuller et al. sanctified. Despite all the technicalities of modern warfare and the burdens of management, divisional commanders also felt impelled to lead their troops, especially after the First World War. Generals like Montgomery or Rommel certainly went forward to the front to be in the optimal position to make decisions but they were deeply conscious that they could provide leadership best by their visibility in the zone of danger.

One of the most impressive recent studies of this phenomenon has been conducted by Emmanuel Saint-Fuscien. Saint-Fuscien focuses on small-unit leadership up to the battalion level in the *3e Division d'Infanterie* in the First World War. He is less concerned with divisional leadership itself. However, his findings are so instructive that they are worth considering in some detail. Significantly, Saint-Fuscien explains the continuing motivation of French Army units in the First World War not by reference to the threat of punishment, but by the positive example of leadership. While the French Army did employ discipline, including capital punishment, to coerce its troops, coercion became less effective the closer troops were to the front and it was utilized less the longer the war went on. The war disproved the notorious declaration of Adolphe Messimy, the minister of war until 26 August 1914: 'Let me have the guillotine and I guarantee victory'.[30] As a republican army of citizens, Frenchmen could not ultimately be forced to fight, as the mutinies of 1917 showed. They had to be inspired and, here,

---

[30] Emmanuel Saint-Fuscien, À Vos Ordres?, 206.

the exemplary leadership of the officer was critical. The officer did not simply command his men in the First World War; he actively led them, caring for them out of combat and physically leading them during it.

Saint-Fuscien documents the central importance of physical presence and contact to effective leadership in the First World War. With a refined anthropological eye, Saint-Fuscien records the micro-practices of leadership in the trenches. For instance, almost all officers in the trenches adopted the term 'tu' when referring to their troops; '"Tu" represented an attribute of authority' but it communicated not so much a dismissive superiority but rather a paternalistic familiarity.[31] At the same time, gestures became deeply significant in generating these bonds of leadership: 'to groom or dress, to seize, to close, to push, these gestures of contact moved officers closer to men'.[32] Finally, Saint-Fuscien documents a series of signs and objects which symbolized the authority of the officer; 'the watch, binoculars, the telephone and compass became emblems of authority', as did revolvers and canes.[33] These objects were exclusive to officers and, in the case of the revolver and the cane, they were, strictly speaking, 'weapons of constraint of authoritarian force' and a 'threat against [one's] own soldiers'. They were formally issued to officers as a means of punishing or coercing their troops. Yet, the pistol and cane quickly became symbols of courage and warrior valour and, therefore, of combat leadership, precisely because an officer could not defend himself effectively with them. Moreover, other objects were shared by both men and officers in the trenches; the pipe became a great unifying symbol.[34] The authority of French officers was formally unquestionable but the effective exercise of command required companionship with their troops. French officers had not merely to order their men but also to lead them by personal moral example.

The Second World War afforded the French Army much less opportunity to demonstrate leadership of this kind; it collapsed in six weeks in May 1940. Nevertheless, among the Free French forces, exemplary personal leadership was plainly evident especially in the cases of Generals Charles de Gaulle and Philippe Leclerc. Both adopted theatrical postures and props as aids to their leadership; Leclerc, for instance, wore a Kepi and never carried more than a cane throughout

[31] Ibid., 83.
[32] Ibid., 87.
[33] Ibid., 88.
[34] Ibid., 92.

his campaigns in North Africa and Europe, deliberately communicating a Gallic hauteur to his troops.[35] In this way, especially when he was in command of *2e Division Blindée* in France and Germany in 1944 and 1945, Leclerc was able to inspire a fierce loyalty from his subordinates, who called him 'Le Paton' or 'Pere le canne'.[36] Jacques Massu, one of his battalions commanders who would go on to command 10 Parachute Division in Algiers in 1957, was utterly entranced by Leclerc, whom he tried to imitate closely. Massu noted the way in which Leclerc had always developed a close relationship with his regimental commanders and was very visible to them and to the troops in combat.[37] He was equally solicitous of his men. In Normandy, for instance, Leclerc drove around in a jeep to visit his combat units wherever possible, dismissing the concerns of his staff: 'If you are killed who will command the division?'[38] Leclerc's reply was instructive: 'I have a lot of people who do not know how to fight and I have to show them.'[39] For Leclerc, ensuring high morale was worth the risk that he might be killed.

The pattern was repeated in Britain. Montgomery specifically stressed the importance of personal leadership at the divisional level, where the character of the commander could still impress itself directly on the formation.

1. A Divisional Commander must have certain personal qualities if he is to command successfully in battle. He must have qualities of leadership, he must have initiative, and he must have the drive to get things done and to get the last ounce out of tired troops...
2. His first task is to create an 'atmosphere' and in that atmosphere his staff, subordinate commanders and troops will live, work and fight.
3. A Divisional Commander has a unique opportunity to influence personally the morale of his Division. The surest way to get high morale is to instil confidence. If troops have complete confidence in their Commander, then all is well, since they know he will see to everything. He should be known to as many as possible of all the ranks serving under him. This can be achieved by short talks to all

---

[35] W. Moore, *Free France's Lion: the life of Philippe Leclerc, de Gaulle's Greatest General* (Philadelphia, PA: Newbury, 2011), 275.
[36] Ibid., 275.
[37] Général Jacques Massu, *Septs Ans avec Leclerc* (Monaco: Libraire Plan, 1997), 97.
[38] William Mortimor-Moore, *Free France's Lion: the life of Philippe Leclerc, de Gaulle's Greatest General* (Philadelphia, PA: Newbury, 2011), 265.
[39] Ibid., 275.

ranks during periods out of action on subjects which he wishes to put across himself, by frequent visits to Brigades and units both in and out of action, and by personal messages on special occasions. If every man in his division can be made to feel that he is a member of one happy and successful family, and that the honour of the good name of his unit and the Division are worthy of any sacrifice which he may be asked to make, a Commander can be sure that his division will respond to every call made upon it.[40]

Michael Howard has affirmed Montgomery's observations. As a serving officer in the Second World War, he personally experienced the distinctive leadership style adopted by many British commanders: 'British officers above the rank of company commander seldom carried arms, apart from pistols issued for personal protection, and even those were normally discarded by general officers'. Howard notably singles out a series of divisional commanders, who were especially adept at leadership, such as Herbert Lumsden, 'Strafer' Gott, John Harding, Douglas Wimberley and Francis Tuker, for special praise: 'These men were of attractive and often unusual personalities, with mild eccentricities in behaviour and dress that awoke amusement and imitation among their followers. Their fly-switches, silk scarves and desert boots became the trademark of officers in the Eighth Army'.[41] It is noticeable that in his memoirs of his service with 47th Division in the First World War, Charles Carrington also emphasized the leadership of his General Officer Commanding, Major-General Andrew Fanshawe, who would regularly visit frontline trenches, 'wearing an old raincoat over his rank badges so that the men were not intimidated'.[42] In each case, these officers were adept at projecting their personalities onto their troops in order to motivate them. They were able to motivate their troops through staged self-presentations.

There are a number of American generals who embodied the principle of personal leadership in the Second World War, General George Patton being at the very forefront here. However, at the

---

[40] 21st Army Group, *Some Notes on the Conduct of War and the Infantry Division in Battle*, 13–14.

[41] Howard, 'Leadership in the British Army in the Second World War', 123–4.

[42] Charles Carrington, *Soldier from the Wars Returning* (Barnsley: Pen and Sword, 2006), 103.

divisional level, Matt Ridgway, commander of 82nd Airborne Division from 1942 to 1944, was perhaps the most famous, not least because he led the division during D-Day and the Normandy Campaign. He was, indeed, the stuff of 'instant legend'. Throughout his command, Ridgway was highly sensitive to the requirement to fulfil the leadership needs of his men, even though they were all volunteers. Before D-Day, as tension and frustration mounted in 82nd Airborne, Ridgway made a point of touring his units. Subordinates noted his 'impressive appearance', with a visage like a 'Roman emperor and very sharp'.[43] Ridgway, in fact, took considerable pains to construct this effect. For instance, on Sicily, Ridgway had arrived by sea – rather than parachute – and had been slighted by the British Airborne General Frederick 'Boy' Browning for this demeaning entry into the theatre. Accordingly, he decided to parachute into Normandy. Since deploying even by glider would have been an 'ego destroyer'; it would not have conformed to the 'symbol he was trying to create'.[44] The result was that his men found him inspiring; 'He was brilliant' and 'intense' and was viewed with 'awe'.[45] Benjamin Vandervoort, who commanded 2nd Battalion, 505th Parachute Infantry Regiment in Normandy, simply stated: 'I love the man'.[46]

Despite considerable tensions between them, Brigadier James Gavin, Ridgway's Assistant Divisional Commander in Normandy and eventual successor as commander of the 82nd Airborne Division, always affirmed Ridgway's extraordinary performance as a leader. He described Ridgway as a 'frontline soldier's soldier'; 'We'd follow him straight to hell'. In Sicily, Gavin recorded that Ridgway's effect on his men was electric and he earned a reputation 'of the intense commander for whom war was a Manichean crusade'.[47]

> It was always Ridgway versus the Wehrmacht in my mind. He'd come up to the front and go around the road bend and stand and urinate in the middle of the road. I'd say, 'Matt, get the hell out of

[43] Guy Lofaro, *The Sword of St Michael: the 82nd Airborne Division in World War II* (Cambridge, MA: Da Capo), 194.
[44] Clay Blair, *Ridgway's Paratroopers* (Annapolis, MD: Naval Institute Press, 1985), 216.
[45] Lofaro, *The Sword of St Michael*, 49, 50.
[46] Ibid., 50.
[47] Ibid., 123.

there. You'll get shot.' No, he was defiant. Even with his penis he
was defiant.[48]

This was not mere posturing. It was Ridgway's command principle
always to display himself histrionically at the decisive point. There was
an executive dimension to this; he could make better decisions. Yet, it
had equally important moral effects. By being up at the front, Ridgway
could be seen by his troops and he could bodily impose his personality
upon them; he could *lead* them.

One of the most celebrated examples of this style of leadership occurred three days after D-Day. It is worth considering in some
detail. By the evening of D-Day, 6 June 1944, 82nd Airborne Division
had taken and held St Mere Eglise, its most important objective.[49]
Nevertheless, partly as a result of a dispersed drop,[50] 82nd Airborne
had failed to secure the decisive crossing over the Merderet River at
La Fière. Despite intense fighting, the Germans still held the crossing
two days later. Consequently, under intense pressure, Ridgway
decided to seize the causeway on the morning of 9 June.[51] However,
when Lieutenant Colonel Charles Carrell, the commander of 2nd
Battalion 401st Regiment, was ordered to attack on that morning, he
visibly blanched at the prospect of charging into intense enemy fire,
stuttering: 'I don't think I can do it; I'm sick'. He was relieved on the spot,
replaced by Major Arthur Gardner, his operations officer. The attack
went ahead and the troops from the glider regiment were ordered forward. Yet, even with the additional deployment of a company of 507th
paratroopers, the attack stalled in the face of ferocious enemy opposition. At this point, Matt Ridgway and his assistant commander, James
Gavin, advanced to the eastern end of the causeway, where they stood
exhorting and physically pushing their troops across: 'in the midst of
the bloody chaos, as much exposed to danger and imminent death as

---

[48] Ibid., 123.

[49] Indeed, Major-General Matt Ridgway would subsequently be sensitive to any
suggestion that this critical mission had not been achieved. He insisted that the first
draft of the US Army Official History of the Second World War, *Cross-Channel
Attack*, be amended to include this important fact; it was a point of honour both for
him as commander and his division.

[50] Clay Blair, *Ridgway's Paratroopers* (Annapolis, MD: Naval Institute Press, 1985), 230.

[51] Lofaro, *The Sword of St Michael*, 235.

any man that day, were the two most recognizable figures in the division – Ridgway and Gavin'.[52] Although he rarely underestimated his importance, Ridgway's description of the event is illuminating:

> We lost a lot of men there and I think the assault unquestionably would have failed if all the commanders from division to battalion had not been there in person to shove troops across ... Some of them began to go down and others hesitated. Then they turned back and started back, instinctively recoiling from the sheer blasting shock of the concentrated enemy fire. I jumped up and ran down there. These men were milling around in the cut. Jim Gavin, my Assistant Divisional Commander, was there with the regimental commander, Harry Lewis, and his battalion commanders. And there in the cut, we grabbed these men, turned them around, pushed, shoved, even led them by the hand until we got them started across.[53]

It seems plausible to suggest that as a result of Ridgway's leadership, 82nd Airborne secured La Fière, opening the way out of the bridgehead for VII Corps. The episode at La Fière was striking but it represented only a manifestation of a leadership strategy which both Ridgway – and other successful American generals – had long adopted. He drove reluctant citizen soldiers across the causeway with the force of his own personality.

James Gavin was, in fact, little different. In order to establish himself not only as a commander but also as a leader, Gavin was also extremely conscious about his appearance. A tall man, he sought to impose himself physically upon his men by his impressive demeanour; he paid his close attention to his dress. Even in combat, he wore tailored shirts, his jacket smartly done up and a helmet; he always carried a rifle.[54] 'He just didn't act like a general, more like one

---

[52] Ibid., 238.

[53] Matt Ridgway, *Soldier: the memoirs of Matthew B. Ridgway* (New York: Harper and Brothers, 1956), 14.

[54] Gavin used a diary to collate an eighty-seven-page miscellany on leadership. The miscellany, which seems to have been developed from the 1940s, consists of famous and predictable quotations; the very first cutting is from Shakespeare's *Henry V* but it includes numerous other diverse sources such as Heraclitus, Thucydides, Polybius, Nietzsche, Napoleon, Montgomery, Frederick the Great and Hannibal. The themes

of us' and his presence had a physical effect on his troops, 'as though an electric shock going through the whole group'.[55] Both Ridgway and Gavin entranced their troops with an elaborate and impressive ideal of martial masculinity. They believed personal exemplary leadership was essential in modern warfare. Only leadership provided the normative motivation which the dangers of industrial warfare demanded. The performance of their Division under them suggested that there was some evidence for this. Indeed, on Operation Market Garden, it might even be claimed that Gavin's leadership, which included firing at and killing German soldiers himself, compensated for a mission which was neither brilliantly conceived nor expertly managed.

Unsurprisingly, personal leadership was revered in the German Army too. Erwin Rommel was, perhaps, the greatest embodiment of this principle. It is noticeable that commentators have highlighted the importance of his physical bearing. Ralf Reuth, for instance, noted that war correspondents invested great significance in his physique:

> His head shows a high, smooth forehead, a strong energetic nose,
> prominent cheekbones, a narrow mouth with tight lips above
> a chin of dangerous determination. The strong lines around
> the nostrils and corners of the mouth would ease into smiling
> mischievousness. His clear and blue eyes, cool in a ponderous
> glance, penetrating and focused, revealed the cunning which
> marks this man, and if it broke through, imbued his Colleoni
> head with lovely warmth.[56]

Rommel seemed to embody leadership physically. His extraordinary performance as the commander of 7th Panzer Division during the Battle of France has been discussed but it is worth re-considering it, specifically in relation to leadership. Certainly, he positioned himself at the front at Avenses and Arras in order to expedite decision-making and, therefore, his responsibilities as a commander. Nevertheless, the psychological effect of his actions was unignorable. As he helped engineers, stripped

---

of Gavin's miscellany are closely compatible with the works of Liddell Hart et al. James M. Gavin, Papers, Personal Diaries, Box 10, Army Heritage and Education Centre, Carlisle, Pennsylvania.

[55] Lofaro, *The Sword of St Michael*, 194-5.

[56] Ralf Reuth, *Rommel: end of a legend* (London: Haus Books, 2008), 127.

to the waist, bridging the Meuse, he was consciously seeking to lead his troops by example: 'he was a natural leader, and he relied both instinctively and deliberately on his personal leadership'.[57] Rommel's deportment and his deliberate ploy of exposing himself prominently were highly effective methods of leadership.

In the citizen armies of the twentieth century confronting mass industrial warfare, personal exemplary leadership played a vital role for all combatants. Young, often inadequately trained and poorly motivated, soldiers needed not just commanders but leaders. In many cases, they craved the guidance and support of an individual who, in their imaginations, assumed the role of a father figure. In their celebrated work on cohesion in the Wehrmacht, Morris Janowitz and Edwards Shils highlighted the psychological role which combat leaders played in motivating troops; German soldiers would be encouraged to fight, as long as they enjoyed 'the provision of paternal protectiveness by NCOs and junior officers and the gratification of certain personality needs'.[58] The psychological effects of leadership on individual soldiers was plainly important but generals also exerted an important collective influence. By establishing themselves as totemic beacons, recognized and admired by all their soldiers, they acted as a collective reference point for them. They became a shared ideal by means of which soldiers could unite themselves into dense interpersonal fraternities. The brief exchanges with the general which the soldiers experienced together became powerful collective memories for them, unifying them as a community and committing them to common endeavours. At this point, command did not require mere intelligence and administrative skill. It required empathy, charisma and emotional intelligence. Indeed, the best commanders were adept at the dramaturgy of generalship, skillfully staging their leadership with the use of various gestures, postures and physical props. In this way, the most successful commanders became a unifying symbol for their divisions and an emotive collective reference, encouraging the very highest levels of sacrifice from their soldiers. They embodied the principles articulated in the voluminous leadership literature of the period.

---

[57] Mark Connolly, 'Rommel as Icon', in Ian Beckett (ed.), *Rommel Reconsidered* (Mechanisburg, PA: Stackpole, 2014), 165.
[58] Morris Janowitz and Edward Shils, 'Cohesion and Disintegration in the Wehrmacht in World War II', *Public Opinion Quarterly* Summer 1948, 315.

Failed Leaders

The exceptional leaders discussed up to this point demonstrate the ideal. Of course, most commanders could not hope to demonstrate the extraordinary leadership of Ridgway or Rommel. Nevertheless, the existence of lesser leaders does not deny the significance of personal leadership. On the contrary, the importance of personal leadership to citizen soldiers in the twentieth century is, perhaps, demonstrated most clearly in its absence. Commanders who failed to inspire their men highlighted the expectations of leadership in this era with special clarity.

There, of course, are a large number to choose from here. Although he does not reveal his identity, in his account of France's defeat in 1940, Marc Bloch recounts a striking episode involving a failed general:

> It had been one of the most degrading spectacles of human weakness that it has ever been my lot to witness. As the morning wore on we became aware of the figures of a man slumped in a chair close to the door. Dull-eyed and gloomy, he sat there chewing innumerable cigarettes. He wore no badges of rank on his sleeve, and the personnel of the office pushed past him with no more consideration than they would have accorded to the lowest orderly. He was, in fact, a general of division who had been deprived of this command a few hours previously – for drunkenness, it was said.[59]

While the circumstances of his demise might have been strange, Bloch's divisional commander was by no means unusual. Many divisional commanders failed in the First and Second World Wars and were removed.

It is unnecessary to discuss a large number of examples but two particularly well-known cases conveniently illustrate the importance of leadership: namely, Major-General Charles Bullen-Smith, 51st Highland Division, and Brigadier General Jay Mackelvie, 90th Infantry Division. Bullen-Smith is, particularly, useful because his failures facilitate a discussion of Douglas Wimberley. Bullen-Smith and Mackelvie commanded their formations briefly in Normandy before

---

[59] Marc Bloch, *Strange Defeat* (London: W.W. Norton and Company, 1999), 14–15.

their removal in July 1944. There is little doubt that both commanders lacked expertise in combined arms operations; Mackelvie was an artillery officer, while Bullen-Smith had only served as a staff officer in the Second World War. However, contemporaries explained and, indeed, demanded their removal primarily because they failed as leaders; neither could motivate their men.

The example of Mackelvie and 90th Division was striking. 90th Division landed on Utah Beach on 8 June 1944 and was subsequently committed, alongside 82nd Airborne, to the Cotentin Peninsula. From the outset, their performance was woeful. They failed in every operation they were given and suffered severe casualties. William Depuy, who would go on to command 1st Division in Vietnam and, in the 1970s, would be the first commander of the US Army's new Training and Doctrine Centre, was a young lieutenant in the division. He was scathing about command in the division. Before D-Day, Mackelvie had proved ineffective. He insisted on implementing petty rules and had isolated himself from his staff; remaining aloof and silent, he became known as 'Oral Non'.[60]

His performance did not improve in Normandy. The division was unlucky in losing a disproportionate number of regimental and battalion commanders in its opening actions. However, MacKelvie failed to inspire the formation and, indeed, in the face of problems of straggling and desertion, he displayed a 'dispirited, defeatist attitude'.[61] He was relieved by General Lawton Collins, VII Corps Commander, on 13 June: 'I understand that General MacKelvie only recently assumed command of the division. However, he has not demonstrated his ability to correct existing conditions, perhaps because he lacks familiarity with the problems of infantry combat. While personally brave, he has been unable to instil a determined aggressiveness in his men'.[62] In fact, Collins' description of MacKelvie's personal valour was more than a little generous. His Assistant Divisional Commander, Brigadier-General Sam Williams, found MacKelvie lying in a furrow against a hedgerow on 12 June, the day before his removal: 'Goddamit, General, you can't lead this division hiding in that goddamn hole'.[63]

[60] H. Jack Meyer, *Hanging Sam: a military biography of General Samuel T. Williams* (Denton, TX: University of North Texas Press, 1990), 4.
[61] Ibid., 71.
[62] Ibid., 72.
[63] Ibid., 73.

The experiences of Bullen-Smith and the Highland Division bore some resemblance to 90th Division. Having performed well in North Africa and Sicily under Douglas Wimberley, the division failed under Bullen-Smith. His failure pointed to the importance of personal leadership. Wimberley was a competent divisional commander, but not a brilliant one. However, Wimberley was an extremely skilled and admired leader, revered by his soldiers as 'Tartan or Long Tam'. Wimberley was replaced by Charles Bullen-Smith in August 1943 as the division returned from the Mediterranean. The appointment was met with dismay: 'No understandable reason was given. The Jocks reacted with amazement that their "Tartan Tam" was leaving: the man they knew, the man they trusted. The man who had made every single one of them believe he was a Highlander. When he came to say farewells to the Bn [5th Battalion Black Watch], tough battle veterans had real tears in their eyes'.[64] The soldiers were demoralized by the loss of a proven commander; it would take an exceptional replacement to make good that loss. In fact, Wimberley's leadership generated difficulties for his successor that are instructive.

In order to project himself onto the division, Wimberley had emphasized the distinctive ethnicity of the Highland Division; he insisted on recruiting only Scottish soldiers. Indeed, even after 7000 casualties in the Mediterranean theatre, 81 per cent of officers and 72 per cent of other ranks remained Scotsmen.[65] Even soldiers who were not Scottish were accorded a pseudo-ethnic status; Wimberley 'made every single one of them believe he was a Highlander, whatever else his birth certificate said to the contrary'.[66] To this end, he insisted that all troops wear their regimental tartan dress whenever possible and he was enthusiastic about unit and divisional sign-posts, which he wanted prominently displayed. The famous 'HD' symbol of the division was painted almost ubiquitously on vehicles and buildings.[67] He attached this divisional pride to a sense of political and national purpose and claimed that 'the inherent belief in a worthy cause made such things as the inculcation of synthetic "hate" [of the Germans, often encouraged

[64] Delaforce, *Monty's Highlanders*, 116; also Salmond, *The History of the 51st Highland Division*, 132.
[65] Salmond, *The History of the 51st Highland Division*, 133.
[66] Delaforce, *Monty's Highlanders*, 116.
[67] Salmond, *The History of the 51st Highland Division*, 22–3.

by other commanders] entirely unnecessary'.[68] The Scottish ethno-national identity which Wimberley deliberated cultivated in the division was, at least, partly the 'invented tradition'[69] of an 'imagined community'.[70] Nevertheless, it was deeply effective in motivating his troops. Wimberley reinforced this corporate identity by his frequent visits to his soldiers so that each one 'felt he had a personal acquaintance with the General'.[71] He was not a headquarters general but, like Leclerc, was constantly driving around in his jeep. As one officer in the Division noted; 'The Jocks fare better if it is under somebody they know'.[72]

Wimberley was able to generate a strong corporate identity in the Highland Division, but his very success caused Bullen-Smith major problems. Although some officers had served with Bullen-Smith when he commanded the 15th Scottish Division, Bullen-Smith was English and he had served only in the lowland Kings' Own Scottish Borderers. He was a Highlander neither by birth nor by service and he had never served with the division. Indeed, he had not commanded a unit in combat in the Second World War at all; he had served on Montgomery's staff in 3rd Infantry Division during the Battle of France in 1940. This role brought him to Montogmery's attention.

Given this biography, he could not exploit the common ethnicity that had been so powerfully invoked by Wimberley. It was very difficult for Bullen-Smith to project himself onto the division and establish himself as a reference point. Bullen-Smith tried to generate a sense of divisional pride before D-Day and to encourage his troops in Normandy. Before the Normandy Campaign, he enjoined them to

---

[68] Ibid., 23. Highlighting the importance of ethnicity to the division, the racist element of Wimberley's identity politics needs to be noted here. His memoirs include several passages in which Wimberley reveals that he did not want Africans or Jews in the Division: 'On another day I came across a big South African "buck" Nigger wearing a Balmoral Bonnet with a red hackle up. I was so angry that I did what I should not have done, and there and then removed it off his head. I think he was rather surprised, and no doubt he really meant no harm, but our morale was pretty high, and I was having no black Africans in the Highland Regiment, or wearing the uniform of a Highland Regiment', Douglas Wimberley, *The Memoirs of Major-General Douglas Vol 1 and 2*, IWM PP/MCR/182, 35.

[69] Eric Hobsbawm and Terence Ranger, *The Invention of Tradition* (Cambridge, MA: Cambridge Unversity Press, 1983).

[70] Benedict Anderson, *Imagined Communities* (London: Verso, 2016).

[71] Salmond, *The History of the 51st Highland Division*, 21.

[72] Martin Lindsay, *So Few Got Through* (London: Collins, 1946), 18.

uphold the traditions of the Division and was careful to communicate congratulations to his units from his superiors. Yet, he failed. It was very noticeable that his dismissal was not mentioned in any of the War Diaries either of 51st Highland Division or any of its subordinate Brigades or Battalions.[73] His subordinates wanted to erase him from their memory. By contrast, the arrival of his replacement was greeted with pointed enthusiasm: 'The new divisional commander has arrived: Major General Tom Rennie. He is Black Watch who escaped in 1940 when the Division had to capitulate at St Valery and subsequently commanded a battalion and then a brigade in the reformed Highland Division in North Africa. Everybody is delighted with the appointment'.[74] Another officer in 5 Black Watch reaffirmed the point, usefully highlighting the importance of the Highland connection:

> To the Battalion it [Rennie's appointment] was especially welcome; he was their CO who had taught them so much; had led them into their first battle at Alamein; had then commanded 154 Brigade with distinction and, more recently, had taken the 3rd Division into the D-Day landings and secured his final objectives. He was "one of their own" and a real successor to General Wimberley. The effect on Divisional morale was immediate and lasting and the Battalion noted with pride that they were one of the first units to received a visit from General Rennie.[75]

For this battalion, Bullen-Smith was an aberration, rectified by the appointment of Rennie; crucially, Bullen-Smith was never considered *one of their own*.

The contrast between successful divisional commanders like Ridgway, Gavin, Rommel and Wimberley and failed ones like MacKelvie and Bullen-Smith is striking. However, the reasons invoked to explain the failures of the likes of Bullen-Smith and Mackelvie were even more interesting. Their tactical expertise was clearly inadequate; they did not understand divisional manoeuvre. They failed in their executive duties to define and manage missions effectively. However,

---

[73] 5 Black Watch, War Diary, 25 July 1944, WO 171/1266, TNA.
[74] Lindsay, *So Few got Through*, 32.
[75] Robert Doherty, *None Bolder: the history of the 51st Highland Division in the Second World War*, 167.

they were primarily removed because they failed to motivate their soldiers. For instance, when Montgomery met with Bullen-Smith on 26 July to relieve him of his command, he explained himself in significant terms: '"You must go, the men won't fight for you".'[76] It is a useful summary of the central importance of morale and leadership in the twentieth century. Citizen soldiers required active personal leadership from their divisional commander. In this period, that leadership was provided by the exemplary personal example of the commander. Leadership was understood to be a manifestation of the character of the commander and was demonstrated through theatrical displays of courage and solidarity with the troops.

The Father Figure

Mass citizen armies in the twentieth century faced a major organizational problem. The battlefield had become so lethal that not only were casualty rates very high but troops also had to disperse in order to avoid the increased firepower which armies had at their disposal. In this situation, as many commentators such as S.L.A. Marshall noted, inertia was likely to set in. Away from the comfort of close-order dispositions and distant from the immediate observation of peers and superiors, it was easy for soldiers to shirk and to straggle. Exemplary personal leadership was identified by all the major Western powers as the central means of overcoming battlefield inertia and ensuring combat effectiveness even in an era of industrial firepower. In particular, contemporary narratives espoused a psychological model of leadership based on the personality and character of the commander. Leadership was possible insofar as generals projected their personality out onto their troops to form a bond with them. For the soldiers, themselves, this relationship was substantially imaginary since they would actually interact with even the most forthcoming general only infrequently. Troops did not really know their commanders personally; they saw them only at these rare, thaumaturgical moments. However, these brief but effervescent exchanges were invested with huge social significance in the subsequent memories of the soldiers. Soldiers imbibed the charisma of their commander and were sustained by its sacred mantra long afterwards.

---

[76] Delaforce, *Monty's Highlanders*, 145.

Accordingly, and especially after the apparent command failures of the First World War, divisional commanders were supposed to lead, if not from the front, then at least to provide leadership at the front. It was expected that they should inspire their troops by their own calmness under fire. The most successful commanders displayed a heroic form of generalship. They may have been the unusual actions of a particularly forceful and driven commander but they represented a wider norm which was established by the mid-twentieth century; the divisional commander had a duty to lead – personally. The divisional commander was personally responsible for the motivation of his troops and for overcoming the potential inertia which was always a recurrent possibility on the modern battlefield. Of course, in the latter part of the twentieth century, especially in the 1960s and 1970s, personal leadership became less important. Despite obvious exceptions like Hank Emerson or David Hackworth, American leadership failed catastrophically in Vietnam.[77] Moreover, the operational conditions of the Cold War, when armies only ever exercised, and the professionalization of Western armies in this period altered its significance. Professional troops were not so dependent on father figures; they took their motivation from the duty of their vocation, realized at the small-unit level. Nevertheless, for most of the short twentieth century, personal exemplary leadership was an essential characteristic of divisional command.

In the twentieth century, then, the divisional commander occupied a singular position at the top of a steeply graded military hierarchy. Dominating decision-making and surrounded by only a small coterie, they were potentially remote and distant figures. However, the best commanders circumvented the formal rank structure to form a direct bond with their troops; they became highly emotive collective references for the troops, inspiring love and affection. They created an intimate solidarity with their soldiers. These commanders were imagined as father figures by their troops, who, in most cases, were twenty or even thirty years younger than them. Troops wanted to earn the respect and affection of leaders like this. Paternalistic leaders were

---

[77] Paul Savage and Richard Gabriel, *Crisis in Command* (New York: Hill and Wang, 1978); Paul Savage and Richard Gabriel, 'Cohesion and disintegration in the American Army: an alternative perspective', *Armed Forces & Society* 2(3) 1976: 340–70; Edward King, *The Death of an Army* (New York: Saturday Review Press, 1973).

revered, especially in the first half of the twentieth century, and troops were often willing to fight and to die for them.

It is notable that, in terms of understanding the broader regime of command, there was a close elective affinity between the practice of leadership and command in this era. In the previous chapter, it was argued that commanders monopolized decision-making; they defined the mission and supervised its execution personally. Leadership, too, was a similarly individualist practice at this time. This does not seem to be coincidental. On the contrary, while the individualistic practice of command and leadership developed organically without higher direction or intent, there were definite organizational benefits to this convergence of practice. The best commanders did not merely order missions abstractly from above but, through leadership, actively embodied the will to accomplish them, embracing the risks they involved. Precisely because these leaders enacted their own orders, missions were imbued with the compulsion of the commander's personality. Missions attained a moral force and troops felt obliged to accomplish them or to fail their leader. At the same time, exemplary personal leadership legitimated individual decision-making. By leading their troops through personal example, generals arrogated the right to make potentially fatal command decisions. They were allowed to practise command individualistically, issuing orders on the basis of their intuition and instinct and by means of the force of their personality, precisely because they also led their missions personally. A heroic leader was also an individualistic commander.

7 THE COUNTER-INSURGENTS

The division played a critical role in conventional interstate warfare from 1914 to 1991. The previous chapters claimed that the practice of command might be best understood as a form of individualism. With the help of a very small staff, commanders personally monopolized decision-making responsibility both for the determination of the mission and also for its subsequent coordination and were expected to demonstrate exemplary personal leadership. Clearly, because the division was primarily designed for warfighting, the identification of a command regime which might be called 'individualist' is a significant finding for this type of operation. However, it does not yet demonstrate that an individualist regime of command existed in the twentieth century. Divisional operations were, of course, by no means limited to conventional combat in the twentieth century. On the contrary, divisions were also simultaneously employed on many counter-insurgency missions throughout this period.

For instance, British divisions were involved in the Irish War of Independence in 1919–22, the Arab Revolt in 1936–9, Malaya, Kenya and Cyprus in the 1950s and, of course, the Troubles in Northern Ireland from 1969 to 1996; French divisions were involved in Syria and Morocco in the 1920s,[1] Africa in the 1930s, Indochina from 1945 to 1954 and Algeria from 1954 to 1962, while American divisions were heavily committed to Vietnam from 1965 to 1973. If command

[1] Martin Thomas, *Fight or Flight: Britain, France and Their Roads from Empire* (Oxford: Oxford University Press, 2014), 27–32.

individualism really were a general paradigm of military decision-making in the twentieth century, it is imperative to understand how command was exercised on these pacification operations.

Self-evidently, these pacification operations were quite different to warfighting. These conflicts were typically of low intensity; combat was normally small-scale and localized against bands of often poorly equipped insurgents. By contrast, military operations became highly politicized. Soldiers interacted immediately and directly with the population and commanders at a low level were engaged with local civil and political agencies. The Anglo-French counter-insurgency literature, which emerged out of their experience of the wars of decolonization from the 1940s to the 1970s, demonstrated this complexity very clearly. Both Robert Thompson's and David Gallula's now-classic texts on counter-insurgency prioritized the political goals of the campaign and, therefore, the requirement of commanders to consider the non-military implications of their actions.[2] Thompson's fourth principle of counter-insurgency stated that 'the government must give priority to defeating the political subversion, not the guerrillas'. Similarly, Gallula argued that 80 per cent of counter-insurgency campaigns were political. Politics became primary. On a pacification operation, a commander aimed to secure the civilian population and, therefore, the political, civil and informational implications of any military operations became salient. In addition, the military had to cooperate closely with indigenous security forces.

The geometry of the battle space also changed radically on counter-insurgency operations. While the twentieth-century division fought on a small front in combat, it sought to pacify large areas during a stabilization mission. Its area of responsibility expanded dramatically. In Algiers, 10th Parachute Division was responsible for a city of 600,000[3] and the surrounding area. In Vietnam, the US Army's 9th Infantry Division was responsible for a huge and complex area in the Mekong Delta in 1968–9. It consisted of four provinces: Long An, Dinh Tuong, Kien Hoa and Go Cong, inhabited by a population of 1.8 million and covering an area of over 6000 square kilometres. It

[2] David Galula, *Counter-Insurgency Warfare: theory and practice* (Westport, CT: Praeger, 2006); Robert Thompson, *Defeating Communist Insurgency: experiences from Malaya and Vietnam* (London: Chatto and Windus, 1974).

[3] Göran Therborn, *Cities of Power: the urban, the national, the popular, the global* (London: Verso, 2017), 128.

was 'about the size of New Jersey' and included several major towns.[4] Divisional areas were huge.

The organizational problems which confronted a counter-insurgent were then of a quite different order to high-intensity conventional warfare. In their work on Vietnam, Julian Ewell, the commander of 9th Infantry Division in 1968–9, and his chief of staff, Ira Hunt, for instance, noted:

> The Vietnamese War was so complex, so varied and so changeable that these high level approaches tended to be very difficult to use with any confidence ... The strategy and grand tactics of the Vietnamese War will probably not be well understood for years. In general, the war and its total environment were so foreign to classical western experience, military and civilian, that one could not grasp it at the time much less understand it.[5]

Stabilization operations involved the support of an indigenous regime, a colonial or postcolonial government, against an internal insurgent faction. In stark contrast to the major conflicts of the twentieth century, these confrontations were not wars of fronts but wars 'among the people'; the threats were asymmetric and internal. They were, therefore, complicated and confusing operations.

Pacification operations, consequently, represent an important test case in terms of understanding the regime of command in the twentieth century. On conventional operations, command might be characterized as individualist. By contrast, it could be argued that on a counter-insurgency campaign, a quite different practice of command was required. It might be claimed that the individualism, so evident on conventional missions, was replaced by more collaborative systems of commands as decision-making became more diverse and dispersed. Increased complexity demanded an alternative system of command. Plainly, if this were the case, it would represent a serious blow to the argument of command transformation proposed here. Collective

---

[4] Julian Ewell and Ira Hunt, *Sharpening the Combat Edge: the use of analysis to reinforce military judgement* (Washington, DC: US Government Printing Press, 1973), 9.
[5] Ibid., 5, 7.

command would not be a distinctive historical regime related to the special conditions of the twenty-first century but would merely reflect contingent operational conditions. On this account, while warfighting optimizes command individualism, pacification operations always require a more collective, collaborative method. In order to maintain that divisional command has become distinctively collective only in the twenty-first century, it is necessary to show that there was a common practice of command in the twentieth century across the operational spectrum. This demonstration is possible only by assessing command of counter-insurgency operations in the postwar period in detail.

The Evidence

To argue for a common practice of command on pacification operations in the twentieth century is challenging. Ideally, the analysis would consider French, British, German and American examples in order to align the evidence with Chapters 4 and 5 and the discussion of warfighting. Of course, this is not possible. After the First World War, Germany was stripped of its relatively modest empire under the provisions of the Treaty of Versailles. It became a purely continental power and was, therefore, involved in no pacification operations in the twentieth century. It might be possible to describe German actions against partisans and guerrillas in the Second World War especially in Central, Southern and Eastern Europe as a form of counter-insurgency. Yet, it was so closely associated with their purely military campaigns that such a definition would be artificial. Moreover, these campaigns were often closer to elimination than pacification operations. Accordingly, it is necessary to focus on the remaining powers – France, Britain and America. Nevertheless, the question of case selection remains.

The American selection is self-evident. Notwithstanding the banana wars of the 1930s, the case of Vietnam has to be considered in understanding divisional command in the twentieth century. It was an intense, large-scale and enduring campaign; the US eventually deployed a force of 500,000 and fought a nine-year campaign, in which 58,000 troops were killed. It was also a war in which numerous innovations of profound future importance were implemented; precision-guided munitions, sensors and helicopters all appeared.[6] No serious study of divisional command could ignore Vietnam. Accordingly, this chapter examines the Vietnam War. Yet, here, naturally, there is a requirement for selection. The United States deployed ten divisions to Vietnam in total (1st, 4th, 5th, 9th, 11th, 23rd, 25th, 1st Cavalry, 101st Airborne and 1st US Marine Divisions), as well as several independent brigades between 1965 and 1973. These divisions were involved in numerous operations in that time, and with commanders serving for one-year rotations, there are many generals from which to choose. As Ewell and Hunt noted above; it is difficult to claim that there was a typical US division in Vietnam. The operating environment was different in each area and the war evolved drastically. The Tet Offensive of February 1968 constituted an important fulcrum in the war when tactical conditions changed substantially. Having suffered a major defeat, the Viet Cong, supported by the North Vietnamese Army, were reduced to smaller unit actions than they had been between 1965 and 1968.

In Vietnam, it is impossible to select a truly representative division but that does not mean that the analysis of a particular division is nugatory. Eric Burgerud's brilliant work on the 25th Infantry Division focuses solely on that formation but it has some profound things to say about the war more widely.[7] Precisely because he attains a deep understanding of one formation, he is able to highlight fundamental operational problems faced by US forces as a whole, and the methods by which they sought to resolve them. Burgerud's strategy is followed here. Rather than investigating numerous formations, this analysis focuses on one; it employs the 9th Infantry Division, which deployed to the Mekong Delta in 1968, as a focus.[8] Its operations were particular but it may usefully illuminate wider practices. Moreover, there is good supporting evidence because the commander and his chief of staff wrote a monograph about their operations, which was itself challenged by one of their battalion commanders, Colonel David Hackworth. While not perfect, these resources do mean that the command technique of Ewell and the 9th Division is better documented than most other formations. In addition, the Division was engaged in a series

---

[6] The British and French had begun to use helicopters in the 1950s, yet on nothing like the scale of the Americans in Vietnam.

[7] Eric Burgerud, *The Dynamics of Defeat: the Vietnam War in Hau Ngia Province* (Boulder, CO: Westview, 1993).

[8] I am grateful to Eric Burgerud for recommending this formation as a focus of study.

of operations against the Viet Cong using tactics which had been developed by 1st, 25th, 1st Cavalry and 101st Airborne Divisions over the previous three years. The Division, commanded by the controversial and extremely aggressive Major General Julian Ewell, represented the culmination of an operational approach common across the US forces in Vietnam, which it refined very considerably. As Ewell himself noted: '9th Division did not do anything differently'.[9]

Although the environment in the Mekong Delta was unique – quite different to the central highlands or the north near the DMZ – with among the worst climate and conditions in Vietnam, 9th Division's area of responsibility was closely compatible with those of 1st and 25th Division operating contiguously in or near War Zones D and C. In addition, although it was involved in very intense combat at company and battalion level, deploying in 1968 after Tet, it was involved in smaller-scale operations than its sister divisions before 1968; the Viet Cong's forces had been decimated and were still recovering. Consequently, while highly – perhaps excessively – kinetic, its operations were somewhat closer to conventional pacification than wholesale warfighting, which had characterized the pre-Tet environment. The Mekong Delta was also the most heavily populated part of Vietnam. Accordingly, it becomes easier to align 9th Infantry Division in the Mekong Delta with British and French colonial operations of the same period. There is no typical Vietnam division but 9th Infantry Division represents a plausible example of divisional command during this war. This study will focus on the Division's operations from spring 1968 to early 1969 when Ewell was in command.

As Britain retreated from empire, its forces were involved in numerous campaigns. In his work on British counter-insurgency, David French examines ten military operations between 1945 and 1967: Malaya, Kenya, Cyprus, Oman, Aden, Nyasaland (Malawi), Borneo, Palestine, Rhodesia and the Canal Zone.[10] Any of these might provide a good example of divisional command in a pacification operation. In the case of the Malayan campaign, there is an extensive literature on military operations. Nevertheless, this chapter

[9] Senior Officers Debriefing Programme: Conversations between Lieutenant General Julian Ewell and Mr Robert Connelly and Lieutenant Colonel Norman Bissell, Carlisle Barracks PA 17013, Army Heritage and Education Centre, 70.
[10] David French, *The British Way in Counter-Insurgency 1945–67* (Oxford: Oxford University Press, 2011).

uses the Mau Mau uprising in Kenya (1952–8) to illustrate British approaches to counter-insurgency. There are a number of reasons for this. In suppressing the Mau Mau uprising, the British authorities and the armed forces, under General George 'Bobbie' Erskine, who was appointed military commander, Commander-in-Chief East Africa, in June 1953, explicitly drew upon methods which had been used in Malaya. The British military effort eventually focused on the forests with the army hunting small insurgent groups and their leaders in their refuges away from the population. These operations assumed a fairly conventional military form, involving extensive use of air power; they are not particularly indicative about the distinctiveness of pacification operations in this era. However, in April 1954, the British launched Operation Anvil to clear Nairobi of Mau Mau with a force the size of an army division. It has been widely and properly regarded as the decisive operation of the campaign which ultimately ensured the defeat of the Mau Mau, driving them into the forests. Operation Anvil is, then, a pertinent and conveniently discrete operation conducted at divisional level and precisely because of its importance there is sufficient evidence from which to develop a picture of divisional command.

In some ways, Operation Anvil represents an ideal example; it was an urban divisional operation. However, there is an obvious caveat here. Erskine was not a divisional commander in Kenya. He was a lieutenant-general who was Command-in-Chief East Africa and he did not have a formal division under his command. Moreover, on his appointment, Major General William 'Loony' Hinde, who had been directing military operations up to that point, became the Deputy Director of Military Operations.[11] Hinde was concerned with the implementation and monitoring of the purely military campaign. Strictly speaking, Hinde rather than Erskine should be the focus of analysis here. However, although Hinde commanded a divisional-size force in Kenya against the Mau Mau and, as Deputy Director Military Operations, was formally responsible for all military operations, he played a subordinate role in Operation Anvil itself. It is accepted that the selection of Erskine, as an example of divisional command on a pacification operation, is not optimal; he was not formally a divisional

---

[11] Hinde had served as the commander of 22nd Armoured Brigade, 7th Armoured Division, under Erskine in Africa and Normandy. After a disappointing performance, he was relieved by Montgomery in early August, on the same day as Erskine.

commander. Yet, his performance during the Mau Mau uprising seems minimally illustrative of divisional command since Operation Anvil involved a security force which was broadly equivalent to a light division. Moreover, because it was such an important operation, Erskine supervised its execution very closely. He effectively commanded a division on this operation.

France was involved in two infamous and disastrous postwar campaigns of de-colonization: Indochina and Algeria. Although pacification was critical, Indochina substantially involved conventional operations against the Viet Minh, often in remote locations, culminating in the Battle of Dien Bien Phu.[12] In order to understand the distinctive French approach to stabilization, the Algerian War (1954–62), represents a better example, therefore. Indeed, it is too important a campaign militarily, politically and historically to ignore. However, the Algerian campaign was both long and diverse geographically and, after the implementation of the Challe plan in 1958, assumed a different character; French combat forces were then committed outside population centres, often to remote parts of the desert along the Moroccan border. Accordingly, a similar problem of selection that attended the Vietnam War affects the Algerian campaign. There are a number of operations and divisions which might be analyzed. This chapter examines the notorious performance of 10th Parachute Division under the command of Brigadier-General Jacques Massu in Algiers in 1957.

There are some methodological disadvantages here. Many of the files remain closed.[13] However, Massu, himself, and three of his most important subordinates, Roger Trinquier, Paul Aussaresses and Marcel Bigeard, have all written accounts of the conflict which are deeply illuminating about command on this operation. Moreover, the very fact that it was executed in a city within and, in fact, on a civilian population differentiates it markedly from the conventional divisional operations, described in the previous chapter. The methods which 10th Parachute Division used may have been extreme but, like 9th Infantry

---

[12] Bernard Fall, *Hell in a Very Small Place* (Cambridge, MA: Da Capo Press 2002); Bernard Fall, *A Street Without Joy* (Mechanicsburg, PA: Stackpole 2005); Martin Windrow, *The Last Valley* (Cambridge, MA: Da Capo Press, 2004).

[13] All the main 10th Parachute Division files at Chateau Vincennes, which are now open, were examined. However, the material in them refers primarily to the less controversial operations in rural Algeria.

Division and Erskine's force in Nairobi, it was operating in a densely populated civilian environment.

Indeed, the parallels between Operation Anvil and the Battle of Algiers are close; both involved a divisional clearance of a major city. In each case, the operations played a vital role in breaking the insurgency, to be followed by more expansive clearance operations in rural areas: Erskine's operations in the forests of the Aberdare mountains in Kenya and the French operations conducted as part of the Challe Plan in the mountains, deserts and hinterland of Algeria. 9th Infantry Division's operations were more dispersed and rural, but they too involved the attempt to drive the Viet Cong out of population centres in the Mekong Delta in order to protect Saigon. The similarities between the operations – and especially between Operation Anvil and the Battle of Algiers – assist the comparison with counter-insurgency operations in the twenty-first century. In Chapter 9, the struggle for Kandahar City in 2010 will be considered and Anvil and Algiers represent an instructive contrast to that operation. This chapter discusses mission definition in all three cases before going on to examine the way in which Ewell, Erskine and Massu managed and supervised military operations in Vietnam, Kenya and Algeria. Clearly, the aim is to trace the practice of command in the two executive functions thematically across the case studies. However, for the sake of clarity it is easier to discuss each case in turn chronologically, identifying similarities and finally summarizing these at the end of the section. Accordingly, the discussion begins with Erskine's command in 1954, before moving onto Massu's in 1957 and finally to Ewell's in 1968–9.

Operation Anvil

The Mau Mau[14] emerged among the Kikuyu, Embu and Hera populations in and around Nairobi and the White Highlands during the 1940s in protest at the distribution of land. From the 1930s, accelerating after the end

---

[14] The origins of the term Mau Mau are contested. Some claim it means 'out, out' referring to the goal of independence. Others claim that it is a corruption of the formal title of a Kikuyu oath. The most plausible translation is that Mau Mau means 'greedy eating', a reference to the consumption of goat meat during oathing ceremonies; see Daniel Branch, *Defeating the Mau Mau, Creating Kenya* (Cambridge: Cambridge University Press, 2009), 23.

of the Second World War, increasingly large sections of the Kikuyu population were being alienated from their lands and turned into squatters.
Among the Kikuyu, land ownership was critical to full political status.
Consequently, in addition to the economic disenfranchisement, landless
young Kikuyu men were stripped any political recognition and could not
even marry. Consequently, the Mau Mau began to 'oath' poor Kikuyu
from the late 1940s; individuals swore – or were compelled to swear –
allegiance to the movement, to resist British imperialism and to regain
their lands. The Mau Mau uprising was certainly ultimately an insurrec-
tion against the British Empire and white rule but its immediate targets
were predominantly conservative Kikuyu leaders and their followers,
whose interests lay with colonialism. The Mau Mau's terror campaign
began in the early 1950s. In March 1953, the Mau Mau launched their
most murderous attack, at Lari, killing and mutilating seventy-four
loyalist Kikuyu, including Luku Wakuhangame, a local leader. This crisis
led to the appointment of Erskine as military commander three months
later, responsible for suppressing the insurgency.

Erskine quickly defined a mission for his forces. Erskine
was not especially racist. He was highly critical of the settlers, des-
pising them as a sybaritic elite. Above all, he wanted to prevent the
Mau Mau rebellion turning into a general Kenyan rebellion against
British rule. He feared that a local uprising might become a race war
between white settlers and black Kenyans: 'the Mau Mau programme
visualized the complete unanimity of the Kikuyu tribe, strong support
of neighbouring tribes and violent action to exterminate the European
and later the Asian'.[15] Erskine's identified his principal mission as
re-imposing imperial order on the Kikuyu rebellion in support of the
white land-owning population in the highlands and loyalist Kenyans.
Consequently, Erskine rejected the extreme measures which the
security forces had implemented before his arrival, when summary
executions and random brutality had been accepted practices. On
23 June, he issued a directive stating: 'I will not tolerate breaches of
discipline leading to the unfair treatment of anyone'.[16] He stopped
the use of score-boards, recording the number of Mau Mau who
had been killed, among British Army units. These scores encouraged

[15] Lieutenant General George Erskine, 'The Mau Mau Rebellion', lecture given by
General Erskine to 1955 course, Army Staff College, Camberley, 1.
[16] Huw Bennett, *Fighting the Mau Mau: the British Army and counter-insurgency in the
Kenya Emergency* (Cambridge: Cambridge University Press, 2013), 112.

competition between units and, therefore, increased the chances of indiscriminate shootings:[17] 'There have been a lot of indiscriminate shootings before I arrived and one of the first things I did was to stop the casualty competition which had been going on. The second thing I did was to issue a letter of direction of all officers'.[18] The British Army and local units had also cut off the hands of Mau Mau who had been shot, ostensibly in order to fingerprint them. Yet, the practice was gruesome and descended quickly into trophy-taking. Erskine banned it.

Erskine also endeavoured to reduce the incidence of abuse and murder by the security forces. Much of his effort concentrated on the notorious Major Gerald Griffiths; a British officer and an embittered colonialist, he killed and wounded a number of innocent Kikuyu and sanctioned, even encouraged, abuse among his subordinates. In his personal records and letters, Erskine revealed his contempt for Griffiths, who was eventually found guilty of murder and torture. Erskine described him as 'this blasted man';[19] he was 'astonished' Griffiths was originally acquitted[20] and dismayed by the lenient sentence he eventually received. Erskine also sought to bring the Home Guard, a Kenyan militia, under control, since its brutalization of the population was a major factor in Mau Mau recruitment.[21] In reality, Erskine had limited success in reducing the excesses of the security forces, not least because to discipline every infraction would have been to undermine the cohesion and morale of the force.[22]

At the same time, Erskine demanded that the insurgency had to be crushed. Moreover, Erskine's understanding of the Mau Mau itself was crude. Influenced by Louis Leakey, John Carothers and the 'Committee to Enquire into the Sociological Causes and Remedies for the Mau Mau', Erskine dismissed the Mau Mau uprising as a form of primitive psychopathology. The Mau Mau had succumbed to savagery.

---

[17] Ibid., 118.
[18] Letter to wife, 28 Nov 1953 from GHQ, The Papers of General Sir George Erskine, IWM 75/134/1 Official Records of Service 1915–1964.
[19] Letter to his son Philip, 2 February 1954, IWM 75/134/1 Official Records of Service 1915–1964.
[20] Letter to wife, 28 November 1953, IWM 75/134/1 Official Records of Service 1915–1964.
[21] David Anderson, *Histories of the Hanged: Britain's dirty war in Kenya and the end of empire* (London: Weidenfeld and Nicolson, 2005), 257.
[22] Bennett, *Fighting the Mau Mau*, 267.

At the same time, Erskine also paradoxically recognized that the Mau Mau rebellion was 'no sudden outburst but a cold blooded unfolding of a carefully prepared programme' to unite the Kikuyu against British rule.[23] Erskine never resolved the contradiction but, concerned by the immediate threat they posed to the colony, he adopted a remorseless approach.

In her polemical analysis of Britain's suppression of the Mau Mau rebellion, Caroline Elkins has claimed that the British colonial authorities were engaged in a deliberate programme of Kikuyu genocide.[24] In the light of Erskine's extensive efforts to moderate the behaviour of his forces, this assertion cannot be sustained. Erskine rejected indiscriminate killing and had no intention of perpetrating genocide. Nevertheless, as Elkins' work usefully illustrates, the harshness of the repression cannot be underemphasized. There were 24,000 deaths during the Mau Mau rebellion, including 11,500 excess killings.[25] Accordingly, although perhaps more sensitive than other counter-insurgents of the time, Erskine executed a remorseless campaign of repression.

In response to this emergency, Erskine not only defined the general mission against the Mau Mau but also conceived Operation Anvil almost immediately on his arrival to the theatre. In a report written to the Chief of the Imperial Staff on 29 September 1953, Erskine highlighted that Nairobi was critical to the Mau Mau and that the elimination of the movement in the city would constitute a decisive defeat; the Mau Mau movement drew its resources from the city and was able to advance its political programme, mobilizing the Kikuyu population there most effectively. Operation Anvil would be his decisive operation.

However, in order to execute Anvil, Erskine had to create a command structure which was able to manage the execution of the operation. He found existing arrangements wanting. When Erskine arrived in Kenya, he was given the option of assuming full responsibility for the colony and enforcing martial law. He declined to implement such a drastic measure:

[23] Lieutenant General George Erskine, 'The Mau Mau Rebellion', lecture given by General Erskine to 1955 course, Army Staff College, Camberley, 1.

[24] Caroline Elkins, *Britain's Gulag: the brutal end to empire* (London: Jonathan Cape, 2005).

[25] Bennett, *Fighting the Mau Mau*, 190.

> Fortunately I found that the Government of Kenya were
> determined to use the very considerable powers at their disposal.
> They could and did pass Emergency regulations of severity and
> entirely appropriate to the military requirements. There was
> never any question of the Government of Kenya breaking down
> although it clearly needed it needed active military support in a
> number of areas.[26]

However, Erskine did revise the command structure considerably. Up to this point, the military, civil and police efforts had not been sufficiently integrated, with the Director of Military Operations assuming too much responsibility for the overall campaign. Consequently, Erskine established a War Cabinet, consisting of himself as Commander-in-Chief, Evelyn Baring as the Governor, Frederick Crawford as the Deputy Governor and Michael Blundell as the settler representative (the Minister without Portfolio). In February 1954, he established a special command structure for Operation Anvil, appointing a dedicated Joint Operations Committee. This Committee consisted of the 'Joint Commanders of Operation Anvil':[27] Mr R. Turnball, the Deputy Governor, as the civilian authority, Brigadier G. Taylor, commander of 49 Independent Infantry Brigade, and M.S. O'Rorke, Commissioner of Police. This committee was given responsibility for Nairobi, Kiambu and Thika and reported directly to the War Cabinet; their functions were replicated at the higher level by Baring (civil), Erskine (military) and the Blundell (police). At the same time, a small Anvil staff was also appointed to administer the respective civil, military and police efforts.

The Joint Commanders were instructed to produce an outline plan by 23 February.[28] The operation was directed by the Anvil Area Joint Commanders together – a point about which Erskine was insistent. However, especially in the decisive first phase of the operation, Brigadier Taylor and his 49 Independent Infantry Brigade headquarters played a vital role in writing the military plan, ordering the construction of detention camps, the cordoning of key areas in Nairobi and screening the population. This headquarters commanded 20,000 troops, supported by the police and Home Guard: five British

[26] Erskine, 'The Mau Mau Rebellion', 3–4.
[27] Emergency Directive No. 12 Operation Anvil, WO 276/189, TNA.
[28] Anvil Area Operation Instruction No. 2, 8 April, WO 276/188, TNA.

Army battalions (1 Buffs, 1 Royal Northumberland Fusiliers, 1 Royal Inniskilling, 1 Black Watch, 6 Kenyan African Rifles), one Kenyan regiment, eleven European, six Asian and four African Police Platoons (about 300 personnel) and a local Home Guard of 1500 European and 1000 Asians;[29] 49 Brigade deployed these forces to surround the suburbs so that by 4:30am on 24 April every road was sealed. By 06:00, Eastlands, where the Kikuyu population was concentrated, was cleared by police, Kenyan Police Reserve and British Army units. The sweep apprehended all illegal inhabitants in the city. In the first forty-eight hours of the operation, 11,600 Kikuyu were screened, with the help of hooded 'gikunia' informants; 8300 were identified as 'black' (committed Mau Mau) or 'grey' (suspected Mau Mau) and detained, of whom 206 were deemed to be active terrorists. Eventually, by the end of Anvil on 26 May 1954, 50,000 Kikuyu had been screened, 24,100 of whom, including 2150 women and 4000 children, were detained.[30] They were processed through a detention camp system. As Elkins has made clear, the scale of the repression was shocking. Although the subsequent villagization programme played an important role, Operation Anvil is widely taken to be the turning point of the Mau Mau campaign from which the insurgency never recovered.

Anvil was a large-scale and decisive operation which processed thousands of Kikuyu in a matter of weeks. Yet, in command terms it demonstrates some striking features. Above all, although the operation involved six infantry battalions and a 20,000-strong security force in total, the military element of Anvil was commanded and controlled by no more than the 'considerably augmented'[31] 49 Independent Infantry Brigade. It is perhaps surprising that such a small headquarters could command a major urban clearance. Certainly, in the twenty-first century, as Chapter 8 will show, the armed forces have required far larger headquarters for equivalent operations. However, although Erskine stressed throughout that Operation Anvil was a 'joint' operation, the jurisdiction of Taylor's Brigade Headquarters was very limited. It remained a purely military command. It did not have to integrate civilian and police actions into its plan or, indeed, the operation. Taylor wrote a purely military plan, which was then coordinated with civil and

[29] Ibid.; Anderson, *Histories of the Hanged*, 201.
[30] Ibid., 202–5.
[31] Operation Instruction 17, WO 276/189.

police authorities. Somewhat ironically, the creation of a Joint Anvil Committee allowed the three agencies – civil, military and police – to collaborate effectively precisely insofar as they remained quite independent of each other; 49 Independent Infantry Brigade's units were not engaged in civil or quasi-police work (which would become typical of the military in the twenty-first century) and they did not assume civil powers, even unofficially. On the contrary, they remained a resolutely military organization, albeit closely linked to civilian authority and the police. The clearance of Nairobi was commanded from a brigade head-quarters, with an augmented but still very small staff.

There was a second feature to the command architecture which Erskine established. He personally supervised 49 Brigade very closely throughout. For instance, on 6 March 1954, Erskine and Baring confirmed their approval of the outline plan for Anvil, which they had received from 49 Brigade and the Joint Anvil Commanders. However, they simultaneously provided a very detailed commentary, para-graph by paragraph, which identified fifteen necessary amendments to the plan. Erskine played the prime role here, overseeing the mili-tary element of the campaign with the greatest diligence. When there was a suggestion that the military element, 49 Brigade, should take the overall lead, Erskine objected: 'CINC says it does not set out his understanding which was Joint Command, Civil, Police and Military, with Brigadier Taylor in charge during the mop-up. He would arrange for the matter to be clarified in GHQ'.[32] It is worth clarifying what Erskine meant here. The 'mop-up' referred to the initial screening and detention operation. Erskine was affirming that 49 Brigade was respon-sible for the security element of Anvil. However, it was incumbent upon Brigadier Taylor to coordinate closely with his civil and police part-ners on this and subsequent elements of the operation. Erskine's micro-scopic examination of Taylor's plan shows that the military chain of command for Anvil ran directly from Erskine down to Taylor at 49 Brigade Headquarters. Consequently, a major divisional operation – the decisive act in this campaign – was commanded from a brigade headquarters, closely overseen by a Commander-in-Chief.

The command arrangements on Anvil were, of course, unique. However, it does not seem excessive to highlight a parallel with con-ventional warfare. It was noted in the previous chapter that despite the

---

[32] Letter to Brigadier Taylor from GSO1 DD Ops, 26 February, FCO 141/5696, TNA.

burdens of divisional manoeuvre, headquarters remained very small because their functions were limited and simple. Consequently, while the staff played a crucial role in administering the mission, the commander was, nevertheless, able to monopolize decision-making with little assistance. A similar pattern seems to be observable in Kenya during Anvil; 49 Brigade headquarters coordinated the operation, with the closest oversight from Erskine. He defined the mission, 49 Brigade refined the plan and then managed its execution. However, Erskine always monitored progress carefully, intervening periodically when it was necessary to make the critical decisions. Clearly, it is necessary to assess whether such a sparse command arrangement, in which one commander played such an important role, was an unusually British arrangement. The Battle of Algiers may provide an answer to that question.

Algiers

The Algerian War began on All Saints Day, 1 November 1954, when fighters from the National Liberation Front (FLN) launched a series of attacks across Algeria. The violence escalated in the following months, climaxing in August 1955 in the Philippeville massacre, when the FLN murdered 123 civilians, including women and children, seventy-one of whom were Europeans. The massacre provoked an intense reaction from both the security forces and the 'Pied Noir' community, which conducted a pogrom against the Muslim Algerians thought to be FLN sympathizers; 12,000 are estimated to have died. Exploiting the deployment of troops to Suez in October and November 1956, the FLN also began to increase operations in Algiers, taking control of the Casbah and mounting a bombing campaign which included notorious explosions at the beach and the Milk Bar. By the end of 1956, the FLN were preparing a four-day general strike in Algiers, starting on 28 January 1957, as a mass, popular revolt against colonial rule. As in Kenya in 1953, the French authorities faced an emergency in 1957. At this point, they decided to act. The 10th Parachute Division was ordered to Algiers under the command of Brigadier-General Jacques Massu. The following section will examine how Massu defined his division's mission and then managed it until October 1957.

The Battle of Algiers began with the January strike and concluded with the death of Ali la Pointe on the 8 October 1957. It consisted of two clear phases. Between January and March 1957, 10th Parachute Division broke apart terrorist commander Yacef Saadi's bomb network and captured the FLN leader Ben M'Hidi through the systematic use of detention, torture and assassination. Most of the units from the division were then withdrawn from the city, providing Yacef with an opportunity to renew the offensive with bombs, most notably in the casino Corniche on 9 June, which killed nine and wounded 85. At this point, 10th Division units, notably Bigeard's *3 Regiment Parachutiste Coloniale*, were recalled to the city to defeat the FLN finally. From June to October, 10th Division destroyed the remaining FLN infrastructure in Algiers, killing or capturing all the major leaders and operatives, including Yacef Saadi, Ali Boumendjel, Djamila Bouhired, Ramel, Mourad and, finally, Ali la Pointe.

When he was appointed on 7 January 1957, General Salan gave Massu three objectives: the hunting and annihilation of militant rebel groups, the destruction of the political structure of adversaries and beneficial action on the population.[33] Massu was effectively also given the authority to introduce martial law; he had the power to control circulation and goods, detain anyone whose activities might be dangerous, regulate public meetings and authorize searches of homes by night and day. As he defined his division's mission, Massu was not totally insensitive politically. Like Erskine, a central principle of his mission was that both Arab and European populations were to be protected. He wanted to avoid an all-out civil war, which was a genuine threat. The Pied Noir population was engaging in recurrent pogroms against the Arab population, typically in response to an attack, and had their own counter-terrorist groups. Indeed, it became apparent as 10th Division deployed that some of these groups had planned a mass attack on the Casbah; they were preparing to release the petrol from some fuel tankers from the top of the Casbah in order to start a massive conflagration which might have killed 70,000 occupants.[34] However, while comparable in intent, Massu adopted far more draconian methods than Erskine.

As Martin Thomas has demonstrated, France adopted a quite different policy to its imperial possessions than Britain in the

---

[33] Jacques Massu, *La Vraie Bataille d'Alger* (Evreux: Librairie Plon, 1971), 33.
[34] Paul Aussaresses, *The Battle of the Casbah: counter-terrorism and torture 1955–57* (New York: Enigma Books, 2010), 73.

postwar period.[35] Algeria was not just a French colony but, as a department of metropolitan France, regarded as an integral part of Republic. Its strategic importance was compounded by the series of crushing defeats and embarrassments which France had suffered in 1940, in 1954 in Indochina and in 1956 at Suez. Massu and his officers were intensely conscious that further defeat was unacceptable. As he deployed to Algeria, Colonel Marcel Bigeard, for instance, noted that he wanted 'to save the honour lost at Dien Bien Phu'.[36] Even more so than Erskine, Jacques Massu concluded that he had to suppress the FLN in Algiers urgently, using maximum military force. Indeed, the defeat of the FLN in the city was achieved in a remarkably short time; the Battle of Algiers lasted only ten months. The repercussions of 10th Parachute Division's campaign reverberate today but, in a tactical military sense, they had achieved their mission with the explosion which killed Ali la Pointe on 8 October 1957.

Massu deployed 4600 paratroopers into the city to fulfil these tasks. In the first instance, the paratroopers broke the strike simply by physically apprehending important public workers in their homes and forcing them to work, and pulling off the shutters on shops to 'open' them for business. In addition, he imposed a curfew and ordered his paratroopers to arrest suspects (normally at night) for interrogation. In a ten-month campaign in the city, 10th Division arrested some over 20,000 Algerians, many of whom were subjected to torture and 3000 of whom subsequently disappeared. At the same time, 10th Division introduced an old Napoleonic system of numbering all the houses in the Casbah and assigning an identified 'responsable' to each house or block. This individual would be responsible for recording the inhabitants and notifying 10th Division of any movement. In this way, the division was able to identify suspect individuals. The methods, then, which Massu personally sanctioned, were brutal.

Erskine supervised Anvil very closely through 49 Brigade. Massu similarly controlled 10th Parachute Division's operations during the Battle of Algiers: 'The experience of Algiers proved to me only that the counter-terrorist conflict is before all else an organizational matter,

---

[35] Thomas, *Fight or Flight*.
[36] Marcel Bigeard, *Ma Guerre d'Algerie* (Baume-Les-Dames: Éditions du Rocher 2010), 11.

of will and responsibility, and therefore a matter of command'.[37] He emphasized his personal authority over the 10th Division mission: 'I had to maintain constant control on the most diverse activities relating to the life of a large city, without neglecting any essential aspect of the mission'.[38] Of course, Massu did not manage the entire operation on his own. His subordinate regimental commanders, his 'colonels', played an important role in supporting Massu throughout the operation. Indeed, 10th Division was unusual even in the 1950s in the exceptionally close bonds between Massu and his subordinates, many of whom had fought together in the Free French Forces or in Indochina as paratroopers.[39]

At the same time, Massu was supported by his headquarters, located at Chateau Pelzer, or 'Hydra'. The structure of this headquarters was extremely interesting. In his memoirs, Massu identified Colonel De Roquiny, his assistant, Lieutenant Colonel Godard, his chief of staff, and Lieutenant Gerard Garcet as his principal aides.[40]

In fact, although unmentioned by Massu, Major Paul Aussaresses and Lieutenant-Colonel Trinquier played the critical role in Algiers.[41] Massu personally selected both officers and was very close to Roger Trinquier, with whom had had been commissioned; 'Trinquier was Massu's comrade-in-arms and his closest confidante'.[42] The relations between Massu and Aussaresses were more distant. They had not served with each other before Algiers.[43] However, Massu had seen the results of Aussaresses's work when the latter was serving in 1955 as 1 *Regiment Colonial Parachutiste*'s intelligence officer. Massu had personally requested Aussaresses to work for Trinquier's counter-subversion campaign. Instructively, Aussaresses's office at Hydra was immediately next door to Massu's.

In effect, then, the Headquarters of 10th Parachute Division consisted of an official part and an actual part, the official acting as a front for the latter. All of the most important operations were commanded from Trinquier's cell, under the daily direction of Massu.

---

[37] Massu, *La Vraie Bataille d'Alger*, 149.
[38] Ibid., 95.
[39] Bigeard, *Ma Guerre d'Algerie*, 11.
[40] Massu, *La Vraie Bataille d'Alger*, 112.
[41] Ibid., 113.
[42] Aussaresses, *The Battle of the Casbah*, 67.
[43] Ibid., 71.

While Trinquier developed the plan and oversaw the strategy, including the system of 'responsables', Aussaresses executed operations. For instance, although the regiments conducted many interrogations, Aussaresses directed the divisional interrogation programme at Villa Tourelles; he was implicated in many of the 3000 deaths of detained suspects, passed on by the regiments. He claimed personal responsibility for the murders of Ben M'Hidi and Boumendjel, of which he kept Massu closely informed.

Meanwhile, Trinquier also created a network of 'pseudo-workers', the notorious 'bleus de chauffe' in reference to their blue overalls, who worked in important services and provided critical intelligence on the FLN. Run by Captain Paul-Alain Leger, they planted incriminating forged documents and spread false rumours about FLN operatives, precipitating fratricide between suspicious Algerian activists.[44] At the same time, Aussaresses ran two other counter-terrorist networks. The first consisted of two groups of specially selected NCOs who acted as night squads, apprehending suspects and bringing them back to Villa Tourelles for interrogation. Aussaresses ensured that neither group knew about the other so that their activities could always be covered up. Aussaresses also ran a network of agents who by the summer of 1957 had so thoroughly infiltrated the FLN command structure that Yacef Saadi was himself being handled by a French agent.[45] The primacy of Trinquier and Aussaresses to Massu's management of the operation can be seen by the fact that whenever there was a serious setback, Massu blamed Trinquier and Aussaresses; indeed, he was furious with them following the Corniche bombings on 9 June.[46] In his view, as his principal intelligence and counter-terrorist officers, they – not the rest of the headquarters – were responsible for interdicting FLN attacks and for ensuring that his orders were enacted.

Massu commanded the Battle of Algiers through two principal assistants, then: Trinquier and Aussaresses, who together operated a clandestine counter-terrorist cell. Massu presumably omitted to mention Aussaresses crucial role in the campaign in his memoirs because to do

---

[44] Martin Alexander and J.F.V. Keiger, 'France and the Algerian War: strategy, operations and diplomacy', in Martin Alexander and J.F.V. Keiger (eds), *France and the Algerian War 1954–62: strategy, operations and diplomacy* (London: Frank Cass, 2002), 6–7.

[45] Paul Alain Leger, 'Personal Account of Chef de Batallion', in M. Alexander, M. Evans and J. Keiger (eds), *Algerian War and the French Army, 1954–62*, 241.

[46] Aussaresses, *The Battle of the Casbah*, 147.

so would invalidate his sanitized version of the campaign. By contrast, Godard and the official headquarters played a subordinate, even marginal, role. As Aussaresses noted: 'Apart from a few people in Massu's entourage and a handful of officers in 10th DP [Parachute Division], no else knew that I was the main organizer of counter-terrorism ... Even in the headquarters of 10th DP many officers did not understand what was going on. Godard's attitude had kept them apart from the hard core of repressive units and they resented that isolation'.[47] Although Aussaresses probably exaggerated the redundancy of the official headquarters and Godard himself, whom Aussaresses personally detested, there is little doubt of the central role of the cell which Trinquier and he administered to the Battle of Algiers. It was the nerve centre of Massu's command. Like Erskine, Massu defined the mission himself, essentially following Salan's orders, and then managed it through a very small – indeed, tiny – staff.

The Delta

In both Kenya and Algeria, Erskine and Massu defined a simple, even savage, military mission and then dominated decision-making, supervising operations through a diminutive headquarters. A similar pattern was observable in the Mekong Delta. US conventional forces had deployed to Vietnam in March 1965 in response to the increasing threat posed by the Viet Cong. However, despite extensive fighting, the Viet Cong launched the Tet Offensive in February 1968. Ewell was deployed with his 9th Division into the Delta in February 1968 in immediate response to Tet. Even after Tet, the situation was bad in the Delta, with Viet Cong dominating much of the rural population; Ewell estimated that only one-third was under government control at the beginning of his tour.[48] Close to Saigon, the Mekong Delta was strategically vital. Like Erskine and Massu, Ewell confronted a crisis.

Ewell's preparation for his tour of the Delta was instructively cursory. General Weyand, the Field Force II Commander of III Corps, instructed him: 'You get down there [to the Delta] and take as much of

---

[47] Ibid., 94.
[48] Ewell and Hunt, *Sharpening the Combat Edge*, 9.

the Division as you can and get those VC out of there'.[49] Moreover, not only was Ewell unfamiliar with the Mekong Delta, but he admitted his ignorance of Vietnam itself: 'I didn't know Vietnam from Singapore'.[50] Nevertheless, Ewell identified a clear mission very quickly. The mission of the 9th Division in the Delta was to attack Viet Cong units continuously, loosening their grip on the population and allowing the Government of the Republic to re-assert control.

In order to accomplish this mission, Ewell developed a concept of operations which he called 'the constant pressure concept'. Between 1965 and 1968, the American campaign in Vietnam had involved a series of major search and destroy operations, in which designated areas of presumed enemy concentration had been assaulted and cleared. Between these operations, US forces remained operationally on the defensive, responding only when the Viet Cong attacked. There was an obvious weakness to this approach, which Ewell noted. Although major operations had some attritional effect on the Viet Cong, their intermittence allowed insurgents safe-havens from which they could prepare major assaults, or, as Ewell called them, 'high points':

> In 1968, the problem became one of bringing evading enemy units to battle during quiet periods and limiting their damage during high points so that they could not interfere with the pacification program, which was just going into a high gear. This was particularly true at divisional level.[51]

Major operations were themselves not optimal since they typically attacked the Viet Cong on ground of their own choosing and, indeed, most of these actions were initiated by the Viet Cong as they ambushed the lead American elements. Casualties were, therefore, unnecessarily high.

9th Infantry Division adopted a different approach. Instead of infrequent large 'search-and-destroy' operations, which typified the American approach pre-Tet, the division engaged in incessant small

---

[49] Senior Officers Debriefing Programme: Conversation between Lieutenant General Julian Ewell and Mr Robert Connelly and Lieutenant Colonel Norman Bissell, Army Heritage and Education Centre, 57.
[50] Ibid.
[51] Ewell and Hunt, *Sharpening the Combat Edge*, 9.

platoon-, company- and battalion-scale missions designed to force the Viet Cong main force to fight. The Division was engaged in offensive operations all the time, constantly seeking to bring the VC to battle in decisive areas of the Delta: 'Communist doctrine was to control the people through force. Unless you can get that force out of there nothing else can happen. Oh, for three or four months things might look like Sunday at the beach, but if you didn't really clobber the Communists they'd regenerate and come back and pull the rug out from under you'.[52] In 9th Division, the constant-pressure concept prioritized the 'kill ratio', the number of Viet Cong killed for every US soldier, as the decisive indicator of success. For Ewell, the kill ratio became the focus of the divisional effort, taken as the best signifier of whether constant pressure was being applied properly. His efforts as commander were concentrated on increasing the kill ratio.

He seems to have been very effective. As General Creighton Abrams, the commander of the Military Assistance Command Vietnam from 1968 to 1972, observed: 'The performance of this division has been magnificent and I would say in the last three months, it's an unparalleled and unequaled performance'. Although critical of Ewell in his memoirs, David Hackworth, who commanded 4th Battalion 39th Infantry in 1969, recorded a rapid transformation in the ratio of enemy to friendly casualties as a result of the implementation of Ewell's concept. When Hackworth assumed command of the battalion in January 1969, it had suffered twenty-four killed and 485 wounded while inflicting no casualties on the Viet Cong: 'no wonder morale was lower than whale-shit'.[53] During the months he commanded the battalion, 'our body-count figures were more than twenty-five hundred VC KIA [Viet Cong killed in action] in exchange for twenty-five battalion lives. 100:1'.[54] This was unusually high. Between January and June 1969, the division recorded a kill ratio of 43.8:1, reaching a high of 84.9 in April 1969.[55] With the constant pressure concept, Ewell defined a clear military mission for his headquarters.

[52] Senior Officers Debriefing Programme: Conversation between Lieutenant General Julian Ewell and Mr Robert Connelly and Lieutenant Colonel Norman Bissell, Army Heritage and Education Centre, 82.
[53] David Hackworth and Julie Sherman, *About Face* (London: Pan Books, 1989), 649.
[54] Ibid., 703.
[55] Hunt and Ewell *Sharpening the Combat Edge*, 135; Nick Turse *Kill Anything that Moves: the real American war in Vietnam* (New York: Henry Holt and Coy, 2013), 209.

In order to determine which was the most efficient in terms of kill ratios, 9th Division analyzed alternate tactical methods. Here, Ewell fully acknowledged his own debt to other commanders in Vietnam, above all Brigadier Hank Emerson. Emerson had commanded a brigade from the 101st Airborne Division in the highlands in 1967 and had introduced a number of tactical innovations such as 'jitterbugging' precisely because he rejected the efficacy of large unit sweeps. Jitterbugging involved the insertion of a battalion by helicopter into a designated area in which Viet Cong had been detected. The aim was to insert the force as close to the Viet Cong as possible and to fix them in a firefight while other elements sealed off their escape routes. At this point, firepower was concentrated on the enemy to inflict maximum casualties, with minimum American losses. No attempt was made to clear the enemy in a conventional way, as infamously occurred on Hamburger Hill in A Shau Valley. Emerson recognized that terrain itself was irrelevant. Ewell was impressed by the concept and he described Hank Emerson as 'the greatest brigade commander in Vietnam'.[56]

Emerson's jitterbugging technique proved very effective but, in fact, 9th Infantry Division implemented a number of its own tactical innovations as a result of its systems analysis, including bushmaster, checkerboard and night hunter operations each involving smaller units than jitterbugging. Checkerboard and bushmaster operations generated 0.27 and 0.22 contacts per operation, in contrast to jitterbugging's 1.80. However, 'although the company-sized operation produced more contacts per operation on a percentage basis than did platoon-sized ambushes, for the number of troops involved the platoon ambushes were 60 per cent more effective than the company-size Bushmasters and Checkerboards'.[57] In each case, operations were tested by means of systems analysis. Those techniques which produced the highest kill ratios were supported and expanded. The methods which Ewell employed to increase efficiency echo some of Monash's techniques in the First World War. Like Monash, Ewell managed military operations as an engineering problem, pursuing quantifiable improvements in performance by isolating certain critical metrics – above all, the kill ratio.

[56] Senior Officers Debriefing Programme: Conversation between Lieutenant General Julian Ewell and Mr Robert Connelly and Lieutenant Colonel Norman Bissell, 90.
[57] Ewell and Hunt, *Sharpening the Combat Edge*, 128.

The constant pressure concept was aggressive and there seems little doubt that it resulted in high numbers of civilian casualties. For instance, between, June 1968 and June 1969, the division killed 22,047 Viet Cong but recovered only 2000 weapons. The latter fact has been widely taken to provide categorical evidence that the division was wholly negligent about collateral damage. On Operation Speedy Express between December 1968 and April 1969, 7000 civilians were officially recorded as killed, while 13,000 civilians were wounded in the first six months of 1969. Ewell claimed that the division stressed 'discriminate and selective use of firepower'. Yet, there were claims that anyone who ran from a helicopter during an operation was assumed to be Viet Cong; since 9th Division used CS gas canisters to flush suspected Viet Cong from their positions, it was likely that in many cases civilians also fled – to be presumed insurgents.[58] Elsewhere, Ewell was recorded as wanting '4000 of these little bastards [VC]' a month and remonstrating with his subordinates: 'What the fuck are you people doing down here sitting on your asses? The rest of the brigade are coming up with a fine body count?'[59] The performance of the division earned Ewell the soubriquet of the 'Butcher of the Delta'.

The constant pressure concept identified a robust objective and some refined methods of achieving it. The concept also required some distinctive management techniques, which had close parallels with those of Erskine and Massu. Ewell claimed, not without evidence, that Vietnam was an immensely complicated theatre and that 9th Division operations were highly sophisticated, with the heavy use of aviation, airpower and the latest tracking technology. The sparseness of Ewell's command system is, therefore, particularly striking. In order to administer actual operations, to carry out systems analysis and to run a G-5 civil affairs branch, 9th Division Headquarters and the Divisional Administration Company consisted of 300 personnel, though Ewell's staff was smaller. Moreover, Ewell commanded mainly through a tight executive, with Ira Hunt, who held 'Rasputin-like power' over him,[60] as his crucial aide. It is even more telling that despite the apparent complexity of the Mekong Delta, Ewell was never exercised by the problem

---

[58] Turse, *Kill Anything that Moves*, 211.
[59] Ibid., 206.
[60] David Hackworth, *Steel my Soldiers' Hearts* (London: Simon and Schuster, 2003), 349.

of decision-making. On the contrary, he found the management of the mission relatively straightforward.

The next chapter will examine counter-insurgency campaigns in Iraq and Afghanistan, focusing in particular on the experiences of ISAF's Regional Command South in Kandahar in 2009–10. The complexity of this operation challenged the headquarters; the decision-making capacity of the divisional command was almost overwhelmed. By contrast, the example of 9th Division in the Delta reveals a rather different phenomenon. Here, there was, in fact, an excess command capacity. The tactics which 9th Division employed – jitterbug, bush-master etc. – were complex and required considerable coordination of troops, helicopters, air power and artillery. However, these operations were small-scale; they never involved more than a battalion and often involved less. In addition, because the constant pressure concept demanded repetitive tactical actions, the coordination of the assets became a staff routine which required little genuine decision-making at the divisional level. Their management became almost automated. Ewell, as he intended, created a formation which operated like an efficient machine, standardizing military operations. Accordingly, once Ewell had set his priorities and instituted means of monitoring performance, the executive function diminished into supervision. On any specific operation, Ewell had very few decisions to make.

As a result, in 9th Division, as elsewhere in Vietnam, a peculiar phenomenon emerged in which battalion commanders on the ground were monitored by their brigade commanders or chief of staff in a helicopter above, while Ewell also oversaw the action in his own helicopter. Ewell claimed that his close supervision served a useful function. It prevented the execution of prisoners, which Ewell had personally witnessed in the Second World War: 'I didn't tell anybody that, but that was my objective – so they wouldn't shoot prisoners.[61] Perhaps Ewell did save some prisoners. However, the problem in Vietnam was that because, after Tet, the level of the fight was as low as the company and platoon level, little decision-making was required at the divisional level: 'In Vietnam you had a sort of assembly line war; it was repetitive operation, day after day, and you could fine-tune the operation.

---

[61] Senior Officers Debriefing Programme: Conversations between Lieutenant General Julian Ewell and Mr Robert Connelly and Lieutenant Colonel Norman Bissell, Carlisle Barracks PA 17013, Army Heritage and Education Centre, 97–8.

Anybody could do it. I mean all you had to do was to keep fine-tuning it'.[62] Consequently, Ewell himself admitted:

> Of course, in a big war, like World War II, you don't get this because as a regimental commander you had plenty to do. You didn't have time to fool with running the battalions. You had a full plate. The battalion commander and everybody had a full job so you didn't get this pressing down. The difficulty in Vietnam was that at division and perhaps brigade, the commanders did not have anything tangible to get their teeth into and there was the temptation to go down and interfere.[63]

Ewell tried to avoid interfering but, in the Mekong Delta, management was radically simplified. The daily orchestration of operations was almost automatic. The constant decision-making, which was such an integral and constant part of the divisional commander's function in manoeuvre warfare, became unnecessary. The level of the fight was too low to require genuine formation-level decision-making.

The relative ease of mission management in the Delta is surprising. As Ewell repeatedly emphasized, Vietnam was a hugely challenging campaign, involving political, civil, psychological and informational elements in a heavily populated and complex area. Operational reports and orders included paragraphs on both activities and provided instructions about how they had to be coordinated into purely military activities. However, although in an area of intense political activity by the Communist Party, Ewell himself engaged in no significant interactions with political leaders. His mission was military and psychological and civil actions were subordinated to that conventional mission. Political and civil concerns about pacification only began to become relevant to the Field Force commanders operating at corps level. Below that, US forces, like the 9th Division, were involved in military operations against irregular forces rather than genuine pacification. Ewell was essentially fighting a small war in the Delta and, consequently, his decision-making process accorded much more closely with those of conventional commanders. Having defined the mission, he supervised its management closely with the assistance especially of one principal staff officer, Ira Hunt.

---

[62] Ibid., 96.
[63] Ibid., 94.

Counter-Insurgent Command

The cases of Erskine, Massu and Ewell may not be definitive, but they are surely instructive. They represent three different campaigns conducted by three Western militaries in quite different theatres over two decades. Yet, despite the evident differences between them, the command practices of these three generals bear close similarity with one another. The counter-insurgency operations to which Western forces were committed in the 1950s and 1960s were potentially more complex than conventional warfighting. Erskine, Massu and Ewell had large, densely populated areas of operation and often had to coordinate with local security forces and civil and political agencies. Yet, in each case, these commanders operated executed highly militaristic campaigns with the assistance of a very sparse staff. They commanded through one or two aides and a small headquarters.

The evidence of similarities between the command practices of Erskine, Massu and Ewell is perhaps not altogether surprising when the biographies of these three commanders are considered. All three were experienced and decorated combat veterans who had long experience of high-intensity warfare in the Second World War. Erskine had commanded 7th Armoured Division in the desert and, until his removal in late July 1944, in Normandy. Massu had fought with Leclerc in North Africa and then commanded *2eme Regiment du Marche de Tchad*, in Leclerc's *2eme Division Blindée*, participating in the Normandy campaign and the liberations of Paris and Strasbourg. Indeed in his memoirs about Algiers, Massu described himself in telling terms: 'What was I in sum? Easy with human contact, keen to be friendly, but a soldier always ready to fight, if I could not avoid it'.[64] He was not known for his intellect. Julian Ewell commanded 3rd Battalion, 501st Parachute Infantry Regiment, 101st Airborne Division, in Normandy and Holland, eventually assuming command of the 501st's Regiment during the Battle of the Bulge. He commanded a regiment in Korea. It seems likely that their experiences of high-intensity conventional operations, conducted only a decade before, were influential in how they commanded in Kenya, Algeria and Vietnam. With formative command experiences in the Second World War, it was perhaps predictable that they seem to

---

[64] Massu, *La Vraie Bataille d'Alger*, 84.

have commanded low-intensity conflicts, like conventional divisional commanders.

Yet, of course, the commensurability between Erskine, Massu and Ewell and the conventional commanders discussed in Chapter 5 went well beyond personal experience. Organizational and operational imperatives were at work which recommended the instrumentalist and individualist method of command which all three adopted. Erskine, Massu and Ewell monopolized decision-making because they were able to define their mission in military terms and to apply military force to more or less to its fullest extent. Thompson and Gallula were presumably correct when they argued that counter-insurgency campaigns were primarily political struggles. Yet, at the divisional level, Erskine, Massu and Ewell conducted conventional military operations against insurgents in a civilian population. They simply employed their divisions in small-force packages to match the level of the fight. Yet, in these small-unit engagements, each commander sought to exert maximum force to eliminate the insurgents they faced. In each case, each of these generals employed military force with a robustness which would become quite impossible in the twenty-first century precisely because strategic, informational and legal constraints would come to impress profoundly upon commanders. Unencumbered by legal or political concerns which would later become the norm, Erskine, Massu and Ewell were able employ the full force of their divisions.

As a result, while the operations were plainly distinctive, the command challenge on counter-insurgency operations was not inherently different from those of conventional warfare at this time. Mission definition and mission management remained unidimensional problems; they involved the application of force against insurgents in a still relatively simple environment. Civilian casualties, collateral damage and abuses were close to immaterial. Consequently, with no imperative for precision and proportionality, these three commanders were able to define a simple mission very quickly and to execute it aggressively with the support of a very small staff. The Anvil Joint Command and Hydra were miniscule headquarters and even Ewell's 9th Division was not a particular large enterprise, especially since only a small part of it was dedicated to current operations. Each of these commanders supervised military operations very closely, even directly. Like their conventional peers, they were able to monopolize decision-making.

Command Individualism

The last four chapters have analyzed divisional command in the twentieth century. They have explored how the three critical functions of command – mission definition, mission management and leadership – have been exercised by Western generals on both warfighting and counter-insurgency operations. The case for command individualism has been made as persuasively but also as carefully as possible. In particular, an attempt has been made to take a wide and diverse enough sample to ensure a degree of representativeness. Although the discussions mentioned commanders like Kneussl, Balck, Leclerc and McAffery, the analysis was primarily based on the evidence of twelve divisional commanders – Rommel, Montgomery, Monash, Smith, Ridgway, Gavin, Wimberley, Bullen-Smith, Mackelvie, Erskine, Massu and Ewell. The preceding chapters have examined both warfighting operations and counter-insurgency campaigns from across the era in order to ensure that no false conclusions were drawn about command regimes on the basis of extrapolating from one kind of campaign. The evidence would seem to be suggestive. However, it is fully recognized that operating on an inductive method, the social sciences can only ever forward interpretations which are probable – never apodictically certain. There are always potential counter-examples which might demand a qualification or even the refutation of the theory. However, the cases analyzed demonstrate that, for these commanders at least, a distinctive practice of command existed in the twentieth century which might be termed individualist. Moreover, because of the diversity of the cases in terms of the types of division, the different theatres and the coverage of both warfighting and counter-insurgency operations, it is suggested that it is plausible to claim that a command regime – a recognizable and stable practice of generalship – is observable throughout the twentieth century from 1914 to 1991; the sample, after all, includes two armoured divisions, four infantry divisions,[65] two parachute divisions and an air assault division. In short, it is claimed here that the

---

[65] 7th Panzer Division (1940), 1 Armoured Division (1991), 3rd Division (1940), 51st Highland Division (1942–4), the Operation Anvil division (1954), 82nd Airborne (1944), 10th Parachute Division (1957) and 9th Infantry Division (1968–9). This figure becomes five infantry divisions if the command of 51st Highland Division by Bullen-Smith and Wimberley is counted separately.

cases surveyed in this sample indicate that a paradigm of individualist command existed as the preferred institutional method from the First World War to the Gulf.

Despite evident operational and national differences, then, the material discussed in these chapters points to a close convergence across the major military powers. The central explanation for this convergence seems to be not personal but organizational. The geometry of counter-insurgency and manoeuvre operations was certainly very different. Yet, while the range of operations increased on counter-insurgency operations, the level of the fight also diminished radically. Instead of peer combined arms divisions, of more or less equal combat power, the counter-insurgent commander normally faced small bands of lightly armed guerrillas. Increased complexity was mitigated by a the low enemy threat and the slow operational tempo. In both cases, the aim was to apply the combat power of the division to maximum effect.

Because of the character of military operations at this time and the structure of the division as an organization, command problems were relatively simple, then. Mass, not precision, was the priority. Charged with an instrument of industrial and homogeneous military power over a geographically limited area, individual divisional commanders were able to define their division's mission very quickly. Moreover, because the number of subordinate units was limited and their orchestration lineal, commanders also tended to be able monopolize the management of missions. Certainly, commanders required a small staff to assist them with administration; the staff collated information and intelligence, and prepared and disseminated orders. It is true that Montgomery created something like a command team in 3rd Division in France in May 1940, when subordinates were trained to enact set drills on order. In the Gulf War of 1991, Rupert Smith went even further, actively seeking to devolve decision-making in the early stages of the campaign. In the cases of highly professional commanders like Montgomery and Smith, it might be argued that they adopted practices which anticipated the twenty-first century. Through intense training and instruction, they sought to integrate their subordinates into a cohesive executive group, capable of enacting their superior's intent independently. However, even in these cases, commanders were normally able to make the major tactical decisions and, significantly, monitored their execution personally. Monash and Smith supervised by means of radio, phone and other forms of signalling; Rommel and

Montgomery physically oversaw their subordinates. Of course, the propinquity of units facilitated this close personal direction. In order to accelerate decision-making, executive authority was exercised personally by the commander, who typically required support only from a principal staff officer or deputy and a small staff.

Even on counter-insurgency operations, divisional commanders adopted very similar techniques. Because of the political context, they were able to apply force with little constraint. Operating in a politically permissive environment, they similarly coordinated operations with the support of a small – sometimes tiny – staff. At the same time, this chapter has shown that generals were also expected to lead their troops and to be physically present at the front. In all three functions, Western armies displayed a distinctive regime of command. Of course, command at this time was a collaborative enterprise; every commander needed aides, advisers, staff and, of course, willing and capable subordinates.

However, although the term is relative, the evidence affirms that a distinctive regime of command persisted throughout the short twentieth century. This regime was certainly professional in its own right. It would be difficult to dispute that commanders like Monash, Rommel, Montgomery and Smith were anything other than consummate professionals. They were highly competent experts in military practice, who used standardized bureaucratic procedures to their fullest effect. Yet, the professionalism they displayed differed from that which has subsequently emerged in the early twenty-first century. While these commander's professionalism lay in their monopolization of the decision-making process, their successor's expertise has resided in their ability apportion, systematize and align decision-making within a closely integrated collective. The continuities are obvious. There is no definitive rupture between the two eras but, at the same time, an alternate paradigm is now apparent. The rest of the book will define the precise nature of this new regime of command.

8 KANDAHAR

Beyond Individualism

Chapter 1 discussed the recent works by Tony Zinni and Stanley McChrystal. Both generals argued that command in the twenty-first century is in transition. Specifically, while a heroic, individualist practice of command had been idealized in the twentieth century, both promoted nascent collaborative command. However, while deeply suggestive, they never fully described the practice of command in the twentieth century; plausibly, they presumed it was individualist. The previous chapters have tried to rectify this assertion and provide extensive evidence about the regime of command in that period. Up to now, therefore, this book has examined command in the twentieth century to argue that, because of specific organizational and operational conditions, an individualist regime of command attained dominance in this period. The analysis of commanders like Gavin, Rommel, Montgomery, Massu and Ewell was intended to demonstrate how individualist command was practised differentially in this era.

In order to recognize how command has changed in the twenty-first century, a detailed account of the preceding regime was required. There must be some comparator against which to evaluate contemporary practices. However, naturally, since this study proposes that a reformation of command has occurred, the focus must be the twenty-first century. Consequently, it is now necessary to examine command today in order to elucidate the specific ways in which command has evolved in the last two decades. The following chapters attempt to do this by a close examination of command in the early twenty-first century. This period has been extended back to 1992, although the following analysis focuses on the period since 2000, and especially after 2003. The examination of contemporary command demands detail and specificity. Precisely because of the evident continuities in divisional command, it is very easy to miss critical transformations and to assume that nothing has changed if too general a view is taken. It is vital that the analysis operates at a sufficiently large scale that apparently diminutive but nevertheless decisive shifts in the morphology of command are detectable.

Consequently, the following chapters attempt to dissect the lifeworld of the divisional headquarters; they describe current command methods, the interactions of the staff and the emergence of new structures and processes which have informed and influenced the decision-making process. They aim at a 'thick description' of divisional command, which defines this practice in the terms of military professionals themselves. The chapters will explore the transition of command, management and leadership from the individual regime of the twentieth century to an alternate paradigm today. Clearly, as noted in Chapter 3, an argument for the emergence of a new regime of command requires evidence from both recent stabilization and warfighting operations, optimally with data from all four major powers, when possible. A command regime can be said to exist only when a common practice of generalship is observable across the spectrum of conflict, among several different powers. Using the work of Zinni and McChrystal as a starting point, the following chapters will analyze the contemporary practices of divisional command in detail across warfighting and pacification operations, contrasting them with already-delineated twentieth-century methods. The analysis will start with recent examples of divisional command in action on stabilization and warfighting operations. In later chapters, the precise character of this command regime in its various manifestations will be discussed through the examination of recent divisional exercises, as the West has prepared for new threats after Iraq and Afghanistan. These chapters attempt to show how the collaborative command, which McChrystal and Zinni advocate, is practised in reality. According to this argument, while commanders remained central to the mission, they have administered multiplying and diversifying decision-cycles only through a professionalized team of empowered subordinates and staff.

Stabilization Operations

The division was originally invented for manoeuvre warfare; it was a response to the industrialization of warfare in the early nineteenth century. Consequently, in order to explore the emergence of a new command regime, it will eventually be necessary to examine conventional warfighting operations. The next chapter, which discusses 1st Marine Division's invasion of Iraq, will address this issue. However, over the past fifteen years, Western divisions have primarily been involved not in warfighting, but in stabilization operations in both Iraq and Afghanistan; they have specialized in counter-insurgency. Indeed, while five American and British divisions were involved in a three-week manoeuvre operation in March and April 2003, thirteen regular American and British divisions as well as numerous National Guard divisions were engaged in stabilization operations in Iraq and Afghanistan for eleven years from April 2003 to December 2014. Excepting the 25th Division, nine of the US Army's ten divisions and both of the US Marine's two divisions served in Iraq and/or Afghanistan in some capacity; most have been deployed more than once. Britain deployed both 1 and 3 UK Divisions recurrently to Basra and employed other divisional-level headquarters, including 6 UK Division and the Combined Amphibious Force Headquarters. From 2001 to 2014, all of these American and British divisions were primarily involved in stabilization operations. Consequently, these operations provide the most extensive evidence about contemporary command practices. Precisely because divisions were used most often on stabilization operations, it is rational to begin the analysis of contemporary command with these missions.

There is a further advantage. As the following chapters will make quite clear, contemporary stabilization operations have contrasted most strongly with twentieth-century operations. Not only have they manifestly differed from conventional manoeuvre warfare of the twentieth century but, in fact, they have also been quite distinct from classical counter-insurgency operations of the 1950s and 1960s. The politicization, multinationalization and informationalization of the Iraq and Afghanistan campaigns, as well as the requirement for precision and proportionality, distinguish them from Kenya, Algeria or Vietnam. Counter-insurgency operations in Iraq and Afghanistan offer a relatively easy point of access into considering contemporary command reform. Since these operations were so unusual, it would be expected that a distinctive practice of command emerged in response to them. They represent a potentially easier case with which to initiate an argument for command transformation.

Stabilization operations have evident methodological advantages, therefore. However, they also present some challenges. The number of divisions which have been involved on stabilization operations in the past decade presents a problem of selection. It is impossible to analyze all these divisions and their operations. A sample is required but, of course, any sample faces a problem of representativeness. Conditions within and between Iraq and Afghanistan differed markedly; commensurability across operations cannot be assumed. At the same time, a convincing account of command requires a deep interpretation which focuses on the micro-activities of commanders and their headquarters. Such a focus precludes the discussion of numerous examples. The problem of representativeness against depth has to be accepted and this chapter makes no attempt at comprehensiveness. It aims for evidential depth. This chapter, consequently, examines an example of a British-led divisional headquarters in Afghanistan; NATO's ISAF Regional Command South in October 2009 to November 2010, Combined Joint Task Force-6, commanded by a British major-general, Nick Carter. There are some disadvantages to this example which have to be admitted. It might be argued that Carter's command is not a good example of divisional command because Regional Command South was not really a division at all; it was at best only a divisional-sized force commanded by a headquarters designated as a two-star command. In this, it was compatible with Erskine's ad hoc Operation Anvil Division, comprised of a composite of infantry battalions and commanded by a brigade headquarters.

Yet, there are also some advantages to selecting Kandahar as an example. Nick Carter commanded Regional Command South during the McChrystal-led surge in Afghanistan in the decisive phase of the Western intervention. Moreover, with responsibility for Kandahar and Kandahar City, Regional Command South was designated the Main Effort by the ISAF commander General Stanley McChrystal. At this point, between the autumn of 2009 and the high summer of 2010, Regional Command South was the focus of NATO efforts in Afghanistan. Regional Command South was in command of the most important province at the most critical time in the entire Afghan campaign, after the initial elimination of the Taliban regime in late 2001. As a central element of the surge, the headquarters commanded an operation in 2010, Operation Moshtarak III (Hamkari), whose purpose was to secure Kandahar City and its environs.[1] Although the differences will become starkly apparent, there are consequently some intriguing parallels between Nick Carter's Regional Command South and the divisional operations of Erskine, Massu and Ewell, not least because in two of those cases, the operations involved securing cities. The Kandahar operation was historically significant and provides a very useful insight into contemporary counter-insurgency operations at the divisional level, then. It fused civil, governmental, informational and military efforts into a single operation. Consequently, it represents the exercise of divisional command in the twenty-first century very clearly.[2]

Kandahar is pertinent for another reason. As discussed in Chapter 2, the experiences of Nick Carter in Kandahar have had a material impact on the British Army since 2014. Kandahar convinced Carter that, in the current era, the divisional level was critical in integrating the multiple levels of today's military operations and, accordingly, as Chief of the General Staff, he re-structured the British Army around the divisional level. Kandahar is, therefore, immediately relevant to the divisional reforms which will be discussed in Chapters 11, 12 and 13.

---

[1] Operation Moshtarak, which means 'cooperation' in Dari, consisted of three phases; the first involved the reorganization of Regional Command South (October–November 2009), the second the securing of Central Helmand (February 2010) and the third the securing of Kandahar City (July–September 2010). Phase III became known as Hamkari ('together'), which referred to a broader civil and political development programme.

[2] At the same time, the operation and the headquarters has some clear evidential advantages; it is a well-documented operation and I was a member of the headquarters in 2009–10. Consequently, I was exposed to the working of the headquarters and had developed a personal relationship with the commander and some important staff members who were willing to give testimonies about their experiences. In addition to documentary material (including my own notes), the analysis is based on interviews with the commander, Major-General Nick Carter, the Chief of Staff (Brigadier Dickie Davis), the DCOS Operations (Brigadier Ben Hodges), the Head of the Prism Cell (a Colonel), the SO1 of the Joint Planning Branch (J5), one of the SO2s in the Joint Future Operations Branch (J3/5) and one of the official historians, as well as my own experiences of working in the HQ between 2009 and 2010.

At the end of the chapter, the Kandahar case study will be briefly supported by evidence from General David Petraeus and the 101st Airborne Division in Mosul to demonstrate that, although certainly distinctive, Carter's experiences were not, perhaps, entirely unique. In Mosul, a devolution of command authority of the type that Carter effected in Kandahar was also evident. Finally, in Chapters 11 and 12, further evidence from 1st Marine Division during the Fallujah operation in 2004 will be discussed, which would also seem to reinforce the interpretation of Carter's command. The aim of this chapter is, therefore, to document the reformation of command at the divisional level in Kandahar as a way of initiating the analysis of twentieth-century command more widely.

Situation

In April 2006, NATO began to assume responsibility for southern Afghanistan, establishing the new Regional Command South at Kandahar Airfield to direct operations in Kandahar, Uruzgan, Zabul, Nimruz, Daykundi and Helmand. At that point, the command was only a one-star or brigade-level command, shared by the three main contributing nations to the south – Canada, the Netherlands and the United Kingdom; it was primarily responsible for operations in Helmand, Kandahar and Uruzgan. From 2006 to 2008, command rotated unsatisfactorily on a six-monthly basis. Although eventually designated a two-star divisional level of command in 2008, the headquarters was still under-resourced and lacked authority. It was incapable of coordinating or supporting operations at the provincial task-force level. For instance, in the summer of 2009, Task Force Helmand launched an operation called Panchai Palang which proved to be the bloodiest of Britain's entire campaign in the theatre; nine soldiers were killed in one week in June 2009.[3] It was subsequently widely claimed that the difficulties of this operation stemmed very substantially from the lack of divisional-level resources.

In response to these difficulties and in the light of an anticipated US surge in Afghanistan in 2009/10, NATO began to re-organize its command structures. This involved a number of innovations, including

---

[3] Theo Farrell, *Unwinnable: Britain's war in Afghanistan* (London: Bodley Head, 2017).

the empowerment of Regional Command South. This headquarters was re-constituted as a 'Combined Joint Task Force'. This change of title denoted an increase of command authority and resources. Regional Command South no longer merely coordinated the operations of the Provincial Task Forces in Helmand, Kandahar and Uruzgan, but actually commanded them. To reflect this increased authority, command and staff tours were lengthened to a year to ensure continuity. It was possible that the first Command Joint Task Force in Kandahar could have been commanded by a Canadian, Dutch, British or American general. However, having committed most heavily to the south and being the only force capable of expansion, the United Kingdom was awarded the first command of the newly reinforced Regional Command South.

In addition, certain personal factors came into play in selecting the British as the initial lead nation for this headquarters. Nick Carter's personal reputation with the Americans was decisive here: 'It was a precondition of the US Surge to have a credible two-star headquarters and Nick Carter's credibility with the US was crucial'.[4] Carter had already commanded in Kosovo and Iraq. The UK was, therefore, appointed as the lead nation. Normally, the UK may have deployed one of its two established divisions for this operation. However, 1 and 3 UK Divisions had already been heavily committed to Basra and, consequently, the UK selected 6 Division as Nick Carter's headquarters. Traditionally, 6 UK Division was a static territorial headquarters based in York – not an operational one. However, despite this status, 6 UK Division was assembled and reconstituted to provide the core staff for Regional Command South in 2009–10. Eventually, it expanded to a size of 800 staff officers. Accordingly, because it was based on 6 UK Division, Regional Command South was given the title Combined Joint Task Force-6 or CJTF-6, where the 6 referred to its divisional designation; subsequent rotations were CJTF-10 (10th Mountain Division) and CJTF-82 (82nd Airborne Division).

Combined Joint Task Force-6 represented a major departure for ISAF, when compared to Regional Command South. Although nominally re-established as a two-star headquarters in 2008, when it was commanded by a British general, Regional Command South at that point was 'underpowered'; 'it had not trained collectively'.[5] As a result

[4] OF-5, British Army, Prism Cell, interviewee 054, personal interview, 12 March 2015.
[5] Ibid.

the commander had little ability to coordinate the campaign: 'I was there with Jacko Page [Regional Commander South, 2007–8]; he had no authority over Task Force Helmand'. Combined Joint Task Force-6 was a quite different construct; it had the resources and authority to command at regional level.

Regional Command South in 2009–10 was an unusual divisional headquarters by twentieth-century standards. The Command's area of responsibility over Kandahar, Uruzgan, Helmand, Daykundi, Zabul and Nimruz covered approximately 78,000 square miles[6] of complex terrain, including numerous towns and cities. The environment was as demanding and the politics as dynamic as anything which Ewell had faced in Vietnam. While the Mekong Delta's population in 1968 was 1.8 million, over 1 million Afghans lived in Kandahar city and its environs alone; the total population of southern Afghanistan was approximately 4.2 million. Instead of planning missions over days or, maximally, weeks, Regional Command South conducted a year-long campaign in southern Afghanistan, planning its signature operation, Moshtarak, for months. In addition, it was a very large formation, consisting of some 60,000 soldiers in eight brigade combat teams. The formation was also a diverse multinational force, including American, Canadian, British, Australian, Dutch, Estonian, Danish, Czech, Lithuanian and, of course, Afghan troops – with all the political sensitivities this involved. Nick Carter had to negotiate with the armed forces and even the governments of the troop-contributing nations. Adding to its suite of responsibilities, Regional Command South also coordinated Special Operations Force operations, with their evident delicacies.

Moreover, it was not simply that Regional Command South commanded a large military force. The headquarters had to manage a multiplicity of functions: intelligence feeds, surveillance platforms, artillery, helicopters, drones, fixed-wing planes in a crowded airspace, media, information, psychological operations, development and civil projects and political engagement. Officers were well aware of the challenge: 'We had to think upwards and above in a way I had not seen'.[7] He continued: 'There was, for instance, a vast increase in the

---

[6] Lieutenant-General Nick Carter, 'The Divisional Level of Command', *British Army Review* 157 Summer 2013.

[7] OF-6, Brigadier (now Major-General retired) Dickie Davis, Chief of staff, interviewee 049, personal interview, 2 December 2014.

flow of information, including classified national intelligence, that the headquarters had to collate, analyse and fuse'. As a result, in Regional Command South, the intelligence cell (J2) comprised some 25 per cent of the entire headquarters: 'the volume, the level of information and the information technology allowed a divisional headquarters to fuse information to a level that has never been seen before'.[8] In addition, Carter also had to negotiate with non-governmental and international organizations to coordinate governance, aid and development projects.

Finally, in stark contrast to Kenya, Algiers or Vietnam, NATO had to exercise extreme discretion in the use of force. Precision was absolutely critical to political legitimacy, exerting very considerable pressure on Nick Carter as a commander. Throughout his command, Carter was extremely careful about the use of force, not least because ISAF Commander General McChrystal had identified it as one of his priorities. The principle of 'courageous restraint' was central to McChrystal's strategy of gaining the support of the Afghan people, many of whom had been casualties of NATO strikes. The one scandal, involving 5th Stryker Brigade, which Carter's command suffered illustrated the extreme sensitivity of Western forces about collateral damage and civilian casualties. Disparaging McChrystal's concept of courageous restraint, 5th Stryker Brigade under Colonel Harry Tunnell was responsible for a number of unnecessary civilian casualties and indirectly culpable for the murders of others. Tunnell was later censured, when it emerged that a sub-unit within the Brigade had gone rogue. In the Maiwand District of Kandahar in January and February 2010, five soldiers from 2nd Battalion, 1st Regiment, 5th Stryker Brigade murdered three Afghan civilians in separate incidents, allegedly collecting body parts as trophies. However, while in no way diminishing the deplorableness of the incident, one of the most striking features of the scandal was the prominence which it achieved. As the previous chapter showed, in the Mekong Delta, Algiers or Kenya, incidents of this type were routinely ignored; indeed, there were many more egregious cases during those campaigns where civilians were killed indiscriminately that received no publicity at all. The 5th Stryker episode demonstrated the absolute requirement for

---

[8] Ibid.

discretion on twenty-first-century operations. Precision and proportionality were paramount.

These changing operational conditions placed special demands on the commander. Indeed, Nick Carter fully recognized the challenges of the role of divisional commander and the unique responsibilities it imposed upon him in Kandahar.

> The pervasiveness of information has changed the Character of Conflict. The distinction between peace and war is now blurred. We live in an era of constant competition, or warfare short of war, where it is increasingly difficult to call out a 'hostile act'. Home and away are now merged, with foreign and domestic policies progressively aligned to meet the challenge of a networked world. Our enemies are now masters of concealment, invariably amongst the populations we are seeking to protect; they avail themselves of the Internet to identify our weaknesses and then utilise commercially available technology to exploit them. As a commander you now live in a fish bowl; war is a theatre and you are a producer of a spectacle that must appeal to a range of audiences. For success is invariably defined by the triumph of the narrative. Terms like 'defeat' and 'victory' do not resonate as they once did.[9]

Nick Carter's predicament contrasted rather markedly with the situation of Erskine, Massu or Ewell. This mission was itself very complex, involving numerous military and political constituencies and Carter also had to exercise extreme sensitivity in order to sustain Afghan and international support. Because of the complex political context of conducting coalition operations in Afghanistan, the objectives were sometimes elusive and unclear – in stark contrast to the 1950s and 1960s – and Carter was subject to a level of scrutiny which his predecessors never experienced. Precisely because it was so different from a twentieth-century operation, Kandahar represents a good example of the changing topography of military command in the twenty-first century. The chapter will explore these changes by analyzing the way in which Nick Carter defined and then managed the mission in Kandahar.

---

[9] OF-7, Major-General (now General Sir) Nick Carter, interviewee 080, personal interview, 29 September 2015.

Regional Command South: Mission

In order to conduct divisional operations, Erskine, Massu and Ewell had to develop a campaign plan. It would be wrong to ignore the difficulty of their task. Nevertheless, as the previous chapter made eminently clear, the operational situation which confronted them was relatively straightforward; they had to eliminate insurgencies through naked military force and were given very wide latitude to do so. They could apprehend anyone at will and kill with few repercussions. Mission definition was, consequently, not difficult, even if they knew very little about the local political and social conditions. In addition, the chain of command above them was relatively straightforward, not least because they operated under a purely national military hierarchy. Indeed, both Massu and Ewell were given their missions.

Although Nick Carter was appointed to his command in Kandahar some time earlier, his headquarters was only formally assembled in April 2009, six months before deployment. From the moment of his appointment as commander, the first major task for Carter was to establish the mission. He identified the city of Kandahar and its environs as critical to his campaign since this was the economic, political and, indeed, cultural hub of the south; Kandahar City was a Pashtun capital of Afghanistan and, therefore, held huge symbolic significance for the Taliban. Indeed, Zhari and Panjwai districts were considered to be the heartland of the Taliban. Mullah Omar had been born in Zhari, a district some ten miles southwest of Kandahar City along the Arghandab River, and had paraded in the cloak of Mohammed in Kandahar when he came to power in 1996. A Taliban reversal here would represent a major advance for NATO and Hamid Karzai, the President of the Government of the Islamic Republic of Afghanistan. Especially for a British officer, this was a bold decision because generally as a result of their operations in Helmand, British personnel viewed southern Afghanistan, and indeed the entire NATO campaign, through the provincial prism of Helmand. Carter inverted this perspective and recognized that his centre of gravity was Kandahar City and its surrounding districts along the Arghandab valley.

In the summer of 2009, Carter developed a concept for southern Afghanistan which eventually crystallized into a schematic which

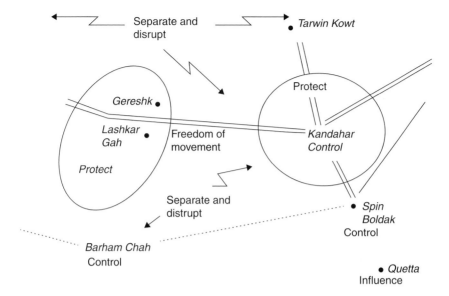

Figure 8.1 Campaign Schematic, CJTF-6 Kandahar.

represented the basic design for Operation Moshtarak.[10] This schematic became a basic reference point for the headquarters in Kandahar throughout the operation and it provided the framework for all the planning and the subsequent execution of Operation Moshtarak. The schematic depicted the main 'effects' – the outcomes – which Carter identified as central to his mission. It was a constitutive act of mission definition, which would play a hugely important role as a reference point throughout the campaign.

Carter's Schematic identified three critical tasks of which the mission comprised (see Figure 8.1). First, as the main effort, Nick Carter's aim was to control Kandahar City by the end of Operation Moshtarak in late 2010, securing it from the Taliban and improving governance and development there. Second, as a subordinate effort, Central Helmand had to be protected; a degree of security and control was required in and around Lashkar Gar, the provincial capital, but at a lower level than Kandahar City itself. While the British were fixated on Sangin, because of the heavy losses they had suffered there, Carter regarded the town as peripheral in operational terms. Finally, in order to improve conditions in Kandahar, Carter identified

10 Ibid.

freedom of movement on the roads and highways as critical. In the south, insurgents and local militias targeted the roads for attack and illegal taxation, alienating the population and impeding business and trade. At the same time, major routes had to be secured so that the Taliban could not use them to move fighters and materiel around the south. Although its implementation proved to be extremely complex, requiring extensive coordination between NATO forces, the Afghan Army and the Afghan Police, as well as many other agencies, Nick Carter's schematic was simple and clear.

Although not specified on the schematic, Carter also developed a mature concept for his operation, involving the construction of security rings around Kandahar City. In the event, Operation Moshtarak inserted three rings around Kandahar City; a composite US Brigade from 101st Airborne Division provided the outer ring of defence. They would be principally engaged in fighting and clearing the Taliban out of the Arghandab Valley. 205 Corps of the Afghan Army, commanded by General Zazai, secured the outskirts of the city, while the Afghan National Police were to secure Kandahar itself with a series of new checkpoints at decisive locations in the city. Meanwhile, 5th Stryker Brigade protected freedom of movement on the highways. These security circles were, after consultation with Afghan partners about an appropriate and understandable term for locals, called the 'cummerbund'. Nick Carter could not have envisaged many details which his concept of operations involved. However, the security cummerbund, eventually constructed around Kandahar City in 2010, was entirely consistent with the original schematic which Nick Carter had developed back in early 2009. The eventual deployment of Carter's forces during Moshtarak demonstrates very clearly the importance of his mission definition and the schematic to his command of this campaign (see Figure 8.2).

It was noticeable that Carter invested considerable efforts in communicating his schematic to his subordinates in order to impress his concept on them. Nick Carter first exposed his concept of operations with the schematic at Westdown Camp on Salisbury Plain to his deputy commanders soon after their appointment to Combined Joint Task Force-6 in July 2009.

> I assembled all of my one stars at Westdown Camp on Salisbury Plain with Buck Bedard, my USMC mentor in late June. We did this on the back of training we were delivering for the next Task

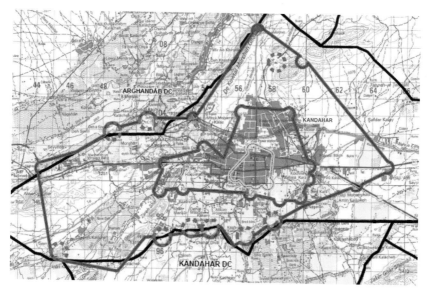

Figure 8.2 Kandahar City, Operation Moshtarak. Deployment of NATO, Afghan Army and Police Units.

Force Helmand. It provided the ideal opportunity to bond as a command team and to expose my emerging operational design – a simple Effects Schematic that designated where force would be concentrated and economy of effort would be applied. It became the basis of Operation MOSHTARAK which endured throughout my tour, that of 10 Mountain Division, 82 Airborne Division and is still recognised by the Afghan 205 Corps today.[11]

The campaign schematic was, then, a decisive moment of mission definition for Carter. Specifically, he was able to unite his deputies – and, subsequently, his staff – around this concept. Indeed, his staff emphasized the importance of Carter's role in impressing the mission on his headquarters.

Nick Carter defined an ambitious and comprehensive mission for his command, especially in comparison with the classical counter-insurgents of the twentieth century. The operation was projected to take place over months, across a very wide area, involving a large, multinational force and requiring the support of governmental and non-governmental organizations. There were further challenges. As he

[11] Ibid.

assumed command of Kandahar, Nick Carter was confronted with a complex situation. In 2009, ISAF was undergoing significant reform. In June 2009, replacing the relieved General David Mckiernan, Stanley McChrystal was appointed ISAF commander with specific responsibility to conduct Obama's eventually short-lived surge. McChrystal began to develop the ISAF campaign plan for the surge immediately. However, this plan only began to crystallize late in the summer of 2009, to be issued in November. Nick Carter was, consequently, developing his own divisional mission concurrently with his superior's plan. Moreover, as Carter and his headquarters deployed, McChrystal established the new ISAF Joint Command in the autumn of 2009 under General Rodriguez. This command was designed to manage the campaign, while McChrystal and his ISAF HQ concentrated on coordinating activities at the political level. By the summer of 2010, ISAF Joint Command was working effectively. Yet, as Nick Carter prepared for his deployment and, indeed, for some of his time in Kandahar, ISAF Joint Command was not functional; even in December 2009, it was still in some disarray. Accordingly, as a divisional commander, Carter did not operate within a clearly defined chain of command, under a corps commander, as Massu and Ewell did, or alongside a governor, as Erskine had done in Kenya. The command architecture was complex, sprawling and inchoate and infused with divergent, even contradictory, political directions and interests. There was, in short, no plan when Carter took over.

Consequently, even though he was only a divisional commander, Carter had substantially to design his own mission. Indeed, he seems to have influenced General McChrystal and the ISAF campaign plan; 'I spent time with McChrystal in August'.[12] At this point, with the ISAF plan still in genesis, Carter came to an agreement with McChrystal that Kandahar – and its population – should be NATO's main effort and that a concentration of forces was required in southern Afghanistan as a result. This was a major change for US forces, which had always focused on Regional Command East and the anti-terrorist mission there. In addition, a central element of McChrystal's campaign plan was the identification of eighty 'Key Terrain Districts'. The alliance did not have the troops to secure every district and, consequently, NATO security efforts were focused on the most important

---

[12] Ibid.

districts. Carter seems to have played some role in the development of the idea of the Key Terrain District:

> In a multi-national command you are far more likely to develop your mission statement iteratively. My RC (South) mission statement was the product of a discussion, indeed a negotiation with General McChrystal. I was fortunate to have served with him in Afghanistan before and we trusted each other completely. He wanted me to provide my assessment of the problem and then recommend the scheme of manoeuvre to him. He recognised that concentration of force and economy of effort would be key principles in our operational design, and that we would need to sequence tactical battles in distinct phases as resources became available. Hence we decided to deal with Central Helmand first followed by Kandahar.[13]

It is, of course, important not to overstate Carter's role. He was but one of many individuals from whom McChrystal took advice as he developed his plan and, certainly, Carter himself made no suggestion that he exerted the only – still less the decisive – influence. However, there was a distinctive level of negotiation and flexibility. With a still-solidifying chain of command above him, Carter, only a divisional commander, exercised an unusual level of responsibility in defining Regional Command South's mission, then.

Moreover, although he played a decisive role in defining his command's mission, Carter did not conceive his operation in Kandahar independently. On the contrary, external influences and his relations to a number of key actors played a decisive role in the germination of his operational concept and the schematic. He developed his mission in response to a diversity of political and military actors both in NATO and Afghanistan, sensitive to each of their interests. Indeed, Nick Carter was himself fully aware of the collaborations out of which the schematic arose:

> I was fortunate to be very well prepared. I assumed my role as GOC 6 (UK) Div in early 2009 and I had responsibility for training the task forces for Helmand. This gave me the chance to

---

[13] Ibid. The United States Marine Corps decided to invest in Helmand and eventually created their own Regional Command South-West in July 2010.

travel regularly with my COS [chief of staff], Colonel Bob Bruce to Afghanistan and engage with the Afghans. Thus I was able to test my emerging operational design on the Commander of 205 Corps, General Zazai who encouraged me to focus on the population centres of Central Helmand, Kandahar and Tarin Kot in Uruzgan. I began to understand the importance of freedom of movement for the Afghans, the need to connect the population to governance, and the complex political dynamics that required analysis before one blundered into kinetic clearing operations. The big question for me was 'who is the enemy'. And the lesson I learned was that you must understand the political context before applying force.[14]

The contrast with the narrow chains of command in which Erskine, Massu and Ewell operated was striking. Carter was influenced by a wide range of interlocutors and the military force was just one of his problems.

The pre-deployment preparations of Combined Joint Task Force-6 to Kandahar illustrate some important features of contemporary command, then. In terms of mission definition, Nick Carter exercised greater responsibility than his typical twentieth-century predecessors. He had to orchestrate a complex operational nexus which included not only multinational military forces but also political and civil elements. In order to define a mission, Carter interacted widely with an international politico-military network in order to gain some understanding of the balance of preferences and interests. He established collaborative relations with Generals McChrystal and Zazai and a diversity of other political and military actors in NATO. Mission definition was Carter's sole responsibility but in order to develop a coherent operation, he had to form partnerships with a diversity of other actors. His command and his definition of his mission reflected the interests of a network of allies and supporters.

Managing Moshtarak

In the twentieth century, because operations were primarily military, Erskine, Massu and Ewell were able to manage instrumentally. They

---

[14] OF-7, Major-General (now General Sir) Nick Carter, interviewee 080, personal interview, 29 September 2015.

determined the best way to employ their forces and employed their staff to organize the details. These commanders issued and supervised their orders. Managing operations in southern Afghanistan, involving a multinational force of 60,000 troops, was significantly more complex. This put significant pressure on Nick Carter and forced him to adopt a more onerous and oblique system of decision-making. Every commander, and especially Afghan officers, required substantial attention. Carter had to explain his operation to them and enjoin their comprehension and support for it. At the same time, because of the political complexity and multinationality of the campaign, Nick Carter had to invest significant amounts of time negotiating with his immediate superiors and with political and military leaders in the broader NATO nexus. Consequently, Nick Carter 'did an enormous amount of stuff upwards'.[15]

> Nick Carter spent a vast amount of time dealing with the Afghans. With the Governors of Kandahar and Helmand, with the Corps Commander. In February 2010, General Zazai and then with Zazai's replacements and then the police chiefs. And then every single country wanted to see the Commander. For instance, Lithuania had 90 SOF soldiers in the south; so Nick Carter was 90 per cent up and out with Afghans, Coalition Senior Representatives and so on.[16]

Other officers confirmed the point: 'Why was he out on the ground? He needed to get to know the commanders, especially the ANA partnered Corps which was another part of the dynamic. He got to know the Afghan corps commander and all his brigade commanders and knew them all well'.[17]

Yet, Carter's decision-making was not limited to his military subordinates. Rather than a purely military commander, he also assumed the role of a pro-consul, influencing military, political and civil domains. Indeed, many of his decisions were purely political.

---

[15] OF-6, Brigadier (now Major-General retired) Dickie Davis, Chief of Staff, interviewee 049, personal interview, 2 December 2014.

[16] OF-6, Brigadier-General (now Lieutenant-General) Ben Hodges US Army, Deputy Chief of Staff Operations, interviewee 058, personal interview, 7 April 2015; OF-3, SO2 J3/5, British Army, interviewee 046, personal interview, 11 December 2014.

[17] OF-6, Brigadier (now Major-General retired) Dickie Davis, Chief of Staff, interviewee 049, personal interview, 2 December 2014.

Strikingly, he defined his most important decision not as a military one at all, but rather as, 'which Afghan to make district governor in the Arghandab with the support of the elders and Wesa [the Governor of Kandahar]'. The identity of the district governor was likely to be far more significant in terms of suppressing the Taliban than any specific military decision.

This work was a prodigious managerial load for Carter. There were further factors which complicated the management of Moshtarak. In the 1950s and 1960s, counter-insurgents commanded through very small staffs. Their role was limited but they executed it effectively. One of the problems for Nick Carter was that in Kandahar, the utility of the staff was severely limited. His staff sometimes played an important role in 'speeding things up'. They had a 'short-cutting effect', providing information, evidence, metrics and details. 'They have the facts. They should be assembling facts to support decision-making'. However, in Kandahar, because of the lack of helicopters and the concerns about protection, the staff often struggled to leave the headquarters. Consequently, their understanding – and, even more, their judgement – was very limited. The staff sometimes provided crucial information but they could not recommend actions in the conventional manner or do any significant liaising work:

> I was able to get out and about. In many ways I was our best
> ISR [intelligence, surveillance and reconnaissance] sensor. I could
> see much more easily than anyone in the HQ that some courses
> of action would be unworkable. That's why it is often said that
> the commander has a monopoly on good ideas; it's easy for
> him because he has access to everything, he has aviation and
> security.[18]

It was difficult for Carter to be instrumental, then; he could not conventionally simply issue orders with the assistance of his staff. Carter was forced to adopt a different approach, which was onerous for him. He engaged directly with his subordinates and a series of partners.

This practice had serious implications for Carter's management of the operation: 'We wanted Afghans to own the decision-making and

---

[18] OF-7, Major-General (now General Sir) Nick Carter, interviewee 080, personal interview, 29 September 2015.

that required political engagement to encourage the right Afghan to say the right things'. Often, Carter improvised:

> I would look for opportunities, I didn't know precisely how things were going to play out, but if I was on the ground providing encouragement there was a reasonable chance the Afghans would take the lead. In this case, I took Governor Wesa to western Zhari at a critical moment for the Afghan population and the media. He needed to be demonstrating leadership as the Provincial Governor. That was decisive. But he would not have taken the risk if I had not travelled with him in his car that day.[19]

Rather than defining objectives and assigning forces to achieve them in standard military fashion, Carter had to be more subtle in his approach. Rather than a clear objective which was attained by rational means, Carter observed that 'You have to know what success looks like'; 'Decision-making requires much more shaping … You need to understand where the blockers might be. The good old days of End-State, ways/means and ends, they are gone'.[20]

Consequently, in place of instrumentalism, Carter engaged in conditional, cooperative and experimental management: 'I think strategy has evolved with the pervasiveness of information, you know broadly the next step to take, and as you do, you build alliances and hedge your opponents'. In Kandahar, Carter discovered that in order to execute his mission and implement his concept, he required the support of numerous agencies and actors who were not always in his chain of command. They were not under his control. Accordingly, in order to achieve success, he could not simply develop and implement a plan and order his forces to execute it, as Ewell or Erskine had. He had to manipulate the situation and align important actors at each point to accomplish his ends, even though he could not compel anyone to perform them.

There are some instructive examples of Carter's circuitous method of decision-making. For instance, in order to conduct the operation and secure Kandahar City, Carter needed an Afghan Army Kandak (battalion) from Uruzgan to be redeployed from the Dutch Task Force. The Dutch would resist such an order from Nick Carter

[19] Ibid.
[20] Ibid.

through the NATO chain of command. Accordingly, Nick Carter massaged the Afghan 205 Corps Commander so that he, not Carter, gave the order for this re-deployment. Since ISAF were there to support the Afghans, the Dutch could not reasonably object to this order. Carter subtly de-politicized the issue. Similarly, in response to a crisis in the Argandab in August 2010 when the Taliban deposed a district governor, rather than using Western troops Carter brokered an intervention by Colonel Abdul Razziq, the Chief of Police in Spin Boldak, with the assistance of Ahmed Wali Karzai, the President's half-brother and the Chair of the Provincial Council in Kandahar. The situation was resolved with only minimal violence, in which two Afghan policemen were wounded. However, this oblique method of decision-making was hugely time-consuming. Carter had to manipulate, negotiate and enjoin. He had act as a diplomat and an ambassador, asking for support, rather than simply commanding in traditional military fashion.

Chapter 7 showed how Erskine, Massu and Ewell managed their missions as military commanders, issuing orders and personally overseeing their execution. In the face of counter-insurgent threat, they simply applied force aggressively. Decision-making was instrumental. Nick Carter was compelled to employ a quite different approach. Operation Moshtarak was a complex and large-scale operation which sought to align military efforts with a wider civilian, informational and political programme.[21] This long-wavelength, multi-chorded approach superseded traditional military decision-making:

> Decision-making is for a crisis. It is to change a plan. But once committed to an operation, the commander normally has only one option, whether to commit a reserve. Nick Carter had no reserve. Did he have a political reserve? Possibly. But he had no military reserve. Hamkari was a six-month programme ... There was lots of tactical stuff but there was no traditional decision making at the divisional level'.[22]

Carter had to address political issues and to engage in a time-consuming management and indirect manipulation.

---

[21] OF-5, British Army, Prism Cell, interviewee 054, personal interview, 12 March 2015.
[22] Ibid.

The Disciples

Chapter 7 described the headquarters of Erskine, Massu and Ewell. In each case, these generals commanded major divisional operations with a small, even tiny, staff, relying on one principal aide: Taylor, Trinquier or Hunt. The command structure of Carter's headquarters in Kandahar was profoundly different. Indeed, even by contemporary military standards, it was unusual, even bizarre. According to contemporary doctrine, in a US Army divisional headquarters, a commander is supported by two one-star assistant commanders. In a British divisional headquarters, by contrast, the Chief of Staff, a colonel, typically acted as the commander's executive deputy.

Combined Joint Task Force-6 was a quite different construct. Above all, it was significantly over-represented at the senior level. Because it was a NATO headquarters, troop-contributing nations expected to have command representation at the senior level if they had forces on operations: 'The top structure of the headquarters was built around the NATO flags to post process that created rather more one star positions than function required'.[23] Remarkably, the headquarters, therefore, had six flag officers at one-star, brigadier rank: 'a USMC deputy (Tom Murray), a British Chief of Staff (Dickie Davis), a US Army Deputy Chief of Staff-operations (Ben Hodges), a Dutch Deputy Chief of Staff-support (Emile van Duren), a Canadian Deputy Chief of Staff-ANSF (Afghan National Security Forces) development (Craig King) and a British Deputy Chief of Staff-Stability (Richard Berthen, civilian)'.[24] At the beginning of the operation, it was widely believed that there were too many senior officers.[25]

Predictably, the flag to post policy generated friction. 'We had a crowded one-star space' as a result of which 'there were many low-level dramas, mainly Dutch, and one officer did not fit'[26]; it 'took a while to work out how to use all the one-stars'. The deployment of so many senior officers was clearly not optimal. An illustrative stress

---

[23] Carter, 'The Divisional Level of Command', 8.

[24] OF-6, Brigadier (now Major-General retired) Dickie Davis, Chief of Staff, interviewee 049, personal interview, 2 December 2014.

[25] OF-6, Brigadier-General (now Lieutenant-General) Ben Hodges, US Army, Deputy Chief of Staff Operations, interviewee 058, personal interview, 7 April 2015.

[26] OF-6, Brigadier (now Major-General retired) Dickie Davis, Chief of Staff, interviewee 049, personal interview, 2 December 2014.

point here was the relationship between Dickie Davis, the Chief of Staff, and Brigadier (now Lieutenant-General) Hodges, the Deputy Chief of Staff-Operations. Davis and Hodges developed very good personal and professional relations during the course of this operation. However, there were some initial misunderstandings in Kandahar. In a US Army divisional construct, the commander was supported by an Assistant Divisional Commander-Operations and an Assistant Divisional Commander-Support, both one-star posts. They hold genuine command authority in these respective areas, supporting and acting for the commander. The Chief of Staff is a colonel, who, while occupying a critical staff post, did not enjoy the same executive powers as the Assistant Divisional Commanders; the Chief of Staff post was primarily an administrative and organizational one involved in directing and coordinating the staff work of the Headquarters. By contrast, as already noted, in the British divisional construct, where there were traditionally no Assistant Divisional Commanders, the Chief of Staff assumed far greater authority. In a British Headquarters, the Chief of Staff not only coordinated the staff but also exercises significant command authority, playing an important role as an adviser and executive deputy to the commander. The doctrinal difference between the US and UK divisional headquarters about the relative role and authority of particular posts generated some confusion in Regional Command (South) between Ben Hodges and Dickie Davies.[27]

There were further institutional tensions between the US Army and the US Marine Corps. Indeed, Nick Carter was warned of the possible difficulties before he deployed by one of his mentors: 'You are in a fight between the USMC and the US Army'.[28] The issue generated frictions in the headquarters. As Regional Command South deployed, the US Marine Corps were seeking to take on a major mission in Afghanistan after the draw-down from Iraq. Eventually, in August 2010, they established their own divisional area of operations, Regional Command South-West, with responsibility for Helmand, Farah and Nimruz, dividing themselves from Regional Command South. However, until that time, the US Marines in Helmand were under the command of Carter. Consequently, Brigadier-General Ben Hodges and

---

[27] OF-5, British Army, Prism Cell, interviewee 054, personal interview, 12 March 2015.
[28] OF-7, Major-General (now General Sir) Nick Carter, interviewee 080, personal interview, 29 September 2015.

Tom Murray became the representatives of this institutional struggle. Once again, they eventually developed a close working relationship but the initial problems were real.

The command structure in Kandahar was top-heavy, then. There were initial concerns that this would create problems during the campaign. Rather than helping Nick Carter to manage the mission, the excess of deputy commanders potentially impeded coherent command. The danger was that there were too many senior officers with inadequate work to do. This would inevitably generate tensions and frictions. However, as the operation developed in late 2009 and early 2010, the over-representation of flag officers actually became useful: 'we worked it to our advantage'.[29] Indeed, Carter's deputies began to be indispensable at this point. It has been noted the Carter quickly found himself over-committed and incapable of monitoring and supervising important parts of the campaign. He required additional capacity to manage the mission.

It was here that the over-appointment of one-star generals to his headquarters became serendipitous; a NATO necessity became an operational virtue. Gradually, over the first months of the deployment, the one-stars officers in the headquarters improvised a division of labour between themselves. Accordingly, the Headquarters took on a distinctive structure. It consisted of 800 personnel but within it there was a core command group, at the centre of which were the six one-star officers:

> There was a HQ within the HQ. The core was less than 15 people. David Orr Ewing [SO1 J5 Plans] was the secretary of that group. There was a super-tanker approach to all the other stuff; routine business, planning and executing Moshtarak and Hamkari but inside that were about 10–15 people: Dickie Davis, myself, Bob [Bruce], Tom [Murray], Ben Hodges and David Orr Ewing. It was UK-US-centric.[30]

The flag officers formed themselves into a command federation around Nick Carter, assisting him with decision-making and the management of Moshtarak.

[29] OF-6, Brigadier (now Major-General retired) Dickie Davis, Chief of Staff, interviewee 049, personal interview, 2 December 2014

[30] OF-5, British Army, Prism Cell, interviewee 054, personal interview, 12 March 2015.

It is possible to delineate the responsibilities of the flag officers more precisely here. Dickie Davis, the Chief of Staff, ran the headquarters; Tom Murray, a US Marine brigadier, was the deputy commander. Ben Hodges became Deputy Chief of Staff-Operations, responsible for current and future operations (the J3/5 and J3 branches), Craig King (Canadian Army brigadier) commanded Plans and Policy (J5) and Emile van Duren, a Dutch air force officer, was responsible for the logistics of national support elements. Each of these deputies had a very large staff, for whom they were responsible. However, the Deputies were not primarily engaged with organizing their respective staffs as branch chiefs. In each branch, full colonels provided that function. Rather, the deputies pointedly acted as proxies for Nick Carter himself. The flag officers were not simply Carter's aides or representatives, they became active agents for him exercising decision-making authority in specified areas: 'There was no doubt about it: Nick Carter was the boss. We were his disciples'.[31]

Having been inducted into the planning process early, especially through the dissemination of the schematic, Carter's deputies understood intimately what their commander wanted. However, they did not simply support Nick Carter, relieving him of administrative burden. They assumed significant executive authority to ensure that the operation progressed. They acted for him – or rather *as* him – when he was not present: 'Nick Carter spent loads of time on the ground. But when you added up where Nick Carter was to be on any day, he could have reasonably been in four of five places. When Nick Carter was struggling for time, he would use Tom [Murray] and Ben [Hodges] so that he could turn into three people'.[32] While Carter was pre-occupied with oblique diplomatic management, his deputies increased his capacity to make timely decisions.

In the quotation above, Chief of Staff, Dickie Davis, noted the role which Ben Hodges and Tom Murray played in multiplying Nick Carter's authority, acting as substitutes for him. It is worth exploring how they did this in greater detail. Tom Murray, the deputy commander, for instance, stood in regularly for Carter in meetings in the Headquarters and often represented Carter on video-tele conferences

---

[31] OF-6, Brigadier (now Major-General retired) Dickie Davis, Chief of Staff, interviewee 049, personal interview, 2 December 2014.
[32] Ibid.

to subordinate and superior headquarters; 'if Nick Carter needed to be in ISAF, Tom Murray would do that'.[33] However, Murray played a more important role than simply sitting in for Carter in meetings: 'The Deputy Commander, Tom Murray, was the stay-at-home guy. He had decision authority. For instance, SOF hit targets every night and that would require approval. He would approve at 0100am. Having a US officer doing this was helpful because it would mainly be US SOF [Special Operations Forces]'.[34] This is a significant observation in understanding how Moshtarak was managed. Special Operations Forces raids were a very important and highly sensitive part of the campaign and the decision to launch one was, perhaps, the most tactically significant decision a commander could make. It required the highest level of authority not least because the intelligence on which a decision was based was always highly classified. A Special Operations raid would, therefore, normally be the sole responsibility of the commander. However, had Carter monopolized this decision, as he might have done, he would have had to have been awake until one or two o'clock almost every single night. Such a regime would have exhausted him and jeopardized his ability to command. Consequently, it was imperative that a trusted and empowered deputy stood in for him at this point to take on this duty. As an American flag officer, Murray was authorized not merely to oversee this decision but actually to make it. At the same time, Murray ran a number of other projects, including courageous restraint, and he was often in the field. In short, 'he deputized for Nick Carter across all functions'.[35]

Ben Hodges took on a very interesting and, perhaps, the most important role as Carter's disciple. He was the leading US Army officer in the south, with command authority over American troops there. As one officer noted: 'I would not overplay the role of all the one-stars in the HQ. The key was Ben Hodges'.[36]

> He was not just one other one-star with no influence and no resources. Access to Ben Hodges was crucial because he had

---

[33] Ibid.

[34] OF-6, Brigadier-General (now Lieutenant-General) Ben Hodges, US Army, Deputy Chief of Staff Operations, interviewee 058, personal interview, 7 April 2015.

[35] OF-6, Brigadier (now Major-General retired) Dickie Davis, Chief of Staff, interviewee 049, personal interview, 2 December 2014.

[36] OF-5, British Army, Prism Cell, interviewee 054, personal interview, 12 March 2015.

resources. He had the ear of COMISAF [Commander ISAF] and COMIJC [Commander ISAF Joint Command]. Whether he had a formal role as a Senior National Representative, I do not know but he felt personally responsible for Nick Carter's decisions for his troops. Effectively, Regional Command South was a US Division, entrusted to Nick Carter with Hodges as the control measure.[37]

Hodges was Deputy Chief of Staff Operations and, therefore, doctrinally, it might have been expected that he would position himself in the Operations Centre in the Headquarters able to observe and make decisions about current operations, organizing and controlling his staff. In fact, this role was principally taken by the Chief of Staff and by the staff officers in the Operations Centre.

During Moshtarak, Ben Hodges spent much of his time on the ground with United States troops and their commanders in the Arghandhab. His presence there was important. Although Regional Command South was based on a British divisional headquarters and was commanded by a British general, the vast majority of troops under it were American and they were engaged in the most dangerous and difficult operations, clearing and securing the Arghandab Valley in Panjwai and Zhari. They were the decisive force. As an American officer who had commanded a brigade in 101st Airborne Division during the Iraq invasion under General Petraeus, Hodges was ideally positioned to liaise, communicate with and coordinate American ground troops: 'As director of operations, I dealt with the brigades and a fair amount with the Afghans. I would not approve a CONOPS [Concept of Operations] without the Afghans. I would distribute ISTAR and work out how to allocate that. Most of the force was US and I was dealing back to the US and incoming Aviation and US rotations'.[38] However, while Hodges enjoyed a high level of autonomy, he 'was brilliant at supporting him [Nick Carter]';[39] he was able to 'talk in American but he realised what Nick Carter wanted; he was the national support bloke with Title 10 Authority. He knew what Nick Carter wanted'.[40]

---

37 Ibid.
38 OF-6, Brigadier-General (now Lieutenant-General) Ben Hodges, US Army, Deputy Chief of Staff Operations, interviewee 058, personal interview, 7 April 2015.
39 OF-4, SO 1 J5, British Army, interviewee 046, personal interview, 11 October 2014.
40 OF-6, Brigadier (now Major-General retired) Dickie Davis, Chief of Staff, interviewee 049, personal interview, 2 December 2014.

An unusual division of labour emerged in Carter's headquarters during Moshtarak. Hodges himself highlighted the distinctiveness of the command arrangement in Regional Command South: 'Kandahar had something which approached a command board. The span of control and the area of command dwarfed the Second World War or Korea. The types of thing going on were utterly different. It was not a case of two regiments up and one back. The brigades were in different areas. It was not just kinetic stuff. There was partner activity – a whole range of things'.[41] Because of the diversification of functions, Carter required far more assistance than the classic counter-insurgents in the 1950s and 1960s. As Chapter 7 showed, commanders, then, were able to focus more or less exclusively on military matters; they concentrated on suppressing the insurgencies through the maximum use of military power.

In Kandahar, Nick Carter consciously shared authority with his deputies, whom he licensed to make decisions for him. They assisted him in the critical role of managing the campaign.

> RC (South) showed me the value of deputy commanders. Given the span of command, the need to designate the main effort and lead it, it is obvious that the commander has to have his back properly covered. I was fortunate to have a real deputy, USMC Brigadier General Tom Murray, who shared the load and freed me to focus on what really mattered. We must embrace this idea in the British Army.[42]

After the first few months, this command team worked effectively to support and represent Nick Carter.

There seem to have been two critical factors in the generation of an effective command team in Regional Command South. First, Nick Carter drew his deputies into his command process early and they remained central to it throughout. He brought them together for a command group meeting on Salisbury Plain early in 2009. Although the outlines had already been developed and socialized, he provided them with detailed operating instructions as guidance and used a

---

[41] OF-6, Brigadier-General (now Lieutenant-General) Ben Hodges, US Army, Deputy Chief of Staff Operations, interviewee 058, personal interview, 7 April 2015.

[42] OF-7, Major-General (now General Sir) Nick Carter, interviewee 080, personal interview, 29 September 2015.

campaign schematic to communicate to them what he intended.[43] He, therefore, united his deputies around his definition of the mission. They thoroughly understood and agreed with the mission. This vertical cohesion from commander to subordinate was plainly important. However, Nick Carter and his deputies were also able to form a close federation of commanders once they had deployed. In theatre, Carter actively maintained the unity of this group. For instance, one of the official historians in the headquarters observed the formation of a tight team around Nick Carter, including Craig King, Ben Hodges, Emile van Duren and Colonel Bob Bruce (strategic communications). 'When I would go past his office, I would see Dickie Davies chatting in there; they used to talk a lot'. Tom Murray was also in his office frequently. 'Nick Carter would discuss his intent striding around the room with people taking notes. David Orr Ewing captured what he said and would write one to two pages'.[44] The command of Moshtarak, consequently, involved 'a small band of determined people'.[45] There were no obviously favoured advisers but a principal planning group consolidated into a command collective, each of whose members supported Carter in his designated area. It is noticeable that very close relations developed between the deputies themselves; 'you need the command team being tight. There was lots of friction early in the year. However, we became very tight. Even now, we are tight. I am very close to Ben Hodges now. The commander relies on everyone and you respect and emphasize competence'.[46] The contrast with the tiny command cells through which Erskine, Massu and Ewell conducted their operations is striking. In Kandahar, Carter certainly dominated the campaign but he commanded through a more collaborative and highly professionalized team of deputies. Once unified around his mission definition, they were able to manage important elements of Moshtarak while Carter was committed to the complex work of negotiating and sustaining partnerships and alliances.

[43] Carter, 'The Divisional Level of Command', 9.
[44] OF-5, British Army, Prism Cell, interviewee 054, personal interview, 12 March 2015.
[45] Ibid.
[46] OF-6, Brigadier (now Major-General retired) Dickie Davis, Chief of Staff, interviewee 049, personal interview, 2 December 2014.

King David

Throughout this chapter, the distinctive operational conditions in Kandahar have been stressed. At the beginning of his tour, ISAF command architecture and McChrystal's own plan were still undeveloped; Carter enjoyed a rare freedom of manoeuvre in terms of mission definition. In addition, throughout 2010, he was the main effort of the American-led surge. There were special local conditions too. The very fact that Combined Joint Task Force-6 was a multinational force complicated command significantly. The headquarters was overpopulated with flag officers. Moreover, Carter had to consider alliance politics to a far greater degree than other commanders. Consequently, in Kandahar, it might be claimed that a wholly distinctive method of command was forced upon Nick Carter. Kandahar is an interesting case study, but not a representative one on this account.

Undoubtedly, the special characteristics of Kandahar were not replicated elsewhere. Consequently, it is worth briefly considering a counter-example which might confirm – or deny – the interpretations drawn from the example of Regional Command South. American divisions in Iraq are highly pertinent here because, especially in the early years of the campaign, they were homogeneous standing formations. Many of the multinational issues that distinguished Carter's command were absent from them. It is, therefore, conceivable that command in these American divisions assumed a quite different form. There are clearly a great number of divisions which could potentially be the focus of attention here. Once Saddam Hussein was deposed in mid-April 2003, American forces spent the following five years in Iraq engaged exclusively in counter-insurgency. However, as an illustration, it is worth considering one of the most well-known examples: General David Petraeus and the 101st Airborne Division in Mosul in 2003.

After the invasion, 101st Airborne Division was redeployed north to Mosul, a city of two million, where it engaged in stabilization operations. While the issue of security remained critical, Petreaus sought to engage in a political and civil reconstruction; he prioritized governance and development projects. He put up posters in the Division's base reading: 'What have you done to win Iraqi hearts and minds today?'[47] Petreaus' actions in Mosul have been widely taken to be the basis for the American counter-insurgency revolution from 2006 and for the celebrated *Field Manual 3–24*, which Petraeus himself was instrumental in writing. In Mosul, Petraeus became known as 'Malik Daoud', King David. Like Carter, he dominated the operation and was instrumental in defining his division's mission and ensuring it was executed. Initially, Petraeus was involved in small-scale offensive operations against remaining regime elements. These operations were more conventional in their execution and assumed the character of counter-terrorist operations, concerned exclusively with defeating, capturing or killing opposition fighters.

> Once we got up to Mosul, we just had a main and an assault headquarters. We pushed out a small [assault] HQ for raids into Anbar Province when our forces would fly helicopters in there with our troopers at night. We would use Al Assad airfield which was huge and we could generally hide our aircraft in remote areas. We did three of those operations and then another north of the Euphrates into a major wadi network where insurgents had established large caches and bases. I used the Assault Command Post for these three operations. A brigade commander ran the operation and I monitored it from my command and control helicopter. We had TACSAT [tactical satellite communication] and blue force tracker. I would go with the air assault element.[48]

In the first phase in Mosul, Petraeus commanded operations through the established architecture of divisional command: a main headquarters and a small deployed assault command post, with which he would deploy.

Nevertheless, once the final elements of the Saddam regime had been eliminated, the character of the operation began to change fundamentally. At this point, the existing structure of command in 101st became inappropriate to the challenges of stabilization. Petraeus, consequently, reorganized his division and its headquarters to meet the new operational requirements. Specifically, the division was no

---

[47] Fred Kaplan, *The Insurgents: David Petraeus and the plot to change the American way of war* (London: Simon and Schuster, 2013), 71–8; David Cloud and Greg Jaffe, *The Fourth Star: four generals and their epic struggle for the future of the United States Army* (New York: Three Rivers Press, 2009), 117–22.

[48] General David Petraeus, interviewee 096, personal interview, 7 January 2016.

longer engaged merely in combat; it had to take responsibility for a multiplicity of functions, many of which were not genuinely military concerns at all. A new distribution of responsibilities was required.

> What ultimately happened in the north, as a single division took control of all provinces north of Baghdad starting around 2003, the divisional headquarters was at an airfield near Tikrit, with one-stars and small HQs in Mosul and Baqubah.[49]

While Petraeus maintained his main headquarters in Tikrit, he established a series of subordinate commanders for his deputies around the region. Petraeus devolved command responsibility to his Assistant Divisional Commanders. His Assistant Divisional Commanders became quasi-autonomous governors in their respective areas in Mosul and Baqubah, operating under Petraeus's direction but independent of him.

At the same time, subordinates were assigned specific areas of specialist responsibility in this new division of labour. For instance, in Mosul, Petreaus assigned subordinate commanders to each of the decisive functions in the city.

> When the 101st was in Mosul, I assigned a unit to every single ministry to help re-establish the ministry office in Mosul. The divisional signal battalion was the partner for the Department of Telecommunications. It was the first that had an international phone system in Baghdad. We had two aviation brigades; the assault Brigade HQs helped to re-establish the university. The Divisional artillery headquarters ended up running the veterans employment centre. I mentored the Governor and established a cell at the Provincial HQs. The engineer brigade re-established the Ministry of Public Works. It also rebuilt the police academy. The medical battalion rebuilt the medical hospital. And so on. The divisional HQ was responsible for overseeing all these initiatives.[50]

The result was that in Mosul, Petraeus developed a command system which was not completely dissimilar to Carter's in Kandahar. As his span of command expanded geographically and functionally, Petraeus devolved command authority to his deputies and subordinates, assigning them decision-making powers over designated areas or

---

[49] Ibid.
[50] Ibid.

specialisms. At this point, Petraeus began to revise his initial method of command.

> At the divisional level, you oversee. You might make an
> occasional tactical or operational decision, allocate forces,
> designate priorties, etc. But we had big divisions in Iraq. There
> were 25,000 troops in Multinational Division North – not
> counting the Iraqis. My focus was two levels down to the
> infantry battalion commanders. Most got it; they got COIN.
> Two of ours did not; they just wanted to do raids. They needed
> additional oversight. The Assistant Divisional Commanders
> visited them. Their Brigade Commanders mentored them. Then,
> their hearts were in it. Eventually we had approximately forty
> battalions, including ten aviation battalions. Goodness knows
> how many others, as well as two civilian affairs battalions.[51]

This account of 101st operations in Mosul is plainly cursory; it is indicative rather than definitive. However, adjacent to the account of Kandahar, it becomes suggestive. While Petraeus affirmed that the divisional commander retained responsibility for all divisional operations, in Mosul, he distributed decision-making authority outwards to assistant and subordinate commanders. The latitude that was extended to them was increased. The scope of command had simply expanded too widely for even a commander as capable as Petraeus to manage the operation alone. Yet, Petraeus' system remained integrated and closely coupled, united around his leadership. Like Regional Command South, command authority was distributed across a tightly articulated command team, with Petraeus, of course, at its centre, closely supported by a group of subordinates.

The Coindinistas

Focusing on the example of Kandahar, this chapter has explored the transformation of divisional command on stabilization operations, comparing Nick Carter's performance with those of his predecessors, Erskine, Massu and Ewell. On the basis of the evidence presented, a divide between them seems to be evident. On recent counter-insurgency

[51] Ibid.

operations, decision-making became more complex as a result of the expansion of military and non-military functions of a division, the vast increase in divisional areas of responsibility, and the imperative of precision and proportionality. Carter and Petraeus could not be concerned only with military affairs. They conducted complex and heterogeneous operations over greater distances and longer periods. Because CJTF-6 and 101st Airborne were involved in so many activities, the span of decision-making increased and diversified. The scope of counter-insurgency command increased. There was no longer simply one divisional decision-making cycle relating to the current and immediate operation against terrorists and insurgents, though these remained critical. A divisional commander could no longer simply order his subordinates to 'get off their asses' and start killing insurgents, as Ewell declaimed in the Mekong Delta.

The division had to synchronize a diversity of simultaneous short- and long-term decisions. Many of these cycles referred to highly specialized spheres of activity, of which no single commander could possibly be the master. At the same time, commanders manipulated and negotiated with partners and allies; they did simply order action. Consequently, the problem in Kandahar was not, as Ewell recalled in the Mekong Delta, that there was not enough action for the divisional commander 'to get his teeth into' but, rather, there was too much; divisional operations threatened to exceed the decision-making capacity of the commander. The command capacity of the division had to increase to address the multiplication of decisions. Deputies began to play a crucial role here, assuming responsibilities for specific jurisdictions while their commander was committed elsewhere. In both Kandahar and Mosul, it is possible to see the emergence of federated command teams, in which decision-making was sub-contracted out to deputies, who were closely integrated into a unified executive body around the commander. Clearly, great care needs to be taken here and claims must be correlated against the evidence. However, on the basis of the Kandahar study, supported by Petreaus's experiences in Mosul, it would seem plausible to suggest that a significant command reformation took place in these theatres. Specifically, a distribution of command authority especially in the domain of mission management seems to be apparent. The rest of this book will seek to elaborate upon this finding.

It is important to stress a final point. The distribution of decision-making authority which seems to have been evident in

Kandahar does not imply that somehow commanders have become mere bureaucrats who make decisions by the consent of a command board. On the contrary, while responsibility for the management of military missions may be increasingly shared, commanders remain solely responsible for mission definition. As one member of Regional Command South observed: 'General Carter's personality and intellect seemed to dominate the whole show'.[52] Indeed, the case of Nick Carter shows that commanders' responsibilities for mission definition have increased. Carter was solely responsible for mission definition. The increasing complexity of the operational environment has accentuated the importance of this command role, not diminished it. Nick Carter, for instance, was no longer simply in a *singular* position in a military hierarchy as his predecessors had been; he occupied a *unique* location where civil, political and military networks converged. He was at the centre of a politico-military nexus. David Petraeus has himself emphasized the point: 'Contemporary operations are commander-centric, network-enabled. The network is not the centre. The commander is'.[53] On recent counter-insurgent operations, the military chain of command has been superseded by an operational politico-military orrery. As a result, the role of the commander in mission definition has become pronouncedly more important.

Through the example of Nick Carter, this chapter has argued for the appearance of a system of collaborative decision-making which might be termed a command collective. Without defining the mission personally, Nick Carter could not have hoped to unite this command collective, which was imperative to his successful management and leadership of the mission. In order to create a command team, it was necessary for Carter to assume a level of individual responsibility and accountability quite foreign to Erskine, Ewell and Massu. Yet, despite his evident talents, Carter also needed a team of capable deputies in order to execute it. Especially when contrasted against classic counter-insurgency operations, Kandahar seems to show that a morphological transformation of command has occurred. It seems to suggest that the command individualism favoured in the twentieth century may be in the process of being displaced by more collective and collaborative practices.

---

[52] Official historian, CJTF-6, interviewee 048, email communication, 14 November 2014.
[53] General David Petraeus, interviewee 096, personal interview, 7 January 2016.

9 THE MARCH UP

1st Marine Division

A transformation of command seems to have been evident during the stabilization campaigns in Iraq and Afghanistan. In comparison with their predecessors in the 1950s and 1960s, when Erskine, Massu and Ewell directed operations closely, Nick Carter and David Petraeus consciously distributed their decision-making responsibilities with deputies to form tightly coordinated command collectives. Clearly, this adaptation is of evidential and historic significance in and of itself. The revision of counter-insurgent command in the twenty-first century is a notable development. However, it is also important not to overstate the significance of this transformation or draw false conclusions from it. The changing character of counter-insurgent command does not mean that a similar transformation has been evident on warfighting operations. It might be argued that on warfighting operations, traditional, more individualist practices of command remained optimal.

Indeed, when he commanded 101st Airborne Division during the invasion of Iraq, and notwithstanding his distribution of decision-making authority in Mosul, David Petraeus stressed that the commander remained the sole decision-maker: 'There is one commander. He is the guy. Everyone else is in support of him. Having two one-stars makes sense – one on operations and one on support. But be very clear, Assistant Divisional Commander-Operations do not generally issue orders'.[1] On this account, even in the twenty-first century, high-intensity manoeuvre warfare demands an individualist method of command. The command groups observable in Kandahar or in Mosul were mere contingencies, the result of the special conditions which pertained to those operations.

In order to demonstrate that there has been a genuine organizational reform of command rather than merely contingent adaptation on counter-insurgency operations, it is imperative to consider the case of warfighting. Just as in the twentieth century, it is possible to argue for a historical transformation of command only if a similar reformation of decision-making has been observable on conventional operations too. There are some evident challenges here, however.

While Western forces have been heavily engaged in stabilization operations since 2003, they have participated much more infrequently in manoeuvre warfare. Indeed, there is only one example of conventional divisional manoeuvre in the last two decades: the invasion of Iraq from 20 March to 12 April 2003.[2] Any consideration of contemporary command practice must consider this unique case. Even then, it might be claimed that in comparison with the First and Second World Wars, the invasion has limitations; the Iraqi Army represented a feeble opposition in comparison with the belligerents of those earlier conflicts. Indeed, following his experience in Iraq, General James Mattis coined a memorable aphorism for military success: 'It's easy to look brilliant when the enemy generals are dumber than a bucket full of rocks'.[3] Neither the Iraqi soldiers nor their commanders proved themselves particularly adept opponents; the Feyadeen were a more formidable enemy. Consequently, because the United States enjoyed vastly superior combat power, the fighting, although periodically

---

[1] General David Petraeus, interviewee 096, personal interview, 7 January 2016.

[2] The invasion officially ended on 1 May 2003, when President Bush made his now-notorious speech on the deck of the USS *Abraham Lincoln* that major combat operations were over. However, fighting ceased in Baghdad on 12 April and the date is generally taken to mark the moment when the regime fell. Consequently, this date is taken as the end of the invasion.

[3] General James Mattis, interview by Dr Gary Solis, 18 June 2007, interview 052, Transcript, United States Marine Corps History Programme, Marine Corps History and Museum Division, Quantico, VA, 35; General James Mattis, interviewee 113, personal interview, 4 June 2016.

heavy, was not as prolonged or as intense as the major battles of the twentieth century.

Nevertheless, although its legality and strategic wisdom remain questionable, the invasion of Iraq, brief though it may have been, was a notable military enterprise. Whatever the opposition, V (US) Corps and 1st Marine Expeditionary Force advanced over 300 miles, securing numerous towns and cities and eventually seizing Baghdad itself, integrating closely with air, maritime and special operations forces. All of this was achieved in less than three weeks. The invasion of Iraq may not have involved fighting of the intensity and scale of the Second World War or the breakout from Normandy, for instance.[4] Yet, neither can it be dismissed as an evidential irrelevance. It was a far more ambitious and dangerous undertaking than the Gulf War of 1991, which has been consistently used to assess Western warfighting capabilities, even though Allied ground forces engaged a mismatched, depleted and demoralized army for less than four days during that war.[5] The Iraq invasion is the only true warfighting example which is available in the twenty-first century and it must, therefore, be selected for this study. For all its particularities, it is by no means a bad example of contemporary divisional command.

The invasion of Iraq was conducted by five divisions: the American 3rd Infantry, 101st Airborne (Air Assault), 82nd Airborne, 1st Marine Divisions and 1 (UK) Division. Of these divisions, 3rd Infantry Division played the central role and was designated the main effort of the entire operation; 3rd Infantry Division advanced on a western corridor all the way to Baghdad, eliminating the Saddam regime with a series of bold 'Thunder Runs'. Meanwhile, as part of the 1st Marine Expeditionary Force (a US Marine Corps), 1 (UK) Division advanced only a short distance from the Kuwaiti border, eventually securing the by-then-benign city of Basra. By contrast, 1st Marine Division advanced on the eastern axis up Highways 1 and 7, eventually entering Baghdad over the Diyala River from the east. 101st

---

[4] In reference to the breakout from Normandy, Operation Cobra, the CENTCOM plan for the Iraq invasion was given the codename Cobra II.

[5] Stephen Biddle, *Military Power: Explaining Victory and Defeat in Modern Battle* (Princeton, NJ: Princeton University Press, 2004); Daryl Press, 'Lessons from Ground Combat in the Gulf: the impact of training and technology', *International Security* 22(2) 1997, 137–46.

Airborne and 82nd Airborne were tasked with the subordinate roles of securing the lines of communication along Highway 8, between Samaweh and Karbala.

Although all of the divisions were involved in intense local fights, two of these divisions immediately recommend themselves as the best example of manoeuvre warfare; 3rd Infantry Division and 1st Marine Division. Only these two formations were involved in genuine manoeuvre warfare at a tempo, range and scale which makes comparison with the twentieth century possible. Consequently, it would seem to be appropriate to focus on these divisions in order to ascertain the character of command in conventional warfighting in the current era. Either division would be a good example of conventional divisional manoeuvre. However, this chapter focuses on 1st Marine Division to draw some conclusions about command in the twenty-first century. The selection of the Marines is justified on three grounds. First, any consideration of Western command in the twenty-first century has to consider the US Marine Corps, as one of its most potent fighting forces. Second, the archive on the 1st Marine Division is well-developed. In addition to a number of memoirs, journalist accounts and an official history, the Marine Corps conducted a series of illuminating interviews with key commanders in the division after the operation. Finally, and most importantly, if Kandahar represented an easy case for testing a theory of collective command, 1st Marine Division and its commander, Major-General James Mattis, surely constitute a hard case. The Marines have disparaged overly technical and bureaucratic methods of command, emphasizing instead the human element. It is an organization which empowers commanders, demanding decisiveness and personal leadership from them. Moreover, of all contemporary Marine commanders, James Mattis represents this ethos at its most developed. He was a hugely capable divisional commander who dominated his division both morally and intellectually. The single case of 1st Marine Division will not in and of itself definitively prove that a regime of collective command has appeared. However, a demonstration that even James Mattis adopted a practice of professionalized, distributed command would significantly advance the argument for a transformation of command in the twenty-first century. Accordingly, this chapter concentrates on the 1st Marine Division and James Mattis.

The Mattis Paradox

The previous chapter claimed that on contemporary counter-insurgency operations, the scope of command had increased dramatically. Consequently, in order to address the proliferation of decision cycles, it was possible to see the emergence of command collectives. Carter and Petraeus shared their authority with chosen subordinates. Any suggestion that James Mattis shared his command authority in Iraq seems counter-intuitive and even absurd. General James Mattis was widely regarded to be one of the most charismatic, powerful and competent generals of his generation. Indeed, James Mattis himself rejected any notion that he could share his command authority. Indeed, the organizational mission of the US Marine Corps has demanded a command-centric system. Because the Marines are relatively light force, which must fight ashore from its own shipping with limited support, it has to be aggressive and adaptable against its enemies; 'you can't solve the problem with mass. You can't put all the stuff on ships or do it all with artillery. You need deception. That requires a commander; an individual with the most experience'.[6] For Mattis, the special amphibious mission of the US Marine Corps demanded a command-led system of decision-making in which the commander was always the central reference point. Consequently, Mattis rejected any notion that command might be exercised bureaucratically or, indeed, collectively: 'I disagree if you are trying to do decision-making in boards. The enemy will dance around you'.[7] In the Marines, there has to be a single point of command and, ideally, a dominating personality filling that position, who plays the decisive and sole decision-making role.

Mattis's own staff in 1st Marine Division concurred. For instance, Mattis was described as 'the master' who exercised 'command influence' throughout the campaign; 'there was no question that General Mattis was *the* single commander'.[8] Another officer was equally forthright: 'If the commander is not invested in ownership of the mission, there is no vision. If he is just a board member, the mission does not get actualized'.[9] For him, Mattis exercised unique authority

[6] Ibid.
[7] Ibid.
[8] OF-4, Anonymous, 1st Marine Division, interviewee 098, personal interview, 15 March 2016.
[9] OF-4, G3 Plans, interviewee 100, personal interview, 22 March 2016.

over 1st Marine Division which was utterly critical to its performance: 'Mattis created a fraternity and a Cult of Personality'.[10] Other
prominent officers affirmed the point, such as Lieutenant Colonel
Clarke Lethin, who became one of Mattis's most trusted staff officers.
Having served with him as his operations officer in Task Force 58 in
Afghanistan in 2002, Lethin was one of the officers whom Mattis
used as a 'directed telescope' or 'eyes officer'. Eventually taking over
as Assistant Chief of Staff Operations on 5 April, Lethin played a
crucial role in the March Up. Although he recognized that sharing
decision-making might be possible, he stressed Mattis's inalienable
authority: 'The general is a pretty talented individual. He's probably unique. We were fortunate'.[11] He described Mattis's extraordinary facility to process a great mass of information, from which he
extracted the salient points relevant to his own decision-making: 'He
was not influenced by one particular staff officer. He was his own
artificial intelligence. He collected information and then made a
decision'.

Mattis exercised an extraordinary authority over his entire
formation, throughout the three-week campaign. He was central to
the decision-making process. Mattis and his subordinates unanimously
emphasized that he was in sole command of 1st Marine Division. On
this account, there was no distribution of decision-making responsibility. Mattis represents a direct challenge to any theory of collective
command in the twenty-first century. He was a traditional commander
in the classic heroic mould.

Nevertheless, there was a potential paradox at the heart of
Mattis's method of command. For, while all were agreed that he was
the sole decision-maker in the division – his authority was unquestionable – both Mattis and his subordinates also stressed that he was
fastidious in the distribution of command authority; he was an active
proponent of 'mission command'. This paradox is important because
it offers an opportunity for reconsidering Mattis as a commander and
of questioning the programmatic statements that he was self-evidently
a traditional Marine general in the classical mould.

---

[10] Ibid. See also Bing West and Ray Smith, *The March Up: taking Baghdad with the 1st Marine Division* (London: Pimlico, 2003), 253.
[11] OF-4, Lieutenant-Colonel Clarke Lethin, Deputy and then Assistant Chief of Staff Operations, G3, interviewee 125, personal interview, 19 July 2016.

As noted in Chapter 2, mission command was first formally established in US doctrine in the 1982 edition of *Field Manual 100–5: Operations* as a means of responding to the challenge of the Warsaw Pact, which numerically overmatched American and NATO forces. In order to accelerate the tempo of operations and, therefore, combat effectiveness, centralized direction was no longer the optimal command system. Local commanders had to be liberated to make decisions rapidly in the light of fleeting opportunities, rather than wait for higher direction. The US Marine Corps adopted this new approach at the same time (which accorded with its own traditions anyway) and the philosophy of mission command has now become highly developed: 'it is essential that our philosophy of command support the way we fight. First and foremost, *in order to generate the tempo of operations we desire and to best cope with the uncertainty, disorder, and fluidity of combat, command and control must be decentralized*'.[12] Consequently, the US Marine Corps manual, *Warfighting*, instituted a system known as 'mission command' in which subordinates were expected to make decisions without consulting their superiors. This system was not based on technology but 'on human procedures'.[13]

Mattis absorbed the lessons of *Warfighting* very deeply and sought to implement is precepts into practice:

> His style of command is a function of the Mission Concept concept from Army and Marine manoeuvre warfare laid out in *Warfighting*. He follows those tenets to a T. It is all about intent and guidance. Everything that can possibly be done by direct communications with commanders should be done that way – through his intent and guidance. Opportunities are fleeting and you have to make sure that commanders are in a position not to have to second-guess their decisions [i.e., to require direction from above].[14]

Indeed, Mattis consciously understood himself to be implementing the precepts of mission command on the March Up. He consciously sought to devolve decision-making to his subordinates, authorizing them to

---

[12] US Marine Corps Staff, *Warfighting* (United States: Renaissance Classics, 2012), 50.
[13] Ibid., 50.
[14] OF-4, Lieutenant-Colonel Clarke Lethin, Deputy and then Assistant Chief of Staff Operations, G3, interviewee 125, personal interview, 19 July 2016.

exercise genuine command initiative. In order to facilitate this distribution of authority, Mattis has always emphasized the importance of a definitive mission statement, the 'Commander's Intent', which united subordinate commanders around Mattis: 'Commander's Intent is straight out of Marine Corps doctrine, as written by Al Gray, 10 years ago. It demands a higher level of discipline'.[15]

On the basis of this evidence, there was an apparent contradiction in Mattis's method of command, then. On the one hand, both he and his subordinates asserted his unique authority. Yet, on the other, they also stressed the way in which Mattis systematically distributed decision-making responsibility to his subordinates through mission command. His juniors were actively licensed and encouraged to make decisions independently. In order to resolve this apparent contradiction between the centralization and decentralization of decision-making authority, a closer analysis of Mattis's technique is plainly required. Only such an analysis will show how Mattis actually commanded the 1st Marine Division. This chapter intends to demonstrate that, in fact, the paradox of command articulated here can be resolved once the distinctions between the executive functions are recognized. While Mattis utterly monopolized the responsibility to define the mission, he was punctilious in his distribution of management authority and the command of specific tasks. Mattis positioned him at the very centre of the mission precisely so that he could distribute decision-making authority to his subordinates in the sphere of mission management. This adaptation is very significant in understanding and refining a concept of collective command. At this point, and despite his undoubted virtuosity as a commander and the force of his personality, the deeply collaborative and, indeed, collective character of Mattis's command method can begin to be appreciated. In stark contrast to most twentieth-century commanders, Mattis did not supervise his subordinates directly. Nor did he run a laissez-faire system which allowed them freedom to make local decisions as they saw fit. On the contrary, he designed an integrated command architecture which aligned decisions across the echelons, each one united around his intent.

[15] General James Mattis, interviewed by Dr Gary Solis, 18 June 2007, interview 0052, Transcript, United States Marine Corps History Programme, Marine Corps History and Museum Division, Quantico, VA, 14.

Mattis's Intent

Mission command carries with it obvious risks; if they are not coordinated, the de-centralized, local decisions of subordinate commanders might undermine an operation. Subordinate units might pursue incompatible, contradictory actions. In order to mitigate against this risk, the principle of the 'Commander's Intent' became of paramount importance: 'subordinate commanders must make decisions on their own initiative based on their understanding of their senior's intent';[16] 'We achieve this harmonious initiative in large part through the use of the commander's *intent*, a device designed to help subordinates understand the larger context of their actions'. Because subordinates understand their Commander's Intent, their decision-making will be aligned with organizational goals rather than undermining them. The Commander's Intent is absolutely vital to mission command, articulating local mission-management with overarching mission definition; local decisions represent the commander's authority.

In his description of the practice of mission command, Mattis continually emphasized the importance of his intent to the March Up: 'The Intent has to be written so that it doesn't constantly change'.[17] If not the supreme function, then one of the most important functions of command is the act of mission definition. It was argued in Chapter 4 that mission definition on conventional operations in the twentieth century was relatively simple; operations were a problem of scale. Divisional commanders were purely tactical commanders located in a strict military hierarchy, answering to corps and army commanders above them. They were given a mission. The fronts on which they operated were very small and the tactical problems linear. Throughout the twentieth century divisional commanders certainly enjoyed some freedom to negotiate and refine their mission with their corps commander. Yet, their latitude for action was limited. Consequently, the task of mission definition, while important, required only a focused effort; they had, in many cases, already been handed a definite mission. The divisional commanders' role was to ensure its optimal execution;

---

[16] US Marine Corps Staff, *Warfighting*, 50.
[17] General James Mattis, interviewed by Dr Gary Solis, 18 June 2007, interview 0052, Transcript, United States Marine Corps History Programme, Marine Corps History and Museum Division, Quantico, VA, 14, 29.

they concentrated on the question of mission management and also crucially, as Chapter 7 demonstrated, leadership.

Mattis confronted a quite different situation in Iraq. There, the operational problem was far more complex and ambitious and Mattis was given far greater latitude by the chain of command in defining his mission. The uncertainty surrounding the invasion of Iraq has been fully documented elsewhere and there is no need to rehearse the disputes between different factions within the Pentagon about force numbers and other issues.[18] However, even at the divisional level, these strategic debates became relevant because 1st Marine Division was never provided with a clear mission for Operation Iraqi Freedom from US Central Command. The US Army's 3rd Infantry Division were designated as the main effort of the advance and they were tasked to seize Baghdad. It was never clarified whether 1st Marine Division, advancing on a subordinate axis to the east, was to reach Baghdad as well. The formation received orders which defined a mission only up to An Nasiriyah: 'We were only told we were going part-way. We were not told our full mission [by CENTCOM]. It was ludicrous. We had to be prepared to go beyond Baghdad. But in the CENTCOM plan we were only ordered to cross the Euphrates'.[19] Consequently, Mattis had to design a campaign which involved an advance of over 300 miles through a number of major cities, with several possible route choices, almost from scratch. In the absence of adequate direction from CENTCOM, the requirement for mission definition and its parameters were substantial.

Consequently, Mattis decided early on that 1st Marine Division would advance all the way to Baghdad and participate in its seizure. From the very start, he planned the mission as a 300-mile advance. It was a major decision. From this interpretation of his mission, Mattis drew out a number of significant deductions on the basis of which 1st Marine Division designed its entire campaign. First, Mattis identified a clear objective: 'Everything we do must be focused on the destruction of the Iraqi Army'.[20] In particular, 1st Marine Division prioritized the Republic Guards units south of Baghdad which, it was presumed,

---

[18] Michael Gordon and Bernard Trainor, *Cobra II* (London: Vintage, 2007).

[19] General James Mattis, interviewee 113, personal interview, 4 June 2016.

[20] Michael Valenti, *The Mattis Way of War: an Examination of Operational Art in Task Force 58 and 1st Marine Division* (Fort Leavenworth, KS: US Army Command and General Staff College Press, 2014), 38.

would block their advance. In order to advance to Baghdad, Mattis accepted significant levels of exposure on each of his flanks and also presumed a heavy dependence on air power: 'My right flank was open. I put Recon Marines there to screen that flank. We also became the most aviation-centric Marine division in history. That was my decision. No one said to leave a 170-kilometre flank open. However, I knew if I had enough reconnaissance forces there, they [the Iraqi generals] would not do it. I'd fought them before'.[21]

Mattis was certainly advantaged by the Iraqi generals he faced but, even with a significant risk mitigated, the mission of assaulting all the way to Baghdad was clearly a very serious enterprise. Consequently, Mattis has to identify a central focus for the division: 'We knew that the centre of gravity was speed'. He repeated this point in orders: 'The division scheme of manoeuvre – speed equals success'.[22] When asked why he selected speed as his centre of gravity he replied: 'If you don't get the big waves right, you are in difficulty. You have to find something about the enemy which you concentrate on'. For Mattis, his analysis of the enemy recommended that speed was his centre of gravity for two central reasons. First, 1st Marine Division as an amphibious force simply could not sustain a long fight; the advance was unprecedented in US Marine history. If the attack were to be successful, it had to be executed quickly, before the division ran out of supplies. To this end, Mattis introduced a number of important innovations to save on weight, fuel and space: 'I was concerned about the culminating point. I got logistics to push off the culminating point by introducing gypsy racks, turning off vehicles [when they were stationary to save fuel], making it a court-martial offense to throw away a half-eaten MRE [Meals Ready to Eat, standard US military rations]'.[23] In addition, no one was allowed cot beds, saving eight medium-lift vehicles. The division accepted the exposure of its lines of communication and expected Marines in support forces to be prepared to defend themselves as well as combat troops. The division also reduced its artillery so that it did not have to transport so many shells and relied, rather, on aviation and air, which constituted no logistics burden on the division itself. Speed

---

[21] General James Mattis, interviewee 113, personal interview, 4 June 2016.
[22] Valenti, *The Mattis Way of War*, 46.
[23] General James Mattis, interviewee 113, personal interview, 4 June 2016.

would also reduce the risk to its lines of communications and flanks because the Iraqi Army would be defeated before it could exploit these vulnerabilities.

However, there was a second reason why Mattis prioritized speed and here he moved from merely tactical command to an operational or even strategic level: 'We had to get there quickly or the enemy would adapt and there would be demonstrations. I had too few troops like Xenophon when he tried to establish civilization there. If we did not take control immediately, the country might rise up'.[24] By contrast, if the invasion were slow, there would be potentially severe political and informational repercussions: 'Saddam would portray us as a Christian crusade. So it had to be done quickly and finally'.[25] Indeed, the political difficulties were not just within Iraq or the Arab world but in the West as well: 'We knew the centre of gravity was speed because the political world might unite against us. We had to get it done quickly so that the political opposition did not short-change us, though on the strategic level, we did not actually know what the US wanted'.[26] At this point, the demands of mission definition were of a different order to the twentieth-century divisional commander, discussed in Chapters 4, 5 and 7. Operating at apparently the same tactical level, Mattis had to define a mission with genuinely political and strategic considerations in mind. He had to develop a plan which did not simply maximize the combat power of his formation but one that was sensitive to the Iraqi, regional and indeed global political context.[27] Clearly, in terms of mission definition and the setting of intent, Mattis retained exclusive authority. Indeed, his responsibility for mission definition and its scope had increased considerably in comparison with his predecessors in the twentieth century.

[24] Ibid.
[25] Ibid.
[26] Ibid.
[27] In contrast to Mattis, in Korea, Major General O.P. Smith was given a mission of advancing to the Yalu by General Almond, X Corps commander. Smith nominally followed this mission but in fact slowed the advance of 1st Marine Division so that he could concentrate his forces around the Chosin Reservoir in anticipation of a Chinese counter-attack. It was an important amendment but not the constitutive act of mission definition performed by Mattis; Lynn Montross and Nicholas Canzona, *The Chosin Reservoir Campaign, Volume III: US Marine Operations 1950–1953* (Washington, DC: HQ United States Marine Corps, 1957), 133–4.

Managing the March up

During the March Up, Mattis proved that in the twenty-first century the commander is more important than ever. Even on a warfighting operation, Mattis was in a privileged position in establishing the mission for his formation, as Nick Carter was in Kandahar; he enjoyed a latitude – or a responsibility – which twentieth-century divisional commanders never exercised. Nevertheless, the individual responsibility of the divisional commander for mission definition was not necessarily incompatible with a distribution of decision-making. The Commander's Intent was manifestly integral to Mattis's command of 1st Marine Division. Mattis has to impress his intent upon his subordinates and ensure that they fully understood and were committed to it. Moreover, 1st Marine Division's attack involved a far more ambitious operation than those which were typical in the twentieth century. The Division planned an advance of unprecedented range which required close integration of heterogeneous air power, aviation, surveillance assets and Special Forces. The operation required the synchronization of a multiplicity of simultaneous decisions at a number of potentially critical points. In order to implement Mattis's intent, there were prodigious issues of coordination, management and supervision. Realistically, even a commander as talented as Mattis could not administer all of this work; it would have exceeded his capacities as a commander and a decision-maker. Here subordinate commanders – and Mattis's relationship to them – began to play a critical role.

It has been noted that Mattis tried to implement the principles of Marine doctrine articulated in *Warfighting*. In addition to the intent, *Warfighting* also emphasized the importance of the relationship between the commander and subordinates to mission command:

> First, we should establish long-term working relationships
> to develop the necessary familiarity and trust. Second, key
> people – 'actuals' – should talk directly to one another when
> possible, rather than through communicators or messengers.
> Third, we should communicate orally when possible, because we
> communicate also in how we talk – our inflections and tone of
> voice. Fourth, we should communicate in person when possible
> because we communicate also through gestures and bearing.[28]

---

[28] US Marine Corps Staff, *Warfighting*, 51.

Somewhat ironically, the decentralized decision-making of mission command in the twenty-first century required not a laissez-faire system in which subordinates were given licence to make tactical decisions without consulting their superior. Rather, it involved the closest integration of commanders across echelons. The interactions between commanders became more frequent and intense, their relations deeper and thicker. Subordinate commanders could know what their superiors intended only if they truly understood them, while superiors trusted their subordinates to make independent decisions only if they truly appreciated their situation; dense bonds between them were essential.

Exemplifying the principles of *Warfighting*, Mattis sought to create a close federation of subordinate commanders in the 1st Marine Division. They were thoroughly committed to his intent and his definition of the mission but expected to manage their missions within specific parameters. Consequently, Mattis emphasized the importance of communication and interaction with them in order that they could clarify their mission collaboratively. Mattis described his command system distinctively: 'It is not so much command and control but command and feedback in the Marines. It is not based on technology. It is a similar system as in Nelson's navy'.[29] He elaborated: 'I'm sure that Wellington did not command directly. If my intent is not clear to the deck plates, then that is a problem. With command and feedback, mistakes will be brought home. Command is always distributed to the correct level. Look at Jutland or Trafalgar. You always share command responsibility'.[30] It might be assumed that communication between commanders – feedback – is self-evident or automatic. In fact, genuinely open communications required a great deal of effort and training. Mattis, in effect, had to create a command team around himself, whose members were thoroughly at ease with their superior. The way Mattis constructed this community was both fascinating and also immediately pertinent to the question of collective command in the twenty-first century.

Before deploying to Iraq on 2 August 2002, Mattis issued his 'Commanding General's Staff Guidance' both to his regimental and battalion commanders and also to his divisional principal and special staff; it consists of a series of bullet points, written out in truncated

---

[29] General James Mattis, interviewee 113, personal interview, 4 June 2016.
[30] Ibid.

note form. The guidance was also communicated orally in a series of visits to his units; indeed, the guidance constituted his notes for these speeches. It is a deeply interesting document which provides a privileged insight into Mattis's command technique and especially his application of mission command. One of the most striking and significant themes is the special status that he accorded to commanders in 1st Marine Division; it shows how he created a feedback system. He fostered a solidarity between commanders across the ranks, linking 'actuals' at each echelon together. The commanders formed a golden thread throughout.

The Guidance includes a striking, even radical statement: 'All of us are MAGTF [Marine Air Ground Task Force] leaders'.[31] This is a remarkable claim. The armed forces operate on the basis of a strict rank hierarchy which defers absolutely to superiors. In a division, divisional commanders are supreme and, precisely because they have responsibility for the formation, they are acknowledged to be completely different from everyone else. Yet, here, Mattis consciously highlighted not his distinction but what he and all his subordinate commanders shared. Commanders in 1st Marine Division down to company and even platoon level might have a different rank, they might all be subordinate to Mattis, but every single one of them bore the same responsibility of command; at their echelon, they had decision-making responsibility. In order to facilitate feedback, commanders at each level were invested with a distinctive status. They were recognized as decision-makers. Crucially, this status as commanders accorded them a privileged access to Mattis himself; they could communicate with him in ways denied to the rest of the division. As one of his officers noted: 'Commander to commander was a special relationship'.[32]

In order to effect mission command and to create a genuine feedback system, Mattis sought to replace a traditional military hierarchy with an integrated command team. Indeed, Mattis explicitly employed sporting metaphors to communicate this unity. Rather than a general directing operations form above, he conceived of himself as a coach or perhaps a quarterback, calling plays from within the action: 'CG [commanding general] = head coach. Each of you

---

[31] General James Mattis, Commanding General's Staff Guidance, 14 August 2002, 1.
[32] OF-4, Anonymous, 1 Marine Division, interviewee 098, personal interview, 15 March 2016.

is a coach'.[33] Mattis was the undisputed commander of 1st Marine Division but, with his commanders, he sought to create a relationship in which he was a *primus inter pares* rather than an absolute superior.

Naturally, subordinate commanders in this team were not formally equal to Mattis. Mattis alone commanded 1st Marine Division and bore the command responsibility for the formation. However, Mattis's commanders constituted a decision-making elite within the division, separate and distinct from everyone else. In one of the most interesting notes in his Guidance, Mattis confessed that he had in fact been criticized for becoming too close to his subordinates: 'Accused of making subordinate commanders my equal – that is good – I stand guilty! I don't need to call the plays so long as the plays will gain my Endstate/Intent. I don't want subordinates on a string like puppets, but I expect them to energetically carry out my intent'.[34] The cohesiveness of the division relied on the alignment of decision-making at every level. Such coordination was possible only if all commanders were completely unified as an executive body.

It should be noted that Mattis's concept of the command relationship far exceeded a traditional concept of mere delegation. Mission command has been practised periodically in the nineteenth and twentieth centuries, especially by the German Army; von Moltke, for instance, had famously used such a system during the Franco-Prussian War. However, at that point, the system had involved a loosely coupled, liberal system of devolution. In the light of poor communications, subordinate commanders made tactical decisions autonomously.[35] During the Gulf War, Rupert Smith distributed decision-making to brigade commanders empowered within his operational framework, in a way which certainly presaged Mattis. However, his system was relatively loosely coupled, with brigade groupings operating autonomously, as Smith coordinated the deep and close battles; although, in fact, after the first day of the advance, Smith was forced to concentrate on the contact battle. Mattis's method did not involve a laissez-faire system in which junior commanders were free to make instinctive decisions more or less independently of their superiors if the situation required.

---

[33] General James Mattis, Commanding General's Staff Guidance, 14 August 2002, 2.

[34] General James Mattis, Commanding General's Staff Guidance, 14 August 2002, 4.

[35] Eitan Shamir, *Transforming Command: the pursuit of mission command in the U.S., British and Israeli Armies* (Stanford, CA: Stanford University Press, 2011).

On the contrary, in 1st Marine Division, subordinate decision-making depended on the integration of command echelons. Close orchestration was necessary. For instance, Mattis surprisingly demanded that his commanders display 'love' for and earn the 'love' of their own subordinates and their Marines; 'Reflect my personality in your own way, humanizing operations, winning trust and affection'.[36] In the armed forces, discipline has been typically enforced by discipline and mistakes have been punished by reprimand and sanctions. Mattis recommended another approach: 'If your unit is screwing up – love 'em more'. Mattis's unconventional, even archaic, appeal to love was intended at one level to generate close cohesion within 1st Marine Division, all of whose members were uniquely committed to each other. Subordinates who were merely fearful of their superiors would not feel confident enough to make independent decisions: 'Hug 'em a little, liberating them to maximum degree so they can move freely and with maximum support against the enemy'.[37]

Yet, 'love' was also an important facilitator of Mattis's concept of mission command. It became a means of integrating his commanders and establishing trusting communication – feedback – with them. While Mattis was ostensibly telling his commanders to love their Marines, he was also performatively demonstrating his own 'love' for his subordinate commanders; he was displaying precisely the affection and, therefore, fostering the trust, which was critical to delegation. He was effectively telling his commanders that he loved them. As long as they 'screwed up' trying to fulfil Mattis's intent, they would not be subjected to reprimand. On the contrary, they would be embraced even closer until their mistakes were rectified. In particular, Mattis's profession of love united his subordinates as partners in an elect, of which Mattis was the captain and play-maker. In this way, Mattis reformed a chain of command into a command ensemble. He created an intense and dense collective of commanders across the division, from his own level down through his Regimental Combat Team commanders, to his battalion and company commanders. In contrast to a traditional military hierarchy, Mattis constructed a command team, united by his intent, around himself. As result, his subordinates were sensitive to the resonances emanating from him, while he was also attuned to them.

[36] General James Mattis, Commanding General's Staff Guidance, 14 August 2002, 3.
[37] Ibid., 8.

Mattis committed his subordinates to his intent by close and continual personal contact. He conceived his relationship to them and their relationship to their subordinates at a form of mentoring. Yet, it would be wrong to think that Mattis united decision-making merely by enjoining 'love' between commander. His technique of command was far more rigorous and professional. At the same time, he invested significant effort in teaching his subordinates how and when to make a decision autonomously and when to seek guidance from him:[38] 'There are three bundles of information which a commander has to handle. Firstly, housekeeping: how many precision guided munitions or how much fuel do you have and need? Secondly, decision-making information left or right. Finally, alarms. You are constantly making housekeeping decision. But the commander is the sentinel, watching his units from being caught out'.[39] Accordingly, Mattis's educated his officers to recognize the difference between a limited risk and a gamble. While they were allowed to take reasonable risks (in line with his intent), they had to recognize a course of action which constituted a gamble and might put the entire division in danger. Such a decision had to be referred to him. He gave an example of this distinction in practice:

> One night a private in the army at the Command Port was observing a feed on a monitor from a JSTAR. We were trying to decide which route to take from An Nasariyah to Al Kut. The division was toe-to-tail at that point. He noted an unfinished road and was watching a local Iraqi riding along it on a motorbike. I asked how fast he was going. He was averaging 45 kilometres an hour. On the basis of this information I made an immediate decision: 'Gentleman, shift 1500 marines from Al Kut road to this unfinished road'. However, this decision rose to the level of a gamble. When you take a risk you have to know the difference between a risk and a gamble. A corporate-level decision comes to me unless there is a disaster going on. No gambles by my subordinate commanders.[40]

By aligning his subordinates to his intent and training them about decision-making, Mattis created a command federation intimately

[38] Valenti, *The Mattis Way of War*, 67.
[39] OF-4, Lieutenant-Colonel Clarke Lethin, Deputy and then Assistant Chief of Staff Operations, G3, interviewee 125, personal interview, 19 July 2016.
[40] General James Mattis, interviewee 113, personal interview, 4 June 2016.

bound together by mutual trust. By creating a decision-making team, Mattis had effectively created proxies who enacted his will, even when he was not present.

There was another side to this community, however. Once inducted into Mattis's command fraternity, Mattis's subordinates had demonstrated their professional and personal commitment to the plan and to Mattis himself. They were morally obliged to make the anticipated command decisions on the operation, no matter how difficult that might be. They had to follow his intent. Indeed, Mattis warned his subordinates: 'Don't screw with higher Commander's Intent, missions, tasks'.[41] This was not an idle threat. It was extremely noticeable that Colonel Joe Dowdy, commander of Regimental Combat Team-1, was deemed to have failed to follow this intent. Dowdy's Regimental Combat Team had been slow and overcautious from the start of the operation and became increasingly indecisive as it approached Al Kut.[42] Crucially, understandably worried about casualties, Dowdy failed to prioritize speed – the central element of Mattis's entire operation. He failed to fulfil Mattis's intent. Consequently, he was recalled to Mattis's command post and personally relieved of his command on 4 April by Mattis himself. It was a sad episode. Once the commanders had committed themselves to Mattis's intent, they were expected and obliged to make decisions which were consistent with it. For all his qualities, Dowdy failed to fulfil his contractual obligations as a member of the command collective; he had to be relieved, therefore. By creating a dense command collective, Mattis was able to inculcate his intent in his subordinates, distributing decision-making authority while at the same time ensuring command unity.

Mattis's intent was directed primarily at his subordinates with a view to creating a close-knit command team. At this point, it is possible to begin to overcome the apparent paradox of command centralization and decentralization. Mattis certainly monopolized the responsibility for setting the mission and establishing his intent. However, in order to manage the operation, Mattis distributed decision-making

---

[41] Commanding General's Staff Guidance, 14 August 2002, 4.

[42] OF-4, G3 Plans, interviewee 100, personal interview, 22 March 2016. Joe Dowdy has himself disputed his performance. He has claimed that he received conflicting orders around Al Kut as a result of which he was reluctant to enter the city: see Christopher Cooper, 'How a marine lost his command in the race to Baghdad', *The New Yorker*, 5 April 2004. www.wsj.com/articles/SB10811198028 5073875.

authority to subordinates. In short, he sought to implement a system of mission command, united around his intent but simultaneously devolved in execution. In order to achieve this simultaneous centralization of mission and decentralization of management, he invested in his relationships with his subordinates. He explained his intent carefully to his subordinates, trained them to make decisions in line with it, ensuring them of his professional trust – his 'love' – for them. In this way, he ensured both that he remained as the paramount leader within the Division but also that executive authority was also coherently distributed throughout the formation. He had, in effect, created a tightly integrated command team.

The Talking Jims

So far, the discussion has focused only on Mattis's subordinates. There was, however, another important member of his command group: Mattis's peer, Major-General James Amos, commander of 3 Marine Air Wing. James Mattis has repeatedly stated that 1st Marine Division was 'the most air-centric division in the history of warfare'. 101st Air Assault had more helicopters than 1st Marine Division but it did not enjoy anything like the fixed-wing support. Indeed, it is incorrect to conceive of 1st Marine Division as comprising only the ground units, which were formally in its order of battle; namely Regimental Combat Teams 1, 5 and 7, 11th Marine Artillery Regiment and so on. 1st Marine Division effectively also consisted of 3 Marine Air Wing as part of its organic assets. Mattis and the rest of the division were explicit that 1st Marine Division simply could not have conducted its advance on Baghdad without 3 Marine Air Wing's constant and close support. 1st Marine Division's ground units were reliant on close air support throughout the mission, especially since they had to dispense with some of their artillery support on the March Up. Moreover, as mentioned before, the Air Wing reduced the Division's logistic burden so that they could move more quickly. This was deeply significant because it shows that even in the formulation of the mission itself, officially Mattis's sole responsibility, he, in fact, conferred with James Amos. Like Carter in Kandahar, Mattis's mission was not a pristine individual production but a collaborative effort, developed jointly with Amos. In the end, it is impossible to understand and explain 1st Marine

Division's operations without considering 3 Marine Air Wing as an integral part of the formation and Mattis's command.

1st Marine Division was not so much a conventional land formation but an integrated air-ground task force, then. This peculiar organizational arrangement demanded a special command construct. Rather than two separate land and air commanders, each under the authority of a corps commander at the level of the Marine Expeditionary Force, the joint air-land formation which the 1st Marine Division and 3 Marine Air Wing had become was commanded collaboratively by two generals of equal rank, Amos and Mattis. Officially, Mattis was the primary commander whom Amos had to assist; in military lexicon, Mattis was the 'supported' commander while Amos was the 'supporting' commander. However, their partnership was much closer than this. Amos and Mattis were longstanding friends who had been promoted to Brigadier General together.[43] Both had a huge personal and professional regard for the other and, having been trained as a Marine from the Basic School, Amos understood that the primary mission of all Marine air forces was to support the ground troops in close combat: 'I focus on Marines. I take care of them; they take care of me. I set the conditions so they can succeed. I love the Marines and there is nothing I would not do for them'.[44] Mattis and Amos shared, then, a close personal and professional bond. As a result, they were completely aligned as commanders on the operation: 'There was never one time that he and I were out of accord with one another, out of sync'.[45] The collaboration between them in terms of mission definition has been noted. There were many practical demonstrations of this close cooperation in the management of the mission too. For instance, 1st Marine Division prepared a series of landing strips and forward air refuelling points for the Air Wing as they advanced up to Baghdad. At one point, the Division cut down the lamp-posts on a highway so that 3 Marine Air Wing's planes could land on the carriageway.

In order to generate this synergy between 1st Marine Division and 3 Marine Air Wing, Amos and Mattis engaged in constant discussions with each other. On one occasion Amos flew up to visit

---

[43] General James Mattis, interviewee 113, personal interview, 4 June 2016.

[44] General James Amos, 3 Marine Air Wing, recorded interview, accession number 2003-07-26-0063, United States Marine Corps History Programme, Marine Corps History and Museum Division, Quantico, VA, 17 March 2003.

[45] Ibid.

Mattis in order to assess whether the selected highway could be used as a landing strip. Most notably, one marine colonel who had served in the Gulf War twelve years before noted the deepening of the relationship between Mattis, as ground commander, and Amos, as air commander, and the increase in communications between them:

> There was twice daily ... VTC [video-teleconference], They also talked on the phone a lot. That really struck me. Compared to Desert Storm ... they talked far more than their predecessors ... [they] often talked late [into the night] ... about ... the latest developments and what kind of air support the Division would need the next day ... they were called the 'Talking Jims' by their staff.[46]

In order to manage the operation, Mattis and Amos relied on each other. Mattis may well have been the priority in this relationship but in order to enjoy the air support which he did, he acknowledged 3 Marine Air Wing's requirements. Mattis's decision-making could not be said to be genuinely autonomous, therefore. At every point, he had to consider the position of his peer, Jim Amos, negotiating closely with him. In the end, it is difficult, even impossible, to define precisely where the authority of Mattis ended and that of Amos started. While Mattis was the designated and sole Commanding General, he actually shared command of 1st Marine Division and 3 Marine Air Wing with Jim Amos; Amos was his joint commander of this dual formation.

The distinctiveness of the Mattis-Amos partnership can be most clearly demonstrated by historical comparison and, conveniently, there is an obvious and almost direct one available: the Chosin Campaign in Korea in November and December 1950. For instance, during this campaign, the 1st Marine Division, commanded by O.P. Smith, had been closely supported by 1 Marine Air Wing, commanded by Field Harris. Relations between the men were good, not least perhaps because Harris' son was an officer in the division. After the campaign, O.P. Smith wrote to Field Harris thanking him for his support, to which Harris replied confirming there was 'a bond of understanding'

---

[46] Nick Reynolds, *Basrah, Baghdad and Beyond* (Annapolis, MD: Naval Institute Press, 2005), 96.

between them.[47] However, communications between them were very limited. Smith met Harris by chance as they advanced up to the Chosin Reservoir; they then met at Hugaru-ri to discuss the completion of a runway there. Thereafter, Smith and Harris, who was based in Hungnam, communicated by radio. The intense intercommunication which characterized the relations between Mattis and Amos simply did not occur. This was primarily a function of the different operational circumstances in Korea and how the Marines organized air support at that time. In Korea, there was no intimate, multi-layered coordination then; air and land forces were not genuinely integrated. Rather, a five-mile perimeter was drawn around the road up to Chosin; inside this area, 1st Marine Division used their artillery, while the entire battlespace outside this corridor was owned by Harris's Marine Air Wing. Forward Air Controllers attached to 1 Marine Division called in air strikes to that area, cuing in the Air Wing's squadrons which were on station in daylight.[48] Consequently, although the Marine Air Wing was in close support of 1st Marine Division, the air-ground integration which was required in Iraq, because of the complex airspace management, was simply not necessary; air and artillery had their own pre-designated sectors.

Air and land power was coordinated in 1950, not integrated. Consequently, the command arrangements were quite different, then. While Smith commanded 1st Marine Division, and Field Harris his Air Wing, Mattis and Amos commanded as a partnership. There were many decisions which they had to make which were independent of each other, relating exclusively to their own formations. Yet, many decisions about the deployment of ground forces implied, and in fact presumed, the availability of air power. Consequently, the operation required the closest cooperation between them. At the same time as Mattis formed an integrated command team with his subordinates, he formed a close partnership with his peer, James Amos. Both adaptations represented innovative solutions to the complexities of warfighting in the twenty-first century. They allowed Mattis to manage a mission of unprecedented complexity.

[47] Major-General Oliver P. Smith, Oral History Transcript, US Marine Corps History Programme, Marine Corps History and Museum Division, 11–12 June 1969 byBenis M. Frank of the Historical Division, at General Smith's home in Los Altos, CA, 295.
[48] Ibid., 283.

Roc Drills

Mattis invested heavily in building relationships with his subordinate and peer commanders. This involved extensive discussions about the operation. However, in order to ensure that decision-making was integrated on the operation, Mattis employed more formal military techniques to ensure that his intent could be enacted. He drew on existing command techniques. Before the operation began, 1st Marine Division conducted a series of Rehearsal of Concept (ROC) drills, initially in the United States at Camp Pendleton and then in the desert in Kuwait in January and February 2003. These drills took place on scale models of Iraq on which 1st Marine Division's manoeuvres were rehearsed. Of course, Mattis was in no way unique in using tactical models or ROC drills to prepare his troops for battle. At both Messines and El Alamein, Monash and Wimberley had employed models to communicate their plans to their divisions.

Nevertheless, Mattis's use of ROC drills was distinctive and worthy of significant attention, not least because these rehearsals were regarded as an essential factor to the performance of 1st Marine Division in Iraq: 'They were critically important. We had no previous experience of that in United States Marine Corps history of moving 22,000 men and 7000–8000 vehicles on a march like that. We'd never done it before. We were not familiar with it. We had to work out what it looked like. We had to image it'.[49] Mattis confirmed the point: 'The ROC drills were enormously valuable'.[50]

Consequently, in August 2002, when 1st Marine Division were first warned that they were to be deployed in the event of the planned invasion of Iraq, Mattis conceived the idea of conducting an initial ROC drill with the help of his aide Captain Cook and his G3 operations officer, Lieutenant-Colonel Clark Lethin. They decided to conduct a rehearsal on a scale model of Iraq, constructed in front of the 'White House', the Commander's Headquarters of 1st Marine Division at Camp Pendleton. It was not clear how this should be done, especially since Mattis wanted a full demonstration of how his formation could move, but eventually it was decided that every vehicle of the

---

[49] OF-4, Lieutenant-Colonel Clarke Lethin, Deputy and then Assistant Chief of Staff Operations, G3, interviewee 125, personal interview, 19 July 2016.
[50] General James Mattis, interviewee 113, personal interview, 4 June 2016.

division would be represented by a piece of Lego. It is not entirely clear where the idea came from and, initially, it seems to have been proposed as something of a joke. Having seen his children playing with Lego blocks, scattered 'on the floor of his house', Clarke Lethin suggested: 'Why don't we buy some cheap blocks?' Mattis agreed and Clarke was tasked to procure the requisite quantity: 'I bought 8000 Lego blocks in division sizes. We drew a map in front of the CP and laid them out on the hard flat landing zone'.[51] Each of these Lego blocks was then marked with its call-sign and arranged in battle order on the model: 'We brought the whole divisional staff out and showed the staff what a division looked like in attack formation; it was 90 miles long'.[52]

The Lego Drill, conducted on 5 December 2002,[53] allowed 1st Marine Division Headquarters to see the physics of the problem and its challenges were made apparent to Mattis and his staff for the first time. They could actually plot the way the division would move, how many vehicles could realistically move along the selected highways, their speed and the location of choke points. As a physical enactment of the plan, the Lego Drill depicted the operation visually in time and space. Consequently, it eliminated presumptions about the division's movement. Mattis noted that: 'When we did it at Pendleton, we could see when three units were at one place. It was a wonderful way to see what to do'.[54]

The Lego Drill was not merely an important orienting exercise. On the basis of it, Mattis and his staff were able to draw definite deductions about those schemes of manoeuvre which might be possible and others which were impractical. Some ignored these findings. For instance, having formulated its plan for the invasion by January 2003, 1st Marine Division was told that an additional force, Task Force Tarawa, would be assigned to 1st Marine Division's area with a mission of securing its lines of communication around An Nasariyah. Task Force Tarawa was a brigade-sized force from 2nd Marine Division, commanded by Brigadier Richard Natonski; he would take over 1st Marine Division for the battle of Fallujah in July 2004. Mattis opposed the order on the basis of the Lego Drill: 'Adding Tarawa which was crossing in front of the divisional line of march and stopping in

---

[51] Ibid.
[52] Ibid.
[53] Michael Groen, *With the 1st Marine Division in Iraq 2003: no greater friend, no worse enemy* (Quantico, VA: History Division Marine Corps University, 2006), 111.
[54] General James Mattis, interviewee 113, personal interview, 4 June 2016.

the middle of it; it was going to conflict with RCT-1. It was going to create friction. We knew that was going to occur but we didn't know how much. We had covered that one though. When we saw Task Force Tarawa briefing their move to the MEF, I said: "You won't be able to do that. We are on the Main Effort and you are now on the same road at the same time"'.[55] Mattis was condemnatory:

> The ROC drills argued against Task Force Tarawa being inserted at An Nasariyah. It was a very bad decision; we knew that from the ROC drill. It was a passage of lines in a built-up area with only one bridge with Chemical Ali potentially threatening to strike. Then you are asking my guys to open the gap and you drive through. You don't know what that is like. This only looked good in staff work. It was a disaster of 2 MEB's making. It holds me up and I lose a Regimental Commander [Colonel Joe Dowdy] as a result.[56]

The Lego Drill allowed the division to enact Mattis' intent concretely. Yet, it did more than depict the operation. It anticipated the friction points in his concept of operations and the likely points at which decisions would have to be made. It was unfortunate that one of the obvious friction points was ignored by 1 MEF and Task Force Tarawa.

Once 1st Marine Division had deployed to Kuwait, they did two further ROC drills in the desert on 7 and 27 February 2003, constructing two 'Olympic swimming pool-size'[57] model pits in the sand with bulldozers – the first one 800 meters square, the second 1000 metres square. In these drills, Marines representing each of 1st Marine Division units were deployed onto the model, standing on their start positions and then physically moving through their scheme of man-oeuvre in turn. In order to distinguish the units from each other, each unit was given a distinctively coloured football jersey inscribed with the unit's call sign. The primary leadership of the division were present to observe this exercise as well as leadership from 3 Marine Air Wing, 1 UK Division, to which 1st Marine Division would hand over the south, 1 MEF and other supporting elements: 'It allowed pilots,

55 Ibid.
56 General James Mattis, interviewee 113, personal interview 4 June 2016.
57 OF-4, Lieutenant-Colonel Clarke Lethin, Deputy and then Assistant Chief of Staff Operations, G3, interviewee 125, personal interview, 19 July 2016.

logistics elements, higher and lower staff to see what the operation looked like'.[58] Indeed, Lethin recorded that the ROC drills had an evidenced impact on personnel during the operation: 'Pilots told me that when they were flying over it [the Division], they saw it, exactly the way they had seen it during the ROC drill. They could see which units were which'.[59]

The ROC drill familiarized the Division and its supporting forces with the Commander's Intent and generated a shared understanding of what the force as a whole and each element was trying to achieve at each moment. It graphically enacted the role which each unit had to perform and, therefore, facilitated the accomplishment of their mission; everyone was clear about what they had to do. For instance, as a result of the ROC drills and the close cooperation which developed between 1st Marine and 1 UK Division, 1st Marine Division handed over to the British formation seamlessly, even though this manoeuvre was complex: 'In the Opening Gambit, 1 Division were to take over Southern Iraq from us. That's why we worked closely with them. We had their forward CPs [command posts] and artillery in our units where their forces were going. Their command elements were in our forces. They understood what was happening so that it was a seamless turnover of the battlespace and so that units could carry one without pausing'.[60] At the most basic level, the ROC drill simply clarified roles so that each unit knew what it was supposed to do and what its neighbours were also supposed to be doing. In this, the ROC drills served a traditional function which Monash or Wimberley would have recognized.

Yet, the ROC drill had a more profound impact in terms of managing the mission. As a result of the ROC drill, 1st Marine Division was not only able to identify friction points but also, crucially, to anticipate possible 'decision points'. A decision point is a doctrinal term, which refers to a predictable moment on an operation where a commander will have to make a decision about how to proceed. Decision points are normally attached to decisive points in an operation and relate typically to the deployment of a force or a reserve. By anticipating alternative scenarios, the two jersey drills allowed 1st Marine Division to predict when a decision might have to

[58] Ibid.
[59] Ibid.
[60] Ibid.

be taken, therefore accelerating or even eliminating decision-making on the actual operation. The identification of decisive points was indispensable to the application of mission command because these points effectively presented subordinate commanders with pre-digested, anticipated decisions; they were already cued to the kinds of situations they would face, the sorts of decisions which they might have to make and the way that General Mattis and 1st Marine Division wanted the decisions to be made; 'Commanders knew the 2nd and 3rd order effects of their possible decision, based on the commander's intent and guidance'.[61] The ROC drills impressed the intent upon commanders, orienting them collectively to a precise pattern of action even when they were not co-present. This is what Mattis meant by 'discipline'. In order to facilitate accurate and coherent decision-making in line with the Commander's Intent, 1st Marine Division also deployed nominated staff officers to those decision points in Iraq: 'We gamed out where the friction points were likely to be. Myself and Colonel Kennedy performed that function of the division. We would be at the friction point; for instance, when the Division was splitting on its line of march. I was free to roam to a friction point when they needed someone there to assist'.[62]

1st Marine Division's ROC drills were specifically designed to align decision-making preemptively across the formation. The collective performances of the Lego and jersey drills facilitated a higher level of common understanding. Above all, these drills allowed each commander at every echelon in the Division to understand the whole operation and to see their own individual role in it. The drills integrated commanders. As a result, knowing what they were trying to achieve as a corporate body, commanders had already rehearsed many of the decisions which they thought they might have to take on during the operation. Crucially, the options from which commanders would have to decide as they made their decisions were already informed by the Commander's Intent. Whatever choice a commander made, it was already in line with Mattis's concept of the operation. In some circumstances, the ROC drills attenuated or even eliminated the need for genuine decisions, because what a commander should do had already been collectively discussed and decided in advance. Decisions

[61] Ibid.
[62] Ibid.

were regularly devolved to subordinates in the twentieth century, but there was little equivalent of this intensely rehearsed collaboration.

No one would deny that James Mattis was a powerful and effective commander. He played a critical role in defining the mission for 1st Marine Division. However, in order to manage this mission, Mattis's command cannot be explained entirely by reference to his individual agency. In order to integrate decision-making across divisional, brigade and battalion echelons, an elaborate series of collective rehearsals were necessary. The participants in these rehearsals were not golems, directed by Mattis's will, but active participants who helped Mattis identify friction points and decision points which were implicit within his plan. Through the course of these drills, staff officers and subordinate commanders were collectively and mutually able to develop solutions or anticipate likely options which commanders would face. At this point, Mattis's role as a commander became distinctive. He no longer directed from above. He became, rather, a conductor in the midst of his orchestra – or the quarterback on the pitch with his football team, as he described himself. 1st Marine Division's command and staff teams ensured that he and his intent were always the key reference point. His command then was collaborative and 1st Marine Division was effective because he was able to distribute decision-making authority in full knowledge that subordinate commanders would make decisions in line with his intentions. Through the process of ROC drills, Mattis sought to unify his commanders, sharing his authority with subordinates in his command network.

The Staff

For Mattis, commanders – at every level – were special and he invested his relationship with each one of them with significance. Through the ROC drills, he coached them intensely about how and when to make particular kinds of decision. This might imply that in 1st Marine Division, the headquarters staff were irrelevant to Mattis's command. Mattis was certainly always insistent about the requirement for a small staff:

> a smaller staff has more shared situational awareness. They are fast reacting. Decision makers are not emasculated by a

bureaucratic process. It's less procedurally driven. It's more based on situational awareness so it's more agile. It also has more of a human face on it rather than an amorphous mask that as you try to figure out who does what in it, it just becomes confusing. It's hard, it's fatiguing, but a smaller staff is much more nimble.[63]

Thus, when he commanded Task Force 58 in Afghanistan in 2002, Mattis reduced the staff of a brigade-sized force to only thirty-five officers, though, in fact, only eight to ten staff officers were ever in one location because the task force was spread around over the region.[64] It is also true that he prioritized his commanders over his staff. An officer who was a battalion commander in 1st Marine Division in Iraq and subsequently worked on Mattis's staff noted the difference; 'With the relationship commander to commander, you have responsibility. You are placed there for the commander. He gives you his will, personality, force – and trust. That was not his relationship with his staff. It is much more demanding to work for him as staff. It was a privilege to be both. But he had a different relationship with his staff'.[65] Specifically, Mattis impressed upon his staff their duty to his commanders. Their role was to support and assist commanders at every point; 'His guidance to us was to support commanders no matter what. He was harder on his staff than on commanders. It was their plans that needed to be executed. He rarely circumvented or countermanded commanders'.[66] Another staff officer confirmed the point: 'For Mattis, commanders were cardinals and the only person who could say no to a regimental commander was Mattis himself'.[67] Indeed, Mattis was absolutely explicit about the subordination of the staff. As his guidance noted: 'Harder on staff than on subordinate commanders'.[68]

---

[63] General James Mattis, Interview by Dr Gary Solis, 18 June 2007, interview 0052, Transcript, United States Marine Corps History Programme, Marine Corps History and Museum Division, Quantico, VA, 3–4.

[64] Lieutenant-Colonel Clarke Lethin, Deputy and then Assistant Chief of Staff Operations, G3, personal interview, 19 July 2019.

[65] OF-4, Anonymous, 1st Marine Division, interviewee 098, personal interview, 15 March 2016.

[66] OF-4, Lieutenant-Colonel Clarke Lethin, Deputy and then Assistant Chief of Staff Operations, G3, interviewee 125, personal interview, 19 July 2016.

[67] OF-4, G3 Plans, interviewee 100, personal interview, 22 March 2016.

[68] Commanding General's Staff Guidance, 14 August 2002, 4.

A Lieutenant-General, who played a very important role as an operations officer during the March Up, illustrated this command-staff hierarchy graphically. He recalled his first briefing with Mattis. This officer was an east-coast marine who had worked with 2nd Marine Division based in Camp Lejeune, rather than 1st Marine Division from Pendleton, California. His first briefing to Mattis did not go well and he ended up 'showing his ass'; he felt his 'head was on the block'. Indeed, afterward, Brigadier John Kelly, the Assistant Divisional Commander, noted wryly that the officer 'had one foot in the grave and the other on a banana peel'.[69] The episode showed that Mattis was typically more demanding and less tolerant of his staff than his commanders; it is very noticeable that he never advocated hugging or loving staff officers more. The staff formed a secondary echelon in 1st Marine Division, whose role was to service and support the commanders.

Yet, it would be seriously mistaken to think that because Mattis preferred a small staff, delineated their responsibilities carefully and subordinated them to commanders, the staff were not critical to his command method. They were; 1st Marine Division headquarters issued thirty-five fragmentary orders during the March Up and the staff were essential to his decision-making process. Mattis rejected proceduralism. However, it would be wrong to believe that he eschewed staff work. On the contrary, 'Mattis insisted on orders'; he was punctilious. For instance, during the March Up, Mattis issued formal orders to his staff, which were written up and disseminated through Blue-Force Tracker, the digital communications system.[70]

In order to create a small staff that was capable of operating at this speed, Mattis was extremely careful about whom he chose. Mattis was heavily influenced by Jim Collins' best-selling work on management, *Good to Great*, whose central claim was that outstanding companies share a common strategy. Before even deciding upon their core business, they hire the very best personnel; 'they get the right people on the bus'. Especially when selecting his staff, Mattis followed this injunction closely. He chose officers with a proven capability and with whom he had typically worked before: 'He selected people from the past – folk he had trust in. They were people I knew and I recommended some

[69] OF-4, G3 Plans, interviewee 100, personal interview, 22 March 2016.
[70] OF-4, Lieutenant-Colonel Clarke Lethin, Deputy and then Assistant Chief of Staff Operations, G3, interviewee 125, personal interview, 19 July 2016.

more'.[71] For instance, Lieutenant-Colonel Clarke Lethin, who proved to be one of the most effective and influential staff officers in 1st Marine Division, had served with Mattis as a principal staff officer on Task Force 58. The rank profile of his staff was also distinctive; it was low with a distinct lack of full colonels. In addition to Clarke Lethin, who would become his Assistant Chief of Staff G3 (operations) when Dowdy was removed, his G1 (personnel) and G4 (logistics) were both lieutenant-colonels. Mattis has claimed that this lack of full colonels was due to a general shortage in the Corps of colonels with the right specialism. Others have suggested that it may have been a deliberate policy: 'There were a lot of lieutenant-colonels on his staff. We were able to work. We were not colonels with all that entails. There were a lot of hungry folk on the staff.'[72] Whether accidental or not, the preponderance of lieutenant-colonels on the staff was beneficial to Mattis. As Lethin observes, lieutenant-colonels were more eager to please and perhaps more flexible than an already-promoted full colonel who, therefore, had the rank to question and oppose Mattis more. It was consequently easier to build a cohesive staff in 1st Marine Division.

The staff issued orders but it also played a critical role in enforcing Mattis's intent. As 1st Marine Division advanced northwards to Baghdad, the staff operated the main and forward command posts, which leap-frogged each other, alternatively taking command of the division. Mattis's staff was critical to this process, gathering information and coordinating movement. The Combined Operations Centre, the G3 cell, played a crucial role here. This cell was a networked situations room which consisted of a series of screens depicting the location of friendly and enemy units, around which staff officers from each branch were organized in a horseshoe. The centre became known as the 'killing U', consisting of a configuration of staff officers oriented to the situation map and Blue-Force Tracker. The 'killing U' and its staff played an essential role in the operation, cuing missions and strikes.

In Iraq, Mattis normally commanded from his jump command post of three vehicles, often accompanied by Lieutenant-Colonel Paul Kennedy, his G3 Plans. Typically, they would be located between the division's vanguard 3 Light Armoured Regiment under

---

[71] Ibid.
[72] OF-4, Lieutenant-Colonel Clarke Lethin, Deputy and then Assistant Chief of Staff Operations, G3, interviewee 125, personal interview, 19 July 2016.

Lieutenant-Colonel Clarity and the main body of the division to their rear. Mattis was deliberately close to the front throughout the operation: 'We were right behind LAR; there were no battalions in between'.[73] Mattis spent most of the advance a long way forward, therefore. However, although he quickly dismissed the utility of formal daily update briefs, he returned daily to his main headquarters; 'That was the way he functioned. He accepted that risk. He had to be out gathering information. And then he would come back to main and to forward and get briefed up and make a decision'.[74] 'He would use the staff to confirm and control things. He would give guidance to us.'[75]

However, Mattis's staff themselves were not confined to the command post coordinating operations from the Current Operations Centre. Selected staff officers were instructed to intervene directly into the management of the operation: 'General Mattis – any commander – needed a few disciples. He needed an inner circle. These disciples conveyed and had confidence in his intent. If there was any misunderstanding, we clarified his intent'.[76] Thus, staff officers like Clarke Lethin, Paul Kennedy and a few others circulated across the battlefield assessing the situation on the ground while their subordinates manned the headquarters. Mattis's staff disciples acted as a monitoring system ensuring that his intent was being followed. Indeed, following Montgomery's practice of having 'ghosts' or 'phantom' officers in 21st Army Group, who would report independently back to him, Mattis introduced the concept of the 'eyes officer'. The 'eyes officers' acted as informants for Mattis. 'The eyes officers were never a formal thing. There were also very few: his aide, the PAO [public affairs officer]. This was not part of their primary duties. They were folks that he would be out circulating with. For instance, Captain Cook [Mattis's aide] would circulate and pick up information'.[77] Clarke Lethin was another officer designated as an 'eyes officer'; indeed, he has been described as Mattis's 'hatchet man'[78]. Concerns about Dowdy's RCT-1 were raised and then confirmed by these staff officers.

---

[73] OF-4, G3 Plans, interviewee 100, personal interview, 22 March 2016.

[74] OF-4, Lieutenant-Colonel Clarke Lethin, Deputy and then Assistant Chief of Staff Operations, G3, interviewee 125, personal interview, 19 July 2016.

[75] Ibid.

[76] Ibid.

[77] Ibid.

[78] OF-4, G3 Plans, interviewee 100, personal interview, 22 March 2016. Lethin's call-sign, perhaps significantly, was 'Sheriff'.

It is now possible to summarize Mattis's command method and to resolve the paradox described at the beginning more fully. Mattis's command consisted of two interlocking circles, his commanders and his staff, each forming a densely bonded team; they operated as two closely articulated networks, one focusing on the close fight, the other overseeing the division as a whole. Mattis located himself between these echelons, animating both teams and constantly connecting the particular situation of his RCTs with the overall position of the Division. Clearly, as the statements underscore, Mattis commanded 1st Marine Division as a powerful and charismatic leader. He was critical in defining the mission. However, the management of this mission could not be directed exclusively by a single commander even of Mattis's talent or, as occurred in the twentieth century, a commander assisted by only a principle staff officer and a miniscule staff. The March Up was too ambitious and complex an operation to be managed in this way. Mattis developed an integrated staff to support his command team.[79]

The Mattis Way of War

The analysis of Carter's method of command in the previous chapter gained much of its force from contrasting his techniques with those of twentieth-century counter-insurgents Erskine, Massue and Ewell. Similarly, the distinction of Mattis's command style can also perhaps be best appreciated by comparing it with his predecessors, discussed in Chapter 5. There are, of course, evident continuities in divisional command across the two eras, especially in the era of manoeuvre warfare. Some of the basic structures and functions of a division have remained broadly constant when it comes to warfighting. It is vital to avoid exaggeration, arguing for rupture and revolution where there is a subtle but, nevertheless, decisive evolution of practice. For

---

[79] The comparison with 1st Marine Division in Korea and especially during the Chosin Reservoir campaign is instructive, not least because the campaigns involved long road moves. It is noticeable that at Chosin in 1950, Major-General O.P. Smith, the commander of 1st Marine Division, relied on one principal staff officer, his G3, Lieutenant-Colonel Alpha Bowser, and a severely reduced staff at Hugaru-ri. He monopolized decision-making supported by a small staff. His method of command was consistent with that of his contemporaries, like Montgomery, Monash, Rommel and Balck.

instance, Mattis's practice of command certainly had some affinity with Montgomery in France in 1940 when he commanded 3rd Infantry Division, and even more so with Rupert Smith in the Gulf in 1991. Montgomery alone defined the mission, preserving the sole right to give orders. At the same time, Montgomery prioritized a series of divisional drills and appointed commanders whom he could trust to enact his plans and to execute these drills, although he was careful to oversee those tasks which he regarded as critical to the operation. In short, although decision-making was limited to simpler and shorter manoeuvres, it might be suggested that Montgomery established a proto-command collective in 3rd Division during the Battle of France. He united his subordinates and staff around his plans and trained them extensively so that they could execute them. Under the influence of the new philosophy of manoeuvrism and mission command, Rupert Smith went yet further and implemented an initially devolved, yet integrated system which anticipated Mattis's method. Yet, of course, Smith had to assume much closer directive control as the campaign proceeded and he lost control of the deep battle.

Notwithstanding continuities with unusually capable commanders like Montgomery, Mattis, nevertheless, demonstrated a step-change from twentieth-century command. In contrast to his twentieth-century predecessors, Mattis commanded an integrated air-land division, consisting of 20,000 troops and 8000 vehicles, which made a complex, multiple-axis advance of 300 miles through and into major cities. At any point during the operation, 1st Marine Division's column extended over ninety miles on the ground, from reconnaissance forces in the vanguard to its logistic units at the tail, and with air support up to 20,000 feet in the air. Mattis had to coordinate air, aviation, unmanned aerial vehicles, artillery and mechanized units into his scheme of manoeuvre, while coordinating closely with 1 UK Division, 3rd Infantry Division and Special Operations Forces. In response to this situation, Mattis displayed three distinctive command elements: a comprehensive definition of his division's mission, an integrated command team to manage that mission, including both James Amos and his subordinate commanders, and a cohesive staff to facilitate, coordinate and oversee the operation.

This chapter began with a paradox. James Mattis and his subordinates asserted both that he utterly dominated throughout the March Up and that, at the same time, he rigorously distributed decision-making authority. James Mattis is one of the most charismatic and competent commanders of the recent era. There is no question that he dominated 1st Marine Division during the March Up. He was the reference point for this formation. Yet, there also is little doubt that he successfully devolved important decision-making duties to his subordinates, whom he empowered. The preceding analysis showed that the paradox was only apparent and can be resolved once the different functions of command were recognized. Mattis played a critical role in defining the mission and he reserved most important decisions for himself. However, on a mission of this ambition and complexity, it was impossible for Mattis to oversee its management entirely. In order to conduct this operation, he constructed a command team which directed the division at each level, uniting it around Mattis's intent. As a result of exhaustive preparation and training, commanders at each level were able to align their decisions, accelerating the tempo of the formation. At the same time, the staff monitored and supported commander. The Division was animated by commanders who constituted a neural network, myelinated by staff who informed, coordinated and confirmed decisions.

There is, therefore, an irony to James Mattis's command method. Mattis conceived himself in traditional and historical terms. He saw his command method as consistent with great commanders from the past such as Nelson, whose practices he sought to imitate on the basis of extensive study. It was certainly true that Mattis did not invent any new techniques of command; personnel selection, the intent and ROC drills have long been part of the military repertoire. Rather, like Monash, Mattis exploited the potential of existing methods and techniques. Yet, while learning from military history, Mattis's command method was, in fact, distinctive. Specifically, Mattis integrated his decision-makers into a tight and cohesive ensemble; commanders at each level were intimately attuned to Mattis and to each other. Decisions were practised repeatedly and closely tuned so that even improvisation would not disturb the overall harmony. As a result, decision-making in 1st Marine Division was simultaneously both dispersed and also aligned because commanders across the formation were so closely integrated. Mattis was a powerful commander precisely because he distributed his command authority so effectively.

The previous chapter discussed command on a recent counter-insurgency operation. This chapter has explored the question of command on a manoeuvre operation. In some ways, Mattis's methods were very different to Nick Carter's. Certainly, they confronted alternative problems; Carter had to adopt a pro-consular role, diplomatically enjoining the support of a politico-civil-military alliance, while Mattis had to mount a rapid and aggressive military attack. Mattis commanded a highly cohesive and exclusively Marine division, in contrast to Carter's heterogeneous stabilization force. Drawing on marine culture, Mattis was able to create a fraternity of commanders and staff officers in a way which was impossible for Carter. Yet, in the end, in the face of organizational complexity, both developed systems of command which might be seen as congruent. In particular, there were affinities in the way in which they fulfiled executive functions of mission definition and mission management. Carter and Mattis assumed sole responsibility for mission definition. They were uniquely positioned in a complex politico-military hierarchy and were both sensitive to the influence of key partners. Both exercised an unusual latitude in defining the mission of their respective forces, ascending from purely tactical to operational and even strategic considerations. In terms of mission management, they both developed sophisticated techniques of sharing command authority, devolving significant decision-making duties to designated subordinates. They authorized immediate subordinates to act as proxy decision-makers for them, having been carefully united around a common concept of the mission. Command authority was distributed in order to manage increasingly expansive and complex missions. In the end, both Carter and Mattis relied on the formation of a command team around them, to support and assist them. Stabilization and manoeuvre operations are distinct and, yet, these two examples suggest that a distinctively professionalized and collective practice now seems to be required to command either.

10 THE NEW HEADQUARTERS

The two previous chapters have examined command on stabilization and manoeuvre operations in Afghanistan and Iraq. In both cases, it has been suggested that in contrast to the twentieth century, Mattis and Carter adopted a more collaborative, professionalized method of command in which they relied on dense command teams which they took great efforts to construct. The two cases would seem to constitute minimally relevant evidence about the transformation of command in the twenty-first century. However, both examples are derived from the first decade of this century; Nick Carter left Kandahar in November 2010. Any serious account of the reformation of command has to consider the most recent adaptations which have occurred in this decade. Indeed, following the campaigns in Iraq and Afghanistan, Western armed forces have committed themselves to a series of reforms; they have developed considerably. Consequently, a sustainable account of command transformation must consider current developments to army structures and practices.

Since the withdrawal of major combat forces from Iraq and Afghanistan, Western powers remain involved in both these theatres with Special Operation Forces and with conventional mentors. They have also fought air campaigns in Libya, Iraq and Syria. 1st Infantry, 82nd Airborne and 101st Airborne Divisions have all provided a command and staff element in the US Headquarters in Baghdad to oversee the campaign against ISIS, coordinating airpower and administering mentoring teams. These are important missions. However, since 2014, Western divisions, as unified formations, have not been used. Rather, in all four major Western powers, army divisions have been trying to re-learn how to conduct conventional manoeuvre warfare after a decade or more of stabilization operations. These powers have been trying to redevelop their ability to conduct high-intensity, large-scale warfare. Chapter 2 suggested two historical counter-points, 1916 and 2016, which are mnemonically useful for understanding divisional command. By 1916, the modern division had emerged as a response to the special organizational problems of industrial warfare. A divisional head-quarters and command system was constructed to coordinate artillery and infantry, synchronizing fire and manoeuvre. The central function of a divisional headquarters today remains coordination. However, the twenty-first-century division faces new organizational challenges. The new divisional headquarters still orchestrates fire and movement but does so at greater ranges and with greater precisions than in the twentieth century. In addition, it also integrates a multiplicity of other activities and assets. The new divisional headquarters is, like its predecessor, a solution to an organizational problem, then. However, because the coordination problem has expanded, the headquarters too has assumed a quite different shape.

The rest of this book examines the implications of this reconstitution of the Western division for command today. Specifically, the following chapters try to delineate the precise character of contemporary command. In order to attain a level of evidential adequacy, the next three chapters will focus on the round of exercises and training which selected divisions in the UK, US, France and Germany have been undergoing as they try to reform themselves as warfighting formations. Chapter 2 discussed the current restoration of the Western division. The following analysis examines this renaissance in depth, as it has been enacted. In particular, the analysis will focus on the headquarters of these divisions, as the primary locale of command, and it will try to show how the evolution of staff structures and processes have transformed the practice of command. The aim eventually is to show the precise mechanics of collective command through an exploration of the lifeworld of the headquarters. However, before this more critical and analytical work can take place, it is once again necessary to describe the object of study: the new divisional headquarters.

This chapter will focus exclusively on the structure of the new divisional headquarters. It will examine the novel architecture of the divisional headquarters. It has to be admitted that the following two chapters are primarily descriptive. The actuality of command is only addressed obliquely in them. At this point, some patience is required on the part of the reader. However, it is simply impossible to understand some of the new micro-practices of command without a recognition of the context in which they take place. In order to understand the transformation of contemporary command, it is essential to understand how the headquarters and its staff have been re-organized. Only once this framework is established is it possible to go into the mechanics of command and decision-making itself. Some suspension of disbelief is required until Chapter 13, when the actual practice of command, mission definition, mission management and leadership, becomes once again the exclusive focus of analysis.

Operations in the Twenty-First Century

By 1916, Western armies had established the combined arms divisions as a means of prosecuting industrial warfare. Today, the major Western powers are reconstituting their divisions in order that they are fit to engage in high-intensity warfare of the twenty-first century. However, while many of the skills of the late Cold War are being re-learnt, the American, French, British and German division of the twenty-first century is not simply a reversion to the twentieth-century division. The major Western powers have the aspiration to fight intense engagements at scale but, even in a future war against a hostile state like Russia, the operating environment is likely to be quite different from the Cold War.

During the Cold War, NATO fielded a force of about one million soldiers, stationed along the inner German border in a nine-corps 'layer cake'. Even after the revision of Western doctrine in the 1980s, with the introduction of Air-Land Battle and Follow-On Forces Attack, NATO still conceived of any land warfare against the Soviet Union in lineal terms; it would have been a war of fronts. Today, Western forces have diminished to about one-third of their Cold War size and the mere reduction in force size has in and of itself had a very significant effect on Western forces and their military operations. As force densities have diminished, the geometry of the battlefield has changed.

The Iraq invasion showed this very clearly, especially when compared with the Gulf War of 1991. The Gulf War involved a conventional lineal assault across the Iraqi and Kuwaiti borders in order to drive out Iraqi forces positioned on the frontiers. In fact, it followed NATO doctrine closely, imitating how Western forces might have counter-attacked against a Soviet strike. During the 2003 invasion, US divisions no longer formed a contiguous front; there were simply not enough troops. 3rd Infantry Division and 1st Marine Division advanced on two widely separated axes, engaging enemy forces simultaneously along the line of advance across the depth of the battle space, from Basra in the south to Baghdad in the north. Typically, in the twentieth century, divisions defended or attacked a front of about ten miles. In Iraq, 3rd Infantry Division and 1st Marine Division were engaging the enemy across a depth of nearly 100 miles.

The extension of ground operations has itself generated a series of further coordination problems. Lines of communication have become radically extended, complicating logistics management and posing challenges for rear-area security. Precisely because ground forces are operating at greater distances and are, therefore, more vulnerable, increased support from air and maritime forces has been essential. Increased air-land integration has demanded enhanced coordination. The demand for closer air-land integration was particularly demonstrated by 1st Marine Division but it is a widespread phenomenon. Ground forces have been distributed only insofar as they remain under an envelope of air cover. Of course, air power has itself diversified to involve support, attack and medical helicopters, unmanned aerial vehicles of various types to provide intelligence and strike capability, ground attack aircraft (A-10s), gunships and fast jets. Ironically, as forces have reduced in size and, therefore, dispersed more on the battlefield, the complexity of commanding them has increased. Fewer troops have, somewhat ironically, increased command problems.

There are other equally profound changes. Many commentators have rightly observed that urban warfare has become increasingly likely, so much so that it has replaced open warfare as the dominant mode of fighting. Armies increasingly campaign in cities, not in the field. With the exception of the Kargil War of 1999 between India and Pakistan and the enduring stand-off on the Korean Peninsula, the last open warfare occurred in the Gulf War of 1991. By contrast, the litany of urban battles since 1990 indicate not a mere series of contingencies but a trend: Mogadishu (1993), Grozny (1994–5), Sarajevo (1994–5), An Najaf, Al Nassariyah and Baghdad (2003), Fallujah (2004 and 2014), Ramadi (2006), Kandahar (2009–10), Donetsk (2014), Aleppo

(2014–16), Sana'a (2014–17), Mosul (2016–18) and Raqqa (2017). Armies are increasingly fighting in and for cities. Alice Hills and David Kilcullen have plausibly argued that urban warfare has become more prevalent in the twenty-first century primarily because of demographic changes.[1] In 1960, the world's population was 3.2 billion, of which half a billion lived in cities; by 2020, 3.5 billion of the world's population of 7 billion will live in cities.[2] Since more people live in cities, which have consequently become key nodes of connectivity, conflict is ever more likely to occur in them. The mere reduction in the size of the military has also played an important role here. The armed forces are now simply too small to form the fronts which typified the twentieth century. Instead, they converge on and in cities, for whose control they struggle. Contemporary urban conflict dramatically complicates the battle-space, increasing coordination problems.

Technology has also played an important role in this evolution, in a somewhat unexpected way. The most significant innovation for command in the last two decades has been the introduction of secure digital communications which have allowed for the transmission of a hitherto-inconceivable quantity of information at previously unachievable ranges. As David Petraeus has noted: 'Now all of a sudden, it vastly increased the ability to communicate and to achieve situational awareness'.[3] Equipped with a satellite radio and a digital situation map on a laptop computer, commanders have been theoretically enabled to control the entire battle in real time, communicating immediately with all their subordinates. Theoretically, the introduction of digital satellite communications should have reduced the number of staff and even eliminated some command echelons and headquarters.[4] In fact, the opposite has happened. Digital technology has certainly facilitated an extension of the range and precision of operations. Yet, this extension of operations has also generated new problems for commanders, burdening rather than liberating them.

---

[1] Alice Hills, *Future Wars in Cities: re-thinking a liberal dilemma* (London: Frank Cass, 2004); David Kilcullen, *Out of the Mountains: the coming of age of the urban guerrilla* (London: Hurst and Company, 2013); Sean Edwards, *Mars Unmasked: the changing face of urban operations* (New York: Rand, 2000); Stephen Graham, *Cities under Siege: the new military urbanism* (London: Verso, 2010).

[2] Mike Davis, *Planet of the Slums* (London: Verso, 2006), 1.

[3] David Petraeus, personal interview, interviewee 096, 7 January 2016.

[4] Ibid.

There are a number of obvious ways in which new communications technology has merely altered – perhaps even exacerbated – rather than obviated the problem of command. First, digital communications have increased the amount of information coming into the headquarters from a diversity of sources. Indeed, commanders are now in danger of being suffocated with information, not only about military operations but a diversity of other civil, political and cultural issues, fed in, often randomly, from media and social media sources. This overload was plainly evident in Kandahar. Second, the increased range of network-enabled operations has accentuated the difficulties of administration and control. In the twentieth century, the divisional area was highly circumscribed and competent commanders were in physical contact with most of their formation on a daily basis. They could visit their subordinates and personally assess the situation. That physical contact has now become impossible. Consequently, precisely because forces can operate at a greater range, commanders cannot be everywhere. More staff are now required to supervise and coordinate their units' activities, in place of immediate direction from the commander. Third, digital communications have enabled air, land and maritime forces to be coordinated ever more closely with each other. This integration imposes a huge coordination cost on any commander.

In addition, even conventional, high-intensity military operations now involve civil, political and informational engagement, which were all but irrelevant at the divisional level in the twentieth century. Indeed, Chapter 7 demonstrated that, even on counterinsurgency operations, divisional commanders in the 1950s and 1960s were not overly engaged in civil and political action. This is not the case today. Frank Hoffman's concept of 'hybrid war' has been very influential in military circles and it usefully describes the likely scenario in future conflict. Hoffman fully recognizes that irregular warfare has been a constant feature of wars historically. However, he suggests that in the twenty-first century it has become increasingly impossible to separate irregular from regular conflict; high- and low-intensity conflict have fused. Increasingly, even apparently conventional wars against a peer involve highly politicized, irregular activities at an ever lower level: 'These hybrid wars blend the lethality of state conflict with the fanatic and protracted fervour of irregular

Table 10.1 *Twentieth- and Twenty-First-Century Operating Environments*

Twentieth-Century Operations	Twenty-First-Century Operations
Scale	Scope
Conventional	Hybrid
Homogeneous	Heterogeneous
Fronts	Battlespace
Field	Urban
Mass	Precision
Single-service	Joint
National	Multinational
Alliance	Coalition
Citizen	Professional
Operations	Campaigns
Military	Inter-agency
Intelligence	Understanding
News	Information

warfare'.[5] Every conflict has become, in effect, hybrid. As a result, commanders even at a low level now have to engage with political and civil leaders; operations have become inter-agency. While the scale of operations has diminished drastically – the armed forces are numerically miniscule in comparison with the million-men armies of the twentieth century – their scope has expanded radically. Divisional operations have become truly multi-dimensional. In the twentieth century, divisional operations constituted a problem of scale: the coordination of mass forces on simple missions over a short range. Today, they have become problems of scope: the precision coordination of heterogeneous forces at range.

In 1916, all the major Western powers published dedicated divisional doctrine for the first time. These manuals demonstrated that the belligerents had recognized an epochal shift in the character of warfare and had institutionalized organizational reforms to adapt to the new challenges. Today, Western powers are similarly aware of the profound transformation of warfare. New doctrine has appeared which has sought to define the central problems which forces now face and, in the case of Western armies, to reconfigure their divisions so that they are capable of meeting contemporary challenges.

---

[5] Frank Hoffman, 'Hybrid Warfare and Challenges', *Joint Forces Quarterly* 52 (1st Quarter) 2009: 37.

Of course, American armed forces have led the way here. For instance, the *US Army Operating Concept: Win in a Complex World* represents a leading contribution to contemporary debates, describing the current predicament very clearly. There is absolutely no doubting the centrality of traditional firepower and manoeuvre, in either this manual or contemporary American doctrine more widely; the US Army aims to develop combat power *en masse*. War remains a battle of wills and the army division retains its central role in delivering raw combat power. Yet, the central idea of the concept is illuminating: 'The Army, as part of joint, inter-organizational and multinational teams, provides multiple options to the Nation's leadership, integrates multiple partners, and operates across multiple domains to present adversaries with multiple dilemmas and achieve sustainable outcomes'.[6] While combat superiority remains a priority, the US Army cannot rely on firepower alone:

> Future armed conflict will be complex, in part, because threats, enemies, and adversaries are becoming increasingly capable and elusive. State and non-state actors employ traditional, unconventional, and hybrid strategies that threaten US security and vital interests. The complexity of future armed conflict is due to increasing momentum of human interaction, threats emanating from dense and weakly governed urban areas, the availability of lethal weapon systems, and the proliferation of CBRNE threats.[7]

The manual provides specific guidance as to how this might be achieved and emphasizes the requirement to understand and, therefore, to be able to exploit the environment.

(1) Develop and sustain a high degree of situational understanding while operating in complex environments against determined, adaptive enemy organizations.

(2) Shape and influence security environments, engage key actors, and consolidate gains to achieve sustainable security outcomes.[8]

In the twenty-first century, even conventional war has developed quite unconventional aspects. Indeed, the US Army has claimed that in order to be militarily significant, forces will have to engage in 'unified

---

[6] *US Army Operating Concept: Win in a Complex World*, www.tradoc.army.mil/tpubs/pams/tp525-3-1.pdf, vi.

[7] Ibid., 15.

[8] Ibid., 31.

action'. They will have to fuse military activities with civil and political action: 'Unified action is the synchronization, coordination, and/ or integration of the activities of governmental and nongovernmental entities with military operations to achieve unity of effort'.[9]

More recently, the US Army has been developing a new concept of 'multi-domain battle'. Multi-domain battle is not totally original; it is best seen as a revision of the US Army's Air-Land Battle of the 1980s. Air-Land Battle was developed at that time as a means of offsetting the numeric advantages of the Warsaw Pact. Air-Land Battle sought to exploit American air superiority to compensate for the deficiencies in land forces; it added a second dimension to ground warfare. The doctrine also introduced the concept of 'deep', 'close' and 'rear' and, while ground forces continued to fight the close battle, air power would be employed to strike the enemy in depth. Air-Land Battle represented a significant reconfiguration of the battlespace.[10] Extending the depth of the battlespace, it was a step towards twenty-first-century operations. Yet, multi-dimensional battle represents a radical extrapolation of Air-Land Battle not only in the range but also in the domains of military operations: 'Modern information technology makes the information environment, inclusive of cyberspace and the electromagnetic spectrum, indispensable for human interaction, including military operations and political competition'.[11] The US Army has sought to operate simultaneously not only in the physical nor even land-based dimensions but also in the virtual, informational and electro-magnetic spheres: 'Multi-Domain Battle is not unprecedented, rather it is about using capabilities in more innovative ways to overcome new challenges. Multi-Domain Battle allows US forces to outmaneuver adversaries physically and cognitively, applying combined arms in and across all domains'.[12]

Multi-domain battle has demanded that the US Army is capable of conducting military operations characterized by a quite novel

[9] US Army Combined Arms Centre, *Army Doctrine Reference Publications ADRP 3-0 Operations* (Washington, DC: Headquarters Department of the Army, 2016), 1–5. www.apd.army.mil/epubs/DR_pubs/DR_a/pdf/web/ADRP%203-0%20FINAL%20 WEB.pdf.

[10] US Army, *Field Manual 100–5 Operations* (Washington, DC: Headquarters Department of the Army, 1982).

[11] US Army Combined Arms Centre, *Army Doctrine Reference Publications ADRP 3-0 Operations* 1-1, 1-2. www.apd.army.mil/epubs/DR_pubs/DR_a/pdf/web/ADRP% 203-0%20FINAL%20WEB.pdf.

[12] Ibid.

'simultaneity, depth, synchronicity and flexibility'.[13] The re-configured US Army division will play a critical role in multi-domain battle. Chapter 2 described how the US Army was currently reconfiguring its divisions. The demands of Iraq and Afghanistan had disturbed the structure and coherence of American divisions. Yet, the restoration of the American division has not simply been a matter of administrative reconstitution. On the contrary, the American Army division has been identified as the critical command echelon for high-intensity warfare in the twenty-first century. The division has been identified as playing a crucial role because only this formation and this command echelon has the capacity and size to coordinate the heterogeneous elements which are required to conduct multi-domain battle. Just as in the First World War, the division is being reorganized in order to resolve a command problem.

Following the United States closely, the British Army has also recognized that warfare today displays highly distinctive features: 'The operating environment is likely to be volatile and unpredictable with threats ranging from terrorism, hostile states, fragile and failing states, and hybrid threats and adversaries ... In this environment, threats to UK interests will be politically rooted and nuanced, fed by, or exploiting, complex problems'.[14] As noted in Chapter 2, the Army has identified the division as the primary formation for the prosecution of high-intensity warfare. Only the division has the sufficient resources and capabilities to coordinate contemporary operations.

In 1916, SS 135 described how the division was uniquely configured to coordinate mass artillery and infantry. Today, the division is required to coordinate not just fire and manoeuvre but a diversity of other activities. Thus, according to the June 2014 edition of the British Army Field Manual, a division must engage in what it initially defined as 'Joint Action'. Joint Action involves the orchestration of four levers of action:

(1) Information activities to manipulate perceptions and affect understanding.
(2) Fires to achieve or threaten physical effects.

---

[13] US Army Combined Arms Centre, *Army Doctrine Reference Publications ADRP 3-0 Operations*, vi. www.apd.army.mil/epubs/DR_pubs/DR_a/pdf/web/ADRP%203-0%20FINAL%20WEB.pdf.
[14] Army Field Manual Volume 1 Part 1A: *Divisional Tactics*, 1-1.

(3) Outreach, including stabilization, support to governance, capacity building, as well as regional and local engagement.

(4) Manoeuvre, to gain advantage in time and space.[15]

The aim of coordinating these four levers is to exploit the physical, cognitive and virtual vulnerabilities of enemies: 'The military contribution to people-centric operations is exercised through Joint Action, by which the division blends manoeuvre (physical), fires (real and EMS), information activities and outreach to achieve influence through effects in the physical, virtual and cognitive domains.[16] In the most recent version of British doctrine, joint action has been renamed 'integrated action', to denote that the British Army is not simply referring to inter-service and, therefore, 'joint' activity but to inter-agency action involving civil and political actors.

The British Army has identified the division as the optimal level of command to implement integrated action: 'Key to A2020 (Army 2020) is the intent to re-set and resource the division level after a decade of stabilization operations focused predominantly, nationally, at the brigade level. Command is a capability where each level offers particular utility. The re-set acknowledges the unique characteristics of the divisional level of command'.[17] The division uniquely has 'the capability and capacity to conduct manoeuvre across the virtual and cognitive domains, as well as the more traditional physical domains'.[18] The primacy of the division has been widely affirmed by senior British officers: 'The division is the first level of combined, joint, government and interagency integration; it is therefore, the first level for the current environment. It is involved in the integration of kinetic and non-kinetic effects for political outcomes'.[19] As military operations become hybrid, operating in new domains, the challenge of command has changed. In Britain, the renascent division has been seen as means of addressing new operational challenges.

The French Army is currently developing its doctrine but it concurs with the general position advocated by both the United States and the United Kingdom. It recognizes the new operating environment

[15] Ibid., 1-7.
[16] Ibid., 1–7.
[17] Army Field Manual Volume 1 Part 1A: Divisional Tactics, 1-1.
[18] Ibid.
[19] Anonymous, British Army, 1 July 2015.

in which complex, hybrid operations are likely to be the norm. Consequently, because of the fusion of increasingly precise firepower and softer forms of influence, the French Army has also accepted that the divisional level has become primary. The views of commander of *État Major De Force 1* converge closely with those of his partners in 3 UK Division: 'I can't conceive of an operation where there would not be people you would be fighting in the population. Therefore, the divisional headquarters requires expanded functions. In the past, when I was a junior in the 1980s, a division had four infantry regiments and one armoured regiment, engineers etc., and that was it. There was no brigade level. Now the division headquarters is a matrix coordinating many functions'.[20] The deputy commander of *État Major De Force 1* made a similar argument:

> What is the main difference between the twentieth and twenty-first century? The major factor is the environment; the threat. The main factor is that we have lost our traditional enemy, a hostile state. We therefore lost our notion of the border. The threat has no border, it not outside our border. In a permissive world without borders and linked by the internet, it is not just the ground on which we fight – but perception as well. Our terrain is not the same as in the twentieth century. There are many dimensions to this terrain.[21]

Like its allies, the French Army is similarly reinvesting in the division as a means of coping with hybrid, high-intensity warfare.

The Bundeswehr has similarly recognized the changing operating environment. This is very evident in the 2016 *Weissbuch*. The *Weissbuch* is, of course, directed at the strategic level; it is the statement of security policy, not of specific operational requirements at the divisional level. The central principle of the document is to affirm Germany's commitment to the international rules-based order, human rights and to its allies in NATO and the EU. Nevertheless, prominent within the document is the recognition of the emergence of new hybrid threats: 'All areas of social life can be the target of

---

[20] OF-7, Major-General, Commander EMF 1 French Army, interviewee 023, personal communication, 15 May 2015.
[21] OF-6, Brigadier, Deputy Commander EMF 1 French Army, interviewee 097, personal interview, 3 February 2016.

hybrid attacks: through cyber attacks and information operations (propaganda for instance), economic and financial pressure as well as attempts at political destabilization'.[22] This changing strategic context has had an immediate effect on the Bundeswehr:

> Conventional territorial and alliance defence has clearly changed its character in comparison with the time of the Cold War; it must operate today diversely at short notice against a spatially focused threat through military forces under and above the threshold of open war. This is ever more frequently embedded in a hybrid strategy, which is marked by the whole bandwidth of the threat spectrum all the way through to orchestrated operations of military and non-military means.[23]

In response to these new threats, the Bundewehr has identified the need to operate in informational and cyber domains.[24] It aspires to become flexible and agile, capable of multi-functionality and adaptability.[25] The prime mission of the German Army may be the territorial defence of Germany, Poland and the Baltics, a mission which looks similar to its role in the Cold War. Then it defended the inner German border; now it defends the Polish and Baltic borders against Russia. In fact, territorial defence has assumed a quite different form. Following its allies, Germany has recently begun to reorganize and reinvest in its three remaining divisions. They have been identified as the critical formations for the mission of territorial defence. Yet, like other Western formations, German divisions will have to operate in the virtual, civil and political domains in order to be militarily effective in the Baltics.

Indeed, the Bundeswehr is well aware of these new challenges. It published a new concept for future war in September 2017 which described these new operating conditions very clearly.[26] Written under

---

[22] *Die Bundesregierung Weissbuch 2016: zur Sicherheitspolitick und zur Zukunft der Bundeswehr.* https://m.bundesregierung.de/Content/Infomaterial/BMVg/Weissbuch_zur_Sicherheitspolitik_2016.pdf;jsessionid=B363C8A762E222DF5C229B41D5B52 A5F.s1t1?__blob=publicationFile&v=2, 38.

[23] Ibid., 88.

[24] Ibid., 93.

[25] Ibid., 98.

[26] Kommando Heer, *Thesenpapier I: Wie kämpfen Landstreitkräfte künftig?* (Bundesamt für Infrastruktur, Umweltschutz and Dienstleistungen der Bundeswehr, 2017); For an excellent commentary see Bjorn Muller, 'Wie die Bundeswehr den Landkrieg der

the direction of Lieutenant General Frank Leidenberger, the document was intended to highlight potential equipment shortfalls in the Bundeswehr but it has been pertinent to the question of divisional command. The paper envisaged how the German Army might participate in a NATO conflict against a peer opponent (presumably Russia), in 2026. The starting point of the paper was the observation that mass forces have disappeared; the current 'lack of mass' has fundamentally change the nature of military operations.[27] The armed forces will need to be better networked so that they can work more closely with other forces and partners across the dimensions; a 'Comprehensive Approach' (i.e., inter-agency) will be required.[28] With the proliferation of sensors, the battlespace will be increasingly transparent and theatre entry will be ever more difficult as opponents become more capable.[29] The threat of indirect, long range precision fires and airstrikes will be an increasing threat.[30] Although armour will remain important, tanks have become vulnerable to discovery and destruction by drones and long-range fires. Consequently, they will have to operate in highly dispersed formations, avoiding direct tank duels, with special armour and defence systems.[31] The paper focuses practically on the Bundeswehr's procurement needs but it demonstrates that the German Army has adopted a similar vision of future conflict as its allies. Wars will be fought at a range and depth and across domains quite different from the twentieth century. The new challenges of twenty-first-century warfare have profound implications for German Army divisions.

The major Western powers are, then, reinvesting in the divisional level not only as a means of regaining lost warfighting capabilities but also, primarily, as a way of responding to the challenges of the new operating environment. These armies all recognize that the mission of a division in the twenty-first century has changed radically. In contrast to the modern combined arms division, the current division no longer simply attacks or defends a small front.

Zukunft gewinnen will'. www.pivotarea.eu/2017/09/22/thesenpapier-des-deutschen-heeres-so-will-die-bundeswehr-kuenftige-landkriege-gewinnen/.

[27] Kommando Heer, *Thesenpapier I: Wie kämpfen Landstreitkräfte künftig?*, 8.

[28] Ibid., 8.

[29] Ibid., 8.

[30] Ibid., 10–11.

[31] Ibid., 14, 11.

It does not simply mass firepower in support of its manoeuvre brigades. The geometry of the battlespace has been revised – if not revolutionized. The division operates over much larger areas in a dispersed battlespace, coordinating heterogeneous assets, while operating in the informational, cyber, political and civil domains as well. Its mission has become truly multi-dimensional. The division has to synchronize simultaneous activities, each executed with precision.

It is apposite to highlight the contrast with the twentieth-century division here. Chapters 4 to 6 described the highly circumscribed mission of the modern division. Divisions, then, were large but simple organizations which fought on small fronts. They were solutions to the problem of mass, industrial warfare. Even on counter-insurgency operations, their functions remained almost exclusively military. Consequently, divisions were homogeneous, vertically integrated hierarchies. In stark contrast, the divisional level has evolved into a mechanism for articulating joint and integrated firepower, manoeuvre and influence. The division has become the means of applying precise and graduated force to complex operational problems. In order to defeat an adversary, the division has had to assume responsibility for a spectrum of activities which were quite irrelevant in the twentieth century. The core of the division's fighting power remains in place: three combat brigades and a brigade of artillery. Yet, divisions now routinely draw upon air, maritime and special operations forces while interacting with numerous other agencies. In place of a vertically integrated Fordist hierarchy, the division has become a sprawling, heterogeneous and loosely coupled system, consisting of a multiplex of units, resources and partners. Chapter 4 described how the modern structure of the divisional headquarters was an adaptation to the problem of coordinating artillery and infantry. Coordination remains the central function of the division but the transformation of divisional mission has demanded a radical reform of its headquarters. The Western division is now expected articulate a host of heterodox military and non-military capabilities. This reformation has profound implications for the practice of command. The following passages will provide a detailed description of the emergent structure of the divisional headquarters in order to investigate the transformation of command in the last decade.

Headquarters

Size

Chapter 4 described how the modern divisional headquarters was institutionalized in the First World War and remained broadly stable throughout the twentieth century. One of the most obvious features of the reconstituted twenty-first-century division is simply its size; the divisional headquarters have grown inordinately in the last two decades. Although professional and careerist factors are certainly not irrelevant here and will be discussed below, contemporary military doctrine shows that the growth of the headquarters has been substantially propelled by new operational, informational and organizational demands. As the division has assumed new functions, it has required additional staff to administer the increased demands. This proliferation of staff functions was especially evident in Kandahar when Regional Command South assumed a diverse portfolio of responsibilities. The headquarters was massive: 800 staff. The Chief of Staff of Regional Command South emphasized the changing demands on the division: 'It is the nature of conflict. In World War I, there were goodies and baddies, it was not a war among the people. The divisional frontages were narrow. The division was set simple problems. Take the extreme example of Kandahar: 60,000 troops. It was verging on a corps. The question is: what am I comparing? You are fighting over a bigger area among the people. The nature of the problem has changed.'[32] As a result, he noted that even with 800 personnel in Kandahar, they struggled to manage all the information flows.[33] Even during the March Up when James Mattis strenuously limited the size of his staff, his headquarters still grew to over 250 personnel, double the size of a divisional headquarters even at the end of the Cold War.[34] Functions simply could not be fulfilled without more staff. In response to the expanding scope of military operations, the divisional headquarters has expanded radically.

The trend of headquarters expansion is clearest in the United States. The standard US Army divisional headquarters today is

---

[32] OF-6, Brigadier, Chief of Staff CJTF-6, interviewee 049, personal interview, 2 December 2014.

[33] Ibid.

[34] Lieutenant-Colonel Clarke Lethin, Deputy and then Assistant Chief of Staff Operations, 1st Marine Division, interviewee 125, personal interview, July 2016.

approximately 450, although there are exceptions. The 82nd Airborne Division has a staff of 700; as the Global Response Force, 82nd Airborne requires a great number of staff to be ready to coordinate the rapid deployments to anywhere in the world. Yet, on operations in Iraq and Afghanistan, US divisional headquarters have tended to be huge by twentieth-century standards; for instance, when 1st Infantry Division was stationed in Bagram as Regional Command (East) in 2012, the headquarters consisted of 1700 personnel. Clearly, this was unusual, reflecting the special character of the Afghan campaign. Yet, it demonstrates that while larger than other divisions, 82nd Airborne's headquarters is not a complete anomaly. The US Marine Corps has retained its preference for small divisional headquarters. Nevertheless, on the March Up, as already noted, the staff of 1st Marine Division was not small.[35] 1st Marine Division currently has a staff of 250 officers, which would almost certainly expand on any operation. A typical American divisional headquarters is at least four times the size of its Cold War predecessor and some ten times the size of a 1940s headquarters; it consists of 400 staff officers, rather than forty.

The permanent establishment of British, French and German divisional headquarters are predictably smaller than their American counterparts. 3 UK Division's permanent staff is much smaller, for instance. Despite being the central element of British Army reforms, 3 UK Division is badly under-staffed. In 2013, 3 UK Division had a staff of just over 100 officers. However, over the following two years, its permanent staff complement declined to 88 officers – about the same size as a late twentieth-century division. However, when 3 UK Division has exercised or if it were deployed on an operation, its staff has increased to 400; 250 staff officers with a further 150 supporting signals officers and other personnel. The radical augmentation of 3 UK Division on exercises has been a major weakness which has been the cause for significant concern in the organization.[36] Nevertheless, on operations 3 UK Division would consist of at least 400 staff.

The French Army has adopted a different model to the British Army. *État Major De Force 1*, for instance, has a permanent staff of 270, though this is augmented to about 400 on major exercises and on

[35] Ibid., personal email, 30 May 2017.
[36] Anthony King, 'Corroding the Iron Division: personnel problems', *British Army Review* 168 Winter 2017: 59–63.

any operations on which it might deploy.[37] Similarly, 1 Panzer Division has a permanent staff of 280, though on exercises this figure is likely to expand too.[38] 82nd Airborne is unusual then; it has a truly massive divisional staff required by its special mission of very rapid airborne deployment. However, there is a clear pattern here. The Western divisional headquarters now typically consists of some 400 staff when it is exercising or if it were deployed on operations. The brute increase in staff size is the most obvious feature of the new divisional headquarters of the twenty-first century; these organizations are vast in comparison with their predecessors.

At one level, this increase is simply a product of the functional complexity with which a division now has to deal; new intelligence, information and outreach cells have been created. As the scope of military operations has expanded, the size of the headquarters has increased. However, the expansion of the headquarters has attracted much criticism from commentators and, indeed, from professional soldiers themselves. For instance, Jim Storr, a British military studies scholar, regards the increase in staff not as a necessary or rational response to complexity but driven by institutional imperatives alone: 'We should be doubtful that any increase in the apparent complexity of modern war is justified by the increase in staff numbers'.[39] Storr invokes Brooks's Law to show that as an organization increases in size, it expends more of its time coordinating its employees rather than actually conducting useful work. The result is that, according to Storr, decision-making in a modern headquarters has decelerated, while the staff has grown.[40] Jim Storr regards the insatiable desire for information as a central cause of expansion: 'Underpinning this whole issue is a major fallacy. It is that more information leads to better decisions'. Storr dismisses this attitude: 'You don't need much information to make decisions which are "about right"'.[41] Yet, alongside these pressures, internal, careerist or organizational factors, which have nothing to do with combat performance, also impel expansion. Especially in peacetime, when organizational interests predominate over operational ones, generals can

---

[37] Fieldnotes, EMF 1, Besancon, 24 May 2016, Volume V, 102–112.
[38] Fieldnotes. 1 Panzer Division visit to 3 UK Division, Bulford UK, 30 August 2016, Volume VI, 53.
[39] Jim Storr, *The Human Face of War*, 135.
[40] Ibid., 151.
[41] Ibid., 140.

augment their reputations simply by expanding their organizations; indeed, for some, it is a major focus of effort. In addition, a larger staff provides professional opportunities for officers and increases the visibility and importance of particular arms, branches and services. Arbitrary and irrational pressures have sometimes encouraged unnecessary expansion.

All of these points are valid and there is much evidence for them both now and in the past. Storr's scepticism is further affirmed by the fact that there might be alternate ways of responding to increased complexity. Instead of expanding a headquarters, it might be more efficient to increase the expertise of individual staff officers, enhancing human capital rather just increasing the number of personnel. Indeed, following Jim Collin's injunction about 'getting the right people of the bus', this is precisely what Mattis tried to do in both Afghanistan and Iraq in 2003. Yet, while Western forces certainly try to appoint trained specialist staff, they have not implemented this policy with any rigour. They have preferred to increase the size of the headquarters. Institutional factors cannot be dismissed here as an explanation for the expansion of the divisional headquarters.

Certainly, size generates very considerable problems for the new divisional headquarters. Problems of internal coordination, sustainability and vulnerability are all magnified with a large staff; a large headquarters requires prodigious protection and represents a huge logistical and communications burden. For instance, between 2013 and 2015, 3 UK Division conducted three major Command Post exercises in the UK in which the whole headquarters deployed under tentage. It took the division's signals regiment two weeks to construct the headquarters and its communications infrastructure and it required a full infantry battalion to protect it.[42] On this model, 3 UK Division would have absorbed an unfeasible quantity of manpower before it had even started to have a military effect on any theatre.

These anomalies have to be acknowledged. Even if operational imperatives have been paramount, other less-rational factors have sometimes impelled the expansion of the divisional headquarters. However, the expansion of the divisional headquarters cannot be dismissed simply as a bureaucratic imperative, driven by institutional interests. Professional soldiers are well-aware of the problems of size

---

[42] Fieldnotes, Exercise Iron Triangle 2013, St Mawgan, 21 November 2013, Volume I, 5.

and, yet, even the most experienced senior officers, while acknowledging a preference for a small headquarters, affirm the requirement for capacity and, therefore, size. The commander of 82nd Airborne Division admitted that he was 'shocked by the lack of staff' in 3 UK Division; this provides very clear evidence of the point.

In order to coordinate the activities of its units, a divisional headquarters must replicate all the functions of a division in the staff. The staff requires the expertise to collate information about every element of the division and its activities so that they can provide direction and guidance to those subordinate units and inform the commander's decision-making about each function. Clearly, it is important to be sensitive to the inevitable politics behind any army reform; organizational and professional interests are almost always at work. Yet, it would be misleading to suggest that the expansion of the contemporary divisional headquarters fulfils no organizational function and will inevitably undermine the effectiveness of the division. While fully accepting the problem of size, both staff officers and commanders affirmed that the size of the divisional headquarters had increased because of a proliferation of functions. Complex operations have required complex headquarters. There does not seem to be any other way to coordinate operations.

Structure

The re-invigoration of divisions has involved not only a dramatic increase in the size of the headquarters but also some major restructuring. Today, as the functions of a division – and, therefore, its staff – have increased, the traditional Napoleonic structure of the division has been very substantially revised. A new structure has appeared in the divisional headquarters. As one retired British officer, who had served in divisional headquarters in the 1980s and 1990s, observed: 'The division headquarters of the Cold War was nothing like what you've seen in Afghanistan or 3 UK Division; nothing like it at all. The divisional headquarters was derived from the Second World War and traced its lineage back to World War I'.[43] By contrast, the divisional headquarters has changed so much in the last decade that it is difficult to see its

---

[43] OF-7, Major-General (retired), British Army, interviewee 139, personal interview, 30 May 2017.

lineage at all. The United States has, of course, led this process and was the first to initiate many of the changes. However, 3 UK Division and *État Major De Force 1* have followed the US model closely. In place of the old Napoleonic system, the new divisional headquarters consists of a spine of three interrelated cells: Future Plans (G5), Future Operations (G3/5), and Current Operations (G3). These cells are known as the integrating cells since their purpose is to fuse all the functions of the division into a unified plan. The three integrating cells have defined functions. G5, Future Plans, receives orders from the higher headquarters and conducts mission analysis and design to generate a detailed operation plan. Functionally, Future Plans has expanded very significantly from the Cold War. In 3 UK Division, for instance, the cell consists of about thirty staff officers organized into a number of 'Operation Planning Teams'.[44] On recent exercises, these teams consisted of about five staff officers but they drew on the wider expertise of the headquarters to ensure that every function – and every unit within the division or supporting units outside it – were represented in the plan.

Although a division is nominally only a tactical formation, its span of command has increased so that in some cases Future Plans is involved in operational- or theatre-level planning; Future Plans does not just plan immediate missions but also designs divisional campaigns, involving numerous subordinate operations. Accordingly, although the Future Plans cell plans up to ninety-six hours before execution, the horizon of the cell has now typically extended to weeks and months; its role is to design a divisional campaign as part of an Operation Plan followed by a series of missions through Operation Orders. At the same time, the physical range of operations has expanded dramatically to potentially hundreds of kilometres; 82nd Airborne uniquely conducts operations at a range of thousands of miles. Future Plans represents a major development for the divisional headquarters from the G5 cell of the 1980s which focused only on the next mission on a small divisional front.[45] Of course, with the expansion of the temporal and spatial horizon in which a division now works comes a diversification of the functions which the formation seeks to coordinate.

---

[44] Fieldnotes, Exercise Iron Triangle 2013, St Mawgan, 21–29 November 2013, Volume I, 6–62.

[45] Fieldnotes, Exercise Iron Triangle 2013, St Mawgan, 21 November 2013, Volume I, 9; OF-3, Royal Marines, 3 UK Division, interviewee 008, personal interview, 27 November 2013.

The Future Plans cell allows the divisional headquarters to look beyond purely tactical considerations about the next mission. It allows the division to consider a multi-dimensional environment over a much longer timeframe. However, by expanding the time horizon of the division, further reforms of the headquarters have been necessary. Chapters 4 and 5 showed that, throughout most of the twentieth century, divisions had only G3 or current operations cells (or their equivalent); divisions conducted one fight at a time, normally within twenty-four hours. The G3, operations cell supervised operations and issued orders for the following day's activities. By the end of the Cold War, there had been some extension of this frame. However, since the plan involved only a limited number of subordinate units, simple actions and the mission were to be executed almost immediately – there was little requirement to refine the plan any further. With the emergence of the Future Plans cell in the new divisional headquarters, the gap between the issuing of the plan and its execution has grown to ninety-six hours. Consequently, there is a significant delay between the production of the original order and its eventual execution. Conditions will almost inevitably change in the meantime; new details will emerge which require refinement and revision of the plan. Consequently, an intermediate cell has been required between G5, planning, and G3, operations, to fulfil this function: the so-called G3/5 or Future Operations cell. The designation G3/5 denotes that the cell sits between the G5 and G3 cells. The G3/5 cell's role is to refine the plans and orders disseminated from the Future Plans cell. In 3 UK Division, G3/5 currently consists of about thirty officers organized into operation planning teams. Specifically, the Future Operations cell refines the plan in the light of immediately changing conditions and in its final exchanges with superior, adjacent and subordinate echelons. Like the Future Plans cell, the Future Operations cell represents all the functions and, therefore, units of the division. The Future Operations cell is divided into multi-functional operation planning groups which match those in Future Plans. Indeed, in some headquarters the planning teams cycle between Future Plans and Future Operations.

G3, Current Operations cell is the last integrating cell. Although it has been significantly transformed by the introduction of digital communications which allow for live displays of the battlefield, the Current Operations cell is perhaps the most recognizable branch within the new divisional headquarters. As discussed in Chapter 4, the traditional G3 or operations cell consisted of a map board or a 'birdtable' overlain with acetate overlays or 'talcs' marked with the positions of enemy and friendly forces and with battle-management control measures. At the same time, reports came in by radio or by written message to be collated in a log; where appropriate, markers were moved on the map boards. Today's Current Operations Centre is digitalized – in the US Army totally so. However, the broad structure and function of the Current Operations Centre remain the same. The cell is organized around a digital situation map of the battle area, marked with enemy and friendly units; because these units have digital GPS trackers physically on them, their icons move in real-time on the current operations screen. Instead of written, analogue reports, Current Operations Centres use emails to communicate with each other; other screens record incoming and outgoing messages and reports from subordinate units and higher command.[46]

It is easy to be deceived by the digitalization of the Current Operations Centre; the ability to monitor action in real-time is a significant advance over the old analogue G3 cell with its map. Yet, it performs the same function and the basic procedures of monitoring; confirming and anticipating immediate action are the same. Indeed, in the First World War, Monash ensured that he had a current picture of the battle which was no more than ten minutes behind real-time. The central role of the Current Operations cell is to monitor the mission and to ensure that operations are proceeding in accordance with the plan. As events transpire that may undermine the plan, the Current Operations staff issue warnings of possible difficulties and prepare remedial actions in support of their units. Often, they simply cue additional air or artillery support. Despite impressive modernization, the Current Operations cell is recognizably similar to its predecessor. However, in addition to its digitalization, it demonstrates some functionally important adaptations. Like its sister cells, Future Plans and Future Operations, it is now thoroughly integrated. All the functions of the division, including informational and civil actions, and supporting assets such as air and aviation are represented in the cell. Current Operations explicitly seeks to conduct 'Multi-domain battle' or, in

---

[46] Fieldnotes, Exercise Iron Triangle 2013, St Mawgan, 3 December 2013, Volume I, 80; OF-2, Battle Captain 3 UK Division, interviewee 016, personal communication, 3 December 2013.

the UK, 'integrated action'. In 3 UK Division, the Joint Air Ground Integration Cell (JAGIC) has become a critical sub-department here. This cell has become an important team of artillery, air and intelligence officers who seek to coordinate surveillance with ground and air fires.[47] The Current Operations Cell is coordinated by a Chief of Current Operations. In 3 UK Division, this role has been fulfilled by senior lieutenant-colonels (the old GSo1), who is positioned on a special podium above the rest of the staff in order to facilitate their ability to communicate with and coordinate them (see Figure 10.1).[48] In 82nd Airborne Division, by contrast, the Commanding General or Deputy Commanding General is positioned in the dominating position at the head of the cell, overlooking their subordinates.[49]

As the division's functions and the span of operations have expanded, it has been necessary to distinguish the responsibilities of the divisional headquarters from those of its constitutive brigades more carefully. Consequently, in the United States and United Kingdom, the division now organizes the battlespace into deep, close and rear sectors; these zones refer to designated physical areas, marked on divisional maps with clear and definitive boundaries. UK Divisional doctrine, for instance, explicitly states that the division fights the deep, supports the close and protects the rear: 'The geographic, or physical framework, distinguishes military activity by close, deep, and rear. This framework may be physical, virtual or cognitive. The divisional close battle is likely to be the business of the combat brigades, with the division primarily operating in and controlling the deep and the rear battles'.[50] The close battle has been assigned to the brigades and, while the Current Operations cell monitors their progress to ensure that it is capable of supporting them in a crisis, the division focuses on the deep and the rear. As always, and despite the diversification of functions, artillery has played a major role in the delineation of the battlespace. The close fight of the brigade is normally determined by the range of its own organic artillery. The deep refers to the area beyond the range of brigade artillery, which the division can influence by long-range artillery or by air or aviation attack. However, a very notable addition to

---

[47] OF-4, Major, Chief of JAGIC, 3 UK Division, interviewee 135, personal interview 14 June 2014.
[48] Ibid., 92.
[49] Fieldnotes, Exercise Warfighter, Fort Bragg, 15 June 2017, Volume VI, 102.
[50] Army Field Manual Volume 1 Part 1A: *Divisional Tactics*, 2–10.

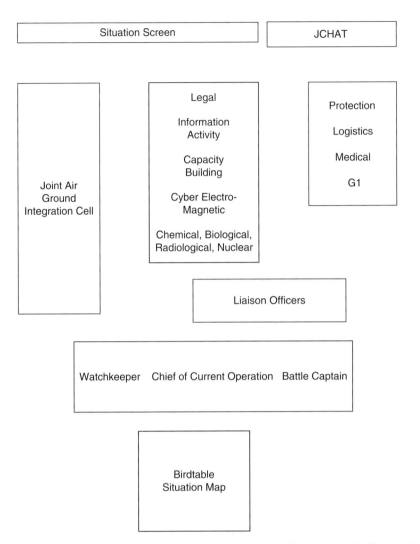

Figure 10.1 3 UK Division, Current Operations Cell, Exercise Warfighter, Fort Bragg, June 2017.

the deep is that it now also involves cognitive and virtual domains; the division now supports the close fight with informational, psychological and cyber operations for which the brigades do not have the resources. Finally, the rear refers to the logistical area. The division's role is to create the conditions in the deep and the rear so that the brigade can win its fight in the close. Building on the work of Future Plans and Future Operations, Current Operations seek to implement Integrated Action in the deep in order to support their brigades in the close fight against an immediate opponent. The Current Operations cell coordinates not just fires and manoeuvres, as the old G3 cell did, but is engaged in outreach and information activities, developed and refined by the planning cells.

3 UK Division has described the three integrating cells of the new divisional headquarters as the 'pistons' of the headquarters; their role is to plan and execute missions which integrate all four elements of 'integrated action', as it is called in the United Kingdom. In addition to the integrating cells, the headquarters includes functional cells consisting of specialist staff dedicated to particular activities and units. 3 UK Division, for instance, has employed six functional cells; fires (artillery), intelligence and understand (G2), air, engineers, sustain (G1 and G4), protect (Military Police), information activity and outreach. In most cases, the functional cells are based on the traditional G1, G4, G2, artillery and engineer cells, though, in each case, there has been a very significant expansion in their activities. The G2 cell exemplifies these changes very well. Traditionally, the G2 cell gathered purely military intelligence; its prime function was to identify the location and movement of enemy forces. In the Cold War, for instance, it plotted the direction and speed of Soviet advance, the so-called Iron Needle. G2 has now expanded as a result of new kinds of military intelligence sources and a widening remit to the human, social domain; the cell's role has expanded from a purely enemy focus to wider understanding. The information activity and outreach cell, which coordinates media strategies and key leader engagements, is completely new. The functional cells also command their subordinate units and assets. These cells play a crucial role in liaising with the division's units, collating specialist information that they feed into the integrating cells, G5, G3/5 and G3. At certain moments, staff from the functional cells have surged into the integrating cells if additional specialism has been required in the development of a plan or on a current operation.

The French Army division has displayed similar changes, although *État Major de Force 1* headquarters has a slightly different structure. In particular, its Fire Support Coordination cell is situated alongside rather than in the Current Operations cell. In addition, it has a dedicated Comprehensive Approach cell which monitors the military and non-military activities of the headquarters in order to ensure a coherent strategy of stabilization. Nevertheless, while there are important national differences, a remarkable feature of the reorganization of the division is the overwhelming similarity between the major

Western powers. The new divisional headquarters has assumed the same basic pattern in all Western armies. At the heart of this structure is the innovation of the three integrating cells, Future Plans, (G5) Future Operations (G3/5) and Current Operations (G3), around which the functional cells (the traditional G1, G2, G4, fires and engineers and new cells dealing with civil and informational action) are organized.

Because of its size and structure, the ergonomics of the new divisional headquarters has become an important issue. Since the headquarters is so large, a poorly conceived layout can undermine the interaction between critical functions. For instance, on a 3 UK Division exercise, Exercise Iron Resolve 14 in October 2015, the Intelligence and Understand cell was separated from both Fires and Current Operations.[51] This was seen as a major disadvantage since Current Operations relied on the latest intelligence information in order to coordinate operations and anticipate crisis. The temporary solution was for the SO1 from Intelligence and Understand to locate himself physically in Current Operations at moments of crisis, sending runners back to his functional cell.[52] On each 3 UK Division exercise between 2013 and 2016, the architecture of the HQs was slightly different depending on the space available and the requirement, but the basic lay-down was consistent (see e.g., Figure 10.2).

The modern divisional headquarters was created on the Western Front in the First World War, as described in Chapter 4; modern staff systems, processes and the physical artefacts of command appeared for the first time at that point. The contemporary divisional headquarters represents a major expansion of the traditional divisional command post. Nevertheless, there are some obvious and important continuities. The Current Operations Centre is recognizably similar to the original divisional command post. Indeed, in the United Kingdom, 3 Division always maintains a 'birdtable' (a situation map marked with the location of units) in its Current Operations Centre in case of a loss of power or communications. In this way, the twenty-first-century divisional headquarters might be compared to some early Gothic cathedrals in Europe. Although these vast structures, with their grand

---

[51] Fieldnotes, Exercise Iron Resolve 2014, Knook Camp, 29 September – 3 October 2014, Volume II, 71.

[52] Fieldnotes, Exercise Iron Resolve 2014, Knook Camp, October 2014, Volume II, 105.

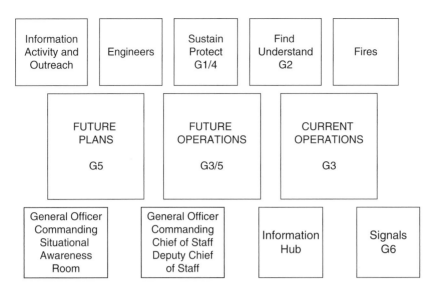

Figure 10.2 3 UK Division Headquarters, Project Horrocks.
Note: Exercise Iron Resolve 2015, Westdown Camp, 29 September–12 October 2015.

naves, vaults and flying buttresses, remain impressive, elements of the original Romanesque chapels from which they grew are sometimes still visible within the existing superstructure. The divisional headquarters of the twenty-first century is comparable. It represents a thorough-going reconstruction of the original divisional headquarters and, yet, at its heart, in its Operations Centre, traces of its original structure remain. Nevertheless, the vast expansion of the headquarters has profound implications for command.

Distributed Command

In the twentieth century, using analogue radio communications, divisional headquarters were typically organized into three echelons, the Forward (or Tactical) Command Post, Main and Rear, normally separated by a terrain feature. Each, especially Forward and Main, was mobile; they consisted of a few vehicles carrying commanders and staff officers who established an operations cell with radios and maps where necessary. Typically, they moved every twenty-four hours or less, taking only hours to reconstruct. A retired British general described the con-struct in the British Army in the 1980s:

> The divisional headquarters consisted of an armoured tactical headquarters: 432/436s APV – the armoured command variety. Three or four vehicles in total. There was the CRE/CRA [Commander Royal Engineers/Commander Royal Artillery] vehicle, the ops, plans and clerks vehicle. But it was only manned for specific operations. It was not like Monty's Army Group headquarters; it was not routinely manned. The second headquarters was Main: ten to fourteen vehicles. They formed a rectangle with a birdtable in the middle: G1, G4, G2, G3, Air Defence and Aviation and GOC vehicles. There were two signals clerks. But it was never more than fourteen vehicles. When the equipment was available it was replicated to form a step-up – an equally manned alternate HQ. In the First Gulf, 1 Division had one of these. In Cold War, you had Main and Step-up, which had a few staff officers in to monitor things. The Divisional HQ moved every twenty-four hours from Main to step-up. An activation party went from the Main to the step-up and once the GOC and COS was in the new headquarters, they assumed control ... The rear was unarmoured.[53]

There is an obvious problem created by the expansion of the divisional headquarters. Divisional headquarters are now so large, they are immobile and, with huge electronic signatures, very difficult to hide. They are an easy target for any near-peer enemy. The very potency of the new headquarters with its multi-functionality is also its weakness. Western forces are well aware of the vulnerabilities of the new divisional headquarters. During 3 UK Division exercises, when the entire staff was recurrently accommodated in a large, unhardened tent, successive commanders of the division highlighted the vulnerability of their headquarters. While they accepted the construct for exercise purposes, they declared that fighting from a tent was, as members of 3 UK Division recurrently noted, 'not an act of war'. In reality, against a near-peer enemy, such a headquarters would be destroyed almost immediately. Accordingly, Western forces have begun to experiment

[53] OF-7, Major-General (retired), British Army, interviewee 139, personal interview, 30 May 2017.

with new systems of command. 82nd Airborne Division has recently experimented with the use of two fully networked but relatively small command tents, one acting as a Main, the other as a Forward, step-up or reserve command post in the event of a strike on Main. Both tents are able to be struck and re-erected in one-and-a-half hours.[54] This solution has obvious parallels with the twentieth century, described by the British general above, but the span and range of command exercised by these nodes far exceeds the previous era.

However, while these continuities are important, it is important not to be confused. A completely new system of command has been introduced. Instead of traditional command echelons, comprised of Main, Forward and Rear, a system of 'distributed command', as the British Army call it, or Mission Command, according to the US Army, is currently being instituted. Mission command here does not mean the devolution of decision-making authority in line with classic military doctrine, although it certainly implies it, but rather the creation and deployment of dispersed command nodes. These command nodes are not located a single terrain feature from each other, but are separated by many miles – or even, exceptionally, by continents. Of course, once again, the United States leads the way here. The US Army now seeks to be able to deploy a small, digitally enabled forward command post to the combat zone, while the main headquarters remains in continental America at the home base of the division. Rear, Main and Tactical are no longer separated by a few miles and a convenient terrain feature but by hundreds, even thousands, of miles.

82nd Airborne is a pertinent example of this command system in the twenty-first century. Although 82nd Airborne has served as Combined Joint Task Force, Regional Command South in Kandahar in 2011–12 and has recently deployed a headquarters element to Baghdad to coordinate a US mentoring operation, the division is primarily focused on warfighting, not stabilization. 82nd Airborne has been in the vanguard of 'mission command' because it is designated as the Global Response Force. The Division is tasked to deploy at short-notice. Specifically, on command from the President, the mission of the division is to be able to seize an airfield anywhere in the world by an airborne *coup de main*, directly from Fort Bragg and its Pope Airfield.

---

[54] Fieldnotes, Exercise Warfighter, Fort Bragg, 15 June 2017, Volume VI, 102.

This airfield will then be used to feed in following forces in order to expand the mission. 82nd Airborne has an airborne battlegroup on standby at all times able to fly from Pope Airfield at three hours' notice. Theoretically, the division could have troops on the ground anywhere in the world within about twenty-four hours of an order. Indeed, on exercises in 2015 and 2016, having mounted at Fort Bragg, paratroopers from 82nd Airborne parachuted directly into Spain and Poland as part of NATO exercises. The division is able to mount a full brigade combat team within eighteen hours of an order to deploy. 82nd Airborne has, then, a unique role in the US Army and as such it benefits from the highest levels of investment. Typically, it is receives new equipment after the Special Operations Forces and, in terms of digital communications, it has been significantly privileged. Indeed, the idea of commanding operations from a main base in the continental United States seems itself to have been a Special Operations Force innovation.[55] The result is that 82nd Airborne has been able to implement an advanced system of mission command so that operations can be coordinated from Fort Bragg.

Accordingly, 82nd Airborne has constructed an 'All-American Joint Operations Centre' inside its standing headquarters at Fort Bragg, North Carolina. This represents a radical reformation of the command-and-control architecture. In the past, the standing headquarters of a division served a purely administrative function. Located at the garrison of the division, the headquarters provided office space for the commander and staff to organize the division in peacetime and coordinate itself with the army hierarchy. On operations, a divisional headquarters deployed under canvas or armour, typically leaving a small standing rear element at the base to provide a supporting administrative function. 82nd Airborne have now instituted a quite different Command Post system in which operations are actually commanded by a Division Main headquarters at Fort Bragg and a deployed tactical headquarters. Divisional Main is no longer an administrative centre but an active operational command post. Consequently, in addition to the normal offices of a divisional headquarters, 82nd Airborne now has the capacity to monitor, control and to assist in the command operations from Fort Bragg as a result of the construction of a large,

---

[55] Fieldnotes, 82nd Airborne, Fort Bragg, 16–21 April 2015, Volumes III–IV.

secure and digitally connected operations centre within the headquarters building itself.[56]

The All-American Joint Operations Centre (JOC) is a remarkable and very recent innovation which has harnessed the potential of secure digital satellite communications; the centre was opened in 2013 after the division returned from its deployment to Kandahar.[57] As one officer noted: 'If you knew what this building looked like before, you would realise the importance of technology'.[58] The All-American JOC consists of a very large amphitheatre, equipped with ranks of computer terminals for staff officers, facing three very large screens. The central screen projects a digital situation map; other screens provide additional feeds. Adjacent to the All-American JOC is the Secret Compartment Intelligence Fusion (SCIF), which receives classified information from the national intelligence community, including the CIA and the NSA, which it is then able to share both with the JOC and subordinate units. The All-American JOC has allowed 82nd Airborne to implement its concept of mission command because staff back in Fort Bragg are able to maintain direct, constant and current awareness of the situation in theatre anywhere in the world. Consequently, 82nd Airborne has been able to divide its huge headquarters into two elements; the majority of the division's 700 staff, including the Plans (G5), Intelligence (G2) and Logistics (G1 and 4) elements, remain in situ in North Carolina, benefiting from working out of a properly founded and secure headquarters on continental America with a full complement of staff.[59]

Since its construction, 82nd Airborne has experimented and tested its new JOC in a series of demanding exercises which culminated in Exercise Warfighter in December 2014. The Warfighter series is perhaps the hardest examination to which the US Army submits its units, involving – as the name implies – high-intensity warfare. 82nd Airborne's officers confirmed the intensity of this exercise, noting that the division came close to losing on several occasions in its fight against an armoured division.[60] The exercise pressurized the headquarters and

[56] Fieldnotes, 82nd Airborne, Fort Bragg, 16–21 April 2015, Volume III, 115–16.

[57] Ibid.

[58] OF-3, Major, G2 82nd Airborne Division, interviewee 073, personal interview 21 April 2015.

[59] OF-5, Colonel, Chief of Staff, 82nd Airborne Division, interviewee 068, personal interview, 20 April 2015.

[60] Ibid.

its staff by creating a scenario in which its ground forces were subjected to multiple simultaneous attacks. Not only did the All-American JOC perform well but, because it has almost unlimited bandwidth, the Joint Operations Centre often has better situational awareness than the deployed tactical headquarters: 'We now have better awareness sitting back here – we have UAV etc – we know better than the DTAC [Divisional Tactical Command Post]. On the current fight, we have the next target; we have incredible situational awareness. They don't have the bandwidth and they don't have the cultural components'.[61] The All-American JOC is equipped to fight the deep battle.

82nd Airborne Division's All-American JOC has become critical to current operations. Indispensable staff elements now remain permanently in Fort Bragg where they are coordinated and controlled by the Deputy Commanding General-Support and the Chief of Staff. However, no matter what the fidelity of the intelligence in the Joint Operations Centre, a forward command element and headquarters has remained essential for the division. Because the division deploys by parachute, the construction of a forward command post on the drop zone is especially challenging; it severely limits its size and communications equipment which the division can employ, especially in the initial entry phase. However, the division signals team has enabled the Commanding General to have communications with Division Main by means of a satellite phone and personal laptop throughout any flight.[62] Consequently, the Commanding General is theoretically out of communications with Division Main only for the minutes required for him to hook up, jump from the aircraft and to land. The division has, then, built its forward headquarters in a three-stage process. The Assault Command Post is established immediately on the landing of the Commanding General and fifty staff officers on the drop zone. The Assault Command Post provided an almost immediate ability for Commanding Generals to exercise control over the division, by connecting them with their supporting staff and commanders back at Fort Bragg.

Four hours after setting up the Assault Command Post, a Main Assault Command Post becomes operational. Depending on the situation and the operation, the Divisional Tactical Command Post, a

[61] Ibid.
[62] OF-5, Colonel, G6, 82nd Airborne Division, interviewee 067, personal interview, 20 April 2015.

full forward headquarters consisting of 100 staff, can be established between twelve and twenty-four hours; some of the equipment for this headquarters is air-landed by plane rather than parachuted into the drop zone. Since 82nd Airborne are configured to seize an airfield, the formation has presumed that they will be able to fly in subsequent waves of support. The Divisional Tactical Command Post operates from specialist tenting and has its own Joint Operations Centre and supporting cells (see Figure 10.3) and a full suite of capabilities with supporting bandwidth; there is essentially no limit to the amount of data it can receive, process and disseminate. The 82nd Airborne Divisional Tactical Command Post is an example of the US Army's command post of the future. Consequently, its Joint Operations Centre includes a digital near-time location finder and has the software to install battlespace management tools, such as phase lines, onto it, which can be disseminated immediately to subordinate units. The command post is currently experimenting with a new digital tracking system.[63] This is a system which is already operational in the All-American Joint Operations Centre.

With 100 staff officers, the Divisional Tactical Command Post is itself as big as a divisional headquarters at the end of the twentieth century and is substantially more capable. For instance, on the Combined Joint Operational Access Exercise at Fort Bragg in April 2015, 82nd Airborne commanded not only their own forces from the Divisional Tactical Command Post at Landing Zone Sicily, but also a United State Marine Corps Marine Expeditionary Unit (an amphibious battle group) which was conducting an amphibious exercise on the coast some 100 miles away. The creation of a transcontinental command-and-control system has required some procedural reforms. For instance, the fidelity of digital communications which allows divisional commanders to observe small-unit actions in real-time potentially encourages micro-management, while there is a danger that the All-American JOC will simply duplicate the Divisional Tactical Command Post because it has the same or, in some areas, even better situational awareness. The Division has tried to avoid these problems by delineating responsibilities between Deep, Close and Rear, discussed previously. The Division Tactical Command Post has been tasked to

[63] OF-3, Major, Current Operations, 82nd Airborne Division, interviewee 063, personal communication, 16 April 2015.

Figure 10.3 82nd Airborne Division TAC HQ: LZ Sicily, EX CJOAX, April 2015.

fight the close fight in the present, while the All-American JOC, back at Fort Bragg, has focused on the future, planning operations ninety-six hours ahead or more; ninety-six hours is designated as the change-over from Division Main to Division Tactical because the Air Tasking Order has to be prepared four days in advance of execution. Of course, Division Main prepares a mission potentially weeks ahead of current operations. There is a division of command in the headquarters on the basis of time and space. Chapter 4 included a description of the 82nd Airborne's headquarters by a sergeant, Len Lebenson. It is instructive to compare 82nd Airborne's current headquarters and its capacities with Matt Ridgway's command post in Normandy in June 1944, in which Lebenson worked. That headquarters, which consisted of forty personnel, was easily accommodated in a small tent in the corner of a field just outside St Mère Eglise. Once it was established on 7 June, it allowed Ridgway to supervise and communicate with his formations, none of which was located much more than a mile away.

82nd Airborne has a unique mission in the US Army and enjoys a privileged position in terms of resourcing. Yet, it is not the only formation to have introduced mission command. 4th Infantry Division is currently committed to Europe with a specific mission of protecting the Baltic states. In the last two years, it has trained and exercised for this mission. In particular, like 82nd Airborne, it has introduced and tested a system of mission command so that while its brigades deploy forward into Europe under a forward divisional command post, the main divisional headquarters remains in Fort Carson, Colorado, at the division's home base. Mission command is a novel development in the US Army but it is not limited only to the Special Operations Forces and 82nd Airborne. It is a new command system across the Army. Indeed, like the US Army, the Marine Corps is experimenting with its maritime version of mission command. In the light of the increased likelihood of urban littoral operations and the dangers they pose for command posts, 1st Marine Division has experimented with situating the Main Headquarters off-shore on over-the-horizon amphibious shipping. Indeed, they have practised commanding urban operations at the 29 Palms training area from Camp Pendleton some 120 miles away.[64] As the US Army contemplates future wars, especially in urban environments, it is widely believed that an even greater dispersal and disaggregation of the headquarters will be necessary. It is likely that the processes which have been observable over the last few years will be accentuated rather than reversed.

The capabilities of 3 UK Division are a long way behind 82nd Airborne but, partly in response to the obvious vulnerabilities of its new headquarters, it too has begun to experiment with the concept of 'distributed command'. The concept of distributed command is derived directly from the US Army's mission command; it refers to the separation of main and tactical command posts. Indeed, there are close

[64] OF-7, Major-General, Commanding General 1st Marine Division, interviewee 098, personal interview, 15 March 2016.

links between 3 UK Division and 82nd Airborne and as 3 UK Division sought to re-structure from 2013, it visited 82nd Airborne repeatedly, took advice and sought to implement the American division's model of mission command. 3 UK Division has had to try and implement its model of distributed command on a much smaller budget than 82nd Airborne and, consequently, the innovations have been slower and less impressive. However, developments have taken place which represents a significant transformation of the traditional divisional headquarters in the United Kingdom. 3 UK Division is based at Picton Barracks, Bulford, on Salisbury Plain. Its headquarters has served as an office for its commander and staff from where the division has been administered during peacetime. However, as with other divisions, during exercises or on operations, the division's headquarters has deployed into the field, leaving a party at Picton to administer the rear. The headquarters at Picton Barracks has never been employed for operational command.

However, following the example of 82nd Airborne, the British Army has recently invested in Picton Barracks, constructing a new command facility, the Iron Division Operations Centre, adjacent to the existing headquarters building. This operations centre was officially opened in March 2017.[65] This building is, of course, far smaller than the All-American Joint Operations Centre but it is a fully networked, permanent and secure headquarters. The Iron Division Operations Centre includes a Joint Operations Centre and a series of offices and desk-spaces allowing staff officers to contribute to operations from their normal workstations. Before its construction, 3 UK Division has sought to implement the concept of distributed command on a number of exercises. For instance, in November 2014, 3 UK Division conducted its first full experiment of distributed command by flying a forward command post – Division Forward – to Cyprus to conduct an exercise using a reachback capability at the headquarters in Picton Barracks, which had been temporarily equipped with the requisite informational technology. A staff of fifty-eight personnel and equipment was flown forward in two C-17 transport aircraft to conduct the exercise, supported by intelligence, planning and logistic cells which remained in the UK.[66]

---

[65] Fieldnotes, 23 March 2017, Bulford, Volume VI, 70–1.
[66] Ibid.

The division experimented with distributed command on two further exercises, Joint Horizon in December 2015 and then Joint Venture in July 2016. In these cases, Division Forward was deployed to RAF St Mawgan in Cornwall, 170 miles from Bulford, while a temporary Division Main was created in the existing office space at Picton Barracks. There are certainly a number of obstacles which confront 3 UK Division. For instance, unlike the US Army, the British Army does not have one unified secure communications system. It has an operational communications information system and a tactical one. The interface of these two systems is at the divisional level so information cannot be disseminated seamlessly across command echelons, generating very considerable inefficiencies. The British Army also lacks a real-time system of unit identification and location like the American Blue-Force Tracker system above the tactical level. Yet, even with these problems and within its relatively constrained budget, 3 Division has proved its capacity to implement distributed command. Indeed, the signals branch of the headquarters does not see any significant technological impediments to distributed command. The problem is, in fact, primarily financial. One megabyte of data costs 3 UK Division £1000. On Exercise Joint Venture in July 2016, 3 UK Division procured two megabytes per day, which – although not optimal – was adequate for an exercise. However, a genuine operation would require much more bandwidth; eight megabytes – or £8000 per day.[67] The result of this budgetary constraint is that 3 UK Division has not been able to test distributed command as thoroughly as 82nd Airborne. Nevertheless, staff in the headquarters are confident that the system of distributed command is functionally viable and will become a real capability once the Iron Division Operations Centre is fully operational.[68] British distributed divisional command represents the budget version of the US Army's mission command. A British division is unlikely to possess the ability to command military operations globally in the foreseeable future; indeed, the aspiration to deploy a division globally and to command it from the Iron Division Operations Centre may be over-ambitious. Nevertheless, the Iron Division Operations Centre is a radical rupture of command arrangements from even the recent past.

[67] OF-3, Major, G6 3 UK Division, interviewee 122, personal communication, 5 July 2016.
[68] Fieldnotes, 23 March 2017, Bulford, Volume VI, 70–1.

État Major De Force 1 has no plans to institute an equivalent system of distributed command. Although it aims to exploit the benefits of digital communications to coordinate operations at greater range, it plans to deploy the divisional headquarters in a more conventional fashion. Recent French operations illustrate their thinking. In January 2013, the French Army conducted a major and very successful operation against Islamicist insurgents from MUJAO, Ansar Dine and Al-Qaeda in the Magreb in northern Mali, in Operation Serval. The operation involved about 6000 troops in total, commanded by a joint two-star headquarters, with a smaller land component. The land component involved the deployment of a composite land force of approximately two battlegroups (2000 soldiers) under a composite brigade headquarters of 100 staff and soldiers, including force protection, provided by *3eme Brigade Mecanisé* and *11 Brigade Parachutiste*.[69] The headquarters elements at both Joint Task Force and Land Component deployed into theatre. There is no ambition within the French Army to implement a system of distributed command and certainly, as Serval also showed, their digital communications systems are currently insufficient for such a system of command. Indeed – and Serval potentially indicates the point – the French Army may have developed EMF 1 and EMF 3 as their divisional headquarters not primarily with a view to deploying them as organic divisional headquarters on future operations but to provide a higher-level command and staff capacity. It has been suggested that parts of the divisional staff are most likely to be deployed to form an ad-hoc headquarters, just like the land component headquarters on the Mali mission.

1 Panzer Division is currently undergoing a radical programme of reform which will involve digitalization and the incorporation of a Dutch brigade into the formation. This will absorb its attention until 2020, when it is seeking to achieve full operating capacity. The division is also tasked to operate over a much smaller area: northern Germany, Poland and the Baltics. However, it seems likely that in the face of the changing character of warfare, 1 Panzer will have to implement a version of distributed command in order to fulfil its mission. It cannot be assumed that the other European powers will follow the British Army with distributed command. Yet, especially since the major European powers want to remain closely interoperable with the United

---

[69] www.rand.org/content/dam/rand/pubs/research_reports/RR700/RR770/RAND_RR770.pdf.

States, it seems likely that in the coming decade, some form of mission command will be promulgated and imitated much more widely.

The Globalized Headquarters

In order to command complex, multidimensional operations, the divisional headquarters has undergone a profound transformation in the last few years. These organizations have dramatically increased in size and the old Napoleonic structure has been superseded by integrated planning cells. At the same time, and perhaps most strikingly, they have institutionalized a radically dispersed system of command so that the Main and Forward elements of the headquarters, once only miles apart, are now potentially on different continents. In this way, the new divisional headquarters has assumed a surprising organizational form, which has some parallels with the commercial sector. In her work on financial institutions, Saskia Sassen has highlighted a profound reconfiguration of these companies from the 1970s as stable domestic markets evaporated. Specifically, in order to respond to competition and market volatility and to coordinate their increasingly globalized activities, these corporations reorganized management. Companies expanded their headquarters in major financial centres in a few global cities, while subordinate regional offices were closed down. In place of a national hierarchy of main and regional offices, corporate headquarters emerged. These nodes coordinated subsidiaries globally, attempting to respond more quickly to local opportunities. Sassen records a dual process of concentration of executive authority and simultaneous expansion of its responsibilities to a global scale:

> The geographic dispersal of economic activities that marks globalization, along with the simultaneous integration of such geographically dispersed activities, is a key factor feeding the growth and importance of central corporate functions. The more dispersed a firm's operations across different countries, the more complex and strategic its central functions – that is, the work of managing, coordinating, servicing, financing a firm's network of operations.[70]

---

[70] Saskia Sassen, 'The Global City: introducing a concept'. www.saskiasassen.com/pdfs/publications/the-global-city-brown.pdf.

Existing national hierarchies have condensed, while the reach of empowered corporate headquarters has expanded globally.[71]

Mission command and the new divisional headquarters seems to represent a military version of this distinctive double movement. In place of mass, industrial warfare on stable fronts against a conventional opponent, Western forces are now engaged in dispersed, informationalized operations against diverse, hybrid opponents in challenging urban areas. Western forces have attempted to coordinate military action at greater range and precision through the integration of heterogeneous forces. Command structures have been profoundly reformed to enable such synchronicity and simultaneity. At the divisional level, command capacity has been vastly increased at the home base, enabling divisions to conduct operations on an increasingly global basis through subsidiary forward command posts, connected with a continental Division Main through secure digital satellite communications. In the light of new operational conditions and facilitated by digital technology, there has been a profound revision of the divisional headquarters.

---

[71] Saskia Sassen, *The Global City* (Princeton, NJ: University of Princeton Press, 2001).

11 | DISTRIBUTING COMMAND

In the twenty-first century, the scope of military operations has expanded dramatically. They are now conducted over ranges, with diverse assets and in multiple domains, quite at odds with twentieth-century manoeuvre. The emergence of the new divisional headquarters has been a response to these new conditions. The staff has been expanded and command posts restructured as a result of increased coordination problems. Of course, the expansions of the divisional headquarters points only to a more fundamental issue. The increasing scope of operations has placed enormous pressures on the commander and, ultimately, demanded a reform of the practice of command. It is increasingly difficult for a single commander to monopolize decision-making. This transformation has already been plotted in the cases of Nick Carter and James Mattis in the first decade of the twentieth century. In both examples, it was possible to see an evolution of command. A new morphology was appearing. Mission definition has become ever more critical and the burdens of mission management have multiplied.

Since the withdrawal from Iraq and Afghanistan, the problem of command already evident in those theatres has only been accentuated. In the light of hybrid, informationalized conflicts, decision-making has become very challenging for divisional commanders. Command has become ever more complex and, as already noted, the reformation of the Western division should be substantially understood as a response to these challenges. In this new construct, as the span and the range of operations has increased; the number of decisions a commander has to make has proliferated. Coordinating a divisional operation and synchronizing its heterogeneous activities has become an intricate task. The new divisional headquarters represents an adaptation to these new pressures. Yet, the reformed headquarters has itself sometimes exacerbated the problems of command. The vast size of the divisional headquarters and its potentially intercontinental dispersal generate difficulties in themselves. Where divisional staffs were once small co-located bodies, the coordination of the staff has itself become a major managerial issue. Command breakdown is eminently possible.

Consequently, as the major Western powers have reinvigorated the divisional level, they have introduced a number of innovations in order to facilitate coordination and to assure unity of command. In order to increase the decision-making capacity of the division, Western armies have explicitly sought to construct a system of deputies to support and assist the commander. Effectively, the ad-hoc innovations which were observable in Kandahar in 2009 have been institutionalized and the deputy commanding general has become a critical figure at the divisional level. At the same time, as the divisional headquarters has enlarged, there have been systematic efforts to enhance the cohesiveness and professionalism of the staff. Precisely at the moment when the divisional headquarters has been extrapolated and diversified, the armed forces have tried to ensure, and indeed to deepen, levels of cooperation within the staff. Of course, neither of these adaptations is new. In the twentieth century, divisional commanders often had deputies and staff were also often professional. Yet, despite the continuity, the relative roles of the deputies and the staff have developed. The transformation of operations and the concomitant reorganization and expansion of the divisional headquarters itself has quite altered the role of the deputy and the staff. This chapter will examine the new significance of the deputy commander and the staff and their implications for contemporary command. It will be claimed that the rise of the deputy commanding general with executive powers and the professionalization of the staff constitute important elements of increasingly collective command at the divisional level.

The Deputy

Assistant commanders and deputies are not new. Chapter 5 discussed how many successful commanders employed a principal staff officer to help coordinate operations in the twentieth century. Some of these officers could assume the role of a deputy; Kienitz might well be described as Balck's deputy and Montgomery's GSO1, Victor Brown, was clearly a hugely capable staff officer. Montgomery himself was made Chief of Staff of 47th Division by Major General Gorringe in the First World War. In his memoirs, he recorded how his divisional commander had given him some executive authority over the division's units. Yet, the principal, indeed, exclusive, responsibility for decision-making still lay with the commander. The primary responsibility of the principal staff officer, even when assuming the role of deputy, was to disseminate and supervise the orders of their commanders, rather than to actively manage the mission.

The US Army formally employed Assistant Divisional Commanders from the early 1940s. However, the traditional Assistant Divisional Commanders often had only a subsidiary role, normally with little managerial authority. For instance, Brigadier General 'Dutch' Cota, Assistant Divisional Commander of 29th Infantry Division in Normandy, was certainly one of the most notable soldiers to perform this role. He landed on Omaha Beach in one of the first waves and, encountering inertia among his shocked troops, personally led the break-out through the Vierville Draw.[1] Even though he was a one-star general, he conducted himself as a platoon or company commander on that beach, directing his troops and physically leading the attack. Later, he taught platoons how to clear houses; this was important but hardly constituted executive decision-making. He led rather than commanded troops in the division.

Brigadier General Sam 'Hanging' Williams played a similar role in the troubled 90th Infantry Division in Normandy, on the Cotentin Peninsula.[2] General William Depuy, who served in the 90th Division in Normandy as a platoon commander and then a battalion executive officer, affirmed his qualities as a combat leader: 'he was helpful and very brave'.[3] Pointedly, however, Depuy never mentioned Williams' decision-making acumen and he was later sacked along with Brigadier General Mackelvie in July.[4] The examples of Cota and Williams are

---

[1] Joseph Balkosi, *Beyond the Beachhead: the 29th Infantry Division in Normandy* (Mechanicsburg, PA: Stackpole, 1999), 138.
[2] H. Jack Meyer, *Hanging Sam: a military biography of General Samuel T. Williams: from Pancho Villa to Vietnam* (Denton, TX: University of North Texas Press, 1990), 77–80.
[3] Ibid., 100.
[4] See Chapter 6.

suggestive. Both were involved in infantry assaults at the company and battalion level, not in executive decision-making at the divisional level. They were dedicated more to local leadership than divisional command.

The twenty-first-century deputy has assumed a quite different significance. As the previous chapter described, the scope of contemporary operations has expanded massively. As a result, mission management has become extremely complex; the number and range of decisions which a commander has to make have multiplied. It has become impossible for any commander to fulfil this executive function alone. Consequently, the role of the deputy has assumed a new importance. Deputies have been increasingly invested with circumscribed but genuine decision-making responsibility to increase the command capacity of a division. Nick Carter's experiences in Kandahar showed how important the deputy had become in contemporary warfare. His deputies did not just support him but acted as agents and proxies for him; they were actively engaged in decision-making.

The enhanced role of the assistant divisional commander, as an executive decision-maker, has been observable in other formations. For instance, during the invasion of Iraq in 2003, Major-General Buford Blount, the Commanding General of 3rd Infantry Division, shared his command with an Assistant Divisional Commander for manoeuvre (Brigadier Lloyd Austin) and an Assistant Divisional Commander for support (Brigadier Louis Weber). They acted as proxies for him on the battlefield, coordinating and directing everyday action, allowing Blount to focus on wider issues.[5] James Lacey's account of 3rd Infantry Division's war documents this distribution very well: 'Great commanders don't decide all the time. They know when to keep their fingers out of the pie and whey they decide, they made sure it was important things with the biggest impact. Blount was the master of this'. Specifically, 'the man General Blount trusted to make minute-to-minute decisions was Brigadier General Lloyd Austin'; described as an 'awesome, great leader', he drove from 'hot spot to hot spot in a small but efficient assault command post'.[6] Meanwhile, Louis Weber sustained the division;

[5] Jim Lacey, *The Take-Down: the Third Division's twenty-one day assault on Baghdad* (Annapolis, MD: Naval Institute Press, 2007), 8-9.
[6] Ibid., 8

'all three generals made major impacts on the conduct of the war'.[7] Integrated into decision cycles, Blount's deputies were far more active and empowered than the Assistant Divisional Commanders of the twentieth century. The current reorganization of the division has only accentuated this distribution of command authority to deputies. As the new headquarters has emerged and integration on the multi-domain battlefield has become the central command problem, deputy commanders have become increasingly important and prominent with enlarged decision-making responsibilities. They have assumed increased executive responsibilities; they have acted as proxies for their commanders, arrogating some of their authority.

The emergence of empowered deputies has been demanded by the changing operating environment. However, the need for deputies is further accentuated by internal organizational developments and, above all, by mission command or distributed command. When the divisional headquarters is so widely dispersed, commanders simply cannot physically be in the presence of all their staff or subordinates at any one point. They cannot give them direction personally, nor interact directly with them, as they did daily in the twentieth century. Digital communication has, of course, become critical here. Satellite communications have allowed commanders to communicate with their staff at range and the video-teleconference has mitigated the tyranny of distance to a degree. Commanders have been able to impress their intent on their staff through these means. Yet, virtual command of this type is regarded as far from optimal. Communicating digitally and talking with staff, even by live teleconferencing, is not the same as being physically co-present with them. Against the advocates of virtual communication, who presume that digital communications eliminate the problem of distance entirely, some American officers have warned: 'Virtual presence means actual absence'.[8] On this account, digital communications are no substitute for real presence. Indeed, according to these sceptics, if commanders are not physically present in a headquarters, they are not there at all. They cannot exert influence over their staff and subordinates. Personal interaction remains essential to the exercise of command.

---

[7] Ibid., 9.
[8] OF-7, Lieutenant-Colonel, III Corps, US Army, interviewee 137, personal interview, 16 June 2017.

At precisely this point, when headquarters have been dispersed, the deputy commanding general has played an increasingly important function. The deputy fulfils the need for command presence. A distribution of command authority has become especially necessary; commanders have increasingly utilized deputies, as their designated agents at each of the divisional headquarters' dispersed locations. Consequently, while commanders have not been able to maintain an immediate connection with their vast staffs in such dispersed systems, they have been able to retain a very close relationship with their deputies, who can actively ensure that the Commander's Intent is followed. Deputies have acted as the incarnation of the commander at each command node. Ironically, while digital communications have theoretically eliminated the need for command echelons by placing commanders in apparently instant contact with their subordinates, in fact, additional management has been required. Consequently, commanders rely on a designated team of local subordinates to enforce their intent. While commanders have to define the mission, as they ever did, the management of the mission and the suite of subordinate decision-making which that necessarily entails requires a distribution of command authority, if not responsibility. The proliferation of deputies is the manifestation of this reconfiguration of command.

The requirement for executive deputies can be seen in most of the new Western divisions. As with many other developments, 82nd Airborne has been at the forefront of developments here. The central problem of command in the 82nd Airborne is radical dispersal; operations are conducted intercontinentally. Because of mission command, the Commanding General will be on the objective in the Division Tactical Command Post. It is, therefore, impossible for Commanding Generals of 82nd Airborne to exert any personal influence over the vast majority of their staff or to communicate directly with them. This is plainly a major problem. In the twentieth century, more or less constant communication between the commander and staff was seen as essential. Accordingly, 82nd Airborne has developed a distinctive command system. As part of the reform of divisions, the US Army redesignated Assistant Divisional Commanders as Deputy Commanding Generals. At one level, the change in title was semantic. Yet, the alteration also highlighted the growing executive significance and status of the Deputy Commanding General in the division. In 82nd, the Commanding General has been formally supported and assisted by three deputies – all brigadiers: Deputy Commanding Generals-Operations, -Support and -Interoperability. These Deputy Commanding Generals have played a critical role in 82nd Airborne.

The emergence of the Deputy Commanding General does not imply that decision-making has become a matter of consensus or that the commander's authority has been attenuated. On the contrary, the Commanding General of 82nd Airborne Division retains total command responsibility over the formation. Indeed, the formation is typically commanded by a highly competent and experienced officer with a very powerful personality. Above all, Commanding Generals have retained responsibility for mission definition; any operation was always their responsibility. Critical decisions that might affect the entire division or the direction of the whole operation were directed to them.

The Commanding General 82nd Airborne Division, from 2012 to 2015, was fully apprised of his inalienable duties as a commander. In particular, he emphasized his responsibility to produce an intent for the division and to ensure that his subordinates adhered to it: 'My intent lays out the division's mission, the commander's priorities, emphasizing those and coming back to them all the time. From day 1 in command, this is the first thing I did. I produced a division policy letter. This is the first thing I did: Policy Letter No. 1. It provided my guidance and priorities.'[9] Policy Letter No. 1 laid out the commander's priorities very clearly: 'This policy establishes my commander's vision, enduring priorities and leadership philosophy. This is the enduring policy from which all other division policies will flow'. The intent then defined the division's mission: 'On order, the 82nd Airborne Division (-) rapidly deploy by Airborne Joint Forcible Entry (if required) to conduct specified mission in Support of Combatant Commands to accomplish US National policy objectives'. To this statement, the Commanding General appended a vision: 'The Division is rapidly deployable, scalable, tailorable and can easily operate in a Joint, Interagency, Intergovernmental and Multinational environment. The Division will train to provide our Nation with Paratroopers who are physically and mentally fit; extremely disciplined; and possess an expeditionary

---

[9] OF-7, Major-General, Commanding General 82nd Airborne Division, interviewee 137, personal interview, 20 January 2015.

mind-set'.[10] Finally, the Commanding General established 'five enduring priorities': readiness, leader development, training, professionalism and interoperability. Only the Commanding General of 82nd Airborne could establish divisional policy and issue an intent.

However, although the commander affirmed his sole responsibility for the division and the priority of his intent, he also underlined the importance of his Deputy Commanding Generals. They had the authority to implement the intent, manage significant parts of the mission it laid out and to take significant decisions in the coordination of operations. The Commander's Intent became a critical reference point for them.[11] However, the Deputy Commanding Generals managed the manoeuvre and support units. The Commanding General of 82nd Airborne summarized the command construct: 'The commander himself has to be at the heart of the decision-making process. You have to be careful not to get bogged down in coordination. You can't forget the essence of command. For bigger decisions, it goes to you. However, there is delegation of lesser decisions to the DCGs [Deputy Commanding Generals] and COS [Chief of Staff]'.[12]

On this model, the new Deputy Commanding Generals in the 82nd Airborne have sometimes acted as decision-makers with executive authority: 'Our deputies are deputies in big macro sense'.[13] However, they have not, of course, displaced the Commanding General's supreme authority. Rather, they have been assigned jurisdiction in specific areas: 'The Deputy Command General Operations handles the manoeuvre brigades, the parachute infantry brigades. The Deputy Commanding General Support deals with Artillery and attack helicopters'.[14] In these domains, the Deputy Commanding Generals have taken responsibility for these lower-level decisions, especially in relation to the management of specific aspects of the mission. In addition to a specific role, each Deputy has also been given a location. Deputy Commanding Generals-Operations have been located forward

[10] Commander 82nd Airborne Division, *Memorandum for all Paratroopers Assigned to or Attached to 82nd Airborne Division*, 20 October 2014, 1-1.

[11] See the following chapter for a discussion of the Decision Points.

[12] OF-7, Major-General, Commanding General 82nd Airborne Division, interviewee 051, personal interview, 20 January 2015.

[13] Ibid.

[14] OF-7, Major-General, Commanding General 82nd Airborne Division, interviewee 051, personal interview, 20 January 2015.

in the Divisional Tactical Command Post, responsible for the close battle and the coordination of the brigades. There they have worked closely with the Commanding General. Meanwhile, the Deputy Command General-Support and the Chief of Staff have managed the mission from the digitalized All-American Joint Operations Centre at Fort Bragg. There, the Deputy Commander-Support has fought the deep battle. In 2012, a further Deputy Commanding General-Interoperability post was created and assigned to a British officer. The purpose of this role was to coordinate the integration of the UK's 16 Air Assault Brigade into the division. From 2016, the British post was converted from Deputy Commanding General-Interoperability to Deputy Commanding General-Plans.

The result of this distribution of command is a clear division of labour: 'They [the Deputy Commanding Generals] actually go out more often than I do. They are unencumbered compared to me'.[15] Deputies have not relieved the commander of the burdens of command but they have helped share the managerial role, in a way which has clear echoes to Kandahar:

> My deputies give me, as GOC, additional eyes. The commander of 3 UK Division was here. We had an interesting discussion. He was asking, how/what do I do with my one-star deputy. My counsel to him was that you have to empower him. You have to give him direction and guidance. He is the senior guy – your deputy. The DCG is the direct boss of the brigade commanders. How do you take a one-star and use him to be value added and not just a staff officer? Both DCGs have their own lanes; they have their terms of reference. Specifically, it spells out the responsibility of senior leaders. The 3 DCGs and RSM get an understanding of how to divide the effort.[16]

In the face of increased complexity, the commander of 82nd Airborne has shared decision-making authority with his deputies in designated areas. While he retains sole responsibility for the formation, he has created a division of managerial labour, parcelling out decision-making authority to his deputies.

---

[15] Ibid.
[16] Ibid.

Significantly, staff officers in 82nd Airborne have also noted the importance of this distribution of command authority.

> There is a difference between 'heroic' World War II legacy and today. People going into command today don't think like that anymore. We have tried to change it [command style] through Mission Command. When you go back to WWII, when the commander tried to keep his hands on things, it actually disrupts operations now. There are too many data points for any one person to manage. There are all the warfighting functions and other operations and when they do [try to command individually], they break the system. They break the system which was explicitly developed for complex operations.[17]

While the responsibilities of the commander are unalienable, according to this officer, commanders now have to share and distribute decision-making authority. Indeed, on this account, an overly individualistic commander, intent on monopolizing managerial decisions, would undermine the coherence of divisional operations. Successful commanders in 82nd Airborne have to know when and how to share their executive responsibilities and to give deputies genuine decision-making authority. In 82nd Airborne, the Deputy Commanding Generals have become indispensable.

The high-quality training and extensive experience of Deputy Commanding Generals is immediately relevant here in illustrating this expansion of authority. Because of the complexity of planning, the division required greater experience and authority below the Commanding General. In the twentieth century, Assistant Divisional Commanders were not necessarily of the highest quality. Cota was an excellent leader but he struggled with the burdens of being divisional commander when he was eventually appointed to the 28th Infantry Division;[18] Williams was relieved. By contrast, American Deputy Commanding Generals today have already commanded a brigade successfully before they take up their post in a division. Moreover, the selection process for Deputy Commanding General is very intense. For instance, to command one

---

[17] OF-3, Major, G3, 82nd Airborne Division, interviewee 075, personal interview, 22 April 2015.

[18] Robert Miller, *Division Commander: a biography of Major-General Norman Cota* (1989).

of the thirty-two regular brigades in the US Army, an officer has to be regarded as in the top sixteen officers in an original cohort of 4000.[19] Deputy Commanding Generals are also likely to go on to command a division; David Petraeus, for instance, was an Assistant Division Commander in 82nd Airborne, while General Richard Clarke, a former Commander, served as a Deputy Commanding General before assuming command of the division.

82nd Airborne is clearly a privileged formation and may be extreme, even in the US Army, in terms of its distribution of decision-making authority. Yet, the division is not unique. The important role of Deputy Commanding Generals in 3rd Infantry Division in Iraq in 2003 has been noted; they exercised actual command authority. Other US Army divisions – like 4th Infantry Division – have the standard two Deputy Commanding Generals, one for operations and one for support. In each case, Deputy Commanding Generals have been appointed to augment the command capacity, and specifically the management and leadership, of the division. The Commanding General has defined the mission and laid out the intent but the Deputy Commanding Generals have ensured that managerial decisions are enacted and the forces motivated to execute them across diverse locations.

A British general who served as a Deputy Commanding General-Support in a US corps on Operation Inherent Resolve in Iraq in 2016 explained that while command responsibility always lay with the commander, the deputy now wielded critical authority: 'The Deputy Commanding General has no intent, no synchronization matrix and no commander's critical information requirements. But he acts as oil to drive the Commanding General. To quote my commander: "you do what I don't have time to do. Or I don't want to do. You set me up for success when I don't have time to set the conditions".'[20] As Deputy Commanding General-Support, this officer described his role in preparing the conditions for operations, especially in terms of logistics and infrastructure: 'My decisions were way back here [before the operation began]. He can't micromanage this. But only a General Officer

---

[19] OF-5, Colonel, Chief of Staff, 82nd Airborne Division, interviewee 068, personal interview, 20 April 2015.

[20] OF-7, British Army, Deputy Commanding General III Corps US Army, interviewee 138, personal interview, 16 June 2017. Although the officer's experiences referred to his time in III Corps, he described them because he believed they were illustrative of compatible developments at divisional level.

can do it. Only a General Officer can do the "oiling"; a full colonel can't.[21] According to this officer, only the flag rank carried the requisite status and authority to exercise genuine command. As a result of his rank, this general 'fluffed' various partners. He negotiated with, cajoled and encouraged various individuals who were essential to the operation, but whom the Commanding General did not have time or the inclination to manage. Decisions have been extrapolated so far across time and space that it is simply impossible for a single commander to manage a mission.

In Chapter 9, the distinctive command culture of the US Marine Corps was highlighted. The US Marine Corps idealizes a highly personalized system of command, which James Mattis embodied during the March Up. In 2015, 1st Marine Division had only one Assistant Divisional Commander post and it was not even filled for the first part of that year. However, it would be a mistake to presume that the US Marine Corps is entirely distinct or that it has responded to the operational pressures in a completely different way. The experiences of Major General Richard F. Natonski, commander of 1st Marine Division in Anbar in 2004, illustrate the importance of the deputy, even in a very command-centric organization like the US Marine Corps. Natonski took over command of 1st Marine Division from James Mattis in August 2004. He was responsible for ground operations in the whole of Anbar Province but his most immediate task was to seize and secure the city of Fallujah, which had become a haven for insurgents and threatened the Iraqi national election in January 2005. The 1st Marine Division was one of the most homogeneous and integrated of any Western formation; it was contrasted markedly, for instance, with the ad-hoc, multinational force which Nick Carter commanded in Kandahar, discussed in Chapter 8.

However, despite the initial divergence between their own formations, there were clear parallels between both commanders in the attack on Fallujah. Like Carter's force in Kandahar, Natonski eventually commanded a diverse multinational force for Fallujah, which required additional leadership investment by him. Four Iraqi battalions were integrated into Regimental Combat Teams 1 and 7, while an Iraqi battalion and 2 Brigade Combat Team, 1st Cavalry screened the city to the east. Indeed, the attack was preceded by the

---

[21] Ibid.

assault of 36 Iraqi Commando Battalion, which seized the hospital, being used by insurgents as a command node, on the west bank of the Euphrates. In all, six Iraqi battalions were under Natonski's command. There was also a significant element from the US Army, including 2nd Battalion, 2nd Infantry and 2nd Battalion, 7th Cavalry Task Forces, while 2 Brigade Combat Team, 2nd Infantry Division and 2 Brigade Combat Team, 1st Cavalry, supported the assault into Fallujah. Finally, a British Army battalion, The Black Watch, was redeployed from Basra to Northern Babil to replace US Marine units which had been assigned to the attack of Fallujah. Generating cohesion in such a diverse force was a considerable challenge.

There were further challenges. Although Natonski was focused entirely on the Fallujah operation during the assault into the city, this was not the exclusive mission of 1st Marine Division at that time. On the contrary, while fighting in Fallujah, the Division was still responsible for the whole of Anbar Province, including such difficult locations as Ramadi, Hit and Al Qaim. Although it was necessarily the focus of attention for the commander, 1st Marine Division could not concentrate entirely on Fallujah. It also had to continue to command and control forces in the rest of the province. 'The Main Effort of the Division was Fallujah but I was not relieved of responsibility for the rest of Anbar, so I had to split the Division staff'.[22] Accordingly, Natonski employed his Assistant Division Commander, Brigadier General Joe Dunford, to provide additional command capacity while he was committed to Fallujah. Natonski was fortunate here and he certainly emphasized the competence of his Assistant Division Commander. Joe Dunford had commanded Regimental Combat Team-5 during the invasion of Iraq and he was widely regarded as the most successful of the regimental commanders in the division at that time. He has subsequently gone on to command ISAF and serve as the Commandant of the Marine Corps and Chairman of the Joint Chiefs of Staff. Natonski relied upon Dunford to continue to oversee operations in Anbar Province during the Battle of Fallujah.

> Anbar is the size of North Carolina; Fallujah is just one city.
> I had the best Marine and officer in the armed forces in Joe

---

[22] Lieutenant-General Richard Natonski, interviewee 101, personal interview, 22 March 2016.

Dunford. He is brilliant, humble and a true warrior. In the days
before the assault, I took my Jump Command Post, with certain
of my staff principals, and displaced to Camp Fallujah. I gave
Joe the rest of Anbar Province, including Ramadi. In this way
I narrowed my span of control. The bulk of the staff remained at
Camp Blue Diamond and continued to conduct operations.[23]

In order to maintain command coherence across 1st Marine Division
and its multinational partners in Fallujah and across Anbar, Natonski
had to devolve decision-making authority to Dunford and subordinate
commanders.[24] Natonski, of course, remained ultimately responsible
for 1st Marine Division's action, playing a critical role in defining
the mission and making the most important decisions. However, in
order to orchestrate a complex, dispersed operation, he required the
assistance of subordinate commanders who acted as his agents, making
decisions for him when he was committed elsewhere. Even in the US
Marine Corps, deputies have played an increasingly important role in
managing operations.

Somewhat like the US Marine Corps, the British Army has
traditionally displayed little interest in deputy commanders; they too
have idealized a personalized command-centred system. At the divisional level, up to the recent past, a major-general normally had a
deputy, but the role was often filled by a 'passed-over' officer who had
no possibility of further promotion. Indeed, it was commonplace for
the deputy commander to have never even commanded a brigade; the
deputy role was often reserved for officers deemed to be trustworthy
but second-tier. It was a subsidiary and secondary appointment and the
British Army assigned an officer of this type to the deputy role precisely
because the position was regarded as undemanding. The deputy commander in the British Army had little, if any, operational role and was
usually employed in administering the home base or divisional rear
area. A senior British general was scathing about his Army's negligence
of the role of the deputy: 'In the UK we are really bad at it. Deputies
are seen as "hangers-on"'.[25] Indeed, he noted how this disdain for deputies had sometimes generated problems for the British. For instance,

[23] Ibid.
[24] Ibid.
[25] OF-8, Lieutenant-General (retired), British Army, interviewee 114, personal communication, 31 May 2016.

during the NATO IFOR intervention into Bosnia in 1995, a British commander and his chief of staff collapsed and needed two weeks off during the operation. They were trying to do too much precisely because there were no deputies: 'You need the capacity to take the pressure and work and decision-making off them'.[26] By contrast, when this senior officer was working in a three-star NATO appointment, he operated as a fully executive deputy. His German superior gave him a clear area of responsibility and affirmed to this British officer that in those areas, 'You are me!'[27]

Even today, the British Army is often unclear about the role and status of a deputy commander. For instance, in 2015, Joint Force Command established a new two-star command, capable of conducting joint operations. In 2015, this joint headquarters began an exercise regime which was intended to bring it up to full operating capacity. On one of these exercises in November 2015, a British brigadier was assigned the position of playing the deputy commander of this head-quarters. Because of the traditionally peripheral status of the deputy, he regarded the role as difficult and even demeaning. He summarized his attitude towards his new role bluntly: 'I hate it'. The problem was that, for him, no clear distinction had been drawn between the roles of commander, deputy and chief of staff; 'there was no purity'. He found it frustrating to stand in for the commander and then to make decisions, only for the command to return to say, 'that is not quite what I want'. He concluded: 'I am used to command. I am an alpha male. And suddenly I am someone else's servant'.[28] The specific problems of this officer and the Standing Joint Task Force are not particularly relevant here. However, his predicament usefully illustrates the traditional status of the deputy in British military culture. It has been a low-status role, given to unambitious officers

However, the status of the deputy is beginning to change. Following his experiences in Kandahar, Nick Carter came to recognize the value of deputies: 'We [the British] think of deputies as irrelevant. But in Regional Command South, I needed two empowered deputies, one US Army (Hodges) and one US Marine Corp (Murray)'.[29] Indeed,

[26] Ibid.

[27] Ibid.

[28] OF-6, Brigadier, Royal Marines, interviewee 095, personal interview, 29 November 2015.

[29] General Nick Carter, presentation, interviewee 080, 23 June 2015.

Chapter 8 describes how Carter eventually utilized all six of his deputies in different roles. Partly as a result of Nick Carter's intervention, 3 UK Division eventually institutionalized a permanent Deputy Commanding General. In 2015, an American brigadier who had already commanded at brigade level was appointed to the role. Since that time, 3 UK Division has been determining how best to employ this deputy in order to improve the managerial capacity of the division. It has taken advice from 82nd Airborne.[30] Nevertheless, even in 2017, when a deputy commander had been formally appointed, his role was still unclear. Moreover, the divisional chief of staff retained his traditional position of primacy with genuine executive authority. Not only did the chief of staff continue to organize the headquarters, coordinating the staff work, but he was intimately involved in the decision-making process.

The precedence of the chief of staff has been recurrently observable on exercises. For instance, during Exercise Warfighter in June 2017, the division was attacking a river line so that it could attain one of its major objectives. As the advance proceeded, one of the division's two assault brigades approached the river crossing more quickly than expected. It was ahead of the schedule and began to become misaligned with the other brigade to its left. Not only did this mean that the brigade was exposing its flank and might reach what was thought to be the main line of enemy resistance on its own but additional supporting assets were not prepared for early execution. The Current Operations Centre became concerned with the situation and requested a decision from the Chief of Staff and the Deputy Commanding General as to how to proceed.[31] Intense discussions followed over the birdtable in the Current Operations Centre. While the Deputy Commanding General was involved in these discussions about what to do, in the end the Chief of Staff – not the Deputy Commanding General – decided to stick with the initial plan and to order the forward brigade to wait until the other unit had caught up. He concluded decisively: 'It's a problem but not enough to change the plan'.[32] Even today, 3 UK Division has residues of the traditional headquarters, where the relationship between the

---

[30] OF-7, Major-General, Commander 82nd Airborne Division, interviewee 137, personal interview, 20 January 2015.
[31] Exercise Warfighter, Fort Bragg, Fieldnotes, Vol VI, 14 June 2017, 93–5.
[32] Ibid., 95.

commander and the GSO1 was critical. In this context, the Deputy Commanding General is an anomaly.

Nevertheless, despite these cultural preferences, 3 UK Division has begun to formalize the role of deputies. For instance, when he was Commander Field Army, and as part of his programme of reforming the divisional level, General Nick Carter institutionalized a system where the commander of 3 UK Division was supported in the way he had been in Kandahar. 3 UK Division's new headquarters has included the formal designation of a 'Principal Planning Group' comprising all the senior officers in the headquarters. The Principal Planning Group is designed to support and enhance command in the division. The senior officers in the group are, somewhat confusingly, designated as Deputy Commanders of their specialist functional area, though they should not be confused with the actual Deputy Commanding General. This Principal Planning Group has consisted of four Deputy Commanders for Fires (the old CRA; a brigadier), Engineers (the old CRE; a colonel), Intelligence and Understanding (a colonel) and Information and Outreach (a brigadier), as well as the Chief of Staff, the Deputy Chief of Staff (both colonels), the heads of the integrating and other functional cells and a military legal adviser (lieutenant-colonels). In addition to this military staff, the Principal Planning Group has also included a civilian political adviser and stabilization adviser. The Principal Planning Group constitutes an executive body which has been called a command board. The group attends all the major meetings during the planning and targeting process to ensure unity across the diverse lines of activity and to offer expert opinion. It has explicitly been conceived as possessing 'enhanced wisdom' to assist commanders in making their decisions. The Principal Planning Group has provided the commander with a 'hierarchy of wisdom to deal with the complexity based on professional experience and staff capacity that is a step change from the brigade'.[33] Consequently, in marked contrast to the twentieth century, the divisional command is now advised by three brigadiers (the Deputy Commander and Deputy Commander Fires, Information and Outreach), four colonels and five lieutenant-colonels. 3 UK Division may not have genuine Deputy Commanding Generals, equivalent to the US Army, but it has introduced structures to augment its decision-making capacity.

---

[33] Army Field Manual Vol 1 Part 1A Divisional Tactics, 1-1.

The French Army also has a command-centric system.[34]
However, in response to complex contemporary missions, the
emergence of a board to support the commander, which has some
parallels with 3 UK Division's 'hierarchy of wisdom', is evident.
French officers highlight the distinctiveness of the twenty-first-
century operating environment and, therefore, the requirement for
increased managerial capacity. In terms of command representation,
the French divisional headquarters is perhaps somewhat closer to
the American model than the British. The commander is supported
by a one-star deputy commander, a chief of staff (colonel), an
assistant chief of staff (colonel), a deputy chief of staff-operations
and -support (both colonels), as well colonels and half-colonels in
charge of the various functional areas.[35] As in the UK, the chief of
staff has occupied the critical position in coordinating the headquarters, connecting the commander with the staff: 'The chief of
staff is the pivot. The Chief of Staff is aware of everything in this
situation, both up and down'.[36]

The military functions performed by the staff, managed by
the chief of staff, are crucial. However, because of the changing operational environment, these officers have been augmented by various
non-military specialists to form a command group:

> The environment has changed. There are other stakeholders.
> You are not alone. You are not alone when you arrive
> in theatre. There are political actors, social actors, HA
> [Humanitarian Assistance], economic, IGOs, NGOs, media.
> You have to interact with these agencies all the time; it is
> always inter-something. It is different from the twentieth
> century. It is now inter-service, -agencies, -government. To
> face these combinations/complexities, the commander asks to
> have many advisers around him: the Polad [Political Adviser],
> Legad [Legal Adviser], Ecoad [Economic Adviser], Culad
> [Cultural Adviser]. That is your board.[37]

---

34 Fieldnotes, EMF 1, Besancon, 24 May 2016, Volume V, 104.
35 OF-5, Colonel, Chief of Staff, EMF, 1 French Army, interviewee 107, personal interview, 24 May 2016.
36 Ibid.
37 OF-6, Brigadier, Deputy Commander, EMF, 1 French Army, interviewee 097, personal
interview, 3 February 2016.

In some cases, especially with civilian advisers, these individuals see their role as actively challenging and questioning the presumptions of the commander to confirm the rectitude of the decision-making.[38]

The commander is at the centre of a complex organizational network in the new French divisional headquarters, retaining command responsibility. However, there is an explicit institutional attempt to improve command decisions by ensuring that they are properly informed by experts representing all the activities of a division: 'His [the commander's] main job is to anticipate. Perhaps you can do that alone, but today to do that it is important to share that with your command group. Every day, you have to share questions of the day and to do that continuously. For me the command group is very flexible; it consists of the army deputy, the Polad, some advisers, the Legad, the COS, depending on the situation and if he is not caught up in the current action'.[39] However, the commander nevertheless plays the decisive role:

> When you are in command you work with a command group
> and a chief of staff. But you are not the commander because
> you have many advisers. The more advisers you have, the more
> you have to command. Your advisers ask what you would
> like to know in their areas of expertise. But they are not
> responsible. You are the only one who is responsible. You are the
> only one with the overall view. Only you are responsible for the
> consequences of military action in all these areas.[40]

The officer continued: 'The great commander has to be really strong in his attitude and demeanour and to absorb this pressure [from the media and from the strategic and political level]. He has to protect his subordinates from that; if he doesn't do that, he's a failure'.[41]

Clearly, in a French division, the commander has to be helped with decision-making because the operating environment has become more complex but the requirement for decision-making assistance

[38] Political Adviser, EMF 1 French Army, Exercise Rochambeau, interviewee 033, personal interview, 16 May 2014.

[39] OF-7, Major-General, Commander, EMF, 1 French Army, interviewee 108, personal interview, 24 May 2016.

[40] OF-6, Brigadier, Deputy Commander, EMF, 1 French Army, interviewee 097, personal interview, 3 February 2016.

[41] Ibid.

could not be confused with a devolution of the fundamental command responsibility:

> We have to collect information on the enemy. At the present moment, it is more complex but we have many assets to help us make decisions. But the leader – he is the one to take the decision. You can't share the decision. Especially today with the pressure of justice, all the time you have to explain what you have done. You are the only one responsible. You can exchange a lot before orders. But once you give orders, you are responsible.[42]

The chief of staff emphasized the point: 'The commander decides every time. But the staff has the responsibility to show to the commander all the criteria of the decision. Commander decides the COAs [courses of action] etc and decides the *Effet Majeure* and the mission. The staff prepares the decision to ensure that the decision fits all the criteria: enemy, terrain, logistics'.[43] In the French division, the commander retains sole responsibility for mission definition and all major decisions. However, no commander has expertise in all the functions which are now required to conduct divisional manoeuvre and, consequently, requires the counsel of advisers to ensure the validity of major decisions and to assist with the management of operations.

France certainly has a different command culture to either the US, which tends to be more formal, hierarchical and specialized, or the UK, which tends towards more informality and a devolution of responsibility to surprisingly low levels, but the appearance of collective executive bodies parallels the American and British experience closely. Indeed, the claim that the increased responsibilities of commanders have required a board of deputies to assist in decision-making accords closely with the findings of Chapters 8 and 9. There it was shown that while Mattis and Carter assumed far more responsibility than their predecessors for mission definition, they relied on a team of subordinates and staff – a command collective, it was suggested – to manage operations in Kandahar and Iraq. Similarly, in recently reformed Western divisions, although responsibility for the decisions resided exclusively with the commander, who retains sole

---

[42] Ibid.
[43] OF-5, Colonel, Chief of Staff, EMF 1 French Army, interviewee 107, personal interview, 24 May 2016.

responsibility for mission definition, the process of decision-making has been shared collectively with senior officers, staff and deputies. In these divisions, commanders have defined the mission but they have increasingly invested deputies with executive authority in order to manage and coordinate it.

The Staff

In his memoir of his service as the operations sergeant in the headquarters of 82nd Airborne Division in the Second World War, Len Lebenson describes the irascibility of one of the branch chiefs in the headquarters, Colonel 'Rusk'. Lebenson had served under this officer in the G3 branch in Sicily and loathed him. He was delighted when this officer was reassigned to G2 for Overlord. Indeed, in Normandy, Lebenson described how he could hear this officer berating his subordinates in the G2 cell through the canvas of the tent. At one point between bombardments on D-Day, the martinet Rusk ordered his sergeant to clear up all the discarded carbon paper and tissue slips on the ground, from incoming and outgoing messages: 'Vines, this is a direct order, police up the area!' Vines refused: 'If one can imagine a hush coming over an area under fire, one came to our apple orchard'.[44] The incident demonstrates the intimacy of the divisional headquarters in the 1940s. All the staff of Ridgway's headquarters were immediately colocated. Close cooperation – or conflict – was simple, almost inevitable.

The situation is now quite otherwise. Headquarters have expanded dramatically so that, even if officers are in the same Command Post, they are often not sharing immediate office space. Moreover, under the system of mission command or distributed command, the staff has been radically dislocated. They may be hundreds of miles, even continents, apart. There are clearly very serious implications here for the situational awareness and collaboration of the staff. The function of a staff is to collate and analyze information coherently in order to inform a commander's decision-making. The dispersion of the staff threatens their unity and, consequently, jeopardizes their ability to fulfil their prime function. The disaggregation of the staff potentially

---

[44] Len Lebenson, *Surrounded by Heroes*, 117.

undermines command. At a time when decision-making is ever more complex and necessary, this is a serious organizational problem.

Chapter 9 described how James Mattis had taken great care to build a cohesive staff in order to conduct the March Up. He kept his staff small, selected trusted officers and minimized the rank profile in order to engender a sense of unity and purpose. However, the expansion of the distances over which operations are now conducted, the multiplication of functions within the division and the appearance of dispersed new headquarters has demanded an even higher level of cohesiveness among the staff. Professionalization has been critical here. In his work on the officer corps in the late 1950s, Samuel Huntington defined professionalism as expertise – 'specialized knowledge and skill in a significant field of human endeavour'; responsibility – the service is 'essential to the functioning of society'; and corporateness – 'the members of a profession share a sense of organic unity and consciousness of themselves as a group apart from laymen'.[45] It remains a very useful way of understanding professionalism and is immediately relevant to understanding the staff in a contemporary divisional headquarters. On the basis of Huntington's definition, a professional staff can be defined by three essential features: specialist knowledge of both particular functional areas and staff procedures themselves and a corporate ethos. In response to the increased complexity of divisional operations, the engorgement and dispersion of the divisional headquarters, divisional staff have been forced to become more professional. Their expert knowledge has increased and diversified, while the solidarity between them – precisely because they no longer enjoy the contiguity which Lebenson described – has been intensified.

Of course, in the twentieth century, a divisional staff always contained some professional staff officers; the Ia, GSO1 or Chief of Staff were almost always career soldiers, with specialist staff training, and some of the other important staff positions were also occupied by professionals. Once the British and American armies abandoned conscription in 1960 and 1973 respectively, the entire staff of a division was, of course, professional. However, from 1914 to 1991, and especially during the First and Second World Wars, staff expertise in many divisional headquarters was often low. Before the First World War, the

---

[45] Samuel Huntington, *The Soldier and the State* (Cambridge, MA: Belknap Press, 1957), 8–10.

British Army was deeply concerned about the lack of qualified staff officers who had passed staff college; by 1910, the Staff College at Camberley had increased its number of graduates to forty-nine a year. In 1914, 1443 British serving officers had passed staff college. This was more than sufficient to staff the BEF; the *Army List* for January 1908, for example, records that *psc*-qualified officers occupied every GSO1 appointment in the divisions.[46] However, it was quite insufficient to provide qualified staff to the sixty-five divisions of the expanded British Expeditionary Force.

The US Army suffered the problem in the First and Second World Wars even more acutely, because their expansion was even more pronounced that the British. The inexperience of Gavin's staff for Market Garden demonstrated the point very clearly. There was a general shortage of qualified staff officers. Yet, even the supposedly highly professional Wehrmacht demonstrates precisely the same problem. Rommel was never staff-trained at all. Erich von Manstein observed that as Germany prepared for the invasion of Poland in 1939, it was difficult to train new divisions. He implied a shortage of adequate staff officers at divisional level.[47] It was simply very difficult of train enough staff officers for mass citizen armies, especially when they expanded rapidly during the First and Second World Wars.

Chapter 5 showed how commanders like Monash, Montgomery, Balck and Smith operated very professional headquarters. They and their staff were highly competent, hugely adept at managing the complexity of divisional operations at the time. However, in the twenty-first century, the increasing complexity of operations and the size and dispersal of headquarters have demanded ever higher levels of professionalism from the staff. It is notable that, in contrast to most of the twentieth century, the staff, all of whom are now professional career officers, are now trained more thoroughly in common procedures and, in many cases, are deep specialists in their area of expertise. Increased numbers of officers now attend staff college and are staff-trained. Higher command and staff courses, like the German General Staff Service Course, remain highly selective across the Western powers. However,

---

[46] Douglas Delaney, *The Imperial Army Project: Britain and the Land Forces of the Dominions and India, 1902–1945* (Oxford: Oxford University Press, 2017), 50–4, 123–4, 268–71.

[47] Erich von Manstein, *Lost Victories*, 86.

where staff college was once the preserve of an exclusive elite, almost all officers now attend at least junior staff training at the rank of captain or junior major and a significant minority, and certainly all those who are going to hold important jobs in a divisional headquarters, typically attend a further course for senior majors and lieutenant-colonels. They understand the intricacies of staff work and all the technical terms associated with it, having practised it extensively both in the classroom and on exercises. In the United States, a selection of officers from each cohort have also completed a School of Advanced Military Studies course, which involves historical education and professional training. [48] The general level of staff training has increased notably as a result. There were certainly outstandingly professional staff officers in divisional headquarters in the twentieth century; there are some poor ones in today's headquarters. However, across the officer corps, the corporate level of expertise has increased. It is, of course, necessary to define the key characteristics of this professionalization.

Expert knowledge is nothing new in a staff, as Chapters 4 and 5 demonstrated. However, in the current era, with the proliferation of military technologies and the increasing interdependence of the services, headquarters require a greater number of specialist staff officers. Staff officers must have expert knowledge of the specific military function for which they are responsible – artillery, drones, human intelligence, mapping, cyber, information. For instance, many of the functions in the 82nd Airborne's intelligence cell simply did not exist in the twentieth century; some surveillance techniques were not invented, while others, such as the human terrain, were irrelevant. The new headquarters is a conglomeration of experts covering a range of disciplines which quite dwarf the twentieth-century divisional headquarters.

The following chapter will analyze a specific piece of modern staff work, the Decision Point, to demonstrate the professionalized practice of today's divisional staff in detail. There, the mechanics of contemporary staff work and the way in which it informs decision-making will be analyzed in depth. As an introduction to the lifeworld of the modern divisional headquarters, it is necessary at this point to record the special ethos of these institutions today. Divisions have actively sought to enjoin unity in their staffs.

---

[48] http://usacac.army.mil/organizations/cace/cgsc/sams.

Precisely because of its extreme dispersion, 82nd Airborne has been deeply conscious of the problem of staff unity. It has instituted specific methods in order to try to maximize the cohesiveness between the deployed and rear elements of the division. For instance, during the Exercise Warfighter in December 2014, the Chief of Staff insisted not only that Division Main was in communication with the forward command post but that there was genuine cognitive cohesion across the staff: 'I want you to be psychologically deployed. You are to consider yourself deployed'.[49] Exercise Warfighter was set in Africa under Africom with the deployed headquarters element actually in that theatre. Accordingly, throughout the exercise Division Main at Fort Bragg worked on African time so that they were synchronized with the deployed units and their headquarters; the working day started at four o'clock in the morning. However, staff in Division Main found that they had to wake up much earlier than this as the exercise proceeded:

> In the morning there was an update brief. We had intelligence guys and girls in J2 [joint intelligence branch] behind the eight ball [they were not current with the situation]. It was a nightmare. So the solution was to get up earlier; three hours before the brief, not one hour, so that we could get a solid, clear intelligence picture. This meant that Forward and Rear [Main] and outlying CPs were all on the same page. If not, you base your assessments on impressions. It was a positive advance. We were always on the same page: Forward and Rear. But we needed time to do it. We got started at 0400. We were on Africom time. So we got up at 0100.[50]

To facilitate this reorganization of the working day, the division brought camp cots into Division Headquarters at Fort Bragg so that the staff could align their sleep with the battle rhythm. In pursuit of shared awareness, 82nd Airborne synchronized the staff even though they might be separated by an ocean.

Teamwork of this kind is essential for divisional operations today but, in fact, divisional headquarters have tried to inculcate a deeper corporate ethos, which Huntington described. This ethos refers

---

[49] OF-5, Colonel, Chief of Staff, 82nd Airborne Division, interviewee 068, personal interview, 20 April 2015.
[50] Ibid.

not just to cooperation but to the moral obligation of the staff to support the commander and each other, individually and collectively. A professional staff is one that feels compelled to produce precise and detailed staff work on time, even in difficult and stressful conditions. The ideal of professional performance and the respect which it earns are motivating in and of themselves. Divisions have consciously tried to overcome the problem of the enlargement and dispersal of head-quarters by accentuating this professional ethos. They have tried to encourage commitment and loyalty by impressing on staff their professional obligations. Staff are, in fact, very susceptible to this encouragement. Staff officers want to be esteemed as effective and professional officers by both their commanders and their peers and this desire for approbation motivates them to work hard for each other – even when they are not co-present.

This professional ethos is particularly pronounced in 82nd Airborne, where its elite status inspires and pressurizes the staff to perform:

> Staff here are motivated by the fear of failure. The span
> of command is so large that the commander relies on his
> subordinates. We have responsibility for any failure. 3/3 [Current
> Operations Cell]: we're responsible; we don't want to fail. So
> the fear of failure is motivating. It is fear. It's like mum and dad
> looking at you and saying: "I'm disappointed". With the leaders,
> it is the fear of letting them down. They put all their trust in
> you. It goes into the realm of personal relations. It is a familial
> organization.[51]

One officer highlighted the pronounced ethos of 82nd Airborne by comparison with the British Army. He regarded some elements of British planning doctrine as superior to the United States and admired the professionalism of the British officer. Yet, he also noted a stark difference in terms of work ethos:

> In my dealings with the British Army, they are struck by the
> aggressive nature in our approach to work: "You guys are
> nuts". They go home at 1800. But here there is an expectation

---

[51] OF-3, Major Current Operations, 82nd Airborne Division, interviewee 065, personal interview, 20 April 2015.

for products: "I'm not going to disappoint the boss". There is
another level of expectation. I'm the busiest I've been in my
career. Expectation drives performance. I'm proud to be part of
this organization.[52]

The chief of staff confirmed the point: 'It is competitive. The competition here is the strongest. What we do: we're competing. There is a
healthy byproduct of that. There are some bad ones too; the need to be
seen and heard and being effective creates problems'. Nevertheless, the
elite status of 82nd Airborne Division and the expectation that it must
be the best motivated the staff to perform. Precisely because they saw
themselves in a competitive environment both externally and internally, they were determined that the division should succeed and that
they themselves should be viewed as highly professional and competent
officers by their peers and superiors.

Global Response has demanded ever higher levels of collaboration and teamwork from staff in the 82nd Airborne headquarters
precisely because they can no longer always rely on face-to-face interaction. In place of interpersonal commitments, an aggressive professionalism now unites the staff so that each officer is determined to
perform well out of a fear of corporate and individual failure. As a
result, officers can collaborate at distance, even if they do not necessarily know each other. Although many of the staff cannot know each
other, they are committed to the same organizational endeavours by a
common commitment to their profession and to the organization as
a whole.

Although 3 UK Division does, perhaps, not demonstrate the
elitist ethos of the 82nd Airborne, the importance of professional
teamwork within the staff has become ever more important to the
division, as it attempts to implement distributed command. Indeed,
3 UK Division staff have themselves recorded that the division of the
staff between the Iron Division Operations Centre and the Forward
Headquarters has demanded higher levels of teamwork from them. In
particular, on some exercises, the separation of the headquarters has
induced a feeling of alienation among the deployed staff, if they have
not already been closely unified.

---

[52] OF-3, Major, Current Operations, 82nd Airborne Division, interviewee 066, personal
interview, 20 April 2015.

For instance, during Exercise Joint Venture in July 2016, 3 UK Division's most recent experiment with distributed command, the intelligence (G2) cell was split between the Main Headquarters at Bulford and RAF St Mawgan. The team at Bulford analyzed the deep battle beyond forty-eight hours while the intelligence staff in Forward HQ focused on the close fight in the near future. Bulford Main (which would later become the Iron Division Operations Centre) passed the intelligence materials to Forward forty-eight hours in advance. The system had worked well. However, one of the officers in the intelligence cell in Bulford Main noted a potential problem: 'Forward can think that the rear is not busy. You need to develop a unified team; more so than if you are all present in the same headquarters'.[53] He stressed the importance of teamwork to overcome the potential tensions. Other officers affirmed the point: 'Distributed Command needs teams to avoid a feeling of us and them'.[54]

A permanent member of the targeting team provided a useful insight into the specific character of this corporate ethos. This artillery officer was based at the Iron Division Operations Centre and was engaged in deep targeting potentially working weeks out from execution. In order to develop a targeting package, fires had to be integrated with the Information Activities and Outreach cell and with the Political Adviser to generate 'Integrated Effects': 'The key meeting is the Integrated Effects working group. There is no problem here with the Main/Forward split. We can do it on lync (3 UK Division's digital communications system). In this headquarters, this is what you would do [even if you were in the same building]. So it makes no difference'. However, the officer did notice that the separation demanded better collaboration: 'It requires good working relations and teamwork'. She observed that the former staff officer in Information Activities and Outreach had just moved to a new post and been recently replaced. Her successor did not yet understand the system so well. Consequently, the limitation of the system was not technical, it was human and specifically social. Distributed command requires a higher level of teamwork; staff members need to be more attuned to each other and they must

---

[53] OF-3, Major, G2, 3 UK Division, interviewee 120, personal communication, 5 July 2016.

[54] OF-3, Major, Fires, 3 UK Division, interviewee 123, personal communication, 5 July 2016.

have all internalized common procedures more thoroughly. However, if these conditions existed, the officer thought that 'you could have the whole of targeting back in Picton Main [the name for the Iron Division Operations Centre before its opening]'.[55] The physical disaggregation of the headquarters has required ever higher levels of collaboration among the staff.

Professionalization

The dispersion of the headquarters presents major challenges for the unity and effectiveness of command. At precisely a time when decision-making has accelerated and proliferated, the very structure of the command post has jeopardized its ability to assist the commander. The divisional headquarters has simply become so big and dispersed that the unity of command has been compromised. Western armies are in something of a predicament and they have sought to resolve this situation through two critical innovations: the appointment of executive deputies and the professionalization of the staff. Divisional commanders have remained inexorably at the centre of operations. Their definition of the mission – their intent – has remained primary; it has been essential to the coordination of such a complex system. Indeed, mission definition has become ever more decisive and demanding in the current era. Major decisions have come to the divisional commander, as the commander of 82nd Airborne Division made clear. However, in order to maintain organizational unity and operational tempo, commanders have devolved very significant managerial responsibility to nominated deputies. In many cases, commanders have not been within miles, or even continents, of significant parts of their staff and troops. Commanders have shared their command authority and allowed these deputies to make decisions for them. In order to sustain organizational unity, commanders have devolved and shared their decision-making authority. The dispersion of the headquarters has involved a distribution of command; mission command has required an accentuated form of 'mission command'.

---

[55] OF-3, Major, Targeting, 3 UK Division, interviewee 124, personal communication, 5 July 2016.

At the same time, the staff has become more professionalized, in Huntington's sense. They have become both more expert across a range of specialisms and in relation to staff procedures; impersonal process has become increasingly important to coordinate an enlarged, dispersed headquarters in which staff do not always know each other well – or even at all. Yet, in order to overcome the increased scope of operations and the tyranny of distance, the staff has also become increasingly united as a professional body. They have displayed a heightened form of corporate ethos, united with and committed to each other even when they are not co-present or have not had the luxury of developing close personal relations. The result is that highly professionalized team have appeared consisting of commanders, deputies and staff.

It is easy to deplore the emergence of complex headquarters with their proliferating structures, command boards, deputies and enlarged staffs. It is not certain whether these divisional headquarters will be able to conduct high-intensity operations against peers, as critics complain; there is no definitive evidence to prove their utility. It is possible that these swollen headquarters would be easily defeated in a conflict against Russia and China.[56] On the other hand, American and British divisions have tested the arrangement on a number of very demanding exercises which imitate war against peers like Russia. The artificiality of exercises has to be recognized. The system of deputies and professionalized staff described in this chapter has been tested on exercises. The evidence from these exercises suggests that the new headquarters, with its distributed and collective systems of decision-making, has been effective. Moreover, forward elements from the headquarters of 1st Infantry Division and 82nd Airborne have already been deployed to support military operations in Iraq and Syria. These were not genuine divisional operations; in each case, the US Army divisions commanded training missions and assisted in coordinating the military operations of indigenous forces against ISIS. However, they have tested the new divisional headquarters and the concept of mission command and shown it to be functional on genuine military operations. Paradoxically, in order to maintain the unity of command as they headquarters disperse, Western generals have increasingly had to distribute their decision-making authority.

[56] See Chapter 14. There is evidence that Russia and China are adopting a compatible command system.

Of course, todays' divisional headquarters share many features with their twentieth-century predecessors. Although reformed, traces of the twentieth-century headquarters, institutionalized in 1916, remain in their basic structure and procedures. Yet, the appearance of the new divisional headquarters, with its deputies and command boards and its professionalized staff, suggest that, continuities notwithstanding, a new regime of command might now be appearing. A more collective practice of command seems to be superseding the more individualist methods of the twentieth century.

12 THE DECISION POINT

Garbage-Can Thinking

Divisional headquarters have sought to enhance the professionalism of their staff in the face of new operational and organizational challenges. The previous chapter mentioned how headquarters have increased the specialist knowledge among the staff. However, the chapter focused primarily on the ways in which the staff's corporate ethos has been developed in order to overcome the problems of enlargement and dispersion. The chapter tried to show how, at precisely a moment when routine face-to-face cooperation has become difficult, that a higher level of teamwork among the staff has become necessary and the staff have worked hard to sustain cooperation between themselves. The professional commitments of the staff have played an important role here. However, in order to coordinate complex contemporary operations, divisional headquarters have also instituted new staff techniques to assist in the planning and coordination. Of course, as Chapter 4 showed, standardized procedures, plans, orders and maps were always important to the divisional staff. These artefacts proved essential for the conduct of divisional operations from the First World War and had been thoroughly institutionalized by 1916 by all belligerents. However, in the twenty-first century, existing techniques have been refined and augmented; new methods have been introduced to facilitate planning and managing operations. This chapter examines one new staff technique, the 'Decision Point', in order to illustrate how a professionalized staff has played an increasingly important role in decision-making.

Commanders face an obvious but intricate problem; with the help of their staff and deputies, they must make decisions. This is very challenging. In their celebrated work on decision-making in organizations, James March and Johan Olsen demonstrate the difficulty, even impossibility, of organizations making good, still less rational, decisions. March and Olsen claim that there are four currents which inform any decision in an organization: problems, solutions, participants and choice opportunities. Organizations recurrently face problems which a decision-making body resolves through the choice of one solution from a suite of possibilities. Ideally, the four elements of decision-making constitute a rationally managed sequence. Indeed, organizations employ bureaucratic procedure to separate and sequence these four elements and, thereby, ensure coherent decision-making. Protocol, agendas and the structure of meetings are designed to try to ensure that problems and their solutions are assessed properly. Yet, very frequently, this segmentation fails and the rationality of the process begins to collapse. Choice, opportunities and solutions precede problems; the wrong people are on executive boards. The mere timing of each of the four elements in the decision cycle becomes critical to the influence it exerts: 'The process is one that often looks capricious to the observer. Many of the outcomes are produced by distinct consequences of the particular time phasing of choices, problems and participant availability'.[1] Instead of a rational sequence of assessment, decision-making assumes the form of a garbage can. Factors randomly thrown into the process have a disproportionate influence on the chosen outcome. In this situation, the actual problem disappears from view and is not solved at all. Important choices are made, rather, by oversight or by flight; decisions are taken which either ignore the problem or, alternatively, which address a quite different but more easily resolvable issue than the specified problem.

Of course, the armed forces are by no means immune to these problems. On the contrary, precisely because of the extreme uncertainty of decision-making during a military operation, when actions must be taken under duress with insufficient information, the military have been well aware of the likelihood of false, 'garbage-can' decision-making. Indeed, in the current era of complex operations and enlarged,

---

[1] James March and Johan Olsen, *Ambiguity and Choice in Organizations* (Bergen: Universitetsforlaget, 1976), 35.

dispersed headquarters, they would seem to be particularly vulnerable to garbage-can thinking. However, although eliminating faulty decision-making is impossible, the armed forces have introduced methods which might at least mitigate its risks. They have introduced formal administrative methods, Standard Operating Procedures, designed to organize decision-making.

Indeed, March and Olson are aware of these techniques and have produced a volume which is dedicated to the question of decision-making in the armed forces. There, Roger Weissinger-Baylon usefully discusses the problem of ambiguity in naval command. Weissinger-Baylon fully accepts that navies are susceptible to garbage-can thinking; in battle, they operate under conditions of 'organized anarchy'. There is always inadequate information, commanders are distracted and time is limited. However, in the light of these conditions, navies have developed a number of techniques of reducing garbage-can thinking. He describes how decentralization can ensure that decisions are assigned to the level with the best information. Alternatively, he notes: 'Decision load can be shifted in time to earlier periods of reduced activity. There are at least two approaches: (1) standard operating practice (SOPs), which are rehearsed, organizationally approved decisions of broad applicability; and (2) operation plans, which are tailor-made for specific tactical objectives and therefore have narrow applicability'.[2]

By developing a set of pre-established drills and anticipating likely decisions in the planning process, naval commanders have sought to offset garbage-can tendencies. By pre-emption, decisions can be analyzed slowly, calmly and more fully in order to determine the most effective courses of action. In this way, the problem of deciding by oversight or by flight can be minimized. The actual problem is more likely to be addressed properly, if the headquarters has already prepared itself for the kinds of decision it is may make: 'therefore, naval commanders and their organizations have devised unique mechanisms for matching problems and solutions during the organizational anarchy of naval warfare. This approach reduces the decision-making load on commander by prematching problems and solutions at lower levels in an

---

[2] Roger Weissinger-Baylon, 'Garbage-Can Decision Process in Naval Warfare', in James March and Roger Weissinger-Baylon (eds), *Ambiguity and Command: organizational perpectives on military decision-making* (Marshfield, MA: Pitman, 1986), 40.

organization or by planning, which prematches problems and solutions before peak loads actually occur'.[3]

Anticipatory techniques like these have, in fact, been institutionalized at the divisional level for a long time. Chapter 5 discussed the emergence of bureaucratic methods in the modern divisional headquarters. Specifically, it noted the appearance of the situation map and the standardization of the planning and orders process. These innovations were an attempt to organize and systematize decision-making by ensuring that all the relevant information had been considered coherently. Yet, although standard operating procedures often accelerated decision-making, staff work was rarely conceived as a means of addressing the problem of garbage-can thinking. The planning methods at this time were primarily designed not so much to anticipate decision-making as to provide a mnemonic for staff and commanders. Plans, estimates and orders were all structured so that commanders did not forget important factors as they made decisions. However, as the scope of military operations has increased and the new headquarters has itself become larger and more complex, staff processes and procedures have been revised and refined. In some cases, new techniques have been invented to coordinate operations and support the commander more effectively. Specifically, in the light of heightened complexity, new processes have been developed in order to overcome the problem of ambiguity and garbage-can decision-making. Administrative processes have been introduced to accelerate, improve and even automate decision-making. As Weissinger-Baylon suggested, standardization has been a means of pre-empting decision-making in periods of lower stress.

The development of these apparently mundane new administrative techniques is deeply relevant to understanding the transformation of command. Commanders are responsible for any decision they make but the introduction of these new methods, which presage decisions, means that while they lack formal authority, the staff now play a critical role in structuring decisions. Chapters 8 and 9 showed how Mattis and Carter distributed their decision-making authority to subordinate commanders who acted as their deputies. The administrative reforms in the new divisional headquarters may have an even more radical implication. They suggest that the contemporary divisional

[3] Ibid., 47.

commander has increasingly shared decision-making authority with the staff itself. Indeed, as a result of techniques like the Decision Point, the staff have effectively appropriated an executive function. Through the medium of new procedures, the staff have now quietly become part of the command team itself, informing, directing and channelling decision-making. As a result of professionalization, the staff actively collaborates in decision-making.

In order to analyze the professionalization of the staff and its impact on command, this chapter focuses exclusively on one small, but important, device, the 'Decision Point'. The Decision Point is defined in NATO doctrine in the following way: 'A point in space and time, identified during the planning process, where it is anticipated that the commander must make a decision concerning a specific course of action'.[4] US Army doctrine uses somewhat different terms but the meaning is plainly the same: 'Execution decisions implement a planned action under circumstances anticipated in the order. An executive decision is normally tied to a decision point – a point in space or time the commander or staff anticipate making a key decision concerning a specific course of action (JP 5-0)'.[5] A decision point refers, then, to an envisaged moment in the future when the commander will have to make a decision.[6] This chapter will explore the mechanics of the Decision Point and its implications for command in the twenty-first century.

---

[4] Ministry of Defence, *Allied Joint Planning Doctrine 5-00* (Swindon: The Development, Concepts and Doctrine Centre, 2013), 3–43.

[5] US Army Combined Arms Centre, *Army Doctrine Reference Publication (ADRP)-5 The Operations Process* (Washington, DC: Headquarters Department of the Army, 2012), 4-4.

[6] Recently, the US Army has been experimenting with a planning method called 'Decision Point Tactics' which is currently used by the opposition forces on Command Post exercises. This procedure involves developing not a single plan in conventional military fashion but rather multiple plans for a variety of possible scenarios, each of which might be activated. 'Decision-point tactics, as defined by the OPFOR, "is the art and science of employing available means at a specific point in space and/or time where the commander anticipates making a decision concerning a specific friendly course of action. This decision is directly associated with threat force activity (action/reaction) and/or the battlefield environment"' (www.globalsecurity.org/military/library/report/call/call_97-4_chap1.htm). Decision Point Tactics has not been formally introduced into US military doctrine but the practice usefully illustrates how important the concept has become in contemporary staff work.

A final observation is necessary before beginning the analysis. It will be argued below that the Decision Point has become an important tool in decision-making today. Yet, the limitations of the Decision Point as a tool have to be acknowledged. Specifically, the Decision Point has often improved and accelerated decision-making by mobilizing the expertise of the staff more fully and including them in the practice of command. However, the Decision Point is primarily directed to periods of normal decision-making when events are broadly predictable. The Decision Point functions most effectively when operations are going to plan. Then, it has been effective in augmenting routine decision-making. Of course, the real challenge of command is when things do not go to plan. When there is a crisis, the Decision Point has not proved so useful precisely because it has been adapted to deal with predictable events. Then, when the unexpected occurs, alternative forms of decision-making are required. In the following chapter, crisis decision-making will be discussed. This chapter will focus solely on predictable, normal decision-making as a way of initiating the analysis of the micro-practices of command. Taken together, the two chapters are intended to provide a comprehensive, if inevitably incomplete, account of contemporary decision-making in the divisional headquarters. The chapters intend to show just how many actors participate in decisions at the divisional level today.

The Research

This chapter is based on research conducted on the divisional headquarters of the three major Western powers – the UK, the US and France – and specifically 3 UK Division, 82nd Airborne Division and *État Major de Force 1*. However, the most important ethnographic material is derived from 3 UK Division; indeed, the central analysis of how the Decision Point is used to aid decision-making draws exclusively on British evidence. Specifically, this chapter draws upon a series of exercises which 3 UK Division underwent between 2013 and 2016, focusing in particular on two divisional exercises in 2014 and 2015: Exercise Iron Resolve 14 and 15. These exercises were large-scale 'Command Post' exercises involving the entire staff of 3 UK Division and its augmentees, some 400 officers, working from a large tented headquarters for two weeks. The exercises took place respectively in October 2014 and September and October 2015 at Knook and West Down Camps on the British Army training estate on Salisbury Plain. During the exercises, the headquarters tested out its procedures against a simulation of a real operation.

The prominence of the British material is a simple product of research access; the longest and best periods of ethnographic research were conducted on 3 UK Division. In order to understand the Decision Point fully, close observation is imperative. Only at this level of detail will it be possible to show how Decision Points – and the increasingly professionalized staff utilizing them – inform decision-making. However, there are obvious disadvantages to this dependence on ethnographic evidence from one site; the findings at 3 UK Division are not necessarily replicable in the other headquarters. This is a danger of all 'thick' research. Nevertheless, while the findings from 3 UK Division cannot be assumed to be automatically replicated in the other headquarters, French and American allies are converging ever more closely on the same planning and staff doctrines; the United Kingdom's national planning doctrine, Joint Doctrine Publication 5-00, has been superseded by NATO's Allied Joint Doctrine-5, which is followed by all NATO member states. In addition, observations of 82nd Airborne and *État Major de Force 1* as well as interviews with French and American staff officers and commanders at both divisions suggest that the practices of 3 UK Division are not unique. Indeed, the Decision Point is an American invention.

However, before beginning the discussion, some further introductory remarks about 3 UK Division's recent sequence of exercises and their format are necessary here. As part of the divisional reformation, 3 UK Division has undergone an intense programme of exercises since December 2013. To maximize the utility of this training cycle, the British Army procured the US 'DATE' scenario based on the central Caucasus, focusing on Azerbaijan. Although the DATE scenario has fictionalized the country names and the conflict situations, the data on which it is based are real. Consequently, the exercise scenario has a fidelity and depth which is often lacking in completely constructed scenarios; economic, political, social and cultural factors are richly represented. The British Army procured DATE primarily because of its quality but it also aligned the UK with the US Army, which also uses this scenario and, therefore, aided inter-operability. 3 UK Division utilized the DATE scenario over the two consecutive exercises, Iron Resolve 14 and 15. Moreover, it allowed 3 UK Division to participate in the US Army Warfighter Exercise in June 2017 and April 2018. Warfighter is the most important and demanding command post exercise to which the US Army submits its forces and it is deeply significant that the British Army uniquely has been invited to participate in it.

The DATE scenario involves a fictitious conflict between two Caucasian countries, respectively renamed Atropia and Minaria. The scenario involves a conventional military invasion of Atropia by Minaria, alongside ethnic conflict and terrorism by ethnic Minarians in Atropia. As part of a NATO intervention force, 3 UK Division was ordered to drive Minarian forces out of Atropia and restore its ter-ritorial sovereignty. Having landed in Baku, Exercise Iron Resolve 14 involved an initial advance eastwards against Minarian forces; Exercise Iron Resolve 15 focused on the seizure of the major city of Mingechevir and its hydroelectricity plant in north-eastern Atropia from Minarian forces. This Exercise followed Exercise Iron Resolve 14 directly, restarting the operation – and the planning – from where the previous exercise had ended: with 3 UK Division advancing on the city of Mingechevir. The operation to seize the city provides the empirical focus for the discussion of the Decision Point below.

The Decision Point is, of course, the focus of this chapter. However, in order to explain the significance and function of the Decision Point to command, it is necessary to discuss some other staff products and the planning process more widely; namely, the Commander's Intent, the 'effect', the Decision Support Matrix[7] and the Synchronization Matrix. The Decision Point is created once the headquarters has gone through each of these planning processes and produced the related staff work. The analysis of the Decision Point will begin with an examination of the Commander's Intent, followed by a description of the concept of the effect, the Decision Support Matrix, concluding with a discussion of the Synchronization Matrix

---

[7] To simplify the argument, the Decision Support Overlay, which is closely related the Matrix, is not discussed.

and, finally, the Decision Point itself. Some patience may be required with this preliminary but essential material. The aim throughout these discussions is to show how the complexity of new operations has propelled a professionalization of the divisional staff and its procedures. In order to improve command, the staff have sought to develop new techniques, like the Decision Point, whose purpose is to anticipate, preempt and accelerate decision-making. The staff have tried to prepare decisions for their commanders. As a result, decision-making has been increasingly shared. In contrast to the twentieth century, when individual commanders monopolized decision-making, decision-making has become an increasingly collective, professionalized activity in which commanders, while remaining the critical reference point, are increasingly supported, guided and cued by their staff.

The Commander's Intent

One of the most important artefacts produced at the early stages of the planning process is a document called the Commander's Intent. The Commander's Intent may not strictly initiate planning but it is a decisive moment in the process, without which staffwork cannot proceed. Indeed, the analysis of both Nick Carter and James Mattis demonstrated the importance of the Commander's Intent to contemporary operations. It is the primary reference point for all subsequent decisions. Indeed, staff officers unanimously underscored the significance of the Intent to all their work. British officers in 3 UK Division described it as 'critical' and 'fundamental'[8]: 'The critical thing is understanding where the boss wants to go: to get his intent. Then any divergence from the plan is done in the light of the fact that you know where the boss wants to go'.[9] American staff officers in 82nd Airborne shared a similar view:

> The Commander's Intent is a general narrative on how he sees the environment, the enemy and ourselves. When it is complete we

[8] OF-4, Lieutenant-Colonel, Chief of Future Plans 3 UK Division, interviewee 102, personal interview, 18 November 2016; OF-3, Major, Future Operations 3 UK Division, interviewee 129, personal interview, 18 November 2016.
[9] OF-4, Lieutenant-Colonel, Chief of Current Operations 3 UK Division, interviewee 45, personal communication, 1 October 2015.

[G5] and 3/5 look at it to work out the key tasks for the division.
ADRP-6 describes Mission Command and we work under that
construct. The commander gives you the Mission Statement and
the Intent. That is where you get your main effects – defeat for
instance – who, what, when, where and why'.[10]

Quite independently of each other, staff officers in the UK and US
described how their everyday working practice has been continually
informed by the Commander's Intent; it has become a critical point of reference for them. They could not plan without it. The guidance provided
by the Commander's Intent is regarded as critical by staff officers, then.
Even in the immediate absence of their commander, the Intent informs
all the work of the staff officers; they consciously seek to operate within
the guidance provided. The commander bears sole responsibility for
the Intent; only the commander can define the mission and the Intent
constitutes the triangulating point for all subsequent planning.

The concept of a commander's intention is certainly not a
new departure in military practice. For instance, as early as the First
World War, commanders typically included their intent in their orders,
followed by the missions and tasks for subordinate units. For instance,
General Leclerc's orders to *2eme Division Blindée* normally included
a paragraph entitled, 'The General's Intentions'; it involved a sentence
or two about what Leclerc wanted the division to achieve from the
operation.[11] It was followed by 'particular orders' to his subordinate
combat commands about their tasks. Today, mission statements, the
Intent, have become more elaborate. Moreover, there are some notable
features to the contemporary Intent. Specifically, as a mission statement,
the Commander's Intent relies heavily on the concept of the 'effect'.

The effect is a relatively recent planning concept for the military emerging in the 1990s. Instead of focusing on the target or the
action, the concept of the effect focuses on the achieved outcome of
a mission or task: 'Effects are the change brought about in a target
by the consequence of action or activity. Effects are therefore the
commander's desired outcome in relation to the enemy, population,
terrain or friendly forces'.[12] The central purpose of the Intent is for

[10] OF-4, Lieutenant-Colonel, G2, 82nd Airborne Division, interviewee 070, personal
interview, 20 April 2015.
[11] Op Order 248/3, 29 November, *2eme Division Blindée*, GR 11 P 224, SHD.
[12] The British Army Staff Officer's Handbook (Land), 2014, 4.1.2-1.

commanders to specify the major effects which they want to achieve. Indeed, the Commander's Intent is substantially a list of the effects which a commander wants to achieve with an account of the context which explains their sequencing and prioritization. It is ultimately of a series of 'effects' linked together by a narrative: 'Within orders, effects are articulated in the commander's intent and in the unifying purpose of subordinate's mission'.[13]

Commanders do not typically invent their own effects. Rather, when commanders write their Intent, they draw on an established effects lexicon which lists a series of accepted definitions. The words specify a particular kind of military activity and outcome. The current edition of British Army Staff Officer's Handbook (Land) records 101 effects words; e.g., deter, coerce, destroy, screen, secure, seize, delay, disrupt, protect, block, deceive, deny etc.[14] Thirty-four of these effects words have their own designated 'tactical graphic', a recognized sign which staff officers insert onto operations maps. The concept of the effect has become an integral part of the Commander's Intent, then.

A qualification is necessary here. Naturally, the major Western powers have incorporated the concept of the effect into their planning processes somewhat differentially. For instance, the French Army have employed a distinctive concept called the *Effet Majeure*. The *Effet Majeure* (major effect) refers to the decisive effect which has to be achieved in order to a mission to be successful; it refers to a decisive action, typically against a critical element of the enemy force, which will inevitably lead to the success of the operation. Anglophone armies do not have an exact equivalent of the *Effet Majeure*. British and American headquarters will identify a centre of gravity (normally the most potent enemy force) and a Main Effort (the most important friendly force element). Typically, the centre of gravity is targeted by the Main Effort, the destruction of whose centre is likely to accelerate the collapse of the enemy force. Consequently, an *Effet Majeure* is implied in British and American planning processes; the *Effet Majeure* would be the decisive action of the Main Effort against the enemy's centre of gravity. However, no explicit concept exists in the United Kingdom and United States.

[13] The British Army Staff Officer's Handbook (Land), 2014, 4.1.2-1.
[14] Ibid., 4.1.2-2-16.

Similarly, British and American headquarters tend to use the concept of the effect somewhat differently. The British refer to general outcomes, not to specific actions: 'The British are more free-flow. With the British, they identify a series of conceptual effects which they want to achieve in specific places and times. It is not events-driven. They are influenced by an idea of what the commander wants to achieve. In the United States, it is events-driven. If none of these have happened, we then ask: what do we do?'.[15] According to this officer, in an American head-quarters, the planning process focuses more pragmatically and directly on specific actions which subordinate units have to execute. Of course, the effect is presumed but the planning is more directed to the comple-tion of activities (which will produce that effect). Notwithstanding an awareness of the alternative application of the concept of the effect in British, American and French headquarters, there is also manifest unity across these forces. The differences between them are nuances rather than fundamental; exchange officers or officers from different head-quarters working together on multinational exercises have no difficulty in adapting to other systems. The effect is central to contemporary Western planning processes and has been thoroughly incorporated into divisional procedures. It refers to the outcomes which a commander seeks to achieve through military actions. The effect constitutes the substantive content of the Commander's Intent.

The importance of the 'effect' in the Commander's Intent could be seen very clearly on 3 UK Division's Exercise Iron Resolve 14 and 15. For instance, on Iron Resolve 15, the commander of 3 Division wrote an Intent for the forthcoming operation to seize the city of Mingechevir, Objective Eagle, as the staff began to plan the operation in detail. The city was held by an enemy 'Minarian' force, 393 Brigade, which was the main obstacle to retaking the town. A large printed copy of the Commander's Intent was reproduced in poster size and displayed prominently in every planning cell in the headquarters. Crucially, the key effects which the commander wanted to achieve appeared in the Intent in capital letters.

The purpose of this phase of the operation is to secure Critical National Infrastructure in Mingechevir giving Atropian forces

---

[15] OF-3, Major, G3/3, 82nd Airborne Division, interviewee 066, personal interview, 20 April 2015.

a visible lead in liberating their own city. The key to achieving this is the removal – by whatever legal means necessary – of 393 Brigade from Mingechevir. In our **Shaping Operations**, we will seek to *isolate* 393 Brigade (the Minarian force in the city of Mingechevir) and its commander physically and psychologically, underpinned by a series of preliminary actions, including raids and fires to *degrade* his capability and to *undermine* his Lines of Communication, that will leave him uncertain as to the final timing and method of our **Decisive Operations** to *compel* 393 Brigade withdrawal, or if its commander decides to stand and fight, to *defeat* it in detail. At all stages, I will be prepared to offer terms to 393 Brigade's surrender in an effort to save lives … Throughout we must *maintain* our legitimacy, *preserve* our cohesion with Atropian forces, *protect* Internally Displace Persons (refugees) and the civilian population and *neutralize* and *marginalize* malign irregular forces. Initially the Main Effort is the information activities to ISOLATE the Commander 393 Brigade. Switching to DEFEAT of 393 Brigade in the city.[16]

The Commander's Intent designated two main effects: the isolation and defeat of enemy forces in the city, written in capitals. However, it included ten other subordinate effects (marked in italics): the reassurance and protection of the civilian population in and around the city, the protection of refugees, the screening and interdiction of the area west of Mingechevir against other Minarian forces and the securing and control of the areas which 3 UK Division had already seized during Exercise Iron Resolve 14.

The Commander's Intent is a very important moment in the planning process. Detailed planning of the selected course of action cannot proceed without it. It is, therefore, an assertion of the commander's authority over the mission. However, the Intent is but the beginning of the planning process. Once it has been presented by the commander, the Intent has to be operationalized and applied by the staff. At this point, the staff actively appropriate the Intent, deconstructing it to identify all the tasks and actions which it implies and constructing schemes of manoeuvre for their commander. While the commander retains formal responsibility, the work which the staff do

---

[16] 3 UK Division, Commander's Intent, Mission 1, Securing Mingechevir, Exercise Iron Triangle 15, Fieldnotes, 30 September 2015, Volume IV, 60.

on the Intent informs all subsequent decision-making. In this way, the staff become an integral element in the decision-making process. They play a critical role in the management of the mission and, indeed, begin to discipline and structure their own commander's decision-making, in line with the Intent which they have been given. The Decision Point plays an important role at this point. However, in order to understand how it is used and how it allows the staff appropriate decision-making authority, it is necessary to analyze how the staff apply the Intent in detail.

The Decision Support Matrix

The Commander's Intent initiates detailed planning. On the basis of the Intent, the staff produce a number of artefacts, one of the most important of which is the Decision Support Matrix.[17] The British Army's Staff Officers' Handbook describes the Decision Support Matrix as a diagram which shows 'where the formation will have an effect against the enemy, and where and when the commander needs to make a decision'. The Decision Support Matrix depicts the intended effects which the commander wants to achieve to complete the mission. It consists of a schematized map of the operating area onto which the staff draw a series of boxes. Each of these boxes is marked with an effect word derived from the Commander's Intent and, consequently, the Decision Support Matrix is sometimes known simply as the 'Intent Schematic'. In this way, the effects that the Commander wants to achieve are depicted graphically in physical space on a map of the operating area. Consequently, the headquarters can see precisely where and when the commander wants to achieve the decisive effects.

In line with this procedure, on Exercise Iron Resolve 15, following the dissemination of the Commander's Intent, 3 UK Division staff produced a Decision Support Matrix for the approaching operation against the city of Mingechevir. The critical effects were placed

---

[17] The Decision Support Overlay depicts 'areas of interest' on the operating map. These areas, consisting of a series of imaginary boxes, focus on the activities of the enemy. From the information derived from these areas, the staff attempt to anticipate what the enemy will do in order to assist the commander to make timely decisions.

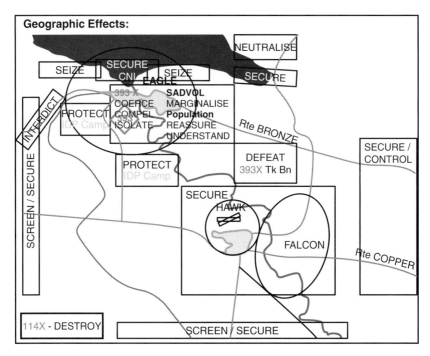

Figure 12.1 Decision Support Matrix, Exercise Iron Resolve, 2015.

physically on the locations where they were to occur. For instance, Objective Eagle, the city of Mingechevir, had a large effects box drawn around it defined by the term SEIZE denoting the prime mission of 3 UK Division during this phase of the operation. This effects box also included subordinate effects against 393 Brigade and the civilian population; the city was to be seized by coercing, compelling and isolating 393 Brigade, while the civilian population were reassured and understood and refugees were protected. At the same time, rear areas and lines of communication were to be secured, while the area west of the city was to be interdicted and screened. In a simple schematic, which could be understood immediately by any trained military personnel, the Decision Support Matrix lucidly summarized the Commander's Intent and a highly complex divisional operation. It graphically depicted the critical tasks of the operation and where and when they would occur. In this way, illustrated by the Decision Support Matrix (Figure 12.1), the Commander's Intent condensed an intricate mission involving numerous units and prodigious coordination problems while preserving the autonomy of subordinates. The close relationship between the Commander's Intent and the Decision Support Matrix is clear. The effects from the Intent were laid out by the staff in the specific places they were to be achieved.

The Decision Point

Once the staff had produced the Decision Support Matrix, they then developed the Synchronization (or 'Synch') Matrix. It is at this point that the staff invoked the Decision Point. The Synchronization Matrix breaks down all the effects identified on the Decision Support Matrix and converts them into specific tasks, which are assigned to particular units at specified times and places. The Synch Matrix is a standard business spreadsheet, typically produced on Microsoft Excel software. It consists of three elements; a twenty-four-hour timeline, displayed on the x-axis at the top of the matrix, including the phases of the mission. Meanwhile, all the units under command and supporting units and agencies on the y-axis are listed down the left-hand side. The tasks of each unit were inserted into the corresponding boxes against its precise timing, by date, hour and day of the operation. The Decision Support Matrix and the Synch Matrix represent the entire operation graphically. Together, the Decision Support Matrix depicts where, when and by whom tasks will be achieved in order to achieve the effects identified in the Commander's Intent.

The Decision Point is derived from the Synchronization Matrix and first appears in the planning process at this point. The Decision Point refers to a designated point in time on an operation when a commander will – or is very likely to – have to make a decision. As the staff disaggregate the plan into its constituent tasks, they also identify a series of Decision Points on the Synch Matrix. The staff contemplate the operation to determine its decisive moments, to which a Decision Point will be appended. Any operation consists of a series of tasks which have to be completed; effects are achieved through the accomplishment of tasks. Many tasks are relatively small. However, there will be several decisive tasks that have to be achieved in order to for the operation to continue. For instance, in order to be able to advance into a city, a key bridge might have to be taken. Alternatively, there will come a moment on an operation when commanders have to decide, on the basis of current conditions, whether to launch an element of their force according to the plan in order to continue the operation or whether to revise or even abandon the plan. These critical tasks, of which any operation is comprised, are identified by the divisional staff and designated as Decision Points. Decision Points anticipate when a decision will need to be made and what that decision will be; as such, Decision Points are absolutely 'key to effective planning'.[18]

US planning doctrine is explicit about the utility and importance of decision points: 'Identifying decision points and designing branches ahead of time – combined with a clear Commander's Intent – help create flexible plans'.[19] It is echoed by UK and NATO doctrine:

> Sound planning for a campaign and major operations requires
> that JFCs [Joint Force Command] and their staffs truly think
> at the operational level. This means that they need to think
> far ahead to identify possible changes in the situation and
> then determine what decision to make and when, to positively
> influence events before they occur. It mentally prepares the JFCs
> to identify potential Decision Points and focus their thoughts on
> potential branches and sequels.[20]

Decision Points orient the staff to the future by anticipating decisions and alternative courses of action.

On Exercise Iron Resolve 2015, having developed a Synchronization Matrix for the seizure of Mingechevir, the 3 Division staff identified a series of Decision Points for the operation. The staff then physically marked these points on the Decision Support Matrix and on the Synchronization Matrix with a prominent yellow star, numbered in chronological sequence. Each Decision Point was physically placed either on the x-axis at the top of the Synchronization Matrix at the specific time when the headquarters predicted the commander would have to make the decision, or in the box alongside the specific unit and task which would have to execute the decision (Figure 12.2).

---

[18] *ADRP 5 The Operations Process*, 2-2.
[19] *ADRP 5 The Operations Process*, 2-2.
[20] Ministry of Defence Allied Joint Publication 5-00: *Allied Joint Doctrine for Operational Level Planning* (Shrivenham: DCDC), 2–87.

	26 Oct	27 Oct	28 Oct
	G+20 ★	G+25	G+26
Air		Gain control of air	
Division HQ		Tactical bound	
IA and CB		behind 20X BPT exploit Nato	
JHF		gains in MVR BPT insert 16X	
1 Artillery Brigade		Support	
		20X/350X ★	
1 ISR Brigade		Find 393X	
350 Brigade		BPT Secure Obj	
4 Brigade		Bdy/Raid MVR	
16 Air Assault		Secure Yevlahk	
Brigade		Op on Obj Eagle	
3/1 Brigade		BPT to secure	
Combat Team		Obj/Raid ★	
		Eagle	
1 Danish Brigade		Secure Parrot	
20 Brigade		BPT to ★	
		secure	
		Obj/RaidEagle	
101 Logs Brigade		C2 of FSA/Support X	
Protect		Establish in FSA/	
Divisional Troops		Supporting X AD	

Figure 12.2 The Synchronization Matrix, Exercise Iron Resolve, 2015, showing Decision Point 6b.

On Exercise Iron Resolve 15, eight Decision Points were identified by the staff. It is unnecessary to describe all of the eight (most of which had three variants) in detail. Rather, an example will demonstrate what a Decision Point is and how the staff identify one. In order to achieve the prime effect laid out in the Commander's

Table 12.1 *Decision Point 6b, Exercise Iron Resolve, 2015*

'Enemy has not withdrawn'	Green
'Intelligence suggests that enemy will not withdraw'	Green
'Enemy assessed at 60% combat effectiveness'	Amber
'Enemy force has withdrawn'	Amber
'Mass IDP (refugee) movement towards Friendly Forces'	Red
'Friendly Forces not set in H-Hour positions',	Red
'Friendly Forces assessed below 60% combat effectiveness'	Red

Intent – the seizure of the city of Mingechevir – 3 UK Division had, at some point, to launch 3/1 Brigade Combat Team and 20 Brigade into Mingechevir. The operation could not continue without this advance but it was also an action of very significant important since it would almost inevitably lead to street-fighting and some heavy casualties. Consequently, launching the assault to seize Mingechevir was plainly decisive at this phase in the mission. The staff surmised that such an action required a conscious decision by the commander. Accordingly, they created a Decision Point which they designated 'Decision Point 6b'.

The Decision Point predicted that once 3 UK Division had invested Mingechevir, the commander would have to make a decision about mounting the attack. This prediction served a useful cognitive function, preparing the staff and the commander for the operation. However, Decision Point 6b did not merely anticipate that the commander might have to make a decision at this point in the operation, however. Crucially, it also prepared and, indeed, preempted the decision itself by the identification of decision criteria. The criteria referred to the conditions under which a decision could be made.

Consequently, Decision Point 6b was defined as 'Authorize Seize and Hold of Mingechevir @G+26' and a list of conditions were appended on the basis of which the decision would be made of whether to authorize the advance or not. To assist in decision-making, the staff produced a decision criteria table:

The decision criteria table for Decision Point 6b identified seven conditions, listed in the left-hand column, on the basis of which the decision to launch the attack was to be made (Table 12.1). The seven conditions referred to three principal factors; the state of the enemy forces, the readiness of the 3 UK Division's forces and the humanitarian situation. The table identified the status of each decision criteria, which it recorded by means of a colour-code – red, amber, green. The colour coding was somewhat complex. According this traffic light system, the staff tried to depict in short-hand the conditions which had to pertain for an attack to be launched. Thus, as long enemy troops were still in the city ('enemy has not withdrawn'), the condition was green – for go. The third criterion recorded that remaining enemy had to be at or below 60% combat effectiveness; as long as this figure was not above 60%, the conditions for attacking were acceptable, or amber. An amber coding was, therefore, the minimal acceptable level for a decision. At the same time, of course, friendly forces had to be ready to mount the attack and to be minimally at 60-per cent combat effectiveness; this condition had to be green. Similarly, any humanitarian crisis with large numbers of refugees fleeing from the city would undermine the operation and constituted a red light. For each criterion, the staff had denoted what conditions had to pertain for the decision to launch to be enacted by the commander. During the Exercise, when 3 UK Division was in a position to launch the attack, the commander was simply presented with the conditions and told that they fulfiled the established criteria.

The Decision Points created for Iron Resolve 15 worked adequately. However, the staff at 3 UK Division subsequently sought to improve on them. Specifically, they began to recognize that there was some ambiguity about conditional criteria and the colour-coding system. The staff believed that Decision Points could work more effectively if the criteria focused on clearer and more concrete factors. In addition, greater clarity could be achieved if the Decision Point criteria were expressed as simple binary questions rather than as conditionals. Consequently, as 3 UK Division prepared for Exercise Warfighter 2017, the Decision Point format was revised. The plan for the exercise was still organized around a series of Decision Points which referred to the critical activities which the mission would involve but the Decision Point criteria table was much clearer, as 3 UK Division's experiences at Exercise Warfighter in June 2017 show.

Exercise Warfighter was also based on the DATE scenario and involved the ejection of Arianian forces from the Division's area of operations in the south of the country. The mission involved an advance eastwards towards a series of towns. The decisive action was the crossing of a river in an urbanized area, 'Objective Giants', held by the enemy. This crossing was recorded as Decision Point 6 ('Can the obstacle crossing commence in GIANTS?') on the Synchronization Matrix and involved ten criteria – listed not as conditionals but as clear questions. These included:

Has the Corps fixed 19 DTG's [an enemy formation] reserve?
Have the levels of attrition been achieved to set the conditions of success for the Brigades?
Has enemy Air Defence been neutralized/defeated to a sufficient level to allow deep aviation operations?[21]

In contrast to the potential ambiguities of a colour code, each question required only an affirmative or negative response. In order to launch the crossing, the commander required a simple 'yes' to each question. The revision of the decision criteria table was a substantial improvement over the original iteration.

It might be thought that the Decision Point is simply an exercise artefact of no significance on real military operations. This would be a mistake. Synchronization Matrices and Decision Points were used extensively during the campaigns in Iraq and Afghanistan. For instance, during the invasion of Iraq, 101st Air Assault Division employed methods which were recognizably similar to 3 UK Division. Indeed, General David Petraeus himself confirmed the importance of staff procedures to his command of 101st Air Assault Division in Iraq. He emphasized that his divisional operations required a massive coordination effort of air, aviation, guns and ground units. In order to ensure all the elements were coherent, the division produced a 'huge operational Synch Matrix. We had one on a board under plexiglass'.[22] Each unit was listed and its tasks sequenced in time and space. On the basis of the Synchronization Matrix, the headquarters then produced an operations schedule:

> Then the staff turn it into an operations schedule. All the activities are listed by time and you checked each one off in turn. In an air assault operation, it is necessary to be meticulous. To have everything planned to the minute. All the tasks had a codewords and you go through it, checking each one off. It involves very serious professional expertise. The Synch Matrix is crucial – and the map, with operational graphics.

[21] Fieldnotes, Exercise Warfighter wargame, Bulford, Vol. VI, 23 March 2017, 77.
[22] General David Petraeus, interviewee 096, personal interview, 7 January 2016.

He concluded: 'If you have a Synch Matrix and a map – with graphics – you have all you need'.[23] In Iraq, Petraeus's decisions as a commander were pre-structured by his Synchronization Matrix, the code words of which acted as potential Decision Points. Petraeus knew that in the event of the failure of one of these tasks, he would be required to make a command decision about how the operation should proceed.

The Decision Point is an important bureaucratic innovation. It is actually employed in the headquarters on operations to inform decisions and to guide the commander. Staff officers repeatedly stressed the relevance of the Decision Point to their work and to their support of the commander. In 82nd Airborne Division, the staff actively sought to ensure that their work could inform a Decision Point: 'The Decision Points are critical. It drives the assessment. We use those religiously and use them well'.[24] The Chief of Staff of 82nd Airborne confirmed their importance:

> We develop the plan around CCIR [commander's critical
> information requirements], PIR [priority information
> requirements], FFIR [friendly forces information requirements],
> EFIR [enemy forces information requirements]. From these
> we develop his [the commander's] DPs [Decision Points] from
> reviewing all that data. And here's in effect what we present when
> we get to the BUB [Battle Update Brief] the next day. The Decision
> Support Matrix is changing and [we tell the commander] there are
> two decisions which you may have to make.[25]

The Decision Point was not simply useful for staff. Commanders, too, regarded it as imperative in aiding their decision-making. A British officer concurred: 'As a commander, three things are vital to me: Intent, risks and Decision Points'.[26] In the twenty-first century, new staff methods have been introduced which have tried to automate and refine decision-making. The Decision Point is one of the most striking and important of these new techniques.

---

[23] Ibid.
[24] OF-3, Major, G3, 82nd Airborne Division, interviewee 066, personal interview, 20 April 2015.
[25] OF-5, Colonel, Chief of Staff, 82nd Airborne Division, interviewee 068, personal interview, 20 April 2015.
[26] OF-6, Brigadier Royal Marines, interviewee 095, personal communication, 1 June 2015.

Understanding the Decision Point

In order to understand the true significance of the Decision Point, it is necessary to analyze this artefact in detail in order to delineate its precise functions. Weissinger-Baylon's work is hugely helpful here. It will be remembered that in reference to naval operations, he described how plans and Standard Operating Procedures pre-empted decision-making to times of lower stress, when errors were less likely. The Decision Point performs precisely this function. Specifically, the Decision Point is a bureaucratic means of overcoming, or at least mitigating, garbage-can thinking. The Decision Point tries to discipline the four organizational factors identified by March and Olson, holding them in their appropriate sequence. By pre-emptively defining the problem and the criteria for its solution, the Decision Point seeks to prevent irrational, random and individual factors vitiating choice-making at moments of risk.

Although their interest in devices like the Decision Point is practical rather than analytic, many staff officer today are fully aware of its significance. Indeed, they are often eloquent about it utility. For instance, a British staff officer from 3 UK Division detailed the precise functions of the Decision Point in order to explain why it had become so important to headquarters:

> There are five or six reasons for DPs. 1) Agility and subordinate empowerment. 2) Tempo; it increases speed on a federated command model. 3) It gets the sequence in the right place. 4) It allows you to take an opportunity when it is presented. 5) When a risk is being taken, it allows you to assess whether it is acceptable and whether it is mitigated to the pre-agreed level.[27]

This is a very useful and perspective statement; it lays out many of the critical functions of the Decision Point. However, it is also very condensed, and while this officer went on to elaborate what he meant, in the contracted format of a quotation, it is not entirely clear what he meant. In order to understand the true significance of Decision Points, it is necessary to interpret this officer's statement more closely and to delineate its precise functions. This officer argued

[27] OF-3, Major, Future Plans (G5), 3 UK Division, interviewee 119, personal interview, 18 November 2016.

that the Decision Point had five or six functions, although there was plainly much overlap between them. By contrast, in the following section it will be argued that Decision Points can be understood as having four major functions: orientation, acceleration, accuracy and delegation. Specifically, the Decision Point coordinates the staff; it accelerates decision-making; and therefore, finally, it ensures that decisions are delegated to the right command level. Each of these functions will be discussed in turn.

It is evident from the previous chapters that operations today have become complex; they involve many elements over elongated timelines. Consequently, it is potentially easy for the staff, especially because it is so large and often dispersed, to become confused about what is actually happening and the sequence of activities. There are hundreds of timings and events on the Synch Matrix and it is impossible to remember all of them. Some simplification is required. In the first instance, Decision Points structure an operation for the staff. Highlighting the most important elements of the operation, Decision Points act as triangulating points so that the staff collectively knows where they are in the plan and what still needs to be achieved. Consequently, the staff in Current Operations employ Decision Points, not as a prescription, but as a guideline, usefully illustrating the direction of travel without determining in advance what has to be done: 'It is a handrail'.[28] Indeed, a Decision Point could only act as a guide because, as this officer appositely observed, 'I have my orders but the enemy has a vote too'. On any operation, unexpected events occur. However, even though unanticipated action is the norm in war, the Decision Point nevertheless serves a valid coordinating function. As one officer noted:

> You've got to go from A to B. You've got to take crazy roads to get there. DPs navigate you through the crazy roads to get through. For instance, if difficulties arise, instead of going left, you might have to go right at a junction and then take three lefts. The DPs ensure that you stay on track even when you have to deviate.[29]

---

[28] OF-4, Lieutenant-Colonel, Chief of Current Operations, 3 UK Division, interviewee 045, personal communication, 1 October 2015.

[29] OF-3, Major, Future Operations, 3 UK Division, interviewee 129, personal interview, 18 November 2016.

The Synchronization Matrix and its Decision Points provide a constant reference point for the staff. In 3 UK Division, the staff – and especially the Chief of the Current operations cell – actively monitored the progress of the battle against the next Decision Point. The sequence of Decision Points, consequently, allow the staff to assess the progress of the battle and to calibrate their inventions against the Commander's Intent. Decision Points do not have to be enacted but the fact that a decision has been anticipated highlights to the staff the direction in which the operation has to go if it is to be a success. Minimally, the Decision Point provides a collective point of reference against which the staff can adapt and improvize the plan in support of their commander. Even when they do not get enacted, Decisions Point play an important role in orienting the staff to the plan, then ensuring adherence to it even as they adapt it.

However, while this orientating role is very important, Decision Points are not merely passive waymarkers for the staff. They play an active role in decision-making itself. Specifically, the Decision Point has brought two further organizational benefits: speed and accuracy. The Decision Point actively assists commanders not only in preparing for a decision but in the act of decision-making itself. Indeed, rapidity and coherence are its principal advantages. By identifying likely decisions, the staff significantly accelerate the headquarters' decision-making on an operation. The headquarters know when they will require the commander's contribution and what they are asking the commander to decide. The Decision Point reduces the commander's options to normally one or two courses of action. On Exercise Iron Resolve 15, for instance, when the Commander of 3 UK Division was eventually asked whether or not to initiate the assault on Mingechevir, he did not have to cogitate over the decision. The decision was almost automatic. Crucially, the recommended decision was itself effectively demanded by the commander's own Intent at the outset of the planning process. The staff were effectively forcing the commander to follow the logic of his own Intent but, having worked through the implications, they were able to foreshorten the actual decision-making process.

There are some good examples from recent operations which demonstrate how Decision Points have accelerated decision-making. Chapter 10 analyzed James Mattis's method of command and, while his acumen and charisma as a commander were recognized, it was argued that his success relied on the construction of a command and staff team around him. Even in the case of a powerful commander such as Mattis, anticipatory decision-making, embodied by the Decision Point, proved useful in helping him make timely and accurate decisions. Thus, Lieutenant-Colonel Clarke Lethin, James Mattis' operations officer in 1st Marine Division, described the way in which a commander's decisions were anticipated and pre-constructed during the invasion of Iraq:

> Adaptation and agility for a command to react to crisis on unexpected/unanticipated events can be mitigated during the initial planning process. What I observed and experienced was that we did not spend all of our planning time on the basic order. We spent a considerable amount of time looking at branches and sequels. One example of this is a branch that had 1st Marine Division reorganizing the Division to attack and seize Mosul. We thought that branch through in enough detail that the staff and units knew how we would reorganize for combat and send a Division Task Force to seize Mosul. As it turned out, and once we were in Baghdad, we received orders to seize Tikrit. Since we had already thought through the problem, we were able to quickly (within hours) able to adapt our Mosul plans for Tikrit and Gen. Mattis was able to issue the orders to the division through a collective radio call and followed up with the graphics and orders. We reorganized and commenced movement in less than twenty-four hours. The lesson learned: don't spend all of your time on the basic order and spend enough time on branches and sequels so that you're not caught flat-footed.[30]

Lethin does not explicitly discuss Decision Points here. He focuses on branches and sequels but Decision Points are implicit in his discussion because the planning options he describes were activated at important, pre-identified junctures: i.e., at Decision Points. Chapter 9 described Mattis' virtuosity as a commander; he was an extremely capable general who dominated his division. Yet, even for a commander as powerful as Mattis, 1st Marine Division staff were able accelerate his decision-making by using Decision Points and preparing alternative 'branches'.

---

[30] Lieutenant-Colonel Clarke Lethin, Deputy and then Assistant Chief of Staff Operations, 1st Marine Division, interviewee 125, email communication, 8 June 2017.

Mattis was not alone in being guided and helped by a Decision Point. One of the most striking applications of a Decision Point to accelerate decision-making occurred during the Battle of Fallujah in November 2004, when 1st Marine Division retook the city from insurgents. During Operation Al-Fajr, it was necessary for Major General Richard F. Natonski, the Commanding General of the 1st Marine Division, to make a major decision which involved a potentially significant employment of his force. As the Fallujah attack proceeded southwards on 10 November 2004, the Regimental Command Teams advancing south were in danger of becoming misaligned. In particular, RCT-1 clearing southwards through the Jolan District parallel to the Euphrates was advancing more quickly than RCT-7 to the east, which had met stiffer resistance. Consequently, the left flank of RCT-1 was in danger of becoming exposed. Natonski was presented with a sizeable problem. One option was to use 2–7 Cavalry to support RCT-7's right-flank attack.[31] The problem with this plan was that it would take twenty-four hours to realign forces before the assault could be mounted. This was unacceptable, as insurgents would use a pause in operations to escape or to reinforce their defences.

The solution was found as Natonski talked to his G-3, Lieutenant-Colonel Joe Letoille. He reminded Natonski of a branch plan which had been developed before the operation had started. This branch plan had reorganized the battlespace in Fallujah assigning a larger area to RCT-1 and directing them to cross Phase Line Fran and continue the attack south, and specifically relieving RCT-7 of some of their battlespace: 'We scheduled the execution of the branch plan for 1900 on 11 November. Then we briefed the MEF Commander in order to ensure he knew of the change. When one Commander said: "We can go early". I said, "no we'll go at 1900 – there is too much coordination to go earlier". We then continued the attack'.[32] As a commander, Natonski agreed to the implementation of the branch plan; that was his decision. Yet, the substantive content of the decision – the very option of being able to make it – did not reside in Natonski alone but, on the contrary, collectively with his staff and Operation Planning Team. In particular, Natonski enacted a Decision Point and initiated a branch

[31] Lieutenant-General Richard Natonski, interviewee 101, personal interview, 22 March 2016.
[32] Ibid.

plan, which had already been prepared under his Intent but substantially independently of him. A complex decision, which threatened to stall the entire assault, was accelerated by the anticipation of his staff, developing contingency plans in advance.

In addition to accelerating decision-making, the staff have tried to improve the accuracy of the commander's decisions by preparing decision criteria in advance when there is no pressure on them.[33] As March and Olson's work has showed, one of the most difficult elements of decision-making is not, in fact, the decision itself. Rather, it is establishing the proper criteria on the basis of which a rational decision should be taken and committing to those standards. Garbage-can thinking typically arises when participants forget the boundary conditions of their decisions or develop new ones without truly realizing their implications. Decision Points and especially the decision criteria have played a crucial role here. Through standardized tables of the type discussed above (Figure 12.2), the staff have preemptively established the appropriate and rational criteria for decisions. They have then used these criteria to guide and even direct the commander to the correct choice, when the actual situation arises. This is very important because on a military operation when decisions might have to be made at inconvenient moments when everyone is exhausted, anxious and confused, the preparation of the decision eliminates the requirement for extensive cogitation and discussion. Crucially, Decision Points reduce the chances of irrelevant information, distracting the decision. Although it cannot eliminate mistakes, decision criteria minimize the danger of garbage-can thinking by dissecting the problem – and specifically its conditions – beforehand: 'Rather than making a decision in the hectic part of a battle, when you are under pressure, when the enemy has a vote, it enables you to have clarity of thought. Do we have the aircraft to enact that decision? It allows the GOC [General Officer Commanding] to make a decision'.[34] The Decision Point is an ingenious way of automating command decisions, by pre-establishing the grounds for decision-making before the critical moment ever arises. Following the commander's own Intent closely, the staff have pre-structured what decision a commander can make in advance, obviating the need for the complex and dangerous

---

[33] Weissinger-Baylon, 'Garbage-Can Decision Process in Naval Warfare', 40.
[34] OF-2, Captain, Battle Captain, Current Operations, 3 UK Division, interviewee 130, personal interview, 18 November 2016.

exercise of judgement in a crisis. Instead of having to cogitate about a decision under intense pressure, the commander was already channelled along pre-established decision-making tracks.

There are a large number of examples of this distribution of command authority to the staff in order to form a professionalized decision-making collective. For instance, as they prepared for Exercise Warfighter in 2016, 3 UK Division organized their campaign around Decision Points and, on a study day before the exercise, the American Deputy Commanding General emphasized the value of Decision Points:

> We need to anticipate decisions from the Decision Support Matrix/Decision Support Overlay and 'pre-make' them early. The GOC tells us what he wants to do, you we need to tell him what the conditions are there. We need to be able to tell him what our recommendations are on Day 4: 'That will be my decision'. We could pre-make many of our decisions and make them Priority Information Requirements and Commander's Critical Information Requirements. They drive you to decisions, once the criteria have already been met. You don't have to wake up the GOC; the decision has already been made.[35]

The staff of 3 UK Division actively sought to anticipate decisions in order to improve the performance of their commander.

The establishment of conditions is hugely significant. It is a means of ensuring that commanders and staff are not distracted by the fog and frictions of war or by information overload. The criteria focus decision-makers on the important factors which actually inform a rational decision, providing a framework in which the irrelevant is dismissed. Problems, solutions, participants and choice opportunities are held in the correct sequence by the decision criteria.

Discussing his experiences of commanding the 101st Airborne Division in Iraq, General David Petraeus gave a very simple example of how Decision Points mitigated against garbage-can thinking on that operation. Air assault operations rely on helicopters to transport the troops and to provide fire support for them. Consequently, the refuelling of helicopters becomes a major issue. Typically, refuelling is conducted by means of Forward Air Re-Fuelling Points (FARP), which the 101st establishes along its line of march. FARPs were absolutely

---

[35] 3 UK Division, Bulford, 23 March 2016, Fieldnotes, Vol VI, 76.

critical to divisional operations, therefore, because without them the operation could not continue. It was impossible to launch the division further north without them. As such, they were always the cue for a potential decision.

However, as a result of his staff's work, Petraeus' decision was reduced to a simple binary: 'If a FARP is not set up, it is a no-go'.[36] Without a FARP in place, no operation could take place. Essentially, for a FARP to be functional, its fuel bladders had to contain sufficient petrol to sustain the helicopters, communications with it had to be established and a force for its protection had to be in place. If any of these conditions were not in place, the FARP was not operating and no decision to launch the operation could be given. A command decision to launch an operation was reduced to whether or not the fuel, etc. was in place and, therefore, to the criteria which the staff had established. In the end, the staff simply presented Petraeus with a pre-constituted decision on the basis of these conditions. Of course, only Petraeus, as the commander, had the responsibility to activate this decision but the decision itself was pre-conceived for him by the staff. In this way, the staff simplified the decision, pre-identifying the critical factors which should inform any sensible judgement. In the end, although he retained command responsibility, Petraeus endorsed the collective decision of the headquarters, rather than making a pristine individual one.

Petraeus' FARP example is very simple. As such it is extremely useful in showing how the Decision Point has improved the accuracy of his decisions. There were moments on that operation when more complex decisions potentially had to be taken. Once again, Decision Points played an important role. In his account of 101st Airborne Division's campaign in 2003, Rick Atkinson describes Operation Destiny Reach, an aviation attack on Karbala on 28 March 2003. He shows how the entire operation was organized by a Synchronization Matrix into which Petraeus's decisions were already pre-structured. It is worth quoting the description at length:

> Petraeus, Freakley [his ADC], and the battle staff had taken their chairs in the ACP [Advanced Command Post] when I entered at 8pm. Nine maps covered the walls. The voltage in the room reminded me of ringside before a prizefight. I took the only

---

[36] General David Petraeus, interviewee 096, personal interview, 7 January 2016.

available seat – on the floor, against a map board – and studied a two-page 'execution checklist'. Alphabetized female names, beginning with Alexandra, Bonnie and Carol, provided code words for significant events that could be transmitted by radio without betraying vital information to Iraqi eavesdroppers. 'Carrie', for example, signified the formal authorization of the attack by Wallace, at 4:42 pm.[37]

In the event, two Apaches crashed due to the dust: 'At 8:43 pm a voice announced, "Apache down south of Shell. Cause unknown." Alarm and imprecations rippled through the tent'.[38] In fact, the crashes were minor, involving no enemy action or fatalities. No decision needed to be taken. The operation proceeded according the Synchronization Matrix and its code-worded tasks: 'Helen. Hope. India. "Julie, with six aircraft". Another company had taken off'.[39] However, each of these code tasks had a series of options attached to them, between which the commander would choose. As he listened to the code words, David Petraeus was being prepared to have to make decisions at each point. If the crashes had involved fatalities or been due to enemy action, Petraeus would have been asked to select between anticipated courses of action. Yet, he would not have made a command decision *ab initio*, forced to analyze the conditions on which a decision could be rationally made at a moment of crisis. He would have been asked to adjudicate on predetermined conditions. As a result, because decision-making had been consciously collectivized, he was much less likely to descend into garbage-can decision-making, confusing the critical elements of his decision and ultimately avoiding the issue by flight or oversight. Because the conditions had already been preemptively established and he was being asked only to endorse a decision, the chances of errors were reduced.

Decision Points anticipate, accelerate and refine decision-making. They actively incorporate the staff into the decision-making process. Precisely because they do this, Decision Points also facilitate a 'federated command model', as the staff officer cited above noted. Specifically, they allow for a coherent delegation of decision-making. This is very important on contemporary operations, when distributed

---

[37] Rick Atkinson, *In the Company of Soldiers*, 188–9.
[38] Ibid., 189.
[39] Ibid., 190.

decision-making is both essential but also an opportunity for confusion and duplication. In order to maintain coherence, it is vital for staff to ensure that divisional commanders and their subordinates are aligned with the appropriate level of decision-making. On contemporary operations, it is all too easy for a commander to be distracted: 'You can get sucked into chasing the shiny things. For instance, four soldiers are kidnapped and you deploy assets to find them. In fact, the ISR [intelligence, surveillance and reconnaissance assets] should be focused on the deep. You get distracted by the close battle when you should be thinking of the deep – out to five days plus'.[40] The Decision Point has become a means of disciplining commanders and ensuring that they concentrate on the formation level priorities which they have themselves set in their Intent. Similarly, Decision Points authorize the staff to assign lower-level decisions to deputies and subordinate commanders with confidence.

Indeed, staff officers have actively used Decision Points to cue the commander's decisions or to delegate them to deputies and subordinates. The following discussion between two officers in 3 UK Division demonstrates the way in which Decision Points are actively used to steer the commander. Imagining a typical scenario, they described the process of moving towards a decision with the commander by reference to the Synchronization Matrix and the Decision Points:

> OF-3, Future Plans: As you go through an operation you are ticking them [Decision Points] off.
> OF-2, Current Operations: And warming up the GOC [for a future decision].
> OF-2: We are going towards a decision.
> OF-3: 6 of the 9 criteria are set. We are warming up the GOC. On the basis of them [the Decision Points], we confirm or deny the assessment [in order to recommend a decision to the commander].[41]

Here, by chaperoning the commander along plausible avenues of decision-making, the staff ensure that the commander concentrates

[40] OF-4, Lieutenant-Colonel, Chief of Future Plans, interviewee 102, personal interview, 18 November 2016.

[41] OF-3, Major Future Operations 3 UK Division, interviewee 129, personal interview, 18 November 2016; OF-2, Captain, Battle Captain Current Operations 3 UK Division, interviewee 130, 18 November 2016.

on the correct level of decision-making. The commander is not distracted by 'shiny things'. In this way, the staff have ensured that their commander's attention is employed appropriately, however much pressure the general might be under. However, precisely because Decision Points anticipate, accelerate and refine any decisions which need to be made, they also allow nominated subordinates to make decisions for the commander. Indeed, informed by precisely the same decision criteria, Decision Points allow subordinates to act as the commander. General David Petraeus himself emphasized the importance of Decision Points to the delegation of command: 'When the conditions are met, just go ahead. You don't have to ask me at 2am. You have an understanding of the appropriate authorities and what conditions they are delegated under'.[42] In some situations, the Decision Points anticipate decision-making so effectively that delegation becomes automatic. The commander does not need to be there, or even notified; the subordinate, in effect, becomes the commander. Decision Points already express the Commander's Intent and, therefore, any nominated subordinate can enact the decision; its criteria have been established. By anticipating and refining decisions, Decision Points have played an important role in systematizing this delegation. Decision points structure decision-making, so that the staff are able to position a commander in the optimal place to make decisions or to assign decision-making authority to a nominated subordinate, in the absence of the commander. Indeed, sometimes, under a Decision Point, the staff themselves have been authorized to make decisions for the commander. Decision Points have been used to anticipate, accelerate, refine and, finally, delegate decisions. In this way, they facilitate a genuinely collective system of command, where command decisions have themselves become the shared property and responsibility of the staff.

Decision Point Tactics

The Decision Point has become an important device for improving decision-making in a divisional headquarters, unifying the staff and the

---

[42] General David Petraeus, 'Commanding a Combat Division', presentation, Command in the 21st Century Conference, University of Warwick, 6 September 2017.

commander into a single executive community. The commander remains central to the cohesiveness of this collective, of course. Every decision point and all its criteria are consciously linked to the Commander's Intent and the staff are always contemplating their superior's next decision. However, there were some evident weaknesses in the Decision Point, as 3 UK Division, and indeed other divisions, had employed it up to 2017. Decision Points may be useful bureaucratic devices but they can encourage inflexibility. In the face of unexpected enemy action, the work which is invested in them can be a wasted effort. Often the situation can have changed so much by the time a Decision Point is meant to be invoked, it becomes irrelevant.

In response to this problem, the US Army has recently been experimenting with a planning method called 'Decision Point Tactics'. This procedure involves developing not a single plan in conventional military fashion but rather planning multiply for a variety of possible scenarios, each of which might be activated.[43] Conventional planning remains essential in this process. Operations must be based on a coherent framework. However, instead of a single, lineal plan, Decision Point Tactics draws heavily upon wargaming, in which alternative scenarios assume priority, precisely because the enemy's reactions are always unpredictable. Decision Point Tactics aim ideally to anticipate every conceivable decision which a commander might have to make and have courses of action prepared for each of them. Consequently, Decision Point Tactics 'is the art and science of employing available means at a specific point in space and/or time where the commander anticipates making a decision concerning a specific friendly course of action. This decision is directly associated with threat force activity (action/reaction) and/or the battlefield environment'.[44] Decision Point Tactics has not been formally introduced into US military doctrine but the concept has been used as a means of improving decision-making.

Indeed, following a rather scarring experience at Exercise Warfighter in 2017, 3 UK Division has sought to incorporate Decision Point Tactics into its planning process. As already mentioned, Exercise Warfighter is the most testing command post exercise, when headquarters are deliberately pitched against materially superior and highly experienced opponents. The exercise is intended to test US Army

[43] www.globalsecurity.org/military/library/report/call/call_97-4_chap1.htm.
[44] www.globalsecurity.org/military/library/report/call/call_97-4_chap1.htm.

warfighting capabilities against an enemy like Russia, North Korea or China. In 2017, 3 UK Division discovered that their established planning procedures, including the Synchronization Matrix and its Decision Points, were inadequate to the challenge of high-intensity operations in the twenty-first century and the headquarters was disappointed by its own performance. As one staff officer put it: 'Warfighter 17.5 was a wake-up call'.[45]

Following their return from Warfighter in June 2017, 3 UK Division therefore revised its decision-making processes and, specifically, reformed the way in which the headquarters used Decision Points. These reforms did not revolutionize existing practices. The Division still produced a detailed Operation Plan which was organized around Decision Points and from which a Synchronization Matrix could be derived. However, the headquarters recognized that a rigid, time-based Synchronization Matrix with predetermined Decision Points, all scheduled days and weeks in advance, was unrealistic and unhelpful. Consequently, while existing procedures were preserved, they were augmented by several important developments.

The headquarters began to consider the concept of risk seriously. This renewed recognition of risk was a crucial cognitive change in 3 UK Division, facilitating the adoption of Decision Point Tactics. At that time, a new concept of risk was advocated almost single-handedly by the staff officer, commanding the 'protect' function in the headquarters; she was a lieutenant-colonel in the Military Police, whose job was to ensure the security of the Division, especially in the rear area. This officer encouraged the Division to analyse risk – i.e., potential threats – more seriously and systematically. In the past, as evidenced above, the headquarters had tended to develop a plan, noting possible risks but not really analyzing them in any serious depth. The potential of enemy action and the diverse courses which an opponent might take were not truly appreciated. Under the leadership of this officer, the headquarters incorporated risk assessment formally into their planning process for the first time. In particular, she developed the 'bow-tie risk analysis' system for the headquarters, which identified the risks, ranked them in terms of likelihood and seriousness and then specified the means of mitigating those risks, should they arise:

[45] OF-4, Future Operations, 3 UK Division, interviewee 139, personal interview, 14 March 2018.

> The first stage [of bow-tie risk analysis] was gathering the risks. Checking the assumptions that you had made and, sometimes, seeing risks we'd not recognized. The second stage was racking and stacking: working out their likelihood. They were then organized on a diagram in order of consequence with the top two risks highlighted for the commander and mitigated against with additional planning.[46]

This method of risk management was not complex but it had a profound effect on the headquarters: 'It changed the way people were thinking about planning; it was not mechanistic. You were thinking about threats and vulnerabilities'.[47] Because this risk-oriented approach highlighted unexpected events, the way the division planned began to change. Instead of a single, unilineal plan, with its pre-set Synchronization Matrix and Decision Points, the division began to develop a 'flow chart' which was explicitly prepared for unexpected eventualities.[48] The plan now encompassed permutations, changes and revisions: 'We have moved away from blue lines and a singular G5 plan'.[49] Attuned to risk, the staff now actively planned for contingency and alteration.

Following on from its new methods of assessing risk, 3 UK Division then implemented some additional staff procedures to enhance its responsiveness to the unexpected. A revised concept of the Decision Point has been an important feature of these changes. 3 UK Division still generates a full Operation Plan, which is very detailed, especially for the first stage of the operation. The staff still identify the major Decision Points, around which the whole operation is still orientated. However, the Decision Points are no longer rigorously tied to a predetermined Synchronization Matrix; they become 'floating', conditions-based Decision Points. Detached from a prescribed sequence of events, Decision Points provide useful waymarkers for the commander and staff, identifying what they broadly need to achieve, without ossifying decision-making. Instead of an instrumental

---

[46] OF-4, SO1 Protect, 3 UK Division, interviewee 144, personal interview, 14 March 2018

[47] Ibid.

[48] OF-4, Future Operations, 3 UK Division, interviewee 139, personal interview, 14 March 2018.

[49] OF-3, ISR Current Operations, 3 UK Division, interviewee 144, personal interview, 14 March 2018.

implementation of a pre-established Operation Plan, 3 UK Division now concentrates on its contingent revision.

Under Decision Point Tactics, the way the staff plan has materially changed. The staff do not waste time writing detailed plans or orders about events a long time in the future. They sketch out future events, while they concentrate in detail only on the next twenty-four hours, of whose conditions they can be more certain. The twenty-four hours before execution has now become a critical period for the Division in terms of decision-making. At this point, staff from Future Operations assess the most immediately available intelligence about enemy and friendly forces. They ascertain where the enemy is likely to be and what it is likely do; and what friendly forces might be capable of doing in response. On the basis of this analysis, Future Operations (G3/5) issues a 'Decision Support Matrix' to Current Operations for execution. The Decision Support Matrix is a significant revision of the old Effects Schematic, discussed above. It tabulates the schedule of specific activities over the next twenty-four hours, in the light of the most recent intelligence. The Decision Support Matrix is, in effect, a very detailed and specific Synchronization Matrix for the next day's activities. It also includes a number of Decision Points, to direct the commander's interventions about likely and possible decisions in this period: 'There might be seven Decision Points for a whole plan. But there will be five or six Decision Points for one FRAGO [a fragmentary order, typically issued twenty-four hours before an action to the brigades]. The GOC will want a handle on the level of detail which is refined over the coming days. As a concept, the Decision Point is spot on'.[50] Significantly, Decision Points also specify a series of refined decision criteria which inform the commander's decision. Because the information is likely to be more detailed and accurate under the new twenty-four-hour system, the criteria have enhanced the fidelity of decision-making.

The revision of 3 UK Division's procedures has been a deeply interesting process. Tested on a series of exercises in the latter half of 2017, Decision Point Tactics has improved decision-making. By focusing on the next twenty-four hours and considering risks more seriously, it has allowed the Division to react more quickly and coherently

[50] OF-4, Future Operations, 3 UK Division, interviewee 139, personal interview, 14 March 2018.

to surprises. These have been important innovations. However, the central logic behind the Division's new Decision Point Tactics has not changed. As with the previous system, the Decision Point has been implemented to refine and accelerate decision-making precisely at a moment when operations have become more complex and extended. Under the new system, the staff actively prepare decisions for the commander and structure those decisions by reference to pre-conceived criteria, as they have done in the past. Decision Points may now be created for only the next day – rather than some time in the distant future – but the staff are still attempting to automate executive action in order to increase the tempo and accuracy of the headquarters. The new process represents an important revision of procedure; 3 UK Division is confident it has improved decision-making. However, the fundamental aim and method are the same. With Decision Point Tactics, 3 UK Division has sought to facilitate command through the introduction of new concepts, like risk, and new practices and artefacts, such as the Decision Support Matrix. The headquarters has incorporated the staff yet more systematically into the decision-making process.

Checklist Command

The Decision Point has become an important device in the new divisional headquarters. It has fulfilled four essential functions: orientation, delegation, acceleration and accuracy. Using the Decision Point as a tool, the staff has been able to deconstruct decisions in order to align, anticipate and improve decision-making. In the first instance, Decision Points have simply oriented the staff to the plan, acting as triangulating points to guide them through complex operations. The staff have plotted the current operation against the next Decision Point, ensuring that they are working towards it, even when they are forced to temporarily take a different tack.

In addition, instead of being forced to respond to everything, the staff have used the Decision Point to focus the commander on the key issue. Decision Points have insulated the commander from the pressure of events and from excessive information. They have channelled the commander's executive interventions. In this way, decisions have been aligned to their proper level. Minor decisions about subordinate tasks have been properly devolved to subordinates and deputies have been authorized to make decisions for the commander. Under the Decision Point, Deputy Commanding Generals, Chiefs of Staff and key staff officers such as the Chief of the Current Operations Cell have been entrusted to take decisions on the basis of pre-established criteria. In the dispersed division of the twenty-first century, with its distributed command hierarchy, this delegation and empowerment has often proved crucial. It is particularly interesting that the staff officer from 3 UK Division cited above explicitly observed that the Decision Point was consistent with a 'federated command model' in which decision-making authority has been shared by deputies, subordinates and by staff.

In addition, as a result of the identification of decision criteria, the chances of sudden, random and individual decisions on the basis of intuition have been minimized. Decision-making has been accelerated and even automated because the conditions for a decision have already been established beforehand. Decision criteria have also improved the accuracy of decision-making, reducing the chances of garbage-can thinking. Rather than committing the errors of flight or oversight, commanders are forced by their staff to focus on the actual problem. The division has become too complex a system for instinctive, unanticipated decision-making, which was a feature of twentieth-century command when generals typically focused on the close tactical fight. Decisions have been pre-planned and anticipated by the staff so that commanders have been better able to make rapid *and* accurate decisions.

In this way, while commanders have retained sole responsibility for any operation, the staff have assumed an increasingly important role in decision-making. They have begun to share *de facto* executive authority, directing, channelling, participating in the decision-making process and guiding the commander through an operation. The staff have contributed rather more than simply attending to the details of the plan, as they traditionally did. They have been actively engaged in the executive function of management. It is important to stress there that while the staff have played a more active role in decision-making as a result of an artefact like the Decision Point, divisional command has not become bureaucratized; commanders have not been displaced by bureaucracy, still less by the staff.

In the twenty-first century, commanders are still the central point of reference for the staff. Both commanders and their staff regard Decision Points as useful in helping a general to make the best decisions, rather than reducing the commander to a staff cipher. It must be remembered that the entire Synchronization Matrix, the Decision Points and, indeed, the decision criteria are derived from the Commander's Intent and are normally all agreed to by the commander. Decisions Points are therefore in the end a manifestation of the commander's own will. Ultimately, the staff are not trying to subvert the command when they invoke a Decision Point. On the contrary, they are seeking to ensure that in the confusion of battle, commanders enact the courses of action which they have themselves selected as the most likely to bring success. The staff and its procedures have not replaced the commander. The Decision Point does not signify the supersession of the commander but the emergence of a deeply integrated, inter-dependent command collective, consisting of the commander and the staff who together seek to exploit their expertise. The Decision Point marks an important moment in the reformation of the division then. It shows that deep cooperation between the staff and their commander has increasingly displaced the more individualized generalship of Rommel, Monash or Montgomery. Today, commanders are still crucial; they are the decision-makers. However, commanders are systematically assisted to make decisions by a professionalized staff through the use of innovations like the Decision Point.

In Chapter 4, the emergence of the modern division headquarters and its techniques was described. Standardization is not new and the plans, estimates, orders and situation maps of the twentieth century certainly sought to reduce the chances of garbage-can thinking. The Decision Point has an ancestry, therefore. However, while acknowledging this background, the novel functions of the Decision Point have to be acknowledged; Decision Points have professionalized decision-making. They have standardized, improved and accelerated decision-making through the application of collective expertise to the problems of command. They have involved a considerable refinement of the planning process and presumed advanced staff expertise. In order to identify a Decision Point, a detailed deconstruction of the mission into its constituent tasks is required. The staff must then identify the most important tasks and make a series of inductions about them to determine what conditions are required to make them possible. All of this information and analysis must be recorded on standardized charts and forms in order to ensure absolute clarity once an operation starts. This complex work is all directed at a single goal: improving decision-making. In an increasingly complex system, the Decision Point has assisted in the management of missions. It has reduced individual human error by sharing decision-making with a team. Coordination of complex operations is achieved more effectively through professional cooperation. The individualist commander of the twentieth century has been replaced by the collective expertise of a team, operating on the basis of institutionalized procedure. This team includes not only deputies, as Chapters 8 and 9 described, but also the staff itself as a professionalized expert body. Ironically, under the process of professionalization, the staff have become part of the command team too.

The Decision Point is a military device but it has an obvious parallel in the civilian sector; namely, the check list. The checklist first rose to prominence in aviation in order to reduce individual pilot error, which had been a major cause of air accidents. The formulation of established protocols for a variety of eventualities, which are typically enacted by a flight team of at least the pilot and co-pilot, has been proven to reduce accidents significantly. The idea of the checklist has since been disseminated to other spheres, perhaps, most notably to medicine and especially to surgery. There are some parallels between surgery and military command, beyond the fact that both generals and surgeons conduct 'operations' in a 'theatre'. As in the military, the consultant surgeon once dominated the operating theatre and was the centre of decision-making. In the past, the authority of the consultant was broadly functional. However, as medical procedures have become more complex and intricate, the heroic surgeon has been increasingly displaced by an operating team. As part of this collectivization of expertise, the checklist, taken essentially from civil aviation, has played an increasingly important role in medical procedures.

Atul Gawande has played a significant role here in institutionalizing the checklist into modern surgery and his bestselling book, *The Checklist Manifesto*, describes both this reform and its wider significance. He describes a number of clinical mistakes, when simple steps were omitted because surgeons had simply forgotten to check basic procedure. Gawande gives a simple but striking example of a successful implementation of a checklist – the attempt at Johns Hopkins University to reduce central line infections in 2001. The clinical care specialist at the hospital, Peter Pronovost, created a checklist for all doctors:

On a sheet of plain paper, he plotted out the steps to take in order to avoid infections when putting in a central line. Doctors are supposed to (1) wash their hands with soap, (2) clean the patient's skin with chlorhexidine antiseptic, (3) put sterile drapes over the entire patient, (4) wear a mask, hat, sterile gown, and glovers, and (5) put a sterile dressing over the insertion site once the line is in. Check, check, check, check, check.[51]

The result of enforcing this checklist on surgeons was that infections fell from 11 per cent to 0. This case is exceptionally simple but it illustrates Gawande's wider point. As medical procedures become ever more specialized and complex, involving the participation of teams of surgeons rather than one expert surgeon, checklists have become critical to ensure that vital tasks are not overlooked. The checklist is a response to an organizational problem of increasing complexity and, attempting to generate higher levels of performance, it is a manifestation of professionalization. The Decision Point is the military equivalent. It is an attempt to accelerate and refine decision-making through collective expertise. The Decision Point has improved command by submitting decision-making to the collective scrutiny of the staff and the commander.

[51] Atul Gawande, *The Checklist Manifesto* (London: Profile, 2011), 37–8.

13 THE CRISIS

Abnormal Accidents

Through an investigation of the Decision Point, the previous chapter mainly examined normal decision-making in routine situations. There, it was claimed that divisional headquarters have sought to accelerate and improve decision-making by incorporating the staff into the executive function, thereby creating a cooperative command system. Normal decision-making is an important feature of military operations and planning for them. A large military organization has to have some idea of what it is going to do and sometimes operations go more or less according to plan. However, in war, it is very common that unexpected events transpire; things go wrong. Consequently, commanders have to prepare for crises and develop decision-making practices which are capable of functioning even in difficult and confused situations.

The military are by no means alone in worrying about crises; scholars have been equally interested in explaining how organizations respond to unforeseen predicaments. In his analysis of the notorious Mann Gulch disaster, Karl Weick describes the disintegration of an organization in the face of the unexpected.[1] The Mann Gulch disaster of 5 August 1949 involved a team of nine smokejumpers who parachuted into the Cascade Mountains to assess and, if possible, extinguish a small forest fire. Due to a strong wind blowing up from the valley, they found themselves trapped above the rapidly expanding and

---

[1] Karl Weick, *Making Sense of the Organization* (Oxford: Blackwell, 2000), 100–24.

fast-moving conflagration, which threatened to engulf them. Facing this unexpected crisis, the team panicked. Precisely because there was no common 'sense' of what was best to do as a team, cooperation became impossible. In line with emergency procedure, the team-leader ordered the smokejumpers to throw away their tools and make an escape fire. He was ignored by his subordinates. While he made an escape fire and survived, the other members of the team tried to outrun the fire by climbing up and over the ridge-line; only two survived by finding a small gully. According to Weick, the tragedy occurred because inter-subjectivity broke down completely: 'the crew's stubborn belief that it faced a 10:00 fire [i.e., one that can be surrounded and isolated by 10:00 the next morning] is a powerful reminder that positive illusions can kill people. But the more general point is that organizations can be good at decision-making and still falter. They falter because of deficient sense-making'.[2] For Weick, the disaster demonstrated a collapse of cooperation; the smokejumpers had no common understanding of their situation. Instead of reacting as a group, the smokejumpers, therefore, responded individually. With no idea how to cooperate with each other, they became individually confused: 'I've never been here before, I have no idea where I am, and I have no idea who can help me'.[3] The team of smokejumpers fragmented into a collection of panicking individuals.

The Mann Gulch disaster is instructive for military head-quarters and, indeed, raises a significant question for bureaucratic procedures like the Decision Point designed for routine decision-making. Decision Points have been adopted by divisional headquarters to improve the accuracy and speed of decision-making. However, there is an obvious danger with pre-constituted Decision Points; they may actively impede the responsiveness of the staff, trapping them in their own pre-conceptions. Staff officers have been well aware of the problem. For instance, one officer from 82nd Airborne noted that sometimes 'whatever is on a Decision Point matrix could lead to a level of rigidity' when reality is 'more free flow'. A senior British officer confirmed the point: 'I'm not convinced by Decision Points. In the dynamic uncertainty of battle, it's not that useful to tie yourself to DPs rigidly'.[4] Indeed, he observed that on 3 UK Division's Exercise

---

[2] Ibid., 107.

[3] Ibid., 105.

[4] OF-6, Brigadier, Commander ISR Brigade, British Army, interviewee 133, personal communication, 14 June 2017.

Warfighter in 2017, it was almost impossible to know whether the decision criteria had been fulfilled or not. Consequently, the Decision Points were worthless in informing command decisions. Once a Decision Point has been created, it might encourage inflexibility in the headquarters. Indeed, commanders could be encouraged to make false decisions because the events have so changed the situation that the pre-established Decision Point criteria were no longer valid.

Clearly, 3 UK Division has tried hard to overcome the problems attendant with Decision Points, by incorporating the concept of risk into the very centre of their planning process. The Division has deliberately moved away from a detailed, time-based Synchronization Matrix with its inflexible Decision Points to a flowchart with floating Decision Points. The Decision Support Matrix with its immediate Decision Points, prescribed for the next twenty-four hours, has been a central part of increasing the responsiveness of the headquarters. Nevertheless, despite these improvements, no headquarters can rely on pre-planning to mitigate against all crises. The unexpected will always occur.

At this point, as a bureaucratic device, Decision Points may become detrimental, constraining and distorting an accurate assessment of the current situation. Rather than mitigating the dangers of garbage-can collective thinking, they might actually institutionalize it. Decision Points are potentially dangerous, then, making a replication of the Mann Gulch disaster possible. Committed to pre-conceived Decision Points, a headquarters might collectively persist with its erroneous account of reality, against all the evidence. In trying to obviate garbage-can thinking, adherence to Decision Points might encourage group think. Alternatively, faced with a totally unexpected crisis, staff officers and commanders in a division might simply revert to random individualism. Like Weick's smokejumpers, they may be reduced to confusion: 'We have no idea where we are'. In this situation, a division would quickly collapse as a unified formation.

A catastrophic collapse of decision-making is always an eminent possibility on military operations, then, especially in the light of their complexity and uncertainty. Indeed, on military operations, a breakdown is inordinately likely. In his celebrated analysis of accidents, Charles Perrow has developed the concept of the 'normal accident' in 'high risk technologies that suggest that no matter how effective conventional safety devises are, there is a form of accident that is inevitable'.[5] For a normal accident to occur, 'we need two or more failures among components that interact in some unexpected way'.[6] This is most likely in a complex system whose parts are closely interconnected: 'The odd term normal accident is meant to signal that, given the systemic characteristics, multiple and unexpected interactions of failure are inevitable'.[7] The problem is, of course, that 'our ability to organize does not match the inherent hazards of some of our organizational activities'.[8] Perrow includes weapons and 'military adventures' in his typology, as systems particularly prone to normal accidents. Not only is a division, as an increasingly complex organization, exposed to the risk of a normal internal accident when multiple unexpected failures coincide, but it is subject to enemy action that is actively trying to precipitate just such a disaster.

Indeed, it is not only that operations are sometimes confusing, but the division and sometimes the headquarters itself are under direct attack. The physical destruction of divisional forces and their headquarters is, in fact, a recurrent problem. Even during the invasion of Iraq in 2003, when the United States enjoyed complete air superiority, there was an example of precisely this scenario. On 7 April, the 2nd Brigade, 3rd Infantry Division, established its Tactical Operations Centre in the southern suburbs of Baghdad. The Centre was apparently well-sited in a large, warehouse-like building and a second smaller building with a courtyard for vehicles, protected from the main highway by a ten-foot wall.[9] Some cells, including the Fire Support Cell, worked from their armoured vehicles parked in the courtyard. The Brigade believed they had found a secure location and, indeed, many members of the headquarters were not wearing any of their protective equipment on 7 April. However, at 11am a rocket struck the warehouse building: 'Nearly every vehicle in that courtyard had, in one instant, vanished from existence [in all seventeen were destroyed]. All of the communication equipment was gone. At least half of the large warehouse had collapsed and the remaining elements were quickly

[5] Charles Perrow, *Normal Accidents: living with high-risk technology* (New York: Basic Books, 1984), 3.
[6] Ibid., 4.
[7] Ibid., 5.
[8] Ibid., 10.
[9] http://educatedsoldier.blogspot.co.uk/2007/08/destruction-of-2nd-brigade-3rd-id-toc.html.

burning down'. Remarkably, although the Fire Support Cell in their armoured 577 seemed to have taken a direct hit from the rocket, they emerged from the wreckage unscathed with a still-functioning vehicle. The destruction of the 2nd Brigade Tactical Operation Centre is a pertinent reminder of the realities of war and the constant possibility of a 'normal accident' in any headquarters.[10]

Teamwork

Artefacts like the Decision Point or the Synchronization Matrix seem inadequate – and, indeed, misconceived – in the face of events of this type: a complete breakdown of command. Decision Points may work well when everything is going to plan but when a crisis arises in which there are multiple threats or, even more so, when the very presumptions on which the plan was made become invalid, they may have a paralyzing effect. A number of senior military officers are concerned about the emasculation of command autonomy potentially implied by enlarged division headquarters and its new bureaucracy; certainly James Mattis' command method, discussed in Chapter 9, was an explicit attempt to avoid bureaucratization. Others identified the limitations of the Decision Point itself: 'Decision Points are useful when things are going to plan but I'm skeptical they are appropriate since war is dynamic and unpredictable'.[11] In his work on command, Jim Storr proposes the same argument and, indeed, specifically rejects the creation of new bureaucratic devices like the Synchronization Matrix; 'its use was imposed on the British Army in the mid 1990s by a senior officer by decree without any analysis of its value, or the cost of producing it'.[12] The concern is serious. In effect, in an attempt to eliminate garbage-can thinking, divisional headquarters are in danger of exposing themselves to an even more serious danger: complete paralysis in the face of the unexpected.

At this point, headquarters need to turn to other methods if they are to be able prevail in a crisis. Edwin Hutchins' work on

---

[10] It seems likely that the attack was a friendly-fire incident. This is significant in terms of the speed of the headquarters recovery since the command post was struck by the most advanced weaponry.

[11] OF-6, Brigadier, Commander ISR Brigade, British Army, interviewee 133, personal communication, 14 June 2017.

[12] Jim Storr, *The Human Face of War*, 145.

cognition is deeply pertinent here because he, like Karl Weick, specifically focuses on moments of crisis, when cooperation has to be
improvised. Hutchins begins his work with the example of a crisis
involving the USS *Palau*. As it sailed into San Diego harbour, the USS
Palau lost all power and the pilot was unable to steer the ship. The vessel
was in danger of colliding with the dock or with other ships. However,
working closely together in an emergency, the crew were able to improvise and guide the ship into port: 'The safe arrival of *Palau* at anchor
was due in large part to the exceptional seamanship of the bridge crew,
especially the navigator. But no single individual acting alone – neither
the captain nor the navigator nor the quartermaster chief supervising
the navigation team – could have kept control of the ship and brought
it safely to anchor'.[13] Crucially, the crew recognized the crisis together
and experimented rapidly with a variety of solutions, whatever they
were and whoever suggested them. Eventually, they developed a means
of steering the ship into harbour.

Hutchins employs the *Palau* to introduce the problem of collective cognition which he wants to show is a product not of individuals, but of a wider social cultural system. He goes onto discuss how
maritime navigation depends upon scientific theories and a series of
artefacts, especially the chart. These elements structure and facilitate
collective cognition. Some of his discussion has evident echoes with
the analysis of the Decision Point in the previous chapter; artefacts
facilitate shared understanding and can, therefore, improve decision-
making. However, he also shows, in line with his original *Palau*
example, that teamwork – not technology – is finally critical. He
claims that groups are superior to individuals in generating a diversity of options; 'however, having generated a useful diversity, they
then face the problem of resolving it'.[14] Having developed a number
of possible responses, a crew has, then, to decide collectively which
one to choose. That is difficult. For Hutchins, the social configuration of the crew will determine whether its members can cooperate
effectively with each other to define and therefore resolve a problem –
or whether it is able to at all. Solidarity, interaction, hierarchy and
communication play a critical role here. Hutchins' point is that the
social dynamics on the bridge of the *Palau* allowed its personnel to

[13] Edwin Hutchins, *Cognition in the Wild* (Cambridge, MA: Harvard, 1996), 5.
[14] Edwin Hutchins, *Cognition in the Wild* (Cambridge, MA: Harvard, 1996), 262.

arrive together at a solution to a totally unexpected crisis through improvised but ordered cooperation.

Hutchins' work implies that the culture of a headquarters is very important to its ability to improvise in a crisis. In routine periods, normal decision-making processes guided by standardized procedures (like the Decision Point) are adequate but periodically, abnormal situations arise that require an alternative approach. At this point, deeper levels of cooperation are required. The interactions within the headquarters, its social density and the relations between officers are then ultimately likely to be critical to its responsiveness because they will determine how quickly information, ideas and solutions flow between the staff. The configuration of a headquarters, with its internal allegiances, solidarities and animosities, is likely to determine how well a staff is able to cooperate in a crisis. Staff officers and commanders who have worked together extensively and have developed established, inclusive practices which regulate their relations will be most able to communicate and cooperate; they are likely to be able to respond more effectively.

The previous chapter explored the way in which a bureaucratic device, the Decision Point, had been developed to improve routine decision-making. It remains a very important innovation. However, as Huntington emphasized, professionalism involves not only specialist knowledge but also a distinctive corporate ethos. Professionalism involves an individual and collective obligation to cooperate and collaborate in pursuit of organizational goals, irrespective of the situation or an individual's own interests. Chapter 11 showed how at precisely a time when divisional headquarters are expanding and dispersing, this professional ethos has accentuated among the staff to offset distance. A highly developed corporate ethos also plays an important role in the ability of any divisional headquarters to respond to an emergency. Crisis management requires not only refined staff work and elaborate artefacts, like the Decision Point, but also excellent cooperation among the staff and between the staff and commanders. The staff must follow the Commander's Intent collectively so that they are able to develop detailed courses of action which respond coherently to the immediate crisis. Professionalized headquarters have developed interesting ways of trying to ensure that the staff is sufficiently cohesive, that it can respond to a 'normal accident'. The Decision Point and other staff processes are by no means irrelevant here but they are themselves embedded and enacted within a wider professional lifeworld. In order to understand how a divisional headquarters responds to a crisis to engage in abnormal decision-making, it is necessary to explore other aspects of its practices more deeply.

Meetings

In Chapter 2, the work of Peter Drucker was employed to define command. Drucker's work is replete with entertaining insights which are relevant to understanding the headquarters. Throughout his work, Peter Drucker is amusingly disparaging about meetings; 'One either meets or one works, one cannot do both'. Anyone who has had to endure these gatherings, in a university department or elsewhere, would probably agree with him. Especially in the new divisional headquarters, the meeting has become a prominent and, indeed, sometimes oppressive feature of the daily routine, called the 'battle rhythm'. The 'battle rhythm' of a divisional headquarters consists of a constant cycle of meetings: the morning and evening Commander's Update Brief, the Receipt of Orders Brief, the Mission Analysis Brief, the Targeting Working Group, the Integrated Effect Working Group and various video-teleconferences with other commands. At almost any point in the day, someone in a divisional headquarters is in a meeting.

All of these meetings have an overt practical and cognitive function. They are designed to ensure that the headquarters and its staff share an accurate understanding of the current situation and that the decisions which emerge from each of these meetings are coherent. Meetings are a means of ensuring and updating collective 'situational awareness', then. Headquarters invest a very significant, even extraordinary, amount of time and energy in meetings. In 3 UK Division, for example, a typical meeting of the Principal Planning Group to assess each stage of the plan takes some two hours. Involving the participation of the commander, the deputy commanding general, the chief of staff, the deputy chief of staff and about sixteen other senior officers in the headquarters, it represents an investment of at least forty hours, although once preparation is included this figure increases considerably.[15] 3 UK Division is not unusual. In Iraq, when he was commanding

---

[15] Fieldnotes, Exercise Iron Triangle, St Mawgan, 27–29 November 2013, 27–62.

Joint Special Operations Command, General McChrystal spent three hours preparing for his daily 'O&I' [Operations and Intelligence] meeting, which was eventually attended by 7000 personnel.

Clearly, although officers routinely complain that the battle rhythm is too rigid and overloaded, even when they are on operations, it would be surprising if commanders and staff would persist with meetings if they believed them to be utterly nugatory. They may, indeed, be burdensome and boring but meetings are seen to have an important function. Specifically, the meeting is, in fact, one of the central methods by which military headquarters ensure a close bond between the staff and the commander. Perhaps surprisingly, the meeting, in all its mundanity, is, therefore, absolutely essential for the coherence of a division. Of course, headquarters invest significant time and effort in meetings, primarily because an accurate and shared understanding of the environment is regarded as critical. James Mattis is a commander who, perhaps more than anyone, has waged a war against bureaucracy.

Yet, James Mattis's operations officer, Lieutenant-Colonel Clark Lethin, affirmed the importance of meetings during 1st Marine Division's operations:

> I agree with the concept of bringing staff and commanders together periodically during combat to ensure the command is aligned with the commander and his intent. This is also the time that the commander, staff and subordinate commanders can assess each other's mental and psychological state. I think that we had one or two of these type meetings on the March Up. More often than not, General Mattis, General Kelly and a few of the trusted staff would circulate the battlefield and meet with commanders/units to reinforce guidance and intent, answer questions and assess commanders. We fed that information back to General Mattis and trusted staff to maintain our situational awareness and remain alert to any issues that might pop up.[16]

Even a commander as capable and charismatic as Mattis used meetings to unite his staff around a common definition of the mission. The cognitive function of meetings is plainly vital. As one staff officer noted: 'you

---

[16] Lieutenant-Colonel Clarke Lethin, Deputy and then Assistant Chief of Staff Operations, 1st Marine Division, interviewee 125, email communication, 8 June 2017.

have got to zero the staff'.[17] The cognitive function of the meeting is imperative, then. It is a means by which the command can establish a shared understanding of the situation across the headquarters. Clearly, this is crucial in response to unforeseen events. The problem at Mann Gulch was that the smokejumpers had no pre-established understanding of the situation which confronted them. In order to respond effectively to the unexpected, it is vital for a headquarters to have a clear understanding of what the preceding situation was and what it is trying to achieve. The crew of the USS *Palau* were taken utterly by surprise by the loss of power in San Diego harbour but they knew the position of their vessel and they knew what they were trying to achieve. Pre-established cognitive unity facilitates crisis-response very significantly. For all their tedium, by uniting a headquarters, meetings generate a shared understanding and a cooperative atmosphere before any crisis. Meetings are, therefore, likely to assist in the resolution of crises.

Meetings, however, play an important moral role, not simply informing the staff but also motivating them. In the twenty-first century, meetings have become a forum for leadership. Chapter 7 discussed the importance of leadership in the mass citizen armies of the twentieth century. The exemplary personal leadership of commander played a crucial motivational role. The inspiration of the troops is by no means irrelevant today. Before the March Up, James Mattis ensured that he visited all of his units several times. On the operation, he had a galvanizing effect on his troops: 'When we were feeling down, he would come round and say it might be bad for us but it was worse for our predecessors'.[18] However, because troops are now highly professional, the moral – still less the paternal – role which was so vital in the twentieth century has become less significant; troops are typically motivated more by the professional solidarity of their small units than their generals.[19] It is noticeable that generals today eschew the theatrical attire

---

[17] OF-4, Lieutenant-Colonel, Chief of Future Plans, 3 UK Division, interviewee 102, personal interview, 18 November 2016. 'Zero' here refers to the process of ensuring that the sight of a weapon is accurate.

[18] OF-3, Major, Company Commander, 1st Marine Division, interviewee 099, personal communication, 15 March 2016.

[19] For a longer discussion of combat motivation in the small unit see Anthony King, 'Combat Effectiveness in the Small Infantry Unit: beyond the primary group thesis', *Security Studies* 25(4) 2016: 688–728; Patrick Bury and Anthony King, 'The Profession of Love', in Anthony King (ed.), *Frontline: combat and cohesion in Iraq*

of their predecessors; they dress in a neat professional manner so that, apart from their rank badge, they look just like their soldiers.

Moreover, since formations are radically dispersed and divisional commanders are pre-occupied with intensified problems of coordination, it is often very difficult for a divisional commander to provide personal leadership in a traditional way. Nevertheless, this does not mean that the leadership role has evaporated. Rather, it has been re-configured and re-directed. Divisional commanders may not need to act as a father figure to their often poorly trained and inexperienced troops but leadership has become critical in uniting and motivating deputies and staff:

> Modern leadership is not about riding on a horse and waving a sword. It is about personality and relations with subordinates and superiors and key staff. You need mutual respect based on competence, courage (which remains as important as ever) and trust. Moral factors are no easier. Maybe they are harder. Moral courage has not gone away; you do not accept illegal orders if you know which way is up. Personality is crucial but it is confined to a smaller circle.[20]

Leadership is no longer directed primarily at young, citizen troops but rather at deputies and the staff, whose job is to enact the commander's decisions.

Alongside the command function, meetings are for a leadership. They are a venue in which a smaller circle of deputies and staff can be motivated. Leadership is now projected not so much onto the soldiery at large but at this smaller, more exclusive executive body. Indeed, the purely intellectual comprehension of the situation can only be impressed on the staff collectively to generate unity if it has a moral force. Staff officers have to feel committed to their commanders and obliged to abide by their intent. The meeting is crucial here: 'It is an opportunity for the commander to impose his personality and to create the right culture in the headquarters where you want to succeed'.[21]

and Afghanistan (Oxford: Oxford University Press, 2015) 200–15; Anthony King, *The Combat Soldier.*

[20] OF-8, Lieutenant-General (retired), British Army, interviewee 042, personal interview, 2 October 2014.

[21] OF-4, Lieutenant-Colonel, Chief of Current Operations, 3 UK Division, interviewee 045, personal interview, 7 June 2017. Ibid.

Meetings have a moral just as much as an intellectual function and this is very important when the inevitable unexpected event arises. In a crisis, when staff and commanders are exhausted, confused, worried and sometimes physically frightened, more than just cognitive unity is required. The headquarters has to be bonded viscerally so that the staff and commanders are not just theoretically able to develop a solution but are collective determined to succeed. Indeed, sometimes the intense dedication of the staff to the commander and to each other is rather more important than whether they are clever enough to conjure up brilliant solutions. In a crisis, the staff have to be willing, like the crew of the USS *Palau*, to far exceed their formal job specifications. The meeting is crucial in enjoining this basic commitment. Its moral function is, therefore, as important as its intellectual one in impressing the intent upon the staff.

The personality of the commander plays an important role in enjoining these moral commitments. Forceful, competent and attractive commanders are able to impress themselves on their staff better than weak, vacillating ones. They exude charisma which animates and unites the staff. The staff actively want to please them by fulfilling their intent and even dull artefacts, like Decision Points, become replete with the commander's personality. The commander's personality begins to infuse the headquarters. However, it is important to recognize that charisma does not emanate pristinely from a commander's personality. Whatever their character, the emotional significance of commanders is also collectively generated by the staff who communally invest character traits with a special, even sacred, status. Meetings play a crucial role here as they are an arena in which commanders can impose themselves on their staff who, in turn, can collectively display their deference to their commander. Leadership emerges, then, out of a series of formal performances. Staff are motivated by their participation in a round of ritual meetings when the moral and emotional force of the commander is staged and affirmed.

Despite their important moral function, headquarters meetings are typically not very interesting. Nevertheless, although a common experience for even the most enthusiastic staff officer is boredom, meetings are punctuated by moments of heightened emotional commitment; these moments may be small and fleeting but they are, nevertheless, highly significant. Indeed, leadership is exercised in these brief scenes. These moments involve both formal and informal techniques. For instance, before a meeting, staff officers gather in the designated space, often sitting in pre-assigned seats; typically, they will engage in informal discussions with each other. They await the commander, on whose arrival their conversations break off immediately, and they will be ordered to stand to attention until the commander has sat down. It is an apparently trivial, ritualistic moment but the ceremony explicitly marks the unique status of the commander in the headquarters. The commander's primacy over the staff is demonstrated and they are all necessarily oriented to their commander.

Through micro-techniques of this type, the meeting is structured as a self-referential means of affirming the authority of the commander, then. In this way, meetings accord with David Gibson's analysis of Kennedy's Executive Committee of the National Security Council during the Cuban crisis. In his analysis of the micro-dynamics of decision-making within the body, he records a distinctive distribution of conversations. Overwhelmingly, members of the committee addressed their comments to Kennedy himself: 'We might say that Kennedy was the conversational magnetic pole, toward whom everyone else was, in the last instance, oriented'.[22] The micro-structure of the meetings ensured that 'Kennedy's unique role in the ExComm discussions – as presider, decider and principal recipient – was one way in which this was not merely a conversation among equals'.[23]

Headquarters employ additional techniques in the meetings to highlight the commander's primacy. For instance, in a British head-quarters, ironic humour features prominently. The British Army Staff Officers' Handbook observes in its instructions to the staff officer that laughter is important to efficiency: 'He [the staff officer] should be dis-satisfied with himself if he does not make his commander laugh at least once a day. Remember that the commander, great being though he might be, has but limited reserves of cheeriness. This he passes onto the men in the brigade with selfless extravagance. His reserve must be topped up'.[24] Staff officers can often employ humour in meetings but commanders are normally the primary font of amusement. Precisely because they hold authority, they have the latitude to make jokes – or

---

[22] David Gibson, *Talk at the Brink: deliberation and decision during the Cuban missile crisis* (Princeton, NJ: Princeton University Press, 2012), 59.
[23] Ibid., 61.
[24] *British Army The Staff Officers' Handbook*, 2014, viii.

to try to – and for staff officers to find them infinitely entertaining. Of course, humour works best for commanders who are genuinely held in high esteem by their staff.

For instance, on Exercise Griffin Strike in 2016, the commander of 3 UK Division was reviewing some new techniques of how to assess effects. The system had potential but needed some work and the GOC observed: 'We need to guard against measuring what has happened but instead measure against what *will* happen to help us make meaningful decisions'. At this point the commander acknowledged the input of a French exchange officer in 3 UK Division who had helped the staff develop a method for understanding effects: 'Thank you. You turned it from truly shit to slightly shit!'[25] Everyone laughed at the joke, though in fact, it usefully communicated a serious point; the measures of progress were important and the commander acknowledged the work which the staff had done but he was also noting much more work needed to be done. The joke carried an implicit instruction, even a reprimand. It would not have been quite so amusing had anyone else made it; it might even have been regarded as impertinent or insulting. Whatever the structural origins of the comedy in meetings, the laughter, centred on the commander, imbued him with charisma; he became a site of emotional identification.

Humour is by no means absent from 82nd Airborne Division. However, it has instituted an additional means of charging up the moral authority of its commander. In recent years, the 82nd Airborne Division has been commanded by a series of highly competent, powerful individuals. It is notable that these commanders have been physically distinctive and often imposing; they have been fit, lean and, often, handsome. The commander, Major-General Eric Kurilla, who is a celebrated and decorated war veteran from Iraq, is typical of this mould. He has an extraordinarily extroverted personality. Reflecting their comportment and demeanour, the commanders of the division are expected to lead airborne operations physically, jumping in the first wave. Leadership is important to the division.

The division has also used the meeting to reinforce the authority of the commander. In particular, in meetings it has used the micro-method of salutation to affirm moral authority. The Division's motto is 'All the way'; this refers both to the fact that the division is

---

[25] Fieldnotes, Exercise Griffin Strike, 18 April 2016, Volume VI, 77.

known as the 'All-American' (because it recruits nationally) and that it will always seek to achieve its missions. Members of this division always use this salutation at the end of letters and emails before signing their names. Significantly, it is also employed punctiliously in meetings. Staff officers will begin and conclude any briefing to the commander with the words 'All the way' to him personally, in the manner which Gibson described. This is not a luxury dispensed with once the division is deployed. On the contrary, it is a universal practice even on operations – or exercises in preparation for operations.

Thus, on the Combined Joint Operational Access Exercise in April 2015, at the evening Commander's Update Brief in the Division Tactical Command Port, every single staff officer employed the phrase before and after they briefed the commander. At one level, 'All the way' was a simple profession of corporate loyalty. It denoted identification with the division. However, in meetings, staff officers addressed their commander in person and directed the words 'All the way' to him. Their profession of commitment was not just to the Airborne Division but to the Commanding General personally as its commander. It is not irrelevant that the Commanding General of 82nd Division's call sign is 'All-American-6': six is the numeral normally associated with command in the United States, while 'All-American', of course, refers to the division. In these meetings, the phrase 'All the way', consequently, was also profession of personal allegiance by staff officers to their commander, 'All-American-6'. It demonstrated that they saw their work as a manifestation of his intent. It was noticeable that on Exercise Warfighter in June 2017, liaison officers from 82nd Airborne attended 3 UK Division meetings, communicating information about their division to the British commander in more or less the same function. However, these liaisons officers never concluded their briefings with 'All the way'; the salutation was reserved solely for their own commander.[26] The method is, in fact, common in the US forces. For instance, 101st Airborne Division typically use the phrase 'Air Assault' to the same effect, while the US Marines prefer the generic term 'HUA' [Heard, Understood and Acknowledged] or 'Semper Fi' [Always Faithful, the Corps' motto].

The collective submission of the staff in meetings established the commander as the moral focus of the headquarters. Up to now, the role of consensual leadership techniques have been discussed. These

---

[26] Exercise Warfighter, Fort Bragg, 15 June 2017, Volume VI, 99.

are important but it would be quite wrong to ignore the coercive, disciplinary techniques which are frequently employed in meetings. Typically, meetings are cordial, professional events. However, periodically, meetings have been used as a means of criticizing and reprimanding the staff. It is easy to presume that these reprimands are random. Yet, in fact, although specific reprimands are not always predictable, the official reprimand is too common to be dismissed as a mere contingency. In the nine divisional exercises visited in the course of this research, seven involved meetings in which a reprimand of some kind was witnessed at a meeting; the reprimand has become an international command phenomenon used by French, British and American commanders in almost the same way. It is certainly true that in some of these cases, the reprimand was mild; the commanding general subtly raised a question about the staff work which implied a very serious complaint couched as a moderate suggestion. Indeed, a humorous example of precisely this technique was employed by the commander of 3 UK Division, discussed above.

Alternatively, there were other incidents in which staff officers were subjected to sustained questioning and, ultimately, public humiliation by the commander before a large audience. On one 3 UK Division exercise, a reserve staff officer was developing some work on information activities. Inexperienced in this area, the officer had developed a poorly conceived plan involving, somewhat implausibly, the use of loud-speakers mounted on vehicles to tell the enemy to surrender. The commander highlighted the profound weaknesses of the practicality of his plan, pointing out the limited range of the speakers and that the officer had not worked out exactly the route the vehicles would take. The staff officer was exposed in front of a large audience and the commander concluded publicly: 'I'm looking for a worked up plan. I don't believe in the detail of what you are going to do has been worked through'.[27] The commander, a talented individual, was completely justified in his criticism. Yet, it was a humiliating experience for the officer, who was visibly upset after the episode. The example was extreme, perhaps reflecting the pressures of a long and difficult exercise. Yet, the incident was instructive and was repeated, in admittedly milder ways, on successive exercises and it is a common feature of operations,

[27] Fieldnotes, Exercise Iron Triangle, 2013, St Mawgan Cornwall, 2 December 2013, Volume I, 71.

where the instant removal of staff officers, deemed to be inadequate, is not infrequent. The meeting does not serve just a cognitive function; it is also a moral tribunal. The threat of a reprimand accentuated the obligation of the staff to the commander. Staff officers want to please their commander but they are also afraid of being reprimanded and denigrated by him. Their work is then not just bureaucratic and analytic but infused with emotions and specifically their relationship to their commander.

This moral function of the meeting is, in fact, significantly accentuated by its structure. Meetings typically involve a strict agenda, in which staff from each of the headquarters cells report their work in turn. They will identify the current situation in terms of their own specialist area and describe how they are developing their plans for the future. Significantly, each staff addresses not the meeting as a collective body, but the commander personally. It is noticeable that while the whole meeting is meant to listen to each of the specialist presentations, and there is little doubt that collective understanding is improved in the course of a meeting as the cells find out what others are doing, staff officers not presenting do not listen particularly carefully to their peers. Meetings are long; presentations are sometimes irrelevant to other branches and often, especially cumulatively, uninteresting. Staff officers who are about to present are concerned more with their own performance that with the presentations of others. Consequently, the rest of the audience drifts in and out of engagement with any particular speaker. The meeting, then, becomes not a colloquy but a series of dialogues between individual staff officers and the commander, seated in the dominant position in the briefing room at the head of the table, while the staff occupy locations around the periphery further down the room. In effect, each staff officer presents their tribute to the commander in turn, hoping for personal approbation for their efforts; they are constituted as supplicants to him. Yet, this does not mean the meeting is merely a nugatory ceremonial occasion, though it does sometimes have these features. On the contrary, the meeting provides a large audience for this interaction; each staff officer observes the exchanges between all the other officers and the commander. The meeting has a theatrical dimension in which the status hierarchy within the headquarters and especially the dependence of the staff upon the commander is demonstrated. The staff engage briefly in an interaction with the commander but are witnesses to dozens of other exchanges; their own deference and emotional bond to the commander was affirmed by watching all the other staff officers replicate the position.

This process was demonstrated during a meeting during Exercise Joint Horizon in December 2015, when the UK's new joint headquarters was being tested for Initial Operating Capability. The meeting involved an assessment of how far the execution of the plan had advanced and any problems which had emerged. It consisted of about thirty staff officers, the Commander and the Chief of Staff and involved a sequence of individual presentations. Towards the end of this long meeting, the commander challenged the medical plan, which was, in his view, not sufficiently developed because it presumed the establishment of a maritime medical facility: 'It needs remodeling. We need assurance about who has responsibility of caring.'[28] Uncomfortable moments followed. At the end of the meeting the commander concluded: 'From the broad perspective of the kirk, I need to be presented with events which change the plan and what decisions I need to take'.[29] This incident was very similar to the one at 3 UK Division. The commander's point was that the medical plan contained no useful information which might inform his decision-making; it was a vague and partial description of the state of some medical facilities. The commander used the reprimand to one officer to warn the others of their moral and professional commitments.

Because of the structure of meetings, the public reprimands of officers do not simply have a moral effect upon the humiliated individual but on the entire staff. Indeed, because so many staff officers are present, the news of a reprimand spreads through a headquarters very quickly; everybody hears about it. Of course, the vast majority of meetings concern normal business about routine operations, going more or less to plan. They do not address crises. However, by uniting the headquarters around a shared understanding of the situation as it develops and by aligning staff with the commander, meetings serve a vital pre-emptive process in configuring relations so that the headquarters can respond when crises do occur. Meetings reaffirm command and staff relations across the headquarters, maintaining lines of communication which may later be crucial.

---

[28] Fieldnotes, Exercise Joint Horizon St Mawgan, Cornwall, 2 December 2015, Volume V, 12.

[29] Ibid.

All of the incidents considered up to now occurred on exercises. However, while artificial, similar collective processes have been demonstrated on operations. For instance, one British staff officer, working in the Current Operations Cell in the Multi-National Division South-East in Basra, described how he was reprimanded in a morning update brief by his commander. Overnight he had decided to launch the signals reserve of the division following an incident. The unit was subsequently rocketed by insurgents. When the general heard of the incident the following morning: 'I got my arse felt' (i.e., I was castigated). Cursing, the general demanded: 'Who sent this out?' and 'Under whose authority?' The officer had had to admit in public that he had been responsible.[30] The general, who was not entirely popular with his staff, enforced his personality aggressively on them. They may not have liked him but they fully recognized what he wanted.

One of the best pieces of evidence of leadership in meetings is provided by Stanley McChrystal's O&I meetings in Joint Special Operations Command in Baghdad. In order to be able to conduct a complex campaign against Al-Qaeda, McChrystal had to create a shared consciousness. One of the central means by which he overcame these organizational barriers was the daily Operations and Intelligence Brief, at which every representative from every agency involved in the campaign would share their assessment of the campaign. This brief was 'a relatively small video teleconference between our rear headquarters at Fort Bragg, a few DC offices and our biggest bases in Iraq and Afghanistan. Quickly, though, that audience grew'; 'In time, people came to appreciate the value of systemic understanding. O&I attendance grew as the quality of information and interaction grew. Eventually we had 7000 people attending almost daily for two hours'.[31] McChrystal saw the O&I briefing as principal means of generating shared consciousness and therefore exercising distributed mission command. Indeed, he actively adopted certain practices to encourage this sense of collective participation and shared cognition: 'I adopted a practice I called "thinking aloud" in which I would summarise what I'd heard'. 'Thinking out loud can be a frightening prospect for a senior leader' as it risks exposing ignorance and uncertainty. Yet, in

---

[30] OF-4, Lieutenant-Colonel, Chief of Current Operations, 3 UK Division, interviewee 045, personal interview, 7 June 2017.
[31] Stanley McChrystal, *Team of Teams*, 164, 168.

the context of JSOC, it has a salutary command effect: 'The overall message re-informed by the O&I was that *we* have a problem that only *we* can understand and solve'.[32]

Precisely because of his increased visibility in this diverse network, McChrystal self-consciously sought to develop a new style of personal command appropriate to this situation: 'Much of my and my command team's time was spent solidifying partnerships with the half-dozen agencies involved in a single cycle of F3EA [Find-fix-finish-exploit-analyze]'.[33] In order to achieve this McChrystal developed a distinctive command style. At the very beginning of his autobiography, McChrystal documents the inspiration which famous American generals, like Samuel Grant or Matt Ridgway, had provided him. Yet, his style of leadership assumed a quite different form from the self-promotional bombast which typified many of America's most successful generals, especially in the Second World War: 'the role is very different from that of the traditional heroic decision-making'.[34] McChrystal recognized that self-presentation in the O&I meeting was essential. Because of the multiplicity of agencies with which he was working and their geographical distribution, the video-teleconference became a central apparatus of command; 'I found the requirement to be on camera for so long exhausting, but it forced me to be a better leader'.[35] McChrystal sought to encourage by a calm and clinical approach: 'We didn't have time to drive this with emotions, to huff and puff. We needed constant, demanding, driven vigilance and professionalism'.[36] He was highly conscious of his appearance on these VTCs: 'If I looked bored or was seen sending emails or talking, I signaled lack of interest. If I appeared irritated or angry, notes such as "What's bothering the boss?" would flash across the chat rooms that functioned in parallel to the video-teleconference. Critical words were magnified in impact and could be crushing to a young member of the force'.[37] Personal connection became important: 'When their turns came and their faces suddenly filled the screen I made it a point to

---

[32] Ibid., 228.
[33] Stanley McChrystal, *My Share of the Task: a memoir* (New York: Portfolio/Penguin, 2013, 155).
[34] McChrystal, *Team of Teams*, 228.
[35] McChrystal, *My Share of the Task*, 163–4.
[36] Ibid., 164
[37] McChrystal, *Team of Teams*, 228.

greet them by their first name, which often caused them to smile in evident surprise'.[38] He finished every conference with the words: 'Do your job. People's lives are on the line. Thanks, as always, for all you are doing'.[39] Indeed, '"thank you" became my most important phrase'.[40] McChrystal's O&I meetings became a principal means by which he could not only generate shared understanding but how he could also engender a common sense of moral obligation. These meetings were used as leadership tools by which he encouraged and motivated the complex network which he commanded.

Formal meetings are vital in uniting the staff cognitively; they align the staff intellectually to the Commander's Intent. It is imperative that the staff have a common understanding of the situation, so they can develop solutions which are consistent with the Commander's Intent. Yet, the moral function of meetings is no less important; the meeting is a forum of leadership. The theatrical display of leadership in meetings ensures that the Commander's Intent has moral force; they staff feel viscerally committed to it. Fusing both intellectual and moral elements, meetings ensure unification of the headquarters vertically around the commander and, simultaneously, bond the staff together horizontally. In meetings, the cells understand their mutual roles in the operation and their relations to each other. The staff understand how they will have to cooperate with each other and, impressed by the personality of the general, they feel obliged to work together. Meetings unite the staff around the commander. Performed in meetings and addressing a much smaller circle, leadership in the twenty-first century is often rather less histrionic than it was in the Second World War, for instance, when commanders sought to cut a dramatic figure. Yet it is no less significant in ensuring the coherence of an increasingly complex organization.

Current Operations

Meetings unite the staff around the commander both intellectually and morally. Staff understand what the commander wants them to achieve

---

[38] Ibid.
[39] McChrystal, *My Share of the Task*, 165.
[40] *Team of Teams*, 228.

and feel professionally obliged to deliver it. This unity becomes of paramount importance in a crisis, when the staff have to react rapidly and when, as Weick's example of the Mann Gulch disaster shows, intersubjectivity can break down very easily. In a crisis, the staff must already have been committed to a common perception of the mission, to the acceptable and feasible courses of action and motivated to follow the commander's guidance and to cooperate closely with each other. The vertical and horizontal unity which are enjoined by meetings become very important. Clearly, a truly comprehensive analysis of how a divisional headquarters responds to a crisis would analyze the actions of all the cells and the entire staff. After all, if a crisis is big enough, all the staff will be involved in it. Yet, such an analysis would be so cumbersome and involved, that it would become difficult to understand. Consequently, the following analysis of the crisis focuses on the Current Operations Cell. There are good reasons for this. The immediate locus of any crisis is the Current Operations Cell. This cell coordinates operations in real-time and, consequently, crises appear first in this cell. Messages and reports about unexpected events, casualties and enemy actions are typically communicated to the Current Operations Cell first. Even if they are not, the Current Operations has to deal with any crisis. Consequently, the analysis of abnormal decision-making in a crisis is best conducted in the Current Operations Cell. Ultimately, the cohesiveness of this cell determines how successfully any headquarters will respond to the unexpected. The following analysis will try to show how the horizontal unity within the current operations cell, its professional and corporate solidarity, is crucial to its responsiveness. The analysis will also try to show how meetings have played a role in both generating the horizontal solidarity of the cell while also connecting it with the commander. The point is that effective Current Operations Cells are bound both morally and cognitively to the commander.

It is worth once again considering the case of 2nd Brigade, 3rd Infantry Division in Baghdad in 2003. One of the most remarkable aspects of the rocket strike was the speed with which the headquarters recovered as a functional command post, capable of coordinating operations afterwards. The brigade was perhaps lucky that it did not sustain more casualties; two soldiers were killed and fifteen were wounded. However, the uninjured staff officers quickly reorganized themselves and re-established the Tactical Operations Centre in a new location: 'Eventually every soldier on the ground that remained capable would compose their spirits and efforts and join in an amazing display of timely teamwork. The TOC was quickly rebuilt, albeit in lesser grandeur, at a different location in the parking lot'.[41] Although the attack was potentially debilitating and had, in fact, destroyed apparently indispensable equipment, the teamwork and solidarity of the staff were far more important in sustaining the Command Post: 'In this case, a small group of effective staff were able to manage the immediate situation at the Brigade TOC, whilst also continuing to coordinate an armoured brigade and all of its enablers in the fight. The lesson is that equipment is important but staff skill is the critical determinant of a headquarters' effectiveness'.[42] Here, collective understanding and close coordination between staff officers within and between the branches was absolutely critical.

This exploration of abnormal decision-making will examine the Current Operations Cell at 3 UK Division before going onto the case of the 1st Marine Division in Iraq. At 3 UK Division, the Current Operations Centre is integrated into the normal battle rhythm of the headquarters. Normally the chief of the cell attended all the significant meetings of the headquarters, reporting the latest developments, providing assessments about the immediate future, and collating information from the other branches which may have been relevant. The cell was, therefore, immediately exposed to the leadership of the commander.

However, although meetings like the Commander's Update Brief were crucial to the Current Operations Cell, integrating it vertically into the headquarters and tying the staff to the Commander's Intent, the cell also developed a series of technique to ensure that horizontal cohesion between its staff.

3 UK Division has employed several methods to increase the cohesiveness of the Current Operations Cell and foster a professional ethos in it. In Chapter 10, the topography of the Current Operations Cell was described (see Figure 10.1); it was organized as a horseshoe, overseen by the chief and the battle captain. This structure has been adopted to optimize the ability of the specialist functional staff in

---

[41] http://educatedsoldier.blogspot.co.uk/2007/08/destruction-of-2nd-brigade-3rd-id-toc.html.
[42] http://groundedcuriosity.com/less-is-more-the-enabled-combat-brigade-headquarters/#sthash.pVs6mX4r.enP3zpd9.dpbs.

the cell to observe the current operations screens and the intelligence feeds and, also, crucially to communicate with each other. Horizontal interactions between the staff has been deliberately maximized in Current Operations. The headquarters has been constantly trying to improve the ergonomics of the cell. On Exercise Warfighter in June 2017, for instance, the cell included the Joint Air-Ground Integration Cell, consisting of fourteen specialist artillery, intelligence and air officers, dedicated to the identification and prosecution of targets. The cell was situated on a long desk down one side of the Current Operations Cell, very close to the raised platform of the chief of current operations and the battle captain. This location ensured close communications with the command elements within the cell. In the course of the exercise, however, the structure of the JAGIC proved not ideal.[43] Some of the specialists who needed to be able to work together closely were sat too far apart: 'communications – the horizontal passage of information – is the key'.[44] Every attempt has been to ensure that Current Operations was physically organized to facilitate communication and cooperation.

The topography of the Current Operations Cell is certainly important. A poor lay-out can certainly impede cooperation between staff. However, the structure is only a facilitating condition. In responding to crises, the professional ethos of the Current Operations Cell has been vital. Of course, appointing the right personnel has been a priority here. If the cell lacked expertise or experience, then it simply could not function. On recent exercises, the Current Operations Cell of 3 UK Division was staffed by forty specialist officers, coordinated by a battle captain and commanded by the SO1 chief of current operations. All the specialist subject matter expertise was covered but the cell was still sufficiently small to be able to conduct operations. As the Chief of Current Operations noted: 'We got the manning right in 3 UK Division'. Consequently, because the personnel was right, the chief of current operations was confident that the cell could react to an emergency: 'If something like that [a crashed helicopter] happened, we would be OK'.[45] Indeed, this officer contrasted the staff of his Current

---

[43] Fieldnotes, Exercise Warfighter, Fort Bragg, Volume VI, 15 June 2017, 102; OF-3, Major, Chief of JAGIC 3 UK Division, interviewee 135, personal interview, 15 June 2017.

[44] Ibid.

[45] OF-4, Lieutenant-Colonel, Chief of Current Operations 3 UK Division, interviewee 45, personal communication, 7 June 2017.

Operations Cell in 3 UK Division with the cell in 1 UK Division in Basra in 2006 in which he had worked as a more junior staff officer. That cell consisted of a small core of competent, relevant staff but also included unnecessary personnel.

Appointing the appropriate staff is a major factor in generating a professional ethos. Yet, solidarity and cooperativeness is not reducible only to individual appointments. In order to foster cohesiveness, staff had to feel that they could communicate with each other and with their superiors. It was very important that no one was intimated or excluded. The chief of current operations played an important role in instilling this open atmosphere: 'Everyone is a subject matter expert but we worked on the principle that "no idea was crap"'.[46] Of course, because of the expert personnel already in the cell, every staff officer already had a mature concept of what constituted a realistic suggestion. It was very unlikely that even the most junior staff officer would make an absurd suggestion. Indeed, on Exercise Warfighter, it was very noticeable that a very junior lieutenant in Intelligence, working in the JAGIC, contributed fully to discussions, even though she was the youngest and least experienced officer in the cell.[47] The chief of current operations played a crucial role here in encouraging the appropriate ethos in the cell.

Finally, staff officers within Current Operations communicated with each other routinely and regularly; constant exchange was expected and, indeed, demanded by the chief. In the recent past, the cell was relatively loud, with officers announcing developments to others. Today, the staff operate through a shared digital communication system, 'Lync', so they talk with each other quietly. Indeed, in an American headquarters all communication is done by email, so staff officers work in an 'eerie silence'. A current operations room today is very quiet and it is easy to overlook the density of interactions between staff officers. It appears as if they are working at monitors quite independently of each other when, in fact, they are engaged in a constant round of intercommunication.

These constant informal exchanges are punctuated by the formal four-hourly Update Brief. At this brief, the chief of current operations called on each of the branches to summarize what had

---

[46] Ibid.
[47] Fieldnotes, Exercise Warfighter, Fort Bragg, Volume VI, 15 June 2017, 100–1.

happened in the last hours and what was likely to happen in the near future. It was a critical exchange. At the end of each update, the chief of the cell summarized the key events and advised the staff about what was about to happen on the operations and, therefore, the priorities for the next few hours; the staff was therefore in a position to anticipate events and to cue the requisite assets. The four-hourly Update Brief was an important means of enjoining and affirming horizontal cohesion across the staff. This colloquy ensured that the entire cell had a shared understanding of the immediate situation so everyone was already attuned to possible courses of action and was committed to executing it. It also affirmed that routine channels of intercommunication were open. The staff were, therefore, already united and prepared for any crisis.

Exercises are usually designed to test a Current Operations Centre by presenting them with unexpected serials and, if possible, a major crisis. The aim is to test the professional competence of the cell. A good example of how 3 UK Division's Current Operations Centre cooperated with each other to resolve a crisis, occurred on Exercise Griffin Strike in April 2016. The episode usefully highlighted the importance of micro-interactions within the cell and its vertical integration into the headquarters to effective crisis management. This exercise was a combined exercise in which 3 UK Division was augmented with officers from its sister formation, *État Major de Force 1* from Besancon. The exercise was intended to establish the new Anglo-French Combined Joint Expeditionary Force at Initial Operating Capability. Based on a fictional conflict situation set in South Wales, it involved a divisional intervention in support of a small allied power which was being attacked by a hostile neighbour. 3 UK Division acted as the land headquarters commanding a multinational division, which had to defend South Wales from attack.

Towards the end of the exercise, on 19 April 2016, an interesting situation developed. An enemy armoured brigade began an attack along an expected corridor around the Brecon Beacons, threatening to drive a wedge between the whole formation, separating 3 UK Division's western force elements, 7 French Brigade and 16 (UK) Air Assault Brigade, from the rest of the force. It was a potentially very serious situation for the headquarters undermining their entire operation. It is worth recording the decision-making process in some detail since it illustrates the teamwork of the Current Operations Cell.

The situation was first noted at 1110 in the morning when the Current Operations Cell began to pick up the movement of the enemy brigade southwards; Exercise Control had noticed a possible unobserved avenue of advance and wanted to test the responsiveness of 3 UK Division. In their intelligence preparation of the battlefield, 3 UK Division had missed a small but entirely usable 'B' road which contoured around the high ground directly into 3 UK Division's operating area; this avenue of advance was totally unchecked. At this point, news of the enemy advance began to filter into the electronic messaging system, reported by a subordinate unit. A potential crisis was recognized by the staff in the Current Operations Cell almost immediately and was discussed by staff officers in the cell over their personal radio system. At this point, an Engineer Captain from within the cell examined the map on the birdtable in detail and identified two bridges on the small road, on which the enemy brigade was advancing, with the suggestion that they might be destroyed in order to slow the advance. The chief of current operations thought the suggestion plausible but he did not have the authority to make the decision. Accordingly, he summoned the chief of staff and at 1140 they had a short conference at the birdtable.

the chief of staff initially questioned whether destroying the bridges would work but the chief of current operations stated that it would slow the advance, in which time they could attrit the force with air or artillery fires. The problem was then one of decision authority and an interesting discussion followed:

> Chief of Staff: Can you do it? Do you have permission and is the GOC prepared to defy higher authority? It is militarily sensible but is it legal? I will ask the Chief of Staff of the Combined Joint Task Force (the superior headquarters).
> Chief of Current Operations: We have got to create a choke.
> COS: The Deputy Commander said this morning, let's stick with the plan [i.e., block with 7 Brigade]. What are our decision criteria?

At 1215, a target pack on the two bridges had been produced for Current Operations signed by the chief of staff and the deputy commander. The target pack consisted of a proforma identifying the target and then recording a series of military, political and legal criteria which had to be cleared by the appropriate authority. The chief of current operations confirmed that they now had the authority to destroy the two bridges. A quite unanticipated decision had been taken and executed in an hour; in extremis, a decision could have been made even more quickly.[48]

This incident was small and artificial; it is important not to overstate its evidential significance. However, it illustrates how divisional headquarters might respond to unforeseen crises. It is worth identifying some of the salient features of the Current Operations Cell's response. On recognizing a potential crisis, the staff acted quickly. Crucially, the engineer officer, who had the requisite specialist knowledge, quite independently and without senior instruction immediately got up from his allotted desk and went straight over to the birdtable to examine the road on which the enemy was advancing. He was actively looking for potential choke points. He and the rest of the staff relayed the critical information to the chief of current operations, who in turn notified the chief of staff. Eventually, the deputy commander was brought into the decision-making process. In each case, these superiors were not simply presented with a predicament upon which they had to adjudicate blindly, but with the potential implications of the problem. The staff in Current Operations generated a suite of possible solutions (and the criteria by which these solutions might be selected); the practicality of the options – their advantages and disadvantages – were highlighted. The engineer officer initiated this process with his analysis of the map but artillery and air officers subsequently contributed to the nascent plan.

The Synchronization Matrix with its Decision Points were not irrelevant here. The staff applied the deductive model of thinking implicit in the Decision Point to this situation; they explicitly discussed the criteria by which a coherent decision could be made. Moreover, even in this crisis, staff were trying to put the plan back on track. Although the staff knew what they were ultimately trying to achieve, the Synchronization Matrix was temporarily suspended as an active reference point until after the crisis. While the Synchronization Matrix constituted a precisely orchestrated score for military operations, the Current Operations Centre improvised collectively on the central themes of the original plan. They became a jazz ensemble, rather than a classical orchestra, elaborating together on the basis of the existing

---

[48] Fieldnotes, Exercise Griffin Strike, Bulford, 20 April 2016, Volume V, 90–2.

score as they took various 'crazy roads' to advance the plan.[49] They were able to do this because they had developed close horizontal bonds, facilitating open-ended cooperation, and the cell was thoroughly integrated into the headquarters, committed morally and intellectually to the Commander's Intent.

3 UK Division has not deployed on operations recently. Its Current Operations Cell has only responded to crises on exercises. These are surely suggestive. However, it is useful to support the evidence from 3 UK Division with actual operational examples. These reveal that 3 UK Division's practices are consonant with those actually enacted on operations. It was very noticeable that the head of current operations in 3 UK Division had a personal experience of a crisis of precisely this type. In 2006, he had served in 1 UK Division's Current Operations Cell as a G2 (a major) when that Division had deployed to Basra to command Multination-Division South-East on Telic 8. The experience was not easy, not least because this divisional headquarters commanded only one British brigade, 20 Brigade: 'it was a one over one'.[50] Nevertheless, the importance of the divisional level became clear on that operation at a moment of crisis.

On 6 May 2006, a Lynx helicopter was shot down over Basra by Shia militia; it crashed onto the roof of a building, killing the crew and precipitating significant local unrest.[51] 1 Division's Current Operations Cell was faced with a serious crisis; it was initially unclear whether the crew of the Lynx were still alive, so the crash site had to be secured quickly to prevent hostages being taken, to recover the wounded or dead and to carry out a forensic investigation of the helicopter. At the same time 20 Brigade faced a significant civil disturbance. The episode required a complex response, therefore:

> It had to be controlled at the divisional level. We needed ISTAR feeds. There was rioting in the city and so 20 Brigade were in contact there, actually fighting. They were fighting on the streets. At the same time, we were getting divisional assets into Basra. We were trying to get the RMP up the

---

[49] OF-3, Major, Future Operations, 3 UK Division, interviewee 129, personal interview, 18 November 2016. See Chapter 12, 434.

[50] OF-4, Lieutenant-Colonel, Chief of Current Operations, 3 UK Division, interviewee 045, personal interview, 7 June 2017.

[51] https://fas.org/asmp/campaigns/MANPADS/2007/boi_lynx_xz614_main_report.pdf.

Shatt-al-Arab by boats to conduct forensic investigations,
while we were under contact.[52]

As already noted, the Current Operations Cell of his headquarters was
not so well resourced as 3 UK Division would become. There were some
superfluous personnel, while others were not sufficiently experienced or
qualified to be able to contribute to a crisis. Consequently, in order to
respond effectively to the situation, the chief of staff of 1 Division took
drastic action to ensure close cooperation in the Current Operations
Cell throughout the operation: 'He threw everyone out of the Current
Operations Cell except for ten people'.[53] This team of ten officers, then,
worked intensely for six hours to deploy the divisional assets and to
coordinate the operation until the crash site had been secured and the
riot quelled: 'literally, we were on it for the next six hours, conducting
a rescue and recover operation'.[54] For this officer, who had experienced
both the artificial crises of 3 UK Division exercises and a genuine one,
the Lynx crash, there were parallels between the events. In both cases,
close intercommunication and teamwork with the Current Operations
Cell were critical. There had to be a high level of professional teamwork in the cell, so that officers understood their specialisms and could
cooperate with their peers to conduct operations effectively. Indeed,
he believed that 3 UK Division's Current Operations Cell showed a
higher level of cohesion and responsiveness than 1 UK Division in
Basra in 2006.

In discussing the crisis on Exercise Griffin Strike afterwards,
the chief of current Operations in 3 UK Division was explicit that
his role was to connect the cell to the commander to ensure that all
decision-making was in line with the intent and made at the appropriate level: 'I was the touch point to the vertical shafts in the headquarters as head of the Current Operations Cell. I had to ensure that I was
briefing the right people at the right time on my understanding of what
the GOC [general officer commanding] wants'.[55] Here, the round of
daily meetings, which the chief of current operations always attended,

---

[52] OF-4, Lieutenant-Colonel, Chief of Current Operations, 3 UK Division, interviewee
045, personal interview, 7 June 2017.

[53] Ibid.

[54] Ibid.

[55] Ibid.

played a hidden but important part. Through meetings, he became the point of contact between the 'vertical shafts' of the headquarter and the horizontal cohesion of his cell. Meetings ensured that the solutions that Current Operations offered their commanders were already in line with the Commander's Intent. As another officer in the same cell confirmed: 'We must support the GOC's [general officer commanding] Intent, whether we think it is right or wrong'.[56] Even in the deepest crisis, the Current Operations Cell was conscious of the relationship between its immediate responses and the commander's overarching intent. Although crises are not resolved in them, meetings play an important role in fostering vertical and horizontal cohesiveness in the Current Operations Cell.

Meetings tie the Current Operations Cell to the Commander's Intent both intellectually and morally. In the face of a crisis, the staff in Current Operations have an intersubjective understanding of what they are trying to achieve and what responses are likely to be appropriate. Moreover, the demonstrations of leadership displayed in meetings by the commander suffused the staff, encouraging – and indeed demanding – cooperation between them, even in the face of the unexpected. Staff officers feel obliged to cooperate so that they fulfilled their commander's wishes. The importance of meetings in integrating the headquarters vertically has been recently demonstrated by 3 UK Division. As part of its reforms following its experiences at Exercise Warfighter 2017, the headquarters has increased the staff levels in the Current Operations Cell. Specifically, it has augmented the SO1 (lieutenant-colonel) chief of operations with two deputies SO2 (majors). These majors have been given the role of managing the Current Operations Centre; a job once fulfilled by the SO1. One major is responsible for the day, the other for the night so that Current Operations is permanently commanded by an officer of sufficient experience and rank. The division has found the new arrangement advantageous in many ways. However, significantly, it has allowed the chief of current operations to attend all the important planning meetings in the headquarters without the pressure of being pulled back into Current Operations at any moment: 'It has allowed him to take one step back, giving him space to engage with the plan and to gain a better understanding and to feed that into Current

---

[56] OF-3, Major, Future Plans 3 UK Division, interviewee 008, personal communication, 27 November 2013.

Operations'.[57] Precisely because this officer is more closely attuned to the commander, 3 UK Division has found that it has been able to execute operations more effectively.

3 UK Division has not been deployed on operations since 2007. Consequently, most of the evidence about how it might respond to a crisis is drawn from exercises. This evidence should not be disparaged; the division aims to operate as it has trained and practised. However, it may be useful to support it with additional evidence from actual operations. The Current Operations Centre of 1st Marine Division in 2003 provides an extremely good example of how a Current Operations Cell responded to a crisis. The importance of meetings as a way of vertically integrating the staff around the commander has already been noted. Like 3 UK Division, 1st Marine Division also accentuated the importance of teamwork within the Current Operations Cells. Lieutenant-Colonel Clarke Lethin, who was a leading operations officer in the cell during the operation, described this process in detail:

> I agree with Current Ops and the combat staff being a well-oiled machine and tightly linked. In order to achieve this state, you need a physical layout/design of the COC [Current Operations Centre] and rehearsals/practice. The layout must be centered on the most important functions arrayed in the center and every other function or staff aligned inward to the center of attention. For the division, we called this the 'killing U'. It was a U-shaped set of tables, facing the current ops map, briefing screen and intel map. Around the 'U' was the Ops/Deputy Ops watch officers, the aviation officer, fire support officer, and intel ops/deputy officer. All other functional areas were either behind the killing 'U' or on the wings in adjacent tents, with wide openings into the center of the COC. When we had an announcement or key piece of information that needed to be made, we would shout out 'Attention in the COC', and everything went quiet for those brief moments when we needed to pass information that everyone needed to know. Although a simple concept, we were ruthless in ensuring the everything stopped for that brief moment when information needed to be passed. The other critical piece for a COC is practice and drills. We started building, experimenting and training the div staff and supporting functions in August

---

[57] OF-3, Current Operations, 3 UK Division, interviewee 145, personal interview, 14 March 2018.

of 2002. It started in southern California, and continued when we started to deploy to Kuwait. We rehearsed COC battle drills and contingencies from how we would control movement, battle handover with the Brits, to responding to indirect fire attacks and integrated response with our artillery followed by close air support (within five minutes). These drills and rehearsal paid off and provided a foundation for agility and adaptability when faced with something that we had not anticipated.[58]

This description is deeply significant, affirming the evidence from 3 UK Division. 1st Marine Division relied on the teamwork of its Current Operations Centre. Lethin usefully identifies how the layout of the cell and established drills allowed the staff in the Current Operations Cell to communicate with each other quickly and efficiently. The cell's topography and its established procedures engendered close cooperation. As a result they were able to respond to crisis.

There are several examples of the unity of the Current Operations Cell during the 1st Marine Division's invasion of Iraq in 2003. However, the most memorable crisis occurred on 23 March, when the 1st Light Armored Regiment (LAR) was ambushed outside of An Diwaniyah by Feyadeen fighters. This event, more than any other, challenged the teamwork of the cell, as the following description shows:

> As it started to get dark, we could all feel the hair standing up on the backs of our necks. You could tell something was about to happen. Then, with Blackfoot [Bravo Company] in the lead, we began to see scattered tracers flying across the road in front of us from west to east. The scattered shots soon became a torrent of fire and the entire battalion was engaged almost immediately. They opened up on us with mortars, heavy machine guns, and RPGs. The tracers would seemingly explode when they hit the LAVs [Light Armoured Vehicles], it wasn't like the movies where they just bounce off. We later estimated the enemy at about an infantry battalion in size. There was fire coming from everywhere, and they were starting to mass and charge the column in groupings. We were pouring 7.62 and 25mm on them, but they kept coming. There was no communication with DASC [Division Artillery Support Cell], we were outside of artillery range, and

---

[58] Lieutenant-Colonel Clarke Lethin, Deputy and then Assistant Chief of Staff Operations, 1st Marine Division, interviewee 125, email communication, 8 June 2017.

there was no air on station. Unable to reach the CO on the radio and even though we were not in immediate danger of being over-run the Air Officer made the decision to call 'slingshot' over the guard channel.[59]

The situation was very serious. Indeed, the code word 'slingshot' denoted that the unit was about to be overrun and all available air and artillery assets should be immediately assigned to that unit. Subsequent reports suggest that the air controller within the battalion called 'sling-shot' by mistake. Nevertheless, once it had been invoked, the Current Operations Cell went immediately into crisis-management; they believed they were facing the worst possible situation. In the event, the cohesiveness of the Current Operations Cell was critical to resolving the situation. Once again Clarke Lethin, the division's operation officer, provides a compelling testimony about how his cell managed the event:

> As for an example of a specific crisis that could have unhinged our operation, the only one that I think falls into that category is the night that the division was moving north on Hwy 1 and our lead unit, 1st LAR, was ambushed. Gen Mattis and his jump, along with myself and the plans officer, were well forward and away from the Forward CP, which was in control of the battle. When the unit was ambushed, they called 'slingshot', which meant that were in imminent danger of being overrun. Then Colonel Toolan, G-3, was with the Forward, along with the division chief of staff and other principal staff. They were able to coordinate, bringing to bear all of our fire support assets as well as coordinating aviation fire support that started to stack over the battlefield and were immediately available to the unit for employment. The General and his jump CP were able to monitor the Forward CP's actions and provide any guidance necessary, which was minimal, since the Forward had all of the resources and connectivity to support the crisis.[60]

Because it was so rapid and unexpected, Mattis was unable to make any contribution to the episode; he was at his small Jump Headquarters.

[59] Michael Groen, *With the 1st Marine Division in Iraq 2003*, 185.
[60] Lieutenant-Colonel Clarke Lethin, Deputy and then Assistant Chief of Staff Operations, 1st Marine Division, interviewee 125, email communication, 8 June 2017.

Rather, the 'slingshot' air operation was coordinated entirely from the Current Operations Cell in the Forward Headquarters under the command of Colonel John Toolan. Following established drills, staff officers within the cell called in air support onto identified and prioritized targets, assigning aircraft to specific corridors, while deconflicting them with artillery and ground fires. Even though officers made very rapid decisions, they orchestrated and synchronized a variety of their decisions with their colleagues. In the end, the cell was able to coordinate this action successfully because of the close professional teamwork which the cell had developed in training and which Lethin described above.

The teamwork within the Current Operations Cell and its professional ethos has determined whether a headquarters could respond to a crisis. Effective Current Operations Cells have been able to coordinate operations almost independently without the commander's immediate supervision. Officers within the cell have worked together closely to identify the problem, generate solutions and then coordinate the subsequent actions they involve. Horizontal cohesion in the Current Operations Cell has been vital, then. However, although clearly a necessary condition for effective crisis management, the teamwork of the Current Operations Cell is not in itself enough to ensure a proper response to the unexpected. A highly skilled Current Operations Cell could theoretically respond to a crisis effectively but in a manner which was inconsistent with their Commander's Intent. This would be plainly undesirable; it would undermine the cohesiveness of the division and the wider campaign. Consequently, even the most professional Current Operations Cells have been integrated into the vertical hierarchy of the headquarters to ensure that they have been aligned with the Commander's Intent, as it develops. The staff have to understand the Commander's Intent and be committed to executing it. It is at this point that meetings and the leadership displayed in them becomes highly pertinent. Vertical integration is possible only because of the round of meetings which bind Current Operations to the commander. Then, the staff need not merely understand the mission but, under the influence of their commander, viscerally want to executive it. They feel morally and professionally committed to the plan. When crisis and confusion strikes, the raw determination of the Current Operations Cell to prevail is as important as its specialist expertise.

PROFESSIONALISM

Crises are inevitable in military operations; abnormal decision-making is the norm. Consequently, any robust headquarters must be organized to be able to respond effectively to the unexpected. In the previous chapter, it has been shown how the Decision Point has improved the speed and accuracy of decision-making, when an operation was going broadly to plan. By anticipating decisions, the staff tried to reduce the chances of idiosyncratic error and contingency. Decision Points have become very useful in periods of normal decision-making.

Yet, it would seriously misrepresent the new divisional head-quarters if the decision-making process were reduced to automated, bureaucratic procedures. The effectiveness of a divisional headquarters presumes a deeper professional ethos, in which staff officers not only possess specialist knowledge but are willing to cooperate closely with each other and are collectively committed to the mission. Specifically, in a crisis, coherent decision-making requires shared understanding, close interaction and excellent communication between the staff and commanders. As a complex system, the division of the twenty-first century can be coordinated only if commanders, deputies and the staff are unified as a cohesive team. Staff officers must be highly attuned to what the commander wants and deeply motivated to deliver it; commanders must be able to listen to and be advised by their staff. Although perhaps unlikely, the formal meeting is vital to the generation of close vertical integration in the headquarters. Especially with the commander as the charismatic centre of the division, meetings revivify the relationship between the command and staff, orienting both to common goals while maintaining and encouraging communications across the headquarters between the branches. Formal meetings unite the headquarters morally and cognitively around the commander and the Commander's Intent.

A significant transformation of command is evident in the new divisional headquarters. Commanders can no longer direct operations alone or with the help of a very small staff. At Arras in 1940 and La Fière in 1944, Rommel and Ridgway were personally present at the point of crisis. They were able to intervene immediately with instinctive decisions. The chances of a divisional commander solving a crisis by mere physical presence on the frontline is highly unlikely today; the mere distances involved make it improbable. Mattis was notably impotent during the slingshot incident in March 2003. Today, divisional commanders rely upon a large and highly professionalized Current Operations Centre to assist them in their decision-making, to manage operations and to respond to crisis. As this chapter has made quite clear, the commander has remained essential to divisional operations. The coordination of complex military operations has required a single, central point of reference, which only a commander can provide. The commander has defined the mission, made the most important decisions and motivated the staff to deliver the plan together. However, the executive competence of the commander has relied upon the support and cooperation of a now large and intricate staff system, each element of which has become both highly skilled and deeply cohesive. In the new headquarters, as staff play a greater and greater role, the more individualist command practices, often professional in themselves and wholly adequate to the conditions of the twentieth century, have been displaced by a regime of increasingly collective and professionalized command.

14 THE COMMAND COLLECTIVE

A Military Trilogy

All command is collective. No general can command alone since any military operation necessarily involves the cooperation of others. Commanders have, consequently, always required subordinates, staff and soldiers to implement their decisions and to execute their plans. In his memoirs of the 14th Army in Burma, Field Marshal William Slim employs an eloquent metaphor on the irretrievable collectivity of command:

> A clock is like an army,' I used to tell them. 'There's the main spring, that's the Army Commander, who makes it all go; then there are the other springs, driving the wheels around, those are his generals. The wheels are officers and men. Some wheels are big, very important, they are the chief of staff officers and the colonel sahibs. Other wheels are little ones, that do not look at all important. They are like you. Yet stop one of those little wheels and see what happens to the rest of the clock.[1]

However, in different eras, under alternate operational and organizational conditions, command has assumed different forms, sometimes more collaborative, sometimes more individualist. Consequently, while the fundamental nature of command always endures, its specific character is mutable. Command always consists of three functions. It refers

---

[1] Slim, *Defeat into Victory*, 186.

specifically to mission definition but necessarily also encompasses mission management and leadership. In order to conduct an operation, a general must define a mission, manage the tasks of which it is comprised and motivate the troops. The basic anatomy of command is, therefore, universal but its morphology adapts and changes in response to historical conditions.

This book traces the transformation of divisional command in the twentieth and twenty-first centuries. It claims that, notwithstanding evident continuities and recognizing the fact that command is always collaborative, two distinct, if overlapping, regimes are observable over the last century. An 'individualist' practice of command predominated in the short twentieth century, from 1914 to 1991, to be superseded by collective command in the 'early' twenty-first century and, especially, since the millennium. In particular, in order to illustrate this move from relatively individualist to more collective command, this book has dissected the morphology of command over the last century. It has examined the practice of mission definition, mission management and motivation – command, management and leadership – in the Western division from the First World War. It has tried to show that as the burdens of mission management have bloated in the current era, divisional commanders have been forced to share decision-making authority with their subordinates and staff ever more systematically. Integrated and professionalized command teams have emerged.

The rise of collective command in no way suggests that decision-making today is conducted by committee or consensus; still less does it mean that commanders have been subordinated to their staff. It does not denote the derogation of the commander's responsibility in any way. Indeed, in many ways, the role of the commander is more important than ever. The commander is no longer located at the pinnacle of a military hierarchy but at the gravitational centre of a multiverse. Precisely because the division has become such a complex organizational system, it requires a definitive and ultimate point of reference. Only a single identified commander can act as that beacon. Located at a unique position in a politico-military network, only the commander is able to collate all the factors which bear upon an operation to define a mission. The divisional commander has assumed ever greater responsibility for mission definition, then. Divisional commanders have typically had far greater latitude in defining the mission of their formations than in the twentieth century. Their authority in this domain has increased, though, interestingly, in order to define the mission they typically invoke a wide network of politico-military contacts who assist them in its formulation.

However, in the function of mission management in particular, the authority of the commander has been distributed; it is shared by deputies and staff. To fulfil all the functions of command adequately, responsibilities have to be shared with a small team of trusted deputies, supported by a large and expert staff. Collectivism has been particularly pronounced in the sphere of mission management; deputies have assumed decision-making authority which was once the preserve of the divisional commander. Brigadier Ben Hodges, working as Major-General Nick Carter's deputy in Kandahar in 2009 to 2010, exemplified this new method of command. In other cases, the staff has silently appropriated elements of command agency to itself, disciplining, structuring and refining the commander's decisions. Management has become more collective.

By contrast, because divisional operations were circumscribed in the twentieth century, divisional commanders were able to manage operations individually. Rommel, Monash, Montgomery, Erskine, Massu and Ewell monopolized decision-making in this period, with the support of a small staff and one principal staff officer. In 1991, Rupert Smith constituted a transitional example. Fighting the deep, close and rear battles, and, involving significant air assets, he actively sought to implement mission command. He devolved decision-making downwards to his brigade commanders. He trained them to make appropriate command decisions for him. Yet, the operation was a lineal conventional fight and very quickly Smith had to resort to more conventional, individualist command, in which he concentrated on and supervised his subordinates in the close fight.

The situation has now changed. Because of the increasing span of command at the divisional level, the increasing complexity and range of the military operations and the requirement for precision, a divisional commander can no longer direct operations alone. The increased scope of divisional operations precludes it. As the functions of a division have multiplied and the range at which it operates has extended, decision-making has proliferated. Divisional commanders are no longer responsible for a single critical action on a small front, normally resolved by the coordination of their own brigades and artillery. Now, the commander has to orchestrate a long-term campaign, over a large geographical area and incorporating a diversity of activities. In some cases, because these decisions have involved the integration of heterogeneous assets and actions, they have become objectively more complex; commanders require more staffwork and an enhanced wisdom from subordinates to make informed decisions. Consequently, in the twenty-first century, commanders have increasingly had to share or distribute their command authority. Command teams, command boards, principal planning groups and deputies have appeared to assist and to support the commander and to manage discrete decision cycles to which the commander cannot attend. Collective command has emerged as an institutional response to an organizational problem. It is a method of coordinating operations and sustaining organizational cohesion at a time when complexity threatens to overwhelm existing hierarchies and structures.

The practice of leadership has also changed. In the twentieth century, when mass citizen armies were the norm, the challenge of leadership was pronounced. Generals had to motivate often poorly trained, unwilling troops to accept very high casualties. Accordingly, exemplary personal, sometimes heroic, leadership became the norm. Successful generals tried to project themselves as paternal figures in the imaginations of their young soldiers. In a professional twenty-first-century force, leadership remains essential but its dynamics have changed. Notwithstanding the example of Mattis, troops are typically motivated by a professional ethos which is sustained at the small-unit level. However, as headquarters have enlarged and operations have become more complex, divisional commanders have had to unite and motivate their staff and deputies. They have projected themselves onto a small audience and they have typically sought to embody more modest virtues of professionalism and competence rather than exemplary heroism. Indeed, today, modest, ethically committed professionalism has itself become heroic.

To repeat, all command is ultimately collective. Divisional commanders in the twentieth century required a staff and deputies. When Montgomery trained his subordinate brigade commanders to execute drills on his orders, he was forming a proto-command collective. Balck relied on his Ia. Collectivism is relative. Yet, while relative, the extent and the systematization of collaboration today is so pronounced that command has become, in effect, a different practice. A new regime of command is apparent. It is not always easy to recognize the full significance of a relative transformation, precisely because there are evident continuities with the past. It has been repeatedly emphasized throughout the text that the new divisional headquarters manifestly evolved from the modern command post invented in the First World War and still displays many of its features. It is precisely this continuity which allows for any valid comparison to be made between the two regimes and for the distinctiveness of contemporary practices to be realized. However, even then, the analysis has to be conducted at a sufficiently large scale that the true significance of some of the developments is recognized. It is all too easy to presume that nothing has changed and that the individual agency of the commander remains unaffected by the changing character of military operations.

In the twentieth century, the divisional commander occupied a singular location at the summit of a steep hierarchical and internally unified pyramid. The division had clear and very limited vertical and horizontal boundaries; it was a bounded, homogeneous force within a discrete military chain of command. The problem was one of scale. In the twenty-first century, the divisional commander now occupies a unique position at the centre of an increasingly heterogeneous operational complex. In many ways, divisional commanders today are far more powerful than predecessors; the scope of divisional operations has vastly expanded. However, to harness the potential power of the new division, commanders have had to coordinate and unify a multifunctional, heterogeneous and, indeed, often multinational force. Rather simply issuing orders, commanders have often had to negotiate the cooperation of these partners. At the same time, precisely because of these extensive diplomatic burdens, they have distributed authority to deputies who have acted as agents for the commander. Contemporary divisional commanders have become both far more powerful than their predecessors and yet more dependent upon the allegiance and assistance of deputies, partners, staff and proxies. They cannot operate this system alone.

The best divisional headquarters in the twentieth century were certainly professional but, in the last two decades, a process of intense professionalization has been evident. In order to coordinate complex divisional system and to improve the accuracy of decision-making, new forms of specialist knowledge and new forms of bureaucratic expertise have been introduced into the divisional headquarters. These techniques, such as the Commander's Intent, the Synchronization Matrix and the

Decision Point can be disparaged but they have structured the way in which a division now operates and commanders make decisions. At the same time, the teamwork of the staff has been deepened and strengthened.

This book argues for the rise of collective command. As such, it is an independent study of command which can easily be read alone. However, in mapping changing command regimes, this book concludes what has become a trilogy on contemporary military transformation. The first volume, *The Transformation of Europe's Armed Forces*, argued that, in the post-Cold War era, Europe's forces were not so much downsizing as concentrating. Rather than simply diminishing, European forces were condensing into empowered national nodes of military capability articulated into a thickening transnational network. The book examined new Rapid Reaction Corps Headquarters and rapid reaction brigades in France, Britain and Germany. The work showed how these small, but increasingly capable, rapid reaction forces were emerging across Europe, cooperating every more closely with each other.

The Combat Soldier, the second volume of the series, continued with the themes of concentration, transnationalization and professionalization. It examined the infantry platoon, the smallest military unit. It argued that the combat performance of the infantry platoon has undergone a transition in the late twentieth and early twenty-first centuries. In citizen armies in the twentieth century, the Western infantry platoon had performed poorly due to inadequate training and was typically reliant on nominated individuals to execute actions; platoon commanders were expected to lead while soldiers often remained inert. A mass-individual dialectic was evident. By contrast, through intense training in which drills have been inculcated deeply, the professional platoon of the twenty-first century has increasingly performed as a highly tuned team in Iraq and Afghanistan; at the platoon level, collective expertise and teamwork has superseded the virtuosic individual.

The current work on command makes an, in fact, unexpectedly commensurate argument to those two previous books. *The Transformation of Europe's Armed Forces* examined Corps Headquarters. This book focuses on the divisional headquarters, as a concentrated and globalized node of military power. It shows the way in which resources are currently being concentrated on this command echelon to improve the combat effectiveness of land forces. Similarly, it also argues that, in the twenty-first century, command of the division has been professionalized no less than the infantry platoon. Command individualism, utterly appropriate to twentieth-century conditions, has been superseded by increasingly professionalized collective command. In the contemporary divisional headquarters, highly trained command and staff teams, employing refined planning methods, have replaced the heroic individual commander, exclusively responsible for almost all decisions. Rommel has been superseded by Mattis; Ewell by Petraeus and Carter. A differentiated yet parallel development has been evident both at the level of the smallest tactical unit, the platoon, and the largest, the division. In both cases, individual leadership has been replaced by collective expertise; the team has become paramount.

While each volume has focused on quite different issues, there is a common thread which unites them closely, then. Each has described as aspect of contemporary military professionalization. Precisely because they have become so much smaller, Western forces have had to become more efficient – or to try to. Professionalization has been a way of concentrating military power, at a time when the mass armies of the twentieth century have disappeared. The first volume of this military trilogy examined the rise of professionalism in European rapid reaction forces. The second explored the rise of professionalism in the infantry platoon. This volume has examined how command itself has been professionalized. The book claims that the appearance of collective command represents another strand of professionalization. In order to manage proliferating decision-cycles and, therefore, to accelerate and refine decision-making, the emergence of ever more disciplined and cohesive command and staff teams has been necessary. It has been possible to distribute decision-making, only because refined techniques have been developed to coordinate commanders, deputies, subordinates and staff. In short, collective command has involved the professionalization of the headquarters. The bureaucratic expertise of the staff has been improved and their cohesiveness has been condensed so that they are now bound in dense solidarity, even when they are not co-present.

A new regime of command is appearing among the major Western powers, led, of course, by the United States. This transformation, especially in the United States, has been primarily driven by organizational and operational requirements. Collective command is an adaptation to the changing character of military operations and the changing military requirement. Yet, while adaptive in some sense, the emergence of collective command still poses a question of its objective efficacy. The vulnerabilities and inefficiencies of the current divisional construct are obvious. A common criticism is that divisional headquarters are too large, too dispersed and too comprehensive. Trying to do too much, they risk failure on any future operation.

The complaints are justified. Yet, the campaigns in Iraq and Afghanistan and recent exercises suggest that the divisional headquarters is minimally functional; it has worked as a system of command. However, it is important to avoid any suggestion of ameliorism here or to equate adaptation and development with objective progress. The emergence of command collectivism today does not in any way invalidate the relatively more individualized practice of command in the twentieth century. On the contrary, twentieth-century headquarters were capable of conducting operations which would be very challenging today. In August 1914, the British Expeditionary Force deployed two corps to France within six weeks. It is probable that such a feat would be far beyond a British headquarters today. It is not obvious whether 3 UK Division could match Montgomery's manoeuvre on 27 May 1940, when his 3rd Division sidestepped two British divisions to take up a new position in the line; it seems unlikely that 3 UK Division could better. Indeed, many former generals disparage contemporary command as degenerate.

Collective command is not objectively better than more individualist practices of the past, then. These two regimes of command reflect the alternative organizational and operational contexts in which they have emerged. In the era of mass armies, interstate war or conflicts of imperial liberation, individualist command was functionally appropriate. Divisions conducted one immediate mission at a time and, while far less precision and discretion was required than today, decisions were often critical; catastrophic defeat was a distinct possibility. Collective command has emerged to respond to quite different operational demands. While neither method is objectively better, it might be suggested that each is better adapted for the era in which it operated. Yet, in any future war, it is simply unknowable at this point whether collective command is optimal. It is possible that collective command and the operational approach and force structures to which it is a response will be proven to be effective; or they may be disastrous.

NAVAL AND AIR COMMAND

This book has focused entirely on the command of Western land forces: American, British French and German divisions. This raises the obvious question of whether there has been any parallel command reform in the Western navies and air forces. Of course, developments in the other services are likely to be distinctive; each has a quite different mission from the army, with a discrete organizational culture. Yet, a brief investigation of naval and air command would seem to be minimally useful. It may indicate whether collective command is a purely land-centric innovation or whether, in fact, it might be part of a much more profound military transformation. Of course, if navies and air forces have also revised their command practices, that would constitute some useful supporting evidence for the argument propounded in this book. It would add weight to the claim that command has indeed undergone a transformation in the twenty-first century. It is worth examining naval and then air command to establish whether any compatible changes have occurred.

Western armies have reformed themselves primarily in response to changing operational and organizational conditions. It is very noticeable that Western navies have also emphasized the scale of the changes which they have faced over the last two decades. The maritime operating environment and the navy itself have transformed quite radically. In response to these operational and organizational developments, the US Navy has produced a number of doctrinal publications which try to identify the central features of the current environment: 'The Sea Services face a growing range of challenges in gaining access to and operating freely in the maritime commons'. In addition to potentially new adversaries like China, North Korea or Somali pirates, often utilizing asymmetric techniques, the navy now operates not just on the sea but in multidimensional space. Navies have to engage in informational and littoral domains; cyber and electromagnetic warfare have become a reality, while naval fires have become more integrated with non-kinetic effects. At the same time, even the US Navy has had to work ever more closely with its allies to 'advance the global network of navies concept', which does not merely cooperate with allies but 'integrates allies and partner forces into the Carrier Strike Group'.[2] The US Navy's Capstone

---

[2] US Navy, *A Cooperative Strategy for 21st Century Seapower*, March 2015, 8, 32.

Concept for Joint Operations makes precisely the same point. In the light of digital technology, cyber warfare, social media, transnational networks, globally integrated operations and digital technology, naval operations have changed.

As a result, naval command has itself been subject to extensive pressure. Naval officers have confirmed the point: 'the cognitive demands of informational networks all conspire to burden leadership in ways inconceivable less than a generation ago'. Operations are 'complex, multi-cultural, joint and interagency'.[3] As a result, maritime command is evolving and adapting. Traditionally, Western navies centralized the planning and command of maritime operations but decentralized their execution. A traditional concept of mission command was practised, where local commanders were genuinely free to follow their own initiative; their superiors were often not in direct communication with them and certainly had little understanding of the local conditions. This system of simple devolution is changing.

In their work on naval command, Admiral James Stavridis and Robert Girrier have begun to describe the current transformation. At the beginning of their work, Stavridis and Girrier advocate mission command: 'the most successful commanders empower their subordinates as the size of command grows'. However, as their argument develops, it is clear that by mission command, Stavridis and Girrier have a quite novel and distinctive command system in mind. They are not describing a loose system of devolution but, on the contrary, a highly integrated command model whose echelons are intimately connected. This becomes clear as Stavridis and Girrier begin to discuss the example of Aegis destroyers. In this example, the local commander of an Aegis is no longer empowered to act autonomously as in Nelsonian fashion and simply 'to engage the enemy more closely'. In order to conduct tactical missions, the local Aegis commander now has to coordinate local decisions with the chain of command at operational and strategic levels: 'A ballistic missile defence (BMD)-capable ship can simultaneously be involved at the tactical, operational and strategic levels of warfare: tactically employed in a local anti-surface, anti-submarine, or anti-air warfare mission; operationally engaged in theatre missile defence mission; and strategically as part of a multi-time

---

[3] Christopher Hayes, 'Developing the Navy's Operational Leaders: a critical look' *Naval War College Review* 61(3) Summer 2008: 78–9.

zone BMD fire control system providing national defence to our home-land'.[4] Naval platforms simultaneously perform multiple functions which operate at different levels. Consequently, 'coordination requires connectivity at multiple levels of command'.

In the twentieth century, mission command referred to a laissez-faire system in which local commanders were given licence to follow their initiative with little immediate reference to their superiors. Extreme decentralization was typical of navies in the twentieth century due to the limitations of communications technology. By contrast, in the twenty-first century, commanders at different levels have to orchestrate, synchronize and align their decision-making. Senior commanders certainly supervise subordinates more closely: 'Missile defence to cities and population centres will invite senior level scrutiny'.[5] Moreover, 'with the increased capability that technology brings is a complementary capacity for assistance via "reach-back" mechanisms that leverage staff expertise and compiled data from across the globe'.[6] As on land, reach-back headquarters are informing the local naval commander's decision-making. Crucially, these headquarters provide the necessary information to ensure that tactical decision-making is consonant with operational and strategic imperatives. However,

> notwithstanding all the "help" from outside sources, there is still an extraordinary level of responsibility on the shoulders of the captain. The CO will make the decision of whether to fire in an individual engagement; when and how to tactically execute boardings at sea; when and how to undertake a medical evacuation – indeed, the time, method, and ultimate execution of a thousand discrete decisions remains the responsibility of the captain.[7]

In place of the decentralized command of the twentieth century, Stavridis and Girrier are describing the emergence of an integrated command construct in which relations between commanders at each level have been intensified and deepened. This is the domain neither

---

[4] James Stavridis and Robert Girrier, 'Taking Command' in T. Cutler (ed.), *Naval Command* (Annapolis, MD: Naval Institute Press, 2015), 12.
[5] Ibid.
[6] Ibid.
[7] Ibid.

of centralization nor of decentralization but genuinely collaborative, shared command. It involves ensemble not independent decision-making. It does not seem excessive to suggest that in the navy, as in the army, collective command, involving the integration of distributed decision-making authority, is emerging. Indeed, some officers in the navy have noted precisely the point: 'to make the command network effective the commander must be able to interact with all subordinates on a day-to-day basis'.[8] Many naval officers have feared that new digital techniques would introduce a system of extreme centralized control. In fact, the current era has been characterized not by the elimination of local initiative but its ever closer integration with higher levels of command.

Traditionally, the air force has tended to command in a manner which is compatible to the navy. Highly centralized command led to decentralized execution. In the past, the nature of air operations has almost demanded such an arrangement: 'Technology drove airpower to a centralized control and decentralized execution model'.[9] However, in the last two decades, the nature of air operations, like those on the ground and at sea, have also begun to change: 'The macro-environment [consisting of political, economic, socio-cultural and technological dimensions] has become more competitive and volatile. The net result is that doing what was done yesterday – or even doing it 5% better – is no longer a formula for success'.[10] The sheer volume of information has become a problem for air commanders: 'The explosion of technological growth during the past two decades means that the volume and speed of information flow available to a commander is increasing dramatically, thus accelerating the tempo of air operations'.[11] As in the other services, the changing operational environment has transformed command in the air force.[12]

---

[8] John Bodnar and Rebecca Dengler, 'The emergence of the command network', *Naval War College Review* 49(4) 1996: 100.

[9] Phillip Meilinger, 'The Development of Air Power Theory', in Peter Gray and Seb Cox (eds), *Air Power Leadership: theory and practice* (Swindon: JDCC, 2002), 105.

[10] Brian Howieson and Howard Kahn, 'Leadership, Management and Command: the officers' trinity', in 'The Development of Air Power Theory', in Peter Gray and Seb Cox (eds), *Air Power Leadership: theory and practice* (Swindon: JDCC, 2002), 29.

[11] Meilinger, 'The Development of Air Power Theory', 106.

[12] Alan Stephens, 'Command in the Air', in Peter Gray and Seb Cox (eds), *Air Power Leadership: theory and practice* (Swindon: JDCC, 2002), 14; Brian Howieson and Howard Kahn, 'Leadership, Management and Command: the officers' trinity', in Peter

Many practitioners and scholars have feared that the introduction of digital communications technology will eliminate local initiative, centralizing command at the strategic level: 'The technology now exists to permit real-time intelligence gathering and dissemination, as well as real time secure communications, virtually anywhere in the world'.[13] For instance, air operations in Afghanistan were commanded from CENTCOM in Tampa and 'CINCENT was thus able to watch real time feeds from Predator surveillance aircraft orbiting a potential target'; as on land and on the sea, 'the explosion of communications and sensor technology now permits centralized control and execution of air assets'.[14] Traditions of air command have been overturned:

> This was not a situation that air commanders were prepared for, and they chafed at what they saw as micromanagement and the intrusion of higher headquarters into a regime that had always considered the local air commander's prerogative.[15]

Subordinate air commanders no longer have the freedom simply to execute the mission given to them by higher command. They are themselves monitored and supervised.

Although centralized micro-management by higher command might be a technical possibility, command has in fact evolved in a rather different way in the air force. Precisely because air operations have become so complex, higher commanders have themselves been disciplined and constrained by their staff. Because 'the air commander's challenge of making faster, and wiser, decisions is daunting', the staff have to anticipate and automate decisions in order to ensure their accuracy and coherence. They cannot be made by reference to the commander's intuition; there are simply too many working parts.

> CINCENT relied more heavily on his staff, which of course remained with him in Florida, than he did on this air component commander 5000 miles away. Doctrine has

Gray and Seb Cox (eds), *Air Power Leadership: theory and practice* (Swindon: JDCC, 2002), 28; Stuart Peach, 'The Airman's Dilemma: to command or control?' in Peter Gray (ed.), *Air Power 21: challenges for the new century* (London: The Stationery Office, 2000), 147–8.
[13] Meilinger, 'The Development of Air Power Theory', 105.
[14] Ibid.
[15] Ibid.

traditionally stated that command and staff functions are separate entities that exist within lines and boundaries that must not be crossed. Afghanistan seems to be demonstrating that such doctrine, as well as the entire issue of centralized control and decentralized execution of air assets, needs to be re-examined.[16]

Moreover, rather than mere centralization, digital communications have facilitated greater interaction and exchange between higher and local commanders. In place of necessarily devolved command, a system of increasingly intense collaborative command across the levels is observable with higher and lower commanders cooperating ever more closely with each other to harmonize their decision-making, as operations unfold in real-time.[17]

It does not seem to be too excessive to suggest that, as with the example of the Aegis-class destroyer, the challenge of decision-making for an air commander has increased. Air campaigns have been conducted at greater range and with increased precision and they have been integrated not only with the other services but also with an informational, inter-agency approach. Consequently, local decisions have been orchestrated ever more closely with higher levels. In this situation, it is wrong to confuse the emergence of integrated air command across the echelons for mere interference by higher command. Air commanders at each level are working ever more closely with each other, while cooperating with commanders from other services and agencies, to coordinate complex operations. Clearly, air command is specially adapted to the particular requirements of air warfare. Nevertheless, there seem to be some evident parallels between air command in the twenty-first century and the other services. Like land and maritime command, air command has involved the creation of a globally distributed command system in which higher command has the ability to supervise missions in real-time. Yet, simplistic centralized authoritarianism has not emerged to obliterate local initiative. Rather, these distributed command systems have involved the generation of ever more closely integrated command collectives in which air commanders at each level cooperate and collaborate with each other with increasing intensity. In the air force, highly

---

[16] Ibid., 106.
[17] Peach, 'The Airman's Dilemma', 151.

professional, globally dispersed command collectives commensurate with the army division seem to be observable.

It is obvious that considerable caution needs to be exercised in extrapolating the argument for collective command from the land warfare and the army division, in particular, to the other services. Certainly, there is inadequate evidence presented here to sustain such a theory. Nevertheless, the debates within the navy and air force today about the requirement for a reformation of command is surely significant. It indicates a manifest dissatisfaction with existing systems and at least some adaptation of traditional twentieth-century practices. In both the air and naval services, a condensed network of command has displaced the relatively disaggregated and decentralized hierarchies of the past. In the twentieth century, local commanders were necessarily given missions which they had the responsibility to conduct more or less independently; there was no other way of commanding operations. Now, missions commanded at the lower level are simultaneously coordinated in real-time with decisions being made at the higher level. Commanders across the levels are coalescing into an ever more tightly integrated ensemble, disciplined and constrained by staffs who refine and discipline their decision-making. Naval and air operations of the last two decades seem genuinely to suggest not only that command is changing in the other services but that it might be understood as a form of collective command, different from the command collectives observable in the divisional headquarters and, yet, compatible with them. In each case, the armed forces have instituted a system of command which they have termed 'mission command'.

It is important not to confuse contemporary mission command, as a collaborative enterprise, with traditional, twentieth-century equivalents. Then mission command referred to the individualistic devolution of authority to subordinates. It was a laissez-faire system. By contrast, as the analysis of Nick Carter, James Mattis and the new divisional headquarters shows and the reform of naval and air force command suggests, mission command no longer refers to mere devolution and individual licence – typical in the twentieth century – but to the ever closer integration and interdependence of commanders. Crucially, mission command today involves increasing interaction and synergy between commanders and staff. For contemporary mission command, education and shared concepts are required so that commanders at every level are oriented to the systemic effects of their local decisions. Commanders are themselves disciplined and structured by staff procedures and analysis. In contrast with the individualist practice of the last century, mission command today involves collectivism with commanders united around common definitions and a shared consciousness. Command has evolved from individual virtuosity into a professionalized teamwork.

Future Command

Western armies, and perhaps Western forces as a whole, have reformed command in the last two decades. They have moved from a system of individualist command to a collectivist practice involving a heightened level of professionalism; headquarters and staff have expanded dramatically as forces have introduced digital communications technology. On recent operations in Iraq, Afghanistan, Libya and Syria, this new practice of command has been successful, at least at the tactical level. Western, especially American, forces have repeatedly demonstrate their ability to coordinate complex, joint and integrated operations at range. However, it is also impossible to know definitively whether collective command, which is currently emerging in the West, will defend against future military defeat or actually ensure it.

In Iraq, Afghanistan, Libya and Syria, Western forces have enjoyed total air supremacy against highly motivated but very basically equipped opponents. Although Western forces are currently reconfiguring themselves for high-intensity warfare and a cycle of exercises suggest that divisional headquarters may be capable of fighting against a near peer enemy, it is impossible to know definitively whether this system of command will be optimal in the case of a future conflict against a major military power like Russia or China. Against an enemy of equal combat power, when the West does not enjoy air superiority, it is uncertain whether current command systems will be adequate.

Some have suggested that a return to a traditional, divisional command system is necessary and that Western forces have bureaucratized themselves to irrelevance and to defeat. With its reliance on digital technology, the new divisional headquarters is seriously vulnerable to electronic and cyber attack – or even just to power loss. The very elaborateness of the new systems has generated serious frailties. Professionalism itself may even become a problem in this context, since the over-emphasis on analysis, process, precision and detail may retard the speed of decision-making. Defeat is certainly a possibility and a concern for the armed forces. However, 4th US Infantry Division and 82nd Airborne Division have explicitly tested their systems of mission command in demanding exercises practicing deployments against possible Russian threats to the Baltics. It is impossible to know whether collectivized command will be adaptive for any future conflict. Yet, it has now become so institutionalized that Western forces will fight with this system of command for the foreseeable future. Even it if proves to be a false adaptation, the command collective is an organizational reality.

It is notable that both Russia and China, as two major non-Western powers, seem to have also begun to adapt their traditional systems of command in response to changing operational conditions. This is significant. These reforms provide evidential support for the argument of this book. The Russian and Chinese cases seem to confirm that in the light of current operational and organizational conditions, more collective practices of command have proved more effective in the twentieth century and they have been widely adopted, displacing existing hierarchies. Even if these new systems of command are not objectively better, Western forces may take comfort that their peers may at least be adopting systems with similar vulnerabilities to their own. It is worth examining the cases of Russia and China in detail.

Since the end of the Cold War, Russia has been involved in four major military interventions involving ground forces: the First and Second Chechen Wars, the South Ossetia–Georgian wars and, currently, the conflict in Ukraine. Commentators widely note that in the first three of these conflicts, Russia employed traditional, Soviet methods. In each case, the Russian Army employed large armoured columns to effect deep penetrations against their opponents. While disastrous in the First Chechen War in the battle for Grozny, the technique proved successful later in Chechnya and especially in the short fight for South Ossetia.[18]

However, since 2008, the Russian Army has revised its military doctrine and methods very considerably. Extending the reforms initiated

---

[18] Palle Ydstebo, 'Russian Operations: continuity, novelties and adaptation', in Janne Matlary and Tormod Heier (eds), *Ukraine and Beyond: Russian's strategic security challenge to Europe* (London: Palgrave Macmillan, 2010), 156–61.

by his predecessor General Markov, the current chief of the Russian general staff, General Valery Gerasimov, has played an important role in modernizing the army's approach to war. Usefully, Gerasimov has articulated his new concept of hybrid conflict in a now widely circulated document, 'The Value of Science in Prediction', originally published in 2013. This paper is a passionate plea to Russian military scientists to assist the military in adapting itself to the conditions of twenty-first-century warfare. In this essay, observing the Arab Spring and other violent uprisings in Iraq and Afghanistan, Gerasimov described the transformation of warfare. Instead of conventional state-on-state conflict, war has become hybrid:

> the focus of applied methods of conflict has altered in the direction of the broad use of political, economic, informational, humanitarian and other non-military measures – applied in coordination with the protest of the population. All this is supplemented by military means of a concealed character, including carrying out the actions of informational conflict and the actions of the special operations forces.[19]

Accordingly,

> military actions are becoming more dynamic, active and fruitful. New information technologies have enabled signification reductions in the spatial, temporal and informational gaps between forces and control organs. Frontal engagement of large formations of forces at the strategic and operational level are becoming a thing of the past. Long-distance, contactless action against an enemy are becoming the main means of achieving combat and operational goals.[20]

Gerasimov advocated 'perfecting the forms and means of applying groups of forces', which were highly manoeuvrable and which massed precision-guided munitions and SOF against critical national infrastructure, to integrate effects in the physical and the informational space;[21] 'The informational space opens wide asymmetrical possibilities

---

[19] General Valery Gerasimov, 'The Value of Science in Prediction', *Military-Industrial Kurier*, 27 February 2013. http://cs.brown.edu/people/jsavage/VotingProject/2017_03_09_MoscowsShadow_GerasimovDoctrineAndRussianNon-LinearWar.pdf, 24.

[20] Ibid.

[21] Ibid., 25.

for reducing the fighting potential of the enemy'.[22] Gerasimov's argument manifestly echoes developments in Western military doctrine discussed in Chapter 10, paralleling in particular the UK concept of 'Integrated Action' or the American concept of 'Multi-dimensional Battle'. However, Gerasimov insisted that the Russian Army was not simply aping the West: 'We must not copy foreign experience and chose after the leading countries, but we must outstrip them and occupy leading positions ourselves'.[23]

Significantly, in terms of this discussion, although Gerasimov does not describe new command structures, he makes some highly suggestive allusions to changing command practices in order to realize his vision of informational, hybrid war. He notes that in traditional, twentieth-century conflict there was 'command control of groupings of line units within a framework of strictly organizational hierarchical structures'.[24] The implication is that contemporary combat operations will require alternative command methods which are capable of coordinating a multiplicity of functions over a greater span of space and time. The organizational problem which Gerasimov identifies is very similar to the one which has driven Western forces to a model of collective command at the divisional level. As Gerasimov has promulgated a new military concept, the Russian Army has, in fact, conducted a comprehensive review of it command and control structures and its ability to conduct combined arms operations. Specifically, the Zapad exercises of 2008 and 2013 introduced and tested command reforms. As Gersimov noted: 'The Russian military worked on the interoperability of all branches and combat arms and also other agencies mobilized in the exercises'.[25] Clearly, some care needs to be exercised here. It is not absolutely definite how much Russian command structures and methods have changed. Yet, these developments are clearly suggestive, implying a move away from a steep, authoritarian hierarchy in which designated commanders held all the responsibility for decisions, to a more inclusive, collaborative and synchronized system.

The seizure of the Crimea and the Donetsk and Luhansk regions of Ukraine in 2014 seem to demonstrate a significant enhancement

---

[22] Ibid., 27.

[23] Ibid., 29.

[24] Ibid., 25.

[25] Stephen Blank, 'What do the Zapad 2013 Exercises Reveal' (Part 1), *Eurasia Daily Monitor*, Volume 10 Issue 177, 4 October 2013.

of Russian command capacity. In stark contrast to the 2008 war in Georgia, Russia eschewed conventional manoeuvre, exploiting rather 'little green men', Russian Special Operations Forces, to suppress Ukrainian militias and to generate informational dominance. At the same time, the Russian forces supported and partnered with local ethnic Russian militias in eastern Ukraine, supporting them with drones and especially artillery strikes.[26] Raw firepower is by no means irrelevant to Russian's new way of warfare but conventional strike is now dispersed over a wide area and integrated with other activities. Russian operations in Ukraine seem to imply that the new systems of command suggested by Gerasimov and tested on Zapad 2008, 2013 and 2017 are substantially in place.

China has not been involved in major military operations recently and, consequently, the transformations which are evident in the Russian Army are not quite so apparent. Nevertheless, the recent development of the People's Liberation Army is deeply interesting and likely to be of historic significance. Historically, the People's Liberation Army has been the most important element of the Chinese armed forces. It was instrumental to Mao's rise and, as a large continental power bordered by fourteen nations with diverse ethnic populations, the communist state has relied heavily upon it for defence and security. The automatic predominance of the PLA was revoked in the 2004 defence white paper as the Navy, Air Force and the Second Artillery Force were prioritized; China has increasingly looked towards the Pacific and to the South and East China seas.[27] After the Third Plenum of the 19th Party Central Committee of 2015, the PLA was further reduced by 300,000, to 2.3 million.[28] Alongside these reformations, the territorial command structure of the PLA has been revised.

These alterations are noteworthy but the significant command reforms of the Chinese armed forces have taken place elsewhere. Specifically, in the light of the new strategic imperatives, China has focused its attention on joint operations and on military operations other than war. While the 2004 guideline spoke of 'integrated operations,

---

[26] Ydstebo, 'Russian Operations: continuity, novelties and adaptation', 162–6.
[27] Dennis Blasko, 'Integrating the services and harnessing the military area commands', *Journal of Strategic Studies* 39(5–6) 2016: 686.
[28] Ibid., 687.

precision strikes to subdue the enemy', the 2015 white paper described how the PLA would exploit 'information dominance, precision strikes on strategic points, joint operations to gain victory'.[29] The 2013 edition of *The Science of Military Strategy* provides important evidence here for a substantial shift in Chinese thinking. This essay aimed to describe the changing strategic situation in which Chinese forces were to operate, laying out the principles of new military action. It argued that joint operations now relied on a complete linkage of networked military informational systems, the use of informationized weapons and equipment, and appropriate combat methods in land, sea, air, cyber and space.[30] The document made one apparently small but crucial change to military definitions. From 2004, the Chinese military had been oriented to 'winning locals war under informationalised conditions'. In contrast to a people's war, the prime mission of the PLA has become limited local actions against external or internal threats, while being aware of and utilizing the informational domain. The *2013 Science of Strategy* altered the concept of 'local war under informationalized conditions' to 'winning informationized local wars'.[31] While the information domain provided the context for military operations in the former formulation, 'informationized' techniques have now become an intrinsic element of Chinese operational approach. 'Informationized' refers both to the new salience of digital communication and surveillance technology and to the increasing importance of media, cyber, electronic and psychological campaigns to support any operation. The concept of 'informationized' wars requires the integration of a diversity of assets and activities over greater time and space.

The PLA faces a very similar problem to Western forces and, indeed, to Russian ones. The result is a rather radical reform of the PLA from a single-service, land-oriented military engaging in conventional territorial defence into a modern networked military; 'Operational commanders now have many more weapon systems that can strike 100 to 1000 kilometers from their front lines than they did twenty years ago'.[32] Indeed, the proliferation has been remarkable;

---

[29] M. Taylor Fravel, 'China's New Military Strategy: "winning informationalized local wars"', *China Brief*, Volume 15, Issue 13.

[30] Blasko, 'Integrating the services and harnessing the military area commands', 697.

[31] M. Taylor Fravel, 'China's New Military Strategy: "winning informationalized local wars"', *China Brief*, Volume 15, Issue 13.

[32] Blasko, 'Integrating the services and harnessing the military area commands', 698.

Chinese generals now have guided munitions delivered by manned aircraft, UAVs, attack helicopters or artillery as well as rocket launchers, supported by multiple forms of cyber and electronic warfare and Special Operations Forces. This multiplication of functions resembles the reforms at the divisional level among the Western powers. In the face of this diversification, Chinese forces have developed a unified planning and comprehensive command-and-control system. Specifically, because commanders are now threatened with information overload, they and their staffs have been more highly trained to analyze data and to develop timely plans and decisions.

The improvement of command performance is currently a high priority for Chinese forces and is the object of much attention and investment.[33] Significantly, command of joint operations has been pushed down from the army level to divisional and even brigade level. In stark contrast to the previously highly centralized and deferential PLA command culture, command responsibilities are being assigned to relatively junior commanders.[34] Indeed, using exchange officers at Western staff colleges, the Chinese have been deeply interested in learning about contemporary Western command techniques. It would be premature to suggest that China will adopt the professionalized collective command practices described in this book. It would be unlikely in an authoritarian state whose traditions have been heavily centrist and hierarchical. However, it is apparent that Chinese command structures and methods are evolving in order to be able to conduct informationized local wars. In particular, three developments seem to be apparent: closer interaction between command echelons, increased responsibility at subordinate command levels and a more highly trained and professional staff. It is too soon to say that the PLA has adopted collective command as a preferred practice. However, in the West, collective command has emerged under precisely these conditions.

This survey of two major non-Western powers is clearly cursory and inadequate. However, it may be suggestive. Collective command is not yet a global military phenomenon. It is an occidental practice, pioneered by the United States, imitated by its allies. However, there seems to be some evidence that a reform of command is occurring among other armed forces. Russia seems to be clearly

---

[33] Ibid., 698–9.
[34] Ibid., 699.

the most advanced here. The success of its operations in Ukraine and Syria suggest that it has developed a system of command which is capable of integrating a multiplicity of functions and operating at range. China seems to be following rapidly in its aspiration to fight 'informationized local wars' with integrated and joint assets. In each case, the requirement to integrate multiple functions, to coordinate activities more closely across the levels and to engage in precise strikes at range is compelling a reform of command. In short, while non-Western commands will inevitably assume their own form, in line with local traditions of military professionalism, it would seem plausible to suggest that some reforms are occurring which might usefully be described as collective. As in the West, a highly directive, hierarchical and individualized command regime constructed around a single commander is likely to be replaced by more collaborative, professionalized teams of commanders, supported by an increasingly specialized staff, which informs and supports decision-making. Collective command may become a global military practice in the twenty-first century. It means that the West's potential enemies may increasingly adopt a compatible command system, with all its vulnerabilities.

In the early nineteenth century, following their experiences in the Napoleonic Wars, the Duke of Wellington and Carl von Clausewitz both emphasized the importance of command. Successful military operations required a commander who could perceive the dynamics of the battlefield and anticipate events, even in the densest fog of war. The character of warfare has changed dramatically since that era. However, their observations about the primacy of command remain utterly relevant today. Command remains an imperative for the armed forces and, as the often disappointing Western results of the last decade have shown, military success still relies on good generalship. However, while command is still primary, the practice of command has evolved profoundly in the early twenty-first century. Although there are evident continuities, a rupture between twentieth- and twenty-first-century command is now observable; a new regime of command is emerging. As operations become increasingly complex, extrapolated over time and space, demanding the integration of heterogeneous forces with ever greater precision, the executive functions of mission definition, mission management and leadership have been revised. Above all, where an individual commander, with a small staff, was able to monopolize decision-making, highly professionalized command collectives have begun to emerge. The commander is still central to this system. Indeed, precisely because operations have become so complex, there is an even greater requirement for a single point of reference. Above all, commanders have a duty to define a mission, even when its identification has become very difficult. It is still their duty to illuminate the way, even in the 'darkest hour'.

However, command has become a joint activity in which deputies, subordinates and the staff play an increasingly critical role. In his work on contemporary command, which was discussed in Chapter 1, McChrystal disparages the traditional concept of the heroic leader: 'Even the most successful of today's heroic leaders appear uneasy in the saddle, all too aware that their ability to understand and control is a chimera'.[35] McChrystal's argument is ultimately based on one compelling example: his experiences hunting Al-Qaeda in Iraq. Yet, his argument has much wider resonance. The command collective, which he identified as indispensable to the effectiveness of the Special Operations Forces, is increasingly evident in conventional forces. The division, the once elementary cell of industrial warfare, has become a complex, heterogeneous system. As such, it has demanded a new method of command. It can no longer be directed individually by generals like Rommel, Monash or Montgomery, who dominated decision-making, with the support of a few aides and subordinates. The best commanders today, like James Mattis, are easily the peers of their predecessors both in terms of their competence and personalities. However, in order to conduct divisional operations, commanders today have increasingly orchestrated a cohesive command team, devolving and distributing decision-making authority to empowered subordinates and to staff. Of course, it is impossible to know whether the emergence of even the most professionalized command collective among Western forces will be adequate to the challenge of future military operations.

---

[35] Stanley McChrystal, *Team of Teams*, 231.

BIBLIOGRAPHY

21st Army Group *Some Notes on the Conduct of War and the Infantry Division in Battle* (Belgium, November 1944).

Alexander, Jeffrey *The Civil Sphere* (Oxford: Oxford University Press, 2008).

Alexander, Martin and J.F.V. Keiger 'France and the Algerian War: strategy, operations and diplomacy', in Martin Alexander and J.F.V. Keiger (eds), *France and the Algerian War 1954–62: strategy, operations and diplomacy* (London: Frank Cass, 2002).

Anderson, Benedict *Imagined Communities* (London: Verso, 2016).

Anderson, David *Histories of the Hanged: Britain's dirty war in Kenya and the end of empire* (London: Weidenfeld and Nicolson, 2005).

Aussaresses, Paul *The Battle of the Casbah: counter-terrorism and torture 1955–57* (New York: Enigma Books, 2010).

Bacevich, Andrew *The New American Militarism: how Americans are seduced by war* (Oxford: Oxford University Press, 2013).

Washington Rules: America's path to power (New York: Metropolitan Books, 2010).

The Pentomic Era (Washington, DC: National Defence University Press, 1986).

Bagnall, General Sir Nigel 'Concepts of Land/Air Operations in the Central Region: I' *RUSI Journal* 129(3) 1984: 59–62.

Bailey, Jonathan, Richard Iron and Hew Strachan *British Generals in Blair's Wars* (Farnham: Ashgate, 2013).

Balck, Hermann *Order in Choas* (Lexington, KY: University of Kentucky Press, 2015).

Barnard, Chester *The Functions of the Executive* (Cambridge, MA: Harvard University Press, 1953).

Barr, Niall *The Pendulum of War* (London: Pimlico, 2005).

Barry, Ben *Harsh Lesson: Iraq, Afghanistan and the changing character of war* (London: IISS, 2017).

Bean, Charles E.W. *The Australian Imperial Force in France Vol VI: 1918* (Sydney, NSW: Angus and Robertson, 1942).
　The Australian Imperial Force Volume IV: 1917 (Sydney, NSW: Angus and Robertson, 1933).

Bennett, Huw *Fighting the Mau Mau: the British Army and count-insurgency in the Kenya Emergency* (Cambridge: Cambridge University Press, 2013).

Ben-Shalom, Uzi and Eitan Shamir 'Mission Command between theory and practice: the case of the IDF' *Defence and Security Analysis* 27(2) 2011: 101–17.

Betz, David and Anthony Cormack 'Iraq, Afghanistan and British strategy' *Orbis* Spring 2009: 319–36.

Biddle, Stephen *Military Power: Explaining Victory and Defeat in Modern Battle* (Princeton, NJ: Princeton University Press, 2004).

Bidwell, Shelford and Dominic Graham *Fire-Power: The British Army – Weapons and Theories of War, 1904–1945* (Barnsley: Pen and Sword, 2004).

Bigeard, Marcel *Ma Guerre d'Algerie* (Baume-Les-Dames: Éditions du Rocher, 2010).

Bird, Tim and Alex Marshall *Afghanistan: how the west lost its way* (New Haven, CT: Yale University Press, 2011).

Black, Jeremy *War: a short history* (London: Continuum, 2010).

Blair, Clay *Ridgway's Paratroopers* (Annapolis, MD: Naval Institute Press, 1985).

Blank, Stephen 'What do the Zapad 2013 Exercises Reveal' (Part 1) *Eurasia Daily Monitor* 10(177), 4 October 2013.

Blasko, Dennis 'Integrating the services and harnessing the military area commands' *Journal of Strategic Studies* 39(5–6) 2016: 685–708.

Blau, Peter *On the Nature of Organizations* (London: John Wiley and Sons, 1974).
　The Dynamics of Bureaucracy: a study of interpersonal relations in two government agencies (Chicago: University of Chicago Press, 1955).

Bloch, Marc *Strange Defeat* (London: W.W. Norton and Company, 1999).

Blumenson, Martin *Bloody River: prelude to the Battle of Casino* (London: George Allen and Unwin, 1998).

Bodnar, John and Rebecca Dengler 'The emergence of the command network' *Naval War College Review* 49(4) 1996: 93–107.

Boff, Jonathan *Haig's Enemy: Crown Prince Rupprecht and Germany's War on the Western Front* (Oxford: Oxford University Press, 2018).

Bolger, Dan *Why We Lost: a general's inside account of Iraq and Afghanistan* (New York: First Mariner Books, 2015).

Bond, Brian *Liddell Hart: a study of his military thought* (London: Cassell, 1977).

Bonin, John and Telford Crisco 'The Modular Army' *The Military Review* March–April 2004: 21–7.

Booth, T. Michael and Duncan Spencer *Paratrooper: the life of General James Gavin* (Philadelphia, PA: Casemate, 2012).

British Army *Transforming the British Army: an update – July 2013*. www.army.mod.uk/documents/general/Army2020_Report_v2.pdf.

Army Field Manual Volume 1 Part 1A Divisional Tactics (June 2014).

Branch, Daniel *Defeating the Mau Mau, Creating Kenya* (Cambridge: Cambridge University Press, 2009).

Bronfield, Saul 'Did Tradoc Outmanoeuvre the manoeuvrists? A Comment' *War and Society* 27(2) (2008): 111–25.

Brose, Eric *Kaiser's Army: the politics of military technology in Germany during the machine age, 1870–1918* (Oxford: Oxford University Press, 2004).

Brown, John *Kevlar Legions; the transformation of the US Army, 1989–2005* (Washington, DC: US Army Centre of Military History, 2011).

Buckley, John *Monty's Men: the British Army and the liberation of Europe* (New Haven, CT: Yale University Press, 2014).

Die Bundesregierung Weissbuch 2016: zur Sicherheitspolitick und zur Zukunft der Bundeswehr. https://m.bundesregierung.de/Content/Infomaterial/BMVg/Weissbuch_zur_Sicherheitspolitik_2016.pdf;jsessionid=B363C8A762E222DF5C229B41D5B52A5F.s1t1?__blob=publicationFile&v=2.

Burgerud, Eric *The Dynamics of Defeat: the Vietnam War in Hau Ngia Province* (Boulder, CO: Westview, 1993).

Burnham, James *The Managerial Revolution* (New York: Day, 1941).

Bury, Patrick and Anthony King 'The Profession of Love', in Anthony King (ed.), *Frontline: combat and cohesion in Iraq and Afghanistan* (Oxford: Oxford University Press, 2015), 200–15.

Callon, Michel 'Some elements of a sociology of translation: domestication of the scallops and the fisherman of St Brieuc Bay', in John Law (ed.), *Power, Action and Belief* (London: Routledge and Kegan Paul, 1986), 196–223.

Carrington, Charles *Soldier from the Wars Returning* (Barnsley: Pen and Sword, 2006).

Carter, Lieutenant General Nick 'The Divisional Level of Command' *British Army Review* 157 Summer 2013: 95–102.

Chandler, David *The Campaigns of Napoleon* (New York: Macmillan Publishing, 1995).

Chef des Generalstabes des Feldherres *Grundsätze für die Führung in der Abwehrschlacht im Stellungskriege* (Berlin: Reichsdruckerei, 1917).

Chief of Staff *A Manual for Commanders of Large Units Vol 1 Operations* (Washington, DC: US Government Printing Office, 1930).

Chief of Staff *Field Service Regulations Operations FM 100–5* (Washington, DC: US Government Printing Office, 1941).

CINC Home Forces *Doctrine for the Tactical Handling of the Division and the Armoured Division: Part I Introduction Part II: The Division Part III: The Armoured Divison* (October 1942).

Citino, Robert *The German Way of War: from the Thirty Years War to the Third Reich* (Lawrence, KS: University of Kansas Press, 2005).

Clancy, Tom with Anthony Zinni *Battle Ready* (London: Pan, 2005).

Clausewitz, Carl von *On War,* translated by Michael Howard and Peter Paret (Princeton, NJ: Princeton University Press, 1984).

Cohen, Eliot *Supreme Command* (London: Simon and Schuster, 2002).

Cohen, Eliot and John Gooch *Military Misfortunes; the Anatomy of Failure in War* (New York: Vintage, 1991).

Cohen, Yves *Le Siècle des Chefs: une histoire transnationale du commandement et de l'autorité (1890–1940)* (Paris: Editions Amsterdam, 2013).

Colin, Jean *L'Éducation Militaire de Napoleon* (Paris: Librairie Militaire R. Capelet and Cie, 1900).

The Transformation of War, translated by L. Pope-Hennessy (London: Hugh Rees, 1912).

Collins, Randall *Violence: a micro-sociology* (Princeton, NJ: Princeton University Press, 2008).

Interaction Ritual Chains (Princeton, NJ: Princeton University Press, 2004).

The Sociology of Philosophies (London: Belknap Press, 2000).

Condell, Bruce and David Zabecki *On the German Art of War: Truppenführung* (Mechanicsburg, PA: Stackpole, 2009).

Connolly, Mark 'Rommel as Icon', in Ian Beckett (ed.), *Rommel Reconsidered* (Mechanisburg, PA: Stackpole, 2014), 157–78.

Cooper, Christopher 'How a marine lost his command in the race to Baghdad' *The New Yorker,* 5 April 2004. www.wsj.com/articles/SB10811119802 85073875.

Cornish, Paul and Andrew Dorman 'Blair's wars and Brown's budgets: from Strategic Defence Review to strategic decay in less than a decade' *International Affairs* 85(2) March 2009: 247–61.

'National defence in the age of austerity' *International Affairs* 85(4) July 2009: 733–5.

Creveld, Martin van *Command in War* (Cambridge, MA: Harvard University Press, 1985).

Danchev, Alex *Alchemist of War: the life of Basil Liddell Hart* (London: Weidenfeld and Nicolson, 1988).

Davis, Mike *Planet of the Slums* (London: Verso, 2006).

de la Billiere, General Sir Peter *Storm Command: a personal account of the Gulf War* (London: HarperCollins, 1995), 127.

Department of the Army *FM 17–100 Armored Division and Combat Command* (Washington, DC: US Government Printing Office, 1949).

Delaney, Douglas *Soldier's General: Bert Hoffmeister at War* (Vancouver, BC: University of British Colombia Press, 2005).

Delaney, Douglas *The Imperial Army Project: Britain and the Land Forces of the Dominions and India, 1902–1945* (Oxford: Oxford University Press, 2017).

Dixon, Norman *On the Psychology of Military Incompetence* (London: Pimlico, 1994).

Doherty, Robert *British Armoured Divisions and their Commanders, 1939–1945* (Barnsley: Pen and Sword, 2006).

Donnelly, William *Transforming an Army at War: designing the modular force* (Washington, DC: US Army Centre of Military History, 2007).

Drucker, Peter *The Effective Executive* (Oxford: Butterworth Heinemann, 1997).

Managing for the Future (Oxford: Butterworth Heinemann, 1992).

The Practice of Management (Heinemann: London, 1969).

Duffy, Christopher *War in the Age of Enlightenment* (London: Routledge and Kegan Paul, 1982).

Eberbach, Heinrich 'Preface', in Kurt Meyer (ed.), *Grenadiers: the story of the Waffen SS General Kurt 'Panzer' Meyer* (Mechanisburg, PA: Stackpole, 2005).

The Economist 'Losing Their Way' 31 January 2009. www.economist.com/node/13022177.

Edmunds, Tim and Anthony Forster 'Out of Step: the case for change in the British armed forces' *Demos* 2007.

Edmonds, James *Military Operations in France and Belgium 1917 Volume II: 7 June – 10 November* (London: HMSO, 1948).

Edwards, Sean *Mars Unmasked: the changing face of urban operations* (New York: Rand, 2000).

Egnell, Robert and David Ucko *Counter-Insurgency in Crisis* (New York: Columbia University Press, 2015).

Elkins, Caroline *Britain's Gulag: the brutal end to empire* (London: Jonathan Cape, 2005).

Elliott, Christopher *High Command: British military leadership in the Iraq and Afghanistan wars* (London: Hurst, 2015).

Ellis, John *Cassino: the hollow victory* (London: Aurum, 2003), 90–110.

English, John and Bruce Gudmundsson *On Infantry: the military profession* (Westport, CT: Praeger, 1994).

Erskine, Lieutenant General George 'Bobbie' 'The Mau Mau Rebellion', lecture to Army Staff College Camberley, 1955.

Etzioni, Amitai *Complex Organizations: on power, involvement and their correlates* (Glencoe, NY: Free Press, 1961).

Ewell, Julian and Ira Hunt *Sharpening the Combat Edge: the use of analysis to reinforce military judgement* (Washington, DC: US Government Printing Press, 1973).

Fall, Bernard *Hell in a Very Small Place* (Cambridge, MA: Da Capo Press, 2002).

A Street Without Joy (Mechanicsburg, PA: Stackpole, 2005).

Farndale, General Sir Martin 'Counter Stroke: Future Requirements' *RUSI Journal* 130(4) 1987: 6–10.

Farrell, Theo *Unwinnable: Britain's war in Afghanistan* (Bodley Head, 2017).

Farrell, Theo and Stuart Gordon 'COIN Machine: the British military in Afghanistan' *RUSI Journal* 154(3) 2009: 18–25.

Fayol, Henri *General and Industrial Management* (London: Pittman, 1971).

Fergusson, James *One Million Bullets* (London: Bantam, 2008).

Forget, Dominique *Le Général Leclerc et la 2e DB 1944–5* (Bayeux: Heimdal, 2008).

Forty, George *7th Armoured Division: the Desert Rats* (Hersham: Ian Allen, 2003).

Freedman, Lawrence *Strategy* (Oxford: Oxford University Press, 2015).

French, David 'Colonel Blimp and the British Army: British Divisional Commanders in the War against Germany, 1939–45' *English Historical Review* 111(444) November 1996: 1182–1201.

The British Way in Counter-Insurgency 1945–67 (Oxford: Oxford University Press, 2011).

The French White Paper on Defence and National Security (New York: Odile Jacob, 2008). www.mocr.army.cz/images/Bilakniha/ZSD/French%20 White%20Paper%20on%20Defence%20and%20National%20 Security%202008.pdf; www.css.ethz.ch/content/dam/ethz/special-interest/ gess/cis/center-for-securities-studies/pdfs/CSS-Analyses-46.pdf.

Frieser, Karl-Heinz *The Blitzkrieg Legend* (Annapolis, MD: Naval Institute Press, 2005).

Fuller, J.F.C. *Generalship: its diseases and their cure* (London: Faber and Faber, 1933).

The Generalship of Ulysses S Grant (Cambridge, MA: Da Capo Press, 1929).

Galula, David *Counter-Insurgency Warfare: theory and practice* (Westport, CT: Praeger, 2006).

Gat, Azar 'Liddell Hart's theory of armoured warfare: revising the revisionists' *Journal of Strategic Studies* 19(1) March 1996: 1–30.

'The hidden sources of Liddell Hart's Strategic Ideas' *War in History* 3(3) 1996: 293–308.

'British Influence and the evolution of the panzer arm: myth or reality? Part I' *War in History* 4(2) 1997: 150–73.

'British Influence and the evolution of the panzer arm: myth or reality? Part II' *War in History* 4(3) 1997: 316–38.

A History of Military Thought: from Enlightenment to Cold War (Oxford: Oxford University Press, 2001).

Gavin, James *On to Berlin* (New York: Bantam, 1985).

Gawande, Atul *The Checklist Manifesto* (London: Profile, 2011), 37–8.

General Staff, War Office *The Operations of Large Formations*, translated from Field Service Regulations of the French Army, dated 28 October 1913 (London: HMSO, 1914).

General Staff *Summary of the French Instructions for Higher Formations in the Attack* (Washington, DC: Government Printing Office, 1918).

General Staff *The Division in the Attack*, SS 135 (Shrivenham: Strategic and Combat Studies Institute, 1918).

Summary of the French Instructions for Higher Formations in the Attack (Washington, DC: Government Printing Office, 1918).

Gerasimov, General Valery 'The Value of Science in Prediction' *Military-Industrial Kurier* 27 February 2013. http://inmoscowsshadow.wordpress.com.

Gibson, David *Talk at the Brink: deliberation and decision during the Cuban missile crisis* (Princeton, NJ: Princeton University Press, 2012).

Godefroy, Andrew 'The advent of the set piece attack: Major-General Arthur Currie and the Battle of Mount Sorrel 2–13 June 1916', in Andrew Godefroy (ed.), *Great War Commands: historical perspectives on Canadian Army leadership*, 1914–18 (Kingston, ON: Canadian Defence Press, 2010).

Gordon, Michael and Bernard Trainor *Cobra II* (London: Vintage, 2007).

Gouldner, Alvin *Patterns of Industrial Bureaucracy* (New York: Collier Macmillan, 1954).

Graham, Stephen *Cities under Siege: the new military urbanism* (London: Verso, 2010).

Grand Quartier Général des Armées de l'Est *Instruction sur le Combat Offensif des Grandes Unités* (Paris: Imprimerie du service géographique de l'armée, 1916).

Grauer, Ryan *Commanding Military Power; Organizing Victory and Defeat on the Battlefield* (Cambridge: Cambridge University Press, 2016).

Gray, Colin *Strategy for Chaos: revolution in military affairs and the evidence of history* (London: Frank Cass, 2002).

Grey, Stephen *Operation Snakebite* (London: Penguin, 2009).

Griffith, Patrick *Battle Tactics of the Western Front* (New Haven, CT: Yale University Press, 1994).

Grint, Keith *The Arts of Leadership* (Oxford: Oxford University Press, 2001).

Groen, Michael *With the 1st Marine Division in Iraq 2003: no greater friend, no worse enemy* (Quantico, VA: History Division Marine Corps University, 2006).

Guibert, Comte Jacques de *Essai Général de Tactique* (Paris: Economica, 2004).

Hackworth, David *Steel My Soldiers' Hearts* (London: Simon and Schuster, 2003).

Hackworth, David and Julie Sherman *About Face* (London: Pan Books, 1989).

Haltiner, Karl 'The Definite End of the Mass Army in Western Europe?' *Armed Forces & Society* 25(1) 1998: 7–36.

'The Decline of the Mass Army', in Caforio, G. (ed.), *Handbook of the Sociology of the Military* (London: Kluwer/Plenum, 2003), 361–84.

Hamilton, Nigel *Monty: the making of a general 1887–1942* (London: Hamish Hamilton, 1981).

Hammer, Michael and James Champy *Re-Engineering the Corporation: a manifesto for business revolution* (London: Nicholas Brealey, 1995).

Hansen, Marc 'The German Commanders on D-Day', in John Buckley (ed.), *The Normandy Campaign 1944: sixty years on* (London: Routledge, 2006), 35–47.

Hart, Basil Liddell *The Other Side of the Hill: Germany's generals, their rise and fall, with their own accounts of military events 1939–1945* (London: Cassell and Co, 1948).

The Rommel Papers (London: Arrow, 1987).

Sherman: soldier, realist, American (Cambridge, MA: Da Capo Press, 1993).

Hasselbladh, Hans 'Command and the War Machine', in Karl Yden (ed.), *Directions in Military Organizing* (Stockholm: Förswvarshögskolan, 2005), 39–62.

Hayes, Christopher 'Developing the Navy's Operational Leaders: a critical look' *Naval War College Review* Summer 2008: 78–9.

Headquarters, Department of the Army *FM 100-5 Operations*, June 1993. www.fprado.com/armorsite/US-Field-Manuals/FM-100-5-Operations .pdf.

The Armored Division and Combat Command FM 17-100 (1958).

Heeres Division 487 *Führung und Gefecht der Verbundenen Waffen* (1921).

Hersch, Seymour *Chain of Command: the road from 9/11 to Abu Ghraib* (London: HarperCollins, 2009).

Hills, Alice *Future Wars in Cities: re-thinking a liberal dilemma* (London: Frank Cass, 2004).

Hitler, Adolf *Mein Kampf* (London: Pimlico, 1992).

Hoffman, Frank 'Hybrid Warfare and Challenges' *Joint Forces Quarterly* 52 1st Quarter 2009: 34–9.

Howard, Michael *The Franco-Prussian War* (London: Routledge, 2000).

'Leadership in the British Army in the Second World War: some personal observations', in Gary Sheffield (ed.), *Leadership and Command: the Anglo-American Military Experience since 1861* (London: Brassey's, 2002), 117–28.

Howieson, Brian and Howard Kahn 'Leadership, Management and Command: the officers' trinity', in Peter Gray and Seb Cox (eds), *Air Power Leadership: theory and practice* (Swindon: JDCC, 2002), 68–89.

Hunt, Ira *The 9th Infantry Division in Vietnam: unparalleled and unequaled* (Lexington, KY: University of Kentucky Press, 2010).

Huntington, Samuel *The Soldier and the State* (Cambridge, MA: Belknap Press, 1957).

Hutchins, Edwin *Cognition in the Wild* (Cambridge, MA: Harvard, 1996).

Jackson, Ashley 'The evolution of the division in British military history' *RUSI Journal* 152(6) 2007: 78–81.

Jaffe, Greg *The Fourth Star: four generals and the epic struggle for the future of the US Army* (New York: Three Rivers Press, 2009).

Janowitz, Morris and Edward Shils 'Cohesion and Disintegration in the Wehrmacht in World War II' *Public Opinion Quarterly* Summer 1948: 280–315.

Janis, Irving *Group Think: psychological studies of policy decisions and fiascos* (Boston: Houghton Mifflin Company, 1982).

Jennings, Louis J. (ed.) *The Croker Papers: The Correspondence and Diaries of the Late Right Honourable John Wilson Croker, LL.Dm F.R.S, Secretary of the Admiralty from 1809 to 1830* (1884), Vol. III.

Kagan, Kimberley *The Eye of Command* (Ann Arbor, MI: University of Michigan Press, 2006).

Kamiya, Major Jason *A History of 24th Mechanised Division Combat Team during Operation Desert Storm* (Fort Stewart, GA: 24th Mechanised Division, 1992).

Kaplan, Fred 'Challenging Generals', in Robert Taylor, William Rosenbach and Erik Rosenbach (eds), *Military Leadership* (Boulder, CO: Westview, 2008).

The Insurgents: David Petraeus and the Plot to Change the American Way of War (London: Simon and Schuster, 2014).

Kedzior, Richard *Evolution and Endurance: the US Army Division in the twentieth century* (New York: Rand, 2000).

Keegan, John *The Mask of Command* (London: Pimlico, 1999).

Kelleher, Catherine 'Mass Armies in the 1970s: the debate in Western Europe' *Armed Forces & Society* 5(1) 1978: 3–30.

Kilcullen, David *Out of the Mountains: the coming of age of the urban guerrilla* (London: Hurst and Company, 2013).

Blood Year: Islamic State and the Failures of the War on Terror (London: Hurst, 2016)

King, Anthony 'Military Command in the Last Decade' *International Affairs* 87(2) 2011: 377–96.

'Understanding Helmand: British military campaign in Afghanistan' *International Affairs* 86(2) 2010: 311–32.

The Transformation of Europe's Armed Forces: from the Rhine to Afghanistan (Cambridge: Cambridge University Press, 2011).

The Combat Soldier: infantry tactics and cohesion in the twentieth and twenty-first centuries (Oxford: Oxford University Press, 2013).

'Combat Effectiveness in the Small Infantry Unit: beyond the primary group thesis' *Security Studies* 25(4) 2016: 688–728.

'Corroding the Iron Division: personnel problems' *British Army Review* 168 Winter 2017: 59–63.

King, Edward *The Death of an Army* (New York: Saturday Review Press, 1973).

Kiszely, John *Anatomy of a Campaign: the British fiasco in Norway 1940* (Cambridge: Cambridge University Press, 2017).

Klein, Gary 'Overcoming complexity through collaboration and follower-based leadership' *Small Wars Journal* 2017. http://smallwarsjournal.com/jrnl/art/overcoming-complexity-through-collaboration-and-follower-based-leadership.

Kober, Avi 'What Happened to Israeli Military Thought' *Journal of Strategic Studies* 34(5) 2011: 707–32.

Kommando Heer, *Thesenpapier I: Wie kämpfen Landstreitkräfte künftig?* (Bundesamt für Infrastruktur, Umweltschutz und Dienstleistungen der Bundeswehr, 2017).

Kortenhaus, Werner *The Combat History of the 21st Panzer Division* (Solihull: Helion and Co, 2014).

La Bree, Clifton *The Gentle Warrior: General Oliver Prince Smith, USMC* (Kent, OH: Kent State University Press, 2001).

Lacey, Jim *The Take-Down: the Third Division's twenty-one day assault on Baghdad* (Annapolis, MD: Naval Institute Press, 2007).

Latawski, Paul 'A Historical Perspective of the Division in the British Army' Army Field Manual Vol 1 Part 1A *Divisional Tactics* 2014: 4.1–4.28.

Latour, Bruno and Michel Callon 'Unscrewing the Big Leviathan: how actors macro-structure reality and how sociologists help them do so?', in K. Knorr Cetina and A. Cicourel (eds), *Advances in Social Theory and Methodology* (London: Routledge Kegan Paul, 1981), 277–303.

Latour, Bruno *Reassembling the Social* (Oxford: Oxford University Press, 2005).

Laver, Harry and Jeffry Matthews (eds) *The Art of Command* (Lexington, KY: University of Kentucky Press, 2008).

Lebenson, Len *Surrounded by Heroes* (Philadelphia, PA: Casement, 2007).

Ledwidge, Frank *Losing Small Wars: British military failure in Iraq and Afghanistan* (New Haven, CT: Yale University Press, 2011).

Leger, Paul Alain 'Personal Account of Chef de Batallion', in M. Alexander, M. Evans and J. Keiger (eds), *Algerian War and the French Army, 1954–6* (Basingstoke: Macmillan, 2002), 237–42.

Leonard, Robert *The Art of Maneuver* (New York: Ballantine Books, 1991).

Lewin, Ronald *Rommel as Military Commander* (New York: Barnes and Noble, 1968).

Lindsay, Martin *So Few Got Through* (London: Collins, 1946).

Lock-Pullan, Richard 'An Inward-Looking Time' *Journal of Military History* 67(2) (2003): 483–512; 147–73.

Lofaro, Guy *The Sword of St Michael: the 82nd Airborne Division in World War II* (Cambridge, MA: Da Capo, 2011).

MacDougall, Tony *The War Letters of General Monash* (Sydney, NSW: Duffy Snellgrove, 2002).

Macgregor, Dan *Breaking the Phalanx* (London: Praeger, 1997).

Mackay, Andrew and Steve Tatham 'Behavioural Conflict: from general to strategic corporal, complexity, adaptation and influence' The Shrivenham Papers, 9 December 2009.

Macksey, Kenneth *Rommel: battles and campaigns* (New York: Da Capo Press, 1997).

Maginnis, Robert *Deadly Consequences: how cowards are pushing women into combat* (Washington, DC: Regnery Publishing Inc, 2013).

Mansoor, Peter 'The British Army and the Lessons of the Iraq War' *British Army Review* 147 Summer 2009: 11–15.

Manstein, Erich von *Lost Victories* (Minneapolis, MN: Zenith, 2004).

Mantas, Mirjam Grandia *Deadly Embrace: the Decision Paths to Uruzgan and Helmand* (Doctoral Dissertation, University of Leiden, 2015).

March, James and Johan Olsen, *Ambiguity and Choice in Organizations* (Bergen: Universitetsforlaget, 1976).

Marston, Daniel '"Smug and Complacent?" Operation TELIC: the need for critical analysis' *British Army Review* 147 Summer 2009: 16–23.

Martin, Michel 'Conscription and the Decline of the Mass Army in France, 1960–75' *Armed Forces & Society* 3(3) 1977: 355–406.

Massu, Jacques *La Vraie Bataille d'Alger* (Evreux: Librairie Plon, 1971).
Septs Ans avec Leclerc (Monaco: Libraire Plan, 1997).

Maurer, E. 'Schilderung der Operationen gegen die Truppen der US-Armee: die Kämpfe der 253 Inf. Div.' 1946, Bundesarchiv-Militär-archiv Freiburg-im-Breisgau, ZA1/1711, 20.

McCarthy, Peter and Mike Syron *Panzerkrieg: the rise and fall of Hitler's Tank Divisions* (London: Constable, 2002).

McChrystal, Stanley *My Share of the Task: a memoir* (New York: Portfolio/ Penguin, 2013).

Team of Teams (London: Penguin, 2015).

McGrath, John *The Brigade: a history* (Fort Leavenworth, KS: Combat Studies Institute Press, 2004).

McMullin, R. *Pompey Elliott* (Melbourne, VIC: Scribe Publications, 2000).

Mearsheimer, John *Liddell Hart and the Weight of History* (London: Brassey's Defence Publishers, 1988).

Meilinger, Phillip 'The Development of Air Power Theory', in Peter Gray and Seb Cox (eds), *Air Power Leadership: theory and practice* (Swindon: JDCC, 2002), 90–106.

Mellenthin, F.W. von *Panzer Battles*, translated by H. Betzler (London: Futura, 1979).

Meyer, H. Jack *Hanging Sam: a military biography of General Samuel T. Williams: from Pancho Villa to Vietnam* (Denton, TX: University of North Texas Press, 1990).

Meyer, Kurt *Grenadiers: the story of the Waffen SS General Kurt 'Panzer' Meyer* (Mechanisburg, PA: Stackpole, 2005).

Miller, Robert *Division Commander: a biography of Major-General Norman Cota* (Spartanburg, SC: Reprint, 1989).

Ministère de la Guerre *Instruction Provisoire du 6 October 1921 sur L'Emploi Tactique des Grandes Unités* (Paris: Charles-Lourauzelle and Co, 1924).

Instruction Provisoire sur le Service en Campagne. 20 October 1924. Annex No.1 a l'Instruction Provisoire sur l'emploi tactique des Grandes Unités (Paris: Charles-Lavauzelle and Co, 1924).

Ministry of Defence *Allied Joint Doctrine for Operational Level Planning Allied Joint Publication 5-00* (Shrivenham: Development, Concepts and Doctrine Centre, 2013).

Monash, John *The Australian Victories in France* (Uckfield, Sussex and London: Naval History Press and Imperial War Museum, no date).

Montgomery, Bernard *The Memoirs of Field Marshal the Viscount Montgomery of Alamein, K.G.* (St James Place, London: Collins, 1958).

Montross, Lynn and Nicholas Canzona *The Chosin Reservoir Campaign Volume III US Marine Operations 1950–1953* (Washington, DC: HQ United States Marine Corps, 1957).

Mortimor-Moore, William *Free France's Lion: the life of Philippe Leclerc, de Gaulle's Greatest General* (Philadelphia, PA: Newbury, 2011).

Morgan, Patrick 'The Impact of the Revolution in Military Affairs' *Journal of Strategic Studies* 23(1) 2000: 132–9.

Moss Kanter, Rosabeth *The Change Masters: corporate entrepreneurs at work* (London: Unwin, 1987).

When Giants Learn to Dance: mastering the challenges of strategy, management and careers in the 1990s (London: Unwin, 1990).

Müller, Bjorn, 'Wie die Bundeswehr den Landkrieg der Zukunft gewinnen will'. www.pivotarea.eu/2017/09/22/thesenpapier-des-deutschen-heeres-so-will-die-bundeswehr-kuenftige-landkriege-gewinnen/.

Newton, Paul, Paul Colley and Andrew Sharpe 'Reclaiming the Art of British Strategic Thinking' *RUSI Journal* 155(1) February/March 2010: 47; Public Administration Committee, *Who Does UK National Strategy?* www.publications.parliament.uk/pa/cm201011/cmselect/cmpubadm/435/43502.htm.

North, Richard *Ministry of Defeat* (London: Continuum, 2009).

Owens, William 'Creating a US Military Revolution', in Theo Farrell and Terry Terriff (eds), *The Sources of Military Change* (London: Lynne Rienner, 2002), 205–20.

Peach, Stuart 'The Airman's Dilemma: to command or control?' in Peter Gray (ed.), *Air Power 21: challenges for the new century* (London: The Stationery Office, 2000), 123–52.

Pedersen, P.A. 'General Sir John Monash: corps commander on the Western Front', in D.M. Horner (ed.), *The Commanders: Australian military leadership in the 20th century* (Sydney, NSW: Allen and Unwin Press, 1984), 85–125.

  Monash as Military Commander (Melbourne, VIC: Melbourne University Press, 1985).

Perrow, Charles *Normal Accidents: living with high-risk technology* (New York: Basic Books, 1984).

Porch, Douglas *March to the Marne: the French Army 1871–1914* (Cambridge: Cambridge University Press, 1981).

Powell, Geoffrey *Plumer: the soldier's general* (Barnsley: Pen and Sword, 2004).

Press, Daryl 'Lessons from Ground Combat in the Gulf: the impact of training and technology' *International Security* 22(2) 1997: 137–46.

Prior, Robin and Trevor Wilson *Command on the Western Front: the military career to Sir Henry Rawlinson 1914–18* (Barnsley: Pen and Sword, 2004).

Puryear, Eric *19 Stars: a study in military character and leadership* (Novato, CA: Prisidio, 1981).

Radley, Kenneth *We Lead, Others Follow: the First Division 1914–1918* (St Catherines, ON: Vanwell Publishing, 2006).

Reuth, Ralf *Rommel: end of a legend* (London: Haus Books, 2008).

Reynolds, Nick *Basrah, Baghdad and Beyond* (Annapolis, MD: Naval Institute Press, 2005).

Richards, General Sir David 'The Art of Command in the Twenty-First Century: reflections on three commands', in Julian Lindlay-French and Yves Boyer (eds), *The Oxford Handbook of War* (Oxford: Oxford University Press, 2012), 346–56.

  Taking Command (London: Headline, 2014).

Ricks, Thomas *The Gamble* (London: Penguin, 2009).

Fiasco: the American Adventure in Iraq (London: Penguin, 2006).

The Generals: American military command from World II to today (London: Penguin, 2012).

Ridgway, Matt *Soldier: the memoirs of Matthew B. Ridgway* (New York: Harper Brothers, 1956).

Reid, Brian Holden *JFC Fuller: military thinker* (London: Macmillan, 1987).

Roberts, Michael 'The Military Revolution, 1560–1660', in Michael Roberts (ed.), *Essays in Swedish History* (London: Arnold, 1967), 56–81.

Robinson, Linda *Tell Me How This Ends: General David Petraeus and the search for a way out of Iraq* (New York: Public Affairs, 2008).

Rogers, H.C.B. *Napoleon's Army* (London: Ian Allan, 1974).

Ross, Steven 'The Development of the Combat Division in Eighteenth-century French Armies' *French Historical Studies* 4(1) Spring 1965: 90.

Saint-Fuscien, Emmanuel À *Vos Ordres? La relations d'autorité dans l'armée française de la Grand Guerre* (Paris: Edition de l'Ecole des hautes etudes en sciences sociales, 2011).

Salmond, J.B. *The History of the Highland Division* (Bishop Auckland, Durham: William Blackwood and Sons, 1994).

Sassen, Saskia 'The Global City: introducing a concept'. www.saskiasassen.com/pdfs/publications/the-global-city-brown.pdf.

The Global City (Princeton, NJ: University of Princeton Press, 2001).

Savage, Paul and Richard Gabriel *Crisis in Command* (New York: Hill and Wang, 1978).

'Cohesion and disintegration in the American Army: an alternative perspective' *Armed Forces & Society* 2(3) 1976: 340–70.

Searle, Alaric 'Rommel and the Rise of the Nazis', in Ian Beckett (ed.), *Rommel Reconsidered* (Mechanisburg, PA: Stackpole, 2014), 7–30.

Seaton, Albert *The German Army, 1933–45* (London: Weidenfeld and Nicolson, 1982).

Sennett, Richard *The Craftsman* (London: Penguin, 2009).

Together: the rituals, the pleasures and politics of cooperation (London: Penguin, 2013).

Selznick, Peter *TVA and the Grass Roots: a study in the sociology of formal organizations* (New York: Harper Torchbooks, 1966).

Serle, Geoffrey *John Monash: a biography* (Melbourne, VIC: Melbourne University Library, 2002).

Shisler, Gail *For Country and Corps: the life of Oliver P. Smith* (Annapolis, MD: Naval Institute Press, 2009).

Shirreff, General Sir Richard 'Conducting Joint Operations', in Julian Lindley-French and Yves Boyer (eds), *The Oxford Handbook of War* (Oxford: Oxford University Press, 2012), 373–86.

Showalter, Dennis 'The Bundeswehr of the Federal Republic of Germany', in Lewis Gann (ed.), *The Defense of Western Europe* (London: Croom Helm, 1987), 212–54.

'Army and Society in Imperial Germany: the pains of modernization' *Journal of Contemporary History* 18(4) October 1993: 583–618.

'From Deterrence to Doomsday Machine: the German way of war, 1890–1914' *Journal of Military History* 64(3) July 2000: 679–710.

Patton and Rommel: men of war in the twentieth century (New York: Berkley Caliber, 2006).

Simmons, Brigadier General Edwin *Frozen Chosin: US Marines at Changjin Reservoir* (Createspace, 2014).

Slim, Field Marshal Viscount William *Defeat into Victory* (London: Cassell, 2009).

Sloterdijk, Peter *Globes: macrospherology* (Cambridge, MA: MIT Press, 2014).

Bubbles: microspherology (Los Angeles, CA: Semiotext(e); Cambridge, MA: Distributed by the MIT Press, 2011).

Smith, Brigadier Rupert 'The Division' *British Army Review* 144 1990: 77–83.

Smith, Major-General Rupert 'The Gulf War: the land battle' *RUSI Journal* 137(1) 1992.

Sons of the Iron Lady 'Donkeys led by Lions' *British Army Review* 150: 55–8. www.wapentakes.co.uk/donkeys.pdf.

Smithers, A.J. *Sir John Monash* (London: Leo Cooper, 1973).

Stachelbeck, Christian *Militärische Effektivität im Ersten Weltkreig: Die 11 Bayerishe Infanteriedivision 1915 bis 1918* (Paderborn: Ferdinand Schoningh, 2010).

Stanhope, Philip *Notes of Conversations with the Duke of Wellington* (New York: Longmans Green and Co, 1888).

Stavridis, James and Robert Girrier 'Taking Command', in T. Cutler (ed.), *Naval Command* (Annapolis, MD: Naval Institute Press, 2015), 5–12.

Stephens, Alan 'Command in the Air' in Peter Gray and Seb Cox (eds), *Air Power Leadership: theory and practice* (Swindon: JDCC, 2002), 1–14.

Storr, Jim *The Human Face of War* (London: Continuum, 2009).

Strachan, Hew *The Direction of War: contemporary strategy in historical perspective* (Cambridge: Cambridge University Press, 2013).

Sullivan, Gordon and Jim Dubik *Envisioning Future Warfare* (Fort Leavenworth, KS: Army Command and General Staff College Press, 1995).

Swain, Richard 'Filling the Void; the operational art and the US Army' in Brian McKercher and Matthew Hennessy (eds), *The Operational Art* (Westpoint, CT: Praeger, 2006).

Taylor Fravel, M. 'China's New Military Strategy: "winning informationalized local wars"' *China Brief* 15(13) 2015.

Telp, Claus 'Rommel and 1940', in Ian Beckett (ed.), *Rommel Reconsidered* (Mechanisburg, PA: Stackpole, 2014), 30–59.

Teyerman, Christopher *How to Plan a Crusade* (London: Allen Lane, 2015).

Therborn, Göran *Cities of Power: the urban, the national, the popular, the global* (London: Verso, 2017).

Thiebault, Baron Paul *The Memoirs of Baron Thiebault (Late Lieutenant General in the French Army) Volume I and II* (Memphis, TN: General Books, 2012).

Thomas, Martin *Fight or Flight: Britain, France and Their Roads from Empire* (Oxford: Oxford University Press, 2014).

Thompson, Robert *Defeating Communist Insurgency: experiences from Malaya and Vietnam* (London: Chatto and Windus, 1974).

The Times 'The Officers' Mess', 9 June 2010, 2.

Toczek, David 'The Rapido River Crossing' *Infantry* November–December 1993: 18–22.

Todman, Dan 'The Grand Lamasery Revisited: General Headquarters on the Western Front, 1914–18', in Gary Sheffield and Dan Todman (eds), *Command and Control on the Western Front: the British Army's experience 1914–18* (Staplehurst: Spellmount, 2004), 39–70.

Toomey, Charles Lane *XVIII Airborne Corps in Desert Storm: from planning to victory* (Central Point, OR: Hellgate, 2004).

Tradoc Pamphlet 525-3-1 *US Army Operating Concept: Win in a Complex World*. www.tradoc.army.mil/tpubs/pams/tp525-3-1.pdf.

Turse, Nick *Kill Anything that Moves: the real American war in Vietnam* (New York: Henry Holt and Coy, 2013).

US Army *Infantry Division Special Text 7-100-1* (Fort Leavenworth, KS: US Army Command and General Staff College, 1959).

Field Manual 100–5 Operations (Washington, DC: Headquarters Department of the Army, 1982).

US Army Combined Arms Centre *Army Doctrine Reference Publications ADRP 3-0 Operations* (Washington, DC: Headquarters Department of the Army, 2016), 1–5. www.apd.army.mil/epubs/DR_pubs/DR_a/pdf/web/ADRP%203-0%20FINAL%20WEB.pdf.

Army Doctrine Reference Publication (ADRP)-5 The Operations Process (Washington, DC: Headquarters Department of the Army, 2012).

US Marine Corps Staff *Warfighting* (United States: Renaissance Classics, 2012).

US Navy *A Cooperative Force for 21st Century Seapower* (March 2015).

Valenti, Michael *The Mattis Way of War: an Examination of Operational Art in Task Force 58 and 1st Marine Division* (Fort Leavenworth, KS: US Army Command and General Staff College Press, 2014).

Vennesson, Pascal 'Cohesion and Misconduct: The French Army and the Mahé Affair', in Anthony King (ed.), *Frontline: combat and cohesion in the twenty-first century* (Oxford: Oxford University Press, 2015), 234–49.

Vennesson, Pascal and Amanda Huan 'The General's Intuition: Overconfidence, Pattern Matching, and the Inchon Landing Decision' *Armed Forces & Society* 2017. http://o-journals.sagepub.com.pugwash.lib.warwick.ac.uk/doi/pdf/10.1177/0095327X17738771, 1–23.

War Department *Armored Command Field Manual FM 17–100: the Armored Division* (Washington, DC: US Government Printing Office, 1941).

Staff Officers' Field Manual: Part 1 Staff Data (Washington, DC: US Government Printing Office, 1932).

War Office *Operations: military training Pamphlet No.23 Part III – Appreciations, orders, intercommunications and movements* (London: HMSO, 1939).

The Infantry Division in Battle (London: War Office, 1950).

The Armoured Division in Battle (London: War Office, 1952).

Wavell, General Archibald *Generals and Generalship: the Lee Knowles Lectures delivered at Trinity College, Cambridge 1939* (New York: Macmillan, 1941).

Weick, Karl *Making Sense of the Organization* (Oxford: Blackwell, 2000).

Weissinger-Baylon, Roger 'Garbage-Can Decision Process in Naval Warfare', in James March and Roger Weissinger-Baylon (eds), *Ambiguity and Command: organizational perpectives on military decision-making* (Marshfield, MA: Pitman, 1986), 36–52.

Wesbrook, Stephen 'The Potential for Military Disintegration', in S. Sarkesian (ed.), *Combat Effectiveness and Cohesion* (London: Sage, 1980), 244–78.

West, Bing and Ray Smith *The March Up: taking Baghdad with the 1st Marine Division* (London: Pimlico, 2003).

Wilson, J. *Maneuver and Firepower; the evolution of divisions and separate brigades* (Honolulu, HI: University Press of the Pacific, 2001).

Wimberley, Douglas *The Memoirs of Major-General Douglas Vol 1 and 2*, IWM PP/MCR/182.

Windrow, Martin *The Last Valley* (Cambridge, MA: Da Capo Press, 2004).

Woodward, Bob *State of Denial* (London: Pocket Books, 2006).

Plan of Attack (London: Pocket Books, 2004).

Bush at War (London: Pocket Books, 2003).

Ydstebo, Palle 'Russian Operations: continuity, novelties and adaptation', in Janne Matlary and Tormod Heier (eds), *Ukraine and Beyond: Russian's strategic security challenge to Europe* (London: Palgrave Macmillan, 2010), 153–61.

Yingling, Paul 'A Failure in Generalship', in Robert Taylor, William Rosenbach and Erik Rosenbach (eds), *Military Leadership* (Boulder, CO: Westview, 2008), 181–92.

Zinni, Tony and Tony Koltz *Leading the Charge: leadership lessons from the battlefield to the boardroom* (London: Palgrave Macmillan, 2009).

INDEX